Internal Structure of the City

Contributing Authors

William Alonso
Brian J. L. Berry
Hans Blumenfeld
Frederick W. Boal
Larry S. Bourne
Ronald R. Boyce
Edward Brecher
Ruth Brecher
Eugene F. Brigham
Lawrence A. Brown
F. Stuart Chapin, Jr.
William A. V. Clark
Karl W. Deutsch
Robert Earickson
Joseph L. Fisher
William H. Form
Herbert J. Gans
Peter G. Goheen
Britton Harris
Robert O. Harvey
Edward F. R. Hearle
Homer Hoyt
M. E. Eliot Hurst
Dennis B. Johnson
John F. Kain
Edward J. Kaiser
Gerald J. Karaska
Roger E. Kasperson
Kevin Lynch
Duane F. Marble
Harold M. Mayer

John R. Meyer
William Michelson
Eric G. Moore
Richard L. Morrill
Robert A. Murdie
Howard J. Nelson
Bruce E. Newling
John H. Niedercorn
John D. Nystuen
Allan R. Pred
Robin J. Pryor
Andrei Rogers
Harold M. Rose
Leo R. Schnore
John R. Seeley
James W. Simmons
Larry Smith
Wallace F. Smith
Athelstan Spilhaus
Anselm L. Strauss
Michael B. Teitz
Charles M. Tiebout
Charles Tilly
James E. Vance, Jr.
Raymond Vernon
David A. Wallace
David Ward
Melvin M. Webber
Shirley F. Weiss
James O. Wheeler
John Wolforth

Internal Structure of the City

READINGS ON SPACE AND ENVIRONMENT

EDITED BY
LARRY S. BOURNE
University of Toronto

New York
OXFORD UNIVERSITY PRESS
Toronto   1971   London

Contents

VI. ACTIVITIES:
Specialized Activity Patterns and Systems   345

VII. PROBLEMS:
Perspectives on Research and Policy   427

VIII. PROSPECTS:
Toward an Improved Urban Future   491

Internal Structure of the City

Introduction

Urban society is becoming synonymous with society at large. Problems of the latter are increasingly found in the city, so much so that we may have lost sight of those particular problems whose origin is in the city. Greater awareness of the problems of rapid and unplanned urban growth and the deterioration of urban environments has accelerated interest in understanding the complex metropolis. This volume is a response to this interest. The papers collected here are concerned with the internal spatial structure of the contemporary North American city, the environments created, and the way the city changes. Papers are drawn from numerous disciplines which have a common interest in spatial and environmental problems in the city.

The book is problem-oriented. What do we already know and what do we need to find out to understand why cities have taken their present form? What problems arise from this form, and which of these problems are of particularly critical importance? What concepts or theories of the city are essential tools in formulating an urban policy? The concern for urban problems is clearly twofold. Initially, problems in the formulation of theory, and those of analysis and research are considered. Subsequently, attention turns to some of the broader social and environmental problems of contemporary urban life. It is suggested here that implicitly or explicitly these two sets of urban problems are inseparable. A concern for problems also implies a search for solutions. This search leads in two directions. One is toward improving the construction of urban theory, the other toward policy formulation and the planning of improved cities. Solutions in one set will guide our thinking in the other. To use a common expression, there is nothing as practical as a good theory.

Threads of several common problems underlie the following papers. What is the distribution of land uses and activities in a city, are these patterns to be taken as inevitable outcomes of the invisible hand of the market? To what extent are they immutable and to what degree are they subject to revision? What of the conflicts between urban transportation needs and the quality of urban life? By what means does the stock of housing change hands and how do these lead to improved housing quality? What trends are evident in the growth and structure of cities, and do these suggest a further deterioration in the quality of the urban environment? Is there a fundamental conflict between the clean, healthy, and efficient urban environment desired by most urban residents and democratic ideology?

Within this problem context, the present volume has several objectives. First, to provide a perspective on the range of approaches to and problems in the geography of the city, drawing on a diversified body of literature which has a common concern for spatial and environmental aspects and problems of urban areas. The rapid growth of the literature on cities increases the need for anthologies which act to coordinate and synthesize selected examples of published materials in order to reach a wider audience. Second, to introduce examples of recent research findings in urban geography and related fields, and third, to suggest lines of enquiry which may stimulate interest in the geographical bases of urban structure, growth, and environments, and in contemporary problems of urban life generally.[1] It is also clear that the internal structure of a city cannot be viewed in isolation. The city cannot be divorced from its relationships to the external environment, that is, relations with other cities in the urban system, nor from the national or regional urbanization processes of which the city historically is an integral part.[2] But as both of these aspects are adequately covered elsewhere they are not emphasized here.[3] It is felt that to attempt to encompass all aspects of urbanization in one collection of readings such as the present volume will do justice to none.

Themes

The term "internal structure" refers to the location, arrangement, and interrelationships between social and physical elements in the city. This sug-

1. For example, Harold M. Mayer, "Cities and Urban Geography," *Journal of Geography*, LXVIII, 1 (January 1969), 6-19.
2. For example, O. Handlin and J. Burchard (eds.), *The Historian and the City* (Cambridge, Mass.: The M.I.T. Press, 1963, reprinted 1966); Sylvia Fleis Fara (ed.), *Urbanism in World Perspective: A Reader* (New York: T. Y. Crowell, 1968); H. J. Dyos (ed.), *The Study of Urban History* (New York: St. Martin's Press, 1968); Sibyl Moholy-Nagy, *Matrix of Man: An Illustrated History of Urban Environment* (New York: Frederick A. Praeger, 1968); and A. B. Callow, Jr. (ed.), *American Urban History* (New York: Oxford University Press, 1969).
3. Brian J. L. Berry and Frank E. Horton (eds.), *Geographical Perspectives on Urban Systems: Text and Readings* (Englewood Cliffs, N.J.: Prentice-Hall, 1970).

gests that we must be concerned in this book both with spatial distributions and the interaction between these distributions. But this presents a static view of what is obviously a dynamic city. Our images must therefore respect that the key element in understanding the city is change. Further this definition must be expanded to encompass the environments, real and perceived, that residents of the city create and inhabit. These then are the volume's themes.

How should materials on such diverse topics be approached? One view is to conceive of the city as a system, that is, as a set of linked elements. This system comprises a number of interrelated subsystems or subsets of elements. It must be assumed that each of these subsystems is subject to identification, ordering, and analysis. Through the cumulative effects of interactions among these subsystems the city itself becomes a definable system for purposes of geographic study. The principal difficulty most students of the city face is that of ordering the entire urban area into spatial subsystems due to the extreme multiplicity of such subsystems and the complex interrelationships within and between them. These subsystems may represent such diverse elements in a city as the housing and land markets, the networks of transportation and communication, the retail structure, social communities, the diffusion of information, the political power structure, and industrial linkages. The list could be infinite. The papers in this anthology mirror the most important of these subsystems.

Recent themes or currents of change in urban geography, and in urban studies generally, are also reflected in this anthology. At least four themes have been apparent in urban geography in the decade since the important Lund Symposium in Urban Geography was held in 1960 at the Royal University of Lund, Sweden.[4] First, as the study of the city is inevitably an interdisciplinary task, there has been a convergence of interests and methodologies among the social and behavioral sciences.[5] Second, there has been a greater inclination toward more rigorous testing of research hypotheses through the use of scientific methodology, including the use of quantitative techniques,[6] than was the case previously.[7] Third, urban researchers

---

4. Knut Norborg (ed.), *Proceedings of the I.G.U. Symposium in Urban Geography, Lund, 1960,* Lund Studies in Geography Series B. Human Geography No. 24 (Lund, Sweden: G. W. K. Gleerup Publishers, 1962).

5. A recent collection of review papers on urban research in social science disciplines is given in Leo F. Schnore (ed.), *Social Science and the City: A Survey of Urban Research* (New York: Frederick A. Praeger, 1968). An excellent review of recent developments in geography generally is C. Board, R. J. Chorley, and P. Haggett (eds.), *Progress in Geography* (London: Arnold, 1969).

6. Excellent reviews of quantitative applications in geography are Leslie J. King, *Statistical Analysis in Geography* (Englewood Cliffs, N.J.: Prentice-Hall, 1969); Peter Ambrose, *Analytical Human Geography* (Toronto: Longmans, 1969); and

have recognized the necessity of combining traditional studies of population groups with those of the behavior of individuals in the population. The
fourth trend is an increased awareness of the need for direct involvement
in social issues: that is, in research tailored to assist in public policy formulation and decision-making. These trends accord well with the problem-
based approach of this text.

Although the book is intended primarily for beginning students in urban
geography the themes selected are of more general relevance. Many of the
papers are standard references for advanced students in geography and in
urban studies generally. They are also, for example, in scope quite appropriate to students of other disciplines sharing similar interests in the spatial
structure and environmental character of urban areas.[8] In selecting articles
to represent specific themes an attempt was made to avoid overlap with
numerous readings volumes available in sociology,[9] economics,[10] planning,[11] and urban politics.[12]

J. P. Cole and C. A. M. King, *Quantitative Geography* (New York: Wiley, 1969).
For a review of applications in the social sciences in general see M. Dogan and S.
Rokkan (eds.), *Quantitative Ecological Analysis in the Social Sciences* (Cambridge,
Mass.: Harvard University Press, 1969).

7. Harold M. Mayer and C. F. Kohn (eds.), *Readings in Urban Geography* (Chicago: University of Chicago Press, 1959).

8. A collection of papers specifically commissioned to review progress in urban re-
research in the mid-1960's is: Philip M. Hauser and Leo F. Schnore (eds.), *The
Study of Urbanization* (New York: Wiley, 1965). Recent contributions in urban
geography include: Arthur A. Smailes, *The Geography of Towns* (Chicago: Aldine
Publishing Co., reprinted 1968); R. E. Murphy, *The American City: An Urban
Geography* (New York: McGraw-Hill, 1966); J. Gottmann and R. A. Harper,
Metropolis on the Move: Geographers Look at Urban Sprawl (New York: Wiley,
1967); and Emrys Jones, *Towns and Cities* (London: Oxford University Press,
1966). An excellent general overview is provided in B. J. Garner, "Models of Urban
Geography and Settlement Location," Chapter 9 in *Socio-Economic Models in
Geography*, R. J. Chorley and P. Haggett, eds. (London: Methuen, 1967), 303-60.
A critical review of recent developments in urban geography is Nisith Ranjan Kar,
"Research Frontiers in Urban Geography: An Appraisal and Critique of Recent
Trends in Quantification in Urban Geography," *Urban Affairs Quarterly*, Vol. III,
No. 3 (March 1968), pp. 37-68.

9. For example, P. Meadows and E. Mizruchi (eds.), *Readings in Urban Sociology*
(Reading, Mass.: Addison-Wesley, 1968); R. E. Pahl (ed.), *Readings in Urban
Sociology* (London: Pergamon Press, 1968); Richard Sennett (ed.), *Classic Essays
on the Culture of Cities* (New York: Appleton-Century-Crofts, 1969); D. W. Minar
and S. Greer (eds.), *The Concept of Community: Readings with Interpretations*
(Chicago: Aldine Publishing Co., 1969); Terry N. Clarke (ed.), *Community Structure and Decision-Making* (San Francisco: Chandler, 1968); Robert M. French
(ed.), *The Community: A Comparative Perspective* (Itasca, Ill.: F. E. Peacock
Publishers, 1969).

10. H. S. Perloff (ed.), *The Quality of the Urban Environment: Essays on New
Resources in an Urban Age* (Baltimore: Johns Hopkins Press, for Resources for the
Future, Inc., 1969); and H. S. Perloff and L. Wingo, Jr. (eds.), *Issues in Urban
Economics* (Baltimore: Johns Hopkins Press, for Resources for the Future, Inc.,
1968).

Organization

The ordering of papers reflects the definition of the city as a system. The eight section headings connote the broad themes employed in organizing the materials. The internal differentiation of the city is discussed in terms of: Images, Patterns, Processes, Networks, Communities, Activities, Problems, and Prospects. The subtitles describe in more detail the particular emphases contained in the papers within each section. This arrangement in fact represents a flow chart of ideas. Each section develops a theme, building on what has gone before; yet each also leads directly to the materials in all subsequent sections.

The flow of ideas is as follows. To discuss the city we must first define the context in which our studies are set. This involves the specification of images held about cities, the area of interest, and the range of possible approaches utilized in urban research. The papers in Section I attempt to summarize various interpretations or images of what the city is, the geographic unit or units whose internal differentiation is under study, and what aspects or problems within this area should be emphasized. On the basis of this introduction the next two sections represent a broad picture of the city's spatial patterns—and an analysis of the processes which have produced these patterns—as background to all subsequent sections. Section II describes the basic distributions or silhouettes of urban land uses, the location of economic activities and population, land-use change, and the classic

11. A bibliography of similar volumes of readings in urban studies has not been undertaken, but it would be extensive. A few examples of recent anthologies dealing with urban planning and social problems which are relevant to the themes of this volume include Leo F. Schnore and Henry Fagin (eds.), *Urban Research and Policy Planning* (Beverly Hills, Cal.: Sage Publications, 1967); Gerald Leinwand (ed.), *Problems of American Society: The Negro in the City* (New York: Washington Square Press, 1968); James Q. Wilson (ed.), *The Metropolitan Enigma: Inquiries into the Nature and Dimensions of America's Urban Crisis* (Cambridge, Mass.: Harvard University Press, 1968); Warner Bloomberg, Jr. and Henry J. Schmandt (eds.), *Power, Poverty and Urban Policy* (Beverly Hills, Cal.: Sage Publications, 1968); Thomas D. Sherrard (ed.), *Social Welfare and Urban Problems* (New York: Columbia University Press, 1968); Donald Canty (ed.), *The New City: A Program for National Urbanization Strategy* (New York: Frederick A. Praeger, 1970); H. W. Eldridge (ed.), *Taming Megalopolis*, Volume 1: *What Is and What Could Be*, Volume 2: *How To Manage an Urbanized World* (New York: Frederick A. Praeger, 1967); B. J. Frieden and R. Morris (eds.), *Urban Planning and Social Policy* (New York: Basic Books, 1968); and W. G. Bennis, K. D. Benne, and R. Chin (eds.), *The Planning of Change: Readings in the Applied Behavioral Sciences,* second edition (New York: Holt, Rinehart and Winston, 1969).

12. E. C. Banfield (ed.), *Urban Government: A Reader in Administration and Politics,* revised edition (New York: Free Press, 1969); R. T. Daland (ed.), *Comparative Urban Research: The Administration and Politics of Cities* (Beverly Hills, Cal. Sage Publications, 1969); and H. R. Mahood and E. L. Angus, *Urban Politics and Problems* (New York: Scribners, 1969).

Organization Flow Chart

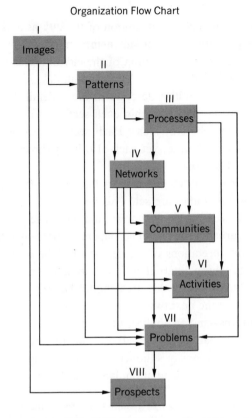

empirical models which have been formulated to generalize these patterns. The processes or determinants summarized in Section III include the operation of the economic real estate market, particularly competition among social and political groups, the influence of public policy, and the behavior of urban residents. The order of these two sections might have been reversed. However, this arrangement follows the methodological approach of most geographic research in attempting to sift theoretical insights from an array of empirical observations.

The specialized aspects of the spatial structure of the city, the networks of interaction, residential areas, and activities, comprise the following three sections. Each of these was described in part at least in Section II. First, Section IV discusses the networks of transportation, communication and linkages which tie the structure of the urban area together as a system. Examples are the links between home and work, the elements of travel behavior and the transportation system, manufacturing linkages and agglomeration, and information flows. Filling in the cells created by these networks, particularly by the transportation system, Section V examines the communities and households that comprise the residential fabric of the city. Specific reference is made to the development of urban social geography, the measurement of different social areas and community types in the city, the evolution of ghettoes and ethnic communities, the housing stock, population densities, and changes in residential location. Section VI identifies the city's major activity subsystems, their spatial structure and their constituent parts. These activities are linked together by the networks of interaction in the city, and they are interrelated in both character and location with the city's communities. These activities support the residential population and provide centers for employment, services, leisure, and other preoccupations. Among the subsystems examined are the core area or central business district as the dominant organizing node of the metropolis, the skeleton geography of retail and service business, industrial patterns, political systems, and public facilities. Finally, attempts to generalize and forecast growth in the spatial patterns of these activities are illustrated in the last paper on urban systems models. Clearly the papers in this section overlap with those in previous sections in the same way that the subsystems they describe overlap.

The last two sections shift the discussion to re-emphasize urban spatial and environmental problems, and planning of the future city. Inclusion of these themes is a slight departure from the more traditional organization of volumes such as this one. It is in fact a direct plea for social relevancy in urban geographic research. The problems represented in Section VII are specifically those which follow as consequences of themes in preceding sections. The concluding section takes a brief look at the prospects for cities of the future, including the social, analytical, and policy difficulties involved in attaining these futures. No attempt is made to summarize the innumerable views or designs of future cities and utopias that have been put forward, nor even to be representative of these views. Rather, the purpose is to encourage an awareness and understanding of the spatial and environmental questions that must be considered before one approaches the study and design of future cities.

Several concluding remarks on the papers are appropriate. First, the broad frame of reference employed means that proportionally fewer contributions are drawn from the geographic literature. Papers were selected from diverse sources including the popular press, to vary the style and current of discussion, and from sources not generally available. Second, because of the large number of themes to be represented only portions or extracts of most papers could be included. Third, an extensive bibliography is given by the reference materials in each of the papers and in the prefatory remarks beginning each section. The latter references are selective, pointing both to major contributions which might not otherwise receive sufficient emphasis, and to papers published more recently than those included here. Fourth, the tenor of the articles selected shows a marked diversity in level of difficulty. Most papers are introductory, but some are not. Those involving statistical techniques are obvious examples which extend beyond the introductory level. Yet it is felt that even in these few cases (the Brigham and Newling papers, for example) the underlying arguments can be appreciated without a grasp of the details of each technique.

This diversity is to be expected. Given the broadening of interests in urban research, the desire to sample from a wide range of social science disciplines, and the increasing improvement of analytical capabilities noted above, it simply reflects the state of the art. A desirable state at that. In those areas of urban research where the type of analysis is particularly advanced, an attempt is made to select articles which summarize the approaches involved or set out a conceptual framework, rather than those that describe more elaborate empirical analyses. The preparatory remarks beginning each chapter should assist the reader in anticipating and adapting to this diversity. These comments are meant to be more than mere descriptions of the papers. They are designed to define a context in which to view the materials that follow, to pose questions for interpretation and research, and to suggest challenges for contemporary planning and social values.

Classroom Use

This collection of readings is intended to be used both as a general reference volume and as a textbook. It would serve well as a text in introductory courses in urban studies, urban geography, urban sociology, planning, and in interdisciplinary programs in the social and environmental sciences. Instructors may find it useful to organize their courses around the broad section headings of the book, as the author himself has done, or they might use these headings as an outline complementary to their own in order to stimulate class discussion on basic approaches to, and underlying principles of, the internal structure of cities. In graduate and more specialized courses, it might serve as a review text and a reference for supplementary reading. The content of the book is also intended to provide considerable freedom and to shift substantial responsibility in the design of courses to the individual instructor. The fact that most papers included here tend to be of a more general nature, rather than empirical and place-specific, leaves to the instructor the task of providing in-depth materials on his own particular region or individual city. Past experience finds that one volume cannot do both, and that students react most positively to examples drawn from the environment in which they live and are most familiar.

I

IMAGES: Defining the Urban Realm

The city has different meanings to different people.[1] For example, to the inner-city slum-dweller the city is perceived as a spatially restricted and oppressive force on his existence, its areal extent limited by his lack of information and by his social and geographical immobility. To the ex-urban automobile commuter the city is an expressway system leading to an office or factory, a city that he samples, often reluctantly, during brief periods away from his semi-rural retreat. To the geography teacher, on the other hand, the city may be conceived as a living textbook and an environmental classroom; to the public-works engineer it is a system of underground utilities; to the suburban housewife it may be an alluring sea of shopping alternatives. These define the city, its structure, and problems in a subjective or perceived manner. But the city may also be viewed in objective terms. It has physical location, geographical extent, internal differentiation, and environmental character. This section summarizes various definitions or images of the city as a spatial and environmental unit for study purposes.

To define the city and to understand its problems necessitate that we view the city in social and political context. The introductory essay by Raymond Vernon is a perceptive review and critique of commonly held

1. See Stephen Carr, "The City of the Mind," in W. Ewald, Jr. (ed.), *Environment for Man* (Bloomington: Indiana University Press, 1967), pp. 197-231; E. W. Bacon, "The City Image," in E. Green, J. R. Lowe, and K. Walker (eds.), *Man and the Modern City* (Pittsburgh: University of Pittsburgh Press, 1963), pp. 25-32; Derek Jonge, "Images of Urban Areas," *Journal of the American Institute of Planners,* XXVIII (November 1962), pp. 266-76; Kevin Lynch, *The Image of the City* (Cambridge, Mass.: The M.I.T. Press, 1960); and S. Carr and D. Schissler, "The City as a Trip: Perceptual Selection and Memory in View from the Road," *Environment and Behavior,* Vol. 1, No. 1 (June 1969), pp. 7-36.

images of the nature and complexity of urban problems. To what extent do these views reflect the particular nature of our democratic system? What are the critical problems in the form and structure of our cities and in the living environments they provide? What is the origin and support of planning directed at these problems? Why have we been unable to deal with urban problems effectively?

Using zoning ordinances and the problem of urban renewal as examples, Vernon points out that the confusion which frequently surrounds the definition of problems and priorities is an obvious handicap in identifying solutions. Yet, is there not a strong degree of subjectivity in the identification of urban problems? Our urban political system has set its own priorities on urban problems. Another implication of Vernon's arguments is that public policies must be based on a thorough understanding of the processes affecting urban form in order to encourage change in the most effective manner.

With Vernon's overview as an introduction, we must then define the contemporary metropolis. The following papers offer different views of the city. What does the word "city" mean in our culture? How do urban residents perceive the environments in which they live? What is meant by the concept of a metropolitan area, and what criteria are employed to measure its areal extent? Is it possible to extend current census definitions to reflect the ever-expanding area utilized by contemporary urban residents? What signals are provided by changes in the nature of urban life styles, and what do these mean for future cities?

The images people have of their cities influence the questions that are raised about today's urban milieu. Anselm Strauss reviews examples of specific images held about American cities, their geography, their problems, and their ultimate destiny.[2] Following on the "problem" theme established by Vernon, Strauss begins by suggesting that the changing imagery of cities influences the way they develop by altering the definitions of problems. What are the implications of the suburbanization image for the vitality of central cities in general and for the downtown area in particular? Are we witnessing the development of new images of city and suburb, and of community and neighborhood? Are we passing through a revolution which is shattering our spatially based views of contemporary metropolitan life? If so, how then do we define the city?

Images of the "city" generally seem more diverse if one examines a broader spectrum of our cultural literature. One impression of this diversity may be conveyed most succinctly by a sample of quotations collected by Harold Mayer. By ranging from the writings of William Shakespeare to

2. Anselm L. Strauss (ed.), *The American City: A Sourcebook of Urban Imagery* (Chicago: Aldine Publishing Company, 1968).

Lewis Mumford it provides one index of the images that have influenced our thinking on cities. It also draws on portions of contemporary literature which otherwise might not be represented in this volume. One theme that permeates these definitions, and the reader is left to establish his own specific interpretations, is that the city is the home of man and the vehicle of civilization. In one author's terms, the city is what we mean by civilization.

Other attempts to conceptualize the city have been made in terms of analogous systems found in the physical or life sciences.[3] In the next essay, sociologist Leo Schnore discusses the frequently cited analogy between cities and organisms. In part, the organismic image arose because of the complexity of system interrelationships which seemed typical of both. For example, the nervous system is compared to the city's communication and transportation networks, and the individual human being in society shares a similar function with the cell in an organism. But the analogy is somewhat limited and is not currently in prominence among urban sociologists and geographers. Schnore puts forward the underlying concepts in a rather light vein, as a basis for discussion and as a means of reviewing various sociological approaches to the study of the city.

One of the principal limitations of the analogy with organisms is that it ignores life styles. Among the pioneer works in the field noted by Schnore, and still a source of considerable debate as Strauss's paper indicates, is Louis Wirth's "Urbanism as a Way of Life."[4] Wirth developed a definition of the city as a dense and permanent concentration of socially heterogeneous individuals. These characteristics led to an urban society significantly different in character from suburban society. Wirth attempted to identify fundamental differences in social and demographic characteristics between inner city and suburban life-styles and attitudes. Schnore's conclusion is that we do not sufficiently understand different concepts of ways of life for use as a conceptual framework for urban studies. Yet Wirth's ideas should encourage greater interest in urban life-styles and images, and thus in what constitutes the city.

3. For example, Mort and Eleanor Karp, "Who Ever Said the City Was a Tree," *Landscape,* 17 (Autumn 1967), pp. 29-33.
4. Louis Wirth, "Urbanism as a Way of Life," *American Journal of Sociology,* Vol. 44 (July 1938), pp. 1-24. This article has been reprinted in numerous volumes including Paul Hatt and Albert J. Reiss, Jr. (eds.), *Cities and Society* (Glencoe, Ill.: The Free Press, 1957), pp. 47-64. One of the most thorough reviews and evaluations of Wirth's paper is Herbert J. Gans, "Urbanism and Suburbanism as Ways of Life: A Re-Evaluation of Definitions" in Albert Rose (ed.), *Human Behavior and Social Processes* (Boston: Houghton Mifflin, 1962), pp. 625-48; and in A. B. Callow, Jr. (ed.), *American Urban History* (New York: Oxford University Press, 1968), pp. 504-18. A more recent discussion is Stanley S. Guterman, "In Defense of Wirth's 'Urbanism as a Way of Life,'" *American Journal of Sociology,* 74 (March 1969), pp. 92-99.

Preceding papers have been concerned primarily, although not exclusively, with broad images of urban patterns. What differences exist in the way individuals react to the city? In what ways do these images affect their behavior? How do we study such images? These are important questions. We have previously noted the increasing interest in people's images of and attitudes toward the city. A paper by Kevin Lynch in the final section of this book illustrates the importance of such research in formulating policies for planning future cities.

As one specific example, Charles Tilly examines how people visualize cities. He suggests that people behave, interact, and react differently to the urban environment in terms of how they perceive that environment.[5] Individuals tend to live within their own personal urban environments which represent images created by their own experience and awareness of the city. He has attempted to measure how people visualize their cities by asking his own children to display their information and images of the city in maps. Each map, of course, will differ according to such characteristics as the individual's age, education, awareness, and interest in his surroundings. Clearly, there are as many images as there are residents, yet there may be crucial identities and common attitudes underlying these images which must be discovered.[6]

As a basis for geographical study our definitions must, in most instances, be susceptible to direct measurement. The most common definition of the urban area is reflected in the census concept of the metropolitan area. There are, of course, other definitions for other urban areas, such as a minimum threshold population to differentiate town from city, and village from town. Political or legislative definitions are also relevant in particular approaches to urban research, such as those involving studies of political behavior. Moreover, within the body of census definitions other urban forms are recognized: the built-up or urbanized area definition, and the central city/central county distinction. In this volume, however, the particular area of interest in studying the internal structure of the city is, in most instances, defined according to the metropolitan concept. In fact, one definition of metropolitan might be that geographic area which displays considerable regularity in its internal structure. Such regularity emerges only in cities of large size and complexity. The paper by P. G. Goheen represents the work of a group of researchers in the Center for Urban

5. For a review see Elizabeth M. Eddy (ed.), *Urban Anthropology: Research Perspectives and Strategies,* (Athens: University of Georgia Press, 1968).
6. The literature on human responses to their physical urban environment is growing. One such paper by William Michelson is reproduced in Section VIII. Another is Peter G. Flachsbart, "Urban Territorial Behavior," *Journal of the American Institute of Planners,* XXXV (November 1969), pp. 412-16.

Studies at the University of Chicago. They undertook a thorough and critical review of the underlying concepts and criteria employed in the definition of metropolitan areas by the U.S. Bureau of the Census in 1960 as part of the preliminary planning for the 1970 census.[7]

The metropolitan area concept defines both an economic and a spatial city. That is, it delimits a geographic area which is economically integrated. The area is tied inwardly to the core area or central business district through commuting to work, and outwardly in terms of the distribution of services and the circulation of information. It is a spatial city in the sense that each metropolitan criterion has a spatial expression. For example, it reflects a spatial continuity of population densities higher than the average level which might be anticipated in uniformly rural areas. The city extends as far outward as densities remain above these rural levels and until commuting into the core area becomes insignificant in the economy of the local area. In the U.S. Census definitions, the metropolitan area is created by combining those counties which are integrated in terms of commuting with the central city and the county in which it lies. Many of the specific criteria are arbitrary, and as cities and society become more synonymous, the use of strict spatial and physical limits in defining metropolitan areas is increasingly brought into question. Numerous arguments and criticisms of both current and proposed procedures are summarized in Goheen's paper, and a set of alternative concepts and proposals is advanced.

Among the alternate concepts is the notion of the geographic city as an urban field. The urban field, which Friedmann and Miller introduced or reintroduced as some would suggest, is defined to reflect the behavioral space of urban residents.[8] It is a much broader zone than that defined in the metropolitan concept, and it is not necessarily coincident with the tributary area or hinterland. It encompasses the entire area utilized by urban residents for diverse activities such as weekend outings and even less frequent recreational travel. It is, in fact, a new kind of city, a product of this era of increasing incomes, more leisure time, wider communities of interest, and greater mobility. Its definition is not dependent on the physi-

7. The definitions of a metropolitan area employed in the Canadian Census parallels those used in the United States in most regards. See Leroy Stone, *Urban Development in Canada* (Ottawa: Dominion Bureau of Statistics, 1967); J. W. Simmons and R. Simmons, *Urban Canada* (Toronto: Copp Clark, 1969); and N. H. Lithwick and G. Paquet, *Urban Studies: A Canadian Perspective* (Toronto: Methuen, 1968).
8. J. Friedmann and J. Miller, "The Urban Field," *Journal of the American Institute of Planners,* Vol. XXXI (November 1965), pp. 312-20. For an earlier use of the term the reader is encouraged to read, and to compare the concepts as used in A. E. Smailes, *The Geography of Towns* (London: Hutchinson University Library, 1953); and "The Analysis and Delimitation of Urban Fields," *Geography,* Vol. 32 (1947), pp. 151-61.

cal expression of urban life in terms of urban land-uses, population densities, or commuting patterns. In the United States, for example, these areas may extend as much as 100 miles in all directions beyond the outer limits of the built-up or developed urban area. Combined, the urban fields of U.S. cities encompass most of the continental U.S. east of the Rocky Mountains. The entire country is then partitioned into sets of metropolitan fields and non-metropolitan peripheries. Concepts such as the urban field are obviously more diffuse than that of the census metropolitan area, and thus much more difficult to measure. Yet in light of the increasingly diffuse patterns of urban activities and households, such concepts may be the most appropriate for further study.

These trends suggest that identifying explicit differences between rural and urban landscapes is now more difficult. But are these differences less important? Robin Pryor summarizes the relevant literature and the variety of definitions pertaining to the frequently cited transitional area in which rural uses are gradually replaced by those defined as urban. In political systems with more rigid planning controls, such as the United Kingdom, defining this area is a less difficult problem than in North America as physical development of the urban area tends to end more abruptly. The fringe area surrounding most North American cities, however, is usually typified by an extensive area of discontinuous, sprawling, unplanned, and generally unattractive urban growth. In any case, there is certainly less agreement about the extent of the urban fringe when it is measured in terms of non-physical influences such as changes in the life style of rural inhabitants. How far beyond the built-up fringes of the metropolitan area does the influence of the metropolis extend? As illustrated by Pryor's summary, land use types rather than social or behavioral characteristics usually serve as the means of identifying limits on the fringe area.

Are our traditional definitions and images of cities outdated? Are we entering a post-city era precisely at the time when the world is only beginning to study the city seriously? Are there not at least two different sets of definitions of the city: the most common one identifiable spatially; the other referring to that part of society's characteristics in general which find their origin or highest expression in the city? Is the importance of space and territory in our society declining? Or is it that space and environment are simply assuming different roles? These are questions which Strauss has already raised and that Melvin Webber picks up again in the concluding section on urban futures. Intervening sections marshal some of the evidence necessary to make such judgments.

RAYMOND VERNON

The Myth and Reality of Our Urban Problems

If a major object of our existence were to create great cities of beauty and grace, there would be something to be said in favor of dictatorship. As a rule, the great cities of the past have been the cities of the powerful city-states in which a dominant king or governing body had the power and the will to impose its land-use strictures upon an obedient populace. Weak or divided local governments, responsive to the push and pressure of the heterogeneous interest groups which make up a city, have rarely managed to intervene enough to prevent the unpalatable kind of growth which typifies our larger American urban areas.

Up to a few decades ago, there was no serious effort by any American city to take a hand in shaping its development. Such efforts in the United States date back to the year 1916 when New York City put America's first comprehensive zoning law on its statute books. By that time, an elite group of New Yorkers could already see the outlines of some of their emerging problems. Land in downtown New York was being used incongruously and wastefully. Fish markets and ancient warehouses stood side by side with temples of finance and giant office buildings. Tiny streets, built for another age, were being choked with traffic and darkened by towering skyscrapers.

The problem was not solely that of downtown land use, however. Real estate taxes were growing, seemingly without a limit. Besides, the difficulties of daily ingress to the shops and offices of the central business district were now beginning to appear as more and more citizens moved off Manhattan Island into the distant reaches of Brooklyn, the Bronx, and New Jersey. And in the other great cities of the country, similar developments were also beginning to take visible shape.

Something had to be done to arrest the deterioration of the community. The closest approximation to the peremptory powers of the ancient kings was land-use planning, planning achieved through the use of zoning ordinances. So the first pioneering steps were taken.

It should not go unnoticed that the strongest support came from a part of the community which the casual observer might have considered least ready for it—

From Raymond Vernon, **The Myth and Reality of Our Urban Problems,** Cambridge, Mass.: Harvard University Press. Copyright © 1962, 1966 by the President and Fellows of Harvard College. Reprinted by permission of the publishers.

the merchants, the financiers, and the daily press, whose ideology seemed almost un-qualifiedly committed to the proposition that the interference of government in the economic affairs of men was unwise and unproductive. The reasons for which these groups were the first to rise in support of so drastic a use of the police power, how-ever, will already be clear to my readers. These groups more than any others—partly because of sentiment, partly because of offended values, partly because of self-in-terest—had the strongest stakes in chang-ing the course of the urban areas' develop-ment pattern.

The wisdom of some kind of land-use planning, however, was also apparent to many groups outside the central business district. Many communities were begin-ning to appreciate that when abattoirs sat alongside high-priced houses, neither ben-efited from the contact. When an industrial area blocked access to a residential neigh-borhood, both were hurt by the propin-quity. When enclaves of land were spoiled by nearby uses, and remained unused, neglected, and overlaid with weeds and trash, no one gained from the loss of pre-cious space. Community after community, therefore, acquired the legal power to reg-ulate the use of land, until today most of our urban areas are blanketed by a patch-quilt of land-use regulations.

But there was slippage, considerable slippage, between the abstract concepts that justified land-use planning and the actual practice of the art. In the older sprawling cities of America, the zoning tool had come too late to have much effect on the style and pattern of urban life. Most of the land of the downtown areas was already covered with structures whose uses were largely fixed until the time when there would be some economic reason for razing the buildings and beginning all over again. And when the opportunity arose to tear down some antique hulk and to use the land once more, the new use proposed by the eager redeveloper, as often as not,

was inconsistent with the zoning plan. In these circumstances, what zoning board could hold out for very long against the pressure and importuning of the redevel-oper? What, after all, was the board pro-posing instead—more decay, more delay? Was it against progress? Surely, some ac-commodation, some flexibility was pos-sible.

Even when the land was not already encumbered by structures, many features of the older cities already were fixed, sub-stantially influencing how the rest would develop. For one thing, the ossified street grid itself was in place, fixing some of the dimensions of homes and industrial sites. For another, the railroad yards, the stock-yards, the power plants, and the garbage dumps had established the general charac-ter of many half-occupied outlying neigh-borhoods. Then, too, there were the poli-cies of the financial institutions which were expected to provide the mortgage money for any proposed new structures. One could hardly expect them to finance a $20,000 home in a $10,000 neighbor-hood; to underwrite the long-term collec-tion of little parcels over a lengthy period of time; to gamble on the possibility that the city fathers might close an old street or open a new one in order to make some venture possible. For large areas of the city, the die was cast; the city was bound to be more of what it already was.

To the extent that land-use planning has much effect, therefore, it has been in open unencumbered territory where, for one reason or another, a determined and united citizenry has sought to impose some clear pattern of use upon the land. The most conspicuous kind of case in which the requisite openness and the requisite determination came together was in the exclusive suburban communities of the very rich.

You will recall my having observed that the growth of the urban areas had an un-kindly effect upon the well-to-do. Their suburban communities had been invaded, their sense of exclusiveness and privacy destroyed by the irrepressible spread of middle-income subdivisions. By the 1920's, however, some exclusive communities were beginning to discover that they had the legal means for fighting back; zoning ordinances, vigorously and scrupulously applied, could arrest or divert the flow. Here and there, one began to encounter such ordinances—prohibitions against structures of less than such-and-such value, prohibitions against lots of less than such-and-such size. Applied in timely fashion, these restrictions managed to preserve the sparse and splendid land-use pattern of a number of outstanding suburban communities.

Later on, following the lead of the pace-setters, various middle-income communities in the suburbs began to play at the same game. In their case, however, the strategy of land use had to be a little different. Unlike the well-to-do, the middle-income group had no desire to exclude members from their communities who might be able to share the mounting tax burdens. Accordingly, they were prepared to admit some industrial plants in their midst, on the assumption that these could help finance the new schools and streets of the growing area. True, the plants could only be those of a certain type—quiet, well-mannered, giving off the aura of a college campus rather than an industrial nexus. But if they met the specifications, they were more than welcome.

Where the middle-income communities could exercise greatest freedom of action, however, was in seeing to it that the poor would be excluded from their precincts. Shacktowns, of course, were already barred; the health and fire ordinances of most towns were sufficient to deal with these. But then there was always the risk that some enterprising builder might divide a site into handkerchief-sized lots, install the basic sanitary facilities, use concrete slabs or other utilitarian materials as his medium of construction, and provide the unaesthetic minimum of decent housing for the upper stratum of the poor. This was a possibility obviously to be avoided, not only for social reasons, but for fiscal reasons as well. Accordingly, the zoning laws and building ordinances were quickly developed to block off the possibility.

Most communities, too, whether middle- or upper-income in their style, have gradually become aware of another clear and present danger—the danger that the older and more commodious structures in their midst, too obsolete to be used much longer by the income group for which they were first designed, may be divided and subdivided into spaces for the poor. At this stage in a community's development, the monolithic façade of community interest is cracked, broken by the internal conflict between the holders of the new homes and the sellers of the old. This development will not easily be prevented, therefore. Here and there, communities will be invaded by the poor.

Once more, the rich will be pushed outward, even further from their jobs and interests in the central city. Once more, the middle-income group will move on, placidly pulling their job market with them. Once more, the poor will spread out, in the expanded leavings of their financial betters.

There are three or four aspects of the pattern which need concern us: whether we are poor or rich, city-oriented or otherwise. The first point to be made, of course, is that land-use planning in any comprehensive sense really does not exist in our larger urban areas. What does exist is a complex game of chess among localities, each attempting to palm off the undesired applicants for space upon their neighboring communities. This is warfare, not planning. Those who are "for" local planning in any community are dubbed altruistic and "good"; those against are "bad." The purposes of those who are against planning may be no less self-centered than the purposes of those who are for; but neither position must be confused with altruism or with the interests of the urban area as a whole.

The kind of land-use planning that is needed for the major urban areas of America is planning which takes cognizance of the total land-use needs of the area. The localities will have to turn in their weapons of war to some authority whose mandate is broader than their own and will have to be prepared to accept the decisions which issue from that higher level. The authority may be made up of local representatives; it may be something less than a court of last resort. But until such an authority exists in some effective form, we shall have to accept the fact that the planning which exists in our urban areas is incapable of doing much to improve the area as an economic or social unit.

We seem so far from having achieved the necessary organization for effective urban planning that it may appear gratuitous to speak about the policies and techniques of a group charged with that objective. So I shall confine myself to no more than a few footnotes on the subject. One of the first objectives of a group of this kind must be that of defining and preserving the land areas which will be needed for public use in time to prevent their being completely pre-empted by private uses. This should not be confused with a plea on my part for more parks and more green belts. I have little knowledge and few convictions on the question of whether the public needs or would use more open space for recreation. It is a much more simple point that I am making. Although each locality concerns itself with land for its immediate public purposes, no level of government really worries about the preservation of land for more general public use, whatever that use may be. The localities usually try to push common land-use needs off their shoulders onto the shoulders of others. "Everyone wants the water, but no one wants the reservoir," to quote a waggish phrase which is particularly apt. . . . Although the localities are too close to the problem, the state government is usually too far away. Few states can be made to concern themselves very much with the detailed land-use needs of their urban areas. So we are back to a familiar problem in government structure, that of creating a body of authority which is bigger than a breadbox but smaller than an elephant—more extensive in its scope than the localities but less extensive than the state.

One more point of general applicability: events of the past few decades, as I read them, are proving that the zoning powers, which are usually reserved to the city or to the suburban community, are simply not enough to insure the use or reuse of land according to any given land-use pattern on which general agreement had previously been reached. The pressures upon a zoning board applied by a private investor who is ready and eager to move ahead on some plan of redevelopment are so great as almost to be irresistible.

This is a problem, of course, which everyone concerned with land-use planning appreciates very well. As a consequence, an old concept is being brushed off and re-examined with considerable interest for its possible application to the current planning problem. This is the notion that the authorities which are responsible for planning the use of land should have the power not only to zone land, but also to buy various kinds of property rights short of outright ownership. This property right could be an easement for limited public purposes; it could be a development right which excluded certain private uses from the land; or any one of half a dozen other forms of interest. In any case, the sacred institution of property —one of the most powerful of symbols among the *lares* and *penates* of our current civilization—could be turned to the end of insuring the effective use of a potentially scarce resource, the land.

Those who have been concerned with transforming our urban areas have not confined their efforts to the use of such feeble tools as zoning and land-use planning. There have been bolder and more spectacular efforts—the rebuilding of downtown New Haven, the rebirth of Pittsburgh's Golden Triangle, the execution of New York's Lincoln Center, and so on. These great schemes of bold and aggressive doers have added hope and cheer to those of us who cherish the vitality of the cities.

In surveying these works, however, there are two debts we must discharge. We have an obligation to the men who conceived and executed these latter-day Herculean labors to express our admiration for their efforts. At the same time, we owe it to ourselves to appraise these results in cold and dispassionate terms, to determine how relevant they may be to the total problem of urban renewal.

To gain this perspective, the best vantage point is a helicopter. Hover motionless over America's major cities and you will shortly be impressed by two facts: As a rule, only minute portions of the older areas of our cities have so far been subjected to rebuilding and renewal in the twentieth century. In New York City, for instance—a city whose activities in this field have been more extensive than those of any other in the nation—all the publicly supported renewal projects undertaken over the past quarter century do not cover as much as three square miles of city surface. Second, the areas of the city which have been the subject of the most intensive renewal activity tend generally to be in or very near the city's central business district. Beyond the comparatively tiny compact central business districts of our giant urban areas, the gray, monotonous jumble of obsolete structures extends almost uninterruptedly in all directions.

The tiny land coverage of the publicly supported urban renewal programs certainly does not result from a lack of crying need. By almost anyone's aesthetic or structural standards, literally hundreds of square miles in the urban areas of America should long ago have been torn down. Yet there have been periods of time when uncommitted federal funds have gone begging for lack of acceptable projects.

Why should acceptable projects have been so hard to find? There are a number of reasons. First of all, one has to understand that an urban renewal project is usually a partnership between governmental and private interests; the government procures the site, using its powers of condemnation as necessary, and turns the site over to private redevelopers at a substantial discount from the acquisition price. The private redeveloper, therefore, must see a possibility for profit; he must see an opportunity to rebuild on the site and to find renters or buyers for the new properties.

At this point, our harassed redeveloper is between the devil and the deep blue sea. Shall he plan to build a little patch of new construction—a small oasis in a sea of decaying structures? If so, although his costs and commitments may be small, his chances of finding renters for his redeveloped properties will be small as well. For who among those capable of paying the $40 to $50 per room for rent would want to wade through the filth and insecurity of the rundown, obsolete neighborhood in order to reach his concrete-and-brick oasis in the city?

Alternatively, then, should our redeveloper cut a wide swath through the city, with a giant redevelopment covering half a square mile or so? But the alternative is just as unprepossessing as the first. It demands the closing of streets, the rerouting of traffic, the reorganization of utilities. It entails staggering financial commitments. And it requires a judgment of market demand for a supply of housing so large as to frighten off the hardiest developer and the most interpid financier. In a word, the problem seems utterly impossible. Almost impossible, anyway. For there is one place in the built-up portions of the old cities where, with energy and imagination, there is just a chance that a good-sized project may be carried off—that place is in or near the central business district.

The reasons for which the central business district should be attractive for redevelopment when the rest of the city usually offers so little attraction are all implicit in what I have said earlier. First, the central business district, unlike the rest of the older portions of the obsolescent cities of America, continues to harbor some elements of vitality and growth. The jobs which demand face-to-face communication in America continue to increase as more of our economic activity is concentrated in financial institutions, central offices, law offices, and the like. Not all cities share in this growth, but many do. As a consequence, a number of large central business districts in America promise to register an increase in jobs. Even those that do not show an absolute increase may experience some upgrading in the jobs they harbor. More executives are likely to appear at the center even if the number of clerks, dishwashers, goods handlers, and factory hands declines. This is one of the forces which explains why it is possible for Pittsburgh's Golden Triangle and Philadelphia's Penn Center to rise out of the ashes and find a basis for survival.

The appearance of a larger number of elite jobs at the center, coupled with the growing remoteness of the exclusive communities and golf courses, stimulates the demand for luxury housing close by the central business district. The amounts involved are not very great, measured in terms of the size of the city as a whole. But the demand is nicely concentrated in a tiny area—in or near the central business district, preferably with a pleasant prospect of river or harbor. When all the elements of demands and subsidy are put together, they sometimes provide the basis for tearing down the structures in the thinned-out slums of the ancient city and building imposing new structures on the site.

There may be another major reason, however, why the central business district tends to capture the lion's share of urban redevelopment projects. If one could plumb the minds of the leaders of any large urban community and look upon the urban area as they see it, I am confident of the image that would emerge. Instead of seeing the central business district as an area containing one tenth the city's land and one twentieth its resident population, they would see the central business district as dominating the image. This is the target of the elite's daily commuting trips. It is the area which contains the city hall, the museums, the theater, the night clubs, and the apartments of friends and associates. It is the area in which the history and the tradition of the city are centered. In short, it is the area that contains almost all that matters in the city for most of its civic leadership.

ANSELM L. STRAUSS

The Latest in Urban Imagery

As the United States progressed from an agricultural nation to a markedly urbanized one, each step of the way was paralleled by Americans' attempts to make sense of what was happening. This ideological accompaniment to the objective facts of national urbanization was shot through, during the nineteenth century, with contrasts drawn between urban and rural styles of life. These contrasts still persist in muted forms.

However, the imagined polarity between country and city or town and city no longer dominates the American scene. It was succeeded some decades ago by a presumed polarity of city and suburb—a polarity which followed in the wake of a vastly increased suburbanization and the flight of great numbers of city dwellers to the suburbs in search of fresh air, safe and quiet streets, genuine communal life, better standards of domestic living, financial profit, and—as sociologists have so often stressed—more prestigeful locales in which to live. But the imagined polarity of suburb and city is already breaking down, and new imagery is beginning to take its place. This imagery suggests some of the kinds of questions that Americans are raising about the destinies of their metropolitan areas. It also points to the particular ways in which Americans are attempting to make sense out of the often puzzling facts of today's urban milieu.

What is going to be the fate of American cities? The envisioned alternatives, in answer to this momentous question, range from the continued dominance of cities to their actual disappearance. The *New York Times,* perhaps only for purposes of provocation, recently raised the alternatives in this way:

One hundred million Americans are now living in metropolitan areas, including their central cities.

Will the new pattern of settlement result in the eventual dwindling of great cities like New York, Chicago and San Francisco? Will they be just islands of national business headquarters, financial clearing houses and other specialized functions within great flat seas in which the other activities of our national life will mingle?

Or will our historic cities sparkle brighter by contrast with the sprawling urbanized regions which they will serve as centers of culture as well as commerce?

Far from dominating the American scene today, the big cities are on the defensive, at least in some ways. Our magazines are full of stories about cities fighting to make a "comeback" and cities are combating "The threat of strangulation by the suburbs." One emerging concept of the fate and function of the metropolis is that it can serve as "the core" of the entire metropolitan area. By "the core," urban planners and civic propagandists may mean either centers of business or cultural functions, or both. For instance, the mayor of Detroit, like many other civic leaders, advocates strengthening downtown districts so that they can serve as strong magnets to attract people from distant suburbs, either for daily visits or for permanent residence. Hence, he advocated building expressways to bring suburbanite shoppers into the downtown area: "If we don't make it possible for them to come back, they will build large shopping areas in the outlying communities and we will lose that business." To some other metropolitan champions, "the new metropolis" connotes somewhat less hardheaded emphasis upon business and more upon cultural and political leadership of cities.

New concepts are also emerging of who shall—or should—live in the central city. Here, for instance, is the view of William Zeckendorf, probably the most influential of American urban redevelopers:

There is a swing back to the cities of the highest-grade type of tenant. He is generally aged 45 and upward. He has raised his children; he has reached the peak of his earning power; his house is now superfluous in size; he is tired of commuting.

That man, if you provide him with appropriate living conditions in the central areas of the cities, can be reattracted on a scale never dreamed of before to a way of life that is impossible to obtain in the suburbs.

He adds, and here we may see how new is the concept involved, that: "For each 10 people that the city loses to the suburbs, it can get 10 times their collective buying power in people who return." In the hands of people like Zeckendorf, the concept of "redevelopment" has now come to mean a combination of things: partly the replacement of slums with upper-income housing; partly the renovation of "downtown U.S.A." But other planners and influential citizens urge—on moral as well as on economic grounds—that the city ought not to be given over only to the wealthier residents; and in fact, others keep pointing to the steady abandonment of the large cities to Negroes, who are thus effectively segregated within the greater urban area.

While cities are "fighting back" against suburbs, the transformation of suburban areas is being accompanied by a reinterpretation of life as it is lived there. In place of a relatively undifferentiated "suburb"— a symbolic area contrasting with an equally symbolic city—a differentiated set of popular concepts is appearing. As those suburbs near the city's actual boundaries become increasingly crowded, virtually parts of the city, the "better class" of residents who live further out refer disdainfully to those older suburbs. They make subtle distinctions among the relative qualities of various communities—knowledge essential when unwanted ethnic groups or Negroes may tomorrow set up residence in certain of those locales. Especially since the enormous extension of the suburban rings all the way into the next states, it was inevitable that someone would make a distinction between suburbs and suburbs-beyond-the-suburbs. Spectorsky's "exurbia" and "suburbia" has met this need. The sociologists themselves, spurred on by William H. Whyte's discovery of a certain kind of suburb, chock-full of youthful transients, are beginning to wonder about different kinds of suburban styles.

In past decades, a momentous aspect of the suburban dream was the wish to reinstate, or establish, the emotionally satisfying bonds of community and neighborhood. For more civic-minded souls, a suburban community also represented a reasonably good way to enter into the political process; something that was much more difficult to effect within the crowded city wards. Both aspirations have attracted much acid comment in recent decades. The imagery of a truer political democracy has not always been easy to put into practice, especially as the suburbs have grown larger or have become the locus of clashes between uncompromising social classes. As for the bonds of community and neighborhood, two kinds of criticism have been directed against these. One is uttered by suburbanites who expected the friendliness and democracy of an ideal small town, but who were bitterly disappointed by the realities of suburban living. They accuse the suburb of false friendliness, of mock neighborliness; they claim that it has not a democratic atmosphere at all, that it is ridden with caste and snobbery. Another kind of criticism is leveled by both suburbanites and outsiders against the achievement of too much "community." It is said that there is not real privacy in most suburbs and that so deadening is the round of sociability that little time can remain for genuine leisure. While most critics are willing to admit that friendship and communal ties are to be valued, they deride the standardization of suburban communities and their all too visible styles of life (the barbecue suppers, the PTAs, the suburban clothing, the commuting). Since World War II, criticism has continued to mount about the suburban way of life. The new kinds of suburbs are too homogenous in population, too child-dominated, too domestically oriented, too little concerned with intellectual or cultural pursuits—or so they seem to the critics.

When conceived in such terms, suburbanization represents to inveterate lovers of the city a genuine threat to urban values —a threat even to the nation. In place of the earlier derision of the suburb as an uncomfortable or inconvenient place to live, and added to the fear of the suburb as a threat to true democracy (because it enhances class distinctions), we now observe an increasing concern over the continued exodus to suburbs. If it is true that suburban life is inimical to much that has made the city exciting, freeing, and innovative, then—it is felt—there is cause for alarm. Despite the counter argument that the suburbs now have theaters and concerts, the city as the great central local for the arts, and for civilized institutions generally, still remains convincing as an image to many city residents. Even intellectuals living in the suburbs betray uneasiness about their abandonment of former habitats and pursuits: and the growing literature of the suburban novel portrays the city as a creative foil to the dull, if necessary, domesticity of suburbia.

The intellectuals, too, are joined by urban politicians and by urban businessmen in despairing of the suburban movement. According to Zeckendorf, "Satellite towns, which are the product of decentralization, are parasites, jeopardizing the entire fiscal and political future of our great municipalities." He like others, argues how it is detrimental to the whole metropolitan community, and thus ultimately to the nation, that suburban cities should refuse to be incorporated into the nearby dominant metropolis.

Such incorporation, or annexation, is one of the burning metropolitan issues of the day. "Does Your Community Suffer from Suburbanitis?" queries *Colliers,* as it publishes the comments of two noted therapists who analyze this civic disease. They argue that cities have always gained needed breathing space by annexation of outlying areas, but that since 1900 the suburban residents have successfully prevented annexation through fears that they would have to pay higher taxes, would be affected by corrupt municipal governments, would be lost in the huge cities. Yet, as these pleaders for annexation say, these arguments are losing force, for annexation, although hard fought by many towns, appears to be a growing movement.

Thus, a new imagery about the city and its suburbs is appearing. The city as an invading malignant force which threatens the beauty of the suburban village has been a fearful image held by suburbanites for many years, an image which has been expressed in antagonism against new kinds of neighbors, in complaints about loss of rural atmosphere, and in a continual flight further outward. But a reverse aspect of the city is supplementing another image—namely, that the former idyllic suburban landscape is, or is becoming, a thing of the past. The services which the central city can offer the nearby communities are inestimable, or at least are better than can be locally supplied, for the suburbs are no longer relatively isolated, autonomous, proud towns. If old, they have been swamped with population, and, if new, they have been erected too quickly and lack adequate services or were built with an eye to future growth of population.

Although most suburbanites still undoubtedly imagine the central city to be different from the suburbs, already some prophets are beginning to visualize very little true difference between the two locales. They delight in pointing out, if they are themselves city dwellers, that the suburbs are fully as noisy as the city; that traffic is becoming as onerous in the towns as it is in the metropolis; that city people are wearing the same "suburban" kinds of informal attire. The suburbanite is beginning to notice these things himself.

The lessening of differences between suburb and city—by the increasing suburban densities and the possibility of planning cities for good living—seems destined to bring about further changes in the urban imagery of Americans. Very recently several new images have appeared. Thus one sociologist, Nathan Glazer, who loves cosmopolitan city life and who is afraid that it cannot flourish in suburbia, has argued that suburbia itself is in danger of invading, in its turn, the big city. This is a new twist, is it not? Glazer's argument is that because redevelopers have combined certain features of the garden city (superblocks, curving paths) and Corbusier's skyscraper in the park, they have in a large measure destroyed "the central value of the city—as meeting place, as mixing place, as creator and consumer of culture at all levels." If poorer classes are better off now than they were in our older great cities, the rich and middle classes are worse off; artists, poets, intellectuals and professors also have less propitious circumstances in which to flourish. The city core itself,

the part that people visit, that eager migrants want to live in, that produces what is unique, both good and bad, in the city, as against the town and the suburb. What has happened to that? Strangely enough, it loses the vitality that gave it its attraction.

Glazer asserts that the very density of nineteenth century cities forced city planners to build towns at the rim of existing cities, rather than to plan for better cities. We have now, he argues, to plan for the metropolis without losing that essential cosmopolitanism which makes it great. A rich and varied urban texture must be created, "and this . . . cannot be accomplished by reducing density." Whatever it is that has gone wrong with our cities, he concludes, "one thing is sure: nothing will be cured by bringing the suburb, even in its best forms, into the city." This is a radically different kind of argument—and imagery—than that of the city boy who merely refuses to take up residence in the suburb because he believes life there is intellectually stultifying.

In either case, though, the critic of suburbia takes the city as his measuring rod: he assumes the city as the locus for a frame of mind, a style of life. The proponent of suburbia reverses the procedure and measures the city against a healthier, saner, more sociable suburban counterpart. There is, of course, another transcending position whereby one may avoid taking sides, saying that both city and suburb have their respective advantages; people who own homes in both locales doubtless subscribe to that particular imagery.

Yet another transcending imagery is possible:

We are going to have to learn a wholly new concept of a city—a great sprawling community covering hundreds of square miles, in which farms and pastures mingle with intense developments, factories and shopping centers, with the entire area run purposefully for the common good. . . . These wonderful new cities, aren't as far in the future as they may sound.

Notice the wording: we have to learn a "wholly new concept of a city," and "these wonderful new cities" that are just around the corner. These terms signify a claim that the dichotomy of city *versus* suburb is no longer defensible in the eyes of some Americans. In its turn, this dichotomy is in some danger of the same dissolution as its predecessor, the country-city polarity. When Americans can maintain no longer that the two locales differ then we can expect new imageries to arise—new interpretations of the latest phases of urbanization.

One can almost see them being born. Only four years ago, *Fortune* magazine published a series of articles on the "exploding metropolis," closing with William H. Whyte's "Urban Sprawl." Whyte begins his report on the state of American metropolitan areas by warning that their fate will be settled during the next three or four years. "Already huge patches of once green countryside have been turned into vast, smog-filled deserts that are neither city, suburb, nor country." That last phrase forebodes the invention in the near future of a less neutral, more descriptive, term than the sociologists' colorless "metropolitan area." Whyte himself coins no new term, but his attitude toward the region eaten into by urban sprawl reflects something new. He reports a conference of planners, architects, and other experts that was convened by *Fortune* magazine and by *Architectural Forum* to tackle the problem of remedying the worst features

of urban sprawl. This group made recommendations, based upon the assumption that large amounts of suburban land need to be rescued before they are completely built upon in distressingly unplanned ways. As Whyte says, "it is not too late to reserve open space while there is still some left—land for parks, for landscaped industrial districts, and for just plain scenery and breathing space." The language—and outlines of these recommendations—are consciously very like that of earlier generations of city planners who were concerned with the problems of urban density; although the current situations, as everyone recognizes, involve a more complex interlocking of city, suburb, county, and state.

Americans are now being told in their mass media that soon they will "be living in fifteen great, sprawling, nameless communities—which are rapidly changing the human geography of the entire country." They are beginning to have spread before them maps of these vast urban conglomerations which are not cities but are nevertheless thoroughly urban: "super-cities" and "strip cities." They are being warned that America's urban regions are already entering upon a new stage of development, "even before most people are aware that urban regions exist at all." And even before the recently coined concept of "exurbia" is more than a few years old they are being confronted with "interurbia," which represents simply all the land not actually within the denser urban strips of land but within the urban regions, an area within which few people live on farms but where almost everybody commutes to work—not necessarily to cities "but to factories and offices located in small towns." As the polar concepts of city and suburb thus dissolve, Americans are being invited to think of urbanization in newer, more up-to-date terms. The new terms, however, technically they may be sometimes used, refer no less than did the older vocabulary to symbolic locales and associated sentiments.

HAROLD M. MAYER

Definitions of "City"

Not houses finely roofed or the stones of walls well-builded, nay nor canals and dockyards, make the city, but men able to use their opportunity. (*Aristides Rhodian Oration.*)

What is the city, but the people? (William Shakespeare, *The Tragedy of Coriolanus,* Act III, Sc. 1, line 198.)

A city is a vast collection of memories and expressions of emotion, with its greatest concentration of human meanings at its center, and a gradual thinning out of emotional value until one reaches the drabness of the fringes. But these are not separate and distinct emotions; rather they build upon and reinforce each other, and thus we get that organization which characterizes a great city. But it is not a biological form of organization, an organism; it is an organization of meanings and values. I believe that the real source of fascination of the city is that it represents the widest and fullest expression of all the types of meaning which man has achieved. The city is what we mean by civilization. (Mason W. Gross, President, Rutgers, The State University, New Jersey, at National Conference on Urban Life, Washington, D.C., March 28, 1962.)

As a type of community, the city may be regarded as a relatively permanent concentration of population, together with its diverse habitations, social arrangements and supporting activities, occupying a more or less discrete site, and having a cultural importance which differentiates it from other types of human settlement and association. In its elementary functions and rudimentary characteristics, however, a city is not clearly distinguishable from a town or even a large village. Mere size of population, surface area or density of settlement are not in themselves sufficient criteria of distinction, while many of their social correlates (division of labor, nonagricultural activity, central-place functions and creativity) characterize in varying degrees all urban communities from the small country town to the giant metropolis. (Eric E. Lampard, *Encyclopedia Britannica*, 1963 edition, Vol. 5, p. 809. Reprinted by permission.)

Enjoying the crowds, the satisfaction of "being there" feeling oneself a part of

Reprinted by permission of the author.

that power complex which is called *city,* freedom from the country, being protected in the world of people, culture, and comfort, more money for less work, and the opportunity to spend the money in a most pleasurable way—all that is the attraction of the city. (Wolf Schneider, *Babylon Is Everywhere: The City as Man's Fate,* p. 318. Copyright 1963, McGraw-Hill Book Company. Reprinted by permission of McGraw-Hill Book Company.)

. . . even before the city is a place of fixed residence, it begins as a meeting place to which people periodically return: the magnet comes before the container, and this ability to attract non-residents to it for intercourse and spiritual stimulus no less than trade remains one of the essential criteria of the city, a witness to its inherent dynamism, as opposed to the more fixed and indrawn form of the village, hostile to the outsider. (Lewis Mumford, *The City in History,* Harcourt Brace and World, Inc., 1961, and Martin Secker & Warburg Limited, pp. 9-10. Reprinted by permission.)

. . . the very essence of urban character is the function of service for a tributary area. . . . The universally distinctive characteristic of the town arises from the mode of life and activities of its inhabitants. The town differs from the village in the occupations of its people, who are not concerned directly with farming, and who live and work in the settlement, sharing in its life and organization. . . . True town character implies some measure of community service and organization— what is sometimes called community balance. . . . It is this grouping of centralized services in a clustered settlement which is the essence of a town and which, at a higher grade, is the hall-mark of a city. (Robert E. Dickinson, *City Region and Regionalism,* Kegan Paul, Trench,

Trubner and Co., Ltd., 1947, pp. 21-22. Reprinted by permission.)

The town in western Europe and North America may be defined as a compact settlement engaged primarily in non-agricultural occupations. (*Ibid.,* p. 25).

. . . the dense clusters of folk, who have no immediate interest in the production of the materials for their food and clothing or general comfort, but are engaged in the transporting, manufacturing, buying and selling them, or in educating the people, or in managing the affairs of the State, or in merely "living in town," become the urban section. (M. Aurousseau, "The Distribution of Population: A Constructive Problem," *Geographical Review,* XI (1921), p. 567. Copyright 1921, American Geographical Society, New York.)

The city, in the widest sense, as it appears throughout all ages and in all lands, as the symbol and carrier of civilization, has certain fundamental characteristics. The first and the most important of these is that it is an institutional centre, the seat of the institutions of the society which it represents. It is a seat of religion, of culture and social contact, and of political and administrative organization. Secondly, it is a seat of production, agricultural and industrial, the latter being normally the more important. . . . Thirdly, it is a seat of commerce and transport. Fourthly, the city is a pleasurable seat of residence for the rulers, the wealthy, and the retired, where they can enjoy all the amenities of civilized life that the institutions of their society have to offer. Fifthly, it is the living place of the people who work in it. (Robert E. Dickinson, *The West European City,* Routledge and Kegan Paul Ltd., 1951, and Humanities Press, Inc. Reprinted by permission.)

. . . we wish to speak of a "city" only in cases where the local inhabitants satisfy an economically substantial part of their daily wants in the local market, and to an essential extent by products which the local population and that of the immediate hinterland produced for sale in the market or acquired in other ways. In the meaning employed here the "city" is a market place. The local market forms the economic center of the colony in which, due to the specialization in economic products, both the non-urban population and urbanites satisfy their wants for articles of trade and commerce. (Max Weber, *The City,* Collier Books, 1962, pp. 72-73. Copyright © 1962, The Macmillan Company (A Subsidiary of Crowell Collier and Macmillan, Inc.), New York. Reprinted by permission.)

The term "city" has been utilized in varying fashions. We see it, in contrast to a town or village, as having greater size, density, and heterogeneity and including a wide range of non-agricultural specialists, most significant of whom are the literati. The information of the latter is . . . crucial for assigning a beginning date to city life. Gideon Sjoberg, *The Preindustrial City,* The Free Press, p. 11. Copyright © 1960, The Macmillan Company (A Subsidiary of Crowell Collier and Macmillan, Inc.), New York. Reprinted by permission.)

The ancient city was primarily a fortress, a place of refuge in time of war. The modern city, on the contrary, is primarily a convenience of commerce, and owes its existence to the market place around which it sprang up. Industrial competition and the division of labor, which have probably done most to develop the latent powers of mankind, are possible only upon condition of the existence of markets, of money, and other devices for the facilitation of trade and commerce. (Robert E. Park, E. W. Burgess, and R. D. McKenzie, "The City: Suggestions for the Investigation of Human Behavior in the Urban Environment" in *The City,* p. 12. Copyright © 1925, the University of Chicago Press. Reprinted by permission.)

Culture suggests agriculture, but civilization suggests the city. In one aspect civilization is the habit of civility; and civility is the refinement which townsmen, who made the word, thought possible only in the *civitas* or city. For in the city are gathered, rightly or wrongly, the wealth and brains produced in the countryside; in the city invention and industry multiply comforts, luxuries and leisure; in the city traders meet, and barter goods and ideas; in that cross-fertilization of minds at the crossroads of trade intelligence is sharpened and stimulated to creative power. In the city some men are set aside from the making of material things, and produce science and philosophy, literature and art. Civilization begins in the peasant's hut, but it comes to flower only in the towns. (Will Durant, *The Story of Civilization,* Part I: *The Oriental Heritage,* p. 2. Copyright 1935 by Simon & Schuster, Inc. Reprinted by permission.)

Needless to say, the urban environment is vastly different from the rural, for in it is always a concentration of services and varied goods. It is a meeting place and melting pot, both a refuge for people and ideas and also a reservoir of new ideas and venturesome populations. It feeds off the land, but nourishes the land with enlightenment and ingenious artifacts. In our world and time, it has begun virtually to absorb the countryside. (Philip L. Wagner, *The Human Use of the Earth,* The Free Press, p. 153. Copyright © 1960, the Macmillan Company (A Subsidiary of Crowell Collier and Macmillan, Inc., New York. Reprinted by permission.)

Cities are the focal points in the occupation and utilization of the earth by man. Cities are also paradoxes. Their rapid growth and large size testify to their superiority as a technique for the exploitation of the earth, yet by their very success and consequent large size they often provide a poor local environment for man. The problem is to build the future city in such a manner that the advantages of urban concentration can be preserved for the benefit of man and the disadvantages minimized. (Chauncy D. Harris and Edward L. Ullman, "The Nature of Cities," *Annals of the American Academy of Political and Social Science,* Vol. 242, November 1945, p. 7.)

The city is a settled aggregation of people who by their density tend toward heterogeneity and impersonality. (E. Gordon Ericksen, *Urban Behavior,* p. 22. Copyright © 1954, The Macmillan Company, New York. Reprinted by permission.)

. . . there is much to love and to admire in the great city. It is the home of the highest achievements of man in art, literature and science: the source from which the forces of freedom and emancipation have sprung. It is the place where the spirit of humanism and of democracy have grown and flourished, where man's quest for knowledge and justice has been pursued most constantly, and truth revealed most faithfully and fearlessly. (William A. Robson, *Great Cities of the World, Their Government, Politics and Planning,* George Allen and Unwin Ltd., 1954, p. 105. Reprinted by permission.)

LEO F. SCHNORE

The City as a Social Organism

In his discussion of the emergence of the first urban areas, Lewis Mumford speaks of "little communal village cells, undifferentiated and uncomplicated, every part performing equally every function, turned into complex structures, organized on an axiate principle, with differentiated tissues and specialized organisms, and with one part, the central nervous system, thinking for and directing the whole."[1] This is the image of the city as a social organism.

What is the justification for such a view? We might begin with some specification of basic terms—"city," "social," and "organism." The term "city," of course, has many meanings, but the most common conception is legal or political; that is, the city is regarded as a kind of corporate entity possessing certain delegated powers. Thus, Eric E. Lampard quite properly observes that "city is the name given to certain urban communities in English-speaking countries by virtue of some legal or conventional distinction."[2] For our pur-

poses, however, such a conception is unduly restrictive.

We are interested in cities around the world, not just in English-speaking countries; and we are interested in cities of many forms, from the earliest urban islands that rose above the seas of agricultural villages, through city-states, through preindustrial and postindustrial cities to the Megalopolis of today. Thus, I think it is well to keep a certain looseness in our conceptions of the city, for the city is many things—political, economic and social, historical and geographic, physical, and even psychological. For present purposes, however, we can think of "city" as referring to a particular type of community—the urban community—a large, densely settled community devoted to nonagricultural activities.

Next, we will have to consider what "social" might mean. How shall we understand this term? It happens that the literature in sociology exhibits a very interesting tension or ambivalence between two fundamentally different views. In the first view, "social" has reference to what we shall call consensus—an explicit or implicit understanding based on some kind of exchange of meaning within a shared frame

1. Lewis Mumford, *The City in History* (New York: Harcourt, Brace & World, 1961), p. 34. image of the city as a social organism.
2. Eric E. Lampard, "The City," an article prepared for a forthcoming edition of *Encyclopaedia Britannica*.

From **Urban Affairs Quarterly,** Volume I, No. 3, March 1966, pp. 58-69. Reprinted by permission of the publisher, Sage Publications, Inc.

of reference or universe of discourse. This view takes man's capacity for symbolic communication of ideas as central, focussing upon mental interpenetration, and a meeting of minds is seen as the critical feature of human conduct. Thus the city, along with such social forms as family and society, is regarded as one expression of a uniquely human capacity for meaningful communication.[3] This view is unquestionably valuable. It points to an aspect or facet of city life that is worthy of study in its own right. Yet, an exclusive emphasis upon consensus misses a more fundamental sense in which the term "social" has a great deal of meaning—a sense that permits us to speak of infrahuman social animals such as the so-called social insects. Such animals may be able to communicate rudimentary "ideas," but they are certainly limited by genetically determined characteristics to exchanges far less complex than those made by human beings.[4]

This second view of "social" stresses symbiosis or interdependence, whether or not it is mediated by the use of symbols. The relevance of such a view to any examination of the city becomes clear when one reminds himself that the city is simply not a self-sufficient or wholly independent entity. Rather, it is dependent—dependent on other areas such as rural areas for food and fiber and (through most of history) for men, or migrants to the cities. When we say that the city is dependent on other areas, whether we are thinking of rural areas or of other cities, we understand it to mean interdependent—especially in an economic sense. Cities offer things in return for still other things received by cities, whether these "things" are tangible goods or intangible services. The city is caught up in a kind of web of exchange relationships, supplying goods and services of a wide variety, including, most importantly, direction, control, integration, and coordination.[5]

All of these things are quite evident on the external side, for the interdependence of the city with other areas is obvious. The internal counterpart is somewhat less obvious. But, interdependence does exist *within* cities as well as *between* cities and other places, especially in the contemporary world. There is a territorial or geographic division of labor between the subareas making up the city. Most broadly, the division is between homes and workplaces, producing and consuming areas, between which there is a continuous flow of commodities, information, and people. It is exemplified by the stream of commuters between home and work. On a finer grain, there is also a division between areas devoted to different land uses—industrial, commercial, and recreational. From the standpoint of interdependence, then, the city is a "social" entity *par excellence,* for it displays both internal and external forms of symbiosis. Simultaneously, it reveals itself as an expression of symbolic communication between men.

It happens that these two faces of the city, the symbiotic and the consensual, were probably most clearly perceived in the 1920's by a sociologist at the University of Chicago, Robert E. Park. Park's thinking laid the groundwork for a singularly creative series of works by a group that came to be called the "Chicago School" of urban sociology. Park himself was a newspaperman before he was a sociologist, and he carried on a lifelong love affair with the city. In fact, he liked nothing better than to roam the alleys of Chicago and other cities, exploring backyards and observing cities from such vantage

3. Anselm Strauss, *Images of the American City* (New York: The Free Press, 1961).
4. Martin Lindauer, *Communication Among Social Bees* (Cambridge: Harvard University Press, 1961).

5. C. J. Galpin, *The Social Anatomy of an Agricultural Community* (Madison: University of Wisconsin Agricultural Experiment Station, May, 1915), "Research Bulletin No. 34."

points as the lobbies of second-rate hotels. This was his style of work. And this is how he achieved his insight, for out of this habit of observation of city life and city ways, Park came to see that the city manifests a high degree of order and a remarkable level of organization *without* a perfect and somehow all-enveloping consensus. That is, the city was seen as an interdependent entity functioning quite effectively in the face of its inhabitants' indifference to and ignorance of the system as a whole. The residents of the city carried on their daily rounds and lived out their lives in their own small worlds, largely unaware of the larger unity of the city. At the same time, the city was exhibiting a life of its own.[6] This leads us quite naturally to the idea of the city as a so-called organism.

The notion of the community or the society as an "organism" is very old. The idea was especially prominent in the late nineteenth century, when biological reasoning, evolutionary and organismic, was in vogue. It probably reached its fullest and most detailed expression in the writings of Herbert Spencer, a British philosopher and sociologist. It has to be added that this mode of reasoning has since been virtually abandoned and, in the minds of many people, it has been thoroughly discredited. The historian Crane Brinton, for example, has asked, "Who now reads Spencer?" His question has been repeated by sociologists and others.[7] Without entering into a debate on the merits and demerits of analogous reasoning, without listing anew all of its uncritical uses, and without enumerating all the questionable purposes for which this particular analogy has been used, let us consider some of the

ways in which the city may be considered *like,* though not identical to, an organism.

This approach is one way of bringing out the city's unit character, and a way of stressing the interdependence of its parts. In the words of Amos Hawley, a sociologist:

The community has often been likened to the human individual organism. So intimate and so necessary are the interrelations of its parts, it has been pointed out, that any influence felt at one point is almost immediately transmitted throughout. Further, not only is the community a more or less self-sufficient entity, having inherent in it the principle of its own life process; it has also a growth or natural history with well-defined stages of youth, maturity, and senescence. It is therefore a whole which is something different from the sum of its parts, possessing powers and potentialities not present in any of its components. If not an organism, it is at least a super-organism.[8]

This quotation sketches the main themes of organismic thinking about the community, and despite the questionable remark about the self-sufficiency of communities, the passage is a valuable summary of the organismic view.

I would like to underscore two points about the city as an organism. First, the parts, the individual human beings making up the city, can be regarded as replaceable and interchangeable. They are very much like cells and, as in the organism, cells may come and go and the organism itself may survive. One might ask if this is radically different from the fact that the city may live on, while people come and go. Secondly, the city may grow and there are young, middle-aged, and old cities. Cities are founded, or born. There are periods of rapid growth, as in "boom towns." Cities live and die. There are "ghost towns," or dead cities.

6. Robert E. Park, "The City: Suggestions for the Investigation of Human Behavior in the Urban Environment," *American Journal of Sociology,* 20 (March, 1916), pp. 577-612.
7. Crane Brinton, *English Political Thought in the Nineteenth Century* (London: Ernest Benn, 1949); quoted in Talcott Parsons, *The Structure of Social Action* (New York: The Free Press, 1949), p. 3.

8. Amos H. Hawley, *Human Ecology: A Theory of Community Structure* (New York: Ronald Press, 1950), p. 50.

If all this seems a bit fanciful, or as simply playing games with words, I would remind you that a reversal of the procedure is frequently used. In other words, a "social-system analogy" is often employed in order to say something about individual organisms. Communication systems, for example, are likened to the nervous system, with wires as ganglia, trunk lines as the spinal cord, etc. Similarly, transportation systems are likened to the circulatory system, with roads representing veins and arteries. The city is compared to the brain and the heart. Consider the following discussion of the "nervous system" of the higher organisms in a popular encyclopaedia:

In the "division of labor" characteristic of multicellular animals, a nervous system has developed as a group of tissues and structures that function to regulate the activities of the body. . . . The nervous system may be compared to an extensive communications system. It transmits messages (impulses) from sense organs (receivers) to a central switchboard (the brain). . . . From the brain or lower centers the impulses are transmitted to the proper regions or organs in such a way that an action appropriate to the stimulus is initiated.[9]

If one compares this passage with Mumford's idea quoted earlier, one sees that the analogy can be turned in either direction.

These considerations lead us to some observations concerning the internal aspects of the cities. Think first about some very simple demographic attributes, or population characteristics, such as the city's size and rate of growth. Without a detailed review of the evidence, one may assert that some of the most imaginative contemporary urban research in sociology, economics, and geography consists of spelling out the implications of variations in growth rates among cities or of identifying the concomitants of differences in size.[10]

Fast and slow growing cities are different structurally, whether regarded from economic, social, or political points of view. Large and small cities are also dissimilar, organizationally speaking. Size operates as a kind of limit upon complexity of organization. Large places are at least potentially more heterogeneous and more complex. Spencer himself observed that "it is a characteristic of social bodies, as of living bodies, that while they increase in size, they increase in structure. . . . The social aggregate, homogeneous when minute, habitually gains in heterogeneity along with each increment of growth; and to reach great size must acquire great complexity."[11] While his language is archaic, Spencer's thought is quite modern, at least in the sense that these problems are still being explored today. These words—complexity, heterogeneity, and homogeneity—are essentially structural or organizational terms.

What do we know about the structural characteristics of cities? We are coming to know a great deal about the internal social and economic organization of cities. In part, the ease of acquiring this knowledge stems from a convenient fact—that some structural features are very clearly represented in the spatial arrangement of parts, the way things are distributed in space. Space acts as a kind of mirror, reflecting structural patterns. Recall our earlier reference to the city as composed of homes and workplaces. There are areas devoted to residential uses and there are others given over to employment or productive uses. You can regard these as multicellular

9. Alden Raisbeck, "Nervous System," in *The American Peoples Encyclopedia* (Chicago: The Spencer Press, 1954), Volume 14, p. 466.

10. Otis Dudley Duncan and Albert J. Reiss, Jr., *Social Characteristics of Urban and Rural Communities, 1950* (New York: John Wiley and Sons, 1956).

11. Herbert Spencer, *Principles of Sociology* (New York and London: D. Appleton and Co., 1920 edition), Volume I, Part II, pp. 449 and 471.

parts or "organs," bound together by flows of every description. In the organism, there are flows of nutrients, blood, and impulses of different kinds constantly being transmitted. In the community, there are flows of commodities, information, and individual persons.

We are also coming to know a great deal about why certain "organs" are located where they are in cities. For example, we are learning why "central offices" are truly central, why manufacturing plants of one type tend to be bound to the city core, while other types tend to move toward the periphery; why there should be selective decentralization of services; and why retailers of different goods take up different locations. We are also beginning to understand why certain units are segregated with others like themselves, as in manufacturing areas and financial districts, as well as why some highly dissimilar units are clustered together, functionally and spatially linked, as in the case of flower shops clustering around hospitals.

This kind of knowledge comes from observations that are very much like those of a laboratory technician examining tissue in a microscopic slide. This represents a static or cross-sectional view. We are also gaining new knowledge in longitudinal or historical terms. For example, we are learning how certain technological eras have left "scar tissue" in cities of a certain age, such as in pre-automobile cities. The street pattern and many of the other contemporary features of cities are residues of the past.[12] We are also beginning to find regularities in the changing shapes of cities.

We know least about a process that might be called "cellular turnover." That is, we don't know much about the appearance and disappearance of households and firms, the entry and exit of individual cells. We have imperfect knowledge, for example, of the absorption and assimilation of immigrants. We know very little about the general impact of the city on the individual. We also know very little about "social selection," the shifting and sorting that goes on, distributing people between occupations and industries, and distributing families through space.

We know a little about residential segregation according to socioeconomic status, and there is a great deal of interest in segregation according to race or color; but research hasn't been pursued to the point that we can speak of these things in any knowledgeable manner.[13] We can't say much about the social-psychological aspects of these problems. One might ask whether or not there is a distinctively urban personality. We have to say we don't know, though we do have a whole family of hypotheses that have been in the literature at least since the publication of a very influential essay by another Chicago sociologist, Louis Wirth, regarding "urbanism as a way of life."[14] In the conventional textbook treatment of this subject, in urban sociology and elsewhere, many of the ideas which Wirth expressed in tentative and hypothetical form have been taken as known facts. We know far less about "urbanism"—the individual in the city setting—than we do about "urbanization," or population concentration. We know a fair amount about the massing of people in cities from a demographic standpoint. We know quite a bit about urban structure, but we have very little in the way of

12. Edgar M. Hoover and Raymond Vernon, *The Anatomy of a Metropolis* (Cambridge: Harvard University Press, 1959).

13. Otis Dudley Duncan and Beverly Duncan, "Residential Distribution and Occupational Stratification," *American Journal of Sociology*, 60 (March, 1955), pp. 493-503; Leo F. Schnore, *The Urban Scene: Human Ecology and Demography* (New York: The Free Press, 1965), Part 4; Stanley Lieberson, *Ethnic Patterns in American Cities* (New York: The Free Press, 1963); Karl E. Taeuber and Alma F. Taeuber, *Negroes in Cities* (Chicago: Aldine, 1965).

14. Louis Wirth, "Urbanism as a Way of Life," *American Journal of Sociology*, 44 (July, 1938), pp. 1-26.

a social psychology of urban life. I should also add that we know more about all of these things in the West than we do for cities in the rest of the world, and we know more about the present than we do about the past.[15]

Though it is being reduced, there is still a kind of cultural bias in our thinking about cities, and I regret to say that there is a kind of historical bias still present in the urban literature, despite the efforts of many historians and others interested in the past. I would submit that the present challenge is to learn more about cities or urban communities and to learn more about societies—both urban and urbanizing societies. We do know enough to appreciate the importance of context. We know of important differences in those societies in which city dwellers are in the majority, as opposed to those in which city dwellers form a small but growing minority.

This matter of context is important. Within cities there are important differences depending on the larger societal setting. For example, preindustrial cities are notably more "segmented," made up of highly similar parts which remain relatively independent of each other. Many cities of Asia and Africa consist of subcommunities which are physically separated from each other by walls and connected only by gates, but which are very much like each other in form and content, containing the same kinds of trade outlets and services.[16] This is in contrast to the closely linked, highly differentiated, yet interdependent form of city in the industrial West. In the United States it is useful to think of the urban community as composed of formerly quasi-independent cities, arranged like a sun and its planets, with a large metropolis surrounded by smaller urban subcenters. It is a community composed of legally distinct cities. In contrast, the segmented type is a city (a legal entity) composed of communities. These social segments or subunits are the true communities in many parts of Asia and Africa.

So much for the internal side. I have stressed the importance of context and I have emphasized the need for understanding cities that are found in different contexts. Externally, too, cities stand in different relations to the outside world. Many entrepôt cities in underdeveloped areas emerging from colonialism actually have closer ties to the cities in Europe and America than to their own hinterlands.[17] In contrast, our cities are intimately linked to rural areas, as well as to other cities, at home and abroad. In a society like our own, heavily urbanized and industrialized, it becomes hard to distinguish the urban from the rural. The diffusion of culture via the mass media has apparently led to a kind of homogeneity that is the counterpart of the heterogeneity we have been discussing.[18]

One cannot overstate the importance of context. To speak of context is only to remind ourselves that any understanding of the nature of an organism, even so complex an organism as the city, requires attention to its environment. We might ask ourselves this question: What is the most salient aspect of the city's environment? After looking at the historical and comparative evidence that is available, I have been persuaded that the critical feature is

15. Eric E. Lampard and Leo F. Schnore, "Urbanization Problems: Some Historical and Comparative Considerations," in *Research Needs for Development Assistance Programs* (Washington, D.C.: The Brookings Institution, August, 1961); Philip M. Hauser and Leo F. Schnore (editors), *The Study of Urbanization* (New York: John Wiley, 1965).
16. Gideon Sjoberg, *The Preindustrial City: Past and Present* (New York: The Free Press, 1960).

17. Hauser and Schnore, *op. cit.*
18. Walter Firey, Charles P. Loomis, and J. Allan Beegle, "The Fusion of Urban and Rural," in Jean Labatut and Wheaton J. Lane (editors), *Highways in Our National Life* (Princeton: Princeton University Press, 1950), pp. 154-163.

the growth of the human species itself. The West has already passed through its rapid growth stage. It is no coincidence to find that the period of most rapid city growth in England and Wales was between 1811 and 1851, when Britain was achieving an unprecedented mastery over a far-flung environment. In the United States, the period of most rapid city growth was between 1860 and 1890; in Germany it was between 1870 and 1910. What about the rest of the world? The most rapid growth in Egypt has been since 1920, in Mexico since 1921, and in India since 1941.[19] These periods correspond very interestingly to the periods of tremendous national population growth in these underdeveloped lands.

As a consequence, there are very striking differentials in city growth around the world today. The cities in the West are growing relatively slowly, while those in the developing areas, themselves more numerous than Western cities, are manifesting explosive growth. Calcutta is an interesting case, because its growth has meant that roughly 650,000 of its inhabitants are "street-sleepers," living on the sidewalks or in the railroad stations. Housing has not kept up with population growth. Calcutta is already the tenth largest city in the world, with a population of 4.5 million. But projections of its current rate of growth would yield a population of between 35 and 36 million people by the year 2000. It happens that if one took such a population and gave it the density of New York City, he would have a city that would envelop an area larger than the entire state of Rhode Island. One may ask if this is really possible. Actually, it may well be impossible, but these figures are really designed to illustrate the magnitude of current growth, the enormous speed of increase in Calcutta and other cities in the underdeveloped areas of the world.

To take another case, there is reason to believe that twenty million people left rural areas to go to the cities of China between 1949 and 1956. This number happens to be nearly equal to the combined population of the Benelux countries, i.e., Belgium, Netherlands, and Luxembourg. Enormous numbers were thus involved in the rural-urban stream. In roughly the same period the cities of China were growing very rapidly.[20]

Such facts underscore the importance of both national growth and world population growth. Consider the difference between the births and deaths that are occurring, i.e., the "natural increase" of world population. At current rates, something like 6,000 persons are added each hour, or around 144,000 persons per day; this is a larger number than the population of Madison, Wisconsin. The world is gaining 4,320,000 people per month, a number larger than the current population of the entire state of Wisconsin. The world is increasing by 52 million people per year; this is roughly the size of the United Kingdom—England, Wales, Scotland, and Northern Ireland.

The emerging picture is one of an ever-more-crowded world, and one finds many expressions of concern about the implications of this "population explosion." It is useful to think for a moment about whether this increasingly crowded world will mean increasingly crowded cities. The answer is clearly in the affirmative. The world is not only growing in terms of human numbers, but these numbers are being more compactly arranged. This holds true for urban communities and for the world as a whole. Cities are multiplying, they are growing larger in area and in population size, and they are containing progressively larger proportions of man-

19. Kingsley Davis, "The Origin and Growth of Urbanization in the World," *American Journal of Sociology,* 60 (March, 1955), pp. 429-437; Jack P. Gibbs and Leo F. Schnore, "Metropolitan Growth: An International Study," *American Journal of Sociology,* 66 (September, 1960), pp. 160-170.

20. "The World's Great Cities," *Population Bulletin,* 16 (September, 1960), pp. 109-131.

kind in every major country throughout the world.

Very generally, with respect to the context of urbanization today, the critical fact is the sheer growth of both urban and non-urban communities. Population increases are being registered not only within cities, but within rural areas, with this latter increase indirectly providing the major source of city growth—rural-urban migration. To state the matter somewhat differently, the most impressive thing about contemporary urbanization is the fantastic proliferation and multiplication of human *and* social organisms.

You may not find the organismic anal-ogy very helpful, but the principal facts that we have been considering remain the same. We should be aware of our growing world and of the fact that it is an increasingly urbanized world. If only to demonstrate that even now someone does read Herbert Spencer, I shall close by adopting as my own the words that he wrote in 1876 in defense of the organismic analogy. As he said, "I have used the analogies elaborated but as a scaffolding to help in building up a coherent body of sociological inductions. Let us take away the scaffolding; the inductions will stand by themselves."[21]

21. Spencer, *op. cit.,* pp. 592-593.

CHARLES TILLY

Anthropology on the Town

Once upon a time, anthropologists were supposed to spend all their time out in the bush, smoking hemp with primitive people. Not any more! Some of them may still be smoking hemp, but the old, ethnocentric division between "primitive" and "civilized" peoples has fallen by the wayside. No one is sure which is which now. And many anthropologists have come to town. Some have followed their subject matter from tribal areas to cities, while others have simply realized that their methods apply to city dwellers as well as to inhabitants of tiny villages.

As an urban sociologist, I greet them with mixed feelings. Have they come to fight for my turf, my city? Yet as a student of cities I have to admit they have something: a style of disciplined, direct observation which gets at the experience of living in different nooks and crannies of big cities.

Now, everyone knows what life is like in his own cranny. The trouble is that we don't know enough about each other's worlds—how they overlap, how they differ, how they add up. Sociologists have done fairly well at adding up pieces of individual lives to get the big picture of land use, or the location of different nationalities within a city, or the distribution of crime. Their development of the sample survey has provided a convenient way of detecting the main trends and major subdivisions in big-city population. They have helped design the biggest survey of them all—the census—and have invented some ingenious ways of using numbers from the census to find out where the city is going. The urban sociologists are great at averaging, at finding the main line. That helps in learning whether the population is getting more mobile, or if one national group is sending more of its children to college, or who is getting what during a general rise in prosperity. It is important to know the averages.

Yet once we know the averages, the deviations from the average begin to matter; so does the way it feels to be at the average, or far away from it. That is where the urban anthropologist shines.

We can see the difference in the study of urban poverty in North America. The sociologists and economists have not done a bad job of finding out how many poor people there are by various definitions of poverty, how the proportions have been

From **Habitat,** Vol. X, No. 1, January-February 1967, pp. 20-25. Reprinted by permission of the author.

changing, and roughly who they are. Where they have often fallen down is in analyzing how people got into their various categories, and what it is like to be there.

Three non-sociologists—an anthropologist, a city planner, and a free-lance writer—played a large part in turning students of cities back toward greater attention to the ways poor people face life in the city. Oscar Lewis, an anthropologist, began his work by studying everyday life in a Mexican village. Later, he followed his villagers to the slums of Mexico City. There he lived with them and let them tell their own stories while his tape recorder turned. The results were a new kind of book, built almost entirely on the oral autobiographies of the people under study, and a new understanding of the distinct way of life Lewis called the "culture of poverty." Since then, the ideas and techniques Oscar Lewis put into such books as *Five Families* and *The Children of Sanchez* have turned up more and more in the study of North American cities.

The city planner was Herbert Gans, who went and lived in the West End of Boston. The West End was a low-income section, with many Italian families, slated for razing and replacement by a tall complex of expensive apartments. His book, *The Urban Villagers,* reporting what he learned, did not appear in time to save the West End from destruction. But it raised prickly questions about outsiders' assumptions that the West End was "disorganized" and a "slum," that it was therefore good only for clearance and that its residents had everything to gain through relocation. Since then, planners in Boston and elsewhere, have taken their responsibility for learning what kinds of communities they are proposing to renew, much more seriously.

Michael Harrington, the writer, tells us himself how he went from a useful, but distant, statistical analysis of poverty to a first-hand exploration of its labyrinths:

After I wrote my first article on poverty in America, I had all the statistics down on paper. I had proved to my satisfaction that there were around 50,000,000 poor in this country. Yet, I realized that I did not believe my own figures. The poor existed in the Government reports; they were percentages and numbers in long, close columns, but they were not part of my experience. I could prove that the other America existed, but I had never been there.

Then he went to the streets of New York and other cities to live with the poor. Harrington laid out the results of his inquiry in a powerful book, *The Other America.* And the American government listened as it established its anti-poverty program.

It happens that Lewis, Gans and Harrington all wrote influential books. But writing books is not all that comes of the anthropological approach to the city. When the group building the big new city of Guayana, in Venezuela, asked Lisa Redfield Peattie to join them as staff anthropologist, they probably thought she would work mainly at feeding back information about sore spots in people's adaptation to the city, and at explaining what

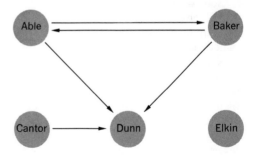

was going on to the natives. With her wide experience in rural Latin America, she certainly could have done this. In fact, she did become a good source of information about what was going on in the poor people's neighborhoods in Guayana, but she did it by settling with her family in the local shacktown, and helping its residents organize a successful protest against living conditions there. Now she is teaching city planners at Massachusetts Institute of Technology, and once again helping poor people—this time in Boston—articulate their demands for planning which will take their needs into account.

It is easy to see the implications for urban action in these investigations of poverty. It may not be so obvious that they contribute to our general understanding of how cities work. The very title of Gans' book, for example, states an important idea: the similarity between the social organization of many of the city's ethnic enclaves—urban villages—and of the small communities from which their members or their members' forebears came. People have been noticing the diversity of cultures in North American cities for a century, but usually under the impression that they were transient residues of old-country customs. Gans establishes the durability of some of these village cultures, and helps explain that durability. Thus a piece of work with direct practical applications contributes to the theory of the city as well.

What do these urban anthropologists do besides settling down in slums? Well, that in itself is an important beginning. It is a way of sharing an important experience and gaining acceptance at the same. The trained participant observer has a chance to see people when they take off their business faces, and to accompany them through the full daily, weekly or monthly round. He makes sure he establishes some contact with all parts of the population he is dealing with, not just the talkative élite. He records what he sees in a systematic way—in classified field notes, in a journal, or perhaps on cards representing different individuals or groups. He may very well take a "sociometric" approach, concentrating on the frequencies and kinds of contact among pairs of members of the group. Those observations he can sum up in diagrams of group structure like this hypothetical, but realistic, representation

of visiting patterns among a group of housewives in adjoining houses, shown above.

Here, Mrs. Able and Mrs. Baker regularly exchange visits; Mrs. Able, Mrs. Baker and Mrs. Cantor regularly visit Mrs. Dunn; and Mrs. Elkin stays by herself. We can do the same diagramming for other members of the families, or for different kinds of contact, like giving help, borrowing tools or going shopping together.

The people actually involved do not need a diagram to tell them that A and B are close, that D is a center of attraction, or that E is an isolate. However, where the observer is a newcomer, where twenty or thirty households are involved, or where the question is whether the same kinds of clusters keep reappearing, only some sort of systematic recording and analysis will bring out the true state of affairs.

This general technique has many versions. It can neatly summarize what groups intermarry in a large city, what kinds of people form cliques in a high school, what individuals talk to each other most in an office.

It is a natural starting point for a study of the flow of communications within a neighborhood. And when done at a scale larger than the pair of individuals, it helps us distinguish three vitally different social arrangements (see next page).

The first might be the structure of a rooming-house district, the second the structure of a Chinese neighborhood, the third a high-rise apartment area.

Sociometric observation can get very complicated. There are simpler and faster ways of getting a sense of social life in one section of a city or another. Very often, all an intelligent observer needs is a stroll through a neighborhood to spot the main points of congregation of the local population—doorsteps, bars, stores, clubs, churches. If they are public enough, he can station himself there and take a small part in local life. Or he can deliberately create his own social situations. When

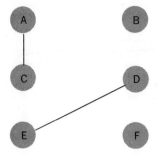
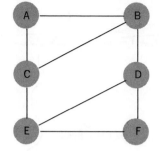
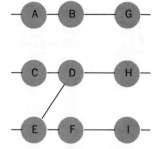

Atomized—pairs and isolates   Tight-knit—overlapping sets   Specialized—extensive chains

Kevin Lynch, the city planner, was trying to find out what kinds of roads and buildings made strong impressions on people, one of his devices was to stop people on the street and ask them directions to other sections of the city, noting what they used as their points of reference.

Lynch also adopted a slightly more formal way of finding out how people visualized their cities. He asked them to draw maps. His instructions went like this:

We would like you to make a quick map of central Boston, inward or downtown from Massachusetts Avenue. Make it just as if you were making a rapid description of the city to a stranger, covering all the main features. We don't expect an accurate drawing—just a rough sketch.

And the interviewer was supposed to note the sequence in which the map was drawn. Everyone marked down Beacon Hill, the Common, the Charles River and the Back Bay, but there were large areas of the central city which simply disappeared from these maps for lack of what Lynch calls "imageability."

With due allowance for skill in drawing and for visual imagination, we have a lot to learn about people's experience with the city from the maps they sketch. As an experiment, I asked my three eldest children to do maps of central Toronto. The seven-year-old's world is the path from home to school and its fringes, with her own block and the play areas she knows

best blown up out of all proportion to their actual size. The nine-year-old (see Figure 1) has grasped the grid pattern of the streets and has had enough experience with the downtown portions of the subway to put some important thoroughfares into the central business district; the appearance of the rivers and of Highway 401 on the map, however, probably comes from booklearning in school. She still gives her own section of the city (from Bloor to Eglinton along Yonge) much more space than its due. The eleven-year-old is aware of too many details for a map on this scale, so many that he gets some wrong and has trouble fitting others together. Each child's view of the city is selective, but the older children can roam mentally through more of its territory, and they select on different principles. It would be fascinating to see how children of the same ages in other parts of the city played this game.

Instead of starting with real cities, sociologist William Michelson of the University of Toronto asked different sorts of people to map out ideal environments. He did this because he happened to wonder what systematic connection there was between the things people wanted out of life in general and what kinds of communities they preferred, but his technique could be used for many other purposes.

The map-drawer began with his own dwelling, placed a number of facilities like schools, movies, shopping centers and workplaces on the map, then drew a line

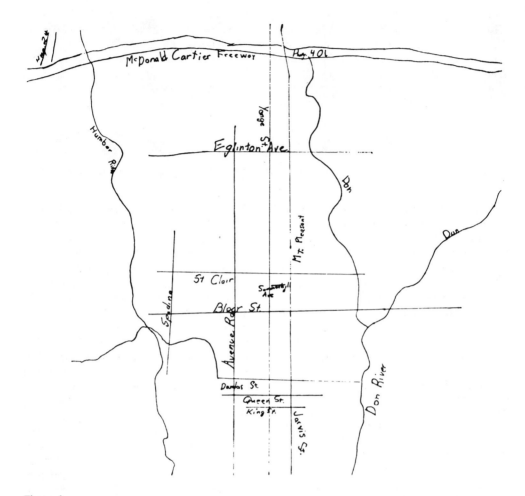

Figure 1

around the area he would consider his neighborhood.

To complement this picture of the ideal world, people can tell us a great deal about what they do with the actual space of the city by simply recounting where they go, what they do and with whom, during an average day. One version of this is the "yesterday interview," in which the interviewer asks the person to give a history of yesterday from 6 A.M. to midnight, including each activity lasting ten minutes or more. Another version is the diary kept under the same rules. Either one produces a valuable picture of how much time different kinds of people spend doing what, where and with whom. If they compared their own "time-budgets" with their wives', many husbands would begin to understand why wives are often eager to talk, talk, talk when they get a chance—for so much of their time is spent alone or with no one but small children. The student of cities has other facts to learn from time-budgets, such as when and where in a city the most people are likely to be in sociable contact with others, how much of all the time available to city-dwellers goes into travelling, what activities most people do alone, what sections of the city are used in the daily rounds of old people, or rich people, or newcomers. How do the daily time-budgets of these individuals fit with the maps of the city they would draw?

Again we have gone from a simple notion to a complicated application. Some parts of these questions about the patterns of activity in the city can be broken off for a separate study. Just who is on the street, and when, is in itself an important fact about local life, and fairly easy to observe. Our students at the University of Toronto have found they can make an informative first contact with a section of the city by going to a local intersection and recording who goes by during scattered five-minute intervals. They set down not only how many people pass the corner, but also a rough judgment of age, sex, and whether they are alone or with others. These distributions will vary sharply and informatively from place to place and from time to time.

If only the process of walking by could be slowed down enough for the observer to take copious notes, there would be many other things to jot down: the objects people are carrying, the way they are dressed, the languages they are speaking, how much they dawdle or gawk. A camera can catch some of these things very effectively.

Here are some ideas culled from different research projects: (1) count the proportion of door-buttons pushed down in automobiles on the street in different areas, in order to see how willing people are to leave their cars unlocked; (2) notice how many backyards in a neighborhood contain grass, how many flower gardens, how many trash piles, and how many vegetable patches, to get an idea of the local style of life; (3) check the percentage of blinds which are drawn, to judge how much people are shutting themselves off from others on the street; (4) notice how many liquor bottles are thrown out on trash day, and what kind, to guess the home drinking patterns; (5) record how many houses have outside Christmas decorations, and how elaborate they are, to gauge how much it is an occasion for public display. In fact, all of us make such observations half-consciously, every day.

Considering how much a part of everyday life these various sorts of observation are, it might seem that "urban anthropology" is nothing but a dressed-up version of common sense. Is it? It does deal with things everyone knows something about. It should build on good, common sense. But it also has more discipline and greater focus than casual observation does. When a woman steps into a roomful of other women, scans it quickly, then mentally ticks off the boutique-bought dresses, the hand-crafted shoes and the genuine pearls, that takes both discipline and focus. It takes training and attention; almost any wife can (and, unfortunately, will) testify that her husband is an ignoramus on such matters.

The urban anthropologist's discipline shows up in his insistence on observing exactly how somebody says something or just how many people gather in a certain place, as well as his faithfulness in recording the observation for future reference. His focus is on social relations, especially on those which reveal something important about the way groups are organized in the city.

Many pressing questions about cities need this systematic first-hand treatment. What difference does it make to people's social lives whether they live in separate houses, chains of garden apartments, or tall buildings? Does the dislocation of urban renewal wound people irreparably? Under what conditions do people have strong attachments to their neighborhoods? When are the dispossessed of the city likely to get together and protest their fate? What does it mean to become poor, and to stay poor? How, and when, does assimilation work? Who, and where, are all the lonely people? Urban anthropology can produce at least some of the answers.

The satisfying thing about the anthropological approach to the city is that it brings theory, policy, action and personal experience into contact with each other. Just as some city planners, uneasy at seeing almost all their colleagues working for governments and real estate developers, have started to organize "advocate planners" to criticize official plans and offer alternative proposals on behalf of the people being planned for, so we need skilled and independent social researchers devoted to scrutinizing the facts and presumptions on which urban policies are based. Like Oscar Lewis, Herbert Gans and Michael Harrington, they will have the chance to deal with vital theoretical issues along the way.

For the same reasons, urban anthropology has an important role to play in education. More so than learning about the history or the government of the city from books, it challenges the student to link his own fate and private experience to the life of the city as a whole. An inveterate city-walker myself, I often send my students out to walk a randomly-assigned section of a city and report back on what they have seen. Even the lifetime residents often find themselves in areas they have never really looked at before. Most of them learn something important about their city, and about themselves.

One final virtue of the methods of urban anthropology is that they still leave room for the gifted amateur. I mean amateur in the exact sense of the word: someone who does something for the love of it. Survey research and much of the large scale quantitative analysis so important to the study of cities depend on teams of specialists and expensive equipment. A few of the techniques I have described here are also easier to use with computers and other machines at hand. But most of the procedures are feasible for a single person with a camera, a tape-recorder, a sketchpad, or just a quick eye and a ready notebook. Many of them consist of making observations most people make anyway, but doing so more systematically. There is nothing wrong with the back-to-nature yearnings of mushroom-hunters and birdwatchers. Why not get back to human nature by watching people?

PETER G. GOHEEN

Metropolitan Area Definition: A Re-evaluation of Concept and Statistical Practice

During the 20th century both the scale and the pattern of the Nation's urban growth have been transformed continuously and with increasing rapidity. Fundamental changes in the American way of life were recognized at the beginning of the century by the Bureau of the Census when, in 1910, it introduced *Metropolitan Districts* to its system of area classification. This marked the first use by the Bureau of the Census of a unit other than the corporate boundaries of a city for reporting data on urban population. The Metropolitan District of 1910, defined for every city of over 200,000 inhabitants and re-applied with little alteration by the Bureau of the Census in 1920, 1930 and 1940 (except that by 1940 MD's had been defined for all cities of 50,000 or more), served basically to distinguish urban population, whether located within the central city or adjacent to it, from surrounding rural population, although not all of the "urban population of the country was included in Metropolitan Districts. The idea behind the definition was in essence that stated in 1932:

. . . the population of the corporate city frequently gives a very inadequate idea of the population massed in and around that city, constituting the greater city, . . . and (the boundaries of) large cities in few cases . . . limit the urban population which that city represents or of which it is the center. . . . If we are to have a correct picture of the massing or concentration of population in extensive urban areas . . . it is necessary to establish metropolitan districts which will show the magnitude of each of the principal population centers.[1]

Almost as soon as the metropolitan concept was introduced to statistical practice, in the attempt to capture "the greater city," several factors led to dissatisfaction with the criteria and operational definitions used, or the results of their application. The definition of any set of statistical areas transcending conventional legal jurisdictions will become the subject of local protest and political pressure. Almost any set of statistics will attract a coterie of

1. U.S. Bureau of the Census (1932) *Fifteenth Census of the United States:* 1930, Metropolitan Districts, 1932.

From B. J. L. Berry, P. G. Goheen, and H. Goldstein, **Metropolitan Area Classification: A Review of Current Practice, Criticisms, and Proposed Alternatives,** Working Paper No. 28, U.S. Bureau of the Census, 1968.

47

users, too, and many of these users find weaknesses in the system for their particular purposes. Criteria used to operationalize something as fundamental and important as the metropolitan concept become the objects of academic evaluation and critique. And because society continues to change, criteria and areas which at one period of time may have been valid representations of conditions and concepts cease to be so with the passage of time.

The resulting response of the Bureau of the Census has been one of successive modification of the definitional criteria, although the original concept has been revised little over the years. Metropolitan Districts were defined in 1940 for each incorporated city having 50,000 or more inhabitants, and included adjacent and contiguous minor civil divisions or incorporated places having a population density of 150 persons per square mile or more.[2] In 1940, however relatively few data were tabulated by minor civil divisions. At the same time, the various government agencies had no set of standardized regions for which they reported statistics. For example, *Industrial Areas,* defined by the Bureau of the Census in the Census of Manufactures, and *Labor Market Areas* used by the Bureau of Employment Security both differed from the Metropolitan Districts by which the Bureau of the Census reported data in the Census of Population.

As a consequence, the *Standard Metropolitan Areas* (SMA's) of 1950 were defined "so that a wide variety of statistical data might be presented on a uniform basis." The SMA consisted of one or more contiguous counties containing at least one city of 50,000 inhabitants. Additional counties had to meet certain criteria of metropolitan character and social and economic integration with the central city in order to be classified within an SMA. Various governmental agencies cooperated to collect and report data by this statistical unit. The SMA was by its very nature a compromise, designed to facilitate uniform reporting of data. It differed from the old Metropolitan District in that it was not defined primarily upon density criteria. The introduction of the *Urbanized* Area in 1950 provided a unit that fit more closely to the idea of the Metropolitan District, although it in turn was a somewhat more restrictively-defined area.

The Standard *Metropolitan Statistical Area* (SMSA) of 1960 represents a slight revision of the SMA concept, the word "statistical" being added so that the character of the area being defined might be better understood.

The primary objective of the SMSA has been stated to be to facilitate the utilization by all Federal statistical agencies of a uniform area for which to publish statistical data useful in analyzing metropolitan problems. The usefulness of the data has been related most especially to the fact that SMSA's take into account places of industrial concentration (labor demands) and of population concentration (labor supply).[3]

Two main claims have been advanced for the SMSA. First, it provides a "standard" area composed of a large city and its closely integrated surrounding area which can be used by the Bureau of the Census and other government agencies for purposes of data gathering, analysis, and presentation. Secondly, the classification provides a distinction between metropolitan and nonmetropolitan areas by type of residence, complementing the older rural-urban, farm-nonfarm distinctions.

Many of the non-Federal users of the SMSA data assume that the areas defined

2. U.S. Bureau of the Census (1941) *Sixteenth Census of the United States:* 1940, Population, Vol. 1, 1942.

3. Otis D. Duncan, "Research on Metropolitan Population: Evaluation of Data," *Journal of the American Statistical Association,* 51 (1956), pp. 591-96.

as metropolitan represent, in some measure, trading areas for the metropolis.[4] Thus, use of SMSA data to establish quantitative indices of potential sales market areas, to set comparative guidelines for contrasting markets and market penetration, and to allocate manpower for sales and promotion efforts is common.

Local and regional planners find SMSA data useful especially because of the quantity of information provided that would be unavailable to them otherwise, and because the areas are ready-made planning regions within which they can study broad trends of change relating to mobility, social and economic patterns of the population, and land use consumption. Recently, as an outcome of the Demonstration Cities and Metropolitan Development Act of 1966, many kinds of requests for federal public works moneys must first be submitted to regional metropolitan planning agencies designated by the federal government. The Bureau of the Budget has been given the responsibility for selecting the appropriate planning agencies, covering the relevant SMSA.

New legal status has thus been given to a set of statistical areas which has been, like its predecessors, subject to intense criticism, and to the pressures of continuing societal change. The purpose of this report is to review this criticism, to evaluate alternative criteria for translating the metropolitan concept into statistical practice, and to illustrate the results of applying the most appropriate of these alternates to a classification of the United States into a set of statistical areas. Primary focus is placed on an exhaustive analysis of the 1960 journey-to-work data tabulated for the Nation's approximately 43,000 census tracts and minor civil divisions or combinations of the latter.

In establishing the SMSA in 1960, the purpose was to set out objective criteria of a quantitative character to define areas "in a manner which reflects the underlying social and economic realities."[5] In the words of the Bureau of the Budget:

The general concept of a metropolitan area is one of an integrated economic and social unit with a recognized large population nucleus. To serve the statistical purposes for which metropolitan areas are defined, their parts must themselves be areas for which statistics are usually or often collected. Thus, each Standard Metropolitan Statistical Area must contain at least one city of at least 50,000 inhabitants. The Standard Metropolitan Statistical Area will then include the county of such a central city, and adjacent counties that are found to be metropolitan in character and economically and socially integrated with the county of the central city. In New England the requirement with regard to a central city as a nucleus still holds, but the units comprising the area are the towns rather than counties. The county (or town in New England) is the basic statistical unit. A Standard Metropolitan Statistical Area may contain more than one city of 50,000 population. The largest city is considered the nucleus and usually gives the name to the area. The name may include other cities in the area. Standard Metropolitan Statistical Areas may cross State lines. . . . One of the basic criteria for measuring economic integration to determine whether additional counties should be included in an area definition, is the relationship of place of residence to place of work, involving outlying counties and the county of the central city. The volume of worker commuting was determined on the basis of data from the 1960 Census of Population.

The definitions presented here are designed to serve a wide variety of statistical and analytical purposes. Adoption of these

4. Allen G. Feldt, "The Metropolitan Area Concept: An Evaluation of the 1950 SMA's," *Journal of the American Statistical Association,* 60 (1965), pp. 617-636.

5. Conrad F. Taeuber, "Regional and Other Area Statistics in the United States," Paper read at the 35th Session of the International Statistical Institute, Belgrade, Yugoslavia, Sept. 1965. (Mimeographed)

areas for any specific purpose should be judged, however, in light of the appropriateness of the criteria by which they are defined.[6]

The Definitional Criteria

The definition of an individual Standard Metropolitan Statistical Area involves two considerations; first, a city or cities of specified population to constitute the central city and to define the county in which it is located as the central county; and, second, economic and social relationships with contiguous counties which are metropolitan in character, so that the periphery of the specific metropolitan area may be determined. Standard Metropolitan Statistical Areas may cross State lines, if this is necessary in order to include qualified contiguous counties.

POPULATION CRITERIA

The minimum population requirements are:
1. Each standard metropolitan statistical area must include at least:
    a) One city with 50,000 or more inhabitants, or
    b) Two cities having contiguous boundaries and constituting, for general economic and social purposes, a single community with a combined population of at least 50,000, the smaller of which must have a population of at least 15,000;
2. If two or more adjacent counties each have a city of 50,000 inhabitants or more (or twin cities under 1b) and the cities are within 20 miles of each other (city limits to city limits), they will be included in the same area unless there is definite evidence that the two cities

6. U.S. Bureau of the Budget (1967) *Standard Metropolitan Statistical Areas.* Washington: United States Government Printing Office, 1967.

are not economically and socially integrated.

CRITERIA OF METROPOLITAN CHARACTER

The criteria of metropolitan character relate primarily to the attributes of the county as a place of work or as a home for a concentration of nonagricultural workers. Specifically, these criteria are:
3. At least 75 percent of the labor force of the county must be in the nonagricultural labor force.
4. In addition to criterion 3, the county must meet at least one of the following conditions:
    a) It must have 50 percent or more of its population living in contiguous minor civil divisions with a density of at least 150 persons per square mile, in an unbroken chain of minor civil divisions with such a density radiating from a central city in the area.
    b) The number of nonagricultural workers employed in the county must equal at least 10 percent of the number of nonagricultural workers employed in the county containing the largest city in the area, or be the place of employment of 10,000 nonagricultural workers.
    c) The nonagricultural labor force living in the county must equal at least 10 percent of the number of the nonagricultural labor force living in the county containing the largest city in the area, or be the place of residence of a nonagricultural labor force of 10,000.
5. In New England, the city and town are administratively more important than the county, and data are compiled locally for such minor civil divisions. Here, towns and cities are the units used in defining standard metropolitan statistical areas. In New England, because smaller units are used and more

restricted areas result, a population density criterion of at least 100 persons per square mile is used as the measure of metropolitan character.

CRITERIA OF INTEGRATION

The criteria of integration relate primarily to the extent of economic and social communication between the outlying counties and central county.

6. A county is regarded as integrated with the county or counties containing the central cities of the area if either of the following criteria is met:

   a) If 15 percent of the workers living in the county work in the county or counties containing the central cities of the area, or

   b) If 25 percent of those working in the county live in the county or counties containing central cities of the area.

Only where data for criteria 6(a) and 6(b) are not conclusive are other related types of information used as necessary. . . . This information includes such items as newspaper circulation reports prepared by the Audit Bureau of Circulation, analysis of charge accounts in retail stores of central cities to determine the extent of their use by residents of the contiguous county, delivery service practices of retail stores in central cities, official traffic counts, the extent of public transportation facilities in operation between central cities and communities in the contiguous county, and to the extent to which local planning groups and other civic organizations operate jointly.

Criticisms of Present Definitions

Each of the criteria used to define the SMSA has been subject to criticism from many points of view. It is clear from these comments that much of the dissatisfaction stems from the compromise nature of the concept as it has been defined. The criti-

cisms are valuable, then, in challenging the bases of the previous criteria and their definitions.

POPULATION CRITERIA

Questions have been raised concerning the basis on which the population criteria should be defined, concerning the necessity of a minimum and/or a maximum limit to population, and regarding the county and distance measures established in Criterion 2 for combining adjacent counties, each containing central cities, into a single SMSA. On a more basic level, there is disagreement concerning the relation of population thresholds and economic organization, as brought out in the work by Fox,[7] and Duncan.[8]

The application of Criterion 2, relating to adjacent counties each having a central city of 50,000 inhabitants or more within 20 miles of each other being included within the same SMSA, has resulted in conflicts with Criterion 6, the commuting criterion. There are 12 cases where cities with 50,000 or more inhabitants within 20 miles of each other do meet the commutation requirements and are classified together within one SMSA. Nine cases occur where cities of 50,000 or more inhabitants within 20 miles of each other do not meet commuting requirements and are classified together as a single SMSA. Seventeen cases exist where cities of 50,000 or more inhabitants within 20 miles of each other are not classified within the same SMSA. In this latter group, one of 17 meets the commuting stipulation. Additionally, there are approximately 40 counties that meet the criteria of metropolitan character and have populations exceeding 100,000 that are not included in any SMSA.

7. Karl A. Fox, "Integrating National and Regional Models for Economic Stabilization and Growth," Paper read at a Conference on National Economic Planning, University of Pittsburgh, March 25-6, 1964. (Mimeographed)
8. Otis D. Duncan et al., Metropolis and Region. Baltimore: Johns Hopkins Press, 1960.

Vandiver has argued that the urbanized area should be used as the population base instead of the central city.[9] A calculation based on urbanized area population would not be difficult since it is already done as a matter of course, but it would involve defining urbanized areas for many cities smaller than 50,000 inhabitants.

The number 50,000 itself has been challenged on several scores. To Fox, that number seems too arbitrary and too large since a great many of the smaller centers of local activity in rural areas will be missed, thus over-emphasizing the importance of size in economic organization of space.[10] Duncan, on the other hand, argues that a city of 50,000 is really too small to constitute a metropolitan center, and that larger areas, with central cities of about 300,000 people, are most meaningful in an economic context today.

CRITERIA OF METROPOLITAN CHARACTER

The criteria of metropolitan character have been subjected to heavy criticism and question. The criticisms arise, for the most part, from the vague and uncertain understanding of the meaning of this concept. No full or adequate apologia for this concept has been enunciated by the Bureau of the Budget, but the social and economic connotations of the criteria have been subject to much debate. There is a need of clarification of the interpretation of the spatial extent of the SMSA. The compromise nature of the present definition has contributed considerably to the confusion.

At the most explicit level, questions about the selection of all particular thresholds have been raised. How does one justify a requirement that 50 percent of the population live in contiguous minor civil divisions with a certain minimum

density? It is no justification to argue, as some have done because this was the density criterion to obtain "metropolitan counties" intercensually in the 1940's as approximations of the Metropolitan District. Specific objections have been raised to the unique definition of the New England SMSA. Critics have suggested raising to 90 percent the proportion of the labor force in a county which must be in the nonagricultural labor force and then dropping Criterion 4 altogether.

In reviewing the comments addressed to it, the Bureau of the Budget has found numerous inconsistencies of application and a bewildering variety of counties rejected from SMSA's because of nonconformance to a few criteria by many counties. For example, the Bureau of the Budget found in a 1966 review, that there were 38 areas in which counties otherwise qualifying as metropolitan have been excluded because of low total population, low total labor force, or insufficiently high population density.

General uncertainties of meaning are accompanied first, by specific questions about the apparent conflicts arising from defining metropolitan character in both economic and social terms. This disjunction is pointed up by the arguments advanced by Fox,[11] and Friedmann and Miller.[12] Second, issues of the urban-rural distinction, a distinction long indistinct, still appear to be built into the metropolitan character criteria in the language of density and size introduced by Wirth.[13] Third, the definition ignores, except in the crudest sense, the question of the necessity for some landscape criteria by which to enunciate metropolitan character. The literature on metropolitan areas reveals a

9. Nels Anderson (ed.), *Urbanism and Urbanization.* Leiden: E. J. Bull, 1964.
10. Karl A. Fox, T. Krishna Kumar, "Programs for Economic Growth in Non-Metropolitan Areas," Ames, Iowa. 1964. (Mimeographed)

11. Fox, *op. cit.*
12. John Friedmann, John Miller, "The Urban Field," *Journal of the American Institute of Planners,* 31 (1965), pp. 312-319.
13. Louis Wirth, "Urbanism as a Way of Life," *American Journal of Sociology,* 38 (1938-9), pp. 1-24.

basic cleavage between scholars relying on some landscape element to form part of their definition and another group who find it unnecessary to include any specific reference to particular landscape features when discussing the concept. Included in the first group are Blumenfeld,[14] Hawley,[15] Pickard,[16] and Schnore.[17] Among those in the second class are Isard and Kavesh,[18] and Webber et al.[19]

Definition of the SMSA with reference both to social and economic criteria has created differing interpretations. It has been implied by some that the county was both a place of work and a home for concentrations of nonagricultural workers while, at the same time, functioning as the primary trading area for the metropolis. Are either or both of these conditions necessary for a county to be metropolitan in an economic sense? Some evidence suggests that wholesale trading territories for large metropolitan areas are conterminous with farm to city migration areas, suggesting a correspondence of boundaries of several indicators of metropolitan economic influence, and that retail trade areas are coincident with commuting areas for smaller places.[20] In agricultural areas and around smaller SMSA central cities, Borchert's findings notwithstanding, others have argued that the general trade area of the central city covers a more extensive terrain than does any kind of extended migration or commutation zone. Further knowledge about commuting patterns will elucidate the unknowns here. It is likely, however, that the patterns will vary for metropolitan areas of different sizes and in different parts of the country.[21] If one refers to a "metropolitan economy," then it is clear that the larger SMSA's are underbounded. If one refers to activity patterns of individuals and groups living within metropolitan areas, then it is clear from research that there is little difference between groups included within metropolitan areas and some of those which are excluded.[22] The differences appear to be more distinct between workers engaged in urban pursuits and those engaged in rural agricultural pursuits.[23] If by metropolitan character of an area we mean the use made of that land by various groups, then it is clear that the sphere of influence of metropolitan dwellers extends far beyond the counties currently classified as metropolitan. At this point the discussion reverts to the problem of interpreting what is meant by "metropolitan."

CRITERIA OF INTEGRATION

A review of the criticisms and comments concerning the criteria of integration reveals a lack of satisfaction with the current definition, based as it is only on commuting to or from the county containing the central city. General comment about the concept of metropolitan areas con-

14. Hans Blumenfeld, "On the Growth of Metropolitan Areas," *Social Forces,* 28 (1949), pp. 59-64.

15. Amos H. Hawley, *The Changing Shape of Metropolitan America.* Glencoe: The Free Press, 1956.

16. Jerome Pickard, "Urban Regions of the United States," *Urban Land,* 21, No. 4 (Apr., 1962), pp. 3-9.

17. Leo F. Schnore, "Metropolitan Growth and Decentralization" *American Journal of Sociology,* 63 (1957-8), pp. 171-80. Leo F. Schnore, "The Growth of Metropolitan Suburbs," *American Sociological Review,* 22 (1957), pp. 165-73.

18. Walter Isard, Robert Kavesh, "Economic Structural Interrelations of Metropolitan Regions." *American Journal of Sociology,* 60 (1954-5) pp. 152-62.

19. Melvin M. Webber et al., *Explorations into Urban Structure,* Philadelphia, University of Pennsylvania Press, 1964.

20. John R. Borchert et al., *Urban Reports,* No. 1-3 (1961-63), Minneapolis: Upper Midwest Economic Study, 1961-63.

21. Donald J. Bogue, *The Structure of the Metropolitan Community.* Ann Arbor: Horace H. Rackham School of Graduate Studies, 1949.

22. Conrad F. Taeuber, Irene B. Taeuber, *The Changing Population of the United States.* New York: Wiley, 1958.

23. Otis D. Duncan, Albert J. Reiss, *Urban and Rural Communities of the United States.* New York: Wiley, 1956.

firms this criticism, with many suggestions that a more precise and detailed statement about economic and social integration within the metropolitan area must be made.

The percentage figures established by the Bureau of the Budget in Criteria 6(a) and 6(b) have been questioned. The discrepancy seems particularly curious and a recent decision has been made by the Bureau of the Budget to eliminate the difference and use 15 percent in both cases. The necessity for direct contact with the central county has been questioned by pointing to the lack of unified labor markets within large metropolitan areas. The achievement of maximum accessibility throughout the metropolitan areas with reductions in the cost and time required for travel has led to the suggestion that a commuting radius be established on the basis of time taken to reach the central county or its central area.

The whole question of integration without what is commonly thought to be metropolitan character is implicit in several of the classification schemes. The classifications suggested by both Friedmann and Miller, and by Fox revolve around a notion of integration without the accompanying population density criterion now closely associated with metropolitan character. The two proposals will be discussed at greater length in the following section of the report, but it is well to note here that these schemes propose a radical alternative to our present definition of the metropolitan concept. Friedmann and Miller see a changing scale in urban life accompanying technological and economic developments. Such an idea rejects as no longer useful the classification distinguishing metropolitan from nonmetropolitan, and it suggests that a new and broad *urban realm* is significant. The argument rests largely on the claim that the area in which a metropolitan population lives and conducts its social activities now encompasses a broad zone around met-

ropolitan centers. This zone, or realm, extends, perhaps, to about 100 miles from the central city, and is defined as the limits for regular weekend or seasonal use. Within this area, the imprint of the urban dweller is of paramount significance. Such realms are largely coincident with areas of general economic health.

Fox is concerned with small, functionally specialized regions which he considers to be the major facts of economic importance in the regionalization of most of the country. Integration here is often without metropolitan character since many of the smaller centers are too tiny to be classed as metropolitan under present schemes or because population densities may be low. Nevertheless, Fox posits such a system of *functional economic areas* as the economic building blocks for a regionalization of the United States.

Commentators are always bound to point out, in any discussion of the criteria of metropolitan character or integration that the issues are bound together and one's understanding of the one can hardly be divorced from the other.

The whole idea of using distance as a major criterion of definition has been challenged by suggestions that time-distance measures ought to be used instead.[24] It has been suggested that selfsustaining economic growth of a region be made the basis of defining one level of metropolitan region and its central city. Researchers who have sought to make trade areas out of metropolitan regions defined by the Census have suggested that selfsufficiency with respect to local services be made the criteria for defining metropolitan areas.

Alternate Proposals for New Classification Systems

The various proposals for establishing new classification systems can be seen as attempts to bring into focus the social

24. Hans Blumenfeld, "The Tidal Wave of Metropolitan Expansion," *Journal of the American Institute of Planners*, 20 (1954), pp. 3-14.

and/or economic aspects of what the research workers consider to be a viable and used concept of the metropolitan area. Definitions of "metropolitan" are often absent from the discussion, but all classifications can be considered as approaches to the regionalization of the country in forms which will highlight what are thought to be the important processes at work in creating the present scene. As an introduction to what follows, three questions can be asked, the answers for which it will be useful to search in the proposed classification schemes:

1. What areal bases are appropriate for defining metropolitan areas? On this point, opinion is generally unanimous that the two aspects represented in the present classification—the economic and social conditions defining metropolitan areas—cannot now be defined meaningfully by outlining one set of regions, occupying a tiny fraction of the total land area, classed as metropolitan and another region, occupying most of the land area, classified as nonmetropolitan.

2. The second question finds less agreement. Can social and economic areas be mapped using coincident boundaries, or must there be a separate classification of territory for each? Some argue that the sphere of metropolitan economic influence is more widespread and general across the country than that of metropolitan social influence. Others, arguing from the facts of the greatly increasing mobility of metropolitan residents, state that the impact of metropolitan dwellers is everywhere evident if one examines areas they visit and use regularly for recreational and other purposes.

3. Can all social communication be subsumed under a single area classification outlining areas of metropolitan residents' social activities? If the journey to work and the weekend holiday involve use and habituation of greatly

differing areas, should not two or more types of social region be defined, at least one based on day to day contact and the other on more extensive territories infrequently occupied by metropolitan population?

From the preceding paragraphs it can be seen that one of the major problems involves the interpretation of the areal boundaries drawn on the map, especially since economic and social area boundaries apparently are so often not coincident. A much more explicit statement of the interpretation of the metropolitan concept and its usage would seem warranted, no matter what decision is reached regarding the classification scheme. The following paragraphs will outline some of the alternative classification systems which have been proposed, considering in each case the implicit or explicit answers provided to the questions outlined above.

Two schemes have been proposed which consider the overall economic organization of the country: one was that of Bogue, emphasizing metropolitan dominance over an adjacent hinterland, and the other was suggested by Duncan *et al.* based on a detailed empirical study of functional specialization in U.S. cities.

METROPOLITAN DOMINANCE

Bogue attempted to examine the hypothesis that the metropolis, by 1950, had come to dominate the social and economic organization of a technologically advanced society such as the United States. Transportation efficiency had, presumably, greatly extended the radius of convenient daily movement to and from the city, diffusing the urban mode of life over ever increasing areas. Distance, therefore, was considered to be the single most important determining factor setting the limits of areas of metropolitan dominance.

In practice, Bogue divided the entire area of the Nation into "metropolitan communities" and abstracted patterns of population distribution from various groupings of these communities. He somewhat arbitrarily began by selecting 67 metropolitan communities, each of the 67 claiming as hinterland all areas lying closest to itself.

Such an arbitrary scheme of division of the area between zones of dominance ignores differences of kind between the largest and smallest of the metropolitan centers. His concept of "metropolitan" was not defined, nor was the selection of the 67 centers justified. Because the distance relationships among the metropolitan centers in the northeast differ from those relationships among cities in other parts of the country, comparisons of the data by distance zones are misleading, for the comparisons are really of different sets of centers.[25] Bogue's work made no reference to data on social interaction and so did not broach the second and third questions posed above. He included and labeled areas as "metropolitan" which are more extensive areally than those so labeled at present. Without providing con- The various proposals for establishing new vincing supporting arguments or evidence Bogue used the concepts of metropolitan area developed by Gras and McKenzie. Gras argued that in defining the metropolis, it was the hinterland that was the important element—and the sphere of commercial dominance that was particularly important.[26] He stressed interdependence of function rather than size. McKenzie sought to explore the dominance of the metropolitan city over social organization in the surrounding areas.[27]

In a later work, Hawley utilized much the same conceptual framework of metropolitan dominance to test the adequacy

25. Hans Blumenfeld, "The Dominance of the Metropolis," *Land Economics,* 26 (1950), pp. 194-6.
26. N. S. B. Gras, *An Introduction to Economic History*. New York: Harper and Brothers, 1922.
27. R. D. McKenzie, *The Metropolitan Community*. New York: McGraw-Hill, 1933.

of the SMA's as population growth poles. He arbitrarily selected a 35 mile radius from central cities and measured population growth within this area to see the extent to which national growth was metropolitan oriented. Over 90 percent of population growth occurred within 25 miles of a central city, but the radius within which this growth occurred increased only slightly from 1900 to 1950.

FUNCTIONAL SPECIALIZATION

Work on functional specialization and areas of metropolitan economic influence was accomplished by Duncan and his associates. Using wholesale trade, bank clearings, business service receipts, value added by manufacture, and retail trade as indicators of metropolitan influence they found the larger metropoli to be much more diversified than the smaller. They concluded that the critical population level for emergence of metropolitan character is 300,000. Above this population, metropolitan areas are, generally, diversified while below it they are functionally specialized. A hierarchy of types of economic relations can be found, but at the highest level the whole Nation is served by one set of metropolitan areas. Concerning a range of higher order goods and services, a metropolitan economy can be discerned which is organized and directed by these great metropolitan centers.

Several suggested schemes of classification have been based on the idea that the country can be divided up into a set of relatively small and somewhat independent local areas which accurately delineate, in economic or social terms, areas of distinct local identity. A few of these schemes will be outlined, briefly, below.

FUNCTIONAL ECONOMIC AREAS

An attempt is made here to set out, ecologically, the labor market areas of central cities, by defining around them a set of small towns and villages and farms which comprise the area of active commuting to the central city. This area forms, according to Fox, the chief proponent of this scheme, a low density city characterized by definite interaction of the various parts with the center. The FEA becomes an independent unit in terms of local services to adjacent population. Fox maintains that the United States, outside the largest metropolitan areas, can be divided into a series of such functional economic areas which will approximate relatively bounded or closed labor market areas.[28] By proceeding to recognize this fact, one can classify workers by place of residence *and* place of work in a way allowing for the minimization of interarea commuting.

To achieve the classification, data needs are considerable. Required is some model of the economy produced by examining the system of structural relations connecting the country and its parts. Flow data are especially necessary for the analysis. The FEA results from local economies of size and specialized management. A central city of the order of 25,000 inhabitants or more is required.

The argument amounts to a statement which asserts that areas of social significance in terms of intimate daily contact are coextensive with areas meaningful in local economic terms.

STATE ECONOMIC AREAS

Bogue and Beale,[29] in setting down a complete system of SEA's for the United States, state that they have subdivided the country into units which are homogeneous with respect to general livelihood and socioeconomic characteristics. They maintain a distinction between metropol-

itan and nonmetropolitan SEA's based on the Bureau of the Budget definitions of metropolitan areas. Their data, evaluated by subjective procedures, consisted of information on land use, industry, social characteristics of the population and the wide range of information available in the various censuses. Their building blocks are counties. The SEA is the basic unit from which a hierarchy of economic areas is built.

The particular areas defined by Bogue and Beale have been called into question by various scholars, as have their methods of delimitation but the idea that the country can be subdivided into a set of relatively selfcontained economic areas, using more rigidly defined procedures, has not been questioned. As defined, however, SEA's provide little insight into any of the questions posed. Vining's answer to this classification is that the arbitrariness of the boundaries established here can be overcome only by examining commodity flows and functional hierarchies rather than by assuming some arbitrary functional grouping of counties each presumed to contain distinctive economies.[30]

URBAN COMMUNITY OF INTEREST AREAS

The premise upon which this argument is based is that the great metropolitan areas are too large to constitute a single labor market area.[31] A new unit is called for which is defined on the basis of generalized areal spheres within which immediate ties of families and communities can be identified. An expectation here is that, at least for the majority of urban dwellers, there is a definably regular pattern of daily activity which can be mapped

28. Charles L. Leven (ed.), *Design of a National System of Regional Accounts.* St. Louis: Institute for Urban and Regional Studies, Washington University, 1967.

29. Donald J. Bogue, Calvin L. Beale, *Economic Areas of the United States.* Glencoe: Free Press, 1961.

30. Rutledge Vining, "Delimitation of Economic Areas: Statistical Conceptions of the Spatial Structure of an Economic System," *Journal of the American Statistical Association,* 48 (1953), pp. 44-64.

31. B. J. L. Berry, W. Garrison, and K. Fox, "Urban Community of Interest Areas." Unpublished paper, 1966.

and generalized. The important activities can be classed as journey to work and immediate shopping and social trips.

This approach provides some answers to the first two questions posed above. It defines social areas within the city which are small and are clearly distinct from areas of economic influence. For the family or community, however, the areas within which regular and frequent social and economic activities are undertaken are coterminous, if the argument is to be accepted.

THE NONPLACE URBAN REALM

There is another argument about social areas that comes to a different conclusion by examining the activities of a different class of urban dwellers. For Webber, the community of interest is no longer conditioned by propinquity. Travel is easy and interests diffuse so that simple mapping procedures can no longer plot the urban spaces which a man inhabits, nor can they separate any urban realm from a rural one adjacent to it. This functionalist view sees the distinction of activity by place of activity exaggerated. Here is a plea for a new meaning of "community" based on an appreciation of the notion of interdependence. Such an argument seems most appropriate when examining activity patterns of upper class, mobile persons whose activities are not conditioned by factory, store or office hours to the degree to which most workers' movements must be.

THE URBAN FIELD

The third of the three questions posed is most directly answered in the propositions outlined by Friedmann and Miller in a discussion of the expanding scene in which urban residents live. The authors argue that increasing mobility has created around areas which are customarily called urban places vast territories which are now integral parts of the widening environment of urban dwellers. These border areas contain the commuting population and also accommodate the weekend travelers from the city. Great reaches of the land have become, in short, economically and socially a part of the urban community. The outer borders of these metropolitan peripheries, in contrast to the traditionally described metropolitan peripheries, are the areas of economic stress and outmigration, and are those places most characterized by substandard educational, health and service facilities. They are, in consequence, characterized also by a declining economic base, an aging population, and low incomes which serve to lock them in and make them helpless in their desire to adapt to changing circumstances.

The urban field is an ecological unit which has been created by the increase in real income, increase in leisure time, and increasing mobility on the part of those people who occupy the country's great metropolitan centers.

ROBIN J. PRYOR

Defining the Rural-Urban Fringe

T. L. Smith's discussion of the "urban fringe" around Louisiana in 1937 marked the first use of this term signifying "the built-up area just outside the corporate limits of the city."[1]

As a landscape phenomenon, the fringe varies from city to city, and from one time to another. Around several cities in the Netherlands a fringe is barely recognizable; Paris is somewhat similar to the U.S.A. in the intermingling and scatter of land use, but there is a closer dependence on public transportation; London is different again, because of its Green Belt, although there is some scattering of land use, and some villages are located *within* this belt. In general, Dickinson concludes that the modern European city "exhibits the same tendency to extend and explode" as the North American metropolis, "but not nearly to the same degree."[2] Conversely, some American writers now question whether the urban fringe *problem* is disappearing, because "laws permit more

cities to supervise zoning within a certain distance of their borders."[3]

Two features characterize the literature on urban fringe over the past 30 years:

1. The general absence of explicit references to the subject outside North America, although there have been studies, for example, in Sydney,[4] Adelaide,[5] Melbourne,[6] and in London[7] and Johannes-

1. T. L. Smith, "The Population of Louisiana: Its Composition and Changes," *Louisiana Bulletin,* 293 (November 1937).
2. R. E. Dickinson, *The City Region in Western Europe* (London: Routledge Paperback, 1967).

3. E.g., R. E. Murphy, *The American City: An Urban Geography* (New York: McGraw-Hill Book Co., 1966).
4. N. R. Wills, "The Rural-Urban Fringe: Some Agricultural Characteristics with Specific Reference to Sydney," *Australian Geographer,* 5 (1945), pp. 29-35; and R. Golledge, "Sydney's Metropolitan Fringe: A Study in Urban-Rural Relations," *Australian Geographer,* 7 (1959), p. 243 ff.
5. D. L. Smith, "Market Gardening at Adelaide's Urban Fringe," *Economic Geography,* 42 (1966), p. 19 ff.
6. R. J. Johnston, "The Population Characteristics of the Urban Fringe: A Review and Example," *Australian and New Zealand Journal of Sociology,* 2 (1966), pp. 79-93.
7. R. E. Pahl, *Urbs in Rure: The Metropolitan Fringe in Hertfordshire* (London: London School of Economics and Political Science, Geographical Papers No. 2, 1965).

From **Social Forces,** Vol. 47, No. 2, December 1968. Reprinted by permission of the University of North Carolina Press.

burg.[8] The relatively integral urban nature (rather than nonoccurrence) of the fringe around European cities emerges from Wissink's comparison of that continent with the American urban scene.[9]

2. The confusion of terminology and lack of clear delineation in case studies. The problem of evaluating and comparing cases is increased by (1) their range in time, as prevailing economic conditions influence the rate of growth and internal characteristics of the fringe; (2) the range in size of the urban center, from a small village to a metropolis or Standard Metropolitan Statistical Area, each with inherent differences in its fringe, according to the rate of growth, functions, and hierarchical relationship of the central place; (3) the variation in type and degree of zoning control of urban invasion beyond a city's corporate limits, so that London's modified Green Belt results in a very different form of guided "overspill" to Eugene-Springfield's "uncontrolled population expansion";[10] (4) the differing social, economic and political contexts of the studies from different countries; and (5) the differing aims and interests of various research workers.

A Review of Related Terms

Because of this diversity, a number of attempts have been made to clarify concepts, and to differentiate between commonly used terms. After reviewing some ten definitions, Kurtz and Eicher[11] differentiate between "fringe" and "suburb"; Wissink[12] defines "fringe," "suburbs," "pseudo-suburbs," "satellites" and "pseudo-satellites"; Schnore[13] distinguishes between "satellites" and "suburbs"; and a number of writers have described different types of suburbs, some of which could be synonymous with the "fringe" of another research worker. Martin discusses satellite rural areas.[14]

Areal differentiations have also been made, qualitatively, *within* the fringe: the "urban fringe" and the "rural-urban fringe";[15] the "limited fringe" and the "extended fringe";[16] the "suburban fringe zone" and the "outlying adjacent zone";[17] and inner and outer fringe areas.[18] American census categories permit the differentiation of urban fringe, rural non-farm (RNF), and rural farm (RF) within the Chicago fringe,[19] and "true fringe," "partial fringe," and "adjacent rural townships" outside incorporated Detroit;[20] the area between the Melbourne Metropoli-

8. G. H. T. Hart and T. C. Partridge, "Factors in the Development of the Urban Fringe North-West of Johannesburg," *South African Geographical Journal,* 48 (1966), pp. 32-34.

9. G. A. Wissink, *American Cities in Perspective: With Special Reference to the Development of Their Fringe Areas,* Sociaal Geografische Studies, Hoogleraar aan de Rijksuniversiteit te Utrecht, Nr. 5 (Assen, Netherlands: Royal Van Gorcum, 1962).

10. W. T. Martin, *The Rural-Urban Fringe: A Study of Adjustment to Residence Location* (Eugene: University of Oregon Studies in Sociology, No. 1, 1953).

11. R. A. Kurtz and J. B. Eicher, "Fringe and Suburbs: A Confusion of Concepts," *Social Forces,* 37 (October 1958), pp. 32-37.

12. Wissink, *op. cit.*

13. Leo F. Schnore, "Satellites and Suburbs," *Social Forces,* 36 (December 1957), pp. 121-127.

14. W. T. Martin, "Ecological Change in Satellite Rural Areas," *American Sociological Review,* 22 (April 1957), pp. 173-183.

15. R. B. Andrews, "Elements in the Urban Fringe Pattern," *Journal of Land and Public Utility Economics,* 18 (May 1942), pp. 169-183.

16. W. C. McKain and R. G. Burnight, "The Sociological Significance of the Rural-Urban Fringe: From the Rural Point of View," *Rural Sociology,* 18 (June 1953), pp. 109-116.

17. M. W. Reinemann, "The Pattern and Distribution of Manufacturing in the Chicago Area," *Economic Geography,* 36 (1960), pp. 139-144.

18. Wissink, *op. cit.*

19. O. D. Duncan and A. J. Reiss, "Suburbs and Urban Fringe," in *Social Characteristics of Urban and Rural Communities* (New York: John Wiley & Sons, 1956).

20. R. B. Myers and J. A. Beegle, "Delineation and Analysis of the Rural-Urban Fringe," *Applied Anthropology,* 6 (Spring 1947), pp. 14-22.

tan Area and Melbourne Statistical Division boundaries in the 1966 Census of the Commonwealth of Australia provides a comparable census zone. The interest of human ecologists in the fringe has added the undefined "rurban fringe" and "rurbanization" to the literature; and "slurb," the "slopped-over suburb," is a more recent deviant from objective terminology.[21]

Definition and Delineation

From a review of some 60 case studies of fringe areas, four major and six minor components emerge from previous definitions, together with a variety of delineation techniques, and these are summarized in Table 1. To date, no definition has successfully integrated these various com-

21. H. Parsons, "Slurb is (sic)," paper presented at the 39th Congress of ANZAAS, Melbourne, 1967.

ponents of the fringe with (1) theories of urban invasion, and (2) practical delineation techniques. It appears to the present writer that these aspects should be integrated, and a proposal for this is made below which will need to be validated quantitatively by future research.

The heterogeneity which writers acknowledge as characteristic of the fringe may be, from one point of view, inconclusive in its very complexity, yet it is better viewed, as *distinctive* in comparison with related urban and rural characteristics. A rural-urban fringe can only exist between a growing urban center and its rural hinterland, so it is no diminution of the concept to view it as the *residual zone* between two more readily defined poles. Characteristics of the fringe need not be intermediate nor on a continuum between rural and urban, yet distinctive location and internal *heterogeneity and transition*

Table 1. The Rural-Urban Fringe: Definition and Delineation

Structural Content		Functional Content	
Definition	*Delineation*	*Definition*	*Delineation*
Location	Census categories (direct or derived) e.g., non-village RNF, urbanized area minus central city	Land use	Specific e.g., market gardens Mixed e.g., between limits of exclusively urban or rural land
	Contiguous census units e.g., "first-tier counties"		Valuation changes
		Employment	Census categories e.g., RNF
Administration	Non-census areal units beyond control of central city e.g., school, voting districts.		Commuting zone beyond central city boundary
		Population density	Rate of growth per year or inter-censal
Population density	Selected parameter e.g., 500 sq. mile		
		Utility services	Area not served by specific services
Zoning regulations	Zoned mixed land use (rural and urban)		
	Lack of subdivision control	Social orientation	Rural location, urban orientation of social activity
Dwelling age	Selected parameters e.g., proportion in recent inter-censal period	"Transition," "dynamism"	Undergoing change e.g., increase in population density or vacant or urban land.

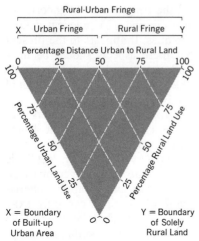

Figure 1. Schematic Diagram of Land Use in the Rural-Urban Fringe

do make possible a unitary if not uniform definition. Figure 1 combines the concept of urban invasion with the heterogeneous land use typical of the fringe; it also introduces the possibility of the "rural-urban fringe" being used as a collective term for the "urban fringe" plus the "rural fringe." The diagram. can also be viewed as a process-response model, with the *process* of urbanization (growth in city size and the percentage of the population urban) resulting in the *response* of land use conversion, transition, and invasion (decline in argicultural acreage and percentage of the rural population). Differentiation of "urban fringe" and "rural fringe" will assist longitudinal studies of the urban invasion of rural areas, particularly in relation to Burgess' zone theory,[22] and Sinclair's recent discussion of the influence of "anticipation of urban encroachment" on rural land in proximity to a growing urban area.[23]

22. E. W. Burgess, "The Growth of the City," in R. E. Park, E. W. Burgess, and R. D. McKenzie (eds.), *The City* (Chicago, University of Chicago Press, 1925).
23. R. Sinclair, "Von Thunen and Urban Sprawl," *Annals of the Association of American Geographers,* 57 (1967), pp. 72-87.

Bearing in mind previous definitions of the rural-urban fringe and the essential components identified by them, the need to take account of the process of urban invasion, and the desirability for the delineation technique to be integral with the definition, the following definition is presented for further testing:

The rural-urban fringe is the zone of transition in land use, social and demographic characteristics, lying between (a) the continuously built-up urban and suburban areas of the central city, and (b) the rural hinterland, characterized by the almost complete absence of nonfarm dwellings, occupations and land use, and of urban and rural social orientation; an incomplete range and penetration of urban utility services; uncoordinated zoning or planning regulations; areal extension beyond although contiguous with the political boundary of the central city; and an actual and potential increase in population density, with the current density above that of surrounding rural districts but lower than the central city. These characteristics may differ both zonally and sectorally, and will be modified through time.

Within the rural-urban fringe it may be possible to identify:
1. *The urban fringe,* that subzone of the rural-urban fringe in contact and contiguous with the central city, exhibiting a density of occupied dwellings higher than the median density of the total rural-urban fringe—a high proportion of residential, commercial, industrial and vacant as distinct from farmland—and a higher rate of increase in population density, land use conversion, and commuting; and
2. *The rural fringe,* that subzone of the rural-urban fringe contiguous with the urban fringe, exhibiting a density of occupied dwellings lower than the median density of the total rural-urban fringe, a high proportion of farm as distinct from nonfarm and vacant land, and a lower rate of increase in population density,

land use conversion, and commuting.

Turning from the general concept and definition of the rural-urban fringe to the detailed findings of the large number of case studies, there is a similar need for clarification, and ample scope for the construction of hypotheses which will subsequently contribute to more objective research. Such hypotheses are subject to the criticism that they attempt to relate findings from a diversity of locales and scales—analyzed and presented by diverse techniques, and frequently unaccompanied by terminological definitions or statements of underlying assumptions. Nevertheless, some generality appears, and hypotheses are presented here for testing in as rigorous a manner and in as wide a field of case studies as possible.

The hypotheses which result from a content analysis of past case studies are summarized in three sections: (a) the residents of the fringe; (b) the factor of accessibility in the fringe; and (c) land and dwellings in the fringe. Unless otherwise stated, the total rural-urban fringe is being considered. In the space available it is not practicable to indicate by footnote the source of each generalization, although the more important references (extracted from a larger study)[24] are included. Similarly, many variables are operative, but cannot be discussed in a paper of this length.

THE RESIDENTS OF THE FRINGE

Demographic and related parameters commonly reflected the attraction of the fringe of an urban area to a particular group—young couples in the early years of married life establishing their first home. The *age distribution* is positively skewed with a greater proportion in younger age groups. The *sex ratio* of the

fringe is higher than that of the urban area itself, but lower than the surrounding rural areas; the degree of male predominance may however vary from place to place within the fringe. This reflects both the high proportion of households with two or more persons (married couples), and more employment opportunities for men.

The *fertility ratio* of the fringe is higher than that of the urban place itself, but lower than surrounding rural areas; one variable is the age of development of a specific location within the fringe. Myers and Beegle[25] concluded that "the substantially higher ratio of the fringe . . . points to the fringe as a significant area where relatively larger numbers of children are produced and a place in which the problems of youth are of major importance." Johnston found the urban-rural gradient unsubstantiated in the case of Melbourne—the differences "probably result from the age of development variations."[26]

The fringe is characterized by a high *proportion of married residents* as compared with the adjacent urban and rural areas. A majority of residents have (a) moved to fringe areas soon after marriage and have no children, or (b) commenced families and can finance newer and/or larger homes. Only Rodehaver[27] appears to have documented the *years married before moving to the fringe*: at least *50* percent of residents move to their fringe residences within 10 years of marriage, with the mean number of elapsed years lower for those of urban rather than rural background. *Size of households:* households in the fringe are on average larger than those of the urban area itself, but smaller than those in surrounding rural areas.

T. L. Smith in *The Sociology of Rural*

24. R. J. Pryor, "City Growth and the Rural-Urban Fringe," unpublished M. A. thesis, University of Melbourne, 1967.

25. Myers and Beegle, *op. cit.*
26. Johnston, *op. cit.*
27. M. W. Rodehaver, "Fringe Settlement as a Two-Directional Movement," *Rural Sociology,* 12 (March 1947).

Life[28] hypothesizes an urban-rural continuum, with a declining proportion of *foreign-born* residents with increasing distance from the central city, and case studies of the fringe have generally borne this out: the proportion of foreign-born residents in the fringe is lower than that of the urban area itself, but higher than surrounding rural areas. Although in a sense "decentralized," residents are usually economically tied to the central city, but there are few consistent findings on social and economic characteristics. The residents in the fringe exhibit a heterogeneous *occupational structure,* with both zonal and sectoral components, and a slightly greater proportion in the commercial and skilled-worker classes than urban or rural areas. *Socioeconomic status,* a complexly derived index, is usually related to occupation and income, but there is a lack of reliable standardized measures. From the varied evidence available, residents in the fringe exhibit wide heterogeneity of socioeconomic status, with sectoral rather than zonal concentrations.

Income distribution, closely related to the two preceding characteristics, does not differ markedly from the central city, mainly because of the heterogeneity already discussed. The residents in the fringe exhibit a positively-skewed income distribution, and a mean annual income per person or per household higher than that of the associated urban and rural areas. Another socioeconomic index analyzed by a number of writers is that of *educational achievement.* For example, Martin[29] concludes from his study of U. S. A. satellite rural areas that there is an upward gradient from rural to urban areas, and this can be related both to exurban invasion, and to the occupational and income characteristics of the fringe:

28. T. L. Smith, *The Sociology of Rural Life* (New York: Harper & Bros., 1947).
29. Martin, "Ecological Change in Satellite Rural Areas."

the residents in the fringe exhibit a lower educational level, by various measures, than residents of the urban place itself, but higher than the surrounding rural areas.

Analyses of length of residence in the fringe, and of the residential background of fringe dwellers, provide consistent evidence for both the instability and transitional nature of this exurban zone, and for the primarily urban source of the population; these characteristics support the concept of invation from a growing urban center, and help to explain the spatial appearance of the fringe, and the motivation of migration.

From studies of *childhood residence location* it is concluded that a higher proportion of residents of the fringe have an urban rather than a rural or rural/urban background. The two variables of sex and socioeconomic status are significant—a higher proportion of males having a rural background, and a higher proportion of middle-class (white-collar) residents having an urban background. While centripetal forces, or rural exodus, and intra- and interstate migration will make a small contribution, it could be expected that the *previous address* of fringe residents would provide even stronger support for the city being the main source of migration, and this generally proves to be true: in a majority of cases the previous homes of fringe residents were in the adjacent urban area, with centripetal and other migration patterns making a varied but smaller contribution. *Length of residence* is a useful index of the dynamism and transitional nature of the fringe, and of its general age of development. While divergent time-periods have been used in various studies, it is concluded that at least *50* percent of the residents have been located in the fringe for less than five years.

The rural-urban fringe is populated by *individuals* who have made personal decisions to migrate, and who subsequently make their own evaluations of their new residential location. In a sense, these individual decisions and motivations are the *raison d'etre* of the fringe as a landscape phenomenon, and in many ways reflect the characteristics which have already been outlined. The most important *reasons for movement to the fringe* are the search for less congestion and more privacy, to be near employment, and for the benefit of children; differences are to be expected between previously urban and rural families, and between individual localities because of differing attractions. As well as the general motivation to move to a new area, specific site characteristics may also be sought, or even take preeminence. The most important *reasons for the choice of a particular site* in the fringe are suitability of the house and desirable lot size. Attraction to the general neighborhood, and access to employment, schools, and the central city will be important to a smaller proportion of households, and differences may be correlated with socioeconomic status.

Because of the varied residential and socioeconomic backgrounds of fringe residents, and the diversity of reasons for moving to the fringe, residential stability and satisfaction will also vary. Studies of the degree of social adjustment, the participation of residents in community organizations and social activities, and of their attitudes toward living in fringe areas, provide some insight into the future stability, or conversely, new intracity migrations, of this low density residence zone. Perceived advantages and disadvantages of the fringe, correlated with other characteristics of present residents, may throw light on future spatial features of the expanding city.

The residents in the fringe exhibit a low degree of *social and community participation* and associational ties. A number of studies of the fringe have documented the residents' *attitudes to living in a fringe area.* Outstanding among these is Martin's study of adjustment to residential location in the Eugene-Springfield fringe.[30] The residents in the fringe are generally well satisfied with their residence location with the exception of unsatisfactory utility services.

THE FACTOR OF ACCESSIBILITY IN THE FRINGE

Distance operates as a major constraint in shaping and facilitating urban growth, and the friction of space experienced by the rural-urban fringe is but a particular example of a principle generally accepted in human ecology and geography: ". . . the layout of a metropolis—the assignment of activities to areas—tends to be determined by a principle which may be termed the minimizing of the cost of friction."[31] This situation is of course complicated where there is not one point of maximum accessibility, but multiple urban nuclei, and where other advantages of residential location, such as the semi-rural environment in the fringe, outweigh sheer physical distance; as Clark and Peters state in a slightly different context "opportunities override distances."[32] The accessibility of services is also a reflection of the stage of development of an area, so that the friction of space may operate via distance from an extending network of services rather than from one or more points at one time. Public utilities and mass transport modes, and the degree of access of an individual to work places, schools and retail centers, tend to be sources of dissatisfaction to fringe residents due to the frequent incomplete range and capacity of such services, at

30. Martin, *The Rural-Urban Fringe.*
31. R. M. Haig, "Toward an Understanding of the Metropolis: Some Speculations Regarding the Economic Basis of Urban Concentration," *Quarterly Journal of Economics,* 40 (1926), pp. 179-208 and 402-434.
32. C. Clark and G. H. Peters, "The 'Intervening Opportunities' Method of Traffic Analysis," *Traffic Quarterly,* 19 (January 1965).

least in the early stages of urban invasion.

It is concluded from case studies that the fringe is characterized by an incomplete range and incomplete network of *utility services* such as reticulated water, electricity, gas and sewerage mains, fire hydrants and sealed roads; this inadequate service sometimes results from difficult physical terrain, and sometimes from inadequate finances to keep capital works in phase with low density urban encroachment. For similar reasons, the fringe commonly has an inadequate network of *public transport modes,* and consequently there may be dissatisfaction wtih this service among some residents; where public transport routes do exist, there is often morphological evidence of their contribution to the formation of the fringe via residential and industrial invasion and ribbon development.

Presumably because of the inadequacy of public transport, and the needs of a commuting population, the fringe area is characterized by relatively high *car ownership* as compared with the associated urban and rural areas. A majority of the *work places* of residents in the fringe are in the city itself, rather than in the fringe or surrounding rural areas, other advantages of residence location outweighing the friction of space involved in commuting. The *accessibility of schools* in terms of distance traveled, and available transport modes, is a problem for households in the fringe. A majority of the *retail centers* patronized by fringe residents are in the urban area itself, rather than in the fringe or surrounding rural areas.

LAND AND DWELLINGS IN THE FRINGE

Land use in the rural-urban fringe is distinctively intermingled and transitional, with an irregular transition from farm to non-farm land. Here too may be found manufacturing or commercial enterprises requiring large acreages; noxious, extractive or other industries zoned-out from the central city; vacant, "dead," or "tax delinquent" land; and scattered urban settlement aligned along highways, in nodes around railway stations, or in other "leap-frog" pockets. Zoning and master plans may assist more orderly invasion of the rural hinterland, cause uneconomic leap-frogging, or if nonexistent, allow totally uncoordinated and piecemeal speculation and the juxtapositioning of incompatible land uses. In rural areas, land values and rates increase with the anticipation of urbanization, and various studies have identified distinctive characteristics in nonfarm dwellings as well as in land use.

On *administration and planning* in fringe areas, case studies have identified (1) excessive and premature subdivision in close proximity to expanding urban centers; (2) the tax delinquency of fringe areas undergoing transition or stagnation in land use;[33] (3) the general need for planning and control, for order and economy in the conversion from rural to land use; and (4) the significance of the urban or rural background of fringe residents in the acceptance of governmental intervention in land use zoning, and in determining the services desired and the attitude toward taxes providing these. It is concluded that the fringe is characterized by inadequate control of subdivision; tax delinquency; zoning inadequately geared to the present and future needs of the expanding urban place; and a conflict of interest in the type and extent of control, between long-established residents and newcomers, and between the central (metropolitan) and local planning or administrative authorities.

Agricultural land use: the fringe area is characterized by a smaller proportion of farm workers than rural areas; by a

33. E.g., H. G. Berkman, "Decentralization and Blighted Vacant Land," in H. M. Mayer and C. F. Kohn (eds.), *Readings in Urban Geography* (Chicago: University of Chicago Press, 1964), pp. 287-298.

relatively high proportion of part-time farmers; by intensive agricultural production in the form of market gardens, poultry farming, and to a lesser degree, dairying and fruitgrowing, by farms considerably smaller in acreage than surrounding rural areas; by land values and rates lower than those of the adjacent urban center, but rising above those of the surrounding rural areas as the urban invasion continues; and by the gradual and irregular conversion of farm to nonfarm to urban land use.

Most studies of the decentralization of *manufacturing land use* have been oriented to "suburbs" rather than the rural-urban fringe; however, the fringe area is characterized by a significant though smaller proportion of manufacturing land use than the urban place itself; by newly established or recently relocated industries, frequently close to major highways; and by the presence of noxious, extractive, and related industries.

Dwellings and allotments reflect a number of features already discussed, for example, income, socioeconomic status, size of household, availability of utility services, and zoning regulations such as those controlling lot size. *Lot sizes* of residential properties in the fringe are characteristically greater, in area and frontage, than in the urban place itself; families who have moved from the urban center tend to have larger lots than other fringe residents. Lower population densities in fringe than in urban areas are a result of both larger lot size and the incorporation of nonurban land. *Dwelling size,* in terms of number of rooms, is lower in the fringe area than in the city. The *value of dwellings* in the fringe area exhibits both a lower mean and a narrower range than the urban area itself. *Land rates* in the fringe are lower than for the urban area, but as urban expansion continues there is a tendency for the gap between the rates, and hence the attraction of lower rates in the fringe, to diminish. Con-

versely, the cost of the primary installation of utility services, roads, etc., means that some fringe areas have higher rates than longer established urban areas.

A higher proportion of *dwellings are fully owned* in the fringe, particularly in the outer parts of the fringe, as compared with the urban area; there is a lower rate of renting or leasing than in the urban area, and a higher rate of renting, leasing, or being-purchased in the inner part of the fringe than in the outer more rural zone. Average *house rents* in the fringe are lower than for the urban place, but higher than for the surrounding rural areas.

Home facilities and the state of repair of the house, more than most other characteristics, reflect the particular time when the study was made. Case studies of the fringe in the 1940's and early 1950's indicated a significant proportion of incomplete and temporary dwellings, and buildings requiring major repairs; fewer inside baths and toilets than in the main urban area; considerable variation in the main fuel used for cooking; and a lower proportion of dwellings with a telephone than in the urban area itself. It could be anticipated that current studies would show less evidence of the postwar housing shortage, and more evidence of technological advances in amenities, and in improved personal spending capacity.

The two major aims here have been (1) to arrive at a definition of the rural-urban fringe which can be integrated with theories of urban invasion, as well as giving some guidance for the delineation of case study areas, and (2) to summarize from previous studies the major characteristics of the fringe. Both the general definition and the subsequent hypotheses have been stated in a form suitable for further testing, with the hope of consolidating the present fragmented body of knowledge of the fringe. In the light of the suggested internal differentiation into "urban fringe" and "rural fringe," future studies may be able to contribute knowledge not only of these two subzones, but of their respective relationships with the urban area and the rural hinterland. There is a need, too, to relate specific fringe characteristics to the size, morphology, economic base, and rate of growth of the associated central place, with the prospect of identifying the key catalysts and functional thresholds which are essential to the invasion process in a specific locality.

II

PATTERNS: Descriptions of Structure and Growth

All cities display a degree of internal organization. In terms of urban space, this order is most frequently described by regularities in land-use patterns.[1] These patterns summarize the distribution of urban activities and populations. What are these basic patterns? How do they change? What concepts have been introduced to explain them? This section reviews some of the traditional concepts of urban form with particular emphasis on land-use distributions and growth, and on the characteristics of residential areas.[2] The following section (III) builds on this introduction and in a more theoretical vein examines the processes which have given rise to these patterns. These two sections could have been combined. Their separation is designed to illustrate the importance of both empirical and theoretical, as well as inductive and deductive, studies of the city.

1. Descriptive summaries of the aggregate land-use composition of North American cities are available in several publications, most of it too bulky to reproduce here. See Allen D. Manvel, "Land Use in 106 Large Cities," in *Three Land Research Studies,* Research Report No. 12, The National Commission on Urban Problems (Washington, D.C.: U.S. Government Printing Office, 1968), pp. 19-59; L. K. Loewenstein, "The Location of Urban Land Uses," *Land Economics,* XXXIX, 4 (November 1963), 407-20. An earlier and classic study is H. Bartholomew, *Land Uses in American Cities* (Cambridge, Mass.: Harvard University Press, 1955).
2. In sociology and human ecology the most relevant references are: A. M. Rose (ed.), *Human Behavior and Social Processes* (Boston: Houghton Mufflin, 1962); G. A. Theodorson (ed.), *Human Ecology* (New York: Harper and Row Publishers, 1961); E. W. Burgess and D. J. Bogue (eds.), *Contributions to Urban Sociology* (Chicago: University of Chicago Press, 1964); and P. Meadows and E. Mizruchi (eds.), *Readings in Urban Sociology* (Reading, Mass.: Addison-Wesley, 1968). A recent summary paper in urban geography is Harold M. Mayer, *The Spatial Expression of Urban Growth,* Commission on College Geography, Resource Paper No. 7, Association of American Geographers (Washington, D.C., 1969).

What are the traditional concepts of urban form? What silhouettes of land use are apparent? In the first essay, Howard Nelson provides an introduction to the classical concepts which have been suggested to describe and explain urban form and patterns of growth: Charles Colby's distinction between centripetal and centrifugal forces, the concentric zonation hypothesis of the urban ecologists Robert Park and E. W. Burgess,[3] the residential sector model of Homer Hoyt, and the multiple nuclei proposal of Chauncy Harris and Edward Ullman. Figure 1 summarizes the latter three of these concepts. Nelson then outlines the major elements in the land-use fabric of the city: the central business district and other components of the city's commercial structure; zones of manufacturing; and the residential districts. One might well ask whether these are, in fact, all the critical elements in the urban structure. Do they represent meaningful classifications of either activities or areas? Might attention not be more appropriately directed to the interaction between the elements rather than on the elements themselves? Questions of definition and clarification such as these should be kept in mind when reading subsequent papers in this volume.

The recent and drastic transformations of urban structure previously referred to have altered both the basic assumptions and the expected outcomes of these classical models. The concentric and sectoral hypotheses of Burgess and Hoyt, for example, predate the major impact of the automobile, the post-war booms in population growth, housing construction, shopping facilities, and in social and industrial mobility. These are developments which most observers would consider fundamental in understanding the form and evolution of the modern metropolis. As the initial contributor to the formulation of the sector concept, Homer Hoyt summarizes and documents those factors which have distorted the traditional patterns which he attempted to generalize in the 1930's. He discusses the effects of rapid urbanization; of widespread ownership and use of the automobile (23 million in 1933, 100 million in North America today); high-rise construction for office and residential use; and other social and technological changes. To this list the reader might well add the effects of changes in attitudes and in political and institutional organization. Hoyt also illustrates that these phenomena of the postwar era are by no

3. R. E. Park, E. W. Burgess, and R. D. MacKenzie (eds.), *The City* (Chicago: University of Chicago Press, 1925). The relevant articles are Robert Park, "Suggestions for the Investigation of Human Behavior in the Urban Environment," pp. 1-46; and E. W. Burgess, "The Growth of the City," pp. 47-62. Two subsequent publications are R. D. MacKenzie, *The Metropolitan Community* (New York: McGraw-Hill, 1933); and E. W. Burgess, "Urban Areas," in T. V. Smith and L. D. White (eds.), *Chicago: An Experiment in Social Science Research* (Chicago: University of Chicago Press, 1929), pp. 114-23.

means limited and their impact is no less severe in the less highly industrialized societies than in North America and Western Europe. The essence of Hoyt's review is that the apparent rigidity of older patterns in the city has been substantially reduced by increases in city size, personal income, and mobility. The apparently conflicting results are that of greater physical dispersion of the urban area, combined with increased internal specialization and concentration of certain activities.

One implication of these trends is the declining relevance of the traditional models of urban structure, and the corresponding increased need for new analytical formulations. In a review paper, Brian Berry synthesizes and gives order to recent findings in three aspects of research on the internal structure of the city to which he has made substantial contributions: urban population densities; the socio-economic patterning of neighborhoods; and the changing structure of retail and service business. Each of these aspects is picked up again in Sections V and VI. Berry begins by outlining those external or exogenous factors which in large part define the initial skeleton of the city. These include regional transportation routes and those city-forming "basic" activities whose locations are determined exogenously to the city. Taking this skeleton as given, empirical regularities in residential, socio-economic, and retail patterns—what he calls the "flesh" of the city—are explicitly defined and illustrated. The intimate relationships between economic and social change in urban neighborhoods and the geography of retail services are also articulated. Stand-

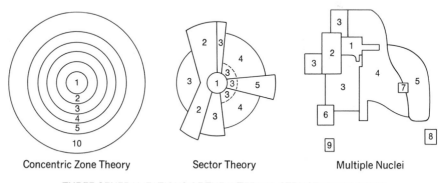

| Concentric Zone Theory | Sector Theory | Multiple Nuclei |

THREE GENERALIZATIONS OF THE INTERNAL STRUCTURE OF CITIES

DISTRICT:
1. Central Business District
2. Wholesale Light Manufacturing
3. Low-class Residential
4. Medium-class Residential
5. High-class Residential
6. Heavy Manufacturing
7. Outlying Business District
8. Residential Suburb
9. Industrial Suburb
10. Commuters' Zone

Figure 1. Traditional Models of Urban Structure

ing out as distinct from these systematic relationships, are the problems
and patterns evidenced by a severely segregated housing market.[4]

The two specific areas where physical growth of the city is most prominent are the downtown and the suburban periphery. Two papers examine
these areas. In the first, Ronald Boyce outlines an interesting analogy between the behavior of the ocean surface and the wave-like patterns of
urban expansion. Boyce argues that this wave analogy appears to be a
useful framework for understanding the dynamic and complicated surface
of the urban landscape. Changes in this surface display regularities in the
form of successive ripples of development moving outward from the center. Each of these ripples selectively alters what development has gone
before. This concept, which has interesting parallels in papers on neighborhood change (Smith) and population densities (Newling) in following sections, seems to offer an interesting avenue for research.

In the second paper, James Vance develops the concept of a series of
historical stages or "lives" to describe the growth of downtown areas over
the history of the city. These evolutionary stages describe changes both in
the internal structure of the core area and in terms of its functions within
the larger urban area. The stages are: the initial inception of the core
area, its subsequent areal expansion and internal differentiation, the continual internal reorganization at later stages of growth, and most recently
the decentralization of core functions to regional centers, and the high-
density redevelopment of the downtown itself. Although the concepts
are not outlined in detail, there are parallels between Vance's evolutionary model of the core area and attempts in other papers (Ward, Pred) in
this volume to outline an historical-development model of city growth. In
summary, Vance notes the dominant trend toward the major restructuring
of the urban area into a different series of what might be described as self-
contained geographic cells. These are similar in some ways to the central
business district, but within which urban residents will act out most of
their lives. As centers they will offer similar combinations of goods and
services.

All of the above papers have referred to city growth and its spatial expression. There is widespread concern, and justly so, regarding the rapid
increase in per capita land utilization in North American suburban growth
apparent in the decade of the 1950's.[5] But it is quite another matter to

4. For example, see John F. Kain, "Housing Segregation, Negro Employment and
Metropolitan Decentralization," *The Quarterly Journal of Economics,* LXXXII,
No. 2 (May 1968), 175-97.
5. For example, R. R. Boyce, "Changing Patterns of Urban Land Consumption,"
Professional Geographer, XV, No. 2 (March 1963), 19-24; Marion Clawson *et. al.,
Land for the Future* (Baltimore: Johns Hopkins Press, 1960), pp. 109-17; Jean
Gottmann, *Megalopolis: The Urbanized Northeastern Seaboard of the United*

measure the physical extent of growth, and particularly to measure changes in the amount of land and space required for different urban activities. Even descriptive analyses of urban land-use patterns tend to be incomplete and inclusive. One attempt at measuring land-use change is reported in a paper by Niedercorn and Hearle. They illustrate the proportions of land devoted to each type of use in a sample of U.S. cities. These data are then employed to document the decline in urban population and employment densities in postwar years and the resulting increase in land absorbed for urban purposes. The extent to which these trends are continuing at present, however, remains to be clearly defined.

Land-use change involves not only the expansion of urban uses at the suburban fringe, but also a rearrangement of land uses within the developed areas of a city. These complex changes occur, in part, through demolition and new building construction. This is the continuous process of rebuilding that has taken place since cities began. It is obvious that older parts of the city are rebuilt and old land-uses replaced. But is there any order in these changes, and what is their net impact? Despite the difficulties of measuring such changes, studies have documented the expected shift in rebuilding from lower to higher density, which means to uses which are able to pay higher rents, and the widespread increase in land area used for automobile-related uses and parking.[6] There is also a tendency for urban land to be frozen into distinct and mutually exclusive types of uses or what we might call "land-use environments," which are seldom altered drastically. The concept of land use or land occupancy environments is useful in that it stresses the interrelationships present in the urban landscape and their effect on inhibiting changes in that landscape. Among the most serious implications of these trends, as Vernon noted, is the apparent inability of existing processes of rebuilding to effectuate major improvements in the structure of the extensive and decaying older parts of the urban area.

The need for more explicit and comprehensive land-use models is evident. As one example, James Simmons outlines a proposal for a multidimensional analysis of urban land use and poses a number of pertinent questions as a guideline for research. What are the appropriate spatial

States (New York: Twentieth Century Fund, 1961); Grace Milgram, *The City Expands: A Study of the Conversion of Land from Rural to Urban Use* (Philadelphia: Institute for Environmental Studies, University of Pennsylvania, 1967); and A. A. Schmid, *Converting Land from Rural to Urban Use* (Baltimore: Johns Hopkins Press, for Resources for the Future, Inc., 1968).

6. L. S. Bourne, "Land Use Succession in Urban Areas: A Study in Structure and Change," *Proceedings of the Association of American Geographers,* Vol. 1 (1969), 12-16.

dimensions of urban land use and what models are applicable? The traditional models of urban structure and growth are basically descriptions of social characteristics in the city rather than of land use. What are the relationships between land-use dimensions and variations in socio-economic characteristics? How should these be measured? Are there certain dimensions of land occupancy that are associated with the age and quality of the building stock in the city, and with ownership and accessibility patterns? Answers to such questions are a necessary descriptive basis for the fruitful development of urban theory and for an understanding of the processes influencing urban form. The next section turns to a discussion of these processes.

HOWARD J. NELSON

The Form and Structure of Cities:
Urban Growth Patterns

The structure of cities in this country has
changed markedly through the years. Today, even small towns with a population
of 1,500 or so show definite internal differentiation. Typically commercial establishments form a closely spaced cluster
along a section of the main street, a lumber yard or other bulk handling facility
is located next to a railroad or highway,
and a small factory or two are attached
to the same transportation lines near the
edge of the town. The residential areas
form their own districts, adjacent to, but
apart from, the rest. And in larger cities
an immensely complicated urban structure has developed, a constantly changing but delicately balanced areal organization composed of many highly specialized districts with complex linkages, the
product of a variety of forces operating
through several centuries.

The casual observer, in today's era of
extensive travel, is perhaps first struck by
the unique features of individual American cities. These characteristics that give
each city a personality are often attributable to the distinctive historic past:
the compact, hilly, water-encircled site of
San Francisco, the level lake plain of Chicago, the charming Vieux Carre section

of New Orleans, or the open squares in
the street pattern of Savannah. But the
more perceptive traveler soon begins to
notice a repetitive pattern in the form
and structure of our cities, and becomes
almost instinctively aware of a kind of
"normal" location of specialized districts,
and of associations of activities within
them. For, in fact, American cities have
developed a highly stylized arrangement
and characteristic, repetitive interrelations
among the specialized areas that constitute their urban anatomy.

Factors in the Growth Patterns
of American Cities

The form and structure of the modern
American city is the result of numerous
economic, social, and cultural factors operating through the many decades since
the evolution of the simple forms like
Williamsburg. The forces contributing to
the contemporary urban structure are
many, some are obvious and strong,
others are more subtle, but all add an important dynamic quality to urban development. Some of the most significant of
these factors include rapid and massive
growth, a heterogeneous population, the

From the **Journal of Geography,** Vol. LXVIII, No. 4, April 1969, pp. 198-207. Copyright ©
1969 by the National Council for Geographic Education, Menasha, Wisconsin. Reprinted by
permission.

persistent desire of Americans for a single family detached house, and the changing forms of urban transportation. The amazing affluence of Americans in recent years has accelerated change.

American cities are the product of rapid and almost continuous growth. In 1790 about 200,000 people lived in urban places (over 2,500 population), by 1890 the figure was 22,000,000, in 1960 it was 125,000,000. The population increase of our cities in the 1950-1960 decade exceeded the total population of all urban places in 1900. Between 1930 and 1969 the urban population has about doubled. As a result, there has been an almost frantically rapid building and rebuilding of the structures that form our urban plant. With increasing populations cities have not only expanded areally in all directions, but urban lands in general, and favored locations in particular, have increased enormously in value, making rebuilding for a "higher use" profitable. Rapid growth has resulted in uncommonly dynamic cities, with constant change, sorting out, and filtering down in every section of the city.

The American urban population has not only been growing but it also has been unusually heterogeneous, resulting in many distinctive neighborhoods and much internal migration. In the past, much of the population variety was the result of a series of waves of migration. There was, for example, a heavy immigration from Ireland after 1847, another wave from Germany after 1852, and a tide of immigrants from other European countries beginning in the 1880's and continuing until about 1920. The ethnic neighborhood was common. Often the newer immigrants replaced the older groups in the oldest sections in the inner city as the earlier arrivals prospered and moved further out to newer homes. During and since World War II urban growth came mainly from migration from rural areas and included both whites and blacks, but with the blacks in many cases moving in typical fashion into the older homes in central locations in neighborhoods being abandoned by slightly more affluent residents. This succession of peoples results not only in shifts in living quarters, but also in changes in shops, schools, and churches. But even where assimilation has taken place, American cities remain heterogeneous, with segregation by income replacing that of ethnic group or race.

The deeply ingrained desire of Americans to own a single family house on a large open lot is a further factor influencing the structure of our cities. Regardless of the psychological origin of this drive—the difficulty European immigrants experienced in owning such a structure in Europe, the pioneer tradition of a cabin in a clearing, the dispersed farmhouse familiar to the rural migrant, or notions about privacy, play space, and the nature and meaning of the family—the detached house has persisted for two hundred years in American cities. Whenever he can afford it, the American urban dweller appears to prefer ample space and a private yard over a short journey to work. Encouraged by governmental mortgage policy, perhaps as many as 15,000,000 single family homes have been built since World War II, mostly in suburban areas. These low density residential neighborhoods, covering vast amounts of space, and affecting patterns of commerce and industry, are a prominent and unique item in the American urban structure.

Urban transport not only laces the urban structure together, but it also profoundly affects the arrangement and function of elements in the structure of the city. In America, the horse-drawn omnibus was important from 1830 to 1860, the suburban railroad from 1850 on in the largest cities, cable cars from 1860 to 1890, and elevated rail lines and subways from around the turn of the century. The most universal transport medium from

1890 to about 1945 in all but the largest cities was the electric "street car." But the revolutionary transportation development of the twentieth century has been the spectacular rise of the automobile. There were only about 8,000 automobiles in America in 1900, less than 500,000 in 1910, about 8 million in 1920, but the number has risen spectacularly from about 25 million in 1945 to more than 70 million cars and 13 million trucks and busses today. And each automobile, on the average, is driven more miles every year. The effect on urban structure of this new private form of transportation, not confined to fixed routes, but with the vehicle requiring storage space near the driver, has been immense.

Impressed with the dynamic nature of the American city even before some of the factors just mentioned were operating at maximum strength, one geographer, Charles C. Colby, felt that two opposing forces could be identified. They were centrifugal forces that impelled functions to migrate from the central areas of the city to the periphery, and centripetal forces that tend to hold certain functions in the central zone and attract others to it.[1]

Centripetal forces, Colby said, are the result of a number of attractive qualities of the central portion of the city. One of these is *site attraction,* often the quality of the natural landscape that invited the original occupance, such as a river crossing or a deep water landing. *Functional convenience,* a second force, results from the possession of the central zone of maximum accessibility, not only to the metropolitan area, but often to the entire surrounding region. The concentration of one function in the central zone operates as a powerful magnet attracting other functions. This is called *functional magnetism.* Thus a large department store may attract a swarm of ladies apparel and accessory shops. *Functional prestige* stems from a developed reputation. One street may become famous for its restaurants, another for its fashionable shops, and doctors often cluster for reasons of functional prestige.

Centrifugal forces on the other hand are not only opposite forces, but are made up of a merging of influences—a desire to leave one part of the city and the urge to go to another. Five forces are recognized. One is the *spatial force,* when congestion in the central zone uproots and the empty spaces of the other zones attract. The second is the *site force,* which involves the disadvantages of the intensively used central zone in contrast to the relatively little used natural landscape of the periphery. Another, the *situational force,* results from the unsatisfactory functional spacing and alignments in the central zone and the promise of more satisfactory alignments in the periphery. Then there is the *force of social evolution* in response to which high land values, high taxes, and inhibitions growing out of the past create a desire to move and the opposite conditions in the newly developing periphery provide an invitation to come. Finally, the *status and organization of occupance* creates a force for change, in which such things as the obsolete functional forms, the crystallized patterns, the traffic congestion, and the unsatisfactory transportation facilities of the central zone stand in opposition to the modern forms, the dynamic patterns, the freedom from traffic congestion, and the highly satisfactory transportation facilities of the outer zone.

Well aware of the importance of human choice, Colby added another factor which he called the *human equation* that

1. Charles C. Colby, "Centrifugal and Centripetal Forces in Urban Geography," *Annals* of the Association of American Geographers, XXIII, 1 (March 1933), 1-21. The article has been reprinted in what may be a more accessible source: Harold M. Mayer and Clyde F. Kohn, eds., *Readings in Urban Geography* (Chicago: The University of Chicago Press, 1959), pp. 287-298.

could work either as a centripetal or a centrifugal force. Although today other forces may also be at work, these concepts are still useful in analyzing the dynamics of cities. In addition, more formal models of city structure have been constructed by other students of cities, sociologists, economists, and geographers. Three of the most famous of these constructs follow.

Classic Models of City Structure

The earliest (1923) and best known of the classic models is the concentric circle or zonal hypothesis of Ernest W. Burgess.[2] The essence of this model is that as a city grows it expands radially from its center to form a series of concentric zones. Using Chicago as an example, Burgess identified five of these. In the center of the city was Zone I, the *central business district* or CBD. The heart of the CBD contained department stores, style shops, office buildings, clubs, banks, hotels, theaters, and civic buildings. Encircling it was a wholesale district. Zone II, the *zone in transition,* surrounded the CBD, and comprised an area of residential deterioration as the result of encroachments from the CBD. It consisted of a factory district as an inner belt, and an outer belt of declining neighborhoods, rooming house districts, and generally blighted residences. In many American cities of the 1920's, this area was the home of numerous first generation immigrants. Zone III, the zone of *independent workingman's*

2. First presented as a paper in 1923, Burgess restated his hypothesis at somewhat greater length five years later. Ernest W. Burgess, "Urban Areas," in T. V. Smith and L. D. White, eds., *Chicago: An Experiment in Social Science Research* (Chicago: University of Chicago Press, 1929), pp. 114-123. An excellent contemporary review of the Burgess model is Leo F. Schnore, "On the Spatial Structure of Cities in the Two Americas," in Philip M. Hauser and Leo F. Schnore, eds., *The Study of Urbanization* (New York: John Wiley and Sons, Inc., 1965), pp. 347-398.

homes was the next broad ring, at the time largely inhabited by second generation immigrants, and characterized in Chicago by the "two-flat" dwelling. Beyond this ring was located Zone IV, the *zone of better residences.* Here lived the great middle-class of native born Americans in single family residences or apartments. Within this area, at strategic places, were local business centers, which Burgess implied might be likened to satellite CBDs. Zone V, the *commuter's zone* lay beyond the area of better residences, and consisted of a ring of encircling small cities, towns, and hamlets. These were, in the main, dormitory suburbs, with the men commuting to jobs in the CBD.

The operating mechanism of the concentric circle model was the growth and radial expansion of the city, with each zone having a tendency to expand outward into the next. Burgess assumed a city with a single center, a heterogeneous population, a mixed commercial and industrial base, as well as economic competition for the highly-valued, severely-limited central space. He explicitly recognized "distorting factors," such as site, situation, natural and artificial barriers, the survival of the earlier use of the district, and so on. But he argued that to the extent of which the spatial structure of a city is determined by radial expansion, the concentric zones of his model will appear. Given the limited data available, the Burgess model was a remarkably astute description of the American city of the time.

A second model of the growth and spatial structure of American cities was formulated by Homer Hoyt in 1939 and is known as the wedge or sector theory.[3] Hoyt analyzed the distribution of resi-

3. Homer Hoyt, *The Structure and Growth of Residential Neighborhoods in American Cities* (Washington, D.C.: Federal Housing Administration, 1939). A suggestive fragment of this classic is reprinted in Mayer and Kohn, *op. cit.,* pp. 499-510.

dential neighborhoods of various qualities, as defined by rent levels, and found that they were neither distributed randomly nor in the form of concentric circles. High rental areas, for example, tended to be located in one or more pie-shaped sectors, and did not form a complete circle around the city. Intermediate rental areas normally were sectors adjacent to a high rent area. Further, different types of residential areas usually grew outward along distinct radii, and new growth on the arc of a given sector tended to take on the character of the initial growth in that sector. In summary, Hoyt argued that "if one sector of the city first develops as a high, medium, or low rental residential area, it will tend to retain that character for long distances as the sector is extended outward through the process of the city's growth."

Although no geometric pattern can be superimposed upon a city to determine the position of high and low rent sectors, some generalizations can be made about their location. The area occupied by the highest income families tends to be on high ground, or on a lake, river, or ocean shore, along the fastest existing transportation lines, and close to the country clubs or parks on the periphery. The low income families tend to live in sectors situated farthest from the high rent areas, and are normally located on the least desirable land alongside railroad, industrial, or commercial areas. Rental areas are not static. Occupants of houses in the low rent categories tend to move out in bands from the center of the city, mainly by filtering into the houses left behind by the higher income groups, or in newly constructed shacks on the fringe of the city, usually in the extension of the low rent section. It is felt by some that because Hoyt's model takes into account both distance and direction from the center of the city, it is an improvement on the earlier Burgess effort.

A third model, the multiple nuclei, was formulated by Chauncy Harris and Edward Ullman in 1945 as a modification of the two previous models.[4] They argue that the land use pattern of a city does not grow from a single center, but around several distinct nuclei. In some cases these nuclei, elements around which growth takes place, have existed from the origin of the city, but others may develop during the growth of the city. Their numbers vary from city to city, but the larger the city the more numerous and specialized are the nuclei.

Urban nuclei attracting growth might include the original retail district, a port, a railroad station, a factory area, a beach, or, in today's city, an airport. The authors identify a number of districts that have developed around individual nuclei in most large American cities. The central business district usually includes, or is adjacent to the original retail area. The wholesale and light manufacturing district is normally located along railroad lines, adjacent to, but not surrounding the CBD. The heavy industrial district is near the present or former edge of the city, where large tracts of land and rail or water transportation are available. Residential districts of several classes are identified with high-class districts on desirable sites, on well drained, high land, and away from nuisances, such as noise, odors, smoke, and railroad lines, the low-class districts near factories and railroad districts. Finally, suburbs and satellites, either residential or industrial, are characteristic of American cities. Suburbs are defined as lying adjacent to the city, with satellites farther away with little daily commuting to the central city.

The rise of separate nuclei and differentiated districts is thought to result from a combination of four factors. 1. Certain

4. Chauncy D. Harris and Edward L. Ullman, "The Nature of Cities," *Annals* of the American Academy of Political and Social Science, CCXLII (November 1945), 7-17. Reprinted in Mayer and Kohn, *op. cit.*, pp. 277-286.

activities require specialized facilities, i.e., a retail district needs intracity accessibility, a port requires a harbor. 2. Certain like activities group together because they profit from linkages. For example, retail activities may cluster to facilitate comparison shopping and financial institutions may locate in close clusters to make easy face to face communication by decision makers. 3. Certain unlike activities are detrimental to each other. Thus extensive users of land, such as bulk storage yards, are not compatable with retail functions, requiring dense pedestrian traffic. 4. Certain activities are unable to afford the high rents of the most desirable sites—low class housing is seldom built on view lots.

Models such as these which emerge from the process of analysis and generalization do not conform to the reality of any city. But anyone familiar with large or medium sized American cities will recognize many elements of each model in the vast majority of our urban areas. Obviously, too, they are not mutually exclusive, for the latter two models are both modifications of the concentric circle theory. Even in Hoyt's concept, residential areas expand outward concentrically. There has been extensive statistical testing of these models in recent years with no conclusive results. They remain as valuable conceptual tools for analyzing the modern city, and provide a basis for cross-cultural urban comparisons.

It is obvious, too, that the American city of the twenties and thirties, which provided the data upon which these models were built, is undergoing important structural changes. The traumatic effect of the automobile was not really apparent in the city studies that furnished the inspiration for these classic models. Other factors forming the basis for the urban form have been discussed previously, and some of their effects will be analyzed in the following section on the elements in the urban structure.

CENTRAL BUSINESS DISTRICT

The most obvious and easy to recognize of the components in the spatial structure of American cities described by the classic models is the Central Business District. Generally located on or near the original site of the city, it became the focus of the city's mass transportation arteries, and was thus the point of most convenient access from all parts of the city. Here, in stylized juxtaposition, were found the largest department stores, women's dress shops, men's clothing stores, shoe stores, "five and ten cent" stores, jewelry stores, drug stores, and similar retail outlets. A visitor to an unfamiliar city could anticipate this arrangement, and when he found it he could also be confident that he had located the heart of the CBD as well as the area of highest land values and the place of heaviest pedestrian traffic.[5]

Other groupings of activities into specialized junctional areas have also been traditional in the CBD's of large cities. These may include financial districts, with banks, savings and loan associations, stock and commodity exchanges, brokerage offices, trust companies, and so on. The civic center with its city and county buildings often attracts lawyers' offices and bail bond agencies. Occasionally a theater district may be present, associated with restaurants and perhaps candy shops. Hotels and office buildings are usually found several blocks from the center of the CBD. Occasionally an office building may specialize in particular services, perhaps housing doctors, dentists, and medical laboratories exclusively, or in the height of specialization, it may house the officials of a single company. The extent of an office building area, though,

5. A more extensive discussion of the CBD is found in Raymond E. Murphy, *The American City: An Urban Geography* (New York: McGraw-Hill Book Company, 1966), pp. 283-316.

depends upon the headquarters quality of the city and may cover a large area or be almost nonexistent.

Although absolute areal growth of the CBD may have essentially come to an end with the invention of the elevator and the skyscraper, this area, like the others in the city, is constantly changing. Shifts in its boundaries have been recognized by Murphy, Vance, and Epstein, identifying a "zone of discard" and a "zone of assimilation" associated with this movement.[6] The area from which the CBD is migrating, the "zone of discard" often is characterized by pawn shops, family clothing stores, bars, low grade restaurants, bus stations, cheap movies, credit jewelry, clothing, and furniture stores. The CBD tends to migrate in the direction of the best residences, and in the area into which it seems to be moving, the "zone of assimilation," are found specialty shops, automobile showrooms, drive-in banks, headquarters offices, professional offices, and the newer hotels.

Not only are the boundaries of the CBD changing, but due to the reduction of dependence on mass transit and the rise of the more flexible automobile, the last several decades have seen the movement away from the CBD of some of its traditional functions. Department stores, once the exclusive possession of the CBD, have been built in large numbers in outlying areas. Other retail activities have followed their lead. The proportion of retail sales of the city credited to the CBD have gone steadily downward, and few new retail stores have been built here. A number of small and medium sized cities have attempted to reverse the declining retail importance of their CBDs by converting the main shopping street into a pedestrian mall. The success of this expedient is as yet unclear.

Many students of cities feel the CBD of the future will change considerably and perhaps will consist of two centers separated by a band of parking. The financial and office section in many large cities remains healthy, attracted to the focus of metropolitan transportation and the advantages of "linkages" with other office functions. As the traditional retail functions of the CBD decline, perhaps what remains will evolve into a separate center of dual services, comprising specialty shops serving the metropolitan area and mass selling stores supplying the needs of the inner part of the city.[7]

OUTLYING COMMERCIAL CENTERS

All cities, in addition to a CBD, have a variety of other commercial areas, and the larger the city the more complex the pattern and the more specialized some of the elements become. The largest of the outlying shopping centers, usually referred to as *regional centers,* are built around one or more department stores, with variety, apparel, and local convenience stores, and repeat in a planned or unplanned way, the retail types found in the very heart of the CBD. Usually these stores are smaller than the downtown counterparts and deal mainly in the staple and most profitable lines of merchandise. Early centers of this class grew at intersections of public transportation lines, but most have been built up recently at points of easy automobile access. Next in order of size are *community centers* with a large variety or junior department store, some apparel shops, plus a supermarket, drug store, bank, and similar establishments. The *neighborhood center,* built around a supermarket

6. Raymond E. Murphy, J. E. Vance, Jr., and Bart J. Epstein, "Internal Structure of the CBD," *Economic Geography,* XXXI (January 1955), 21-46.

7. James E. Vance, Jr., "Emerging Patterns of Commercial Structures in American Cities," Proceedings of the IGU Symposium in Urban Geography Lund 1960, *Lund Studies in Geography,* Human Geography, ser. B. no. 24. Lund, 1962, pp. 485-518.

and with some associated stores, is an al-most ubiquitous feature. Finally, *conven-ience centers,* perhaps consisting of a "pop and mom" grocery, a laundromat, and a service station, lie at the bottom end of the commercial hierarchy. Re-cently this hierarchy of commercial cen-ters within cities has been compared to the centers of various orders in central place theory.[8]

WHOLESALING AND LIGHT MANUFACTURING

Located in the concentric-circle model as a ring at the border of the CBD, the wholesale and light manufacturing activi-ties have shifted considerably in response to newer forces. As the automobile has given mobility to the worker, many firms engaged in light manufacturing have moved away from the center of the city to the suburbs where land is inexpensive and large tracts facilitate one story plants, storage areas, and parking lots. Sites near belt highways are particularly desirable. Many wholesalers, too, have been at-tracted to similar locations.

On the other hand, certain types of wholesalers characteristic of large cities are affected by forces that make cluster-ing advantageous, often in or near the CBD. Clustering of wholesaling estab-lishments normally persists when the buy-ers gather in person at the market, where the goods are nonstandardized, when comparison of quality or style is impor-tant, and when the establishment of the price is an important function of the mar-ket. Wholesalers of jewelry, apparel, fruit and vegetables, or cut flowers are charac-teristic examples.

Similarly, although most manufacturers have moved out of the central part of the

city, a few characteristically remain. For example, large segments of the garment industry are found at the edge of the CBD in cities where it is an important manu-facturing activity. One factor involved in this location is the close linkages of the manufacturing and wholesaling aspects of apparel production. But, in addition, clustering in the garment industry results in "external economies" (economies ex-ternal to the firm). For example, the presence of ancillary firms, such as tex-tile dealers, sponging (shrinking) facili-ties, factors (textile bankers), trucking firms, repairmen, and suppliers of every-thing from pretty models to thread, pro-vides external economies to the apparel firms.

HEAVY MANUFACTURING

Heavy industry has almost entirely moved out of the inner ring as postulated by Burgess, much of it into the specialized sites as implied by Harris and Ullman. Early located adjacent to water transport, the development of railroads and trucks permitted industries to leave the central areas. Seeking extensive sites for sprawl-ing factories, parking lots, and storage facilities, large manufacturing complexes are now characteristically found in outly-ing locations. Some newer industries, such as the aircraft industry, are linked to facilities found only in non-central areas, airports in this instance.

RESIDENTIAL DISTRICTS

Much has been said already about resi-dential districts in American cities. Our heterogeneous urban population has shown a tendency to sort itself out one way or another into relatively homoge-neous neighborhoods. As differences in language and ethnic character have be-come less important, segregation of resi-dence has been mainly by economic status, with little mixing of the homes of

---

8. A discussion of the hierarchy of commercial centers within cities is found in Brian J. L. Berry, *Geography of Market Centers and Retail Distribution* (Englewood Cliffs, N.J.: Prentice-Hall, Inc., 1967), pp. 42-58.

the rich and the poor, as in some cultures. Race remains, however, as a segregating force, seemingly more powerful than economic status.

Another striking characteristic has been the propensity of the American urban dweller for the space consuming, expensive, single family dwelling. There is some indications that isolation and privacy are qualities of increasing importance. The front porch oriented to the street from which the family viewed the passing scene has disappeared from the post World War II house. Too, the room arrangement has been reversed: now the living room often faces the rear yard which has been designed as an addition to the living space. And in southern California, where life-styles often seem to originate, the backyard is now enclosed with a solid wooden fence or block wall, making the family's privacy complete. Continued spread of the traditional house in the middle of a lot (the now non-functional front yard remains, required by zoning ordinances reflecting an earlier era) forecasts continued suburban sprawl.

In contrast to this long term trend toward dispersal, in recent years, there has been a striking increase in the proportion of multiple housing in many cities. Perhaps this is simply a temporary phenomenon reflecting the changing age composition of the population due to the low birth rate of the 1930's; the young and old often choose apartments, those in their thirties choose single family homes. To the extent, however, that this changing construction mix reflects a movement of those who can afford to live anywhere into more central, accessible locations, as urban distances become greater, it may foretell a weakening, at long last, of the American's traditional willingness to trade commuting time for space.

HOMER HOYT

Recent Distortions of the Classical Models of Urban Structure

Since the general patterns of city structure were described by Burgess in 1925[1] and 1929[2] and by myself in 1939[3] there has been a tremendous growth of urban population, not only in the United States, but throughout the world. To what extent has this factor of growth changed the form or shape of urban communities?

While the Burgess concentric circle theory was based on a study of Chicago—a city on a flat prairie, cut off on the east by Lake Michigan—and patterns of growth in other cities would be influenced by their unique topography, his formulation had a widespread application to American cities of 1929. Burgess made a brilliant and vivid contribution to urban sociology and urban geography which in-

spired the present writer as well as the sociologists and geographers who made subsequent studies of city patterns.

In the era of the Greek cities in the fifth century B.C. a city was considered an artistic creation which should maintain its static form without change. To take care of population growth, the Greeks sent out colonies, like swarms of bees, to found new cities on the ideal model. Plato said that the ideal city should not contain over 5,000 inhabitants although he himself was the product of an Athens with a 250,000 population. In the Middle Ages most continental European cities were surrounded by walls and many, like Milan, Italy preserved an unaltered form of hundreds of years.

In the United States, however, there has been a tremendous growth of metropolitan areas since 1930. The number of large urban concentrations with a population of a million or more has increased from 10 to 22. The population in the 140 metropolitan districts was 57,602,865 in 1930, of which 40,343,442 were in central cities and 17,259,423 were outside these cities. In 1940 in these 140 metropolitan districts the population was

1. R. E. Park and E. W. Burgess, *The City* (Chicago, Illinois: University of Chicago Press, 1925), pp. 47-62.
2. E. W. Burgess, "Urban Areas," in *Chicago: An Experiment in Social Science Research,* T. V. Smith and L. D. White (editors) (Chicago, Illinois, University of Chicago Press, 1929), pp. 114-123.
3. Homer Hoyt, *The Structure and Growth of Residential Neighborhoods in American Cities,* (Washington, D.C., Federal Housing Administration, 1939).

From **Land Economics**, Vol. XL, No. 2, May 1964, pp. 199-212. Copyright © 1964 **by the** Regents of the University of Wisconsin. Reprinted by permission.

62,965,773 of which 42,796,170 were in central cities and 20,169,603 were outside these cities.[4] After World War II, in the rapidly growing decade from 1950 to 1960, the population of 216 Standard Metropolitan Areas grew from 91,568,113 to 115,796,265. Most of the growth in the past census decade was in the suburbs, but central city population grew from 52,648,185 to 58,441,995, a gain of only 11 percent, while the population outside central cities increased from 38,919,928 to 57,354,270, a rise of 47.4 percent.[5] The population in the central areas of 12 of the largest American metropolitan regions actually declined in this decade from 22,694,799 to 21,843,214, a loss of 3.8 percent.[6] The population loss in the central cores of these cities was much greater, since some central cities still had room for new growth within the other edges of their boundaries. There was also a displacement of white population by non-white population. From 1930 to 1950 the non-white population in 168 SMA's increased from 4,913,703 to 8,250,210.[7] The chief gain was in the central cities where the non-white population rose from 3,624,504 in 1930 to 6,411,158 in 1950. From 1950 to 1960 the non-white population in central cities increased to 10,030,314. The non-white population in SMA's outside central cities was only 2,720,513 in 1960. On the other hand while 43,142,399 white persons lived in central cities of

SMA's in 1960, 49,081,533 white persons lived in SMA's outside the central cities. While the central city population in these 12 SMA's was declining, population outside the central cities rose from 13,076,711 in 1950 to 20,534,833 in 1960, a gain of 57 percent.

In 1960 the population of the areas outside the central cities in these 12 great metropolitan areas almost equalled the population in the central areas and by 1964 the population in the areas outside the central cities has certainly surpassed the number in the central city.

While the cities of 50,000 population and over have been growing at a rapid rate in the past decade, the smaller cities with less than 50,000 population have been increasing in numbers at a slower pace, or from 27.4 million in 1950 to 29.4 million in 1960.[8] The smaller cities thus would be enabled to maintain their static form with the growth element chiefly affecting the larger metropolitan areas as a result of the shift in population growth from the center to the suburbs and a change in the racial composition of many central cities.

Not merely population growth, but a rise in per capita national income from $757 in 1940 to $2,500 in 1963, with a greater proportionate increase in the middle class incomes, an increase in the number of private passenger automobiles from 22,793,000 in 1933 to 70 million in 1963, and the building of expressways connecting cities and belt highways around cities, were all dynamic factors changing the shape and form of cities since the description of city patterns in 1925 and 1939. Let us examine the different concentric circles or zones or sectors described in the books over a quarter of a century ago and see how the principles then enunciated have been changed by the growth factors.

4. United States Census of Population 1940, Vol. I, Table 18, p. 61.

5. United States Department of Commerce, Bureau of the Census, Standard Metropolitan Areas in the United States as defined October 18, 1963, Series P-23, No. 10, December 5, 1963. (Newark, New Jersey is included in New York Metropolitan Area).

6. Baltimore, Boston, Chicago, Cincinnati, Cleveland, Detroit, Minneapolis-St. Paul, New York, Philadelphia, St. Louis, San Francisco-Oakland and Washington, D.C.

7. United States Census of Population, 1930, 1940, 1950.

central cities was only 2,720,513 in 1960.

8. Harold M. Mayer, "Economic Prospects for the Smaller City," *Public Management,* August 1963.

The Central Business District

In 1929 Burgess wrote: "Zone I: The Central Business District. At the center of the city as the focus of its commercial, social and civic life is situated in the Central Business District. The heart of this district is the downtown retail district with its department stores, its smart shops, its office buildings, its clubs, its banks, its hotels, its theatres, its museums, and its headquarters of economic, social, civic and political life."[9] Burgess thus accurately described the central business district of Chicago and most large American cities as of the date he was writing (1929), a description which would hold true in the main to the end of World War II. Since 1946, extraordinary changes in the American economy have occurred which have had a pronounced effect on the structure of the downtown business districts of American cities.

Burgess had noted in 1929 the existence of local business centers, or satellite "loops" in the zone of better residences: "The typical constellation of business and recreation areas includes a bank, one or more United Cigar stores, a drug store, a high class restaurant, an automobile display row, and a so-called 'wonder' motion picture theatre."[10] I also had noted, in 1939, the extensions of string-like commercial developments beyond the central business districts, and the rise of satellite business centers: "Again, satellite business centers have developed independently beyond the central business district, or on the city's periphery. These are usually located at or near suburban railway stations, elevated or subway stations, intersecting points between radial and crosstown street car lines, or intersecting points of main automobile highways."[11]

9. Ernest W. Burgess, "Urban Areas," *op. cit.*
10. *Ibid.*
11. Hoyt, *op. cit.* p. 20.

In 1964, the central retail district, with its large department stores still remains the largest shopping district in its metropolitan area, and all the outlying business districts at street car intersections, subway or suburban railway stations are still operating, but their dominating position has been greatly weakened by the construction, since 1946, of an estimated 8,300 planned shopping districts, with free automobile parking, in the suburbs or on the periphery of the central city mass. The tremendous growth of the suburban population, which moved to areas beyond the mass transit lines, facilitated by the universal ownership of the automobile, and decline in the numbers and relative incomes of the central city population, invited and made possible this new development in retail shopping.

The regional shopping center—with major department stores, variety, apparel and local convenience stores, practically duplicating the stores in the downtown retail area and built on large tracts of land entirely away from street cars, subways, elevated or railroad stations—was virtually unknown prior to World War II. The first of these centers, Country Club Plaza in Kansas City, had been established in 1925 and there were a few others with department stores and a number of neighborhood centers on commercial streets, with parking areas in front of the stores, but the wave of the future was not discerned by planners or land economists before 1946.

There are many types of these new planned centers; the regional center on 50 to 100 acres of land with at least one major department store; the community center on 20 to 30 acres of land with a junior department store as the leading tenant; and the neighborhood center with a supermarket, drug store and local convenience shops on five to 10 acres of land. But the type having the greatest impact on the downtown stores is the regional center which directly competes with downtown in the sales of general merchandise.

General merchandise stores, that is, department and variety stores, had long been the dominating magnets and attractions of the central retail areas. In this field the CBD stores had almost a monopoly in most cities prior to 1920 and even held a dominating position after the establishment of some outlying department stores at street car intersections or subway stations in Chicago and New York. There had been for years neighborhood grocery stores, drug stores and even small apparel and dry goods stores and some variety stores outside of the central business district but the department store sales of the CBD's were probably 90 percent or more of the total department store volume of the entire metropolitan area.

In 1958 the central general merchandise stores, chiefly department stores, in the largest cities of a million population and over, had a lower sales volume than the aggregate of the sales of department stores in all the shopping centers outside of the CBD, or $3.6 billion compared to $5.65 billion, as Table 1 shows.

Table 1. General Merchandise Sales in C.B.D.'s by Metropolitan Area Size Groups

Metropolitan Area Size	Population	(Thousands of Dollars) 1958		1954		Per cent Increase 1954 — 1958	
		In C.B.D.	Outside C.B.D.	In C.B.D.	Ouside C.B.D.	In C.B.D.	Outside C.B.D.
1,000,000 & Over	61,582,070	$3,577,169	$5,652,995	$3,522,089	$3,837,350	1.6	47.3
500,000 — 999,000	17,021,848	1,422,369	1,151,601	1,387,956	618,203	4.0	86.3
250,000 — 499,000	10,491,540	928,358	513,668	849,474	311,573	9.3	64.9
100,000 — 249,000	2,841,645	279,452	111,774	263,530	62,817	6.0	77.9
TOTAL	91,937,103	$6,227,348	$7,430,038	$6,022,149	$4,829,943	3.4	53.8

Homer Hoyt, "Sales in Leading Shopping Centers and Shopping Districts in the United States." *Urban Land,* September 1961.

There were 125 regional shopping centers in 1958 but many more have been completed since that date and the 1963 United States Retail Census of Shopping Districts will undoubtedly show a still greater increase in the department store sales outside of the CBD.

In 94 metropolitan areas with a population of 100,000 and over and total population of 91,937,103 in 1960, dollar sales outside the CBD's had increased by 53.8 percent, but in the CBD's only 3.4 percent. There was an actual decline in general merchandise sales from 1954 to 1958 in the CBD's of Los Angeles, Chicago, Philadelphia, Detroit, Boston, St. Louis, Washington, D.C., Cleveland, Baltimore, Milwaukee and Kansas City.

These new planned shopping districts, with their ample parking areas, cover more ground than the combined areas of the CBD's in all American cities. I have calculated that there were 30,460 acres or 47.5 square miles in the central business districts of the standard metropolitan areas in the United States in 1960, compared with 33,600 acres or 52.5 square miles in all types of new planned centers.[12] Since 1960, however, many new planned centers have been built and there are now probably 150 regional shopping centers. In 1964 the ground area occupied by these centers, as well as that of the many new discount houses

12. Homer Hoyt, "Changing Patterns of Land Values," *Land Economics,* May 1960, p. 115.

with large parking areas, has considerably increased the space occupied by shopping centers as compared with 1960.

In contrast to the tremendous growth of the planned shopping districts, there has been very limited building of new retail stores in downtown areas; the notable exceptions being Midtown Plaza in Rochester, New York; the redevelopment of the business center of New Haven, Connecticut with new department stores, offices and garages, connected by a new highway to the existing expressway; the location of new Sears Roebuck and Dayton department stores in central St. Paul; and the erection of garages for department stores in other cities.

Office building expansion, unlike retail stores, bears no direct relation to population growth but depends entirely upon the extent to which a city becomes an international or regional office management or financial center. Generalization therefore cannot be made about office buildings which would apply to all cities since the number of square feet of office space per capita in the metropolitan area varies from 2.2 square feet in San Diego to 7.5 square feet in Chicago, 16 square feet in New York and 25 square feet in Midland, Texas.

New York City has become the outstanding headquarters center of the United States, with an estimated 171,-100,000 square feet of office space. It has had a tremendous growth since 1946, with 55 million square feet added since World War II. The trend has been uptown, away from downtown Wall Street to Park Avenue, 42nd Street and Third Avenue near Grand Central Station. The world's greatest concentration of office buildings is in the Grand Central and Plaza districts of New York City. From 1947 to 1962 inclusive, there was a total increase of 50,632,000 square feet of rentable office area in Manhattan, of which 33,839,000 square feet, or 66.8 percent, was in the Grand Central and

Plaza areas. In the same period, in the lower Manhattan area, or the combined financial, city hall and insurance districts, 10,935,000 square feet or 21.6 percent of the total were constructed. A partial reversal of the uptown trend in Manhattan will result from the proposed building of the World Trade Center with 10 million square feet of office space, in twin towers 1350 feet high, on the Lower West Side. This development, by the Port of New York Authority, will be started in 1965 and is scheduled for completion by 1970.[13]

In Washington, D.C. there is approximately 16 million square feet of office space. An estimated 11 million square feet have been built since 1946, of which 9 million square feet are in the area west of 15th Street, in the direction of the high grade residential growth.

The location of new office buildings in central city areas has been determined in part by the slum or blighted areas, with old buildings which could be cleared away, such as in the Golden Triangle of Pittsburgh or Penn Center in Philadelphia, or location in air rights over railroad tracks as the Merchandise Mart and Prudential buildings in Chicago, the Pan Am Building and other buildings on Park Avenue in New York and the Prudential Building in Boston. The ability to secure land at a relatively low cost on West Wacker Drive in Chicago caused insurance companies to build there.

Sometimes these new office districts are not at the center of transportation. In Los Angeles new office building has moved away from the central business districts toward the high grade residential areas. From 1948 to 1960 15,500,000 square feet of office floor space was constructed in Los Angeles, of which only 1,500,000 square feet was built in the 400-acre area of the central business district, although 1,000,000 square feet were erected in the southwesterly and western fringe areas of

13. *The New York Times*, January 19, 1964.

the central business district.[14] This decentralization is in marked contrast to the concentration of offices in New York City.

There has also been a tendency for large office buildings of insurance companies, which conduct a self sufficient operation not dependent on contact with other agencies, to locate on large tracts of land several miles from the center of the city as the Prudential regional office buildings in Houston and Minneapolis in 1951, and the Connecticut General Insurance Company in Hartford. Office centers are also developing around some of the regional shopping centers, as at Northland in Detroit, Ward Parkway in Kansas City and Lenox Square in Atlanta.

In Houston more than 6 million square feet of new office space has been added to downtown areas in the past three years, the growth proceeding westerly in the direction of the high income areas. While the main office building district of most cities is still within the confines of the central area, the office center is not fixed but is moving in the direction of high income areas, as in New York City, Washington, D.C., Los Angeles and Houston. This conforms to the statement I made in 1939.[15]

A tall office building that looms in the sky as a beacon or landmark has been built in many cities of moderate size by banks, oil companies or insurance companies for the sake of prestige, regardless of cost or rental demand. In many cities of growing population few new office buildings have been erected. Thus, generalizations can no longer be made about office building locations which will apply to all cities in the United States.

There is a concentration of hotels near each other in large cities so that they can accommodate conventions but central hotels have declined in importance because of the new motels and motor hotels (with parking) on the periphery of the central business district or in the outskirts of the city. This rapid growth in both intown motels and those on the periphery is a use not anticipated in 1939.

There is a trend to the building of new apartments in or near central business districts, such as the Marina Towers in Chicago, the apartments in redeveloped areas in Southwest Washington, D.C. and as proposed for the Bunker Hill redevelopment in downtown Los Angeles. Hence the statement by Burgess that: "Beyond the workingmen's homes lies the residential district, a zone in which the better grade of apartments and single family residences predominate" must be qualified now, as it was in 1939, when I pointed to the Gold Coast of Chicago and Park Avenue in New York City.[16]

Thus, in view of the shifting of uses in the central business districts, the overall decline in the predominance of central retail areas, the rapid growth of office centers in a few cities compared to a static situation in others, the emergence of redeveloped areas, and intown motels, the former descriptions of patterns in American cities must be revised to conform to the realities of 1964.

The Wholesale and Light Manufacturing Zone

Burgess described the zone next to the central business district as: "Clinging close to the skirts of the retail district lies the wholesale and light manufacturing zone. Scattered through this zone and surrounding it, old dilapidated buildings form the homes of the lower working classes, hoboes and disreputable characters. Here the slums are harbored. Cheap second hand stores are numerous,

14. *Los Angeles Centropolis 1980, Economic Survey.* Los Angeles Central City Committee and Los Angeles City Planning Department, December 12, 1960, p. 19.
15. Hoyt, *Structure and Growth, op. cit.,* p. 108.
16. *Ibid.,* p. 23.

and low prices 'men only' moving picture and burlesque shows flourish."[17] This is a vivid description of West Madison Street and South State Street in Chicago in the 1920's. Since that time the whole-sale function has greatly declined and with the direct sale by manufacturers to merchants the 4-million-square-foot Mer-chandise Mart, across the Chicago River north of the Loop, absorbed most of the functions formerly performed by whole-salers. The intermixture of slums and old dilapidated buildings with light in-dustry is being cleared away in redevel-opment projects and the West Side In-dustrial District in Chicago has been created immediately west of the Loop on cleared land.

Light manufacturing, in the garment industry particularly, still clings close to the retail and financial center in New York City because the garment industry depends on fashion and the entertain-ment of out-of-town buyers.

Other light manufacturing industries have tended to move away from the cen-ter of the city to the suburbs where they can secure ample land areas for one-story plants, storage, and parking for their employees' cars. These new modern plants, in park-like surroundings, which emit no loud noise or offensive odors, are not objectionable even in middle-class residential areas, and workers can avoid city traffic in driving to their place of employment, or they can live nearby.

The Factory or Heavy Industrial District

In 1929 Burgess placed the wholesale district in Zone I, the central business district, and described Zone II as the zone in transition, which included the factory district in its inner belt as follows:

Zone II: The Zone in transition. Surround-ing the Central Business District are areas of residential deterioration caused by the encroaching of business and industry from Zone I. This may therefore be called the Zone in Transition, with a factory district for its inner belt and an outer ring of retro-gressing neighborhoods, of first-settlement immigrant colonies, of rooming-house dis-tricts, of homeless-men areas, of resorts of gambling, bootlegging, sexual vice, and of breeding-places of crime. In this area of physical deterioration and social disorgan-ization our studies show the greatest con-centration of cases of poverty, bad housing, juvenile delinquency, family disintegration, physical and mental disease. As families and individuals prosper, they escape from this area into Zone III beyond, leaving behind as marooned a residuum of the defeated, lead-erless, and helpless.[18]

In 1939 I pointed out tendencies of heavy industries to move away from close-in locations in the "transition zone."[19] Since that time heavy manufac-turing has tended more and more to seek suburban locations or rural areas, as nearly all workers now come in their own automobiles and for the most part live in the suburban areas themselves. Factory location in slum areas is not now desired for the clerks and factory workers no longer live there. All of the reasons I cited in 1939 for industries moving to suburban areas apply with greater force in 1964.

In regard to residential uses, this zone in transition was defined as the slum and blighted area of Chicago in 1943[20] and under the slum clearance and redevelop-ment laws which enabled federal authori-ties to acquire by condemnation, proper-ties in blighted areas, it has been exten-sively cleared and rebuilt with modern apartments, both private and public. The remnants of this area which have not been

---

17. Ernest M. Fisher, *Advanced Principles of Real Estate Practice* (New York, The Macmil-lan Co., 1930), p. 126, citing R. E. Park and E. W. Burgess, *The City, op. cit.,* Ch. II.

18. Burgess, "Urban Areas," *op. cit.*
19. Hoyt, *op. cit.* p. 20.
20. Chicago Plan Commission, *Master Plan of Residential Land Use of Chicago,* Homer Hoyt, Director of Research, 1943, Fig. 89, p. 68.

cleared away still retain the characteristics Burgess described in 1929, and the problems of juvenile delinquency and overcrowding have been accentuated in the last 35 years by the in-migration of low income Negro families to Chicago as well as to other northern cities.

Zone of Workingmen's Homes

Encircling the zone of transition, now the slum and blighted area, is Zone III, described by Burgess as follows:

Zone III: The Zone of Independent Workingmen's Homes. This third broad urban ring is in Chicago, as well as in other northern industrial cities, largely constituted by neighborhoods of second immigrant settlement. Its residents are those who desire to live near but not too close to their work. In Chicago, it is a housing area neither of tenements, apartments, nor of single dwellings; its boundaries have been roughly determined by the plotting of the two-flat dwelling, generally of frame construction, with the owner living on the lower floor with a tenant on the other.[21]

The buildings in this zone, now 35 years older than when Burgess wrote in 1929, were in general classified in The Master Plan of Residential Land Use of Chicago as "conservation."[22] This area is not yet a slum but next in order of priority to be cleared away. In some blocks older structures can be razed and the newer ones rehabilitated. A large proportion of its former occupants, white families with children of school age, have moved to the suburbs and it is now occupied mainly by single white persons, older white families or by Negro families in all age groups.

In some cases these older close-in residential sections may be rehabilitated and become fashionable, as in the Georgetown area of Washington, D.C., Rittenhouse Square in Philadelphia and the Near North Side of Chicago; and this is an exception to be noted to Burgess' theory.

Better Residential Area

Zone IV: The Zone of Better Residences. Extending beyond the neighborhoods of second immigrant settlements, we come to the Zone of Better Residences in which the great middle-class of native-born Americans live, small business men, professional people, clerks, and salesmen. Once communities of single homes, they are becoming, in Chicago, apartment-house and residential-hotel areas.[23]

This zone was classified in the Master Plan of Residential Land Use of Chicago in 1943 as "stable," indicating that the residences were still of sound construction and had many remaining years of useful life. As the second immigrant settlers, now indistinguishable from the native born population, once moved from Zone III into this area, so now many of the former residents of this area have moved mainly from this area into the new areas near the periphery of the city, or into the suburbs. Some of the areas vacated by them are now occupied by the non-white population.

The Commuters Zone

Burgess described the commuters zone as follows:

Zone V. The Commuters Zone. Out beyond the areas of better residence is a ring of encircling small cities, towns, and hamlets, which, taken together, constitute the Commuters Zone. These are also, in the main, dormitory suburbs, because the majority of men residing there spend the day at work in the Loop (Central Business District), returning only for the night.[24]

Burgess thus took into account in his fifth zone the existence of suburban towns. However, he refers to them as a

21. Burgess, "Urban Areas," *op. cit.*
22. Chicago Plan Commission, *op. cit.*

23. Burgess, "Urban Areas," *op. cit.*
24. *Ibid.*

"ring" implying that they formed a circular belt around Chicago. However, at the time Burgess wrote in 1929, there was no circle of towns around Chicago but a pattern of settlement along the railroads with six great bands of suburban settlement radiating out from the central mass of Chicago like spokes of a wheel and with large vacant areas in between.[25] Chicago's early growth had taken the form first of starfish extensions of settlement along the principal highways and street car lines.[26] By 1929 the vacant areas in the city between these prongs had been filled in with homes so that there were then in fact belts or concentric circles of settled areas within the City of Chicago. At that time, however, the suburban area of Chicago conformed to the axial pattern of growth with the highest income sector located on one of the six radial bands—the North Shore, along Lake Michigan. There were other high income areas in the other bands of growth but no continuous belt of high income areas around Chicago. Since 1929 the vacant areas between these radial extensions of settlement along suburban railroads have been filled in largely with homes of middle income residents. Many of the new planned shopping districts are now located in between these bands of original settlement along railroads, where large vacant tracts could be secured.

Beyond his five zones, Burgess later identified two additional zones lying beyond the built-up area of the city: "The sixth zone is constituted by the agricultural districts lying within the circle of commutation. . . . The seventh zone is the hinterland of the metropolis."[27]

Richard M. Hurd, in his classic *Principles of City Land Values*[28] had, as early as 1903 developed the central and axial principles of city growth; yet to many persons, before Burgess formulated his theory many years later, cities appeared to be a chaotic mixture of structures with no law governing their growth. Burgess, with acute powers of observation and without all of the great body of census and planning data that has been made available since he wrote, made a remarkable formulation of principles that were governing American city growth in 1929 and he related these principles to the basic facts of human society. Since 1929, however, not only have the vast detailed city data of the United States censuses been made available for study and analysis, but dynamic changes have occurred in our economy which have had a profound influence on the structure of our cities. Since 1929 over 10 million new houses have been constructed on the suburban fringes of American cities, beyond the old central mass, in areas made available for residential occupancy by the increase in the number of private passenger automobiles in the United States from 8 million in 1920 to 66 million in 1964, and the highways subsequently built to accommodate them.

Apartment buildings, once confined to locations along subways, elevated lines or near suburban railroad stations, are now springing up in the suburbs, far from mass transit. Many families without children of school age desire the convenience of an apartment, involving no work of mowing lawns, painting and repairing, and with the comforts of air-conditioning and often a community swimming pool. Complete communities are now being developed in the suburbs, with a mixture of single family homes, town houses and apartments, and with their own churches,

25. Chicago Plan Commission, *op. cit.,* frontispiece, p. 2.
26. *Ibid.,* Fig. 3, p. 22.
27. E. W. Burgess, "The New Community and Its Future," *Annals of the American Academy of Political and Social Science,* Vol. 149, May 1930, pp. 161, 162.

28. Richard M. Hurd, *Principles of City Land Values* (1st edition 1903, republished by *The Record and Guide,* New York, New York, 1924).

schools, shopping centers and light industries, some even with a golf course and bridle paths, of which the 7,000-acre Reston development near the Dulles Airport in the Washington, D.C. area is an outstanding example. Thus the dynamic changes of the past quarter century make it necessary to review concepts developed from studies of American cities in 1925 and 1939.

The Sector Theory

One concept needs to be examined again —the sector theory of residential development. In 1939 I formulated the sector theory which was to the effect that the high income areas of cities were in one or more sectors of the city, and not, as Burgess seemed to imply when he said: "beyond the workingmen's homes lies the residential district, a zone in which the better grade of apartment houses and single family residences predominate."

In a study of 64 American cities, block by block, based on the federal government's Work Project Administration's basic surveys of 1934, and studies of a number of large metropolitan areas, I prepared maps showing that high rent areas were located in one or more sectors of the city, and did not form a circle completely around it. Has this changed since 1939? In a survey of the entire Washington, D.C. metropolitan area in 1954 it was found that the main concentration of high-income families was in the District area west of Rock Creek Park, continuing into the Bethesda area of Montgomery County, Maryland. There were other scattered high income clusters in the Washington area. In surveys of other metropolitan areas it was discovered that the main concentration of high income families is on the north side of Dallas, west and southwest sides of Houston, northward along the Lake Shore of Chicago, the south side of Kansas City, in the Beverly Hills area of Los Angeles,

on the south side of Tulsa, the north side of Oklahoma City, the west side of Philadelphia, and the southwest side of Minneapolis. In the New York metropolitan area there are a number of nodules of high income in Westchester County, Nassau County, Bergen and Essex Counties in New Jersey, but the predominant movement was northward and eastward.

In a trip to Latin American cities in the summer of 1963 I found that the finest single family homes and apartments in Guatemala City, Bogota, Lima, La Paz, Quito, Santiago, Buenos Aires, Montevideo, Rio de Janeiro, Sao Paulo and Caracas were located on one side of the city only.[29]

The automobile and the resultant belt highways encircling American cities have opened up large regions beyond existing settled areas, and future high grade residential growth will probably not be confined entirely to rigidly defined sectors. As a result of the greater flexibility in urban growth patterns resulting from these radial expressways and belt highways, some higher income communities are being developed beyond low income sectors but these communities usually do not enjoy as high a social rating as new neighborhoods located in the high income sector.

Changes in Metropolitan Areas Outside the United States

Since the rate of population growth, particularly of the great cities of one million population and over, is a most important element in changing city structure, let us examine these differential rates of growth.[30] There has in fact, been a

29. The Residential and Retail Patterns of Leading Latin American Cities," *Land Economics,* November 1963.
30. Homer Hoyt, *World Urbanization — Expanding Population in a Shrinking World,* Urban Land Institute Technical Bulletin 43, Washington, D.C., April 1962. See also "The Growth

wide variation in the rate of population growth in the great metropolitan areas throughout the world since 1940. In England, in London and the other large metropolitan areas, the population has remained stationary; on the Continent of Europe outside of Russia, the growth rate of the great metropolitan areas has slowed down to 20 percent in the decade from 1950 to 1960. In Russia, eight of the largest older metropolitan areas increased in population only 15 percent from 1939 to 1962 but in this period many entirely new cities were built and other smaller cities grew in size until Russia now has 176 metropolitan areas with a population of 100,000 or more. China has had a great urban surge since 1945 to 1950 and reports a gain of 91 percent in the population of 18 great metropolitan areas as a result of its enforced industrialization process. This was reportedly carried too far and city dwellers had to be ordered back to the farms to raise food. Japan's five largest metropolitan area concentrations increased in numbers by 41 percent from 1951 to 1961. Fast suburban trains carry workers to and from downtown places of employment. In India, Dehli and New Dehli have more than doubled in population from 1951 to 1961 as a result of greatly expanded government and manufacturing activity. Other great Indian cities have grown rapidly, with 300,000 or more sleeping in the streets of Calcutta. In Australia, Sydney and Melbourne increased by 32 percent from 1951 to 1961. In Egypt, Cairo has gained 155 percent in numbers since 1940 as a result of being the chief headquarters of the Arab world. African cities like Nairobi and Leopoldville have gained rapidly. In Latin America, the urban population has exploded, with eight of its largest metropolitan areas gaining 166 percent from 1940 to 1962. The Sao

Paulo metropolitan area, jumping from 1,380,000 to 4,374,000, gained 217 percent. Mexico City shot up from 1,754,000 to 4,666,000, a rise of 166 percent, in the same period of time.

While there are some similarities in the patterns of urban growth in the United States and foreign cities, as for example, in the sector theory, there are also some marked differences, as a result of the following five factors:

(1) The chief factor in enabling city populations to spread out, to develop vast areas of single family homes on wide lots far from main transit facilities, to develop so many new shopping centers and so many dispersed factories, has been the almost universal ownership of the private automobile. Only in the United States, New Zealand, Australia and Canada, which have developed city patterns similar to ours, had a high ratio of auto ownership to population in 1955, or from 181 per 1,000 in Canada and 183 in Australia to 339 per 1,000 in the United States.[31] Northern European nations had from 58 to 111 cars per thousand of population but most Asiatic and African nations and most of the South American countries had less than 15 cars per 1,000 population. Argentina and Uruguay had 32 cars per 1,000 population in 1955.

The number of automobiles in northwestern Europe has shown marked gains recently: in West Germany from 1955 to 1963 the rate increased from 58 to 122 per 1,000 persons; in the United Kingdom for the same period the rate increased from 92 to 120 per 1,000 persons; and for the same period in Belgium the rate increased from 60 to 106 per 1,000 persons.

Obviously, in most of the world the urban population must depend upon

of Cities from 1800 to 1960 and Forecasts to Year 2000," *Land Economics*, May 1963, pp. 167-173.

31. Norton Ginsburg, *Atlas of Economic Development* (Chicago, Illinois: University of Chicago Press, 1961), p. 74.

busses or bicycles and live in apartments which can be economically served by subways, street cars or busses. Hence the great expansion into rural areas can take place only when there are suburban railroads as in Buenos Aires, Rio de Janeiro, Delhi and Tokyo, or subways as in London, Moscow, Tokyo, Madrid, Barcelona and Paris. Poor families live in central areas on steep mountainsides in Rio de Janeiro and Caracas, in shacks built by themselves; they live in blocks of tenements in central Hong Kong; sleep on the streets in downtown Calcutta, and build mud huts in Central Nairobi.

(2) The pattern of American cities is the result of private ownership of property, which cannot be taken by condemnation except for a public use or in a blighted area and for which compensation must be paid when appropriated. There is now almost universal zoning control which regulates types of use, density of use and height of buildings; but these controls, first adopted in New York in 1916, had no effect upon early city growth and they have been modified or changed thousands of times. Otherwise it would not have been possible to develop the 8,300 new shopping centers nearly all of which required zoning in depth rather than strip zoning nor could thousands of apartment buildings have been constructed in suburban areas.

Consequently, it is impossible to preserve green areas and open spaces without paying for the right. While the public cannot prevent the private owner from building on his land, zoning ordinances in some communities requiring one to five acres of land for each house have practically limited the utilization to occupancy by wealthy families because the high cost of sewer and water lines and street pavements in such low density areas virtually prevents building of houses for middle- or low-income family occupancy. Urban sprawl, or the filling in of all vacant areas, has been the bane of planners

who would like to restore the early star-shaped pattern. Where the State owns all of the land, as in Russia, or controls it rigidly, as in Finland, dense apartment clusters can be built along subway lines and the areas in between kept vacant.

(3) The central retail areas of foreign cities have not deteriorated as a result of outlying shopping center competition for there are few such centers because very few people own cars. Crowds throng the shops on Florida Street in Buenos Aires and Union Street in Lima, which are closed to automobile traffic in shopping hours. Galerias, an elaborate expansion of the arcade, often extending up to five or six levels, have recently been built in downtown Santiago, Sao Paulo and Rio de Janeiro. Rotterdam has its new central retail area; Cologne its shopping street, a pedestrian thoroughfare. In these foreign cities, residents find the downtown area the chief attraction. The parks of Tokyo, London, Paris, Buenos Aires and Rio de Janeiro are downtown; so are the palaces and government offices, the great cathedrals, the museums, theatres, restaurants and night life of many foreign cities. The Forum and Colosseum in Rome, the Acropolis in Athens, Notre Dame in Paris, Westminster Abbey and the Tower of London are all in or near central areas.[32]

One change is occurring which is altering the skyline of many foreign cities—the advent of the tall office building. Formerly, cities outside the United States prized their uniform skyline broken only by the spire of a great cathedral or an Eiffel Tower. But now tall office buildings loom above London and Milan; they are planned for Paris. Caracas has its 30-story Twin Towers; Rio de Janeiro a new 35-story office building, El Centro; Mex-

32. Homer Hoyt, "The Structure and Growth of American Cities Contrasted With the Structure of European and Asiatic Cities," *Urban Land,* Urban Land Institute, Washington, D.C., September 1959.

ico City its 32-story office building; and Sao Paulo has a great concentration of tall buildings in its downtown area.

(4) The great building boom in the United States has been financed on money borrowed from banks and insurance companies. Despite gradual inflation, most people have confidence in the American dollar. The volume of mortgage credit for building in 1 to 4 family units increased from $17.4 billion in 1940 to $182.4 billion in December 1963. Shopping centers are financed on the basis of guaranteed leases by national chain store tenants which afford sufficient funds to construct the center. In nations like Brazil, however, where the interest rates are 3 to 5 percent a month and the cruzeiro has dropped from 384 to 1300 to the dollar in a year's time, it is impossible to secure long term loans. New buildings can be effected only by paying all cash as the work proceeds. An inflation of any marked extent in the United States would drastically curtail the supply of mortgage funds available for new building.

(5) The federal government in 1952 was authorized by Congress to pay two-thirds of the difference between the cost of acquiring sites in blighted areas and the re-sale price for new development. This has made possible the clearing and rebuilding of central areas which could not be done without both the power of condemnation and the write-down of the difference between the acquisition cost and the re-use value.

The principles of city growth and structure, formulated on the basis of experience in cities in the United States prior to 1930, are thus subject to modification not only as a result of dynamic changes in the United States in the last few decades but these principles, originating here, are subject to further revisions when it is sought to apply them to foreign cities.

BRIAN J. L. BERRY

Internal Structure of the City

External Determinants of Internal Structure

Cities are the central elements in spatial organization of regional, national, and supranational socioeconomies by virtue of the interregional organization in a total "ecological field" of the functions they perform.[1] In a specialized society economic activities are undertaken by design, or survive in the market place, at those locations which afford the greatest competitive advantage. Among these activities, those most efficiently performed in limited local concentrations provide the basic support for cities. The location theorist commonly classifies locally-concentrated economic activities into those which are raw material oriented, those located at points which are intermediate between raw materials and markets, and those which are market oriented.[2] Raw material orientation includes direct exploita-

tion of resources and the processing of raw materials, and its character is that of the developed resource endowment of different places. Activities in intermediate locations are usually of a processing kind, involved in intermediate and final processing and transformation of raw materials, and most frequently locate at some favorable spot on the transport network, such as an assembly point, a gateway, a break-of-bulk point, or a port. Market oriented activities may be secondary (for example, where there is a weight gain involved in the final processing of raw materials on intermediates prior to delivery), but are dominantly tertiary, concerned with the direct service of the consuming population through wholesale, retail, and service functions. The consuming population comprises the workers in the other specialized activities, of course, plus the local population supported by the tertiary trades. Thus, market orientation implies a location best suited to serve demands created by prior stages of the productive process. The three classic principles of urban location derive from the three types of locational orientation of economic activities: cities as the sites of

1. J. R. P. Friedmann and W. Alonso, *Regional Development and Planning* (1964); Pappenfort, "The Ecological Field and the Metropolitan Community," 64 Am. J. Sociology 380-85 (1959).
2. W. Isard, *Location and Space Economy* (1956).

From a symposium, "Urban Problems and Prospects," in **Law and Contemporary Problems**, Vol. 30, No. 1, Winter 1965, pp. 111-119, published by the Duke University School of Law, Durham, North Carolina. Copyright © 1965 by Duke University. Reprinted by permission.

specialized functions; cities as the expressions of the layout and character of transport networks; and cities as central places.[3] All three principles, or some combination of them, may operate in the case of any particular city. However, whereas all cities will have a central business district providing retail and service functions to the city and surrounding populations, the role of the other two principles will vary greatly from one city to another.

In the internal structure of cities these specialized functions have priority. The central business district is a point of focus about which land uses and densities, the spatial patterning of the urban population, subsidiary retail and service locations, transportation and commuting patterns, and the like, have evolved. When other specialized activities are performed, they create supplementary or additional nodes. Thus, cities are supported by "basic" activities ("staples") whose locations are determined exogenously to the city by comparative advantage in larger regional, national, and international economic systems. These always include the central business district, the focus not only of the city itself but also of its tributary region, and may include other specialized activities. The skeleton of the city comprises the locations of these basic activities, plus the urban transport network. Flesh is provided by residential site selection of workers with respect to the skeleton, and blood comes from the daily ebb and flow of commuters. Further patterning is provided by the orientation of subsidiaries and business services to the basic activities, and by local shopping facilities to the workers. Shopping trips create another ebb and flow. Further "second-" and "third-round" effects can be described, but these follow logically from the first. The question to be answered here is that of the nature and

bases of residential, socioeconomic, and retail patterns within cities. Because the discussion is concerned with the internal structure of the city it thus perforce takes as given the exogenously determined skeleton. Further, it will focus upon the flesh rather than the blood, although the latter is implicit in the discussion of the former.

The Residential Pattern: Urban Densities

A simple expression summarizes the population density pattern of cities:

$$d_x = d_o e^{-bx} \qquad (1)$$

where d_x is the population density d at distance x from the city center, d_o is density at the city center, e is the natural logarithmic base, and b is the density gradient. The "city center" is, of course, the central business district, so that when the natural logarithm of population density of small areas within the city is calculated, along with their distance from the central business district, and a scatter diagram is constructed with distance along the abscissa, the points in the diagram lie around a straight line with downward slope b, or:

$$\ln \cdot d_x = \ln \cdot d_o - bx \qquad (2)$$

The gradient b may be considered an index of the "compactness" of the city, just as differences in central density d_o index the overall level of "crowding." Equation (2) has been shown to be universally applicable to cities regardless of time or place.[4] Why should this be so? Muth has shown how this negative exponential decline of population densities with increasing distance from the city center is a condition of locational equilibrium which stems logically from the operation of a·competitive housing mar-

3. Harris and Ullman, *"The Nature of Cities,"* 242 Annals 7-17 (1945).

4. Clark, *"Urban Population Densities,"* 114 J. Royal Stat. Soc'y 490-96 (1951).

ket.[5] Seidman has shown it to be a natural consequence of Alonso's locational theory of land use.[6] The theoretical bases of the empirical regularity are thus readily available.

The density gradient b, like the densities it indexes, also shows consistent behavior. For example, in any country at a particular point in time, it falls consistently with city size as follows:

$$\ln \cdot b_j = \ln \cdot P_o - c \cdot (\ln \cdot P_j) \quad (3)$$

so that cities have experienced progressive "decompaction" with increasing size. Further, since in the United States, recent expected growth of metropolitan areas between two time periods t and t + 1 is a constant proportion of size[7] such that

$$\ln \cdot P_{t+1} = k + \ln \cdot P_t \quad (4)$$

which further implies exponential growth of population with time

$$P_t = P_o e^{kt} \quad (5)$$

then

$$b_t = b_o e^{-ckt} \quad (6)$$

which states that the density gradient diminishes through time in a negative exponential manner, which is the case.[8]

Newling has shown, additionally, that the two generalizations that population

density declines exponentially with increasing distance from the city center and that the density gradient itself falls through time in a negative exponential manner, together leads to a third regularity, which he calls the "rule of intraurban allometric growth."[9] This is that the rate of growth of density is a positive exponential function of distance from the city center:

$$(1 + r_x) = (1 + r_o)e^{gx} \quad (7)$$

where r_x is the percentage rate of growth of density at distance x, r_o is percentage growth at the center, and g is the growth gradient, measuring the rate of change of the rate of growth as distance from the center of the city increases. He goes on to show that since both density and the rate of growth are functions of distance from the city center, the rate of growth may be expressed as a direct function of density:

$$(1 + r_x) = mD^{-q}$$

where r_x is as above, m is a constant, D is initial density and q relates the rate of change of the rate of growth to the rate of change of density. As density increases, the rate of growth drops. Moreover, Newling argues for the existence of a "critical density" above which growth becomes negative, i.e., population declines. In several cases he shows a convergence upon 30,000 persons per square mile as this critical density, and in one study he concludes:[10]

The inverse relationship between population density and the rate of growth, the identification of a critical density, and the observation that negative growth, occurring as it does above the critical density, is not solely attributable to competition between commercial and residential use of land, all lead one to speculate that perhaps there is indeed

5. R. Muth, *The Spatial Pattern of Residential Land Use in Cities* (in preparation).

6. D. E. Seidman, *An Operational Model of the Residential Land Market* (1964).

7. This "law of proportionate effect" may be seen by plotting populations of U.S. cities in 1950 against their populations in 1960. The scatter of points is linear and homoscedastic with a slope of +1.0 on double logarithmic paper. Satisfaction of this assumption means that in steady-state the distribution of towns by size will be lognormal so that Zipf's rank size rule for city sizes holds: $P_r = P_1/r^q$ or $Log \cdot P_r = Log \cdot P_1 - q \cdot Log \cdot r$. In these equations P_r is the population of the city of rank, r, P_1 is thus the largest city, and q is an exponent.

8. Berry, Simmons and Tennant, "Urban Population Densities: Structure and Change," 53 Geog. Rev. 389-405 (1963).

9. Newling, *"Urban Growth and Spatial Structure: Mathematical Models and Empirical Evidence"* (processed, Cornell University, 1965).

10. *Ibid.*

some optimum urban population density to exceed which inevitably incurs social costs. We may speculate that certain events in the history of the city will cause this optimum to be exceeded (for example, heavy immigration without a commensurate expansion of the housing stock and supply of social overhead capital), with deleterious consequences for the areas concerned (such as blight, crime and delinquency, and other social pathological conditions) and leading to an eventual decline in the population of the affected areas. . . .

If this is so, then consistent relationships are available between size of city and the pattern of population densities within cities, between growth of the urban population and change of densities within. Further, there is the strong suggestion that this chain provides direct links between an overall urbanization process and the occurrence of pathological social conditions in particular parts of particular cities.

Social and Economic Patterning of the Residents

The generalizations in the preceding section are strong. Equally strong generalizations are now possible concerning the social patterning of the urban residents who live at the density patterns in the changing ways already described.

There has been a long tradition of research by sociologists, geographers, and economists dealing with the social and economic characteristics of urban neighborhoods. Among the earliest descriptive generalizations were those of Hurd, who related neighborhood characteristics, especially income and rentals, to two simultaneous patterns of growth which he called *central* and *axial* growth.[11] Later, Burgess emphasized the importance of outward growth from the center which

caused concentric zonations of neighborhoods.[12] Change occurred by the outward movement of the wealthier to the periphery, and the continued expansion of inner zones upon the outer in a process of invasion and succession by the lower status groups living closer to the city center. Hoyt, on the other hand, emphasized the significance of axial growth when he developed his sector concept.[13] According to this notion, status differences established around the city center are projected outwards along the same sector as the city grows, thus creating a wedge-shaped distribution of neighborhoods by type with the higher status groups following scenic amenities and higher ground. In addition, the literature of sociology has been replete with studies of the segregation of ethnic groups in particular localities conforming neither to the concentric nor to the axial schemes.

Considerable debate has taken place about the relative merits of each of these models. A succession of large-scale factor analytic studies conducted since the end of the Second World War now make it possible to state definitively that the three models are independent, additive contributors to the total socioeconomic structuring of city neighborhoods. Factor analysis is a multivariate procedure which permits a mass of data (an example would be the 100+ census characteristics of each of the 800+ census tracts of Chicago) to be examined to determine exactly how many dimensions of variation are expressed by it. In each of the studies the answer is the same: there are just three dimensions of variation. These are (a) the axial variation of neighborhoods by socioeconomic rank; (b) the concentric variation of neighborhoods according to family structure; and (c) the localized

11. Richard M. Hurd, *Principles of City Land Values* (1903).

12. Burgess, *"The Growth of the City,"* in Robert E. Park, *The City* (1925).
13. Homer Hoyt, *The Structure and Growth of Residential Neighborhoods in American Cities* (1939).

segregation of particular ethnic groups.

Neighborhood characteristics involving educational levels, type of occupation, income, value of housing, and the like, are all highly correlated, as they should be, for undoubtedly they are also functionally related. Each varies across the city in the same way: according to sectors. High status sectors search and follow particular amenities desired for housing, such as view, higher ground, and so on. Lower status sectors follow lower lying, industrial-transportation arteries that radiate from the central business district and which, together with that district, form the exogenously-determined skeleton of the city. This is consistent with the idea, also, that the lower the income the closer is home to work in the contemporary American city.

Conversely, the age structure of neighborhoods changes concentrically with increasing distance from the city center, along with age of housing, densities, existence of multiple unit structures, incidence of ownership by residents, participation of women in the labor force, and the like. Thus, at the edge of the city are newer, owned, single-family homes, in which reside larger families with younger children than nearer the city center, and where the wife stays at home. Conversely, the apartment complexes nearer the city center have smaller, older families, fewer children, and are more likely to be rentals; in addition, larger proportions of the women will be found to work. This "family structure" pattern is consistent with the ideas of Burgess, and has been called by sociologists the "urbanism-familism" scale.

Thirdly, particular ethnic groups will be found to reside in segregated parts of the city. The most obvious case of segregation today in the American city is that of the Negro, although every new migrant group has also experienced this pattern of living. Along with segregation go such other variables as lack of household amenities, deterioration of housing, overcrowding, and the like.

If the concentric and axial schemes are overlaid on any city, the resulting cells will contain neighborhoods remarkably uniform in their social and economic characteristics. Around any concentric band communities will vary in their income and other characteristics, but will have much the same density, ownership, and family patterns. Along each axis communities will have relatively uniform economic characteristics, and each axis will vary outwards in the same way according to family structure. Thus, a system of polar coordinates originating at the central business district is adequate to describe most of the socioeconomic characteristics of city neighborhoods. The exception is in patterns of segregation, which are geographically specific to the particular city, although segregation is a phenomenon which is found in them all. The three classic principles of internal structure of cities are thus independent, additive descriptions of the social and economic character of neighborhoods in relation to each other and to the whole.

Services for the Residents: Local Business

The central business district provides a range of goods and services for the entire urban population and for the larger tributary region served by the city. In addition, a system of smaller business centers exists within the city to serve the city population with the commodities they require on a weekly or monthly basis. Such purely internal or endogenous business appears even in small towns of less than 1,000 population. It does not begin to assume any identifiable structure until the level of county seats, however, and a variety of internal forms is only clearly distinguishable in the cities which serve as centers for multi-county "functional economic areas." At this stage the structural differentiation of centers and ribbons is clear. Ribbons follow the major section and half-section streets and the radial highways, performing a variety of service functions (building materials and supplies, household requirements), automobile oriented activities (gas, repair, parts), and with many large single-standing, space-consuming stores (discounters, furniture, appliances), in addition to being interspersed with convenience shops (food, drugs, cleaners) for adjacent neighborhoods. Certain stretches of ribbon are devoted to the activities of "specialized functional areas" such as automobile row. At the major and minor intersections of the street system are business centers, differentiated from the adjacent ribbons by the functions they perform, the ways consumers shop in them, and by land values. The centers provide both convenience and such shopping goods as food, drugs, clothing, shoes, and luxuries. Consumers generally shop on foot from store to store, in contrast to their single-purpose trips to ribbon establishments. Land values within the city fall with increasing distance from the city center, but commercial values add extra texture. The ribbons create ridges that rise above the adjacent residential areas. Steeply-rising cones at the intersection of ridges clearly indicate the location and extent of centers. Four levels of outlying centers have been identified beneath the central business district: neighborhood and community shopping centers at the convenience level, and shoppers' and regional centers of a larger kind. The differentiation between these levels is made in terms of the number and variety of functions performed, in the size of trade area served, and the like.[14]

It is axiomatic that retail and service activities are consumer-oriented, since internal business has developed entirely to serve the population residing within the

14. Brian J. L. Berry, *Commercial Structure and Commercial Blight* (1963).

city. Consistent with the earlier sections of this paper, it is also possible to place internal business provision within the same frame. Consider a city divided by the concentric-axial scheme described above, and let R indicate the total retail and service provision of any of the cells defined, with P representing total population of the cell, D the population density, F an index of its family structure, and S an index of its social rank, then

$$R = sP^uD^vF^wS^z \qquad (8)$$

which yields an extremely close fit in every city studied. Moreover, the provision of local business, and local business change, may clearly be related back to the socioeconomic pattern of the city. Similar expressions may be developed for ribbons and centers separately, although in the case of centers certain problems emerge concerning the use of arbitrary cells instead of the market areas of the centers as the units of observation, even though a properly drawn set of circles and radii will, by their intersections, locate the outlying business centers of many cities.

As in the case of socioeconomic structure, however, segregation creates problems for generalization. In Chicago, for example, retail systems assume not one, but two equilibrium positions. In segregated non-white residential areas there is a two-level hierarchy of business centers comprising the neighborhood convenience type and the smaller shoppers' goods type, whereas in the rest of the city a four-level hierarchy of outlying centers exists. All retailing is experiencing changes due to increased scale of retailing, increasing consumer mobility, and rising real incomes. Yet as the non-white residential area expands outwards, still another element of retail change is added. Simply, neighborhood transition means loss of markets, since real income among the non-white population is approximately one-third lower than that of the population displaced. The effects are felt in several stages:

(a) Anticipation of neighborhood transition. In this phase the normal replacement of businesses which fail, or which close because the businessman retires or dies, ceases. Vacancy rates begin to rise. Also, a "maintenance gap" appears because property owners, increasingly uncertain about prospective revenues, reduce normal maintenance expenditures. Dilapidation grows.

(b) During turnover. Demands drop precipitously, especially for higher quality goods, and the specialty shops in the larger business centers fail. Vacancies in centers rise to levels as high as one-third to one-half of the stores.

(c) Stabilization phase. The neighborhood settles down into its lower income character. Because incomes and revenues are lower, it is almost impossible to eliminate the effects of the earlier maintenance gap, and so a general run-down appearance persists. Rents in the business centers drop and activities from the ribbons and new businesses directed at the changed market move in and fill up the centers once again. Vacancies mount in the abandoned ribbons, settling down in excess of twenty per cent of the stores, but concentrated in the older buildings which, through lack of use, deteriorate more. Zones of segregated housing are thus criss-crossed with ribbons of unwanted, blighted, commercial property. Much that is critical to an understanding of business within the city thus depends less upon the structuring implicit in use of a model such as equation (8) than upon the existence and nature of segregation in the housing market.

Although the skeleton of the city is determined by broader regional and supra-regional forces, the flesh shows certain simple systematic regularities which are tightly knit into a locational system of simultaneous concentric and axial dimensions. Segregated housing patterns are responsible for the current inability to develop a single model of the whole covering both spatial structure and change.

RONALD R. BOYCE

The Edge of the Metropolis:
The Wave Theory Analog Approach

A metropolis might be considered to grow in two major respects. It might change in its distribution of internal density of land use, and it might increase in its area by growing about its edges. Although there are a number of theories, both descriptive and analytical, which pretend to describe the present surface and extent of the metropolis—e.g. rent theory, central place theory, density gradient studies, and various descriptive diagrams such as those by Burgess, Hoyt, and Harris—these are all primarily static models.[1] There are very few models which take into account the dynamic nature of metropolitan change and almost nothing is available on the spread, or outward movement, or the urban fringe, or cutting edge of the metropolis.[2]

1. Such models are discussed in many articles and books. The most general references are: Raymond E. Murphy, *The American City: An Urban Geography* (New York: McGraw-Hill Company, 1965); Harold M. Mayer and Clyde F. Kohn (eds.), *Readings in Urban Geography* (Chicago: The University of Chicago Press, 1959); and Brian J. L. Berry and Allen Pred, *Central Place Studies: A Bibliography of Theory and Applications* (Philadelphia: Regional Science Research Institute, 1961).
2. See, for example, John R. Hamburg and Robert Sharkey, "Chicago's Changing Land Use

Knowledge of the magnitude, spread, and other characteristics of this outward movement appears critical both for sound planning purposes and for general understanding of the metropolis. Even so, the growing edge of the metropolis has not even been formally considered as a major concept in urban geography. Some empirical models of outward population movement have been developed for use by the planning practitioner,[3] but little philosophy and theoretical underpinnings

and Population Structures," *Journal of the American Institute of Planners* (November 1960), 317-322; Colin Clark, "Urban Population Densities," *Journal of the Royal Statistical Societies*, Vol. 114 (1951), 490-96; Hans Blumenfeld, "Are Land Use Patterns Predictable," *Journal of the American Institute of Planners* (1959), 61-66; and Willard B. Hansen, "An Approach to the Analysis of Metropolitan Residential Extension," *Journal of Regional Science* (Summer 1961), 37-55.
3. See, in particular, John R. Hamburg and Roger L. Creighton, "Predicting Chicago's Land Use Pattern," *Journal of the American Institute of Planners* (May 1959); Walter G. Hansen, "How Accessibility Shapes Land Use," *Journal of the American Institute of Planners* (May 1959), 73-76; and Albert Z. Guttenberg, "Urban Structure and Urban Growth," *Journal of the American Institute of Planners* (May 1960), 104-110.

From the **British Columbia Geographical Series,** No. 7, 1966, pp. 31-40. Reprinted by permission of Tantalus Research Limited, Vancouver, B.C., and the author.

for such regularity of movement is evident. To put it another way, few analogs such as the spread of innovation waves, as documented and discussed by Hagerstrand, have been developed for the growth of the urban fringe.[4]

The use of analogs in geography is so widespread as to require little justification for further use. For example, Peter Haggett in his new book on locational analysis devotes a section to the analog approach in geography.[5] First, it is almost impossible to compare any two areas without some form of analog procedure. To make inferences about area "X" based on its similarity to area "A" is to use a formal spatial transference type of analog. Indeed, the gravitational formulae, so much in use for potential models and the like, are clearly an analog approach. Most spatial simulation models are likewise attempts to build analogs.

An analog is merely a procedure whereby likenesses between two things are noted and comparisons made. In so doing, the new object is often seen in a clearer light. This is especially the case if a well known thing is found to be analogous to a relatively unexplored phenomenon. Webster's Dictionary defines an analog as a "relation of likeness between two things, or one thing to or with another, consisting in the resemblance *not of the things themselves but of two or more attributes, circumstances, or effects.*"[6] (Underlining mine) From a logic standpoint, an analog is "a form of inference in which it is reasoned that if two, or more, things agree with one another in one or more respects, they will probably agree in yet other respects."[7]

I believe that growth within an urban area might be meaningfully viewed from a wave, or undulatory, analog approach. As indicated by the above definition however, I am not saying that the expansion and change in urban areas is exactly like that of ocean waves; merely, that it appears to have a number of similar characteristics to such waves. Such similarity raises questions for research as well as provides a new framework for analysis. Such aids are particularly helpful when well known things such as ocean waves are compared with a relatively unknown thing, e.g., the moving edge of the metropolis. Thus, this approach should provide still another perspective on changing urban patterns which might prove helpful.[8]

From an undulatory concept, three major waves appear to exist within metropolitan areas: (1) a recession wave, (2) a precession wave, and (3) a wave on the edge of the built-up area, herein called the tidal wave. The recession wave occurs in the outer frame area of the central city.[9] It is characterized by a decreasing change in population over time which moves outward from the central area. Technically, of course, this might be con-

4. Torsten Hagerstrand, "The Propagation of Innovation Waves," Lund Studies in Geography, Series B, *Human Geography,* No. 4 (Lund: The Royal University of Lund, Department of Geography, 1952).
5. Peter Haggett, *Locational Analysis in Human Geography* (New York: St. Martin's Press, 1966), 304-310. For further use of the analog method in geography see William Bunge, *Theoretical Geography,* Lund Studies in Geography, Series C, General and Mathematical Geography, No. 1 (Lund: The Royal University of Lund, Department of Geography, 1962); William Bunge, *Patterns of Location,* Michigan Inter-University Community of Mathematical Geographers, Number 3, February 21, 1964; and Edward L. Ullman, *A Measure of Water Recreation Benefits: The Meramec Basin Example.* Center for Urban and Regional Studies, Reprint No. 5, University of Washington, 1964.

6. *Webster's New Collegiate Dictionary,* Springfield: G. & C. Merriam Co., 1959.
7. *Op. cit.*
8. The importance of multiple perspectives in research is made clear in Edward A. Ackerman, *Geography as a Fundamental Research Discipline* (Chicago: The University of Chicago Press, Department of Geography Research Paper No. 53, 1958).
9. See Edgar M. Horwood and Ronald R. Boyce, *Studies of the Central Business District and Urban Freeway Development* (Seattle: The University of Washington Press, 1959).

sidered merely the following side of a full wave or as a reflection of a downward undulation. Urban renewal and redevelopment is largely an attempt to slow down, if not prematurely reverse, this decline and outward spread of this wave. The recession wave has, of course, been widely discussed in the literature, particularly in many of the recent studies dealing with changing density decline functions over time.[10]

The precession wave, to use an analog to explain an analog, is somewhat similar to a squall line in meteorology in that it precedes by fifteen to thirty minutes travel time the actual built-up edge of the metropolis. In this wave zone there is considerable turbulence in land use, land values, and land ownership. It is a zone characterized by speculative land holdings, paper land plats, farms falling largely into disuse, and by a plethora of real estate agents.[11] This rather wide wave moves ahead of the main advance of the actual urban settlement but may in some instances be considered to be absorbed by it. This wave has been little studied and would certainly provide an interesting basis for a dissertation.

The primary purpose here, is to explore in more detail the third type of wave; the tidal wave or cutting edge of the metropolis. Indeed, this is about the only wave noted by the casual observer and the one which has surely received the greatest amount of public attention. In fact, this is the actual front of urban settlement. It has been referred to in many ways in the literature; for example, as the rural-urban fringe, as outer suburbia, as the cutting edge of the metropolis, and as used here as the tidal wave of metropolitan expansion.

There are, of course, other analogs which might be used to describe this growing edge of urbanization. Wave analogs however, appear to hold the greatest promise in providing a new and hopefully more meaningful research framework. While it might be more entertaining to describe such urban frontal scatteration from the analog of an explosion in the urban center scattering debris over the urban countryside, with a higher amount of "debris" falling nearer the outer edge of the built-up area, this analog soon peters out as a very meaningful research framework. By contrast, the ocean wave analog approach appears to be ripe with as yet uninvestigated opportunities.

Blumenfeld's Contribution

As a background to the tidal wave notion of urban expansion, some of the work by Blumenfeld, in 1954, should be noted.[12] Blumenfeld was not only the first to draw a meaningful and documented comparison between the expanding edge of the metropolis and a tidal wave, but he also found a number of other wave-like characteristics in the urban area.

Blumenfeld examined population change in fifteen concentric zones extending twenty-five miles from downtown Philadelphia over a fifty year time period. First, he found that for any given distance zone from the center of the metropolis, there is a similar type of undulatory pattern. Each zone in succession raises relatively steeply to a peak, or crest, of density then declines more slowly and flattens out; probably to begin a new rise again. (Figure 1) Second, he found that the

10. Such studies are especially numerous. For a good review and for a rather extensive bibliography, see Brian J. L. Berry, James W. Simmons and Robert J. Tennant, "Urban Population Densities: Structure and Change, *The Geographical Review* (July, 1963), 389-405. See also Marjorie N. Rush, "Changing Urban Densities" (University of Iowa, Department of Geography, Master's thesis, 1964).

11. See, for example, M. Mason Gaffney, "Urban Expansion—Will It Ever Stop," *The Yearbook of Agriculture* (Washington: U.S. Government Printing Office, 1958), 503-522.

12. Hans Blumenfeld, "The Tidal Wave of Metropolitan Expansion," *Journal of the American Institute of Planners* (Winter, 1954) 3-14.

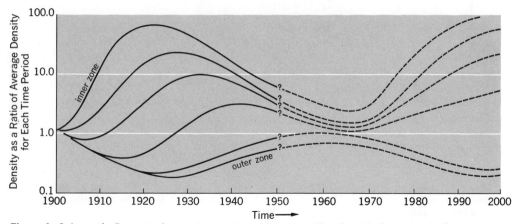

Figure 1. Schematic Presentation of Zonal Undulations over Time in a Typical Metropolis

Source: Adopted and modified from Hans Blumenfeld, "The Tidal Wave of Metropolitan Expansion," *Journal AIP* (1954), 8.

amplitude of each wave decreases as one goes outward from the center of the city. The waves also crest much more steeply in the inner zones. (Figure 1) It should be remembered that we are talking in the above cases of at least a fifty year period and even this was barely enough time to complete fully one undulation in a zone. There is every indication that about a fifty year period is required for an upward and downward movement to occur in a zone. This fits strikingly well the current economic life of structures in a city. Long periods of data are clearly required when one talks about urban waves. Within such a time period however, great undulations are apparent. The current redevelopment of the central city area may actually represent the next upper wave undulation in the area and is therefore perfectly consistent with the wave notions above. (Blumenfeld, however, thought otherwise in this regard.)

In light of this paper, Blumenfeld's tidal wave concept is most important. Blumenfeld argued that in any given time period, there is a particular "zone of maximum growth, . . . which we may define as the crest of the tidal wave of met-

ropolitan expansion." This crest moves slowly and fairly regularly outward from the center of the metropolis to its periphery. In the Philadelphia area, the crest of the wave moved outward at a steady rate of about one mile per decade. (Figure 2) Therefore, he argued that the tidal wave in the metropolis is much like the tidal wave of the sea in that "storm or calm on the surface of the ocean (city) has little influence on the movement of the tidal wave. We are dealing with a secular trend operating with the inexorable consistency of a natural law when we deal with the urban tidal wave," and, still according to Blumenfeld, the tidal wave in the metropolis is a secular trend so powerful that "business cycles are ephemeral agents of secondary interest."[13]

Some characteristics of the ocean tidal wave may perhaps be noted in order to test the analogy. First, the tidal wave has nothing whatsoever to do with tides. Generally, it is a seismic wave caused by an earthquake, an undersea volcanic eruption, or some other major underwater or surface water disruption. The tidal wave on the ocean surface is in fact a very

13. *Ibid.*, p. 11.

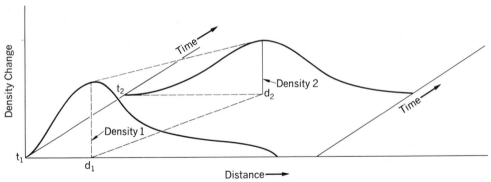

Figure 2. Movement of the Urban "Tidal Wave" Through Space and Time, based on Blumenfeld's discussion on the tidal wave. The author is indebted to William Byers for suggesting this three dimensional diagram.

small wave, being only a few feet in height, but moving at great speeds, sometimes upwards of five hundred miles an hour. The wave lengths of the tidal wave are also very long, approaching about seventeen minutes between wave crests, and therefore largely go unnoticed on the open sea. When they reach shallow water however, they become "rampaging monsters."[14] If one thinks about the analogy of this wave to the zone of maximum population growth in a city, some of these comparisons become dubious. However, if one approaches general change in the metropolis, and particularly the edge of the metropolis, from a general wave standpoint, a number of new approaches and questions become apparent.

Some Wave Analogs

Let's now examine the wave analog approach in greater detail. Imagine the wave effect brought about by dropping a pebble in a pond. The pebble might be

14. For a particularly lucid description see Willard Bascom, *Waves and Beaches: The Dynamics of the Ocean Surface* (New York: Anchor Books, 1964). See also R. C. H. Russell and D. H. MacMillan, *Waves and Tides* (New York: Philosophical Library, 1953) and Albert Defant, *Ebb and Flow* (Ann Arbor: University of Michigan Press, 1958).

analogous to an increase in total urban population and the water waves might represent the spread of this population of the city (pond). One might note the first wave of population to reach the "lakeshore" of the urban built-up area. One might wonder about the magnitude of the wave at any place in the urban area (perhaps dependent on the amount of new population added), the speed of movement, wave length, and other wave features as they apply to the urban scene. One might wonder about the speed of wave in different directions. Perhaps it might be slowed down in some directions by "dragging the lake bottom." This would perhaps be analogous to the friction of population movement over the urban surface. One might wonder about what happens when the wave hits a barrier or the edge of the pond.

The answers and mathematics for ocean waves in these regards are of course known. Even so, general questions about the pebble dropped in the pond analog might be made with regard to an urban unit even though answers are known from a water wave standpoint. If one assumes that the pebble represents population added in an urban area, the type of liquid (water) represents the type of city, the depth of water represents friction of movement within an urban area, and the shore of the pond represents the edge of the built-up area of the city, multiple questions about the nature of urbanization result. For example, how does the amount of population added, and its place of addition, affect the speed, amplitude, cycle, and other characteristics of the resultant waves? How does the particular kind of population affect such a wave? How does the kind of city affect wave movement? What about wave effect (e.g. amplitude and intensity) as distance from the population input area increases? What are the resultant interference patterns if several pebbles (population amounts) are dropped in different locations simultaneously, or in some sequence?

But let's talk in more detail about the edge of the metropolis. One of the most striking characteristics of any metropolis is its form, or shape. Cities differ widely in shape and are rarely circular.[15] They grow outward in different directions at different times; that is, the edge of the metropolis is rarely equidistant from the central core. The usual way in which the shape of cities is explained is by differing accessibilities to the core area or to major employment centers. The outer edge is thereby taken as a crude isochrone. By contrast, consider for a moment such spread from a wave standpoint. Population can move out over the surface with different ease caused by differences in surface friction. Movement might be channelled into particular areas and retarded in others at any given time. Such barriers might by physiographic, based on speculative land holdings, administratively derived by such features as zoning, or transportation network induced.

If such barriers are "hit" by a population pressure wave what will be the effect? A wave from a pebble dropped into the pond which hits a log for example, might be *reflected, diffracted* and *refracted;* that is, the wave can be reflected back with little loss of energy, it can move around the log and fill in behind it somewhat (diffraction), or the wave can be bent by underwater surface friction in such a way that the wave is wrapped around the log barrier. This latter refractive process on the ocean results in far greater energy being focused on shore protrusions. By the same token, point-type barriers to urban development must be receiving far more pressure for settlement than areas further removed. Could one, by use of some orthogonal procedure, determine such population pressure?[16] Or how might one measure the reflective, or clapotis, effect of population pressure on a barrier. In other words, what might be the repercussive effect from such wave hits. One merely has to observe the effects of such urban barriers to residential settlement as water bodies, parks, and rugged terrain to note some major "piling up" effects in some cases and some major aversion in others.

A further analogy to the pebble-generated waves might be made with regard to urban density movement outward. Waves travel in trains, not in single units. As such, the velocity of the train is only about one-half the speed of the individual waves in the train. The first wave is continually being removed because of energy loss in activating particles, an exponential new replacement wave builds up in back of the train. This process results in a loss of energy with distance and, of course, means that the original particles do not actually move much. Instead, the final wave is but a remote descendent of the initial wave. Blumenfeld's work indicates that trains might indeed be involved in urban waves and that such wave substitution of particle matter and loss of wave energy with distance is evident.

When a wave train hits shallow water

15. This is discussed in some detail in Ronald R. Boyce and W. A. V. Clark, "The Concept of Shape in Geography," *The Geographical Review* (August, 1964), 561-572.

16. See Bascom, *op. cit.,* pp. 69-77.

and thereby becomes a series of shallow-water waves—i.e. when the depth of water is less than one-half the wave length (distance between wave crests)—the waves "feel" the bottom and undergo radical changes in length, velocity, and direction. Is it appropriate to talk about "deep" and "shallow" waves within urban areas? Certainly, some movements of population which spread outward "feel" the bottom so to speak much more so than others.

As a final example, imagine the rural area about the metropolis being washed by a series of urban waves. The initial rural settlement and landscape might be analogous to rocks and the like on a beach. As the first urban wave sweeps over the rural surface it will leave deposits of sand behind the rocks and perhaps leave other "beach particles" distributed on the basis of the initial surface condition. In other places, channels might develop and the actual surface changes (analogous perhaps to roads being built, reservoirs developed, etc.). With each successive overlay of waves a new pattern of settlement develops, each pattern being affected by what was there before. If one thinks about the rural-urban fringe in this manner, as a series of waves moving over the area, the scatteration of settlement, indeed the fringe landscape, begins to take on new meaning. This landscape can thereby only be understood as a series of wave-like veneers which have built-up over time. There is multiple evidence that this is indeed how such a landscape emerges. In fact, the familiar sequent occupance notions result in a very similar approach. The sequent occupance notion however, is much weaker than a wave theory approach in that it lacks a meaningful causal element so necessary for complete area understanding.

Toward a General Wave Approach

A more general wave analog to urban morphology and change might be noted by a casual observation of the ocean surface as contrasted with the clear-cut mathematical expressions which have been developed for pure wave forms. If one substitutes the terms city surface for ocean surface, and thinks of wave height as analogous to urban land intensity, or density, he will not great similarities between the urban surface and the ocean surface in the following quote. Bascom describes the sea as follows: "In a sea, waves are merely individual hillocks of water with changing shapes that move independently. The limits of a wave in a sea are indefinable. Each mass of water which the eye selects as a wave has a different direction from the other waves of the sea. The words, period, velocity and wave length have lost the meaning they had in the orderly environment of the wave channel. Thus the surface of the seas is the result of sinusoidal wave trains one on top of another. . . . Individually, the waves in these trains are as true to the classical formulae as those in the model tank."[17] From such a statement, and the inferences made above, one begins to wonder whether the rather erratic surface of the city, with its hillocks and valleys of density and intensity, and its spread outward, might also contain such underlying "wave" orderliness not yet discovered. Perhaps the research approach of oceanographers, which started not with an attempt to understand the complicated sea surface but with a dissection of particular waves, provides a portent for urban analysis.

I appreciate that parts of my discussion may appear to be on the preposterous side. This was not my intention however. The surface of the ocean is equally complex in appearance to the density surface of the city, yet great order has been found in the surface of the sea. Likewise, the surface of the city, which must surely be filled with waves being generated from a

17. *Ibid.,* pp. 45, 47.

multitude of sources and directions, must also contain underlying orderliness; at least, this has been the general contention of urban geographers from the beginning. The oceanographer has been able to make careful study of each wave characteristic under laboratory conditions and has just recently tried to simulate and to dissect the actual surface of the sea. The urban geographer has been grappling with the entire surface of the city from the be-ginning. Perhaps he should be dissecting it into its component parts which, when super-imposed one upon another, will begin to provide a composite more approaching the actual surface reality of the city. When the form, characteristics, causes and consequences of the urban waves discussed here are more clearly understood, perhaps the framework for a new approach to urban research will have been achieved.

JAMES E. VANCE, JR.

Focus on Downtown

When we observe the metropolis as a whole, as if from a plane flying over it, perhaps the simplest way to find the downtown area is to look for the most diverse physical structure. The central area has normally the tallest buildings but also single-storey shops and seemingly vacant land that is used on occasion for parking. If the airborne observer is able to gain any impression of the use that is made of the buildings he sees, the same complexity strikes him.

It is in the core area that most urban uses are juxtaposed, leading social commentators to characterize the single-function suburb as drab and monolithic. Of course, the suburb is monolithic only in contrast with the city center, not in contrast to its outlying agricultural frame, but there can be little doubt that most people's image of the city is the diverse one of the downtown area.

Less obvious to simple observation is the diversity of background of the city's core. When we look at the business district and its surroundings we see activities that grow out of the present demands placed on the city and reflect the character of the present tributary area. But if we ask what ideas shaped the lots and blocks in the business district, or for that matter, what considerations put the business district where it is, the present alone cannot furnish us the answers.

The downtown of most cities was, in the beginning, the town itself, with the result that some parts were laid out to serve commerce but some were not. In the same fashion, the street pattern of central districts tends to have a diversity that makes free traffic flow difficult, not because our ancestors were miserly in their view of what a business district needed, rather they were too modest in their hopes for the city they founded. Conditions of mobility have changed so radically that they have joined with other forces to make the downtown historically complex.

The diversity of the city core comes also from the peculiar status of the central business district as the one area in the city that has traditionally, and continuously, been subject to rebuilding, even in the total absence of planning as we know it today. The value of central space, and the changing function of the core in an expanding and elaborating metropolis, have led to constant renewal and redesign of buildings, and even of large units

From the **Community Planning Review**, Summer 1966. Reprinted by permission of the author and the **Community Planning Review**, Ottawa, Canada.

within the core. Most cities are fortunate indeed that there has been this constant ferment in the downtown as it has created there a physical and stylistic collection that is missing in most other parts of the city. The occasional mistakes that show up in the buildings of the core are less depressing than the transient and uniform newness of the redeveloped area or the outlying shopping center. One may tire of a book but few tire of a library. And half the excitement of the downtown comes in its silent appraisal of our parents' and grandparents' thoughts, which again is more interesting than the thought of a single Saturday morning suggested by the typical outlying shopping center.

Dynamics of Growth

Half the problems that we face in downtown areas today come from the very success of those areas in holding their own. The inadequacy of streets for the loads we put on them, the failure of buildings, or even full blocks, to conform to our notions as to the desirable urban pattern, and the presence of uses that we think demean our city—all can be related to the ability of the central area to maintain its position under a diversity of situations. Elsewhere in the city the problems are usually the spaciousness of neglect rather than the crowding of success.

Placed in such a context, it is clear that the downtown has two qualities that make understanding of its dynamics essential, but far from easy; here we have both the most complex segment of the city, and the most long-lived. And that longevity suggests to us that there we also have the one part of the city that we may fairly confidently assume will be important to our grandsons. Just as we can pick out our grandfathers' quirks in the Napoleonic buildings that frown bulbously over our main streets, and our fathers' up-to-date ideas in the slickly-rounded corners of modernesque car showrooms,

our sons will probably wonder why we thought the surface texture of glass more interesting than that of any other building material, notably so in what will seem to them post-fluorescent times.

If we dealt with an industrial park or a housing estate, we might have the defence of rapid obsolescence, which stems from hustling technology, or from the expanding idea that a house is a machine for living that needs to be replaced on the same cycle as the drill-press. Only in central business districts do we have an articraft that we chip away at—to sharpen now and then, but never throw away.

Assuming, as I do, that there is such a thing as a normal structure for North American cities, and that these cities are shaped by similar forces, it seems reasonable to assume that conditions must be held constant for cities to be similar. Method of land holding, state of technology, attitudes toward the use of capital and resources, and general level of national income are such conditions. Widespread leasehold forms the city differently from small-unit freehold, and still more distinctly in contrast municipalization of land ownership. In the same way we must assume a very rapid spread of technological innovation to think that cities will be similar. Extensive observation of Canadian cities convinces me that the controls of development are sufficiently standard to allow the isolation of a system of general structural forces.

When we set out to understand the growth of downtown areas we may deal with the events in a particular city, or we may try to organize our knowledge so it will apply to a whole class of cities. I personally think that urban problems are nationwide and differ locally only in detail. My own work tells me that 10 years from now San Francisco will seem far more "quaint" than will Boston. So perhaps the place to begin our discussion is by abandoning parochialism and substituting an ecumenical view of urbanism.

The Seven Lives of the Downtown

THE PROCESS OF INCEPTION

As a process, the inception of the city stands alone. Once done, obviously it can never be repeated. And yet the original siting of a town and the decisions that must be taken as to what scale and skeleton its first growth shall have, contain such pervasive influences on the future of the city that we must look at this incipient stage as the most important single force shaping cities, and more particularly, as the one force which is necessarily parochial rather than common to all cities in a particular region.

Admittedly, certain regional consistencies are typical in the process of inception. On the Canadian prairies the rapid expansion of the settlement frontier was associated with the building of railroads, which tended to make the point of attachment to the outside world in all these towns the railroad station. Road connections were later in origin and secondary in structural importance, a condition that contrasts sharply with the order of things in French Canada where the town was the creation of the road and the city the creation of the juncture of several roads. The most obvious result of the single-point attachment in the prairie towns was the ease with which a grid-pattern town could be laid out when there were no fixed and well-traveled trails to interrupt its coherence.

Once beyond the original town-plat, growth normally takes place along alignments that were first external connections of the city. This employment of structures first created for another use is one of the great unbalancing forces in cities, which seem to be capable of change only through the deliberate rewriting of the past that comes with the process of redevelopment. Because the external connections of no two cities can be alike, once growth expands beyond the original town-plat the problems of urban disorder are great and distinct to each city.

The rewriting of the urban past comes through as it were "starting again". By massive destruction we succeed in cleaning the slate so that we may sketch a new "inception" for the city. It is in this context that the notion of urban renewal has its importance for us. Thus, the process of inception, though normally restricted to the initial phase of urban development, may, through the hand of redevelopment, be brought to bear a second time.

THE PROCESS OF EXCLUSION

Once any town has been founded, its residents normally wait impatiently for growth to take place. Such an expansion occurs in the frame of the former town and operates through the mechanism of the rent-gradient, under which a lot at the very heart of the city has the highest value and all lots grading out toward the edge of the city have successively less value. This means that the location of activities tends to be primarily determined by the rent-paying ability of the function. Similar activities tend to have similar abilities at rent-paying, so the high rent area of the city tends to become ever more exclusive in its content. Notably, housing is pushed outward and industry and wholesaling can remain at the center only in the depreciating zone of discard left in the wake of the geographical shift of the core of the downtown.

The agent of exclusion may be rent-paying ability but its results is the creation of the "downtown" or central business district as we know it. Before exclusion has time to accomplish its first resorting, the "town" and the "downtown" tend to be identical and somewhat unstructured. Once the grading mesh of rent has done its job, the central business district has both reality and structure as retail trade and various service functions can buy the more elevated slopes of the rent-gradient, leaving for the manufacturers, wholesalers, and house-seekers the lower, less narrowly-limited slopes.

In the beginning, just after the preliminary sorting has taken place, the core tends to have a number of inherited buildings, built originally for housing, manufacturing, or wholesale trade. As these buildings are taken over by central business district functions they may either enjoy a continued life with a new function in an old form or they will, unit by unit normally, be reconstructed in form as well as function.

This, then, is the evolution of central use and buildings which must be distinguished from the revolution wrought by redevelopment. The evolution of the downtown is a cell-by-cell replacement, similar to the process in wood petrification, while the revolution of the core destroys the structure and uses only the chemical elements, disregarding previous structure.

Because exclusion of non-central functions is the result of a limitation in the supply of central land, evidence of the beginning of exclusion (as a structural dynamic) serves as a fair indicator of the shift of a city from a minor status to that of regional center. As most towns rise to the status of regional center first in retail trade, the process of exclusion shows up first in the retailing core, and only later in other functional areas. But the process applies to all activities given sufficient demand for land. However, as exclusion rests on the idea of the rent-gradient (and the concept of rent is not accepted mechanically where social values are concerned) we have tended, particularly in housing, to substitute restrictions on use for the monetary controls that work to make the downtown largely a selling and service area. The concept of exclusion is consistent, but the agency of its accomplishment may be varied.

Exclusion stands as an essentially negative element in the shaping of the downtown; it throws things out but it does not in itself reform the structure of the city. But the same general forces that worked to reserve the downtown primarily for selling and service also worked to create a completely new structure within the core.

THE PROCESS OF SEGREGATION

Another aspect of location is association. Most things stand in relation to other things and the links between the two may be as important as the outright location. Thus, the tie between a shoe store and a department store is such that the shoe merchant will pay not only for a central site but also for a close linkage with the department store. Exclusion drives uses away from the center but segregation drives groups of uses apart, not necessarily at a greater distance from the center and out of the downtown.

The downtown area differs from any other section of the city in its longer history, but that historical continuity is not mere chance. The manner in which the downtown functions is medieval in many ways. The linkages within the core are often on foot, which places an upper limit on radial extension of establishments that are linked together. This is not the same as saying there is an absolute size above which the downtown cannot go. We have not reached such a ceiling if one does exist. The salvation of the downtown is the ability it has to segregate functions into coherent subdistricts which are manageable in size and shape, whatever the lack of control we may feel with respect to the full downtown.

For example, the financial district of a city can grow only to a certain size before internal segregation takes place, separating the full array of establishments into groups with shared linkages. In New York we find the stock-exchange district around Wall Street, the ship company area on Park Row, advertising several miles away on Madison Avenue, and corporate headquarters, other than those noted, on Park Avenue. This is not a phenomenon of primate cities alone; San Francisco has similar divisions of the financial district. Although in most cities the sub-districts adjoin, there is no absolute need for them to do so, as New York or London show.

As the cluster of any particular type of activity in the core grows, the chances for segregation increase, which in turn may preëmpt downtown space and cause other activities to think of moving out of the downtown. Turned the other way 'round, if a great amount of activity is found in the core, it may ultimately completely exclude any other central business function. The financial district of lower Manhattan is a case in point.

When a firm discovers that it stands as a self-contained unit with relatively few or unimportant external linkages, it may consider moving outside the downtown. Such a move will normally save the firm money as the site selected will be found somewhere down the slope of the rent-gradient. A similar segregation of retailing shows up in the spinning off of specialty shopping. In several cities the high-price specialty shopping area is completely unlinked to the regular shopping district, and essentially outside the downtown, having strong internal ties but links of little strength with the rest of the downtown.

Finally, the process of segregation begins to produce a city for which planning has meaning. Before separate functional districts come into being, the problems facing downtown areas are primarily architectural but once we begin to deal with large interacting functional units, architecture becomes derivative and design begins as spatial planning.

THE PROCESS OF EXTENSION

The assumption on which we have been operating so far calls for minimizing the radial extent of downtown activities. When we look at business districts formed even as late as 50 years ago we find circular edges and a high degree of compactness. But after 1918 business districts began to grow outward in long thin alignments along arterial streets. (Residential land use reflected this type of growth, pushing in tongues into the open country. Before the First World War the typical business district was a compact unit at the focus of routes, whereas the typical residential area was a bead on a string shaped by suburban rail lines.) The shift to linearity came with the introduction of individual mobility in cities. For certain activities access to the mobile rather than the clustered population became the desire.

The growth of the downtown through extension came when some things we now take for granted were new. The sale of automobiles, of food in composite markets, of meals and drink in the suburbs, and of business machines and equipment were introduced in this dawn of mobility. The businesses tended to be set up on those streets that lay in the van of the advance of the downtown, in what we have called the zone of assimilation where style was higher than the rent. In the 40 years since that dawn the arms of downtown-use have grown long and strong. No longer can we think of the core as a completely compact area. Along certain streets there are now distinct land-use districts that represent segregated clusters of activity, which may serve the whole metropolis. Business services and equipment seek such locations as do automotive sales.

THE PROCESS OF REPLICATION AND READJUSTMENT

As the city grows outward, certain of the central functions tend to show up in outlying areas. These replicas occur most often in outlying shopping centers or in massive headquarters offices. As concern here is for the downtown, the importance of replication for us is not these clusters of activity in the vast suburban reaches of the metropolis but the influence that they exert on the city center. That influence may be summed up under the dynamic of readjustment.

In the past, readjustment has been a part of the normal change in the city core but that change came both slowly and in terms of discernible shifts in national economy and culture. Today, readjustment in the central business district must be an adaptation to the secular shifts in disposable income, style, and technology and merchandising that have always affected the downtown, and the quite sudden changes in the locale of shopping and service demand within the metropolis. The slow demise of the "dry goods store" is an example of the first change, whereas the rapid and painful collapse of the small grocery store and meat market on the introduction of outlying supermarkets illustrates the second type of readjustment.

Conditions vary among cities, though certain situations are common. The abandonment of movie theatres, of downtown auto showrooms, of centrally-located food stores, of older rental offices of large corporations, and of central hardware and furniture stores is widespread. The cause of abandonment may differ but the effect on the downtown is similar and the result not of secular economic change but quite rapid development of new facilities in outlying areas.

When a single unit of space is vacated in the downtown, no long-term effect may be felt; but when a number of adjacent uses remove themselves within a short time, urban decay may be critical. In the case of wholesale districts the rapid changes in transportation technology and business organization have caused a number of large firms to shift location over a very short period of time. Sometimes attempts are made to "fill up" the space vacated, but to do so from firms similarly subject to technological change is a pretty sorry palliative in a situation where careful analysis is called for.

There is another readjustment that does not have a direct structural expression but which will ultimately require rebuilding. This is the change in merchandising which comes from the creation of replicas of the downtown in outlying shopping centers. The goods sold in the suburbs will differ considerably from those sold in the main store and ultimately the tendency will be, within the single firm, to apply the dynamics of exclusion and segregation, casting off certain functions from the main store and concentrating them in the suburban branch.

What influence will the growth of the downtown replicas in the suburbs have on trade flowing into the metropolis from its rural hinterland? So long as the main store and the branch stock the same goods, this contest will be in earnest. And the more distant from the downtown outlying shopping centers become, the more real will be the competition. The trip from a farming community 50 miles from the city core may be significantly reduced if an outlying center 15 miles from the core is substituted. As cities grow in areal extent, they approach each other, so the competition among individual cities is made much more complex with these orbitting satellites around each planet of retail gravitation.

The strain òf keeping up is beginning to show with downtowns that lack the relative weight they once had. In such a situation the hierarchical trend continues but it forces more specialized purchasing into a few very large cities and leaves a vast array of quite standard and mediocre centers which can pull customers only weakly, even in competition with what were formerly much less impressive shopping towns.

The realization that trade can be carried on successfully outside the downtown has greatly influenced the rent-gradient. The core has lost relative elevation, and in cities that have experienced strong external replication, the core may not have a market for all its land. Some cities have passed beyond the stage of exclusion to that of readjustment and outright areal contraction. Part of the problem is local competition but another part is an increased intermetropolitan competition introduced by greater individual mobility. Perhaps the future dynamic will be the segregation of retail or service functions among distinct cities rather than within the single city. Where inter-urban distance is not more than 50 miles the movement to another metropolis may be as easy as the movement across the home metropolis.

THE PROCESS OF REDEVELOPMENT

This is both the most powerful influence on cities today and the one most favored by large numbers of planners. There is a neatness and certainty in redevelopment that is missing in the other dynamics that work in the downtown. The financial and operational controls furnished through redevelopment avoid questions of property rights, notably development rights, that plague other efforts to reshape the city through civic design. But two dangers lie hidden in a casual application of the process of redevelopment. The first danger comes from the denial of geographical shift in cities, which seems on the face of it to be a worthy objective as abandonment suggests defeat and decay. The main rub comes over the question whether the provision of particular facilities will effect the end sought. If, for example, we set out to supply new office buildings in the center of a city where replication is widespread, and many firms are moving to take up peripheral sites, the effect of the new offices at the center may be felt mainly on other office properties in the core, not on the new offices in the suburbs. Few cities show a willingness to accept change, expect for the better, in their redevelopment. Thus, the slum is replaced, not by low-income housing, but by middle and high-income housing and apartments for the conditionally prosperous. No doubt a change is worked but only at the expense of the next most vulnerable district in the city.

The second danger that attends a casual use of redevelopment is one that disturbs geographers perhaps more than others. This is the tendency to equate environmental change with social and intellectual improvement, and to argue that we may live in an area in psychological health only if it is "modern" and "well planned". The geographer's concern comes from the recollection of the former seeming simplicity of his own field when it was felt that the environment totally determined what man did and how he did it. That simplicity accepted direct causal ties between the physical environment and human activity—a dubious assumption.

In urban affairs there is danger in settling for physical solutions of complex problems. Physical planning aids health but it does not stamp out social problems, as New York's housing projects demonstrate. Both a more honest and a more compelling reason for good physical planning lies in the improvement of the aesthetic qualities of cities, which we may well enjoy even if we are no less bad for that enjoyment. But so long as the popular mind equates the improvement of the urban physical environment with the solution of problems, it is difficult to find the rational scale to limit the use of the vast and frightening power of urban redevelopment.

IN THE END, A CITY OF REALMS

For a long time students of urbanism have assumed the existence of hierarchical relationships within the city, whereby the downtown was the zone of supreme importance and all other districts sorted themselves into ranks of decreasing eminence. The result was a rather simple economic determinism, under which the rent-gradient was used to measure urban importance and rights. A subsidiary idea was that all uses would chose to locate at the core if they could only afford the rent.

Up to a point these ideas can easily be supported. In the relations between the metropolis and its tributary region there is little doubt that the city core is the focus of attention and the visitor seldom ventures far outside the downtown into the less clearly mapped frontier in the suburbs. And in the past the wholesaling function that bulks so large as the link with the trade area was also clustered around the downtown so buyers coming to town could similarly focus at the center. But the rapid growth of cities and the even greater expansion and elaboration of their functions have been reflected more in the internal structure than in the external ties.

So long as the main support for cities lay in trade with a tributary region, the downtown was alike the focus of the town and of the country. But once the functions included more manufacturing, more service activities, and a larger proportion of non-basic support, the focus of the metropolitan population shifted from complete identity with that of the tributary population and a city of realms began to emerge in which no one district assumed the paramountcy that had held true in earlier times.

I suggest that the system of dynamic processes outlined above is no longer valid in the simple form presented. The major final force that must be noted is tied up with the creation of a city with many cells and without the strong hierarchical ranking that formerly held true. Particularly as a city grows in size, it be-

comes more probable that the resident will live his life largely in only a part of the metropolis rather than in all of it. Even though he has high mobility, he will only use it if he must and will encourage duplication of facilities that are found elsewhere as near his home as possible. Thus, the process of inception, of exclusion and segregation, and of extension will be brought to bear on the development of downtown replicas.

What, then, is the future of the downtown itself? I think the answer is clear, if as yet undetailed. The downtown will continue to be of extreme importance and to serve highly specialized functions. It certainly will remain the center of specialized and mass shopping, but only for that population for whom the downtown is the most convenient place to shop. The center will continue as the nexus of financial operations as much because financial operations are still medieval in linkages as for any other reason. And, the downtown will become the district of civic consciousness and urbanity, the one place in the city where the emphasis will be on the size and complexity of the urban form. Government and culture are the two functions which profit most from the symbolic status of the downtown so I expect that this will be their home.

This symbolic nature of the downtown suggests a final development that we may see come to pass. In the city as a whole the last 40 years have witnessed the determined effort of civic leaders and planners, and of plain homeowners, to shape a city of distinct but neatly specialized realms. Their success has been so great that only one area remains which conveys to us the complexity and excitement that arrived with the urban revolution in the 15th and 16th centuries. That area of urban synthesis is the downtown. In the past we have called it the central business district but that term is hardly adequate today. There is "central business" all over the city at the same time that there is only one "downtown." The distinction rests with the diversity and its outward aspect, urbanity, which exists only in the downtown. It becomes the symbolic summation of the whole city whose loss would leave only a metropolis of realms.

Because we could not create a downtown today, not in totality, we should realize its unique appeal, and not allow it to be made into the image of the simple realms that ring it. If the city is to be made up of consciously structured environments, we must understand the way the downtown came about. That has been our purpose here. All that remains to be said is the appeal to you to plan for complexity in the downtown, allowing some "mistakes" to survive because they may seem less clearly misguided to our children. Just as we have grizzlies in our national parks because we cherish the natural environment, we should have the past in our downtowns to make clear each generation's elation in producing greatest conscious creation.

JOHN H. NIEDERCORN AND EDWARD F. R. HEARLE

Recent Land-Use Trends in Forty-eight Large American Cities

The years subsequent to World War II have brought unprecedented changes in the nation's largest cities. Rapid urbanization of the population coupled with a high birthrate has caused metropolitan areas to mushroom all over the country. Most of the growth has occurred in the suburbs rather than the central cities. In fact, during the 1950-1960 period, 12 of the 13 largest cities in the United States declined in population. Many large cities have also lost varying amounts of employment during recent years.[1] The future role of our central cities seems to be very much in doubt.

A careful examination of land-use, population, and employment trends might help clarify the future prospects of the nation's urban areas. Unfortunately, urban land-use data are hard to obtain, and without such data little objective analysis is possible. This article reports an attempt to overcome this data deficiency.[2]

As part of the research on its Urban Transportation Project sponsored by the Ford Foundation, The RAND Corporation sent questionnaires to the city planning departments of 63 large American cities during the spring of 1963. Usable replies were received from 48 of these organizations, thus supplying enough data to make some analyses of land-use patterns.

The body of this article is divided into three main sections. First, trends in land-use patterns in various subsamples of the 48 cities are discussed.[3] This includes a

Institute Technical Bulletin No. 18, Washington, D.C., May 1952; Harland Batholomew, *Land Uses in American Cities,* Cambridge, Massachusetts: Harvard University Press, 1955; and Lillian Larson Randolph, *Summary of Data From Land Use Surveys Made in 52 U.S. Cities* (dittoed), Seattle, Washington: Seattle Planning Commission, File 1023, June 1956.

3. The 48 cities include Albany, Baltimore, Birmingham, Boston, Buffalo, Chicago, Cincinnati, Cleveland, Columbus (Ohio); Dallas, Dayton, Denver, Detroit, Ft. Worth, Hartford, Houston, Jersey City, Kansas City (Missouri); Long Beach, Los Angeles, Louisville, Memphis, Miami, Milwaukee, Minneapolis, New Orleans, New York, Newark, Oakland, Oklahoma City, Philadelphia, Phoenix, Pittsburgh, Portland (Oregon); Portsmouth (Virginia); Providence, Rochester, St. Louis, St. Paul, Sacramento, San Antonio, San Diego, San Francisco, San Jose, Seattle, Syracuse, Washington, D.C., and Youngstown.

1. See John H. Niedercorn and John F. Kain, *Suburbanization of Population and Employment 1948-1975,* The RAND Corporation, P-2641, a paper presented at the meetings of the Highway Research Board, Washington, D.C., January 1963.
2. Three previous efforts at collecting this type of data have been brought to our attention. See Max S. Wehrly and I. Ross McKeever, *Urban Land Use and Property Taxation,* Urban Land

From **Land Economics**, Vol. XL, No. 1, February 1964, pp. 105-109. Copyright © 1964 by the Regents of the University of Wisconsin. Reprinted by permission.

description of changes over time in the mean proportions of urban land devoted to residential, industrial, commercial, road and highway, and other public uses. Vacant land is also included in the analysis. Second is a discussion of the changes taking place in 22 cities during recent years in both net and gross densities for resident population, and manufacturing and commercial employment. Third, an attempt is made to measure the amounts of land brought into urban use by unit increases in population, manufacturing employment, and commercial employment, respectively.

Land-Use Proportions

The land-use data collected have been grouped into six categories for the purpose of this analysis. These categories are residential, industrial, commercial, roads and highways, other public, and vacant. Residential land includes both single-family and multi-family dwellings; industrial includes both heavy and light industry; and commercial includes wholesaling, retailing, and service uses. The "other public" category includes schools, public buildings, parks, playgrounds, and cemeteries as well as related public and semi-public uses. Although the definitions of these six major categories are not precisely uniform for all cities, they are reasonably comparable and thus suitable for many types of land-use analysis. Railroads and airports have been included in industrial land while agricultural land and parking lots have been considered as vacant land.

Land-use data may be presented in either gross or net terms. The former concept includes in each land-use figure the area of streets abutting the land in question while the latter treats streets as a separate use category. Most of the available data were compiled as net measurements and only these will be used in the calculations which follow.

Table 1. Mean Proportions of Land Devoted to Various Uses in 48 Large American Cities

Type of Use	Proportion of Total Land	Proportion of Developed Land
Total Developed	.770	1.000
Residential	.296	.390
Industrial	.086	.109
Commercial	.037	.048
Road and highway	.199	.257
Other public	.153	.197
Total Undeveloped	.230	—
Vacant	.207	—
Underwater	.023	—

Table 1 gives the mean proportions of land devoted to the various uses in the 48 cities reporting land-use surveys since 1945.[4] Residential uses, roads and highways account for an average of approximately 65 per cent of all developed land within these cities and 50 per cent of the total area. Other public, industrial, and commercial comprise the remaining developed land. Undeveloped land includes both vacant and submerged land.

Although these figures shed some light on the postwar land-use patterns of American cities, nothing about current changes in these patterns can be inferred from them. If the latter is to be accomplished, each city must be compared with itself at two different points in time. This has been done for 22 of the cities which supplied data for two or more years.[5] Data for

4. The 48 cities include all for which data were available except Denver, Houston, Milwaukee and Philadelphia which reported data in gross terms only. The five boroughs of New York City are treated as five separate cities in this table. Means for the different land use categories do not always sum to unity because of rounding. A full set of the raw data appears in RAND Memorandum RM-3664-I-FR.

5. The 22 cities include Boston, Buffalo, Chicago, Cincinnati, Cleveland, Dallas, Dayton, Detroit, Long Beach, Los Angeles, Miami, Minneapolis, New York, Newark, Oklahoma City, Pittsburgh, Portsmouth, (Virginia), Providence, St. Louis, San Antonio, San Francisco and Seattle.

the most recent years have been grouped in the tables under the category "Late Data." Figures shown under "Early Data" are means calculated from earlier land-use surveys.[6] In cases where sets of data for more than two years were available the most recent pair were chosen for the calculations. This same classification scheme is used in Tables 2 and 3 and 4.

Table 2. Mean Proportions of Land Devoted to Various Uses at Different Times in 22 Cities

Type of Use	Proportion of Total Land		Proportion of Developed Land	
	Early Data	Late Data	Early Data	Late Data
Total Developed	.756	.784	1.000	1.000
Residential	.290	.310	.385	.398
Industrial	.085	.085	.110	.104
Commercial	.041	.040	.053	.050
Road and highway	.207	.198	.279	.254
Other public	.133	.152	.174	.193
Total Undeveloped	.245	.216	—	—
Vacant	.233	.204	—	—
Underwater	.012	.012	—	—

Table 3. Mean Proportions of Land Devoted to Various Uses at Different Times in 12 Cities

Type of Use	Proportion of Total Land		Proportion of Developed Land	
	Early Data	Late Data	Early Data	Late Data
Total Developed	.802	.857	1.000	1.000
Residential	.300	.325	.374	.379
Industrial	.100	.106	.124	.124
Commercial	.045	.044	.055	.050
Road and highway	.203	.210	.254	.245
Other public	.154	.172	.194	.202
Total Undeveloped	.198	.143	—	—
Vacant	.184	.129	—	—
Underwater	.014	.014	—	—

6. The early data average 10.2 years older than the late data for the sample of 22 cities and 9.8 for the sample of 12.

Apparently residential and other public land uses have increased relatively both to total area and to total developed land in the 22 cities. Road and highway uses have decreased, and both industrial and commercial uses have remained about the same, although declining slightly as proportions of developed land. Relative amounts of vacant land have decreased even though 10 of the 22 cities made significant annexations during the period intervening between land-use measurements. By deleting these 10 cities from the sample the effects of annexations on the figures presented in Table 2 can be removed.[7]

Table 3 shows that, for 12 cities whose boundaries remained unchanged between land-use surveys, the ratio of land in urban use to the total increased for all categories except commercial, which decreased slightly. The largest increase was in residential and the next largest in other public. The proportion of the total area remaining vacant decreased substantially. Residential and other public uses gained as a percentage of total developed land; industrial remained the same and both commercial and roads declined. However, the proportions of land in each use category relative to developed land remained quite stable, none of the changes being greater than one per cent of all developed land.

Since vacant land in central cities is fast disappearing, substantial growth of central city population and employment will be possible in the future only if net land-use densities can be increased. Trends in urban densities thus become an interesting and important question.

Land-Use Densities

During the late 19th and early 20th centuries the larger cities of both the United

7. The deleted cities are Chicago, Dallas, Dayton, Long Beach, Los Angeles, Oklahoma City, Portsmouth, San Antonio, San Francisco, and Seattle.

States and Western Europe, aided by improvements in construction technology, increased rapidly in net density[8] However, a reversal of this trend was noted before World War II and since 1950 falling densities have become widespread.[9] Manhattan, which has steadily lost population since 1920, was the first area where decreases in density became evident.[10]

Table 4. Net Urban Residential and Employment Densities Measured in Persons per Acre*

Land Use	22 Cities		12 Cities	
	Early Data	Late Data	Early Data	Late Data
Residential	63.23	53.32	76.75	67.25
Industrial	28.42	25.44	36.20	30.85
Commercial	65.80	62.01	81.37	81.82

* Industrial densities were calculated by dividing manufacturing employment by industrial land area. Commercial were obtained by dividing the sum of wholesaling, retailing, and selected service trade employment as defined by the Bureau of the Census by commercial land. Finance, insurance, real estate, and professional services are not included in the calculations since data on these activities are not available. The raw population and employment data used in calculating densities were obtained in most cases by interpolating between census years.

Table 4 indicates postwar trends in population per acre of residential land and in employment per acre of industrial

8. Net density is defined as the city's total population or employment of a given type divided by the land area devoted to residences or employment of the same type.
9. Most authors cite the automobile as the chief cause of urban decentralization. See, for example, Edgar M. Hoover, *The Location of Economic Activity* (New York, New York: McGraw-Hill Book Company, 1948), pp. 210-211.
10. Of course, decreases in density need not be synonymous with population losses. If land is removed from residential use and population declines, increases in density are possible. Nevertheless, this sequence of events is not likely to happen given the present institutional arrangements in the United States.

and commercial land. The data have been calculated both for the sample of 22 cities and the subsample of 12 constant-area cities. Average densities for each type of land use declined in all cases except that of commercial land in cities of constant area. In both samples, declines in industrial and residential densities were substantial.

For the sample of 22 cities, residential densities declined most, followed by industrial and commercial. The constant-area cities exhibited a similar pattern although industrial densities declined more than in the larger sample and commercial densities increased slightly.

As relatively little vacant land remains in the largest cities, declining residential and industrial densities indicate that most of these cities have either attained their maximum levels of population and industrial employment, or will do so in the near future. The same conclusion can be made about commercial employment because commercial densities appear to be approximately constant.[11] Increased employment in the service trades has offset losses in retailing and has consequently prevented commercial densities from falling.[12] The relative strengths of these trends can be seen in the percentage changes in mean net densities which follow.

Land Use	22 Cities	12 Cities
Residential	−15.7	−12.4
Industrial	−10.5	−14.8
Commercial	− 5.8	+ 0.6

Percentage changes in mean population and commercial densities are less nega-

11. As industrial and commercial land uses as here defined constitute only about 60 per cent of total urban employment, possible increases in densities of financial, insurance, real estate, governmental, professional, and transportation uses might lead to increases in total central city employment.
12. See Niedercorn and Kain, *op. cit.*

tive for constant-area cities than for the cities of the full sample, as annexed territory on the fringes of the central city is usually characterized by much lower densities than in the core areas. Annexed residential land is overwhelmingly characterized by single-family houses, often on large lots. Annexed commercial land tends to be used for low density suburban shopping centers with low employment-sales ratios and large parking lots.

Industry may be a somewhat special case. Although annexed industrial land is likely to be of lower density than in the rest of the city, the discrepancy between the two is not likely to be as large as for residential and commercial land. Large amounts of floor space not required by the production process increase costs in the suburbs as well as in core areas. Nevertheless, the data indicate that the relative decline in mean industrial density is greater in the constant-area cities than in those which reported annexations. The explanation is probably that the constant-area cities are typically older centers of manufacturing employment burdened with declining industries and obsolescent plants and equipment. The cities making annexations are younger and have a larger part of their labor force in growing industries that are making fuller use of their plants.

We shall see later how gross densities[13] compare with the net densities. But first, the relationship between gross and net densities ought to be derived. Let L stand for land in a given use category, E the number of people employed on the land and T the total land area of the city. Then, gross employment density can be written as follows:

$$E/T = (E/L) \ L/T. \qquad (1)$$

Taking the total differential,

$$d(E/T) = (E/L) \ (TdL - LdT)/T^2 + \\ (L/T)d(E/L). \qquad (2)$$

The percentage change in gross density

can be obtained for small changes by dividing each term of the equation by E/T:

$$\frac{d(E/T)}{E/T} = \frac{dL}{L} - \frac{dT}{T} + \frac{d(E/L)}{E/L}. \qquad (3)$$

In words, the percentage change in gross density equals the percentage change in land in use minus the percentage change in total land area plus the percentage change in net density. Percentage changes in mean gross densities can now be shown.

Land Use	22 Cities	12 Cities
Residential	− 7.8	− 4.4
Industrial	− 5.1	− 5.9
Commercial	− 4.0	+ 4.3

The relative declines in gross population densities are smaller than in the net because the amount of land devoted to residential use is increasing at a faster rate than total land area in these cities. This would cause gross densities to increase if net densities remained stable. Since net densities are decreasing, gross densities are also decreasing but at a slower rate. The same pattern applies to commercial densities in the sample of 22 cities, and industrial densities in the sample of 12. However, gross commercial densities are increasing faster than net commercial densities in the 12 constant-area cities, and the average fraction of land devoted to commercial use (shown in Table 3) is not increasing. Nevertheless, the mean percentage increase in commercial land is positive because cities with small initial amounts of commercial land have been adding to this use substantially, thus giving high rates of increase which outweigh the decreases in cities with relatively large amounts of commercial land.[14]

---

13. Gross density is defined as the city's population or employment divided by the entire land area of the city.

14. This same kind of distortion is responsible for the percentage decline in gross industrial density being smaller than in the net for the larger sample in spite of the fact that the mean proportion of land devoted to industrial use has not increased.

It is of interest now to investigate the hypothesis that changes in density are roughly proportional to the pre-existing levels of density. This has been done by calculating the simple correlation coefficients between net density and change in density for both samples of cities. The results are shown below.

Land Use	22 Cities	12 Cities
Residential	− .35	− .57
Industrial	− .81	− .83
Commercial	− .05	+ .06

The correlation coefficients indicate that the more densely populated cities and those with high industrial employment densities are losing population and industrial employment most rapidly. Changes in commercial densities do not seem to be systematically related to levels of commercial density. Both samples give similar results. Evidently there is a strong trend toward lower population and manufacturing densities. Urban population and industrial employment appear likely to be less concentrated in the future. Commercial densities do not follow the same pattern; high density centers of wholesaling, retailing, and service activity will probably continue to exist.

Land-Absorption Coefficients

The rate at which vacant land is being absorbed into urban use is a very important matter for city planners and urban economists. In areas where urban densities are stable or decreasing, the amount of available vacant land places upper limits on the city's population and employment. A means of estimating these limits is provided by land-absorption coefficients. A land-absorption coefficient is here defined as the amount of land (measured in acres) brought into urban use by an increase of population or employment of one person. In other words, these coefficients relate increases in population and employment to increases in developed land. Estimates of land-absorption coefficients have been obtained by correlating land-use changes in the sample of 22 cities with changes in population, manufacturing employment, and commercial employment in the same group of cities. The results are presented in Table 5.

Table 5. Land Absorption Coefficients Estimated from a Sample of 22 Cities (Acres per Person)

Type of Land	Population	Manufacturing Employment	Commercial Employment	Standard Error	Coefficient of Determination	Reciprocal of Absorption Coefficient (Persons per Acre)
Residential	.059	—	—	.0009	.86	16.94
Industrial	—	.034	—	.0008	.80	29.41*
Commercial	—	—	.047	.0010	.63	21.27
Road and highway	.006	—	—	.0006	.16	166.66
Other public	.010	—	—	.0004	.46	100.00
Total developed	.091	—	—	.0010	.86	10.99

* This number implies a density higher than would be expected in newly annexed areas. It is biased by business cycle effects caused by the inclusion of some data spanning World War II, and growth occurring nearer the core areas in some cities. The marginal densities for Dallas and Oklahoma City were 9.1 and 10.5. Data compiled by Hoover and Vernon suggest a similar value of about 10.0 for suburban areas within the New York region. See Edgar M. Hoover and Raymond Vernon, *Anatomy of a Metropolis* (Harvard University Press, Cambridge, Massachusetts, 1959), p. 31.

All of the regression coefficients are statistically highly significant. Changes in population, manufacturing employment, and commercial employment account for high proportions of the variance in each of the land-use categories. The low proportion of variance explained for roads and highways probably results from the fact that the road systems of most of these cities have been substantially completed years ago and consequently population changes in the city do not affect them very much.

The reciprocals of the land-absorption coefficients might be called "marginal densities." They indicate the densities at which new development is occurring. Since most of the increases in population and employment in these cities are the result of annexations, both the land-absorption coefficients and marginal densities should be interpreted in the strictest sense as measurements of relationships existing in newly annexed areas at the periphery of the city. A comparison with the net density figures in Table 4 indicates that the marginal densities are far below the average net densities.

This article has discussed changes in land-use patterns over time, changes in population and employment densities, and the relationship between population or employment growth and land absorption. Three important conclusions follow from the analysis.

First, vacant urban land in the larger cities is rapidly disappearing. Second, net manufacturing and population densities are decreasing, and commercial densities are barely holding their own. Third, unless large amounts of vacant land exist inside the city boundaries the average large city appears to have nearly reached its upper limits of population and employment in commerce and manufacturing.

One caveat is in order. The density data presented here are averages. Consequently, individual cities with special characteristics such as New York, Washington, D.C., and important regional centers will not necessarily follow all the trends suggested. For example, increases in central office and service employment in these cities might more than offset decreases in manufacturing and other declining sectors. Therefore, while central city employment densities should decline on the average, a small number of individual cities may follow a different pattern.

JAMES W. SIMMONS

Descriptive Models of Urban Land Use

Urban geographers have long existed in a state of cognitive dissonance in which they have used, simultaneously, three apparently conflicting models to describe the spatial distribution of urban land use.[1] Briefly summarized by Harris and Ullman,[2] these models appear in many discussions of urban land use patterns. They are the hypothesis of "concentric zones," which, attributed to Burgess, says that the land use pattern varies regularly as a function of distance from the city centre (L.U. $= f(r)$); the "sector theory" of Hoyt which has been interpreted to mean that land use varies axially (L.U. $= f(\theta)$); and the multiple nuclei concept of Harris and Ullman, which does not specify a general model of spatial relationships be-tween specific uses but says that there are certain discrete land use nuclei, essentially random, which may be associated with certain other land uses.

Geographers have handled this dissonance by playing down the role of theoretical models in general; stressing one model over the others in a specific situation; or almost subconsciously, recognizing that different models describe different elements of the land use pattern. This paper argues that the final alternative is the correct one; that we cannot abandon models of spatial patterns of land use without throwing serious doubts on our knowledge of the relationships between land value, transportation, and land use, and without reducing our ability to plan, project, or describe land use evolution; and that the solution is to make explicit the different aspects or dimensions of urban land use.

The importance of this approach becomes clearer when the original descriptive models of Burgess (a sociologist) and Hoyt (an economist) are reread. These men are talking primarily about people; about the spatial distributions of people of different social classes and with

1. Cognitive dissonance occurs when one accepts, at the same time, two or more conflicting points of view. This approach is not necessarily bad, in that it may lead to more efficient research in terms of time and money. See Leon Festinger, *Conflict, Decision, and Dissonance* (Palo Alto, Calif., 1964); and Edwin G. Boring, "Cognitive Dissonance: Its Use in Science," *Sci.*, CLV (Aug. 14, 1964), 680-85.
2. Chauncy D. Harris and Edward L. Ullman, "The Nature of Cities," *Ann. Am. Acad. Pol. Social Sci.*, CCXLII (Nov. 1945), 7-17.

From **Canadian Geographer,** Vol. IX, No. 3, 1965, pp. 170-174. Reprinted by permission of the author.

different ways of life.[3] It has been established that there are a number of independent dimensions which combine to describe the social pattern within a city. The theory governing the nature of these dimensions comes from the work of human ecologists on social area analysis, and the empirical evidence comes from the factor analysis of social variables for census tracts within a city.[4] Although the theoretical basis of the analysis has been challenged, the empirical evidence is quite consistent, and for both United States and Canadian cities three major dimensions emerge.[5] Because these dimensions are constrained to be independent by the techniques used, and because they are derived from observations over space, their spatial patterns must differ. In a sense we could reverse the process and seek the social variables which correlate with different specified spatial patterns. Either way a distinct spatial model is required for each dimension. The major dimensions and their spatial patterns are:

(1) *Social Rank,* representing the economic, educational and occupational level of the population. This factor varies axially, producing sectors of high and low income residential areas as Hoyt predicted.

(2) *Urbanization,* reflecting family structure, type of household, women in the labor force, and so forth. When plotted on a map the distribution of this factor varies radially, indicating that this "way-of-life" variable creates concentric zones ranging from working couples in

apartment houses to the sprawling suburbs. Burgess' commuting zone category reflects this social factor.

(3) *Segregation,* associated with ethnic and racial structure of the population. This characteristic of population, like Harris' and Ullman's land use nuclei, is essentially random, cutting across the variation of the other factors.[6]

This multi-dimensional aspect of a common concept should be familiar to geographers who have long coped with a multi-dimensional problem, the region.[7] But what does the above discussion tell us about the models of urban land use? First the traditional models of Burgess and Hoyt explain characteristics of the population and are not necessarily relevant to land use. Secondly, some light may be shed on the problem of land use classifications and models by an attempt to isolate independent dimensions, each of which may be described by an independent spatial model.

Here the suppositions begin. What are the dimensions of urban land use, and, equally important, what spatial models describe their dimensions?[8] A land use map typically contains a set of nominal, mutually exclusive, categories such as commercial, industrial, residential.[9] The spatial model for this nominal variable

3. Harris and Ullman do make explicit that their models deal with the human element, but this fact sometimes becomes confused because the models are grouped with a general discussion of land use.
4. Social area analysis is reviewed in Wendell Bell, "Social Areas: Typology of Urban Neighborhoods," in M. B. Sussman (ed.), *Community Structure and Analysis* (New York, 1959).
5. A study in progress by Robert Murdie for the Metropolitan Toronto Urban Renewal Study confirms the many studies done in the United States.

6. T. R. Anderson and J. E. Egeland, "Spatial Aspects of Social Area Analysis," *Am. Sociol. Rev.,* XXVI (1961), 392-98.
7. Brian J. L. Berry, "A Method for Deriving Multi-Factor Uniform Regions," *Przeglad Geog.,* XXXIII (1961), 263-82; and "Approaches to Regional Analysis: A Synthesis, *Ann. Assoc. Am. Geog.,* LIV (March 1964), 2-10.
8. L. Dudley Stamp defines land use as "literally the use which is made by man of the surface of the land" (*Glossary of Geographical Terms* London, 1961), p. 289.
9. This classification is sufficiently consistent to permit a number of comparative studies for many United States cities. See, for instance, Harland Bartholomew, *Land Use in American Cities* (Cambridge, Mass., 1937); and Louis K. Loewenstein, "The Location of Urban Land Uses," *Land Economics,* XXXIX (Nov. 1963), 407-20.

can be identified if a contingency test is applied to the following matrix of the occurrences of different land uses:

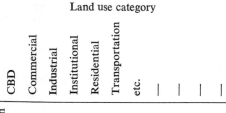

Land use category

The spatial categories may be concentric zones, sectors, nuclei, or combinations of these, and, if knowledge of spatial locations makes a significant contribution to knowledge of the frequency of occurrence of a given land use, an elementary spatial model exists.

Comparative studies by Loewenstein and others have found some consistency in the changing proportion of land devoted to different uses as distance from the city centre increases, but a model at this level leaves room for a great deal of uncertainty within a given city as well as wide variations between cities.[10] Loewenstein's investigations indicate that, given a city site, a city centre, and the size of a city, it is almost impossible to predict the location of these traditional land use categories.

The above approach to a land use model tries to relate a given category of land use to the over-all spatial pattern of the city, but more often we are given, or assume, interaction between specific land uses. Our knowledge of these relationships can be evaluated by converting each

10. Loewenstein, "The Location of Urban Land Uses"; and in transportation studies such as Chicago Area Transportation Study, *Final Report, Survey Findings,* vol. I (3 vols.; Chicago, 1959), chap. III.

of the nominal categories into an independent interval scale variable (for example, the percentage of a given area devoted to residential land use). The spatial association between the occurrences of the different variables can be derived and specified in a correlation matrix, although no spatial model is implied other than the knowledge that, given the spatial distribution of one of two related variables, the spatial pattern of the other follows.

Land use category

	% CBD	% Commercial	% Industrial	%	%	%
% CBD	1.0					
% Commercial	—	1.0				
% Industrial	—	—	1.0			
% —		—	—	1.0		
% —		—	—	—	1.0	
% —		—	—	—	—	1.0

The spatial model emerges from a factor analysis of the correlation matrix, producing independent dimensions, each of which has an independent spatial pattern. These factors are different dimensions of land use which produce *independent* spatial models that are applicable to all cities in the same manner as are the social dimensions.

These land use dimensions will emerge more clearly as we measure the other aspects of land use suggested by Ballabon and Guttenberg,[11] and add them to the correlation matrix. Some of these aspects of land use have considerable regularity. For instance, intensity of use (people per residential acre, workers per hundred

11. M. B. Ballabon, "Aspects of Urban Land Use Inventory in Metropolitan New York," *Can. Geog.,* VIII, 3 (1964), 117-124; and A. Z. Guttenberg, "A Multiple Land Use Classification System," *J. Am. Inst. Planners,* XXV (Aug. 1959), 143-50.

square feet of floor space, proportion of area covered by buildings, and so forth) increases regularly towards the centre of the urban area for nearly all land use types.[12] Other variables relate to the attractiveness of the use (Guttenberg's activity characteristics). There are great variations in the quality of the use in any of the nominal categories: residential includes slums and "Gold Coast" apartments; commercial ranges from skid row to the fashionable *boutiques;* industrial use varies from electronics research labs to steel mills.

Many, many other variables such as ownership pattern, traffic generation ability, age or period of development, and land value, as well as various potential measures of access to total population, daytime population, or employment, could be added to this general analysis. The broader the set of land use variables, the greater contribution to urban land use theory. Once the spatial pattern of each dimension is examined and specified, the whole problem of the relevance of models can be examined. A recent study by Yeates, which investigated the pattern of land values in Chicago over time, found the pattern to be less and less predictable.[13] It is possible that land use patterns are also becoming more irregular, because traditional urban theory links land use and land value very closely. But this latter relationship should also be investigated in order to find just what aspect of land use is sensitive to land value changes. Although land value and intensity of use seem to be related, there is little evidence that land pressures cause extensive shifts among gross land use types, once the initial development has taken place.

12. *Ibid.* See also the review of population density models in Brian J. L. Berry, James W. Simmons, and Robert J. Tennant, "Urban Population Densities: Structure and Change," *Geog. Rev.,* LIII (July 1963), 398-405.
13. Maurice H. Yeates, "Some Factors Affecting the Spatial Distribution of Land Values, 1910-60", *Econ. Geog.,* XLI (Jan. 1965), 57-70.

A most interesting aspect of land use is its age. The general pattern of variation in age of a city is radial, whether it be by means of the growth of a central core pushing rings of population outward, as Burgess suggests, or extension of sectors, as Hoyt predicts. In either case we have a set of concentric rings of different ages of development, each one apportioned and designed in accordance with the socio-economic forces of that period. Variation in the equilibrium conditions may produce changes in the proportions of land devoted to different uses, or a systematic pattern of variation in quality of use.

Finally, what are the relations between the dimensions of social variates and the dimensions of land use? This question introduces a whole spectrum of planning applications. Are there certain dimensions of land use that are associated with the social symptoms of slums? Are there specific dimensions of land use which are incompatible with other dimensions? The results of these analyses could extend the concept of performance standards in land use zoning, identifying the extent of areas affected and the interrelationships of the performance variables with other aspects of land use. The most important theoretical application of a multi-dimensional approach would be the clarification of urban land use models already in use, explicitly or implicitly, in many planning situations. Planners apply these models in urban renewal, zoning, re-zoning, and projecting land use. As Alonso, in discussing the pitfalls of using an incorrect model, has pointed out: "At a time when we are so vigorously rebuilding our cities it is important that we be as intelligent as possible about it. We must make explicit the theories of urban structure under which we are proceeding.[14]

14. William Alonso, "The Historic and the Structural Theories or Urban Form: Their Implications for Urban Renewal," *Land Econ.,* XL (May 1964), 231.

III

PROCESSES: Determinants of Structure, Growth, and Behavior

Urban patterns are simply the outcomes of processes observed at one point in time. What are the processes which give rise to the spatial structure and patterns of growth documented in the previous section? Attempts to understand these processes have taken different directions, of which two are recognized here. The distinction between the two is based on their underlying assumptions.[1]

The first approach is defined by the fundamental role of the "market" mechanism and the natural forces of competition among economic activities and social groups in an urban area. Under severely limiting assumptions, such studies are able to generate useful and testable spatial models. Among the best summaries and examples of the economic market approach to urban structure are *A Model of Metropolis* by Ira Lowry,[2] and the models of urban land use formulated by Lowdon Wingo and William Alonso.[3] One of Wingo's contributions is reviewed in the first paper in this section, and one of Alonso's, "A Theory of the Urban Land Market,"

1. See Britton Harris, "Some Problems in the Theory of Intra-Urban Location," *Operations Research* (September-October 1961), p. 701.
2. Ira S. Lowry, *A Model of Metropolis,* RM-4035-RC (Santa Monica, California: The Rand Corporation, August 1964) and *Seven Models of Urban Development,* P3673 (Santa Monica, California: The Rand Corporation, 1967), pp. 5-13. The latter paper is more readily available in a summary report by the Highway Research Board, *Urban Development Models,* Special Report No. 97, (Washington, D.C.: Highway Research Board), 121-45.
3. General reviews of economic location theory are provided in Harry W. Richardson, *Regional Economics: Location Theory, Urban Structure, Regional Change* (New York: Praeger, 1969).

133

is included as the second paper. In the case of urban communities and the structure of residential areas, these same forces become essentially social and environmental in nature, but the "competitive" market philosophy is still prominent. Interrelationships among and between social groups and communities are similarly viewed as competitive forces. Papers dealing explicitly with these social processes are included in Section V as part of the general discussion of residential areas.

The second approach is concerned with the behavior of urban residents and the decision-making processes which produced urban patterning. It is evident that the city grows and takes a certain form because of decisions made by individuals, corporations, and institutions. These decisions are many and varied. They involve deciding where to live, work, and shop; where, what, and when to build or invest; where and by what means to communicate, and so forth. Who makes these decisions? Is it possible to find similar types of decision-making which would help to explain urban form? What factors influence decisions regarding the location of home and job, for example? Most studies utilizing this approach tend to be oriented by definition to the individual or micro-environmental level, that is, to analyses of the individual agent or unit that makes the decisions. One advantage in operating at this level is that more variables to describe the behavior of the individual agents involved in decision-making may be included than is possible under the limiting assumptions typical of most economic market models. Of course, such behavioral analyses become extremely complicated and the resulting models are as yet inadequately refined. Yet there is a continuum of possible strategies which merge some of the assumptions of the market and behavioral approaches. Both are essential to urban research and to the themes of this volume.

As an introduction, selected examples of this desired range of approaches are outlined by F. Stuart Chapin. Professor Chapin, a planner, begins by suggesting four criteria that are necessary for the derivation of an adequate body of urban spatial theory. He reviews six major theoretical contributions to the recent literature, and evaluates each in terms of meeting his four criteria. The six studies reviewed represent different but related concepts of urban form and growth. The city is alternatively viewed as a system of communication and interaction, as a set of spaces adapted to accommodate human activities, as a means of overcoming accessibility problems, as an outcome of an economic market dependent on transportation, and as a consequence of social values and behavior patterns. Each concept has its own merits and each examines only part of the complexity of processes involved. By summarizing these in one paper Chapin greatly expands the range of the literature that could be represented here, and provides a conceptual framework to which subsequent sections can relate.

The basic arguments in the market-oriented approach are demonstrated by Alonso's theory of urban land-use patterns. This paper is a succinct and non-mathematical overview of his major work, later published under the title, *Location and Land Use*.[4] Arguing from first principles, he assumes a uniform or isotropic plain with equal accessibility in all directions, a single market center, and rational economic man making decisions on the basis of complete information. From these Alonso develops a single theory to explain the competitive locations of both urban and rural land use. The processes of competition are essentially the same among farmers in rural areas, and among business and households in urban areas. Each is based on the rents that users of land are willing to pay for a given location. Thus the locations of urban land uses are related to differences in land rents, the latter decreasing with distance away from the point of maximum accessibility, the city center, to compensate for increased accessibility costs. Those activities which can afford to locate near the city center, and which are capable of operating at higher densities, force other uses increasingly toward the periphery of the city. The result is a sorting out of land uses into concentric zones of differing intensities of use around each rural market and outward from the city center. The pattern of uses and densities are subsequently determined.

The limiting assumptions necessary in the formulation of economic models have nevertheless been severely criticized for what they overlook. Man is not entirely an economically rational animal with a single set of market criteria and with complete information at his disposal. Rather his decisions reflect individual preferences, objectives, ignorance, and errors. It is clear that a complex array of economic forces, technological and transportation innovations, social attitudes, and urban development policies will add greater complexity to the patterns of urban land use than the pure accessibility models.[5] Such factors do not negate the contribution of theoretical models such as those of Alonso and Wingo. Rather they stress the need for their subsequent expansion and improvement.

One outcome of the competitive market processes is that urban land values display a regular zonation. This zonation usually follows a negative exponential decline with increased distance outward from the city center.

4. William Alonso, *Location and Land Use—Toward a General Theory of Land Rent*, (Cambridge: Harvard University Press, 1964).

5. A recent review of the role of accessibility in urban land-use models is Michael A. Stegman, "Accessibility Models and Residential Location," *Journal of the American Institute of Planners*, XXXV (January 1969), pp. 22-29.

One explanation was given in a classic study of New York City in 1903 by Richard Hurd. He concluded that the value of urban land depends on economic rent, rent depends on location, location depends on convenience, convenience on nearness, and thus value depends on nearness.[6] He argued that in the form and growth of the city, land use and land values are intrinsically interrelated. Given that Hurd became a highly successful real estate executive, one is inclined to accept the empirical validity of this generalization.

The determinants of urban land values are usually more complex than can be described solely by distance to the city center. Alonso's model is an example of research in which all spatial variables other than distance are held constant. Parallel to these types of analyses, however, attempts have been made to explain the more localized variations in land values by expanding the number of explanatory variables involved. Brigham's paper is one of the most interesting in this regard. First, he hypothesizes that variations in land (site) values reflect differences in the density of occupance, the value of improvements on the site, size of property, topography, and local amenities, as well as distance to the city center. Second, he tests the statistical significance of these factors using multiple regression analysis in a case study of Los Angeles. The reader unfamiliar with the technique can for the moment skip to the summary and conclusions of the paper. Although there are dissenting views as to the role and measurement of individual factors, the fact that land values reflect a multiplicity of spatial variables acting in concert is not in doubt.[7] Considerable research remains to be done in clarifying the components of the land-value equation particularly as they relate to the costs and character of housing and the future effectiveness of planning.

It should also be recognized that changes occur in the building stock of a city. These changes parallel and augment those in land use and land values. Land uses are in most instances simply the uses made of buildings. The standing stock of buildings provide the physical space for urban activities which in turn serve as the basis for classifying land-use types. One of the fundamental concepts of change, to which reference has been made in papers by Vance and Boyce in Section II, is the rebuilding or

6. Richard M. Hurd, *Principles of City Land Values* (New York: The Record and the Guide, 1903).
7. Considerable debate has taken place on the subject of determinants of spatial variations in land values. The reader is directed to a recent paper which is in some disagreement with the views voiced by Brigham. See Edwin Mills, "The Value of Urban Land," in H. S. Perloff (ed.), *The Quality of the Urban Environment Essays on New Resources in an Urban Age* (Baltimore: Johns Hopkins Press, for Resources for the Future, Inc., 1969), pp. 251-56.

redevelopment process.[8] This process takes its stimulus from the need to adapt individual buildings to suit changes in demands for their use. Most buildings eventually age and deteriorate. As their suitability changes they undergo conversion, usually to accommodate other uses, and eventually most are demolished and replaced. These changes are reflected, for example, in the evolution of the building stock of urban neighborhoods. Large houses are often converted to multi-family use, or to office and retail occupancy. Higher-income families abandon their older homes for the suburbs as lower-income families move in. The transition of urban neighborhoods over time must then be viewed as a complex process in which densities, socio-economic character, and construction history are interrelated, but are not necessarily coincident in space and time.

The movement of activities and households within this building stock is generally described as the filtering process. The varied and often conflicting interpretations of the filtering concept as a process of change are reviewed by Wallace Smith. The concept is introduced in terms of its role of providing housing to low-income groups, a welfare function that is frequently applied to it. The definition is then expanded to include all changes in the quality and occupancy of the housing stock. It is the principal dynamic feature of the housing market. In summary Smith criticizes the usefulness of traditional urban concepts as a basis for understanding the filtering process. Filtering is implicit in these concepts but is seldom clearly identified. Many of these ideas are also applicable to the locational ebb and flow of retail, industrial, and institutional activities in the city. The literature on these aspects, however, is weak.

The argument that patterns of urban land use and activities derive from processes in addition to those of classical economics has already been made. Of direct relevance here are the effects of public policies and of social attitudes and behavior. The effects of public policy on urban development are expressed in two ways. At the municipal level, policy decisions may have a direct influence, through the provision of public buildings, facilities, and services, or an indirect or regulatory influence through the nature and enforcement of public codes and covenants. The latter include the power to determine capital improvement and servicing policies, assessment and taxation, zoning and building codes, school sites, transportation routes, and annexations. These are intermeshed with and influence the

8. The concepts of urban renewal and redevelopment as continuous processes of change in the physical plant of a city were initially formulated in Miles Colean, *Renewing Our Cities* (New York: Twentieth Century Fund, 1953). A recent expansion and application of these ideas is L. S. Bourne *Private Redevelopment of the Central City: Spatial Processes of Structural Change in the City of Toronto,* Department of Geography Research Paper No. 112, University of Chicago, 1967.

development of the urban area at all stages of the growth process. To understand the form of the city one must therefore understand how it functions politically.

What social and institutional pressures influence the structure and evolution of urban land use? William Form argues in support of studies of the specific groups, associations, and institutions, which participate in decisions in the land market. Four components of organizational power and influence are recognized—real estate interests, big business, residents, and government. Each group varies in terms of its resources, motivations, formality, and function, and thus in the strength and direction of its influence in land-use decisions. Although these groups interact in numerous ways, one in particular stands out as of immense importance in the spatial expression of change—the zoning process.[9] The outcomes of the decisions made in this process, or zoning "game" might be a more appropriate term,[10] represent the combined effects of competition among these different spheres of interest. The city then becomes a political animal.

The most important types of decisions influencing urban form are those involving the development of new buildings, facilities, and services and the decisions of public agencies which attempt to influence this development. What is the nature of the decision-making process in urban development? Who makes these developmental decisions? On what criteria are they based? What are the links of decisions which carry land from rural to urban use and through successive redevelopments? What is the importance of public agencies, in terms of direct investment and as a regulating force? What do we know about the attributes of the decision-makers and the impact of their decisions, particularly locational ones on the form of the city?

At present there is limited information on these decisions. It is nevertheless clear from casual observation that such decisions, in both the private and public sectors, tend to be dominated by a few large conglomerates making significantly large investments.[11] As a result the major decisions are essentially market decisions, or at least those based largely on market criteria. The scale question is evident when one thinks of the

9. For a discussion of the role of municipal zoning boards in urban development see Sidney Willhelm, *Urban Zoning and Land Use Theory* (New York: Free Press of Glencoe, 1962).

10. One author has described the community and local territorial systems of the city as an ecology of games. See Norton E. Long, "The Local Community as an Ecology of Games," *The American Journal of Sociology*, LXIV (November 1958), 251-61.

11. William L. C. Wheaton, "Public and Private Agents of Change in Urban Expansion," in M. M. Webber *et al.* (eds.), *Explorations Into Urban Structure* (Philadelphia: University of Pennsylvania Press, 1964), pp. 154-87.

size of most public and private projects, whether they be subdivisions, subways, or new retail outlets. Yet at the other end of the scale there are literally thousands of individual decisions regarding, for instance, the maintenance of housing and the selection of new housing locations which do in the aggregate and over the long run ultimately and substantially affect the growth patterns of the city.

Conceptualizing the decision-making process at work in urban development is a complicated task. E. J. Kaiser and S. F. Weiss examine the individual decision unit, or micro-behavioral unit, in residential development, taking as an example the decisions involved in the location of suburban single-family housing construction. They emphasize the roles of different agents in the process of converting land from rural to urban use: the predevelopment landowner, the speculator, the developer, and finally the household or consumer. The redevelopment process, however, is not included.[12] The important factors at each stage in the process are defined by the authors as the characteristics of the property and of the decision agent, and conditions of the local environment.[13] The behavior of all individual agents are shown to be linked in a complex chain of decisions. Local public policy-decisions are important links in this chain. Their effects, however, tend to be indirect as they are channeled through policies regulating property and environment characteristics rather than in regulating the behavior of the decision-maker. Their effects also vary depending on the degree of enforcement over space and time, as the zoning game analogy suggests.

Location decisions of urban households represent the final link in the residential development process outlined by Kaiser and Weiss. The initial decision to seek a new dwelling and/or a different living environment, and the subsequent decision of where and into what to move, constitute the intra-urban migration process. Lawrence Brown and Eric Moore suggest that each household decision to move is based on an imbalance between needs and aspirations in housing. This imbalance is translated into a stress-strain context in which the household is seen as responding to a stimulus for change. This stimulus is subsequently modified as the search and evaluation of housing alternatives continues, thus reflecting changes

12. See L. S. Bourne, "Location Factors in the Redevelopment Process: A Model of Residential Change," *Land Economics*, XLV (May 1969), 183-93.
13. As yet these groups of decision-makers have not been brought together fully in the context of a single comprehensive study of the residential development process. A framework within which this task might be achieved is outlined in a parallel paper by the same authors. "Some Components of a Linked Model for the Residential Development Decision Process," in *Proceedings of the Association of American Geographers,* Vol. 1 (1969), 75-79.

in the information available to the household, the spatial configuration of this information, and in the feedbacks involved in the decision process. The formulation is still basically conceptual, but a stimulating framework for subsequent behavioral research has been provided.[14]

In the final analysis, there is considerable debate over the most appropriate approach to a theory of urban spatial structure. Andrei Rogers offers a fascinating critique of existing concepts of intra-urban structure. He regards these as deterministic and thus largely irrelevant. The thrust of Rogers's argument is simply that the overwhelming complexity of human behavior, and interactions of all types in urban areas, make futile any attempts to derive deterministic relationships between behavior and resulting spatial patterns. There is a strong random element in the way people behave. He concludes that stochastic or probabilistic techniques offer the greatest potential in assessing interdependent factors in urban growth.[15] The relevance of this argument to subsequent developments in urban research will become apparent in following sections of this book.

14. An indication of the range of approaches to and difficulties in the study of behavioral problems in geography is provided in a recent collection of papers edited by K. Cox and R. Golledge, *Behavioral Problems in Geography: A Symposium*, Paper No. 17 (Evanston: Northwestern University Press, 1969).

15. An imaginative beginning toward the incorporation of concepts of probability in urban geography is by Leslie Curry, "The Geography of Service Centres Within Towns: The Elements of an Operational Approach," in K. Norborg (ed.), *Proceedings of the I.G.U. Symposium in Urban Geography*, Lund Studies in Geography, Series B (Lund, Sweden: C. W. K. Gleerup Publishers, 1962), 31-54. More recent applications include A. Getis and J. M. Getis, "Retail Store Spatial Affinities," *Urban Studies*, Vol. 5 (1968), 317-22; and Andrei Rogers, "A Stochastic Analysis of the Spatial Clustering of Retail Establishments," *Journal of the American Statistical Association*, (December 1965), 1094-1103.

F. STUART CHAPIN, JR.

Selected Theories of Urban Growth and Structure

At the present stage in the field's development, theoretical research for planning is developing along two related lines. One major emphasis is on the process of planning and its relationship to decision-making theory, and the other focuses on the subject matter of this process: urban clusters, regions, and sometimes entire nations. This review is concerned mainly with the second area of specialization, and particularly with urban spatial structure and urban growth. Below I shall first make some general observations on the formulation of theory and on criteria of an adequate theory and then briefly examine six areas in which work has appeared recently. Finally I shall indicate a few of the similarities and distinctive differences in these approaches. It should be noted that utopian concepts are excluded from this review. While constituting an important area of study in the planning field, this area of inquiry does not constitute theory in the usage of this article.

Criteria for an Adequate Theory

Where the objective of theory building is not simply a quest for truth for knowl-

edge's own sake, but includes the eventuality of applying the theory in improving the lot of man (an objective which is characteristic of a profession), we are concerned not only with the conventions of formulating theory, but also with specifying performance criteria. We wish to insure that theory meets the requirements we foresee will be important in its application in the field.

There are at least four criteria of adequacy which will be useful to bear in mind in reviewing the work summarized below.[1] One criterion holds that a theory must have a dynamic aspect if it is to have utility in representing the processes by which cities are structured and by which they grow. A second requirement is that the theory be susceptible of empirical verification, that it be capable of being tested. A third requirement is that the theory have an internal logic and consistency. The rigor of the logic and consistency may vary from a very general and somewhat sum-

1. Adapted from the work of Rosalyn B. Post for the Center for Urban and Regional Studies, University of North Carolina, and summarized in a manuscript entitled "Criteria for Theories of Urban Spatial Structure: An Evaluation of Current Research," 1962.

From F. Stuart Chapin, Jr., Chapter 2 of **Urban Land Use Planning**, "Toward a Theory of Urban Growth and Development," as reprinted in the **Journal of the American Institute of Planners**, Vol. 30, No. 1, February 1964. Copyright © 1965 by the Board of Trustees of the University of Illinois. Reprinted by permission.

mary form where concepts and relationships are very broadly stated to a very formalized presentation where all propositions and relationships are spelled out in detail. Finally, the theory must not be so abstract as to have no relation to reality. Indeed, it should seek to represent the phenomena under study as they actually occur or appear to function in reality.

There are undoubtedly other criteria and certainly other ways of reviewing theoretical concepts. However, these general criteria may be helpful in determining how far advanced the planning field is in theoretical research. For each of six approaches, I shall give a capsule summary of the conceptual framework as I understand it, and then examine it in terms of these four criteria.

A Communications Theory Approach to Urban Growth

Meier approaches the task of a theory of urban spatial structure[2] by asking: What, after all, is the quintessence of the city? Is there a common pattern that holds through time, one perspective in the behavioral sciences that provides a logical basis for building a theory of urban development? After examining human settlements as they emerged from the beginnings of civilization, following the changes as they might be seen by an archaeologist, anthropologist, historian, and natural scientist, and after considering man's behavior in cities, looking at human activities as the economist, social psychologist, human ecologist, and political behaviorist might, Meier concludes that the one common element in all of these perspectives is *human communication*. Whether viewed in very concrete terms of market place transactions or in the more abstract notion of the transmission of culture, he is saying that the human communications process

2. Richard L. Meier, *A Communications Theory of Urban Growth* (Cambridge: The M.I.T. Press, 1962).

possesses all the requirements of an organizing concept for a theory.

Meier conceptualizes the city in terms of systems of interaction prompted by man's urge to maintain communications (in the general sense) with his fellow man. At the present stage in man's state of development, transportation and communications technology supply the principal media of interaction. While noting that cities have always exerted a strong attraction for growth because of the opportunities for face-to-face transactions they offer, Meier holds that technological developments are reducing the necessity for face-to-face interaction, and transportation overloads are imposing limiting conditions on opportunities for interaction through transportation systems. With the substitution of communications for transportation, communication becomes increasingly important as a focus for studying the city. In noting that overload crises in communications systems are in prospect, Meier anticipates control mechanisms being invoked to correct for these overload conditions. Thus, the communications system (in the narrow sense) offers what he considers to be the basis for understanding human communications (in the general sense) and the activity systems that arise out of human relations involved.

Having satisfied himself on the validity of using a communications system as a basis for building a theory of urban growth, Meier develops a set of requirements for the communications process. Specifying that there must be *one,* a sender, *two,* a message, *three,* a channel, *four,* a receiver, *five,* an attention span on the part of the receiver, *six,* a common language, *seven,* time for the process to take place, and *eight,* one or more purposes to be served, he proposes to construct a representation of the city from the information content of communications flows. Information would be measured and recorded in a double-entry accounting system in much the same manner as origin and destination traffic studies record traffic flows today. The unit of measurement for information transmitted would be the "hubit" which Meier defines as "a bit of meaningful information received by a single human being"—a per capita concept of units of information received. According to Meier, by obtaining a sample of communications flows in a metropolitan area, information theory can be used to construct a set of social accounts which can then become the basis for explaining activity systems.

Meier does not indicate fully the manner in which the framework would be used by a planner in a predictive application, say for the year 2000. However, he suggests that his concept of the "urban time budget," which estimates the proportions of a day's time a person would spend in various forms of public communication (as opposed to private or personal communication), would provide a means of making projections. Given an estimate of the population for the year 2000 for a particular metropolitan area, one surmises he would construct a set of sender-receiver accounts of information flows or transactions broken down into "activity sectors" —for example, leisure activity patterns of various forms, wholesale-to-producer or wholesale-to-retailer activity patterns of various types. On the basis of assumed states of technology, presumably he would trace out spatial loci of activities, and once location relationships were established, he would assign space to activities and modes of movement according to standards developed to correspond to the technology assumed. This aspect of his framework will undoubtedly be made clearer as he extends his work further.

On the basis of this all too brief report on Meier's work, it is clear that it possesses a distinct behavioral emphasis on the study of the city, and tends more toward the explanatory than the normative emphasis. His work surely reflects a very strong feeling for the dynamic, not only in the usual time sense but also in his concern for constructing the evolutionary sequence in human behavior patterns. Clearly he is intent on empirical verification of this conceptual framework and builds it with this end in view. Surely there is a compelling logic in this system of thought concerning spatial organization and growth of cities. There is every indication that a formal and rigorous statement of theory will emerge. Perhaps because it is in a working stage of formulation, the internal continuity of the way in which the framework is eventually to be put to use is not entirely clear. How the analysis would proceed from sampling information flows, to identifying transactions, to constructing activity patterns, to defining space use patterns is not yet clearly established. As is perhaps true of any work which is still in progress, there are parts of the schema which are more developed and therefore more easily understood than other parts. Until the work nears a more precise stage of formulation, the exposition of concepts and analytical sequences is likely to remain uneven.

A Framework Emphasizing Human Interaction

Webber also utilizes interaction as the basic organizing concept of his theoretical system.[3] He views urban communities in two related perspectives—one in which human interaction occurs in a particular metropolitan community, and one in which it extends to widely scattered places over the face of the earth. He calls the first a "place community" and the second a "nonplace community." With modern transportation and communications development having the effect of stretching distances, he notes that individuals, firms, organizations, and institutions more and

3. Melvin M. Webber, "The Urban Place and the Nonplace Urban Realm," *Explorations into Urban Structure,* ed. Webber (Philadelphia: University of Pennsylvania Press, 1963).

more have contacts, conduct transactions, and maintain communications on a global basis. Thus their ties may extend to a variety of nonplace communities as well as exist within a particular urban place. To distinguish them from the urban place, he calls these nonplace communities "urban realms."

It is this total concept of the urban community which is the distinctive flavor of Webber's approach. He calls for an understanding of the interaction systems which extend into larger urban realms as well as those which fall within a particular metropolitan area. Thus he holds that the study of systems of interaction within the urban region is no longer a complete and sufficient scope for metropolitan planning. According to Webber's concept, what goes on within the spatial confines of an urban place must be interpreted in the framework of all the ties that the community may have with the world at large. He notes that individuals may or may not engage in all their activities in a place community and, according to whether they are scientists, manufacturers, or writers, their interest communities extend to differing realms. These same individuals may participate in several non work-related interest communities—in the arts, in recreation, in public service, and so on. In contrast, some persons such as the butcher, the factory worker, or the clerk may have interest communities which at present are completely contained within the place community. So today, metropolitan planning requires a view which considers how the place population may also be a part of various realm populations, each with what Webber refers to as its own "space field" for interaction, some global, some national, and some in various regional contexts.

In both the place and nonplace view of the urban community, Webber emphasizes the importance of viewing the city as a "dynamic system in action." This dynamic feature is traced through "link-ages," which he defines as "dependency ties" relating individuals, groups, firms, and other entities to one another. He terms these "the invisible relations that bring various interdependent business establishments, households, voluntary groups, and personal friends into working associations with each other—into operating systems." His spatial counterpart of this aspatial view of linkages involves three related perspectives. First is a view of the city in terms of spatial patterns of *human interactions*—the flow of communications, people, goods, and so on; second is a view of the *physical form* of the city—the space adapted for various human activities and the pattern of networks of communication and channels of transportation; and third is a view of the city as a configuration of *activity locations*—the spatial distribution of various types of activities by economic functions, social roles, or other ways of classifying activities.

Using these three perspectives of the city, Webber develops a cross-classification system for describing urban spatial structure. The interaction, physical, and activity components are classified according to *one,* size of phenomenon; *two,* degree to which phenomenon piles up in major concentric forms around a point; *three,* propensity for phenomenon to pile up at points of lesser concentration; *four,* degree of pile-up per unit (for example, pile-up per 100 contacts between people, per square mile of area); *five,* relative "togetherness" of like phenomena; and *six,* relative degrees of mixture. With the elements of the metropolitan community thus identified, measured, and classified, Webber provides a descriptive framework. But he recognizes that there is still a step beyond, one of using this framework in the investigation of the directions that future growth and development must take. While this step is still to be made, he indicates it would involve an analysis of interaction in terms of the locational behavior of various types of establishments.

In Webber's work we have a conceptual system which is extremely broad in scope but still in a very early stage of development. Presently it consists of a framework for describing the city, one that is explanatory rather than normative. Webber emphasizes the importance of the dynamic aspect of a theory, but how his classification system will be used and how he will develop it in the behavioral approach he favors for the analysis of interaction systems is not yet entirely clear. We know that he places a high premium on making these systems continuous and dynamic, and so we anticipate that some kind of interaction model to represent these as operating systems will become a central concern in the next stages of his theory building. It is premature to examine the empirical content of his work in its present stage, but his concern for the problem of measurement in both the place and non-place aspects of this schema indicates that empirical tests are very much in his thinking. Certainly Webber places heavy emphasis on achieving an internal logical consistency to his conceptual framework, and his concern for the study of locational behavior of the principal agents of interaction would indicate that as his work progresses he will be seeking a close representation of reality.

A Conceptual System Focusing on Urban Form

Lynch and Rodwin view the city as being made up of what they call "adapted space" for the accommodation of human activities and "flow systems" for handling flows of people and goods.[4] Although they differentiate between activities and flows on the one hand and adapted space and flow systems on the other, so far they have devoted their main effort to the lat-

ter level of analysis which they equate with the study of "urban form." The distinctive feature of their conceptual system is the emphasis they place on the formulation of goals as an integral part of their framework. Their work begins with the study of urban form; it then focuses on the specification of goals; and finally it draws upon the goal–form analysis to indicate the nature of the planner's task in efforts aimed at shaping urban form with the goals that have been identified.

In their conceptual framework they are concerned first with a system for analyzing urban form. (Were they starting with activities and flows, they might well focus initially on a system for analyzing *interaction.*) Lynch and Rodwin propose evaluating urban form by six analytical categories: element types, quantity, density, grain, focal organization, and generalized spatial distribution. "Element types" is a category for differentiating qualitatively between basic types of spaces and flow systems; and as might be expected, "quantity" has to do with amounts —a measure of the side of particular types of adapted spaces of flow systems. "Density," expressed either as a single measure or as a range of measures, has to do with compaction (of people, facilities, vehicles) per unit of space or capacity of channel. "Grain" is their term to indicate how various elements of urban form are differentiated and separated. Adapted spaces and flow systems may be fine-grained or coarse-grained according to the extent of compaction or separation in their internal components (houses, skyscrapers, streets) and how sharp or blurred these form elements are at the edges where transition occurs from one element to another. "Focal organization" is concerned with the spatial disposition and interrelations among key points in the city (density peaks, dominant building types, major breaks between forms of transportation). "Generalized spatial dis-

4. Kevin Lynch and Lloyd Rodwin, "A Theory of Urban Form," *Journal of the American Institute of Planners,* XXIV (November, 1958), 201-214.

tribution" is the patterned organization of space as it might be seen from the air at a high altitude. This six-part classification system is the basic analytical tool they propose for classifying urban form.

The second major conceptual problem which the Lynch-Rodwin framework seeks to deal with is the formulation of goals utilizing this analytical tool. They point out that the problem is not alone one of identifying out of the multitude of possible goals those that have significance for urban form, but it is also one of specifying the goals in concrete terms which leave no doubt as to how they are to be realized. The identification of goals is one aspect of the problem, and the specification of content is a second aspect. With respect to the first, Lynch and Rodwin point out that goals must to some extent be determined in the normal democratic processes, with community-held goals being differentiated carefully from the planner's personal goals (which would tend to emphasize the goals of only one segment of society). But at the same time they would give careful attention to the planner's goals as a professional and urban designer where, they point out, he has a proper role to play in seeing that more advanced values take their place in the community value system beside the familiar ones of long standing. They suggest that the choice of goals have first a human and then an economic basis. Thus, goals relating to urban form are fundamentally concerned on the one hand with relationships between man and his environment and between man and man, and on the other hand, with the efficiency of these relationships—maximizing the return and minimizing the cost in both a social and an economic sense. The specification of goal content derives from the analytical framework they devised in the first instance. Thus the goals would be specified in terms of type of adapted space and flow system, quantity, density, grain, focal organization, and the spatial

distribution pattern. Some would have quantitative emphasis, some would deal more in qualitative concepts, and all would be subject to continuing checks as to relevance and reasonableness.

The final aspect of the Lynch–Rodwin framework is concerned with the application of the goal—form statements in the study of the city and in establishing what emphases will be needed in the plan that eventually is to emerge. Through the use of simple cross-classification of the six components of their system of analysis applied to both adapted spaces and flow systems, they demonstrate how these two elements of urban form interact under different goal emphases. In sum, Lynch and Rodwin view the framework as a means for analyzing the urban form in a systematic and logical manner. They think of it as a means of posing the problems for planning but they leave the solution to the planning task which follows from their framework.

This conceptual system has been developed to deal with a particular aspect of what we look for in a total system of theory. Although they acknowledge the important role which the interaction level of study has in theoretical formulations, presently Lynch and Rodwin have limited themselves to urban form, directing their attention to the physical implications of human interaction. Their work is concerned with the rationale of planning for the city rather than a framework for analyzing the structure of the city and explaining how growth occurs. In this sense, they are providing a framework which has special significance for plan-making. In focusing on goal formulation, they have injected an essentially normative emphasis into their schema. However, they do not specify "what should be"; but rather they indicate how goal combinations can be analyzed in deriving "what should be" in a particular locality and how these in turn may be integrated systematically into the planning process. The importance of a theory being a dynamic one is recognized by Lynch and Rodwin, and in the sense that the sequence from goal formulation to form analysis in their conceptual system is seen as a continuous and dynamic interrelationship it is dynamic in conception. But in the sense we have been using "dynamic" to signify the organizing aspect of theory which takes account of the evolutionary process of urban development, their framework is as yet incomplete. Their work reflects sensitivity to the importance of empirical verification. This has since become particularly evident in Lynch's studies of the perceptual form of the city. They have given careful attention to the logical continuity of their conceptual system, and there is clearly a great sense of responsibility for tying their work closely to reality.

Accessibility Concepts and Urban Structure

Although all conceptual systems of the kind we have been discussing sooner or later become concerned with accessibility as an element inherent in the physical organization of space and movement systems, some work gives this concept a more central role in building theory. Much of the recent work on accessibility concepts has been primarily focused on transportation.[5] Although this work has had a very considerable impact on research in urban spatial structure, I do not attempt to include in this summary any report on work which is primarily oriented to transportation.

Guttenberg develops a theoretical approach to urban structure and city growth which utilizes accessibility as an

organizing concept—what he calls "a community effort to overcome distance."[6] In the sense that human interaction is the underlying reason for minimizing distance, he is implicitly viewing interaction as a basic determinant of urban spatial structure. However, his work focuses primarily on the physical facility aspect of a total system of theory. In place of the simple two-part view (space use for activities and interconnecting systems of transport and communications), he identifies three components. He subdivides the first into "distributed facilities" and "undistributed facilities," with these being a function of the third component, "transportation." The rationale states that if transportation is poor, the work places, trade centers, and community services will tend to assume a pattern of distributed facilities; if it is good, these activities will assume more concentrated patterns in the form of undistributed facilities. Thus, Guttenberg maintains that urban spatial structure is intimately tied up with the aggregate effort in the community to overcome distance.

In his framework, he sees the spatial gradation of density outward from distributed and undistributed facilities as a function of access. He points out that his distributed centers of activity acquire a value in accordance with the substitutability of that place for the chief place, with the physical density gradient outward from these centers corresponding closely with, but not necessarily directly coincident with, the economic density gradient. In the context of his framework, therefore, the slope of the economic density gradient is closely related to transport efficiency as it enables outlying locations to substitute for more central locations.

In examining the implications of growth

5. See the work of J. Douglas Carroll and his associates in Detroit, Chicago, and Pittsburgh on metropolitan area transportation studies (for example, J. R. Hamburg, "Land Use Projection and Predicting Future Traffic," *Trip Characteristics and Traffic Assignment*, Highway Research Board Bulletin 224, National Academy of Sciences, 1959).

6. Albert Z. Guttenberg, "Urban Structure and Urban Growth," *Journal of the American Institute of Planners*, XXVI (May, 1960), 104-110.

for his concept of urban structure, he points out that the transportation system holds the key to the way in which growth proceeds. The transportation decisions made from one year to another will result in a constantly changing urban structure, with the emphasis shifting along the continuum between the situation with highly distributed centers to the situation with one major undistributed facility. He implies that there is some limit in the ability of the undistributed facility to continue indefinitely to function as the only major center as compared to the capacity that distributed centers have for absorbing growth. As growth occurs, structural adjustments to overcome distance can take the form of either new centers or improved transportation facilities. Commonly both occur. With the enlarged scale and resulting changed relationships between home, work, and various activity centers, population movements ensue. With these shifts the areas which do offer the accessibility that people seek, develop, and those which do not, decline in a social and an economic sense. With growth, the enlarged scale alters the density gradient. If transport efficiency is improved, favoring the substitution of outlying for central locations (as has been the case in Los Angeles), the slope of the density gradient is flattened, the region spreads out and, depending upon the amount of population influx in relation to the area added, the density may go down.

How may such a view of urban structure and urban growth be used in anticipating urban form in the future? Guttenberg acknowledges that transport efficiency is not the sole variable. He notes that activities may choose a location in relation to a central place for reasons other than time-distance. For example, a change of economic composition in the region may produce new location patterns. However, assuming such other things are constant (similar economic conditions, terrain, tastes, and so on), he

maintains that accessibility in terms of time-distance serves to sort activities spatially. If the additional assumption is introduced that the transportation system remains similar over time, he points out that there will be comparable accessibility and that therefore we may anticipate similar patterns in the distribution of activities in the region. He does not discuss the complexities of prediction involved when constraints are relaxed and one by one the elements held constant are allowed to vary, but it is clear that by introducing differing combinations of assumptions the interplay of these elements quickly becomes exceedingly complex.

In the present stage of its development, this conceptual framework centers mainly on the physical aspects of a theoretical system of urban structure and growth. Its distinctive feature is the emphasis it gives to the interplay between the location of urban activities and transport efficiency. In the sense that activity concentrations and transportation are continuously interacting and that accessibility provides an organizing rationale for urban structure and a regulating concept for urban growth, the framework is a dynamic one, supplying an evolutionary basis for explaining urban form. While it has a well developed logical context and a direct relation to reality, Guttenberg's statement gives no indication as to how this framework is to be translated into an analytical system and given empirical form.

Other works which should be cited here are Hansen's use of the accessibility concept in the analysis of the growth of residential areas and Voorhees' use of the concept in the analysis of other use activities.[7] However, both are primarily concerned with the pragmatic aspects of pre-

7. Walter G. Hansen, "How Accessibility Shapes Land Use," *Journal of the American Institute of Planners*, XXV (May, 1959), 73-76; Alan M. Voorhees, "Development Patterns in American Cities," *Urban Transportation Planning: Concepts and Application*, Highway Research Board Bulletin 293, National Academy of Sciences, 1961.

diction rather than the formulation of a general system of thought governing urban spatial structure.

Economic Models of Spatial Structure

In some respects quite different from the approaches discussed so far, economic models approach the conceptualization of urban spatial structure in the traditions of economic theory. The roots of this work go back to an agricultural land development concept advanced by Von Thünen in the early 1800's and include work in more recent times by Alfred Weber, Lösch, Isard, and others.[8] The economic approaches discussed here make use of what is known in economics as equilibrium theory. Since forms of notation used in equilibrium theory are specialized and some of the technical aspects of the concepts involved in this theory are outside the scope of this discussion, this work is presented in somewhat abridged form. The reader versed in economic theory will want to pursue this line of theoretical development in the original sources of work cited here.

Essentially the view taken in these approaches sees urban development processes as economic phenomena. The organizing concept is the market mechanism and the sorting process it provides in the allocation of space to activities. In the work on urban spatial structure this involves allocation of space in both quantitative and locational aspects to various users according to supply and demand relationships and a least-cost concept in an equilibrium system.

Wingo's work provides perhaps the most systematic and rigorous statement

of urban spatial structure in the framework of equilibrium theory.[9] Traditionally economists have dealt with location as a constant, and there has been a disinterest or an unwillingness to examine location as a variable. In his work, Wingo lifts this constraint. He seeks to give explicit recognition to the way in which policy affects the market and how in turn these effects are reflected in urban spatial structure. In this sense, he is seeking to relate theory to real world situations. However, in addition he seeks to bring developments in spatial models into closer harmony with general economic theory and to relate theoretical work on location to the broader concepts of the urban economy.

Directing his attention mainly to residential development, Wingo develops first a concept of transportation demand, considering the spatial relationship between home and work. With the journey to work viewed as "the technological link between the labor force and the production process," he defines demand for movement as the total employment of an urban area multiplied by the frequency of work—in other words, the number of trips required to support the production process. As Meier has done, Wingo recognizes the propensity for urban society to substitute communications for transportation and stresses the necessity for taking into account technological developments in this respect. The supply aspect is expressed in terms of the capacity of a movement system—a measure of its ability to accommodate movements between home and work. Drawing on a concept of accessibility somewhat similar to that discussed above, he uses as a unit of measurement the cost of transportation based on the time spent in movement between points and out-of-pocket costs for these movements expressed in money equivalents for distance and number of trips.

8. J. H. von Thünen, *Der Isolierte Staat in Beziehung auf Landwirtschaft und Nationalökonomie* (Hamburg, 1826); C. J. Friedrich, *Alfred Weber's Theory of Location of Industries* (Chicago: University of Chicago Press, 1928); August Lösch, *The Economics of Location* (New Haven: Yale University Press, 1954); Walter Isard, *Location and Space-Economy* (New York and Cambridge: John Wiley & Sons, Inc., and Technology Press, 1956).

9. Lowdon Wingo, Jr., *Transportation and Urban Land* (Washington, D.C.: Resources for the Future, Inc., 1961).

The central problem of this kind of economic model is to achieve an equilibrium distribution of households of particular rent-paying abilities to sites with a particular structure of rents. Wingo achieves this location equilibrium by substituting transportation costs for space costs. Thus, on the supply side, he utilizes transport costs to establish the distribution of household sites at varying position rents. He defines position rent as "the annual savings in transportation costs compared to the highest cost location in use." On the demand side, if prices for other goods competing for the household dollar are held constant, the rents households are willing to pay are based on the marginal utility concept, which holds that the greater the unit rent, the fewer the units of space consumed. Clearly this view of space use immediately involves density, and the smaller the quantity of space consumed in the more accessible locations, the higher the density. The spatial distribution of these densities in the urban area involves the density gradient concept noted earlier, with the slope falling off from the center of the city to the outskirts. To get at the characteristics of demand in the spatial context, Wingo constructs a demand schedule and utilizes appropriate position rents from this schedule to determine the point at which prices and densities are in equilibrium.

The economic model Wingo advances functions under the usual behavioral axiom that those who control residential space and households which seek space will each behave to maximize their returns. He specifies as givens: the locations of employment centers, a particular transportation technology, a set of urban households, the marginal value the worker places on leisure, and the marginal value households place on residential space. Wingo then uses his model to determine the spatial distribution of densities and rents, and the spatial distribution, value, and extent of land required for residential use. For the derivation of the elements to

the model as well as the mathematical form, and for his discussion of the empirical advantages and limitations of the model, the reader is referred to the source.[10]

Although it is beyond the scope of this discussion to go further into this work as it relates to economic theory, we may note that as a theoretical system it is the most developed one considered so far. The market mechanism furnishes the dynamic aspect and organizing concept for the theoretical framework. The conceptual system is rigorously stated, and logical consistency is carefully observed throughout. Wingo has sought to maintain a close contact with the real world, and although empirical tests of this work are still to be made, we do have indications from experimentation going on in the use of mathematical models in generating land use patterns that this kind of economic model can be made operational.[11]

Decision Analysis and the Structure of Cities

As still another approach to urban spatial structure, the author has proposed that a conceptual system based on the *values—behavior patterns—consequences* framework developed by a group at the University of North Carolina offers a basic organizing concept for theory development.[12] In its most basic form, and viewing the components in reverse order, this framework seeks explanations for any particular man-induced phenomenon being studied (in this instance, urban growth

10. *Ibid.* See p. 87 for the general form of the model.
11. For example, see Ira S. Lowry, "Location Parameters in the Pittsburgh Model," XI (1962); Roland Artle, *Studies in the Structure of the Stockholm Economy* (Stockholm: The Business Research Institute at the Stockholm School of Economics, 1959).
12. Parts of this approach to urban spatial structure are covered in the "Introduction" and Chapter 13 of *Urban Growth Dynamics,* ed. F. Stuart Chapin, Jr., and Shirley F. Weiss (New York: John Wiley & Sons, Inc., 1962).

and development) in terms of human behavior (patterns of activity), with behavior patterns being a function in turn of people's values (or the attitudes held concerning these activities). A fourth element in the framework has to do with control processes (strategies or plans) that influence the interplay among the first three components.

In common with the view taken by several of the foregoing conceptual systems, under this framework, it is a behavioral axiom that human beings tend to concentrate at various places on the earth's surface in the satisfaction of needs and desires for interaction which, in the framework of the above values-action-outcomes sequence, may be viewed as the middle component (behavior patterns). The term "behavior patterns" is used to refer to rational and overt forms of interaction, both the forms which cluster spatially into duplicating or near-duplicating patterns and remain relatively unchanged for extended periods of time, and the forms which take variable spatial patterns and appear in different locations from one day to the next. Although planners are concerned with both clustering and non-clustering patterns of behavior, to get at the elements of urban spatial structure they are particularly interested in the way duplicating or clustered patterns build up in space. Out of the universe of behavior patterns to be found in a metropolitan area, certain ones have a spatial importance, show a tendency to duplicate in clusters, and occur in rhythmical and repetitive forms in the course of the week, month, or season. These behavior patterns are constantly undergoing adjustments and reformation in response to value orientations, but at the same time some of these behavior patterns have sufficient importance in their spatial, duplicating, repetitive characteristics to produce outcomes in physical structure and form. As in most of the other conceptual systems reviewed here, these physical forms are composed of *one,* spaces adapted to various forms of place-related interaction, and *two,* interconnecting channels for the various forms of movement-related or communications-related interaction. The means by which interaction patterns become translated into these structure-form outcomes is found in the location behavior of households, firms, government, and institutional entities.

Location behavior, then may be thought of as growing out of needs and desires of day-to-day forms of interaction. While location actions occur on a day-in-and-day-out basis, for any particular household or firm, they tend to occur infrequently. The location action constitutes a different type of behavior pattern from the daily activity patterns. But at the same time, the location action is the instrumentality by which the activity patterns of the first type are accommodated in physical form.

The framework we have been developing at the University of North Carolina focuses on the *decision* as the critical point in the behavioral sequence in a location action. Of the many kinds of decisions by which space is adapted and put to use and movement systems established, two groups are differentiated. One group is involved in what are called "priming decisions" in the sense that they are seen to trigger the other group, what are called "secondary decisions," with the two together accounting for development as a whole. Priming decisions are made in both the public sector (for example, those involved in major highway locations or utility locations) and in the private sector (for example, decisions on large-scale investment in land, on the location of industries with large employment or the location of major shopping centers or Levittown-type developments). They set the stage for secondary decisions—for example, park acquisition or street widening decisions in the public sector, or small-scale subdivision, mortgage-financing, lot-purchasing, or home-building decisions in the private sector.

Priming actions tend to develop from single decisions or a mix of discrete decisions of some strategic importance in setting off a chain reaction of development, and secondary actions usually consist of clusters of decisions (for example, clusters of household decisions) stimulated by, but following from the strategic actions. Because it would be impractical to unravel and deal with the separate effects of all kinds of decisions, the emphasis in this framework is on priming decisions—discovering what mix of these actions tends to trigger other actions and thus influence the course of events which accounts for the pattern of development that subsequently emerges. Therefore, under our conceptual system, land development is viewed as the consequence first of certain strategic decisions which structure the pattern of growth and development and then of the myraids of household, business, and governmental decisions which follow from the first key decision.

An experimental model has been developed for testing this conceptual approach.[13] The initial emphasis of this work is on experimentation with household location. In its present form, priming decisions are "givens," and the task of the model is to simulate secondary location decisions—essentially a distribution of households to available land—following an evolutionary sequence of priming actions. While serving to induce secondary location decisions, the "given" priming decisions are seen in part as the result of pressures which arise from daily needs and desires of urban residents, firms, and other entities. Since location behavior is thus viewed as an outgrowth of needs and desires developing from daily-weekly-seasonal forms of interaction, the author places a premium on studying not only

13. F. Stuart Chapin, Jr., and Shirley F. Weiss, *Factors Influencing Land Development* (Chapel Hill: Institute for Research in Social Science, University of North Carolina, in co-operation with the Bureau of Public Roads, U.S. Department of Commerce, August, 1962).

prevailing activity patterns but also attitudes of different population groups for insights they supply into the likely future stability of these patterns. It may be anticipated that future work on this conceptual system will emphasize two lines of research development: *one,* the analysis of activity patterns from data obtained by home interviews, firm interviews, and so on, and *two,* the analysis of attitudes from a paralleling line of inquiry in the course of these interviews. These areas of inquiry are seen as supplying parameters for the location model.

Comparative Aspects of Theoretical Approaches

There are some important similarities in these systems of thought I have been reviewing and some significant differences. Explicitly or implicitly each system is directly concerned with the development of a framework which identifies and describes regularities in patterns of human interaction in space and explains their origins and transformations in time wherever population aggregates in urban areas. Along with these rather fundamental relationships in space and time is a common concern for accessibility, a concept of great importance in spatial relationships. In describing interaction patterns, most of these conceptual systems make a distinction between patterns of intra-place and inter-place interaction, the former having importance for the adaptation of space and the latter involving communications between spaces. "Space adaptation" and "communications," of course, are counterparts for "land use" and "circulation" which are terms common in the vocabularly of the practitioner.

While there is this fundamental common base, other similarities may be found when comparisons are narrowed to two or three approaches. Some similarities are based on acknowledged cross-ties as in Meier's acceptance of Webber's urban realm concept, or Webber's adoption of

Meier's communication emphasis. Some appear to be simply parallelisms among the conceptual systems. Thus, while Wingo sees man's economic behavior in the market place as the medium which regulates location decisions, with adjustments introduced to take account of non-economic factors influencing these decisions, the author's work in effect substitutes the urban social system for the market place as the medium which regulates location decisions, these being determined by the day-to-day interaction needs and desires of urban residents, firms, and other entities.

Yet, with these similarities and parallelisms, there are distinctive differences in approach. The differences are in part a function of the background, specialization, and research biases of the person advancing the approach. Beyond this, one senses differences in conception of what would constitute a proper set of criteria for theory building whether or not they are consciously considered in any particular approach. Meier's work reflects a unique perspective across the expanse of both physical and social sciences, and drawing on this broad scope of interest, he directs attention to the opportunities for synthesizing elements from different fields in a theory of urban spatial structure. Deeply concerned with the implications of technological and social change for patterns of human interaction, Webber emphasizes the placelessness of many new forms of activities and the importance of the dynamic aspect of theory building to take these changes into account. Lynch and Rodwin have focused their attention on one part of the broad area we have been discussing, dealing with this part in some depth and laying particular stress on a normative approach. Wingo's work reflects a strong inclination toward a rigorously classical and systematic approach to theory building. Guttenberg has a sensitivity to the policy implications of theory and the alternatives open to metropolitan areas in making a choice. The author's work with his associates at North Carolina places a strong emphasis on relating theory on urban structure and growth to theoretical work in public policy and decision-making.

It should be clear by this time that there is a significant effort going into theoretical research, a healthy variety to approaches being explored, and a developing emphasis on an experimental view. Some question the present day emphasis in the social sciences on the use of experimental designs. This is in part a reaction against the heavy emphasis in these times on the natural sciences. The advent of symbolic logic and mathematical models is seen by some as a hocus pocus and a dream world of fadism seeking to mystify with esoteric language and mathematical learning. There may be some excesses of this kind, but the real difficulties are more likely to come from the blind hope of formula-hunters who use models without looking into the qualifying conditions which apply in any particular situation. It should be noted, too, that the distrust and occasional eruption of impatience with the use of mathematics in theory building is not peculiar to the planning field. Old-line theorists in economics, political science, and sociology have frequently spoken out on this matter.[14] The planning field has come to this controversy more recently, but the arguments are not too different. Harris offers a cogent brief for the place of models in city planning, and the reader would do well to look up his comments on this subject if he has lingering doubts about the utility of mathematics in planning theory.[15]

14. For arguments pro and con, see James C. Charlesworth, ed., *Mathematics and the Social Sciences,* a symposium (Philadelphia: American Academy of Political and Social Science, June, 1963).

15. Britton Harris, "Plan or Projection: An Examination of the Use of Models in Planning," *Journal of the American Institute of Planners, XXVI* (November, 1960), 265-272.

WILLIAM ALONSO

A Theory of the Urban Land Market

The early theory of rent and location concerned itself primarily with agricultural land. This was quite natural, for Ricardo and Malthus lived in an agricultural society. The foundations of the formal spatial analysis of agricultural rent and location are found in the work of J. von Thunen, who said, without going into detail, that the urban land market operated under the same principles.[1] As cities grew in importance, relatively little attention was paid to the theory of urban rents. Even the great Marshall provided interesting but only random insights, and no explicit theory of the urban land market and urban locations was developed.

Since the beginning of the twentieth century there has been considerable interest in the urban land market in America. R. M. Hurd[2] in 1903 and R. Haig[3] in the twenties tried to create a theory of urban land by following von Thunen. However, their approach copied the form rather than the logic of agricultural theory, and the resulting theory can be shown to be insufficient on its own premises. In particular, the theory failed to consider residences, which constitute the preponderant land use in urban areas.

Yet there are interesting problems that a theory of urban land must consider. There is, for instance, a paradox in American cities: the poor live near the center, on expensive land, and the rich on the periphery, on cheap land. On the logical side, there are also aspects of great interest, but which increase the difficulty of the analysis. When a purchaser acquires land, he acquires two goods (land and location) in only one transaction, and only one payment is made for the combination. He could buy the same quantity of land at another location, or he could buy more, or less land at the same location. In the analysis, one encounters, as well, a negative good (distance) with positive costs (commuting costs); or, conversely, a positive good (accessibility) with negative costs (savings in commuting). In comparison with agriculture, the urban case

1. Johan von Thunen, *Der Isolierte Staat in Beziehung auf Landwirthschaft und Nationalekonomie*, 1st. vol., 1826, 3d. vol. and new edition, 1863.
2. Richard M. Hurd, *Principles of City Land Values*, N.Y.: The Record and Guide, 1903.
3. Robert M. Haig, "Toward an Understanding of the Metropolis," *Quarterly Journal of Economics*, XL: 3, May 1926; and *Regional Survey of New York and Its Environs*, N.Y.: New York City Plan Commission, 1927.

From **Papers and Proceedings of the Regional Science Association,** Vol. 6, 1960, pp. 149-158.
Reprinted by permission of the Regional Science Association, Philadelphia, Pennsylvania.

presents another difficulty. In agriculture, the location is extensive: many miles may be devoted to one crop. In the urban case the site tends to be much smaller, and the location may be regarded as a dimensionless point rather than an area. Yet the thousands or millions of dimensionless points which constitute the city, when taken together, cover extensive areas. How can these dimensionless points be aggregated into two-dimensional space?

Here I will present a non-mathematical over-view, without trying to give it full precision, of the long and rather complex mathematical analysis which constitutes a formal theory of the urban land market.[4] It is a static model in which change is introduced by comparative statics. And it is an economic model: it speaks of economic men, and it goes without saying that real men and social groups have needs, emotions, and desires which are not considered here. This analysis uses concepts which fit with agricultural rent theory in such a way that urban and rural land uses may be considered at the same time, in terms of a single theory. Therefore, we must examine first a very simplified model of the agricultural land market.

Agricultural Model

In this model, the farmers are grouped around a single market, where they sell their products. If the product is wheat, and the produce of one acre of wheat sells for $100 at the market while the costs of production are $50 per acre, a farmer growing wheat at the market would make a profit of $50 per acre. But if he is producing at some distance—say 5 miles—and it costs him $5 per mile to ship an acre's product, his transport costs will be $25 per acre. His profits will be equal to

4. A full development of the theory is presented in my doctoral dissertation, *A Model of the Urban Land Market: Locations and Densities of Dwellings and Businesses,* University of Pennsylvania, 1960.

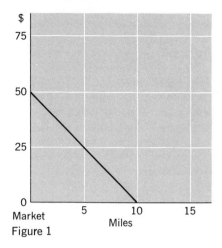

Figure 1

value minus production costs minus shipping charges: $100 - 50 - 25 = \$25$. This relation may be shown diagrammatically (see Figure 1). At the market, the farmer's profits are $50, and 5 miles out, $25; at intermediate distance, he will receive intermediate profits. Finally, at a distance of 10 miles from the market, his production costs plus shipping charges will just equal the value of his produce at the market. At distances greater than 10 miles, the farmer would operate at a loss.

In this model, the profits derived by the farmer are tied directly to their location. If the functions of farmer and landowner are viewed as separate, farmers will bid rents for land according to the profitability of the location. The profits of the farmer will therefore be shared with the landowner through rent payments. As farmers bid against each other for the more profitable locations, until farmers' profits are everywhere the same ("normal" profits), what we have called profits becomes rent. Thus, the curve in Figure 1, which we derived as a farmers' profit curve, once we distinguish between the roles of the farmer and the landowner, becomes a bid rent function, representing the price or rent per acre that farmers will be willing to pay for land at the different locations.

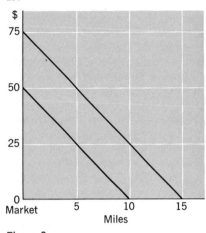

Figure 2

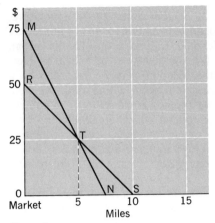

Figure 3

We have shown that the slope of the rent curve will be fixed by the transport costs on the produce. The level of the curve will be set by the price of the produce at the market. Examine Figure 2. The lower curve is that of Figure 1, where the price of wheat is $100 at the market, and production costs are $50. If demand increases, and the price of wheat at the market rises to $125 (while production and transport costs remain constant), profits or bid rent at the market will be $75; at 5 miles, $50; $25 at 10 miles, and zero at 15 miles. Thus, each bid rent curve is a function of rent vs. distance, but there is a family of such curves, the level of any one determined by the price of the produce at the market, higher prices setting higher curves.

Consider now the production of peas. Assume that the price at the market of one acre's production of peas is $150, the costs of production are $75, and the transport costs per mile are $10. These conditions will yield curve MN in Figure 3, where bid rent by pea farmers at the market is $75 per acre, 5 miles from the market $25, and zero at 7.5 miles. Curve RS represents bid rents by wheat farmers, at a price of $100 for wheat. It will be seen that pea farmers can bid higher rents in the range of 0 to 5 miles from the

market; farther out, wheat farmers can bid higher rents. Therefore, pea farming will take place in the ring from 0 to 5 miles from the market, and wheat farming in the ring from 5 to 10 miles. Segments MT of the bid rent curve of pea farming and TS of wheat farming will be the effective rents, while segments RT and TN represent unsuccessful bids.

The price of the product is determined by the supply-demand relations at the market. If the region between zero and 5 miles produces too many peas, the price of the product will drop, and a lower bid rent curve for pea farming will come into effect, so that pea farming will be practiced to some distance less than 5 miles.

Abstracting this view of the agricultural land market, we have that:
(1) land uses determine land values, through competitive bidding among farmers;
(2) land values distribute land uses, according to their ability to pay;
(3) the steeper curves capture the central locations. (This point is a simplified one for simple, well-behaved curves.)

Abstracting the process now *from* agriculture, we have:
(1) for each user of land (e.g., wheat farmer) a family of bid rent func-

tions is derived, such that the user is indifferent as to his location along any *one* of these functions (because the farmer, who is the decision-maker in this case, finds that profits are everywhere the same, i.e., normal, as long as he remains on one curve);

(2) the equilibrium rent at any location is found by comparing the bids of the various potential users and choosing the highest;

(3) equilibrium quantities of land are found by selecting the proper bid rent curve for each user (in the agricultural case, the curve which equates supply and demand for the produce).

Business

We shall now consider the urban businessman, who, we shall assume, makes his decisions so as to maximize profits. A bid rent curve for the businessman, then, will be one along which profits are everywhere the same: the decision-maker will be indifferent as to his location along such a curve.

Profit may be defined as the remainder from the volume of business after operating costs and land costs have been deducted. Since in most cases the volume of business of a firm as well as its operating costs will vary with its location, the rate of change of the bid rent curve will bear no simple relation to transport costs (as it did in agriculture). The rate of change of the total bid rent for a firm, where profits are constant by definition, will be equal to the rate of change in the volume of business minus the rate of change in operating costs. Therefore the slope of the bid rent curve, the values of which are in terms of dollars per unit of land, will be equal to the rate of change in the volume of business minus the rate of change in operating costs, divided by the area occupied by the establishment.

A different level of profits would yield a different bid rent curve. The higher the bid rent curve, the lower the profits, since land is more expensive. There will be a highest curve, where profits will be zero. At higher land rents the firm could only operate at a loss.

Thus we have, as in the case of the farmer, a family of bid rent curves, along the path of any one of which the decision-maker—in this case, the businessman—is indifferent. Whereas in the case of the farmer the level of the curve is determined by the price of the produce, while profits are in all cases "normal," i.e., the same, in the case of the urban firm, the level of the curve is determined by the level of the profits, and the price of its products may be regarded for our purposes as constant.

Residential

The household differs from the farmer and the urban firm in that satisfaction rather than profits is the relevant criterion of optional location. A consumer, given his income and his pattern of tastes, will seek to balance the costs and bother of commuting against the advantages of cheaper land with increasing distance from the center of the city and the satisfaction of more space for living. When the individual consumer faces a given pattern of land costs, his equilibrium location and the size of his site will be in terms of the marginal changes of these variables.

The bid rent curves of the individual will be such that, for any given curve, the individual will be equally satisfied at every location at the price set by the curve. Along any bid rent curve, the price the individual will bid for land will decrease with distance from the center at a rate just sufficient to produce an income effect which will balance to his satisfaction the increased costs of commuting and the bother of a long trip. This slope may be expressed quite precisely in mathematical terms, but it is a complex expression, the exact interpretation of which is beyond the scope of this paper.

Just as different prices of the produce set different levels for the bid rent curves of the farmer, and different levels of profit for the urban firm, different levels of satisfaction correspond to the various levels of the family of bid rent curves of the individual household. The higher curves obviously yield less satisfaction because a higher price is implied, so that, at any given location, the individual will be able to afford less land and other goods.

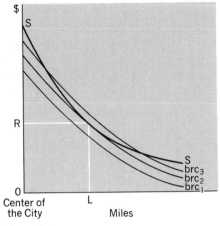

Figure 4

Individual Equilibrium

It is obvious that families of bid rent curves are in many respects similar to indifference curve mappings. However, they differ in some important ways. Indifference curves map a path of indifference (equal satisfaction) between combinations of quantities of two goods. Bid rent functions map an indifference path between the price of one good (land) and quantities of another and strange type of good, distance from the center of the city. Whereas indifference curves refer to tastes and not to budget, in the case of households, bid rent functions are derived both from budget and taste considerations. In the case of the urban firm, they might be termed isoprofit curves. A more superficial difference is that, whereas the higher indifference curves are the preferred ones, it is the lower bid rent curves that yield greater profits or satisfaction. However, bid rent curves may be used in a manner analogous to that of indifference curves to find the equilibrium location and land price for the resident or the urban firm.

Assume you have been given a bid rent mapping of a land use, whether business or residential (curves $brc_{1,2,3}$, etc., in Figure 4). Superimposed on the same diagram the actual structure of land

prices in the city (curve SS). The decision-maker will wish to reach the lowest possible bid rent curve. Therefore, he will choose that point at which the curve of actual prices (SS) will be tangent to the lowest of the bid rent curves with which it comes in contact (brc_2). At this point will be the equilibrium location (L) and the equilibrium land rent (R) for this user of land. If he is a businessman, he will have maximized profits; if he is a resident, he will have maximized satisfaction.

Note that to the left of this point of equilibrium (toward the center of the city) the curve of actual prices is steeper than the bid rent curve; to the right of this point (away from the center) it is less steep. This is another aspect of the rule we noted in the agricultural model: the land uses with steeper bid rent curves capture the central locations.

Market Equilibrium

We now have, conceptually, families of bid rent curves for all three types of land uses. We also know that the steeper curves will occupy the more central locations. Therefore, if the curves of the various users are ranked by steepness, they will also be ranked in terms of their accessibility from the center of the city in the final solution. Thus, if the curves of the business firm are steeper than those of residences, and the residential curves steeper than the agricultural, there will be business at the center of the city, surrounded by residences, and these will be surrounded by agriculture.

This reasoning applies as well within land use groupings. For instance, it can be shown that, given two individuals of similar tastes, both of whom prefer living at low densities, if their incomes differ, the bid rent curves of the wealthier will be flatter than those of the man of lower income. Therefore, the poor will tend to central locations on expensive land and the rich to cheaper land on the periphery. The reason for this is not that the poor have greater purchasing power, but rather that they have steeper bid rent curves. This stems from the fact that, at any given location, the poor can buy less land than the rich, and since only a small quantity of land is involved, changes in its price are not as important for the poor as the costs and inconvenience of commuting. The rich, on the other hand, buy greater quantities of land, and are consequently affected by changes in its price to a great degree. In other words, because of variations in density among different levels of income, accessibility behaves as an inferior good.

Thus far, through ranking the bid rent curves by steepness, we have found the relative rankings of prices and locations, but not the actual prices, locations, or densities. It will be remembered that in the agricultural case equilibrium levels were brought about by changes in the price of the products, until the amount of land devoted to each crop was in agreement with the demand for that crop.

For urban land this process is more complex. The determination of densities (or their inverse, lot size) and locations must be found simultaneously with the resulting price structure. Very briefly, the method consists of assuming a price of land at the center of the city, and determining the prices at all other locations by the competitive bidding of the potential users of land in relation to this price. The highest bid captures each location, and each bid is related to a most preferred alternative through the use of bid rent curves. This most preferred alternative is the marginal combination of price and location for that particular land use. The quantities of land occupied by the land users are determined by these prices. The locations are determined by assigning to each successive user of land the location available nearest the center of the city after the assignment of land quantities to the higher and more central bidders.

Since initially the price at the center of the city was assumed, the resulting set of prices, locations, and densities may be in error. A series of iterations will yield the correct solution. In some cases, the solution may be found by a set of simultaneous equations rather than by the chain of steps which has just been outlined.

The model presented in this paper corresponds to the simplest case: a single-center city, on a featureless plain, with transportation in all directions. However, the reasoning can be extended to cities with several centers (shopping, office, manufacturing, etc.), with structured road patterns, and other realistic complications. The theory can also be made to shed light on the effects of economic development, changes in income structure, zoning regulations, taxation policies, and other. At this stage, the model is purely theoretical; however, it is hoped that it may provide a logical structure for econometric models which may be useful for prediction.

EUGENE F. BRIGHAM

The Determinants of Residential Land Values

Since World War II urban areas in the United States have experienced a gigantic expansion. A number of problems have accompanied the growth—among them are a transportation lag, urban blight, and urban sprawl. Attempts to deal with these problems continually demonstrate our need for a better understanding of the complexities of metropolitan structures. For instance, when an individual selects property in a particular residential area, what influences his choice? Certainly land prices are one of the influencing forces but what determines land values? This paper, which gives results of a study conducted at The RAND Corporation under the sponsorship of the Ford Foundation describes and tests a model of residential land values in Los Angeles County.[1]

An Overview

Essentially, the study is an empirical investigation of residential land values, and

1. Eugene F. Brigham, *A Model of Residential Land Values,* Santa Monica, California: The RAND Corporation, RM-4043-RC, August, 1964.

its structure and methodology are straightforward. First, a very simple theoretical model of land values is developed and used as a frame of reference within which to study the empirical data. The underlying model, described in more detail in the following sections, assumes that the value (V) of a particular urban area site is functionally related to its accessibility to economic activities (P), to its amenities (A), to its topography (T), to its present and future use (U—i.e., industrial, commercial, or residential), and to certain historical factors that affect its utilization (H). Provided these variables can be quantified, the basic land value model of the ith site may be expressed as

$$V_i = f(P_i, A_i, T_i, U_i, H_i) \qquad (1)$$

Since it is likely that accessibility, amenity, and topography will react differently on the value of land in different uses, the basic equation is restated as

$$V_{Ri} = f_1 (P_i, A_i, T_i, H_i) \qquad (1a)$$
$$V_{Ci} = f_2 (P_i, A_i, T_i, H_i) \qquad (1b)$$
$$V_{Ii} = f_3 (P_i, A_i, T_i, H_i) \qquad (1c)$$

where the subscripts R, C, and I designate residential, commercial and industrial land, respectively.

The key variables are thought to be indices, with each index a function of several different variables. A site's accessibility, for example, is a joint function of its proximity to different activities and the transportation system connecting it with these possible destinations. Similarly, the social and atmospheric conditions associated with the site determine its amenity indices.

While the principal analytical tool employed in the study is multiple regression analysis, it was impossible to quantify all important land-value determinants and incorporate them into the regression models. Many of the qualitative forces that shape the structure of urban land values can be considered at an intuitive level, however, especially with the aid of maps. When actual land values and the values predicted by the regression equations are plotted on topographic maps, one quickly sees points where values are high and low, and where qualitative factors cause the model to break down most severely.

The basic data for this study were obtained from tax assessment appraisal records. The sampling method, selected primarily because it was relatively inexpensive yet quite adequate, involved extending arbitrary rays, or lines, out from the Civic Center to the County boundaries. Each block a ray passed through was treated as a sample point, or observation, and the average appraised value per square foot for the block was ascertained. If a block included two or three types of land uses—for example, residential and commercial properties—this fact was noted, and subsequently individual samples of each were obtained.[2]

2. The theoretical model is for residential land only and most of the analysis is concentrated on this sample. The same general relationships, however, were found in each of the samples when they were used in the regression models.

Three rays were selected. The first extends to the northwest through Hollywood, the Santa Monica Mountains, and up the San Fernando Valley to the Ventura County boundary. The second extends to the northeast through Alhambra, South Pasadena, San Marino, the Santa Anita racetrack, and to the base of the San Gabriel Mountains. The third extends to the southeast through the heavily industrialized East Los Angeles area to the Orange County boundary. The rays were selected with the idea of obtaining samples with diverse characteristics.[3]

The Value Determinants

Since land supply is fixed, land value in an urban community is determined by the demand for space. As previously mentioned, the demand function for any site in any given metropolitan area is a function of the site's accessibility, amenity level, topography, certain qualitative phenomena that may be considered "historical accidents," and the value of the land in non-urban uses. Each of these factors is discussed now in order to establish a framework within which to consider the empirical models presented.

Accessibility value. Urban land has a value over and above its value in rural uses because it affords relatively easy access to various necessary or desirable activities. If transportation were instantaneous and costless, then the urban population could spread out over all usable space and all land prices would be reduced to their approximate value in the best alternative use. But transportation is not instantaneous and costless and, since modern life requires the concentration of people in cities, urban land takes on a special accessibility value. The theoretical relationship between accessibility and land

3. The southeast ray did not meet the assumptions of the model, so it was not studied in detail and is not discussed in this paper. See Brigham, *op. cit.,* pp. 51-52.

values has been discussed at length by Wingo and others.[4]

Under very restrictive assumptions it is possible to specify a precise relationship between a site's accessibility and its value relative to other sites in the metropolitan area. Once the simplifying assumptions are dropped, it is no longer possible to specify the accessibility value function. The direction of impact of certain factors can be specified, however, and a number of relationships postulated. Diffusion of trip destinations, especially employment centers, leads to lower travel times and costs and tends to reduce land values in the aggregate. Higher incomes lead to more intensive bids for space, hence to higher land prices. Family characteristics that stimulate greater space preferences also lead to higher land prices. Transportation services vary widely among sites located the same distance from the Central Business District or other major trip destinations. Areas that offer easier access to bus lines, arterial boulevards, or freeways than other equidistant areas may have an accessibility value that influences land value. Finally, cost is not a linear function of distance but increases at an increasing rate as one travels into a congested area.

These relations cannot all be expressed in precise mathematical notation but some can be illustrated with graphs. Suppose a line is drawn from a point near the center of a city to the rural fringe at the edge of the metropolitan area. The ray could be expected to cut across freeways and other arterial roads (where increased ac-

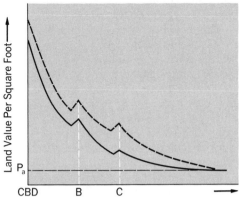

Figure 1. Hypothetical Cross-Sectional View of Land-Value Surface

cessibility brings relatively high values) and through areas close to satellite employment centers that again cause accessibility value peaks. The land value per square foot at each point along the ray could be ascertained and plotted against distance from the city's center, and a graph like Figure 1 would result. A larger city, or one with a wealthier population, might have the dashed rent gradient curve. The dashed line would also represent a city with a population having high space-consumption preferences. A city with decentralized employment might have the lower accessibility value curve but its curve would have some important "blips" and would cross that of the centralized city out on the right tail. A city expected to grow quite rapidly might have the same accessibility *rent* curve as an identical city that expects slower growth, but it expects higher future rents, hence its accessibility *value* curve (measured land prices) will be higher.[5] And a city with topographic or other effective constraints on expansion in certain directions will tend to have longer commutes, higher

4. Lowdon Wingo, *Transportation and Urban Land* (Washington, D.C.: Resources for the Future, inc., 1961); W. B. Hansen, "An Approach to the Analysis of Metropolitan Residential Extension," *Journal of Regional Science,* Summer 1961, pp. 37-55; Herbern Mohring, "Land Values and the Measurement of Highway Benefits," *Journal of Political Economy,* June 1961, pp. 236-249; and William Alonso, "A Theory of the Urban Land Market," *Papers and Proceedings of the Regional Science Association,* 1960, pp. 149-157.

5. Higher land prices would probably force rents up also but this is not entirely clear. Speculators are often willing to rent land at nominal rates while waiting for the land to "ripen" for a higher and better use.

travel-cost savings from living close to the center, and higher values than a city of similar size with no such barriers.

In conclusion, we have an idea about the shape of the accessibility function, but can only specify it under highly simplified conditions far removed from the real world. Many of these simplifying conditions are reassumed in the following subsection where an accessibility variable suitable for empirical testing is formulated and when it is used in a regression model.

The accessibility potential variable. If the CBD is the only work-place, if the journey to work is the only significant trip any household member takes, and if travel to and from the CBD is equally easy in any direction, then the distance from any site R_i to the CBD provides an index of the site's accessibility. If these conditions are not met, then this distance variable is an imperfect proxy for accessibility. It is quite obvious that the necessary conditions are violated in all metropolitan areas and especially in Los Angeles. The following potential model variable makes allowances for many workplaces and is suggested as a possible improvement to distance alone.

$$ P_i = \sum_{j=i}^{N} \frac{E_j}{a + bD_{ij}^{c}} $$

where P_i is the accessibility potential of the ith site, E_j is the total employment in the jth workplace, D_{ij} is the distance between sites i and j; a, b, and c are parameters; and the summation is over all of the N workplaces in the community. Under this formulation, the employment accessibility potential of site i varies directly with the employment opportunities surrounding it and inversely with the distance between it and these employment opportunities. The workplace and residence zones may, of course, be aggregates of sites rather than individual lots; in fact,

census tracts were used in this study. It is obvious that the model could be improved by providing a weighing system in the numerator for different types of jobs—possibly by weighting different types of employment by the mean income in each job category—and by putting a time factor in the denominator to account for differences in the transportation systems connecting different pairs of points. These desirable modifications were not made in the model because the necessary data were not available.

Amenity value. If, for example, a particular site generally has less smog than an otherwise identical site, then it will be a more pleasant place to live in and will have a higher amenity level. Naturally, a site having a higher amenity level is more desirable and more valuable than one with fewer amenities, if all else is equal.

The amenity level is clearly a qualitative factor determined subjectively by different individuals. Its level at a particular site cannot be measured directly as can elevation or temperature but one could measure its value. Suppose a sample of the city's population was selected and allowed to become completely familiar with all the residential neighborhoods in the area. These people could then be asked to rank the residential sites in the order of their relative amenity levels, designating points of indifference by the same rank, and an ordinal set of site amenity rankings could be compiled. Amenity rankings would differ somewhat from person to person—bohemians might find a certain area highly desirable while more conventional types might consider it a slum—but in general these rankings would tend to be very similar.

The ordinal rankings of each individual person participating in the experiment could be scaled from 1 to 100 by assigning his rank percentile to each site—the most desirable 1 per cent of the sites would be given a value of 100, and so on. The percentile rankings of each participant could be aggregated; the final product would be a numerical index of amenity levels in the community.

This composite amenity index would probably be highly correlated with a number of quantitative variables such as the nonwhite proportion of the population, median family incomes, and the extent of dwelling-unit crowding, all of which are readily available on a census-tract basis. Other quantitative factors that are important determinants of amenity, especially in Los Angeles, include the mean and extreme temperatures, and the smog levels in different sections of the metropolitan area.

Since there can be dramatic changes in amenities from one block to the next, it is desirable to have an amenity proxy that is somewhat more sensitive than the census tract-wide variables.[6] Such a variable is the average value of the dwelling-unit structures in a given block. If the average value of the improvements (holding constant the value of the land itself) of each dwelling unit is high, this probably indicates a number of things. First, the buildings are probably more pleasing to the eye. Second, because it will be expensive to live in them their occupants will have relatively high incomes, and high incomes are associated with high levels of education and high social and economic positions. This leads to the feeling that a certain amount of "prestige" is attached to living in the neighborhood, and it is "a good place in which to bring up one's children." It is argued, then, that the value

6. Census tracts consist of relatively homogeneous neighborhoods and contain, on the average, about 4,000 people. Depending on the population density in the area, tracts in Los Angeles generally contain from 20 to 80 square blocks. In the built-up single-family areas of the San Fernando Valley, for example, the average tract in 1960 had about 60 square blocks, while in the densely-populated multiple-dwelling unit area close to the Civic Center, tracts averaged around 25 square blocks.

of dwelling-unit improvements has an influence on and can be used as a rather fine-grained measure of the amenity level in a given neighborhood.

Topography. As used in this paper, the term "topography" means the natural, physical characteristics of a particular site. Foremost among these features are slope, elevation, and soil condition. Topography has two separate impacts on measured land values. First, a site's terrain has an effect on its amenity index. For example, a site situated high up on a steep hill might be above the smog level and might have a commanding view of the city; both factors would tend to increase its amenity level. But, on the other hand, this steep, hilly site might be excessively windy and dangerous for smaller children—factors that create negative amenities for people who dislike wind or who have small children. Thus topography's effect on a site's amenity ranking would vary from family to family depending on their composition and preferences.

Besides its amenity impact, topography also has a bearing on land values through its effect on development cost. Consider a tract of *un-developed* acreage, half of which is quite hilly and half of which is relatively flat. The flat land can be subdivided into residential lots rather easily; while putting in access roads, grading for

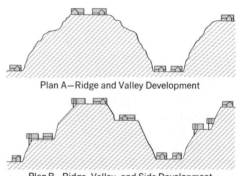

Plan A—Ridge and Valley Development

Plan B—Ridge, Valley, and Side Development

Figure 2. Hypothetical Developments of Hilly Terrain

construction, providing utilities, and so forth, will be quite expensive in the hilly section, whose value will be reduced *vis-a-vis* that of the flat land by these added costs. Similarly, if half the acreage had been on well-drained land and half in a swamp, the value of the swampy half would be reduced by the costs of providing drainage.

Differential values resulting from topography might not be expected with already developed land. In the examples above, if the aggregate accessibility and amenity indices of the hilly sites, after development, are identical to those of the flat sites, then buyers in general will be willing to pay the same price for a developed lot on either the favored or unfavored land,

and measured land values will be identical. This is not necessarily true, however, when land values are computed on a square foot basis. The reason for this can best be illustrated by Figure 2, which shows a cross-section view of a given area under two alternative development plans. In Plan A only the ridges and valleys, which are relatively flat and easy to prepare for construction, are developed. These lots are quite large, but a buyer acquires much unusable space, and most of the purchase price is actually paid for that part of the lot on which a house may be built. Under Plan B (presumably put into effect only if the area's accessibility to employment centers is extremely high) the developer cuts roads into the hillsides

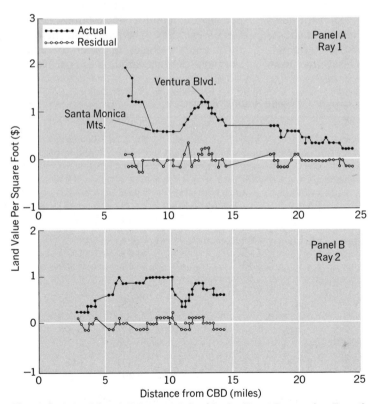

Figure 3. Actual Land Values and Residuals About Regression Equation Based on Data from the Individual Ray Only; Single-Family Properties. (The Equations with CBD the distance variable were used to derive the residuals for panels A and B respectively.)

and uses the entire area. Plan B lots are much smaller than those of Plan A, and are probably about the same price, so the measured value per square foot of lots in the area will be much higher if Plan B is adopted.

Historical factors. In a sense, all factors affecting land values are either historical or physical. An historical accident may have determined the position of a major arterial, hence land values in the area. The lower class residential district of a city may have been located by an historical accident and thus have had a permanent impact on amenity levels and land prices of sites in the city. In this paper, however, a different type of historical factor is considered. As used here, *an historical factor is the employment of land in a way that is no longer suitable.* For example, consider the alternative development Plans A and B in Figure 3. Plan A might be adopted and carried out because, at a particular time, the marginal revenue from

the sale of the hillside lots is lower than the marginal cost entailed in this expensive development. If the acreage had been developed later, after the growth of the city had increased the accessibility of the tract, Plan B might be feasible. Now in a given area some tracts are developed early (like Plan A), others later (according to Plan B); we say that an historical factor—the point in time at which development took place—influences measured land prices. In the long run, redevelopment may occur to equate these land prices but the long run can involve many years in the case of real property.

The Regression Equations

Regression equations were fitted to five-block moving averages of the land value per square foot for single-family properties on each ray. The data were smoothed by moving averages in order to remove as much spurious variation as possible; the

Table 1. The Regression Equations for Single-Family Properties

Sample	Constant Term	Distance to CBD	Acessi-bility Potential	Neighbor-hood Variable[a]	Building Value	Topography Dummy[b]	R^2
			A. Ray 1				
Regression Coef.	1.73	−.051	—	−.15	1.06	−.51	.87
(Std. Error)		(.003)	—	(.13)	(.23)	(.07)	
Partial Corr. Coef.		−.89	—	−.12	.44	−.64	
Regression Coef.	−.29	—	8.80	−.01	.97	−.48	.79
(Std. Error)			(.66)	(.16)	(.30)	(.08)	
Partial Corr. Coef.			.53	−.01	.33	−.53	
			B. Ray 2				
Regression Coef.	1.35	−.041		−4.28	.28	−.70	
(Std. Error)		(.004)		(.31)	(.18)	(.08)	.87
Partial Corr. Coef.		−.68		−.83	.17	−.69	
Regression Coef.	.21		14.90	−5.57	.32	−.91	
(Std. Error)			(1.58)	(.35)	(.17)	(.08)	.89
Partial Corr. Coef.			.73	−.87	.20	−.76	

[a] Median family income is used for Ray 1, and the percentage of dwelling units with more than 1.01 persons per room is used for Ray 2.

[b] A dummy variable set equal to 1 for sites located in the Santa Monica Mountains, through which Ray 1 passes, and the hills about one-third of the way out Ray 2.

purpose of the study was to investigate general, not local, variations in land values and the smoothing process helped make these primary influences more apparent.[7]

Since there are several different proxies for the accessibility and amenity indices and since these proxies are frequently too highly intercorrelated[8] to be used together, a number of different equations are calculated for each of the samples. Table 1 presents the most interesting and useful of these models.

Accessibility. The accessibility variables behave as expected—land values are negatively related to distance from the CBD and the nearest freeway, and positively related to the employment accessibility potential variable. There are differences in the parameters of the accessibility proxies of the several samples but these variations seem reasonable in view of the diverse characteristics of the rays.[9] Ray 1's coefficient for distance to the CBD is slightly larger than that of Ray 2, indicating more distance-sensitivity, but this conclusion should not be pushed too far, considering the differences between the rays. Single-family properties start much closer to the CBD on Ray 2 than on Ray 1. Ray 2 terminates abruptly some 14 miles from the CBD, while Ray 1 continues 25 miles out from the CBD, extending to the point where urban activity has faded away.

7. The data were also fitted in a sample which pooled rays 1, 2, and 3 together. This sample was constructed in order to see the differences between a single-ray and the entire metropolitan area, so the inclusion of Ray 3 is necessary there. The combined ray sample exhibited the same characteristics as those for the single rays. Brigham, *op. cit.,* pp. 50 and 60.

8. See Brigham, *op. cit.,* Appendix C, for a complete breakdown of the simple correlation matrix.

9. The exponent in the accessibility potential equation was determined by experimentation; the value 1.0 was used for Ray 1 and 0.8 for Ray 2. This means that the potential will be higher for Ray 1, *ceteris paribus,* than for Ray 2, hence the accessibility potential regression coefficient should be lower for Ray 1.

The coefficients of the distance variables, all of which exceed their standard errors by 10 times, suggest that land values fall by about four or five cents per square foot for every one-mile increase in distance from the CBD after amenity levels and other value-influencing factors are taken into account. Put another way, the distance elasticities computed at the point of means, values of −1.13 for Ray 1 and −.96 for Ray 2, indicate that a 10-per cent increase in distance from the CBD is associated with a decrease of about ten percent in land values.

In conclusion, we can state that there is clearly a relationship between land values and accessibility to urban activity but that this relationship, even after holding certain other effects relatively constant by the use of multiple regression analysis, is far from stable when different samples are examined.

Amenity. The census tract amenity variables—income for Ray 1, crowding for Ray 2—behave as expected.[10] Neighborhood variables are quite important on Ray 2, relatively less significant on Ray 1. These variations appear to be caused by important differences in ray characteristics. Once the single-family areas have been reached, Ray 1 goes through a series of fairly homogeneous upper-middle class neighborhoods; the mean income is $8,800 and the standard deviation is $1,858. Ray 2, on the other hand, has a mean income of $10,330 in the single-family sections; however, the standard deviation is $4,100, indicating pronounced variations in socioeconomic conditions along the ray. A comparison of means and standard deviations of the other two amenity proxies, crowding and single-family building values, revealed similar tendencies. Naturally,

10. Income has the wrong sign but is less than its standard error in the Ray 1 model when used together with building values. This is because of the high correlation between incomes and the values of single-family homes. Land values are positively related to incomes when building values are removed from the equation.

with so much more amenity variation to be explained, the amenity proxies would appear more important in Ray 2.

Topographic dummy. The coefficient of the topographic dummy is negative and highly significant, indicating that single-family land values are relatively low in very hilly areas. Since all properties included in the sample are developed sites, it is likely that the negative relationship is caused by the inclusion of undevelopable land in hill area lots.

Plots of Land Values and Residuals

Actual land values and residuals about the regression equations were plotted on a large-scale, detailed topographic map of the Los Angeles area. The major peaks and valleys in both actual land values and residuals about the regression lines were then compared with the features shown on the map—the points where the residuals differ greatly from zero are especially significant since they show where the regression model breaks down most seriously. Land values and residuals, plotted against distance to the CBD, are shown separately in Figure 3.

Panel A of Figure 3, which gives the plots for Ray 1, shows very clear peaks and valleys for the actual land values but fewer pronounced patterns for the residuals. The actual values are quite high initially—these sites are on the south slope of the Santa Monica Mountains very close to Hollywood—then fall markedly in the mountainous area, rise in the vicinity of Ventura Boulevard, and tail off rather gradually to the end of the County. The dummy variable adequately accounts for the land value dip in the Santa Monica Mountains but the Ventura Boulevard peak appears on the residual plot. Actual values rise initially on Ray 2 as the very low amenity area is traversed, then follow an irregular pattern to the terminus. The residuals are all fairly close to zero, but there is a tendency, especially toward the tail-end, for the deviations to follow the actual land values rather closely.

One feature of the Ray 2 plots, the pronounced dip in both actual and residual values that occurs about 12 miles out, is partly explained by the map analysis. At this point an "historical accident" occurs—the ray goes through a very fine old neighborhood with large, well-kept-up single-family homes that, over the four blocks responsible for the valley, are situated on lots with an average dimension of 200 x 200. These homes will eventually be removed and the land converted to a more efficient use as the buildings deteriorate and accessibility increases. Assuming a free market exists, single-family homes will be removed to make room for apartments (or other more intensive uses) when the value of the land alone, in the new use, exceeds the value of both land and buildings in the old use. If the old buildings are in very good shape and are therefore valuable in the old use, it is relatively difficult for conversion to occur. The high building values, then, seem to be holding land values down in this instance.

One thing should be made clear—though the *plots* do not reveal clear land value gradients, *these gradients are nonetheless present in the Los Angeles market.* The plots are two-dimensional and do not include the very important amenity factor. When amenities are brought in, as they are in the regression equations, then a very strong negative relation is seen to exist between value and distance from the CBD. This illustrates the inadvisability of looking at simple correlations between value and distance, and probably explain why Frieden found no rent gradients in Los Angeles.[11]

11. Bernard J. Frieden, "Locational Preferences in the Urban Housing Market," *Journal of the American Institute of Planners,* November 1961.

This paper was designed to present the findings of an empirical study dealing with the determinants of residential land values in an urban area. The value of any particular site is assumed to be related to its accessibility index, its amenity level, its topography, and certain historical factors including the way the land is being used. Serious measurement problems are encountered in dealing with these value determinants but they can be approximated by certain quantitative proxy variables. These surrogates are used to fit multiple regression equations to a sample of land values in Los Angeles County.

Accessibility to employment opportunities is positively related to residential land values. This relationship is sometimes swamped by the presence of low amenity levels near the primary work centers and is disturbed by the existence of satellite employment and shopping centers (e.g., Hollywood) located outside the CBD. Amenities are particularly difficult to measure and the most useful proxies vary from section to section depending on the characteristics of the area in question.

The fact that most of the independent variables are correlated with one another, in different degrees, makes it difficult to appraise the significance of the regression models. When the highest inter-correlations are removed, the regression coefficients are consistent with *a priori* expecta-tions and exceed their standard errors by fairly wide margins. The coefficients are not stable from ray to ray and this suggests factors not included in the models are at work.

Several ways of improving the empirical results have been suggested by the analysis. First, it is fairly clear that the potential variable is a better proxy for the accessibility index than is distance to the CBD but the model generating the potential factor must take into consideration travel time between different points. In addition, the analysis area must be defined in sufficient breadth to prevent such problems as the accessibility understatement on Ray 3. Third, considerably more effort could be spent on the construction of a better proxy to the amenity index. The conceptual scheme for ranking areas by their relative amenity levels might be implemented by using real estate brokers who specialize in residential properties; these rankings might be used as the dependent variable and regressed against the quantitative factors thought to influence amenities. Fourth, the number or rays might be increased and cross-town rays sampled in order to increase the representativeness of the study. Finally, the study could be extended to other cities in order to gain insights about the way parameters change in cities of different sizes, with different rates of growth, and so on.

WALLACE F. SMITH

Filtering and Neighborhood Change

"Filtering" is an indirect process for meeting the housing demand of a lower-income group. When new quality housing is produced for higher-income households, houses given up by these households become available to the lower-income group. Though it is a "well-recognized phenomenon,"[1] filtering provides an issue of public policy which has long commanded the attention of housing economists—whether or not it is fundamentally desirable that low-income housing needs be met in this way. The answer to this question can affect the character and pattern of cities, and hence the forecasts of demand for every existing residential neighborhood. In this chapter we show that the filtering concept and the questions it provokes have played important roles in the development of urban analytical technique, shifting this from a cartographic approach to more rigorous matrix analysis.

The filtering issue today can be traced to an empirical study made during the 1930's by Homer Hoyt.[2] That study

1. The phrase is Ratcliff's. Richard U. Ratcliff, *Urban Land Economics* (New York: McGraw-Hill, 1949), p. 321.
2. Homer Hoyt, *The Structure and Growth of Residential Neighborhoods in American Cities* (Washington, D.C.: Government Printing Office, 1939).

offered a concept which would explain and predict the location within a city of certain types of residential uses—the so-called "sector theory." The theory, in turn, implied a succession of occupancy in dwellings originally built for higher-income families. Thus filtering was the dynamic element in the sector theory.

Hoyt's entire study has been subjected to much criticism by other urban economists. In such an important field criticism was nearly inevitable because of the manner in which the sector theory was originally put forward. Hoyt's study called attention to a number of variables affecting the character and evolution of residential neighborhoods, variables such as the distribution of income in the community as a whole, the community's rate of growth and changes in its composition, the quality level of new construction, and, of course, the spatial distribution of socioeconomic groups and of construction activity. Having identified these variables, however, Hoyt failed to present an operational framework in which they might be integrated. He provided only a generalized historical description with vague suggestions about the interrelation among the variables.

Another failing of the original Hoyt

From Wallace F. Smith, "A Review of the Filtering Controversy," Chapter 1 of **Filtering and Neighborhood Change**, Research Report No. 24, pp. 1-16, 1964. Reprinted by permission of the Center for Real Estate and Urban Economics, Institute of Urban and Regional Development, University of California, Berkeley.

study was that it raised policy questions without analyzing their broad implications. The study can be criticized on this score because the work was done for a public agency and was thus to influence public policy. This gave critics of the sector theory even more reason to quarrel with Hoyt and to view his theory as a *justification* of the historical pattern of urban development, a pattern which to many persons seemed undesirable. Rightly or wrongly, Hoyt was soon accused of espousing as "ideal," a form of urban development which he had actually merely described.

Both of these defects in Hoyt's sector theory—the non-operational nature of his concepts and his avoidance of implied policy questions—could be remedied by creating a model of competitive equilibrium. With a theoretical structure for translating any given set of demand and supply conditions into an equilibrium pattern of residential neighborhoods, the implications of policy or other exogenous changes can be worked out.

The present study is an effort to provide and to illustrate just such an analytical framework as a more flexible tool for both forecasting and policy formulation than the sector theory. First, however, we should explore the sector theory and some of its criticisms and developments in some amount of detail.

The Sector Theory

Hoyt's essential notion was that as a city grows the fashionable residential district moves outward from the center, always in the same direction. Obsolete houses left behind by the well-to-do become occupied by the poor, particularly the recent immigrants, so that the wedge-shaped path taken by the high-income group contains both extremes in the income spectrum. This sector is the most vital, the most active, and the most troublesome. Middle-

income families group themselves about the well-to-do, hoping that some of the status of the fashionable areas will rub off on them.

The study in which the sector theory was first presented provided a number of specific rules which seemed to determine the direction which fashionable residential development would take. It moves toward high ground, for example, along the best transportation routes, and avoids "dead ends" which would impede further outward movement. Pre-existing commercial nuclei may exert a pull on high-income residential development, and real estate promoters may succeed in bending the normal direction of this growth.

These points constitute the sector theory "proper." In Hoyt's original study, however, there are at least two other major components. He discusses and illustrates the impact of the community's rate of growth upon the pattern of neighborhood change: ". . . the rapidity of population growth is one of the most important determinants of the differences in the speed with which high-grade neighborhoods move to new locations."[3]

The other major component of Hoyt's neighborhood study is a series of qualifications by which he seeks to offset the inflexibility and the simplification of his model. For example, he explains that: "The rate of neighborhood change may vary even between cities growing in population at the same rate. The component elements of the added population are of extreme importance."[4] Thus, if there were a great wave of poor immigrants, the cast-off mansions of the rich would not suffice to house them; the predetermined pattern of movement within the city would have to be altered in some unspecified way. In this portion of his study Hoyt seems to anticipate, if not to satisfy, some of his later critics.

3. Hoyt, *op. cit.*, p. 84.
4. Hoyt, *op. cit.*, p. 88.

Firey's Cultural Ecology

Hoyt's simplified and "deterministic" description of residential patterns was attacked by Walter Firey in his book *Land Use in Central Boston.*[5] Firey, a sociologist, found the sector theory inadequate as an explanation for the irregular pattern of residential settlement in the Boston area. He wrote: "The spatial distribution of upper class families is apparently more variable than the Burgess-Hoyt theories appreciate. Whatever forces are responsible for it must be sought in less simple and tangible factors than those of inevitable radial extension or inevitable ringlike expansion."[6]

Chief among the "less simple and tangible factors" were "spatially referred values," according to Firey, meaning that cultural attachments could confound the neat determinism of the sector theory. Fashionable districts might spring up wherever an atmosphere of gentility was once centered, and then such districts might persist in or recover such character again and again, long after the sector theory would have moved them into new suburban tracts. Cultural cohesion among low-income minority (especially immigrant) groups might account for their clustering in the slums, rather than a need for hand-me-down housing. The filtering mechanism seemed to Firey too much apart from human volition and non-economic motivations.

Perhaps the most imaginative part of Firey's work is his suggestion of a grand balancing of several objectives from among several cultural groups, within the limited confines of the metropolis. We read:

. . . there is always a problem of allocating space. In such allocation there must always

5. Walter Firey, *Land Use in Central Boston* (Boston: Harvard University Press, 1947).
6. *Ibid.,* p. 55.

be a *proportionalization of ends* [emphasis Firey's]. This arises out of the fact that every community has a multiplicity of component ends, and not merely one or a few ends. Hence it becomes necessary to achieve a certain "balance of sacrifices" in order that every component end of the community will in some degree be attained.[7]

The further exposition of this idea is rather badly bungled by Firey, but it is not too difficult to read into it an appeal for the development of some mathematical programming technique by which the resources of the community, both real and cultural, may be divided among groups of the population in some optimal way.

Filtering as a Source of Low-Income Housing

The concept of filtering certainly antedates Hoyt's study of residential neighborhoods. For example, a British government report in 1929 contained this statement:

When post-war building began, it was hoped that there might be a gradual movement of the working-class population of the slums into better houses. This might occur in two ways, either the slum dweller might go direct into a new house or a process of "filtering up" might occur under which the slum dweller would move from the slum into a better pre-war house, the tenant of which would, in his turn, move into a new house. Both of these processes have, of course, occurred, but on a disappointingly small scale.[8]

By making the filtering process an essential element in his model of residential dynamics, Hoyt implicitly raised an important policy issue. If public policy

7. *Ibid.,* p. 326.
8. "A Policy for the Slums," report of a special committee of the National Housing and Town Planning Council (London: P. S. King and Son, Ltd., 1929), p. 16. (Quoted in *European Housing Policy and Practice,* by Ernest M. Fisher and Richard U. Ratcliff, Federal Housing Administration, 1936, p. 61.)

seeks to raise housing standards among low-income groups, must it—or should it—work through the filtering process? From the standpoint of housing welfare, is the filtering process desirable? Is it even inevitable?

It seems clear that Hoyt originally had no intention of grappling with this issue. In reply to criticism on the filtering issue as it affects low-income housing he said: ". . . the purpose of the study was economic and any appraiser who mixes economic and 'social' factors, or ability to pay and need, will make a hash of both economics and social welfare."[9]

Yet the policy issue was there, the more emphatically because Rodwin could charge that Hoyt's sector theory was developed as a policy tool, to be applied by and through the Federal Housing Administration. The charge is contained in these words:

Perhaps Hoyt may not have intended it as such, but there is a strong emphasis in the study in favor of preserving the better neighborhoods rather than improving the poorer ones. That suspicion is further supported by the fact that the study was made for the Federal Housing Administration whose interest and experience to date have been primarily to protect its insured loans and which has shown little interest in other points of view.[10]

As a reflection on Hoyt's qualifications or his method of attack this remark by Rodwin seems to misfire. An objective, empirical review of urban development cannot be said to be "in favor of" one course of public action as opposed to some other. Hoyt did not even attempt to justify his sector theory as a normative description of ideal competitive allocation.

There is validity to the point raised by

Rodwin, however, in the sense that if the normal market process—i.e., filtering down of older houses—appears to provide only inadequate dwellings for the lower-income population, perhaps somewhat stronger and more direct measures are required. The argument, as developed with particular force by Ratcliff in his *Urban Land Economics*,[11] seems to have evolved in the following way:

1. It is perceived that housing markets usually build new dwellings chiefly for the well-to-do; older dwellings filter down to lower-income families —i.e., Hoyt's empirical generalization is accepted.
2. A social judgment is made that housing of low-income families is deficient. It is proposed to subsidize the construction of new dwellings for them.
3. Some groups—presumably real estate interests—object, point-out that in the course of time houses now being built will be available to the poor through the filtering process. Hence no interference with the market is required.
4. Welfare-minded economists retort that too great a period of time is involved, since the social pyramid is so narrow at the top and so wide at the bottom. In the great length of time needed to transmit a small volume of new housing to families now ill-housed, the filtered units will—in fact must—deteriorate. When they arrive at the lowest income level they will represent no improvement. Hence direct new construction is required to meet the low income needs.

9. Homer Hoyt, "Residential Sectors Revisited," *The Appraisal Journal* (October, 1950).
10. Lloyd Rodwin, "The Theory of Residential Growth and Structure," *The Appraisal Journal* (July, 1950).

11. Ratcliff, *op. cit.* (see especially Chapter 11).

The discussion had about reached this point in 1949, which saw the appearance of Ratcliff's book. It was less specifically developed by Ratcliff and Ernest Fisher as early as 1936 when the two reviewed housing programs in Europe.[12] As part of that review the two economists attempted to test the validity of the theory that housing standards may be improved through filtering. They did this by observing the experience of certain European countries, and their conclusion was:

. . . that no evidence has been adduced . . . that dependence can be placed on this procedure for a substantial improvement in the housing conditions of the lower-income group. Cures of a more positive nature are demanded.[13]

Their "test" of the theory, however, is unconvincing. In England they observed that between 1920 and 1930 there had been a high rate of building, chiefly for upper-income demand. Concurrently, ". . . from 25,000 to 35,000 unfit houses were demolished . . ." and ". . . a total of 5,943,462 dwellings were repaired. . . ."[14] Further, "The 1931 census indicates a definite improvement in the extent of overcrowding in the preceding decade. The average number of persons per occupied house dropped from 4.85 in 1921 to 4.38 in 1931." On the other hand, the doubling rate was unchanged at 1.21 families per occupied house; the average size of families, clearly, had decreased.

In Holland it was noted that construction volume had been stimulated by government aid. A government official was quoted: "Owing to the numerous unoccupied dwellings and the general fall in rents many flats of inferior standard have fallen empty and will be difficult to let." However, the reviewers conjectured that migration back to rural areas could account for some of the vacancy of low-rent dwellings.

The principal "test" of the filtering theory in the Fisher-Ratcliff study turns out to be a theoretical one. With the aid of an abbreviate frequency distribution of dwellings in England and Wales by rent, the authors point out that to supply 10 percent of the lowest group with better dwellings through the filtering process the housing stock at the highest level would have to grow by 45 percent, because the number of units in the former group is four and one-half times that of the latter. The authors considered such a volume of building to be unlikely: ". . . if the producers of housing are well informed of the demand situation there will be no overproduction in any grade of housing, and no surplus will be created."[15] This argument is repeated with only minor embellishments in Ratcliff's 1949 book.[16]

This theoretical argument, that any "surplus" of housing would curtail new construction, could leave the sector theory without its mainspring and would seem to contradict Ratcliff's candid admission that filtering is a "well recognized phenomenon." All new construction for a population already housed is necessarily redundant in a physical sense, but not in an economic sense. But the "no surplus" idea has a more fundamental flaw. A *subsidized* filtering process can indeed provide the requisite surpluses which will permit upgrading of low-income housing. Ratcliff (in particular) has made it appear that to achieve improvement in housing standards the choice is between an unsubsidized market filtering process and a subsidized public housing program. He has said "Filtering cannot be forced."[17] This seems to overlook the fact that public policy can, and often does, stimulate the

12. Ernest M. Fisher and Richard U. Ratcliff, *op. cit.* (especially Part IX).
13. *Ibid.,* p. 66.
14. *Ibid.,* p. 60.
15. *Ibid.,* p. 64.
16. Ratcliff, *Urban Land Economics,* p. 321.
17. *Ibid.,* p. 322. In his book Ratcliff himself contradicts the earlier "no surplus" idea. On page 332 he says: "It has been demonstrated here that filtering cannot take place except in the presence of a surplus."

filtering process. There is the FHA, the Home Loan Bank Board, The Federal Savings and Loan Insurance Corporation, and the legion of freeway builders to lure the relatively well-to-do suburban areas of new housing, leaving their older homes to families of relatively lower income. More direct inducements to accelerate filtering are also possible. Perhaps Ratcliff meant to say that filtering cannot be forced *without some public subsidy or other effort,* though it is difficult to imagine how a market process can be "forced" to accelerate *except* by a public program.

Because of this theoretical lapse Ratcliff (and Fisher) cannot be said to have provided the sector theory with a normative test. They were obviously arguing ex parte for public housing, obscuring rather than creating a set of equilibrium relationships.

Rodwin and the Issue of a Competitive Market

Of course, it is not obvious from Hoyt's work that the filtering process or the working out of the sector theory reflects an efficient, competitive allocation of urban resources by the private market. Perhaps the historical regularities which permitted Hoyt to develop his generalized descriptions of urban development stem from more or less universal imperfections in the housing market. If this be the case the sector theory is robbed of its usefulness as a benchmark of ideal behavior or as an instrument of policy.

Rodwin makes almost this charge in his extensive evaluation of the sector theory which appeared in 1950. He says:

Throughout the analysis, Hoyt has been dealing with the operation of a relatively laissez-faire competitive economy.
Real estate, however, is a notorious and oft cited example of just such market imperfections. Housing, in particular, reflects an additional complication because its long production period and durability contribute to

serious and prolonged marketing errors and maladjustments.[18]

But is the urban housing market so imperfectly competitive? Rodwin mentions the following conditions for "ideal" market performance:

"perfect knowledge and mobility"— but the entire brokerage profession (which some would claim to be overpopulated) and a major portion of newspaper lineage are devoted to the dissemination of knowledge; as for mobility, Hoyt's empirical observations are very largely a documentation of population movement.
"maximization of profit, many buyers and sellers, free entry and departure of productive factors"—but there can be little dispute that these conditions exist in one of the most atomistic of all commodity markets.
"homogenous products"—but product homogeneity is a requirement of two-dimensional *analysis,* not of optimal resource allocation. It is the function, after all, of an economic system to allocate resources among an essentially infinite range of heterogeneous products. The defect of analytical equipment ought not to be attributed to a type of product which is inherently heterogeneous, but Rodwin does so.

There are two other critical estimates of the market process in Rodwin's essay. As noted above, he calls attention to the durability of housing as an impediment to efficient market adjustments. Here he rather spectacularly misses the point of the filtering discussion and the sector theory; the movement of population through the housing stock is the competitive market's way of making use of a durable but deteriorating inventory. This is surely the import of Hoyt's bold

18. Rodwin, *op. cit.*

generalizations. Rodwin presumably would not see in the used car market, or in the markets for used machine tools, passenger airplanes, or household appliances a culpable market organization; why then for used houses? It is the nature of the product to go through a succession of less affluent or less particular users; there is nothing necessarily "imperfect" about the process of handing things down.

Lastly, Rodwin calls attention to the fact that land uses which are determined solely by private market considerations can give rise to notorious external diseconomies or "social costs." Factories produce smoke, and automobiles produce congestion. There are sins of neglect, too:

To compete in the urban land and housing market, uses must be income producing and rather high at that. Uses like playgrounds, parks and good minimum standard housing for low-income groups cannot or at any rate have not been adequately served under such a mechanism.

The need for public remedies for such conditions clearly is a value judgment on Rodwin's part, with which one may agree or disagree. Valid or not, however, the point hardly reflects on the sector theory or the filtering concept as a description of the urban market. One cannot blame a market for acting like a market.

Rodwin's low estimate of the housing market's performance—in which many other economists, planners and urbanists, generally concur—is not based upon a convincing demonstration that this particular market is ineffectively organized. Nor does Rodwin's disillusion with the market place make the sector theory seem less capable of predicting how the clockwork of the market place will tick. Rodwin's complaint is fundamentally with social attitudes, not with the sector theory. His intuition that the filtering process somehow harms low-income people cannot be supported with the analytical tools at his command. It remains an intuition.

Grigsby's Empirical Method

With the publication in 1963 of William Grigsby's *Housing Markets and Public Policy,* the sector theory's cartographic representation of housing market interactions gave way to a matrix approach. Though he concedes that his new formulation is "tentative and exploratory,"[19] Grigsby examines and describes promising new tools for urban analysis. He deals explicitly with the concept of filtering, pointing out that ". . . filtering is, in a sense, the subject of the entire book since, broadly speaking, it is the principal dynamic feature of the housing market."[20] The analytical portions of the book, then, can be construed as a new treatment of the filtering question.

How to define filtering, particularly for purposes of empirical measurement, has been a persistent problem, and Grigsby provides a good review of alternative definitions. The "traditional" definition is Ratcliff's:

This process [filtering] . . . is described most simply as the changing of occupancy as the housing that is occupied by one income group becomes available to the next lower income group as a result of decline in market price, i.e., in sales price or rent value.[21]

This definition has been found to be unsatisfactory in practice.[22]

19. William Grigsby, *Housing Markets and Public Policy* (Philadelphia: University of Pennsylvania Press, 1963), p. 28.
20. *Ibid.,* p. 99.
21. Ratcliff, *Urban Land Economics,* pp. 321-322.
22. For example, Grebler in his empirical study of New York's lower east side writes: "Commonly accepted notions of the operation of the filtering process are found to be ambiguous and inadequate when subjected to an empirical test, and a reformulation of the theory of filtering, which lends itself to verification, is suggested." Leo Grebler, *Housing Market Behavior in a Declining Area* (New York: Columbia University Press, 1952), p. 17.

The specific objection to Ratcliff's definition is that it speaks of changes both in *occupancy* (i.e., income level of occupants) and in *value,* as though the two were necessarily related. But in practice one may fall while the other changes in different degree, or different direction, or remains the same.

A reformulation was provided by Fisher and Winnick.[23] "Filtering is defined as a change over time in the position of a given dwelling unit or group of dwelling units within the distribution of housing rents and prices in the community as a whole." Thus, they chose to measure filtering in terms of changes in relative value rather than in terms of incomes of occupants.

Grigsby who generally seems to prefer the Fisher-Winnick reformulation suggests still another concept—that of filtering as an improvement in real housing standards among low-income families. That is, filtering would be said to occur only if low-income housing standards have been raised. He says:

Such a definition would hold that filtering (changes in house prices and rents) must be measured while holding income, quality, and space per person constant, or in more relaxed form, that filtering occurs only when value declines more rapidly than quality so that families can obtain either higher quality and more space at the same price, or the same quality and space at a lower price than formerly.[24]

This welfare concept of filtering does not play a role in Grigsby's stimulating discussion of market mechanisms. It is not consistent with his expressed belief that filtering is "the principal dynamic feature of the housing market,"[25] for the market may not in fact produce welfare effects.

The welfare issue seems to reduce to this: *optimum use* of given resources should not be confused with *improvement* in the supply or quality of those resources. In the traditional economic jargon, Rodwin, Ratcliff and others have failed to distinguish the problem of allocation from that of growth. Optimization in the use of a durable good requires shifting it about among different classes of users as its relative usefulness declines or rises. The shifting-about, in itself, affects welfare only as it is an efficient or an inefficient reallocation. Other market circumstances being unchanged, filtering in response to deterioration of the housing stock could well leave aggregate and individual housing welfare unchanged.

If filtering is to be understood as a basic pattern of market behavior then it must be defined as a response to any change in conditions of supply or demand—in the number or types of households or in their incomes, in the physical quality of the stock or any portion of it, or in construction of particular kinds of new units. The response must be measured in terms of occupancy of particular houses or neighborhoods by some different class of households.

This is still not a completely precise formulation; such is not required, for the data available to the student of a particular market will usually force him to adopt some workable definition. The important point is that the welfare question is best left either to deliberately contrived (and controlled) empirical tests (unlikely without massive financial support), or to careful deductive reasoning based on an operational model and realistic market data. The former is not yet available. The following chapter of the present study presents a hypothetical example of the latter.

23. Ernest M. Fisher and Louis Winnick, "A Reformulation of the 'Filtering' Concept," in *Social Policy and Social Research in Housing,* Robert K. Merton, ed. (New York: Association Press, 1951). Though Grebler's book (*op. cit.*) was published in 1952 it was available to Fisher and Winnick earlier and is referred to by them.
24. Grigsby, *op. cit.,* pp. 95 ff.
25. *Ibid.,* p. 99.

If filtering is thought of simply as a change in the allocation of housing units among households of different types, the method of analysis most appropriate to this concept would clearly involve a *matrix* of relationships among submarkets. This is precisely the formulation which Grigsby develops in his analytical chapters. Defining a set of submarkets in the Philadelphia metropolitan area, he illustrates flows among these submarkets on the basis of unpublished National Housing Inventory data and certain assumptions about the "second choices" which different households would make if their actual location were not available to them. The object is to provide a "matrix expressing relative degrees of substitutability among submarkets. . . ."[26]

Such a matrix is potentially capable of predicting market responses—i.e., shifts among submarkets, or filtering—which would result from certain essentially exogenous changes in market conditions, such as alterations in the characteristics of dwelling units. The matrix form permits an analyst to give appropriate attention to the *indirect* links between submarkets which might not be directly substitutable; thus,

Bargain house prices in Area A might be completely ignored by potential home buyers in Area C if the latter area were too far distant. These prices might, however, attract a segment of the market from Area B to Area A. This shift might in turn create values in B which would serve to capture a segment of the potential in C.[27]

In this way the entire housing market is seen to be interconnected.

Later portions of the Grigsby book examine issues of new residential construction volume, maintenance of residential structures, and residential renewal. The intention is to make use of the matrix concepts developed in earlier chapters,

26. Grigsby, *op. cit.*, p. 50.
27. Grigsby, *op. cit.*, pp. 34-35.

but the effort is not successful. Grigsby discusses the manner in which the existing stock of houses acts to discourage new construction, the extent to which expenditures on maintenance of the quality of the existing stock (as an alternative to new construction) are justified, and the renewal strategy which will get the best response from the private market.

The problem is that Grigsby's matrix model is not operational (nor does he claim that it is). It cannot simulate market responses to, say, redevelopment of a central slum area, or to development of a suburban middle-income tract. Hence his conclusions with respect to new construction, maintenance, and renewal do not flow out of the model.

The sector theory has been transformed into a matrix. Conceptually the matrix should be able to provide answers to welfare-type questions such as those having to do with the housing standards of low-income families as affected by subsidized or unsubsidized filtering, by renewal or public housing. It may also prove to be a much more precise tool for forecasts of construction activity and neighborhood change. In the following chapters efforts to develop it along such lines will be illustrated.

The sector theory was an empirical generalization which described the experience of many cities approximately but of no cities exactly. It generalized from events that were conditioned on certain social structures, technologies and public policies; wherever or whenever these things differ from those which Hoyt observed his implied forecasts of neighborhood changes are invalidated. The very agency which commissioned Hoyt's study has been as instrumental as any other single force in changing those conditions.

The sector theory was never intended, explicitly, to answer the welfare questions which so concerned its critics. But those questions must be answered as public resources in increasing volume are being directed toward improvement in housing standards. A more flexible means of describing competitive market interactions, particularly in response to alternative hypothetical public programs, was clearly needed.

The basic source of confusion over filtering stems from this close association of welfare issues with patterns of movement in an unregulated private market. This confusion would be heightened by a *definition* of filtering—i.e., of the basic dynamic force—in terms of achievement of a welfare aim.

In a mixed economy, the most effective model for all purposes is one which generates private market responses to all manner of exogenous forces, such as mortgage insurance, rising real incomes, shifts in tastes, public housing, population growth, increased property taxes, or earthquakes. As we are interested in changes in the use made of specific neighborhoods, the model must be considerably disaggregated. Then the impact of any proposed welfare program can be traced through each neighborhood in the community, and its real effect on housing welfare assessed.

WILLIAM H. FORM

The Place of Social Structure in the Determination of Land Use: Some Implications for a Theory of Urban Ecology

Deriving a satisfactory theory of land use change is a pressing problem for both ecologists and urban sociologists.[1] Most of the current thinking on this subject revolves around the so-called ecological processes. A brief inspection of the literature reveals, however, a lamentable lack of agreement on the definition, number, and importance of the ecological processes.[2] It is apparent that the economic model of classical economists from which these processes are derived must be dis-

carded in favor of models which consider social realities.

In studying land use change, this paper proposes that ecology abandon its subsocial non-organization orientations and use the frame of reference of general sociology. Even though the focus of attention of ecology may remain in the economic realm, a sociological analysis of economic behavior is called for. This means that most of the current ecological premises must be converted into research questions capable of sociological verification.

The first step is to analyze the social forces operating in the land market. Obviously the image of a free and unorganized market in which individuals compete impersonally for land must be abandoned. The reason for this is that the land market is highly organized and dominated by a number of interacting organizations. Most of the latter are formally organized, highly self-conscious, and purposeful in character. Although at times their values and interests are conflicting, they are often overlapping and harmonious. That is, their relationships tend to become structured over a period of time. From a study

1. For purposes of simplification this paper will limit itself to a consideration of land use change in middle-size, growing, industrial cities of the United States. Historical analysis of land use change is not within the province of this paper because of the methodological difficulties in reconstructing the ecological processes.
2. One reason for this confusion centers on the controversy whether human ecology should be related to or divorced from biological ecology. Amos H. Hawley claims that the difficulties of human ecology arise from its isolation from the mainstream of ecological thought in biology; see his "Ecology and Human Ecology," *Social Forces,* 22 (May 1944), pp. 399-405. Warner E. Gettys is of the opinion that human ecology should free itself from its primary dependence on organic ecology; see his "Human Ecology and Social Theory," *Social Forces,* 18 (May 1940), pp. 469-476.

From **Social Forces,** Vol. 32, No. 4, May 1954, pp. 317-323. Reprinted by permission of the University of North Carolina Press.

of this emerging structure one obtains a picture of the parameters of ecological behavior, the patterns of land use change, and the institutional pressures which maintain the ecological order.

Four Organizational Congeries in the Land Market

The interacting groups, associations, and relationships which comprise this emerging structure may be identified by asking such questions as: (a) Who are the largest consumers of land? (b) Which organizations specialize in dealing with land? and (c) Which associations mediate the conflicts of land use? Preliminary research suggests that, among the many associations and interests in American society, four types of social congeries or organizational complexes dominate the land market and determine indirectly the use to which land is put.

The first and perhaps most important of these congeries is the real estate and building business.[3] Since they know more about the land market of the city than comparable groups, it is suggested that the study of the real estate-building groups (along the lines of occupational-industrial sociology) would provide more insight into the dynamics of land use change then present studies which are based on the sub-social ecological processes. The analysis of real estate organizations is an especially good starting point to build a sociological ecology because these organizations interact with all of the other urban interests which are concerned with land use.[4]

The second social congeries which functions in the land market are the larger industries, businesses, and utilities. While they may not consume the greatest quantities of land, they do purchase the largest and most strategic parcels. Unknowingly their locational decisions tend to set the pattern of land use for other economic and non-economic organizations. Most of the land use decisions of these central industries and businesses are a response to peculiar historic circumstances in the community. Therefore it would seem fruitless to describe *a priori* the geometric shape of the city as a series of rings, sectors, or diamonds.

The third social constellation in the land market is composed of individual home owners and other small consumers of land. In a sense their position is tangential to the structure or important only under rather unusual circumstances. Most of their decisions on where to buy, when to buy, and what land to buy are fitted into an administered land market and are not, as many would assume, individual, discrete, free, and unrelated. The social characteristics of the consumers, their economic power, degree of organization, and relations to other segments of the community help explain the role they play in the market of land decisions.

The fourth organizational complex is comprised of the many local governmental agencies which deal with land, such as the zoning boards, planning commissions, school boards, traffic commissions, and other agencies. This organizational complex is loosely knit internally, for its segments often function at cross purposes. Their relations to other groups in the community vary with political currents. Unlike other organizations, these governmental agencies are both consumers of land and mediators of conflicting land

3. It appears that an interpenetration of organization and interests of these two groups is increasing so rapidly in American cities that for many purposes they may be conceived as one interest group.

4. This is strongly suggested by strikingly parallel studies in two different types of cities. Cf. Everett C. Hughes, A Study of a Secular Institution: The Chicago Real Estate Board (unpublished Ph.D. dissertation, University of Chicago, 1928); Donald H. Bouma, An Analysis of the Social Power Position of the Real Estate Board in Grand Rapids, Michigan (unpublished Ph.D. dissertation, Michigan State College, 1952).

use interests. Thus political agencies not only acquire land to placate private and public pressures, they are also called upon to resolve conflicts between different types of land consumers. Moreover, some of these governmental agencies try to fulfill a city plan which sets the expected pattern of the ecological development of the city.

These four organizational complexes[5]—real estate, big business, residents, and government—do not comprise all of the organizational entities which participate in land use decisions. However, they are the main ones. Once identified, the problem is to find the nature of the social relationships among these organizational complexes. Is a stable pattern discernible? How does the pattern manifest itself in physical space? In what direction is the pattern emerging as a response to inter-institutional trends in the broader society? To answer these questions, an analytical model is needed to appraise the social relations among the four organizational congeries identified above.

Elements in the Analytical Model

Sociologists have not yet derived completely satisfactory schema to analyze inter-organizational relations, either in their structural or dynamic dimensions. However, ecologists are dependent on such general schema as have already been worked out. Some of the basic elements in the analytical scheme to appraise the relations among the four land consuming groups are described below.

1. The first element in the model is the amount and types of economic resources which each "grouping" has to buttress its land use decisions. Obviously the resources of the four "groupings" differ considerably. Thus, industry has property and capital which are somewhat greater and more mobile than those of the real estate industry. In addition to their tax resources, governmental agencies have the power to expropriate land in their own name or in the name of any interest which can control them. The individual home owner and the small businessman, on the other hand, not only have the smallest but the least organized economic resources. The economic resources of each group must be carefully gauged in each community where there is a contest to control particular parcels of land. However, economic resources comprise only one cell in the paradigm needed to analyze the structural setting of land use changes.

2. The second factors which merit consideration are the manifest and latent functions of each "grouping" in the land market. Thus, the functions of the real estate industry include, in addition to maximizing its earnings, bringing knowledge of available land to different segments of the community. Moreover it tries to organize the land market and control land values to assure itself stability and continuity of income.[6] In the process of so doing, the realtors come into contact with political, citizen, and business agencies.[7] The land interests of big business, on the other hand, are much more specific and spasmodic than those of the real estate business. The desire of businessmen to have large stretches of land under one title, to obtain land additions close to present plant operations, and to dominate the landscape of the community, often

5. Each organizational complex is comprised of groups, associations, aggregations, social categories, and other types of social nucleations. To facilitate communication, the term "grouping" will be used to refer to this organizational complex. I am indebted to Professor Read Bain for pointing to the need for terminological clarification in matters dealing with interaction of different types of social nucleations.

6. See Everett C. Hughes, "Personality Types and the Division of Labor," in Ernest W. Burgess (ed.), *Personality and the Social Group* (Chicago: University of Chicago Press, 1929), especially pp. 91-94.

7. *Ibid.* Hughes indicates that the real estate industry is a loose federation of different types of businessmen. Each type plays a different role to correspond to its clientele and market.

leads them to make diseconomic decisions which are in conflict with those of other groups.

Government agencies have quite different and sometimes conflicting functions to perform. Among these are: protecting present tax values, acquiring parcels of land for specific public or quasi-public uses, altering certain land use patterns to conform to the plan of the "city beautiful," acting as a clearing house and communication channel for those who need land use data. Most important, they mediate conflicts in land use and exercise their legitimate authority for groups which curry their favor.

Individual residents and small businessmen are mostly concerned with preventing changes in land use. They tend to be defensive-minded and sentimentally attached to their neighborhoods and to fight to prevent the encroachment of usages which would threaten present economic and social investments. In general, resident groupings do not play dynamic roles in changing urban land usages.

3. The internal organization of these four groupings differs considerably. Knowledge of this factor is important to assess the degree to which they may be mobilized to fight for control over desired lands. Often small, unified, and organized groups with meagre economic resources can dominate larger, richer, and more loosely knit groups in a land struggle. These four "groupings" differ in their internal structure and external relations. There is an urgent need for research to study the cleavages, cliques, alliances, and arrangements found within and among these groupings. However, certain trends may now be noted.

The real estate industry is slowly emerging from a haphazard aggregation of local agents to a tightly organized professional or fraternal society which seeks to establish control over the land market.[8] Big business and industry, on the other hand,

8. *Ibid.*

have typically bureaucratic structures capable of marshalling tremendous resources in the community for or against other land-interested groups. Municipal agencies, though individually powerful, are often unaware of each other's activities. Therefore they tend to comprise a loosely knit set of bureaus which often function at cross purposes. Since many governmental agencies are tied into the fabric of private associations, they are united to common action only under unusual external pressures. Individual residents and small businesses are the most loosely organized.[9] In fact, they tend to remain unorganized except under "crisis" conditions.

4. Each grouping has an accountability pattern differing in its consequences for action. Each has different kinds of pressures and influences to which it must respond. For example, the real estate organizations are primarily accountable to themselves and sometimes to their largest customers, the building industry and the utilities. On the other hand, the local managers of larger corporations tend to be accountable to other managers, stockholders, and board members who may not reside in the community. Thus, local managers may have to respond in their land decisions to pressures generated outside of the community. Municipal agencies are formally accountable to the local citizens who are, *according to the issues,* realtors, individual landlords, businessmen, educational, political, or any other organized interest.

Each of the four social congeries being considered is organized differently as a pressure group interested in land use policies. Each, in a sense, lives in a power situation which consists of its relation to the other three. Different kinds of alli-

9. Higher status areas of the city are usually more formally organized to protect land uses than are lower status areas. The formation of neighborhood "improvement and betterment" associations stabilizes land use and resists the invasion of other land uses.

ances are made among them and among their segments, depending on the issues. The types of collective bargaining situations which arise among them must be studied in a larger context in order to understand the sociology of land use decisions. For example, businessmen who are sometimes appointed as members of city planning commissions may be constrained to play roles incongruous with their business roles. As members of residential and recreational organizations they may be forced to make decisions which may seem contradictory to their economic interests.

5. In land decisions involving the whole city, the image which each grouping has of the city must be appraised. The realtors are usually the most enthusiastic boosters of the city. They envision an expanding city with an ever-growing land market, for this assures them income and security. Consequently, they exert pressure on the municipal agencies to join them in their plans for the "expansive city."

However, municipal officials do not conceive of the city primarily as a market. They see it as the downtown civic center, the city beautiful, and the planned community. Although desiring an expanding city, they are equally concerned with the politics and aesthetics of locating parks, avenues, schools, and other services. At times their aesthetic-political plans conflict with the boom ideology of the realtors and the industry-oriented plans of businessmen. Indeed this is almost inevitable in some situations, for politicians must secure votes to remain in office. Plans for different areas of the city must be weighed in terms of how they affect votes.[10]

The industrialists' conception of the community tends to be more partial than that of any other group. Since industries often have allegiances to non-community

enterprises, they are not necessarily enamoured by the vision of the expansive city or the city beautiful. They are inclined to view the city primarily as their work plant and residence. They usually regard the existence of their enterprises as economic "contributions" to the city. Therefore they feel that any land decisions they desire as businessmen, golfers, or residents are "reasonable and proper" in view of their "contribution" to the locality. When their demands are not met, they can threaten to remove the industry to more favorable communities.

The citizen's view of the city is also segmental. He tends to envision it as his neighborhood, his work plant, and "downtown." These are the areas he wants to see protected, beautified, and serviced. Since residents do not comprise a homogeneous group, obviously their community images differ. The nature of the intersection of the segmentalized city images of these four social congeries provides one of the parameters for studying their interaction. Needless to say, other nonecological images that these groups have of themselves and of each other have a bearing on their relations. However, since the problems of this paper are more structural than social psychological, this area will not be expanded.

6. Other factors in the analytical scheme may be derived which point to the different orientations and relationships existing among these groups. For example, their primary value orientations differ. For government, community "service" is ostensibly the chief value; for real estate, it is an assured land market; for business, it is profitable operations; for the resident, it is protection. Another distinction may be in terms of the amount and type of land interests of the groups. Whereas real estate is interested in all of the city's land, municipal agencies are more interested in communal lands, and industry is concerned with its private land use. The future task of sociologists will be to select

10. For an illuminating case history of this, see William Foote Whyte, *Street Corner Society* (Chicago: University of Chicago Press, 1947), pp. 245-252.

the most important interactional areas of these groups to locate the forces responsible for land use patterns and changes.

Land Use Changes in a Zoning Context

Following the selection of some of the important dimensions in the paradigm, the task is to characterize briefly the pattern of the relationships among the four "groupings." In the broadest sense, the model to be followed is that used in analyzing the collective bargaining structure and process.[11] An excellent place to begin observing the "collective bargaining" relations among these groupings is in the zoning process of cities. Zoning is recommended because the methodological problems of studying it are minimal, and yet the kinds of intergroup relations found there are not unlike those in non-zoning relations.

Since almost every city of any consequence in the United States is zoned, any significant deviation in a pattern of land use necessarily involves a change in zoning. It would appear then that sociologists and ecologists should study the relations of land-interested agencies to municipal agencies.[12] Most zoning commissions tend to freeze an already existing pattern of land use. If they formulate plans for city growth, these plans tend to correspond to a sector image of expanding areas of ongoing land use. This results in a rather rigid ecological structure which inevitably generates pressures for changes. Since such changes involve obtaining the consent of municipal agencies, a political dimension insists itself in the study of ecological processes.

Traditional ecologists may object to this social structural and political approach to problems of land use change. They may suggest that the ecological concept of "dominance" provides the answer to the question of which group will determine land use or land use change. An examination of this concept in the ecological literature reveals a basic shortcoming. Ecological dominance refers to economic control in the symbiotic sense; it provides no analytical cues to appraise the relations among organizations which comprise the structure dealing with land use changes.[13]

Traditional ecologists may object that the proposal to study the relations of the four land "groupings" in a political context is merely a methodological innovation, in that the *results* of such a study would point to the same pattern of land use change available by recourse to the traditional ecological processes. They may reason that determination of land use after all is an economic struggle or process, in which the most powerful economic interests determine to what use land will be put. While it is true, they may agree, that this process is not as simple and as impersonal as hitherto believed, the end result is very much the same.[14]

The writer has recently been gathering cases of zoning changes that have oc-

11. Herbert Blumer, "Sociological Theory in Industrial Relations," *American Sociological Review,* 12 (June 1947), pp. 271-278. See also the articles in Richard A. Lester and Joseph Shister (eds.), *Insights into Labor Issues* (New York: The Macmillan Company, 1948); William Foote Whyte, *Pattern for Industrial Peace* (New York: Harper and Brothers, 1951); H. D. Lasswell, *Politics* (New York: McGraw-Hill, 1936).

12. Richard Dewey, "The Neighborhood, Urban Ecology, and City Planners," *American Sociological Review,* 15 (August 1950), p. 502-507.

13. See R. D. McKenzie, *The Metropolitan Community* (New York: McGraw-Hill, 1933), pp. 81-131; Don J. Bogue, *The Structure of the Metropolitan Community* (Horace J. Rackham School of Graduate Studies, University of Michigan, 1949), pp. 10-13.

14. In this respect the position of ecologists is not significantly different from the Marxist analysis of land use changes. This may explain the appeal of the ecological approach to some otherwise sophisticated sociologists. I am indebted to G. P. Stone for the elaboration of this idea.

curred in Lansing, its fringe, and in the outlying areas. In addition, cases have been observed where attempts to institute zoning changes have failed. In both types of changes the questions were asked: (a) Did naked economic power dictate the decision to change or not to change the zoning? (b) Could the outcome of these cases be predicted by using a cultural ecology frame of reference? A brief analysis of the cases revealed that no simple economic or cultural analysis could account for success or failure of zoning changes. The actual outcome could be better analyzed on the basis of the paradigm suggested above. Four cases will be briefly summarized to suggest typical kinds of alliances found in attempts to change land use.

In Lansing, the zoning commission may recommend changes in zoning but the City Council must approve of them. This means that all changes in land use must occur in a political context. In 1951, a local metal fabricating plant asked the Council to rezone some of its property from a residential to a commercial classification so that an office building could be erected on it. The residents of the area, who are mostly Negroes, appeared before the Council urging it to refuse the request on the ground that the company had not lived up to legal responsibilities to control obnoxious smoke, fly-ash, traffic, and so on. In addition, they contended that space for Negro housing was limited and rezoning would deprive them of needed space. Moreover, they hinted that the company's request came indirectly from a large corporation which would eventually obtain the property. In short, they urged rejection of the request not on its own merits but on the basis that the company had not lived up to its community responsibilities. Company spokesmen denied any deals, promised to control air pollution, and got labor union spokesmen to urge rezoning. The Council complied. Four months later all of the properties of the company, in-cluding the rezoned area, were sold to the large corporation in question.

Here is a clear case of economically powerful interests consciously manipulating land uses for their purposes. The question arises: why did not the large corporation itself ask for rezoning? Apparently, it realized that greater resistance would have been met. The local company is a medium-sized, old, home-owned enterprise which has had rather warm relations with its employees. The large corporation, on the other hand, is a large impersonal, absentee-owned corporation that has at times alienated local people.[15] Therefore, its chances of getting this property without fanfare were increased by the use of an intermediary.

Yet business does not always win. In another case, a respectable undertaker established a funeral parlor in a low income residential area. The local residents objected strenuously to the presence of the business. The legal aspects of the case remained obscure for a time because the undertaker insisted he did not embalm bodies in the establishment. In a preliminary hearing he appeared to have won a victory. The aroused residents called upon the Republican ward leader who promised to talk to the "authorities." Just before a rehearing of the case, the undertaker decided to leave the area for he was reliably informed that the decision would go against him.

Struggles between businessmen and government do not always work out in favor of the former. Currently, the organized businessmen of East Lansing are fighting an order of the State Highway Commission which has passed a no parking ordinance to apply to the town's main thoroughfare. The retailers are fearful that they will lose business if the order holds. Since business will not be able to expand in the same direction if the order

15. For example, workers insist that during the depression the company recruited Southerners rather than local labor.

holds, pressure to rezone residential areas in the community for commercial and parking purposes will be forthcoming. In a community where residents are a strong, vocal, upper middle status group majority, such pressure may be resisted strongly. Clearly a power struggle involving the State, local businessmen, local government, and the residents will determine the ecological pattern of the city.[16] A knowledge of their relationships is needed to predict the outcome of the struggle and the future ecological changes in the community.

S. T. Kimball has documented a case where the failure to inaugurate zoning involved the same kind of social structural analysis of group relations as suggested above. Kimball studied a suburban rural township where the upper middle status groups failed in a referendum to obtain zoning in the face of an industrial invasion of the area. An analysis of the case showed that the issue would be misunderstood if studied as a struggle of economic interests. In fact, the industrial interests were not an important variable in the case. The failure of the referendum was accounted for by analysis of five types of relationships: (a) those among the suburbanites, (b) those within the township board, (c) those between the supervisor and his constituents, (d) those between the farmers and suburbanites, and (e) those between the supervisor and the informal "leaders" in the community.[17]

This paper has proposed the need to consider social structure in addition to ecological and cultural factors in the study of changes in land use. The traditional ecological processes are no longer adequate to analyze changes in land use. These processes, like most ecological concepts, are based on models of eighteenth century free enterprise economics. Yet fundamental changes in the structure of the economy call for new economic models which in turn call for a recasting of general ecological theory. The new vital trend of cultural ecology does not do this adequately, for it considers the structural realities of urban society only indirectly.

This paper proposes that ecological change be studied by first isolating the important and powerful land-interested groupings in the city. Certain elements in an analytical scheme have been proposed to study the collective bargaining relationships among these groupings. The *forces* that operate in land use change may well be studied in the socio-political struggles that are presently occurring in the area of zoning. A brief survey of some changes in urban zoning points to the greater adequacy of the sociological over the traditional ecological analysis for understanding and predicting land use changes.

16. My colleague, G. P. Stone, suggests that it begins to appear that the State's position will force a very unusual ecological phenomenon: a business district turning its back to the main highway and reorienting itself to the "backyards," as it were.

17. Solon T. Kimball, "A Case Study of Township Zoning," *Michigan Agricultural Experiment Station Quarterly Bulletin,* 28 (May 1946) p. 4.

EDWARD J. KAISER AND SHIRLEY F. WEISS

Public Policy and the Residential Development Process

The land use pattern emerging on the edges of U.S. urban areas is the result of a complex, interdependent, private-public process in which the private realm appears to take most of the initiative. This article focuses on the chainlike nature of the single-family residential development process, with a view toward implications for local planning policy. In order to guide the development process, a mix of policies must affect every decision link in the chain, from the predevelopment landowner's decision to hold or sell his land to the household's decision to move and its selection of a new residence.

If public policy is to be effective in guiding patterns of new urban growth, it must be based on a realistic understanding of the development process. Our conceptualization of the development process is based on empirical research as well as supporting literature.[1] The research in-

cluded in-depth interviews with decision agents and field data from North Carolina Piedmont cities along with some nationally representative data. We focused on the predevelopment landowner, the developer, and consumers of various classifications including white and nonwhite as well as buyers and renters. We feel that the basic ideas about the residential process, the role of public policy, and the modeling approach could be widely applicable. However, the specific relationships found in the analyses and models calibrated on individual cities cannot be generalized to the same extent.

An Overview of Residential Land Conversion

The transition of a unit of land on the periphery of an urban area can be traced

1. For discussion of the nature of the urban land development process, see: William L. C. Wheaton, "Public and Private Agents of Change in Urban Expansion," *Explorations into Urban Structure* (Philadelphia: University of Pennsylvania Press, 1964); Twin Cities Metropolitan Planning Commission, *Determinants of Residential Development*, Background Document No. 1, Series on Determinants of Urban Development (St. Paul: March 1962); Roscoe C.

Martin, Frank J. Munger *et al., Decisions in Syracuse: A Metropolitan Action Study* (Garden City, New York: Anchor Books, Doubleday and Company, Inc., 1965); and Shirley F. Weiss, John E. Smith, Edward J. Kaiser, and Kenneth B. Kenney, *Residential Developer Decisions: A Focused View of the Urban Growth Process*, Urban Studies Research Monograph (Chapel Hill: Center for Urban and Regional Studies, Institute for Research in Social Science, University of North Carolina, 1966).

From the **Journal of the American Institute of Planners,** Vol. XXXVI, No. 1, January 1970, pp. 30-37. Reprinted by permission.

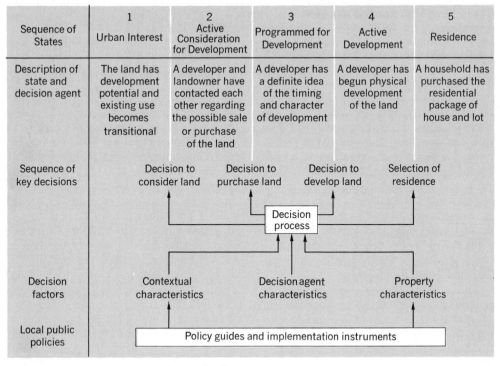

Sequence of States	1 Urban Interest	2 Active Consideration for Development	3 Programmed for Development	4 Active Development	5 Residence
Description of state and decision agent	The land has development potential and existing use becomes transitional	A developer and landowner have contacted each other regarding the possible sale or purchase of the land	A developer has a definite idea of the timing and character of development	A developer has begun physical development of the land	A household has purchased the residential package of house and lot
Sequence of key decisions		Decision to consider land Decision to purchase land Decision to develop land Selection of residence			
			Decision process		
Decision factors		Contextual characteristics	Decision agent characteristics		Property characteristics
Local public policies		Policy guides and implementation instruments			

Figure 1. The Residential Land Conversion Process

from an initial state of nonurban use through several stages of development to a state of active residential use by a household. Such a conception of the land conversion process is illustrated in the top row of Figure 1. Thus, the land could be considered as (1) acquiring interest for urban use; (2) being actively considered by an entrepreneur for purchase and development; (3) being programmed for actual development; (4) being developed; and, finally (5) being purchased and inhabited by a household. Local public policies might be conceived as attempts to control the probabilities of units of land changing from one state to another. That is, the planner could attempt to lower probabilities for development decisions in some areas of the planning jurisdiction (thereby discouraging and postponing de-

velopment) while increasing the probabilities in other areas (encouraging or accelerating the transition from nonurban to urban use).

Land Transition Decisions

Underlying land conversion is a complex set of decisions by assorted individuals and groups, each guided by his own incentives—the household by basic needs and preferences, the developer-entrepreneur by the profit motive, the predevelopment landowner by a mixture of pecuniary and personal motives. These decisions, shown on the second row of Figure 1, are the ones that land use controls must influence if local government is to affect the pattern of change.

Decisions of the Predevelopment Landowner[2]

Land assumes the state of *urban interest* when someone considers it to have urban development potential. At this point, determination of the land's value is based on the prevailing, usually agricultural, use as well as the potential urban use. The existing land use then becomes transitional.[3] Sometimes the transitional nature of the use is obvious, for example, junk yards and used car lots. But sometimes it is disguised as the previous rural use—this is carried on to help the landowner through the transitional period. Meanwhile the old use is becoming increasingly obsolete, due to nearby existing and anticipated urban development.

The landowner's decision to hold or sell the land depends upon income and satisfaction received from the land and his expectations about the land's future value compared to its present market value.[4] The income aspect of the landowner's decision includes such things as net annual holding cost of the land, costs that would be incurred in shifting to another investment, opportunity costs of capital, and time period of the investment.[5] In addition, the landowner's decision also depends on his relative satisfaction from such qualitative aspects as farming as a way of life, the land as a residence, love of the land, or privacy and status.[6] It ap-

pears that these motives are too important to be ignored in the explanation of the predevelopment landowner's decision to hold or sell.[7]

The Developer's Locational Decision[8]

At the next stage, the developer becomes the key decision-maker, taking the initiative by deciding to develop the land as a means of profit rather than relying on land value appreciation for capital gain. If the developer feels that (1) a site may generally fill the specifications for the market he chooses to meet, or (2) there exists a potential demand for housing appropriate to a specific tract and if he can obtain a tentative agreement from one or more landowners to sell, he options the land and proceeds to a purchase decision. This purchase decision represents the most crucial step. The prior decision to consider the land is anticipatory; the latter decision to develop the land is anticlimactic to this decision, for development typically follows within less than five years and probably in a form not much different than the development programmed at the time of purchase.[9]

2. See, Edward J. Kaiser, Ronald W. Massie, Shirley F. Weiss, and John E. Smith, "Predicting the Behavior of Predevelopment Landowners on the Urban Fringe," *Journal of the American Institute of Planners,* XXXIV, No. 5 (September 1968), 328-33.
3. See, Jack Lessinger, "The Determinants of Land Use in Rural-Urban Transition Areas: A Case Study of Santa Clara County, California" (unpublished Ph.D. dissertation, University of California, 1957).
4. Smith, 'Toward a Theory of Landowner Behavior," chap. 3.
5. *Ibid.,* pp. 32-46.
6. *Ibid.,* p. 54.

7. For research on income aspects, see, Sherman J. Maisel, "Land Costs for Single-Family Housing," in *California Housing Studies* (Berkeley: Center for Planning and Development Research, University of California, 1963).
8. The basic ideas of the developer in this paper are derived from Weiss, Smith, Kaiser, and Kenney, *Residential Developer Decisions;* Edward J. Kaiser, *A Producer Model for Residential Growth: Analyzing and Predicting the Location of Residential Subdivisions,* Urban Studies Research Monograph (Chapel Hill: Center for Urban and Regional Studies, Institute for Research in Social Science, University of North Carolina, 1968); and Wheaton, "Public and Private Agents of Change."
9. See, Weiss, Smith, Kaiser, and Kenney, *Residential Developer Decisions,* p. 58, for the experience in the Piedmont Cities of North Carolina; and Grace Milgram, *The City Expands* (Institute for Environmental Studies, University of Pennsylvania, March 1967), pp. 287-9, for the experience in northeast Philadelphia.

The Household's Decisions[10]

In the course of development into residential packages, the unit of property is divided into smaller parcels to accommodate individual dwelling structures. The number of decision-makers involved in this stage of the development process is many times greater than the number involved in earlier stages, but each decision has a smaller impact on the total. However, in the aggregate this step determines the population that will reside in a particular sector of a community's space. By implication, it determines the relative success of the developer's locational decisions in terms of whether the subdivision development proceeds swiftly, slowly, or stalls. It determines, in part, the nature of the demand for urban services. Finally, it establishes linkages, particularly movement linkages, to other spatial, social, and economic sectors of the community.

The household's selection of a residence is actually the second of two related decisions in the residential mobility process. The first is the decision to move. It almost always precedes the selection of a residence in a relatively independent manner. An understanding of the decision to move and its correlations with previous dwelling unit characteristics, geographic divi-

10. The main sources for this paper's ideas concerning the household's residential decisions are: Edgar W. Butler and Edward J. Kaiser, "Prediction of Residential Movement and Spatial Allocation," A Paper presented at the Annual Meeting of the Population Association of America, Atlantic City, N.J., April 11, 1969 (Mimeographed.); The Research Team: Edgar W. Butler, F. Stuart Chapin, Jr., George C. Hemmens, Edward J. Kaiser, Michael A. Stegman, and Shirley F. Weiss, *Moving Behavior and Residential Choice: A National Survey* (Chapel Hill: Center for Urban and Regional Studies, Institute for Research in Social Science, University of North Carolina, in cooperation with the Highway Research Board, National Academy of Sciences, March 1968); and Peter H. Rossi, *Why Families Move* (Glencoe: The Free Press, 1955).

sions within the urban area, and household characteristics can give the planner an estimate of the areas of the city where outmoving and replacement in-moving will occur and where used housing stock will be vacant or turned over and will, at the same time, produce estimates of the composition of households in the market for housing. The second decision, selection of a residence, provides the opportunity to link the residential mobility process with the land conversion process.

Factors Influencing Decisions

Referring to Figure 1, and going one step deeper into our conceptual framework, we introduce three types of decision factors (from interviews, literature search, and statistical tests) to clarify the decisions which explain the transition of property through the land conversion and development process. The lower portion of Figure 1 shows the three types of decision factors: contextual, decision agent, and property characteristics. Each type influences the decision process of each decision agent in an unique way.

Contextual factors include considerations that limit and determine the overall rate and type of change in the urban community and the general structure of decision agent and property characteristics. Contextual characteristics are of two types—socioeconomic and public policy. Some of the socioeconomic contextual factors suggested are economic structure and growth prospects of the urban area, community leadership, condition of local housing market, local development industry concentration and competition, and the prevailing psychology of the period. The public policy context includes annexation powers and the exercise of these powers; capital improvement and services policies affecting quality, gross spatial pattern, and costs of transportation, water, sewerage, and schools; and subdivision regulations, building codes, zoning, and land use plans.

Property characteristics provide an operational means to describe the units of land (sites, parcels, zones, blocks, grid cells) about which decisions are made. It has been useful to distinguish three types of property characteristics. *Physical* characteristics, such as topography and soil conditions, are inherent in the land and cannot be changed except by direct modification of the site itself. *Locational* characteristics, on the other hand, are not inherent in the land but are derived solely from the relative location of the site within the spatial pattern of urban activities. Accessibility to employment areas is an example. Changes in locational characteristics depend on spatial shifts in the surrounding context of community activities and values since the site itself is fixed in space. The third category, *institutional* site characteristics, represents attributes that are applied directly to the site, but that are not inherent in the site. Imposed by social institutions, they include such things as the site's zoning category.

Property characteristics can be changed during the residential development process, so they are not necessarily the same for each decision along the way. For example, the developer in his manufacturing process may change the zoning, or he may build or provide a site for a school, shopping center, or industrial operation, thus changing the locational characteristics of the site. Construction of dwelling units and other improvements adds completely new property variables, such as size of the dwelling unit, type of dwelling unit, and environmental amenity afforded. These were nonexistent for the predevelopment landowner. They became part of the intended market strategy for the developer when he made his locational decision. To the household they are probably the most important of the property characteristics.

Decision agent characteristics, includ-

ing those of the landowner, developer, and household, are the third important set of factors influencing location of residential development. Decision agent characteristics cannot be directly influenced by public policy in the way contextual factors and property characteristics can, but they are too important to be ignored in a discussion of policy-making and the development process, because they play a large role in determining the direction and the strength of the impact of contextual and property characteristics, and hence of public policy, on residential development.

Public Policy, Decision Factors, and the Development Process

The influence of local public policies on the evolution of land is indirect since it is channeled through contextual and property characteristics, as shown at the bottom of Figure 1. The important aspects of public policy are its content, differentiation of the application of this content to properties over space and time, and finally expected variation among different types of decisionmakers' reactions to the policy content. These aspects bear on the decision of the predevelopment landowner to hold or to sell, the locational decision of the developer to develop a property or to look for another location, and the household's decision to move and its selection of a residence.

The landowner's decision to hold or sell. Public policy appears to affect the transition of land through predevelopment landowner selling by influencing (1) the landowner's estimated future stream of income and expenses; and (2) the present or future market value of the land. By decreasing estimated incomes and/or increasing expenses, a policy will lower the value of land to the owner and hence increase the probability that its value to him is less than the current market value. That would, of course, increase the probability that the landowner will either sell or change the use to one creating higher income relative to expenses.

Perhaps the strongest local policy influence on annual expenses is *taxation*.[11] Taxes on raw land may often represent the major cost in holding it as an investment. Smith found that cost of taxes more often than not exceeds current income, even though taxes as a percentage of the land's market value may be minimal.[12] In addition, the impact of taxes is direct; each year the landowner must find the funds to meet this cost. The impact of local policy on the landowner's income is felt through zoning limitations affecting the property's economic use. However, findings from Smith's study suggest that current income considerations are usually not as important as expenses in the transitional landowner's calculus.

The impact of local policy on the estimated future value of the land is less direct than its influence on current income and expenses. Both present and future market values greatly depend on locational characteristics, such as prestige level of the location, as well as accessibility and institutional characteristics, such as zoning protection, availability of public services, and their relationship to subdivision regulations. In general, if all these exist, the present market value may compare very well with the expected future market value.

Because of interactions between decision factors, effectiveness of policy as an influence on transition of land to urban use will depend very much on other contextual and property characteristics as well as on decision agent characteristics. For example, effectiveness of tax policy will depend on general rate of land value appreciation in the area, spatial distribution of decision agent income, and importance of nonpecuniary motives for holding land. First, "in areas with very rapid rates of appreciation, say on the order of 20 percent, only very heavy taxes on land would eliminate the investment potential" of holding land.[13] Second, the impact of heavy taxes on wealthy landowners is not as great because the rate of return on alternative investments may be lower. Third, the impact will be less strong on landowners who have significant nonpecuniary motives in addition to their pecuniary motives for holding land, because these intangible motives increase the present value to the landowner but do not affect market value.

Statistical analyses bear out the importance of decision agent characteristics as a key factor in land sales. In fact, our statistical analyses indicate they are even more important than property characteristics. Least likely to sell are those living on the land, those who are not retired, those who own the land singly, and those who at the start of the study period had held the land longer than ten years but less than forty years. Most likely to sell are absentee owners, along with owners who are retired, own the land jointly, or have had their land either for a very short time or for a very long time.[14] Property characteristics do have some effect—land contiguous to urban development is more likely to be sold than land not so situated. Also, the effect of landowner characteristics is stronger for tracts on the fringe of the urbanized area than it is for tracts within the built-up area or tracts further out.

The developer's locational decision. Again, the influence of local public policy on the residential developer's decision process is primarily channeled through contextual factors and property characteristics. But, just as in landowner and

11. A. Allan Schmid, *Converting Land from Rural to Urban Uses* (Baltimore: The Johns Hopkins Press, 1968), pp. 43-6.
12. Smith, "Toward a Theory of Landowner Behavior," p. 47.
13. Smith, *ibid.,* pp. 74-8, Table 2, pp. 99-100.
14. Kaiser, Massie, Weiss, and Smith, "Predicting the Behavior of Predevelopment Landowners," pp. 329-30.

consumer decisions, the developer's characteristics affect his reaction to property characteristics and contextual factors. Public policy can affect the developer's expected costs, expected revenues, and risk of the investment.

Our study indicates that the effect of contextual, property, and developer characteristics on marketability and revenue tends to make cost considerations secondary to the developer. If this is generally true, local public policy that affects revenues would tend to have more leverage than policy that affects costs. Our interviews indicated that, as an influence in the locational decision, estimated effects of property characteristics on marketability of the residential product far outweigh estimated effects on the cost of producing the product. One reason may be that cost implications for various sites are not as uncertain to the developer nor do they tend to vary as much from site to site. In general, the higher the price range, the more important are the estimated marketability effects of the site characteristics as opposed to cost considerations.

Of the property characteristics affecting marketability, locational and institutional characteristics are clearly the most important. Both the statistical analyses and the reply "location, location, and location" (to the interview question about the three most important factors in the land purchase decision) support the importance of locational characteristics. Of these, social prestige level, a variable little affected by public ·policy other than school location and quality, is clearly the most important. Local public policy may have a substantial effect over a period of time on the accessibility of the site either directly through governmental investment policies concerning transportation improvements and school and recreation facilities, or indirectly through zoning for shopping and employment activities, but these are not as important as social location. More encouraging to the planner is

the finding that institutional characteristics imposed by local public actions, such as availability of urban services, zoning protection, and school district lines that tend to reflect differential standards, appear significant in some developer decisions.

Despite the greater importance of the estimated marketability effects of site characteristics in our study area, the developer cannot afford to concentrate on marketability at any cost. The locational decision still requires weighing of the costs; thus it is possible for public policy to influence locational decisions by affecting change in the spatial pattern of land and physical development costs. This is illustrated by the fact that in spite of the developer's greater concern for marketability, the most influential public policy affecting developer decisions in our major study city, Greensboro, was public facility policy affecting the developer's costs. The city of Greensboro will install streets and water and sewerage systems in residential subdivisions within the city limits for the developer "at cost," up to a maximum charge. If actual costs to the city exceed that maximum charge, the city absorbs the overcost. Further, the city effectively finances the developer within the city limits by allowing up to five years to pay at a nominal interest rate. The effect of this overall policy on residential growth in Greensboro is reduction of scatteration by encouraging a more compact development pattern. Such a policy also tends to eliminate the influence of topographic and soil conditions on subdivision location within the city limits by absorbing the cost of adverse construction conditions.

The developer's assessments of costs, revenues, and marketability are tempered by his consideration of investment risk. A substantial portion of the developer's entrepreneurial activity and strategy while holding an option and considering purchase is directed toward ascertaining and reducing these risks. Part of the risk in the development industry stems from the general rule that analysis of marketability is unsystematic and the facts are weak. This appears especially true of the controlling factors—those concerning estimates of the level of market demand and the proper mixture of house, lot, physical neighborhood, and location to meet consumer preferences in that market.[15] Intensifying the developer's concern with risk are his generally low level of available capital within the firm and the correspondingly strong need for financing by inherently conservative financial intermediaries, first for development and later for homebuying.

Unclear and changeable policies concerning annexation, school district boundaries, extension of public utilities, enforcement or changes in subdivision regulations, zoning regulations, building codes, health codes, and taxation and assessment practices can increase risk, thereby discouraging any but the most conservative type of development and encouraging scatteration. At the same time, clear and relatively stable policies can have the more desirable effect of distinguishing areas where development is to be encouraged from areas where it will be discouraged, rewarding appropriate innovation and reducing some of the fluctuation between shortage and excess in various apartment and single-family housing markets. In addition to stable and clear policies, Wheaton and others have suggested the additional possibilities of information collection, analysis, and dissemination to assist the many decision agents in reducing risks in the city building industry.[16] There is even the more direct approach

illustrated by the development participation policy of Greensboro which reduces uncertainty about the cost of improvements by placing an upper limit on the developer's costs.

Developer characteristics, such as size of firm, entrepreneurial approach, and nature of the production process used, influence locational behavior under similar property and contextual factors by affecting the relative attraction of different kinds of sites. In our empirical tests and modeling efforts, we have found significant differences between the locational decisions of large-scale developers (those developing over 100 lots per year) and the locational behavior of small-scale developers. While both are influenced by property characteristics, large developers are much more responsive to them and therefore to public policy than small developers.[17] Further, the two categories almost appear to be looking for very different combinations of site characteristics. For example, large developers tend to choose sites closer to the CBD, an elementary school, and employment centers, with public utilities available. Small developers tend to select the opposite kind of site.[18]

The price market preferred by the developer also influences his selection of site characteristics and hence the location of his subdivisions. Tests relating site characteristics to the price range of houses indicate that higher priced subdivisions are more sensitive to socioeconomic prestige level of the site than lower priced subdivisions, while middle and lower priced subdivisions are more sensitive to zoning, availability of public utilities, and amount of nearby development.[19]

Policy and the household's decision. In a private market economy the influence of local governmental policies on household decisions is not readily apparent. Excep-

15. This unsystematic approach to decisions by development entrepreneurs appears to be a definite characteristic of the industry. In addition to our interviews, see, Wheaton, "Public and Private Agents of Change," p. 168; and see Twin Cities Metropolitan Planning Commission, *Determinants of Residential Development,* p. 31.

16. Wheaton, "Public and Private Agents of Change," pp. 194-5.

17. Kaiser, *A Producer Model for Residential Growth,* p. 44.

18. *Ibid.,* pp. 27-31.

19. *Ibid.,* p. 44.

tions are open housing laws discouraging private market discrimination practices, therefore removing constraints that affect household locational choice, and financial aids in the form of rent subsidies or mortgage insurance. Also, local public policy can affect the course of change in a developed neighborhood through the level of services provided, housing and health codes, and zoning changes in the vicinity. By providing services, protecting the area from incongruous uses, and discouraging neglect of physical improvements, local government encourages maintenance of a residential area and discourages mobility. However much of the potential for maintenance or deterioration is incorporated in the quality of construction and planning of the original development, and much of the force for change is beyond control of local public policy especially in the socioeconomic context that governs the area's economic vitality, residential and population trends, and federal and state policy regarding financing for used and new housing.

The limited effectiveness of public intervention in the household's decisions suggests that governmental influence could be more effectively applied toward the developer's choice of types of residential packages to be produced in various locations through zoning, for example. Especially important are the developer's decisions about characteristics of the dwelling unit because much of the consumer's moving decision and housing choice appears to be based on the dwelling unit and the neighborhood as opposed to the accessibility portion of the residential package.

Although distance to work is a factor in some planned moves, in our research no difference was noted between prospective movers and stayers in regard to current accessibility in minutes to such services and amenities as grocery stores, shopping centers, downtown, doctor's offices, hospitals or clinics, parks, playgrounds, and elementary schools.[20] With respect to accessibilities of the residences after the moves, there appears to be little difference in time distance to work or services between central city residents and suburbanites, rich and poor, or renters and owners, although there is some between white and nonwhite. The findings relating to the limited role of accessibility in consumer choice suggest two possibilities.

First, that modeling and policy-making based on these research findings would differ substantially from many existing land use planning models in the deemphasis of accessibility as a determinant of residential location. Second, linking the developer and consumer model, as will be suggested below, implies that some of these additional housing characteristics should be part of the description of the developer model output in order to facilitate residential choice, since consumers appear more concerned with the dwelling unit and neighborhood than with accessibility.

Linked Decision Agent Models

Thus far we have discussed three separate decision agents in the residential development process, the predevelopment landowner, the developer, and the household. A possible system linking these decision agent models is illustrated in Figure 2.

In this system, the spatial distribution of new single-family subdivision houses would be estimated by the *developer* model, possibly supplemented by a *landowner* model to simulate the variation in availability of sites from the landowner's viewpoint. An estimate of supply of vacated existing housing units would be created by the residential *mobility* model. The mobility model would also estimate the intrametropolitan movers who, along with estimates of in-migrants and newly formed households, provide the numbers and types of households seeking homes. A

20. The Research Team, *Moving Behavior and Residential Choice*, p. 281.

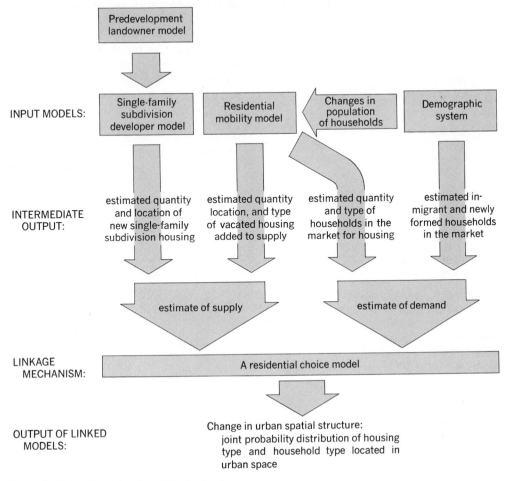

Figure 2. Linked Decision Agent Model System

third model, the *residential choice model,* links housing supply and demand, matching households with housing units. The resulting output could describe distributions of housing and households seeking homes. A third model, the *residential* would provide the planner with estimates of other useful intermediate aspects of the urban residential process, such as the areas of the planning jurisdiction most attractive to developers, the areas most attractive to homebuyers, and the areas most likely to contain predevelopment landowners willing to sell.

Preliminary Results of Producer Model

As an example of such a model, we have developed a pilot version of a producer-oriented model, based on the mathematical form of the discriminant function. Inputs are property characteristic vectors representing a site, and output is the likelihood of the subdivision occurring on that site within a finite time period. Results of some preliminary tests in the use of the model are shown in Table 1. Adequate assessment of the effectiveness of the discriminant model form using site characteristics as predictor variables would require more exhaustive tests in a variety of cities, using a number of configurations for the zones described by site characteristics during several time periods. However, the table

Table 1. Correct Classifications by the Producer Oriented Discriminant Model

Category of subdivision (each category should read "unsubdivided vs . . .")	Per centage of sample cells classified correctly[a]
Subdivided (without regard to developer type or price range)	64.7
Small developer subdivision	51.7
Large developer subdivision	76.0
Low price range subdivision	66.3
High price range subdivision	51.9
Small developer, low price range subdivision	64.0
Small developer, high price range subdivision	77.9
Large developer, low price range subdivision	77.5
Large developer, high price range subdivision	92.4

[a] Applied to the 1961-63 time period sample using coefficients calibrated on the 1958-60 time period sample.

shows that the predictive capacity of the operational model in the 1961–63 time period, using parameter coefficients calibrated in the 1958–60 sample, ranged widely from a rather unsatisfactory 51.7 percent for "small developer" subdivisions to a highly accurate 92.4 percent for "large developer" subdivisions. High price subdivisions and large developer subdivisions were more accurately classified than other types of subdivisions while small developer subdivisions were less accurately classified.

This type of model is more an impact assessment model than a predictive model. It traces the impact of changes in policy

related factors such as zoning, availability of water and sewer, and accessibility. It can map the impact of these policies in a given context by mapping the spatial distribution of likelihood of a particular change in state of the land. However, it is not an allocation model in the sense that it will actually distribute a given number of acres or other units of residential growth. A simulation model for allocation of growth units could be constructed using the probabilities produced by this version of the model.

Conclusions

While recognizing the geographic limitations of the empirical data on which much of this paper is based, we are convinced that a decision agent orientation to studying and modeling residential growth can be extremely useful. It provides an alternative modeling outlook to the more common aggregation of the development process. Using population projection methodology as an analogy, we see the decision agent modeling approach as disaggregating the residential growth process into important components, just as the cohort-survival method of population projection disaggregates the components of population change for separate examinations of the parts and a better understanding of the whole. Further, we feel that this emphasis on disaggregation of the residential growth process will provide insights particularly well suited to the problem of planning and coordinating local public policies. In the end, it is the moving and investment decisions by individuals and organizations that must be influenced if public actions and policies are to effect changes in urban spatial structure.

Along this line, the research suggests that the planner should look toward *mixes* of policies, some of which are aimed at landowners, some at developers, some at consumer households in already built-up areas, and some at households in the housing market. For example, a taxation policy that encourages selling may not necessarily lead to urban residential use of the land unless the site is also made profitable for residential development by other policies. Also, the research suggests that for landowners, policies that affect expenses have more leverage than policies that affect current income, while the reverse is true for developers. Furthermore, property characteristics that seem to have little impact on the predevelopment landowner's inclination to sell have considerable influence on the developer in his purchase decisions.

Analysis of the actions and attitudes of the owners, producers, and consumers of residential land reveals an extremely interdependent pattern, similar to a sort of three-dimensional spiderweb that can be moved by impact in any corner. Local public policies and implementation devices to influence urban residential growth must be determined in terms of a *chain of decisions,* responding to many direct and indirect channels of influence.

LAWRENCE A. BROWN AND ERIC G. MOORE

The Intra-urban Migration Process: A Perspective

In recent years there has been increasing emphasis on understanding the role of the individual decision-making process in influencing patterns of human behavior. When a particular aspect of behavior involves several complex decisions, recognition of interrelations of separate decisions and identification of factors affecting their outcome form an important preliminary step in developing a capability for predicting patterns of such behavior.

The present paper provides a framework for study of residential movements within the urban area by considering the relevant decision-making processes of the household which is the basic decision-making unit.[1] On the basis of existing research a sequence of decisions is postulated and an attempt is made to specify the main factors which influence the outcome of each decision. Particular attention is given to the spatial context in which these decisions are made.

The basic reasons for approaching the study of intra-urban migration in this way are twofold. First, existing aggregate-level

models do not possess a high degree of predictive power; understanding the nature of decision-making processes at the level of the individual may provide a fruitful strategy for identifying variables to be included in subsequent formulations at the aggregate level, and a conceptual basis for the design of such models. Second, and more important, the understanding of the nature of individual responses to environmental conditions will provide a sounder basis for evaluating a number of decisions related to planning of growth, development, and reorganization of urban areas.

Considerable stimulus for the approach adopted in this paper derives from Wolpert's study of the decision to migrate.[2] Wolpert integrates Simon's concept of *intendedly rational* behavior with the field-theory ideas of Lewin and Meier to provide a framework for the study of migration in general.[3] The basic concept developed is that of *place utility,* which es-

1. It is believed that a framework similar to that presented here would be applicable and useful for other types of migration decisions, including those of commercial or industrial enterprises.

2. Julian Wolpert, "Behavioral Aspects of the Decision to Migrate," *Papers of the Regional Science Association,* Vol. 15 (1965), pp. 159-169.

3. Herbert A. Simon, *Models of Man* (New York, New York: John Wiley, 1957); and Kurt Lewin, *Field Theory in Social Sciences* (New York, New York: Harper and Row, 1951).

Adapted by the authors from **Geografiska Annaler**, Series B, Vol. 52B, No. 1, 1970. Reprinted in revised form by permission of **Geografiska Annaler**, Stockholm, Sweden.

sentially measures an individual's level of satisfaction or dissatisfaction with respect to a given location.[4] If the place utility of the present residential site diverges sufficiently from his immediate needs, the individual will consider seeking a new location. The resulting search for and evaluation of dwelling opportunities takes place within the confines of the intended migrant's *action space*. In the context of intra-urban changes of residence, action space is defined as a subset of all locations within the urban area, this subset comprising those locations for which the intended migrant possesses sufficient information to assign place utilities.

In the above context, migration may be viewed as a process of adjustment whereby one residence or location is substituted for another in order to better satisfy the needs and desires of each intended migrant; i.e., in order to increase place utility of the residential location occupied. The nucleus of this paper consists of elaboration and modification of these basic behavioral notions, their explicit extension to the intra-urban case, and their integration with relevant findings of sociologists and psychologists.

The remainder of the paper is divided into two sections: first, an examination of factors leading to the decision to seek a new dwelling, identified as Phase I of the migration decision; second, a discussion of procedures involved in searching for and evaluating a new dwelling, identified as Phase II of the migration decision.

Phase I: The Decision to Seek a New Residence

It is assumed that the members of a household and the activities they perform constitute a simple behavior system.[5] The environment of this system is seen to consist of characteristics of its dwelling unit, its neighborhood, and the location of its dwelling unit in relation to other nodes in the household's movement cycles. This environment both influences the behavior of the household and is influenced by its behavior.

The environment provides a continuous source of stimuli to which the household responds. Certain of these stimuli will constitute *stressors* for a given household. In other words, they will be perceived as either disrupting or threatening to disrupt the established and desired patterns of household behavior. The result is a state of *stress*.[6] It is important to note, however, that both perception of given environmental elements as stressors and the response to stress situations vary from household to household. Appley and Trumbell, for example, note that

It seems likely that there are differing thresholds (of tolerance to stress) depending on the kinds of threats that are encountered,

5. In a *simple* behavior system all elements contribute directly to the system output, whereas in a *complex* behavior system, a separate coordination or control subsystem is included which does not contribute directly to the system output. For an extensive discussion see P. G. Herbst, "A Theory of Simple Behavior Systems," *Human Relations,* Vol. 14 (1961), pp. 71-94, and 193-240.

6. The discussion in this paper maintains these definitions of stress and stressor. It should be noted, however, that different definitions of stress and related concepts abound and that no single definition has yet proved completely satisfactory. For a discussion of this point, see Mortimer H. Appley and Richard Trumbull, *Psychological Stress* (New York, New York: Appleton-Century-Crofts, 1967); or Richard F. Lazarus, *Psychological Stress and the Coping Process* (New York, New York: McGraw-Hill, 1966). Herbst, *op. cit.,* in his discussion of simple behavior systems, and Julian Wolpert, "Migration as an Adjustment to Environmental Stress," *Journal of Social Issues,* Vol. 22 (1966), pp. 92-102, in his discussion of the migration decision both use the terms stress and strain.

4. Geographers have traditionally recognized two sets of attributes of a location: those which relate to the physical characteristics of the *site,* and those which relate to the accessibility characteristics of *situation.* Thus, place utility might be regarded as a composite of site utility and situation utility.

and that individuals would be differentially vulnerable to different types of stressors. In other words, not only must a situation be of a given intensity to lead to stress, it must also be of a given kind for a particular person.[7]

Although individual responses to stress may vary considerably, it is a valid goal of research to attempt to predict in probabilistic terms which people will be adversely affected by a stressful situation.[8] Thus, with respect to intra-urban migration, one might identify the characteristics of households which will perceive given environmental elements as stressors, as well as the relationship between household characteristics and the household's migration response to specific urban environments.

In this paper measures of stress are not discussed. Rather, we seek to specify the role of stressors, stress, and stress-response in the migration decision; and to employ concepts related to these elements to identify pertinent questions in the context of intra-urban changes of residence.

In broad terms stressors relevant to migration behavior derive from disparity between the collective needs of the household and the characteristics of its environment.[9] For any single household, the stress associated with a given situation may be reduced to or maintained at tolerable

limits by: (1) adjusting its needs; (2) restructuring the environment relative to the household so that it better satisfies the household's needs either of which would result in a decision *not* to migrate, or (3) relocating the household, either in part or in whole.[10]

As an example, consider a need with definite spatial expression: access to the place of employment. Suppose that a household head who busses to work is offered a better position at a company whose location is not readily accessible by public transportation from his present residence site. If this situation is perceived as a stressor and if the resulting stress exceeds some threshold level (relevant to that individual), the situation may be resolved by a decision to forego the advancement (adjustment of needs), by purchase of an automobile which will reduce the expenditure of time in journeying to work (restructuring the environment by changing its attributes relative to the household at a fixed location), or by moving the residence to a site which is more accessible to the new employment opportunity (relocating the household).[11] If the last is perceived as a viable alternative and a decision to seek a new residence is made (the terminal point of Phase I), the household proceeds to the stage of search and evaluation of other dwellings. It should be noted, however, that a household may subsequently return to Phase I to consider alternatives to relocation, engaging in some sort of *in situ* adjustment. It may

7. Mortimer H. Appley and Richard Trumbull, *op. cit.*, pp. 7 and 10.
8. Richard S. Lazarus, J. Deese, and Sonia F. Osler, "The Effects of Psychological Stress Upon Performance," *Psychological Bulletin*, Vol. 49 (1952), pp. 293-317, see particularly page 307.
9. Place utility, as defined by Wolpert, would reflect the disparity between household needs and environmental offerings. For a discussion of place utility within the context of a framework such as that proposed here, see Lawrence A. Brown and David B. Longbrake, "On the Implementation of Place Utility and Related Concepts: The Intra-Urban Migration Case," in Kevin R. Cox and Reginald Golledge, eds. *Behavioral Studies in Geography: A Symposium* (Evanston, Illinois: Northwestern University Studies in Geography, Number 17, 1969).

10. Stress reducing behavior which does not involve relocating the household is here termed adjustment *in situ*. The probability of this type of adjustment increases with an increase in the number of years a household has occupied a particular residential site. See George C. Myers, George Masnick, and Robert McGinnis, "The Duration of Residence Approach to a Dynamic Stochastic Model of Internal Migration: A Test of the Axiom of Cumulative Inertia," *Eugenics Quarterly*, Vol. 14 (1967), pp. 121-126.
11. The threshold level referred to may be compared to the concept of *threshold reference point* put forth by Wolpert, *op. cit.*

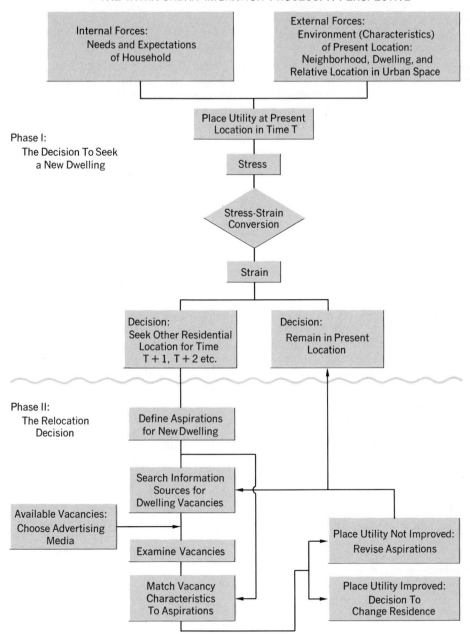

Figure 1. A Model of the Residential Location Decision Process

happen that its search for a new residence is sufficiently frustrating that the household later decides to adjust its need set (1) or restructure its present environment (2) rather than continue to search (Figure 1).

A state of stress is often the result of a significant change in the household's environment or in its needs. On the basis of past research, occurrences significantly affecting individual reaction to the environment include such things as the encroachment and spread of residential and commercial blight in the household's neighborhood; a change in the racial or ethnic composition of the neighborhood; relocation of industrial sites, either closer to or farther from the dwelling; and changes in the accessibility between neighborhoods as a result of changes in transportation technology (the construction of high speed limited access freeways or of modern mass transit lines, etc.).[12] Occurrences significantly affecting the needs of each household include a change in occupation, position (rank or job level), income, or socioeconomic class; an increase or decrease in family size; a change in employment site, a change in marital status; or advancement in one's life cycle. Any of these changes in environment or needs may therefore lead to a situation similar to the employment relocation example in which the household must make a decision as to how it is going to cope with the stress.

Phase II: The Relocation Decision

Having decided to seek a new residential location, the household must search out and evaluate vacancies until a decision is made either to relocate or to abandon the search and adjust *in situ*. The processes of search and evaluation are sufficiently distinct to be considered separately, and this approach is taken in the following discussion. In practice, however, search and evaluation are carried on more or less simultaneously and together constitute *the relocation decision* (Phase II).

12. See, for example, John B. Lansing and Gary Hendricks, *Automobile Ownership and Residential Density* (Ann Arbor, Michigan: Survey Research Center, Institute for Social Research, University of Michigan, 1967); and Peter H. Rossi, *Why Families Move: A Study in the Social Psychology of Urban Residential Mobility* (New York, New York: Free Press, 1955).

EVALUATION PROCEDURES

Until the decision is made to seek a new residence, the household's requirements with respect to characteristics of a dwelling and its environment are considered to be implicit. They are identified only in terms of a transition from an expression of satisfaction to one of dissatisfaction with respect to a given component of place utility at their present dwelling. After deciding to move, however, these requirements must be made explicit in order to provide criteria for evaluating vacancies. Criteria might include environmental prerequisites (such as a neighborhood's accessibility to work or the quality of its schools) that determine the subareas within the urban space which may be profitably searched, and dwelling-specific requirements (such as the number of rooms and purchase cost) that determine which dwelling is finally selected within the searched space. Empirical evidence such as that offered by Lansing and Hendricks and Rossi suggests that such needs are multidimensional.[13] On each dimension, furthermore, upper and lower limits may frequently be defined; for example, too little dwelling space may produce tensions through a lack of individual privacy, while too much dwelling space may create problems of excessive effort in upkeep.

To aid further conceptual development, the notion of an *aspiration region* is formulated. Its boundaries at each time t may be defined by two n-element vectors $A_L(t)$ and $A_U(t)$ which represent the lower and upper limits for the set of n dwelling criteria specified by the household at time t. These vectors are compared to another n-element vector $X_j(t)$ in which each element i represents a measure of criterion i for vacancy j, as judged by each intended migrant. $X_j(t)$ is termed the *vacancy characteristic vector*. A par-

13. John B. Lansing and Gary Hendricks, *op. cit.,* and Peter H. Rossi, *op. cit.*

ticular vacancy at time t, $v_j(t)$ *may* be considered acceptable by a migrating household if the perceived vacancy characteristics lie completely within the household's aspiration region (i.e., for every dimension the observed vacancy characteristic lies between the lower and upper bounds for that dimension).

Many factors have been suggested as influential in determining selection of the new residence.[14] The following list is representative but not exhaustive: (1) Accessibility: to the CBD, major highways, public transportation to place of work, shopping centers, schools, and recreational area; (2) Physical characteristics of neighborhood: physical condition of street and sidewalk, layout of street patterns, quietness, privacy, spaciousness, and beauty of the locale; (3) Services and facilities: the quality of public utility services, schools, police and fire protection, and home delivery services; (4) Social environment: neighborhood prestige, socioeconomic, ethnic, and demographic composition, and perceptions of neighborhood friendliness; (5) Individual site and dwelling characteristics: rental or purchase value, maintenance costs, lot size, spatial configuration, house size, design and state of repair, number of rooms. However, in any given search the individual usually focuses on a small subset of these factors which he considers critical in his own context. In part this restriction also stems from his inability to evaluate choices based on too many attributes.

SEARCH BEHAVIOR

The search behavior of an intended migrant household consists of the utilization of and reaction to a variety of information sources or channels. In this context, a number of critical elements may be iden-

14. See, for example James W. Simmons, "Changing Residence in the City: A Review of Intra-Urban Mobility," *Geographical Review,* Vol. 58 (1968), pp. 622-651.

tified in a given search situation: (1) the information available to the searcher; (2) the information possessed initially by the searcher; and (3) the way in which the searcher utilizes the available information and that which he already possesses. In addition, the passage of time greatly influences the behavior of the search and must be given specific attention.

Information availability. The intended migrant household attempts to acquire information regarding the characteristics of vacancies within the urban area. For each vacancy, such information is disseminated through one or several channels from a set of possible information channels. Each channel is effective over different distances, areas, and socioeconomic groups within the urban area. Channels considered important in previous empirical studies include: (1) *Mass media:* this refers primarily to newspaper advertisements, although radio, television, and billboards also fall into this category; (2) Real estate agents and other *specialized agencies;* (3) *Display of information* concerning the vacancy at its site or elsewhere; (4) The *network of personal contacts* of the owner of the vacancy, the former or current tenant of the vacancy, or other individuals who have acquired knowledge of this vacancy.

The utilization of a particular information channel by the owner of a given vacancy is a function of such variables as his subjective evaluation of success in filling the vacancy by using a given channel, the cost or effort involved in using a given channel and the time remaining until the vacancy must be filled.

From the point of view of search behavior, a significant aspect of information channels is their biases with respect to the information they carry and the audience they reach. Three types of biases may be readily identified:

1. The source is selective with respect to the *types of vacancies* and, by implication, the *type of neighborhood* for which infor-

mation is presented. For example, low rent apartments are more likely to be advertised in newspapers than on real estate agents' lists; furthermore, specific real estate agents specialize in particular residence types, such that some concentrate on high-value single-family dwellings and others prefer to deal in moderate rental apartments.

2. The source is spatially, economically, or socially selective with respect to the *audience* through which information is disseminated. Many newspapers, for example, provide low quality information to an audience within a large area, whereas personal contacts provide much more detailed information to a relatively restricted area. Similarly, some newspapers are directed towards a relatively small and select area (e.g., *neighborhood* newspapers), whereas others are directed to a relatively wide area and audience; real estate agents generally have some spatial range to their territory and socioeconomic selectivity with regard to clientele; and individual households define their acquaintance circles on a variety of social, economic and spatial criteria.

3. The probability of information regarding a given vacancy being available at a specified location decreases with increasing distance from the source of information (which may not be the same as the vacancy location). This *distance-decay* property is highly variable in form, being barely perceptible for newspapers with large circulation, and very marked for information gathered by direct observation of vacancy signs.

In attempting to determine the effect of these various biases, it is evident that the specification of all points at which information is available is not feasible for an entire urban area. However, it is possible to provide aggregate statements for each information channel by recording the density of carriers per unit area (e.g., the number of newspapers, real estate agents, or personal contacts). In this way, the pattern of available information regarding a specific vacancy can be represented by a density surface which, in general, will exhibit distance-decay characteristics, given the spatial properties implicit in the three biases discussed above. The total information available at a given location would then be represented by the sum of the heights of the individual density surfaces. The basic problem then, is to specify the characteristics of the density surfaces for each information channel.

Initial information possessed by the searcher. Prior to the search for information regarding dwelling vacancies, the potential migrant possesses an image of the urban area based on information acquired from previous experiences. This image relates to the characteristics of neighborhoods or even of entire sectors of the city rather than of specific dwellings. It is characterized by a variable surface describing the amount of information possessed by the household about each location. Thus, the household's image of the urban area will be spatially selective insofar as it has no knowledge regarding certain parts of the urban area and some locations will be better *known* than others.

In order to conceptualize this reality, we have adopted the term *awareness space* to refer to those locations within the total urban space about which the intended migrant household has knowledge (or knowledge above some threshold level) before search begins.[15]

Prior knowledge of the characteristics of the urban area derives from two basic sources: the household's day-to-day ac-

15. For the most part, our concept of awareness space conforms to Wolpert's concept of action space. Also it is similar to the psychologist's concept of a cognitive map. See, Julian Wolpert, "Behavioral Aspects of the Decision to Migrate," *op. cit.*, and Edward C. Tolman, "Cognitive Maps in Rats and Men," *Psychological Review*, Vol. 55 (1948), pp. 189-208. Some empirical work in an urban setting is reported in Kevin R. Lynch. *The Image of the City* (Cambridge, Massachusetts, MIT Press, 1960).

tivities which yield information from *direct contact,* and information derived at second hand from such channels as acquaintances' experiences and mass media. The set of locations associated with the first source defines the household's *activity space,* and the set of locations associated with the second source defines the household's *indirect contact space.*

Although there is little empirical research relating directly to household activity space as a composite entity, Chapin has provided a general discussion of activity systems in a spatial context and their relationship to urban structure.[16] Furthermore, work has been undertaken on particular behavior patterns which have a direct influence on the form of the activity space. This includes the household's journey-to-work, urban travel behavior, and the characteristics of acquaintance circles.[17] Although this research does not provide a formal statement of the spatial characteristics of activity spaces, it does indicate that the density of information per unit area for a given household tends to exhibit distance-decay properties with the household's location as the center of the density surface. Furthermore, the activity space possesses a marked orientation along the major transport arteries to the city center.

Utilization of information. Past research on information flows has often taken the view that the recipient of information is a passive element in the spread of information throughout a population.[18] This approach, prevalent in communications research, has influenced the design of migration models attempting to incorporate information availability with respect to vacancies.[19]

The framework presented in this paper suggests a different approach. The receiver of information is seen as an active element who samples available information channels with varying intensity to serve his own interests. Although this approach is at variance with research on information flows in general, it is suggested that it is a realistic representation of information flows as they relate to intra-urban migration.

A basic component of the household's utilization of available information is its *search space.* This is contained within its awareness space and defined by the environmental and locational criteria of its aspiration region or an initial aspiration subregion. Thus, it is explicitly recognized that, on the basis of criteria such as accessibility or social environment, certain neighborhoods will be eliminated from consideration before search begins.

The household's search space, like its awareness space, tends to possess a distinctly social, economic, and spatial character. The household will search only those areas contained within its awareness space that satisfy the environmental and

16. Stuart F. Chapin, "Activities Systems in Urban Structure: A Working Schema," *Journal of the American Institute of Planners,* Vol. 34, (1968), pp. 11-18.

17. See, for example, Edward J. Taaffe, Barry J. Garner, and Maurice H. Yeates, *The Peripheral Journey to Work: A Geographic Consideration* (Evanston, Illinois: The Transportation Center, Northwestern University, 1963); Stuart F. Chapin and Henry C. Hightower, *Household Activity Systems: A Pilot Investigation* (Chapel Hill, North Carolina: Institute for Research in Social Science, University of North Carolina, 1966).

18. See, for example, Lawrence A. Brown, *Diffusion Processes and Location: A Conceptual Framework and Bibliography* (Philadelphia, Pennsylvania: Regional Science Research Institute, Bibliography Series, Number 4, 1968); and Anatol Rapoport, "Spread of Information through a Population with Socio-Structural Bias," *Bulletin of Mathematical Biophysics,* Vol. 15 (1953), pp. 523-534 and 535-547.

19. See, for example, Torsten Hagerstrand, "Migration and Area," in David Hannerberg, Torsten Hagerstrand and Bruno Odevings, eds., *Migration in Sweden: A Symposium* (Lund, Sweden: Lund Studies in Geography, Series B, Number 13, 1957) pp. 25-158; and Eric G. Moore, "Models of Migration and the Intra-Urban Case," *The Australian and New Zealand Journal of Sociology,* Vol. 2 (1966), pp. 16-37.

locational criteria of its aspirations, i.e., its search space. Those locations contained within or near the most desirable areas in the search space are more likely to be viewed than others. Similarly, newspapers may present vacancies from the whole urban area, but many such vacancies will not be considered, either because they are not located in neighborhoods known by the intended migrant household or because they are located in areas considered unlikely to contain acceptable vacancies. Finally, locations of vacancies discovered through interpersonal communication will be spatially, socially, and economically biased by the configuration of the intended migrant household's acquaintance circle and the awareness spaces of the acquaintances contained within that circle.

Some interesting insights into the nature of the information channels utilized in the search for a new dwelling are provided by Rossi.[20] Information sources are rated in terms of the proportion of searchers using each source (A) and the effectiveness of each source in terms of providing information leading to the vacancy selected (B). His indices of effectiveness (B/A) may be seen as estimates of the objective probability of achieving success by using a given information channel. The disparity between the effectiveness of different information sources is the result of differences in quality of available information. For example, information provided by newspapers is far less comprehensive than that obtained by personal contact or direct observation; this observation is consistent with an assertion that the subjective probability of success and the perceived effort associated with the use of newspapers are lower than for other information channels.

The influence of time on search be-

20. Peter H. Rossi, *op. cit.,* p. 161. Rossi examined five information sources: newspaper, personal contact, walking or riding around, real estate agents, and windfall. The proportion of his sample using each source was respectively 63 per cent, 62 per cent, 57 per cent, 50 per cent and 31 per cent.

havior. As the migrant gains experience of the urban area in the course of his search, the search space is likely to be revised. In part this will result from gaining more accurate information about various locations. Thus, some areas in the awareness space but not in the initial search space may come to be included in the latter, while some areas in the search space may be eliminated. The household will also gain information about areas not previously in its awareness space, and these may come to be included in its search space. Finally, as noted previously, the household's aspiration region is likely to be altered in the course of search, and simultaneous redefinition of the search space can be expected.

Time also has an effect upon the choice of information channels and the intensity with which they are used. The household must adjust its search strategy so that as the search time (w) remaining decreases, it intensifies its use of channels carrying increasingly large probabilities of success. In order for this condition to be satisfied, the searcher must be prepared to expend more effort in searching as time decreases, unless he employs the option of revising his aspirations and adjusts *in situ.*

Given an extended search, there is no guarantee that a suitable vacancy will be found within a given time period. In an attempt to avoid such a failure, the household must frequently re-evaluate and possibly restructure its search procedure. Intervals between re-evaluations necessarily become shorter as $w \rightarrow o$. After an unsuccessful interval, a number of alternatives are available: (1) The household may continue with its existing behavior on the assumption that the vacancies available to it will change as $t \rightarrow (t+1) \rightarrow (t+2)$, etc. Thus, later time periods may be supposed to bring a greater probability of success in finding an acceptable vacancy. (2) The household may redefine the vectors $A_L(t)$ and $A_U(t)$. Afterwards, the household might decide to discontinue search for a new residence and attempt to adjust *in situ,* or it may decide to continue search under the restructured aspiration region. The latter decision may prove successful since redefining the aspiration region would likely increase the subset of vacancies designated as acceptable and thus increase the overall probability of finding a new residence. (3) The amount of effort devoted to searching may be increased. This will result in a greater number of information channels being sampled, an increase in the intensity with which utilized channels are sampled, or both. (4) The searcher may attempt to increase the coverage of his search procedure by enlarging the spatial framework in which the information channels are sampled, i.e., by enlarging his search space.

If the time remaining (w) becomes small and no success has been achieved, considerable stress may be experienced by the household. Under such conditions, as Wolpert has pointed out, judgment is impaired, the number of criteria on which a vacancy is judged tend to be reduced, the perception of acceptability becomes ill-defined, and hasty decisions are made. In this situation one might suppose that strategy (2) above is the most likely, and the probability of remaining in the old residence or moving to a highly unsatisfactory residence is large.

Conclusion

This paper has provided a conceptual framework for the study of residential movements within the urban area. Greater research effort is needed if adequate understanding of the decision processes relevant to intra-urban migration is to be attained. A fundamental suggestion is that prime emphasis in data acquisition must be on the utilization of survey studies focusing upon the decision-making characteristics of the individual household, viewed in both a spatial context and a mover-stayer framework. In other words one must be able to compare characteristics of movers and non-movers, rather than focusing on movers alone. Such data should provide valuable guidelines and specifications for the development of more efficient study of intra-urban migration at the aggregate level, including a basis for designing models which are both more plausible and effective than those which are now in use. Of even greater importance, perhaps, is the provision of a framework for evaluating the impact of a variety of planning decisions ranging from direct changes of the urban environment to a restructuring of methods of diffusing information about the environment.

ANDREI ROGERS

Theories of Intra-urban Spatial Structure:
A Dissenting View

The overwhelming problems created by the phenomenal growth of contemporary urban areas have generated increasing efforts to gain a scientific understanding of the organization and distribution of human activities in space, their interlinkages, and the flows of people, goods—and information between them. Researchers from various disciplines have searched for means with which to comprehend the complexities marking the inner workings of the metropolis with the hope that an improved understanding of this city-system will lead to a firmer foundation upon which to base policy decisions designed to effect willful change within it. In short, investigators of urban phenomena have become keenly concerned with the spatial structure of metropolitan areas.

The theory of urban spatial structure is concerned with the disposition of human socio-economic activities in urban areas. Its goals are to discover, explain, and ultimately predict the regularities that exist in man's adaptation to city space. Contributions toward its development have suggested a number of distinct orientations

and approaches, each of which attempts to provide a framework of empirically sound and logically consistent propositions. As Walter Firey has so very eloquently pointed out, however, these give little recognition to social values and focus rather on space as a determinate influence on the distribution of human activities.[1]

Two main streams of thought underlie the voluminous literature on the subject. The basic distinction lies in the orientation with which the fundamental problem is approached. The first point of view is macro and *system-oriented*, focusing on the phenomena of urban growth and change and on the regulative forces acting to promote orderly development. The second, on the other hand, is micro and *process-oriented*, concerning itself rather with the factors that give rise to the phenomena by their collective influence on the decision making of societal units.

A system-oriented approach toward the analysis of urban form and structure is

1. Walter Firey, *Land Use in Central Boston* (Cambridge, Massachusetts: Harvard University Press, 1947), pp. 30-38.

From **Land Economics**, Vol. XLIII, No. 1, pp. 108-112. Copyright © 1967 by the Regents of the University of Wisconsin.

fundamentally one which interprets the spatial pattern of a city in terms of the dynamics of natural, social and economic forces acting within an urban environment. The primary concern of such theories has been to describe and explain why a particular activity is carried on at a given site and how it is spatially related to all other activities of the system. The statement of the problem is presented in a system context and the method of analysis reflects this macro orientation. Typically, the emphasis of such theories lies in the development of a set of general principles which accounts for the urban pattern by reference to factors—such as the role of the city within its hinterland; the social forces which interact to produce segregation; and, most commonly, the land market operating through the medium of rents to promote a greater efficiency in the arrangement of activities in urban space.

A process-oriented approach, on the other hand, focuses on "the events that lead to growth and change in the urban framework."[2] It views these events as the consequences of actions by decision-makers interacting in the urban field. The active role of human volition replaces societal adaption to space as the principal referent. The locational behavior of decision units is examined as it responds to different environmental conditions. Spatial preferences, cost and profit considerations, competition, and accessibility are typical principles which are used to account for observed phenomena.

The System-Oriented Approach

Brief reflection upon the two principal main streams of theoretical thought on the subject of urban spatial structure suggests that their fundamental difference rests on the way in which the phenomenon is viewed. The system-oriented approach focuses on a particular *site* within an overall pattern and is concerned with the forces which determine the activity which will be carried on at that location. The process-oriented approach, on the other hand, focuses instead on a particular *activity* and analyzes the behavior of decision units which seek for it the appropriate location. Both approaches have provided significant insights and understanding concerning urban form and growth. The system-oriented approach, however, in its preoccupation with natural, social and economic forces of change supplies insights which are very general and does not provide the basis for quantitative prediction. The problem is viewed mechanistically. Typically, supply, demand, income and capital are viewed as the principal factors with which spatial structure is concerned. The "behavior of the land market" and the "behavior of rent" are studied as if these are the actors influencing developments and not the human beings who act in the land market or set the rents. "As a result, these concepts are powerless to deal with the prediction of changes resulting from changed conditions; they can in the main only assess the probabilities resulting from a continuation of trends. Thus they are not fully prepared to assist in distinguishing the effects of alternative policy decisions."[3]

Any non-random decision must be based on a prediction and evaluation of the probable effects of alternative actions (inaction being one of them) which are available to the decision maker. The success of such policies is dependent in a large measure on the accuracy of the predicted effects. In short, what is necessary for rational policy making in matters pertaining to urban growth is a reliable theory connecting "instrumental" policy variables with outcome variables by means of a set

2. Britton Harris, "Some Problems in Theory of Intra-Urban Location," *Operations Research,* September-October 1961, p. 701. Harris suggests a different division of theory. His classification identifies three main streams of thought: the design of urban form, the description of urban form, and the explanation of urban form.

3. Harris, *op. cit.,* p. 700.

of relationships between these variables. These typically are specified by means of a model which allows forecasts to be made about particular output variables as a consequence of the manipulation of the "decision" variables included in the input set. Thus, it seems apparent that the principal objective for the development of a theory of urban spatial structure is to provide means of predicting the probable consequences of alternative courses of action in public policy-making. The theory must supply the basis from which planners can establish, with a sufficient degree of accuracy, the implications of various policy "mixes" which may be adopted by governmental authorities.

The system-oriented approach does not offer much promise in ultimately meeting the requirements set forth in the preceding paragraphs. Urban spatial structure is principally influenced by the locational decisions of private and public groups and individuals. These decision units interact in the urban field and create the "events" which lead to change in the metropolitan fabric. Thus, a theory which seeks to cope with the factors leading to growth and change in urban communities must ultimately deal with the behavior patterns of these individual decision units. The process-oriented approach does just that. However, it too suffers from too strict an adherence to the "conventional wisdoms" of parent disciplines.

The Process-Oriented Approach

The body of theoretical work under the process-oriented approach suffers from the implicit belief that methods of analysis which have been so eminently successful in the physical sciences might be applied with equal success to problems in the social field. Two principal tendencies appear in these theoretical attempts to account for the observed regularities in the spatial patterns of urban areas. Both stem from the premise that methods which have explained the behavior of the physical world can be effectively transferred over into the area of human behavior. The first basic tendency is the search for an overall unifying principle which can be used to account for the observed patterns of behavior. The second is the deterministic method of analysis which begins with the definition of quantities considered as overtly observed magnitudes and proceeds to the discovery of the relevant interactive laws of behavior relating these quantities one to another.

REDUCTIONISM

It has become the fashion among process-oriented theorists of urban spatial structure to attempt to deduce all locational behavior in terms of some single all-unifying principle. Like the classical physicists seeking to reduce the explanation of all natural phenomena to the simple laws of mechanics, the investigators of urban structure continue to seek a fundamental *modus operandi* by which people and activities are channeled into their appropriate niches in urban space. Typically, these ultimate determinants of locational choice are expressed as some form of minimization or maximization. Thus "minimization of costs," "maximization of market area," "maximization of profits," and so on, have been postulated as the ultimate unifying principle for a theory of urban spatial structure.

This search for unifying principles of great generality, analogous to those which have had such success in the physical sciences, seems much too premature. The premise that patterns of social behavior may be effectively explained by principles of least or most of something-or-other has been challenged in recent literature. Kendall, for example, in an article on laws in the social sciences offers the following suggestive remark:

The point, for present purposes, is that it may be (and probably is) chasing a will-o'-the wisp to suppose that social behaviour is determined by principles of least something-or-other. Zipf made a gallant attempt, and in the same category I would place efforts by economists to explain business behaviour on the principle of maximizing profits or the tendency on the part of model-fitters to assume that Nature is obliging enough to minimize their errors. Some such principles may, indeed, exist. But if they are to be discovered, I think we must achieve them by synthesis at a later stage and not be over-ambitious about the generality of the patterns which we are studying at the present time. The pathway of knowledge is littered with the wreckage of premature generalization.[4]

The long-standing belief that the explanation of all natural phenomena ultimately rests within the principles of mechanics has steadily declined since the middle of the nineteenth century. The difficulties of extending mechanics into new domains such as electro-magnetic phenomena came to be acknowledged as insuperable and new approaches were proposed. It seems abundantly clear that analogous difficulties, stemming from the overwhelming complexities inherent in human behavior, will ultimately produce the same kind of reaction in the social sciences.

DETERMINISM

There is little doubt that observable regularities exist in urban spatial patterns and may be expressed in quantifiable form. There does, however, seem to be justification for legitimate doubt whether these regularities can be accounted for by methods such as have been used in the physical sciences. Most of the laws of physics may be expressed in terms of fundamental units such as length, mass and

4. M. G. Kendall, "Natural Law in the Social Sciences," *Journal of the Royal Statistical Society,* 1961, p. 5.

time. The behavior of these fundamental observed magnitudes can be studied only by discovering the interactive laws which establish the dependencies of one quantity upon another. The tendency in the social sciences has been to follow this pattern of viewing quantities as overtly observed magnitudes and then proceeding to seek out their interactive laws. Thus, in urban spatial structure, basic conceptual variables have been defined and the search for the laws describing their interaction continues.

The question, therefore, is whether the complex forces, interacting to produce the systematic regularities which have been detected in urban spatial patterns, can ever be explained by deterministic formulations of the kind used in classical physics. Physical processes generally take into account only a few variables between which a functional relationship may be established experimentally. They commonly involve two or three variable situations which are essentially simple in structure. Thus, scientists have been able to develop, with relatively little difficulty, analytical techniques which measure the dependence of one quantity, say gas pressure, on another, say volume. Their essentially simple character has led Warren Weaver to define them as "problems of simplicity."[5] In the studies of urban phenomena, on the other hand, the number of variables that have to be included increases substantially. In addition, a considerable number of these variables reflect features of organization. Thus these phenomena all "involve dealing simultaneously with a *sizeable number of factors which are interrelated into an organic whole.* They are all, in the language here proposed, problems of *organized complexity.*"[6] In the area of urban spatial struc-

5. Warren Weaver, "Science and Complexity," *The Scientists Speak,* (Warren Weaver, editor) (New York, New York: Boni and Gaer, 1947), pp. 1-13.
6. *Ibid.,* p. 6.

ture, in particular, the consequences of a series of interacting activities which vary in space as well as in time must be identified and measured. The problem thus is compounded. The overwhelming complexities associated with analyzing human behavior make futile all efforts to derive relationships between observable factors. The general result is a complex model of reality which defies empirical verification.

What kind of a scientific attack on this problem of "organized complexity" promises an approach which shows evidence of effectively overcoming some of these problems? It is the fundamental thesis of this paper that a mathematized theory of intraurban spatial structure will be stochastic rather than deterministic in nature and, above all, will be addressed to answering questions of the following sort: If a set of observations on an urban system are viewed as elements of the set of all possible observations, "what type of model will enable us to predict observations that as a rule will be elements of a specified subset of the set of all possible observations on the system, while it is possible that the observations will not be elements of the subset?"[7]

This thesis emerges from the experiences of other social and natural science disciplines which recently have turned to probabilistic methods for the very same reasons as are suggested above. Psychological learning theory offers a particularly useful example. A principal problem of learning psychologists is to identify, interpret and analyze the relations between stimuli and response as a function of reinforcement. The major contributions of Pavlov, Thorndike, Guthrie and others developed these concepts in a scientific manner. However, the introduction of mathematical analysis into learning theory was beset with formidable difficulties. The indeterminacies in behavioral processes prevented the discovery of interactive laws

7. A. T. Reid, "On Stochastic Processes in Biology," *Biometrics,* September 1953, p. 276.

analogous to the laws of motion or of gravitation.

As long as behavioral scientists kept wishing there were such laws of behavior, mathematization of behavioral science remained a pious dream. Things began to look different when mathematical psychologists (1) started to describe behavior patterns as sequences of discrete responses; (2) replaced the classical concept of magnitude by that of probability; and (3) took the statistics of the resulting stochastic process as the dependent variables. . . . The result of this re-formulation was the appearance of the first behavioral mathematical model with a large range of application and a large potential for generalization, namely the stochastic learning model, first proposed (I believe) by W. K. Estes and worked out in detail in the first full-length book on mathematical psychology, treating a single theme in depth, Robert R. Bush and Frederick Mosteller, *Stochastic Models of Learning.* . . .[8]

The introduction of the stochastic-analytic approach by Estes, Bush and Mosteller[9] initiated a rigorous but mathematically tractable theory construction. Subsequent investigations such as those by Luce, Suppes and Atkinson[10] have produced the beginnings of a systematic theory of learning which has the same sort of "feel" that theories in physics have. With appropriate

8. Anatol Rapoport, review of *Mathematical Methods in Small Group Processes* (Joan Criswell, Herbert Solomon, and Patrick Suppes, editors), *Journal of the American Statistical Association,* September 1963, p. 830.
9. W. K. Estes, "Toward a Statistical Theory of Learning," *Psychological Review,* 1950, pp. 94-107; W. K. Estes and Robert R. Bush (editors), *Studies in Mathematical Learning Theory* (Stanford, California: Stanford University Press, 1959); and Robert R. Bush and Frederick Mosteller, *Stochastic Models for Learning* (New York, New York: John Wiley and Sons, 1960).
10. R. Duncan Luce, *Individual Choice Behavior* (New York, New York: John Wiley and Sons, 1959); and Patrick Suppes and Richard C. Atkinson, *Markov Learning Models for Multiperson Interactions* (Stanford, California: Stanford University Press, 1960).

identification of the theoretical variables, predictions regarding learning behavior may be derived in a mathematically rigorous manner.

The emergence of urban spatial structure as a definite and important area of research has developed increasing attempts, in the form of theories, to bring conceptual order out of the complex relationships of human activities with physical space. Analysis of these theories discloses that, to a large extent, their differences stem from the point of view with which the problem is approached and the means by which it is analyzed. Common to all theories, however, has been the strict adherence to determinism. This paper suggests that, due to the overwhelming complexities which underlie human behavior, a probabilistic approach may be the only method by which operational models of considerable generality can be developed. The use of the probability calculus as a means for assessing the combined effects of a great number of interdependent factors has proved useful in other disciplines and suggests itself as a possible analytical method in urban studies as well.[11]

11. For example, see, Andrei Rogers, "A Stochastic Analysis of the Spatial Clustering of Retail Establishments, *Journal of the American Statistical Association,* December 1965, pp. 1094-1103.

IV

NETWORKS: Transportation, Communication, and Linkages

The city is first and foremost a center of and for communication. People are brought together in cities and held there by the attraction of improved convenience of contact and by the variety and concentration of alternative channels of communication. The resulting interaction involves an exchange of ideas and information, as well as goods and services. In Christopher Alexander's terms, the city is essentially a mechanism for sustaining human contact.[1]

It follows from this premise that the underlying and organizing framework in the city consists of the media of interaction. The principal means of facilitating interaction of all types are the complex networks of transportation, communication, and linkages. These networks give meaning to the idea of the city as a system. In the first essay, Karl Deutsch introduces a rich array of concepts in defining the components of social communication in the city.[2] A similar approach, Richard Meier's communications theory of urban growth, was discussed in Chapin's article in Section III. To Deutsch, communication specifically means contact and the exchange of information. He argues that the efficiency of the city and the

1. Christopher Alexander, "The City as a Mechanism for Sustaining Human Contact," in W. Ewald, Jr. (ed.), *Environment for Man* (Bloomington: Indiana University Press, 1967), pp. 60-102.
2. Deutsch has also made a substantial contribution in the application of communication models to studies of government. See Karl W. Deutsch, *The Nerves of Government Models of Political Communication and Control* (New York: The Free Press, 1963).

quality of urban life may be measured in the choices of contacts that are available.[3] The city is in effect a gigantic switchboard for all kinds of transactions, and its form is in part articulated by the operation of this switchboard. The author suggests that many of the problems of the congested city can be attributed to a cumulative overload on the available communication and transportation systems. For example, the move to the suburbs may be seen as one outcome of the frustration that results from such overload.

The immediate effects of interaction on the form of the city are most explicit in urban transportation. As several summaries of the enormous literature in urban transportation are now available,[4] the papers included here were selected in order to define a broad context for studies of the interdependence of transportation systems and urban form, and to illustrate related planning problems. Through his long and varied career as a planner and urban critic, Hans Blumenfeld provides the necessary overview.[5] His paper illustrates the critical role of transportation in the form and evolution of the contemporary metropolitan area, and the relationships between traffic volumes and land use. What are the different effects of changing modes and patterns of travel behavior on the spatial structure of the city? What is an appropriate transportation policy? One major implication of the mutual interdependence of land use and transportation is that they must be analyzed and planned together, not as separate entities as is generally the case. Another implication is the need for a balanced transportation system, one which maximizes the potential but minimizes the necessity for travel in general and commuting in particular. The importance of public urban transit in such a system is emphasized in his evaluation of arguments for and against methods of financing urban transportation developments. In designing alternative traffic systems it must also not be forgotten that the city itself is the environment of that system.

3. An interesting general overview of communication is given in Colin Cherry, *On Human Communication: A Review a Survey, and a Criticism* (Cambridge, Mass.: The M.I.T. Press, second printing 1966).

4. For example, recent reviews of urban transportation are provided in International Conference on Urban Transportation Official Proceedings, *Transportation: Lifeline of an Urban Society* (Pittsburgh: Pittsburgh Urban Transit Council, 1969); Canadian Federation of Mayors and Municipalities, *First Canadian Urban Transportation Conference,* A Compilation of Articles, Summaries, and Reviews for the Regional Study Groups, Toronto, February 12-19, 1969; and F. E. Horton (ed.), *Geographical Studies of Urban Transportation and Network Analysis* (Evanston, Ill.: Northwestern University Press, 1968).

5. The interested reader is referred to a collection of published and unpublished articles by Blumenfeld, in which the present essay also appears: Paul D. Spreiregen (ed.), *The Modern Metropolis: Its Origins, Growth, Characteristics, and Planning— Selected Essays by Hans Blumenfeld* (Cambridge, Mass.: The M.I.T. Press, 1967).

The most important traffic generator in any city, and the source of most problems of overload or congestion, is the journey from home to work, and back. Two essays in this collection examine this problem. One is included in this section, the second a critical evaluation of contemporary attitudes and policy problems in urban transportation planning is included in Section VII. In the first, John Wolforth identifies various methods employed in the social sciences in analyzing the journey to work. He illustrates its interrelationships with the spatial structure of the city, and identifies the importance of different demographic and ecological variables in explaining why people travel. He defines the journey to work as both a social and a demographic problem, as well as a problem in the study of urban ecology. Most important, the journey to work provides the critical link between the distribution of urban communities, the subject of Section V, and the location of activities as centers of employment discussed in Section VI. It is both a result of and an inducement to the wide distribution of residential areas typical in the contemporary metropolis.

Transportation in the city is, however, more complex than the journey to work, and its impact on urban structure has yet to be defined. Some documentation exists of the association between travel behavior and the choice of residential location by households in particular,[6] and of regularities in urban travel patterns in general.[7] Equally important, there is growing interest in the differential impact on urban form of the innovations in transportation to which Blumenfeld has referred. Impact studies have examined the effects of highways and expressways and a beginning has been made in evaluating the effects of new mass transit systems that have been recently constructed in several North American cities.[8] But these studies are incomplete.

Is a new spatial ordering of urban activities emerging through changes in transportation and in response to different attitudes to commuting? Is the location of place of work still as dominant in the choice of where to live as planners have assumed? To answer such questions future studies of travel behavior must focus on the individual household or establishment unit, and on factors motivating travel, if they are to provide systematic

6. For example, Duane F. Marble, "A Theoretical Exploration of Individual Travel Behavior," in W. L. Garrison and D. F. Marble (eds.), *Quantitative Geography Part I: Economic and Cultural Topics,* (Evanston, Ill.: Northwestern University Studies in Geography, No. 13, 1967), pp. 33-53.
7. An extensive review of travel patterns in an urban area is provided in John F. Kain, "Urban Travel Behavior," in Leo F. Schnore and Henry Fagin (eds.), *Urban Research and Policy Planning* (Beverly Hills, Cal.: Sage Publications, 1967), pp. 161-92.
8. See Transportation Research Institute, *Urban Rapid Transit: Concepts and Evaluations,* (Pittsburgh: Carnegie-Mellon Institute, 1968).

formulations for both theory and policy.[9] M. E. Eliot Hurst suggests one approach to this type of research. His paper serves several useful functions in this anthology: first, it provides a brief review of the shortcomings of transportation studies, particularly in their dependence on aggregate data; second, a conceptualization of movement patterns and their relation to the subjective and cultural values affecting decisions to travel; and third, an outline for subsequent research on travel motivations, patterns, and impact. The concept of a movement space is introduced to describe the environment in which the tripmaker receives the stimuli for travel and then makes his response. This concept parallels that of the awareness and action spaces previously introduced by Brown and Moore in Section III. The author's suggested strategy for research on the factors affecting travel decisions involves intensive case studies of the households' attitudes and experience. On this basis a clearer understanding of one pattern of urban interaction may be forthcoming.

Ideally one should consider the full array of interactions which permeate the urban landscape. It is these which weave the behavior of social groups and activities into distinctive networks and spatial patterns. Up to this point little has been said explicitly about other types of intra-urban interactions aside from transportation. But the geographic literature is pitifully inadequate in its treatment of such interaction. Nevertheless, there are a number of questions that one might ask. What is the nature and distribution of institutional linkages? What constitutes flows, movements between retail functions, linkages in the spatial agglomeration of industries, flows of political power and influence, the diffusion of information on housing and employment opportunities, and so on? All of these are interaction processes forming a logical part of the analysis of urban spatial structure.

One component of these complex interaction networks is the linkages between manufacturing industries. Gerald Karaska examines one set of linkages leading to the clustering or agglomeration of industrial activity in the Philadelphia metropolitan area. The strength of the linkages among firms, measured in terms of supply or procurement patterns within the local manufacturing system, is assumed to illustrate the importance of agglomeration economies. A matrix of supply and demand patterns, defined as an input-output table,[10] is employed for the Philadelphia region

9. The more advanced reader is referred to a recent article by B. G. Hutchinson, "Structuring Urban Transportation Planning Decisions," *Environment and Planning*, Vol. 1 (1969), pp. 209-20.
10. Techniques of industrial linkages and input-output analysis are probably best exemplified in the writings of Wassily Leontief, Walter Isard, and Werner Hirsch. For references specifically treating the application of input-output to urban areas see a series of articles by Werner Z. Hirsch: "Interindustry Relations of a Metropolitan Area," *Review of Economics and Statistics* XLI (November 1959), pp. 360-

to identify those industrial types most affected by local linkages.[11] The result is a classification of industries in terms of their localization within an urban area. In this example the agglomerative effects are the size and composition of the local manufacturing economy. He concludes that the overall effect of the composition of the local Philadelphia economy appears to be weak. Rather it seems that linkages within the expanding service sectors may provide the key to understanding intra-urban industrial agglomeration.

Flows of information in the city, initially reviewed by Deutsch, are more diffuse and thus more difficult to document. Traditional concepts of the city are inadequate because of their inability to grasp the characteristics of the modern city as a system of rapid information exchange. In part this reflects limitations on the collection and processing of information. If the city is an information processing machine, or as Richard Meier describes it, a transaction-maximizing system,[12] then an understanding of this system must depend on a more adequate analysis of information flows and exchanges. Equally important, public policy must be concerned with the exchange of information among social groups, institutions, and politicians. In light of advancing technology, social alienation and apathy, the future quality of urban life may depend heavily on the encouragement of such exchanges.

The spread of information may be described as a diffusion process. Interest in spatial diffusion problems in general has been considerable, and recently attempts have been made to relate diffusion to the spatial structure of urban areas.[13] Duane Marble and John Nystuen build on the classic work of Torsten Hägerstrand in Sweden in examining the nature of com-

---

69; "Application of Input-Output Techniques to Urban Areas," in Tibor Barna (ed.), *Structural Interdependence and Economic Development* (London: Mac-Millan, 1963), pp. 151-68; and "Input-Output Techniques for Urban Government Decisions," *The American Economic Review,* LVIII (May 1968), pp. 162-70.

11. An earlier paper by the same author is G. Karaska, "Interindustry Relations in the Philadelphia Economy," *East Lakes Geographer,* Vol. 2 (1966), pp. 88-96.

12. Richard L. Meier, "The Metropolis as a Transaction-Maximizing System," in *Daedalus,* Journal of the American Academy of Political Science, Vol. 97, No. 4, (Fall 1968), pp. 1292-1314. See also Arnold Rockman, "The City as an Information Processing Machine," *Habitat,* Vol. X, No. 1 (January-February 1967), 44-47.

13. For example, W. A. V. Clark, "Information Flows and Intraurban Migration: An Empirical Analysis," *Proceedings of the Association of American Geographers,* Vol. 1 (1969), pp. 38-42; R. G. Golledge and L. A. Brown, "Search, Learning and the Market Decision Process," *Geografiska Annaler,* Vol. 49, Series B. (1967), pp. 116-24; R. L. Morrill and F. R. Pitts, "Marriage, Migration, and the Mean Information Field: A Study in Uniqueness and Generality," *Annals of the Association of American Geographers,* Vol. 57 (1967), pp. 401-22. An excellent review of diffusion research is given in Peter Gould, *Spatial Diffusion,* Commission on College Geography, Resource Paper No. 4, Washington, 1969.

munication and information flows within urban residential areas. Their analysis provides a direct lead from the array of interaction networks identified earlier in this section to the analysis of urban communities and their internal structure in the following section.

The relationship between geographical distance and the frequency of face-to-face contact is expressed by Marble and Nystuen in terms of the mean information field (M.I.F.). The M.I.F. is defined as the average spatial extent of a person's short-term social contacts. The concept is then employed in one case study to analyze the travel diaries of residents in Cedar Rapids, Iowa. When mapped the results indicate that a majority of personal contacts do occur over very short distances, and the frequency of contact declines systematically with increased distance from place of residence. This relationship is then approximated with a simple exponential curve (Pareto) similar to that initially obtained by Hägerstrand. Brief comparative studies also suggest that the mean contact distance declines as gross population density in an area increases. This is more clearly apparent when the authors compare studies undertaken in rural and urban areas.

If interaction networks in general are the fundamental means of organizing urban life, their effects should be evident in the distribution of communities and activities. What are the implications of the decline in density of contact over space for the physical structure and social cohesion of urban communities? What is the role of face-to-face communication in defining social areas within the city? What are the associations between the transportation grid and the location of communities? With these questions in mind, the discussion in the next two sections shifts to studies of urban communities and patterns of economic and institutional activities.

KARL W. DEUTSCH

On Social Communication and the Metropolis

Any metropolis can be thought of as a huge engine of communication, a device to enlarge the range and reduce the cost of individual and social choices. In the familiar telephone switchboard, the choices consist of many different lines. Plugging in the wires to connect any two lines is an act of commitment, since it implies foregoing the making of other connections. The concentration of available outlets on the switchboard permits a wider range of alternative choices than would prevail under any more dispersed arrangement. It also imposes less stringent conditions of compatibility. The limits for the potentially useful size of a switchboard are fixed by the capacity of the type of switching and control equipment available.

The facilities of the metropolis for transport and communication are the equivalent of the switchboard. The units of commitment are not necessarily telephone calls but more often face-to-face meetings and transactions. For any participant to enter into any one transaction usually will exclude other transactions. Every transaction thus implies a commitment. The facilities available for making choices and commitments will then limit the useful size of a metropolis.

Contact Choices: The Product of Cities

From this perspective, the performance of a metropolis could be measured in terms of the average number of contact choices which it offers to its inhabitants within, say, one hour of round-trip commuting time, at the prevailing levels of effort and equipment.[1] Efficiency in cities, as in other organizations, differs from effectiveness. Effectiveness is the probability of carrying out a given type of performance, regardless of cost, while efficiency consists in low cost for a given performance. The more persons or services available to a city dweller within a round trip of one hour, the more effective would be his city or metropolitan area, and the cheaper the cost of maintaining a metropolis area; and the cheaper the cost of maintaining a metropolis that places, say 1,000,000 peo-

1. This would be analogous to measuring the performance of a switchboard or of a central telephone exchange in terms of the number of potential calls among which an average subscriber might be able to choose, say, for ten cents, or within thirty seconds time for dialing, automatic switching, signaling, and the first response of the called party.

From **Daedalus,** Journal of the American Academy of Arts and Sciences, Boston, Massachusetts, Vol. 90, No. 1, Winter 1961. Reprinted by permission.

ple and 50,000 public and private institutions, firms or service points within a given commuting radius, the more efficient the metropolis could be said to be. The effectiveness of a metropolis could be measured in contact choices within one hour of travel time, while the efficiency of the same city would be measured by the ratio of such choices to some unit of cost. How many choices will $100 per capita buy for the residents of city X? As in many problems of design, one criterion cannot entirely overide another. Some increases in effectiveness may have to be sought even at the price of rising costs, and some gains in efficiency may be worth some concessions in performance.

According to this view, the essential performance of the metropolis is in the enhancement of the range and number of such choices, and the basic cost is the maintenance of a system of facilities that makes a wide range of choices possible. One might ask: how many choices can an individual buy at a cost he can afford— and how many such choices on the average can the community buy for different groups of people, at prices it can afford? For each type of city and for each type of communication and transport system, it might then be possible to sketch demand and cost curves based either on the best available knowledge, or on prevailing practice.

Large cities, of course, serve many other functions. They offer playgrounds for children, lanes for lovers, shelter for residents and transients. But houses, playgrounds, and lovers' lanes are found in villages as well, and so sometimes are factories, power stations, mills, inns, manor houses and castles. Almost any one kind of installation found in a metropolis can be found in the countryside. It is the multiplicity of different facilities and of persons, and the wide choice of potential quick contacts among them, that makes the metropolis what it is. And this essential character applies to large cities in un-

derdeveloped as well as in advanced countries.

This general function of the metropolis is facilitated by its geographic location at some nodal point in a larger transportation network. The more the arteries that intersect at the site of the city, the greater the opportunities the city has to facilitate a wide range of choice. Again, the larger the city, the more diversified its industries, repair shops, and service installations— hospitals, research institutes, libraries, and labor exchanges—the wider the range of possible choices among them. The larger, the more diversified, the more highly skilled and educated the population, the greater the range of available personal choice either with respect to organizations or to opportunities in the world of culture, recreation and the arts.

In terms of economics, particularly in regard to the location of industrial enterprises, many of these considerations appear as external economies, actual or expected. Roads, port and rail connections, municipal services, the supply of skilled and unskilled labor, and the availability of high-level professional and scientific talent—all appear as so many potential factors of production, and some of them may even appear as free goods, against which no additional items of cost need to be budgeted. As will be evident later, the expectation may not be an altogether realistic one: the effective attractions of the area for new industries may lead after a time lag of some years or decades to substantial problems of congestion and overload. Yet locating in or near a great city is not only an exercise in economic rationality. Often the decision is made in intuitive and human terms; and most often perhaps the economic reasoning and the human preferences for location may seem to reinforce one another. Both tend to seek a widening range of choice at low, or at least tolerable, costs of choosing; and just this is the special advantage of the city. The rising proportions of industrial staff whose jobs are oriented to communication, service or professional functions may reinforce this attraction.

The power of the metropolis as an engine of communication is thus attested indirectly by its power of attraction over people. Though this power has an economic component, in the aggregate it is far more than economic. "How ya gonna keep 'em down on the farm, after they've seen Paree?" asked an old song; and the sociologists and anthropologists of the 1940's and 1950's have been reporting the vast attraction of urban areas in Asia and Africa to former villagers, far beyond any immediate economic or social push. They are held even in the squalor of the shanty towns and *bidonvilles*. If freedom is the opportunity to choose, then the metropolis, in so far as it is an engine for facilitating choice, is also one of liberation. This liberation may be physical, in terms of the visits, the meetings, the sights now possible, or psychological and vicarious, in terms of the choices and experiences which can now be made in the imagination. In either case, it is a liberation whose reality and whose social, political, and psychological relevance cannot be doubted.

Communication Overload:
The Disease of Cities

People come to large cities because there, among other reasons, they find a wider range of choice within their individual limitations than they are likely to find anywhere else. Inevitably this means that every metropolis must offer each of its residents enough freedom for a wide range of choices to be significant to them; and this also means enough freedom so that serious problems of peak loads and of recurrent, possibly growing, overloads are imposed on the city's many but limited facilities. Recurrent overloads are thus not an alien disturbance intruding into the even functioning of the metropolis. They

are, on the contrary, an ever possible result of the essential nature of the metropolis as a device for facilitating a wider range of free choices.

To put it differently, the likelihood of such overloads is a result of the probability of coincidences in human choices and behavior under conditions of freedom. These overloads are not only the occasional loads, for which reserve capacities must be provided, but also the regular rush-hour loads, the result of relatively synchronized hours for work and recreation which in turn permit a larger range of choices than staggered hours would.

Despite their origin, however, recurrent overloads will tend to paralyze many functions, and eventually to blight the very structure of a metropolis. It is for good reason that waiting-line theory has become a fast growing field in operations research and social science. Taken together, increasing overloads of this kind reduce or destroy many attractions of the metropolis as well as the economic value of many of the capital investments in it.

Even in the absence of such overloads, the very effectiveness of a metropolis may produce subtle changes in its culture and in the cast of mind of its residents. A wider range of relevant choices implies ordinarily an additional burden on those who are choosing. Some years ago, Clifton Fadiman wrote a thoughtful article "The Decline of Attention" in modern, and especially American culture.[2] Since then Richard Meier has written of "attention overload" and of the "communication-saturated" society as characteristic problems of modern—and thus particularly of urban and metropolitan—culture.[3] These, too, are overloads in communication, but they occur not in streets and tele-

2. Clifton Fadiman, "The Decline of Attention," in *The Saturday Review Reader* (New York: Bantam Books, 1951), pp. 25-36.
3. I am indebted for the term to Richard L. Meier; see his "Characteristics of the New Urbanization" (multigraphed, University of Chicago, 1953), especially pp. 3-5.

phone lines but within the minds and nervous systems of people.

To increase the range of visible and relevant choices that confront a person usually means to increase the opportunity cost of whatever course he may eventually choose. Whatever he does will necessarily imply foregoing something else that also has appeared relevant and in a sense attractive. The wider the range of relevant choices we put before a person of limited physical and psychic resources and capabilities, the more acute and pressing we make his problem of economy in allocating his own time, attention and resources; and if he has been raised in a "conscientious" culture, such as the American or Northwest European, we are quite likely also to have increased his vague but nagging sense of self-doubt and misgiving as to whether he has made the best choice, and thus the best use, of his opportunities.

Cities therefore may produce a pervasive condition of communications overload. Whereas villagers thirst for gossip, city dwellers with more ample choices may crave privacy. But the internal communications overload of other people makes them less receptive to our needs. Their limited attention or their real need for privacy may tend to exclude us, and in the midst of crowds of neighbors we may experience persistent loneliness. Such loneliness, inflicted on us by others, is the obverse of our own need for privacy; and our own limited capabilities for concentration, attention, and responsiveness will make both their and our loneliness less likely to be overcome.

What people cannot overcome, they may try to gloss over. The poets and the social scientists—both critics of our culture—have catalogued the many rituals of self-deception that men practice: the reading of mass media that purvey illusions of "inside information" to the millions commonly excluded from it; the fancy dress of conformity which they don, from ivy league dress to the black leather jackets of youth gangs, or beatnik beards and sandals. Even these foibles that convey a sense of belonging, of identity, should be seen in perspective. People indulge in them, not necessarily because they are more shallow or stupid than their forebears in a village or small town, but because the commitments the metropolis imposes—of greater freedom, wider choices, greater burdens on their attentions and their powers of response—have temporarily become too much for them.

This temporary overburdening may be particularly acute for newcomers from some radically different cultural background. Then the effects of psychological uprooting through contact with the wider opportunities of metropolitan life are superimposed on the effects of the shock of a new culture and the weakening of the traditional bonds of family and familiar authority.

Communication overloads may be reduced through effective cues for orientation. Consider, for example, the practice of the old city builders, who placed the most important structures of visual attraction, such as cathedrals, palaces, or monuments, at the nodal points in the street network of the city. The nodal points, as the term is used here, were those located at the main intersections of the city's traffic flow, and hence most observed as the city's landmarks, and they were also those points most useful for orientation. The experience of visual beauty in a place of visual usefulness was thus often an inevitable part of a city dweller's daily coming and going. It is perhaps not too fanciful to surmise that this combined experience of perception and clarity of orientation in such cities as London, Paris, Bern, Cologne or Prague contributed, and still contributes to the charm of those cities and to the feeling of their inhabitants that they were members of a deep and rich culture. Bridges can fulfil a similar orienting function: the San Francisco Bay Bridge and the Golden Gate Bridge come readily to mind, together with the Embarcadero Tower of the old ferry building, visible for a long distance along the major artery of Market Street.

In many modern metropolitan areas, however, these conditions are no longer fulfilled. Major intersections in many American cities are often adorned with gasoline stations or car lots, with flimsy, low, shop buildings with large neon signs. At the same time, many of the largest, most expensive, and sometimes most impressive constructions are put on side lots, well away from the main intersections, as for example Rockefeller Center, the Lever and Seagram buildings, the United Nations building or the Museum of Modern Art in New York City. In Boston, the John Hancock building, tallest and most monumental in the city, is tucked away on a side street.[4] Many of our visible landmarks are only of very limited help in orientation, and are best seen from afar or by special visit. At the same time, many of the major intersections passed daily by most of us are either nondescript or appallingly ugly and give subtle but depressing impressions of disorientation, tiredness, or tension.

Such crucial traffic points cannot be easily abandoned. When elegant entertainment and shopping shifted from the central intersection of Times Square to the area of Rockefeller Center, the old subway system became less convenient to users of the Center, who have to make their way there and back by foot, bus, or taxi and who thus have increased congestion. This contrast between the changing fashions in regard to neighborhoods and the unchanging nature of fixed intersections in a major traffic network helps to make the market mechanism such an un-

satisfactory instrument for the development of these crucial sites.[5]

Overloads on some of the public and private services available in an urban area may sometimes be reinforced in their effects by a shrinking, or even an atrophy, of these services. Services vulnerable to this kind of process include service and repair shops, stockrooms, and parts depots, hospitals and clinics, libraries and museums. Many of the services of these institutions might be needed on Saturdays, in some cases, as is true of the cultural institutions, or on Sundays, or often for many hours on each work day. Institutions such as supermarkets and suburban shopping centers provide such longer hours of service, but many others do not, and some now curtail the amount of service previously offered. Much of this situation seems caused by rising labor costs, by fixed budgets, by the rising cost of able managers for small or middle-sized undertakings, or by the difficulty of dividing units of managerial effort so as to obtain management for some extra hours daily or weekly, and perhaps by some subtle development in American metropolitan areas that makes the personnel in service industries prefer shorter hours to more pay. This may be a rational choice, but it may become less so if too much of the new leisure is frittered away in waiting for delayed services. An increase in staff, with additional compensation for staggered hours (already practiced in suburban supermarkets), might be one approach an affluent society could well explore. In any case, free-market forces alone seem unlikely to overcome the persistent gap between the rising need for services in metropolitan areas and the actual volume of services rendered.

4. There are exceptions in many cities, to be sure. The Prudential Building in Chicago, the Coliseum Exhibition Hall at Columbus Circle in New York, and the Liberty Mutual Building in Boston are all at major intersections. These seem to have been exceptions, however, so far as major post-1930 construction is concerned.

5. Many users of the new facilities have employed a new transport system—the taxicab—but the cost to the community includes not only the cab fare but also the surface traffic jams and perhaps the exclusion of a marginal class of customers for the new facilities.

Suburbs: An Escape from Overloads

In the congested metropolis, a major effect of the cumulative overloads on communications, transport, and other urban amenities is frustration. Withdrawal to a suburb offers partial surcease. Taxes play a role in these frustrations. The late Justice Holmes once said he did not mind paying taxes, for this was the way he bought civilization; but exasperated city dwellers may flee to the suburbs from a metropolis where so much tax money buys so little in civilized living. The remedy is but to improve the quality of metropolitan government and metropolitan living by attacking the whole range of overloads. Several lines for such an attack have been proposed, but most are proposals for escape. When put into practice they have not to lower the urban tax cost as such not been markedly successful. For example, the shift in population to dormitory suburbs around the old cities has produced mounting burdens on commuting. A farther shift to some twenty-five or fifty miles from the city would make commuting prohibitive for many; whereas some men have been able to afford the financial and physical costs, their wives have found themselves marooned in a more or less rural environment, deprived of most of the choices and opportunities that make city life attractive.

The schemes for satellite towns are more far-reaching: each would be near the city, with separate though limited facilities for employment, shopping, services, and entertainment. Some towns of this kind have been built, but in Britain, at least, they have proved less popular than expected.[6] Still more far-reaching schemes for decentralization would break up the large cities altogether in favor of a wide scattering of major factories and administrative offices over much greater regions. Such a proposal would require a heavy reliance on medium- and long-distance transport and on telecommunications, as well as the acceptance of rural (or nearly rural) isolation.

All these schemes are unsatisfactory in the same fundamental respect. For escape from the frustrations of the metropolis, they would sacrifice the primary purpose of the large city—a wider range of choice with a low cost. The search for more effective ways of dealing with urban problems cannot ignore this basic function of a metropolis, it must rather be the starting point.

A Strategy of Search for Solutions

The concept of a metropolis as a device for facilitating choice in communications can contribute first of all to answering some general questions, from which one may proceed to more specific surmises and to ways in which both the tentative general answers and the specific surmises can be tested. The first questions might be these: what is the usual ratio of the cost of transport and communications facilities to the cost of shelter? how does this ratio change for different types of cities? how is it influenced by an increase in the scale of a city, as measured by its total population?

There are several ways of exploring this inquiry; they should give us interchangeable indices of the same underlying fact.[7] The proportion of communication costs to shelter costs could be measured in terms of the ratio of total capital investment in communication and transport facilities to the total capital investment in shelter. Or it could be measured in terms of the ratio of current expenditure of com-

6. Lloyd Rodwin, *The British New Towns Policy,* Cambridge, Harvard University Press, 1941.

7. See Paul F. Lazarsfeld's discussion on the interchangeability of indices in his article, "Evidence and Inference in Social Research," *Daedalus,* 1958, no. 4, pp. 99-130 (*On Evidence and Inference*).

munication and transport to current expenditure on shelter; or in terms of the ratio of total manpower employed in communication and transport to the manpower employed in the construction and maintenance of shelter. Doubtless, a range of further indicators of this kind for related ratios might be developed, but those already given should serve amply to illustrate the point.

One could also study the ratios of some appropriate nonmonetary indicators, such as the physical proportions of certain relevant facilities. The known ratio of the area of land that is devoted to streets in a city to the land area devoted to dwellings and gardens could perhaps be used more effectively within the context of the other ratios noted above.

Other types of large-scale organization could be studied. As taller skyscrapers are built, what is the change in the ratio of space devoted to elevator shafts to the total volume of the building? As corporations grow bigger, what is the ratio of telephone calls and written messages to some measure of the total volume of company activities? Such questions are aimed not merely at promoting speculation but also at suggesting a surmise to be tested: as the size and functions of a city grow, the proportion of resources devoted to transport and communications may have to grow faster, or at least as fast, if increasing overloads are to be avoided. It may be that some lag may produce no ill effects. Then the crucial question would be: what lag in the growth of such facilities is acceptable? Research may disclose a range of acceptable or desirable proportions for investment in such facilities and thus offer a potentially useful tool to planners.

What would life be like in an otherwise normal metropolis if its transport and communication facilities had been deliberately somewhat overdeveloped by present-day standards? Suppose its streets and intersections were hardly ever jammed, its parking spaces rarely unavailable, its public transport frequent, rapid, clean and uncrowded, its telephone lines usually free, with quickly available connections? If this sounds too much like utopia, it might still be asked: how much improvement in well-being in a city could be purchased by how large an investment in drastically improved transport and communication?

Some years ago, Sigfried Giedion drew attention to the late nineteenth-century shift to the pavilion system in large exhibitions, away from the earlier practice of centralizing all major exhibits in one giant building of the Crystal Palace type.[8] Giedion suggested that, as the exhibitions and the crowds of visitors grew larger, they gave rise to intolerable demands for more corridors to keep the crowds moving. The solution devised was to break up the exhibition into scattered pavilions, and to let the visitors make their way from one to another across the network of footpaths or across the open ground. People preferred to walk hundreds of yards in the open to the next pavilion rather than push their way for dozens of yards along some crowded corridor or hall. The principle may be relevant perhaps to the metropolis and the problems of urban decentralization.

Again, the question of cost arises. The shift to the pavilion system made the visitors themselves responsible for keeping dry and warm, a cost previously borne by the management of the single central hall. When a shift occurs from a compact city to a spreading network of suburbs, costs are also shifted from the city government to suburban families, who must now maintain one or two cars and pay toll rates for most of their telephone calls. In addition, there is now the financial, physical, and nervous cost of commuting. The decisive factor is the increase in delay in arriving and in the danger and tension. The ten or

8. Sigfried Giedion, *Space, Time and Architecture* (Cambridge, Harvard University Press, 1941), pp. 262, n-11, 725-727, 736-742, 757.

twelve miles between Wellesley and Boston may require twenty-five to thirty minutes with light traffic and good weather, in bad weather or dense traffic, forty-five minutes or more; and there are perhaps a hundred intersections. Over an adequate expressway the same trip might take fifteen to twenty minutes, with less tension and fatigue. A radial and peripheral system of improved expressways, permitting safe traveling speeds of seventy miles an hour—assuming corresponding improvements in the safety features of cars—would permit a city to double its effective radius and quadruple its potential area of integration. Our road experts have told us that "speed kills" if resorted to at the wrong time and place. But our city planners might well remind us that delays, too, can kill when their cumulative burden is added over a long period to an intensive working day.

Safe speed is not cheap. It cannot be achieved except by planned investment under public guidance. But it could do much to humanize life in our cities. The day may come when a profession of specialized expediters may watch over the smooth and quick flow of traffic and communication in our metropolitan areas, to identify and remove bottlenecks and overloads before their effects become cumulative and choking.

The same considerations apply even more strongly to public transportation. Improved and publicly subsidized rail transport—on the ground and underground—offers perhaps some of the most promising opportunities to combine high speed in mass transportation with safety at tolerable cost. The old-style commuting trains that take forty minutes for twenty miles not only exhaust their passengers but also drive more and more people to the somewhat faster highways. A drastic improvement in the speed and caliber of public transportation might relieve the pressure on the road system. Similarly, an extension of local telephone call rates

to the entire suburban area—on the analogy of the successful principle of uniform postal rates—might reduce some of the need to travel back and forth and thus further reduce the pressure on the transport system. Still another step might be the partial staggering of service hours, so that more stores and service facilities would be available for more hours daily, thus reducing the peak loads when all stores open or close. Rotating assignments and staggered hours might require more employees, but it might pay off in higher profits for the stores and in greater freedom for the community.[9]

None of these improvements would be cheap, and none easy to achieve. Such improvements, however, might be a key factor in rehabilitating our metropolitan areas. What is needed is a realistic analysis of the problem of peak loads and of the rising capital requirements for transport and communication. Only a substantial investment in transportation and communications can make metropolitan decentralization practicable, and only a substantial strengthening of public control over strategic land sites can restore beauty to our cities. Ways will have to be found to let planners use the powers of the community to guide urban growth toward a clear and pleasing pattern of new and old landmarks where people can once again feel well-oriented, exhilarated, and at home.

The various lines of research suggested in these pages have a common origin and a common goal. Our inquiry has centered on the function of a metropolis in aiding its residents in their choices and in their search for responses. The ranges and costs of such choices and responses are basic to our analysis. Proportionately ac-

9. For a discussion of some limiting factors and of the forces tending to pull the working hours of the whole community into a single rhythm, see Vilhelm Aubert and Harrison White, "Sleep: A Sociological Interpretation," *Acta Sociologica*, 1960, *4:* no. 3, 1-16.

celerated investment in communications, together with an improved knowledge of the general order of magnitude of these proportions, suggests a possible approach to urban decentralization. It also points up the need for greater clarity and beauty in our cities, and perhaps also for more responsive government, capable of integrating a wider range of metropolitan and suburban services, if the expanded metropolis is to become a genuine home for its people.

HANS BLUMENFELD

Transportation in the Modern Metropolis

Used as we are to thinking in terms of "cities" and "suburbs," we sometimes fail to grasp the implications of the emergence of a new form of human settlement which is going on before our very eyes. For 5000 years and more mankind has lived primarily in two forms of settlement: the town and the rural village. The vast majority of the world's population everywhere lived in "the country" and it was there that most of the world's work was done. Only a small ruling and guiding "élite" and those immediately serving them lived in "the city."

Only about 200 years ago this pattern began to change under the impact of the process known as "the industrial revolution," that is the application of the scientific method to material production, resulting in rapidly growing productivity, ever increasing division and specialization of labour and, as a corollary, ever increasing interdependence and exchange of goods and services.

Transportation played and plays a key rôle in this process. By the middle of the 19th century the new means of long-distance, inter-urban, transportation and

communication—the steamboat, the railroad, and the electric telegraph—made possible the concentration of industrial production in big cities which grew rapidly by a vast migration from the countryside. But within these great agglomerations movement of persons, goods and messages continued to proceed on foot or on hoof, limiting their size generally to a radius of three to four miles. The result was the densely built up "big city" where factories, residences, and all other uses were crowded close together.

Only towards the end of the 19th century did new means of short-distance, intra-urban, transportation and communication become general: electric traction, applied to street cars and to trains travelling on their own grade separated rights-of-way, and the telephone; soon to be followed by the internal combustion engine, applied to passenger cars, trucks and buses, as well as by radio and television. The boundary set by the distance which could be daily travelled on foot and on hoof was broken; the concentrated "big city" proved to be a transitory phenomenon, due only to the half-century time-

From **Queen's Quarterly,** Vol. LXVII, No. 4, Winter 1961. Reprinted by permission of the author.

lag between the impact of the industrial
revolution on inter-urban and on intra-
urban communications.

The country-to-city movement of population continues, all over the world, and
stronger than ever. But this centripetal
wave is now being met by a second, centrifugal "city-to-suburb" wave. The combined result of these two movements is
the modern metropolitan area, or "metropolis" for short, which is emerging as
the predominant form of human settlement in every section of the globe, but has
developed farthest on the North American continent. It differs radically from the
city as we have known it throughout history. As did its precursor, the 19th century "big city," it combines the traditional
"central" ruling and organizing function
of the town with the function of the major
seat of material production. Not only are
the populations of the modern metropolitan areas several times greater than those
of even the largest pre-industrial cities,
but their daily activities are spread out
over a far wider territory; and this territory includes not only "urban," but also
extensive "open" areas: parks, golf
courses, airfields, even farms and forests.
The modern metropolis is indeed "neither
city nor country." Finally, it is characterized by separation of places of residence
from places of work. Corresponding to
the dual function of the metropolis as a
"regional centre" and as a place of industrial production for a national and international market, commercial, governmental, and cultural establishments tend to
locate in a "central area," while manufacturing, warehousing and transportation establishments locate in various "industrial
districts."

The spatial relations between these
four basic land uses: residential areas, industrial districts, central area, and open
(primarily recreational) areas determine
the needs for intra-urban transportation,
while the location of the transportation
facilities in turn determines the pattern of

spatial distribution. Some guiding principles of this pattern can be formulated.

The Functional Pattern of the Metropolis

As stated, the basic "raison d'être" of the
modern metropolis is the need for co-
operation and communication resulting
from the division of labour. Only the
large metropolis offers to the highly specialized worker, in particular in the professional and managerial groups, a wide
choice of employment, and to the employer a wide choice of highly specialized
workers. Primarily the metropolis is a labour market, a place for making a living.
This also sets its limits. It is a commuting
area, extending as far as daily commuting
is possible, and no farther. Under present
North American conditions this means a
radius up to 30 or 40 miles, or an area
100 times as large as that of the 19th century "big city." Within this area the land-
use pattern and the transportation system
should maximize mutual choice of place
of employment and of persons employed
by *maximizing the possibility of commuting*; but should also, in order to minimize
travel time and cost, *minimize the need
for commuting*.

This makes it desirable to provide,
within every major section of a metropolitan area, an approximate equilibrium between resident labour force and places of
employment. Analysis of available data
shows clearly that the percentage of residents of an area who work in different
employment areas, and vice versa, decreases regularly with increasing distance
between places of work and places of
employment. It is therefore evident that
by co-ordination of their location commuting can be minimized; it is, however,
an illusion to believe that it can be eliminated, that planning can create a pattern
in which "everybody walks to work." In
the free choice of place of work (and of
residence) many other motives are far

stronger than the desire to minimize the journey to work. In Hudson County, N.J., for instance, an urbanized area of 44 square miles within the New York Metropolitan Area, there were, in 1960, 244,-000 jobs and 233,000 employed residents, as close to a "balance" as one can ever hope to achieve. But over 35 per cent of those employed in Hudson County commuted "in" from other counties, and 32 per cent of the residents commuted "out." Similar patterns were evidenced by a survey made in 1954 in Metropolitan Toronto, which also found that less than 2½ per cent of all respondents walked to work.

In small towns the percentage of those walking and generally living close to their place of work is, of course, higher. But the percentage of those who have to make very long trips, over 10 miles, is also higher. A survey made by the U.S. Bureau of Public Roads in 1951 in six midwestern and southern states found that in towns of 25,000 and over only 6 per cent had such long journeys to work, in smaller places 14 per cent, and in rural areas 29 per cent. In such small places those who cannot find satisfactory employment locally have only the choice of commuting over long distances to other places or of pulling up stakes and moving to another town. It is one of the great advantages of the metropolis that one can change one's employment without changing one's residence.

But the metropolis is not only a place for making a living, but also for living. Ebenezer Howard, the father of the "Garden City" concept, stated that man is attracted by two "magnets": Town and Country. Whatever one may think of Howard's therapy, his diagnosis is certainly correct. Hence a second pair of contradictory traffic requirements: *access to the city centre and access to the periphery,* to "open country."

The rôle of the centre, usually somewhat narrowly defined as the Central Business District, or "C.B.D.," is changing. In the 19th century with its limited facilities of intra-urban transportation, it had been the preferred location for all activities. Since that time there has been an increasing and still continuing shift from activities dealing with goods—manufacturing and warehousing, and, to a lesser extent, retailing—to those dealing with persons, primarily the wide and growing array of business services and, to a lesser extent, of consumer services. These "tertiary" industries, typically carried on in offices, proliferating with increasing specialization, serving a wide region, and dependent on contact with each other as well as with their widely dispersed customers, are even more characteristic of the modern metropolis than is manufacturing. In view of their rapid growth it is surprising to find that in the largest metropolitan areas in the United States employment in the C.B.D. and traffic into and out of that area has not increased during the last three decades. In Canada this levelling off has occurred later. However, since 1953 the number of persons counted as crossing a cordon line encircling the C.B.D. of Toronto has also remained constant.

The fact that central city traffic—in terms of persons—is not increasing with the growth of metropolitan areas, but levelling off, casts some doubts on the prophecies of doom which predict that "the city will strangle itself by congestion." To a considerable extent the exodus of goods handling activities is, of course, the result of congestion. But it appears to lead not to strangulation of the C.B.D. but rather to its adaptation to those specific functions for which it is best suited.

From the C.B.D. outward the density decreases with amazing regularity in subsequent concentric zones. Over time there is a gradual decrease of residential population density in the inner and a fairly rapid increase in the outer zones. The outgoing wave of population growth has a definite crest, a concentric zone with the highest rate of growth which moves regularly outward. The lines describing the change in population (or density) of all concentric zones follow, one after another, a logistic curve, gradually levelling off after a period of most rapid growth. But —and this is of decisive importance—in each subsequent zone the levelling off occurs at a lower overall density. This regular falling off of densities toward the periphery holds true not only for residential, but for all land uses. Industry and commerce also require increasing land areas per employed person, the farther from the centre they locate. Employment density in new outlying industrial districts may be as much as 20 times lower than in old industrial areas near the centre.

Traffic Movements

This pattern of distribution of land use, population, and employment, the result of transportation, in turn determines the pattern of movement of goods and persons. We will deal here only with the latter. Traffic surveys made during the past few years in Metropolitan Toronto indicate that the inhabitants of that area made an average of 1.6 trips per capita on an average workday, with an average trip length of close to 4½ miles, or about 7 miles per person, within the boundaries of the Metropolitan Municipality. Thus the 1½ million inhabitants of that area travelled, by mechanical means, a total of about 10 million miles daily, an average of over 4000 miles per square mile. By far the most (60.3 per cent) and also the longest, of these trips, were made to or from work. Somewhat less than one-sixth (15.5) were made for social or recreational purposes, only one-tenth were shopping trips, one out of twenty were made for business, and the remaining tenth for other purposes, primarily education. The great majority of these trips were made from or to the home, but about one-sixth

were made between two points other than home. Almost two out of five of these were for the purpose of "work," indicating the great number of persons—presumably businessmen, salesmen, repairmen—who had to travel in performance of their work. Actually there was one of these "second or subsequent" work trips for every six trips from home to work; and their total number exceeded the commonly overrated number of trips from home to shopping. Surveys in the U.S.A. reveal generally similar patterns.

Private and Public Transportation

All these trips are made either by public transit or by private car, and their optimal distribution between these two modes of transportation is the most vexing problem of the modern metropolis.

In an unexpected reversal of a secular trend the invention of the internal combustion motor has led, during the last 40 years, to a growing displacement of public by private transportation. In both the United States and Canada travel by private automobile now absorbs about 10 per cent of the Gross National Product, and in both countries accounts for at least 85 per cent of all person-miles in interurban travel and for a steadily increasing percentage of intra-urban.

The spread of the private automobile has made the operation of public transit more difficult in three ways. First, by depriving it of a substantial portion of its passengers, it has decreased its vehicle load, necessitating either higher fares or a curtailing of service, or both, leading to a further decrease in passengers. Second, by congesting the street surface which it shares with transit vehicles, it has slowed down transit movement, thereby increasing its cost of operation and decreasing its attractiveness. Third—most fundamental and least understood—the private car has created a pattern of low density development which can no longer be served by public transportation because it becomes impossible to assemble a sufficient payload on any one line.

Under the impact of these three factors public transit has lost ground since the end of the war. In the U.S. the number of transit rides per capita dropped by more than two-thirds between 1945 and 1959. In part this was a return to pre-war patterns which had been temporarily disrupted through shortages of cars and of gasoline. But the trend is continuing: from 1954 to 1959 in a period of rapid urban population growth, the number of transit riders decreased by 59 per cent; in towns with a population under 100,000 by 70 per cent. In Canada the decline has been much slower, but equally consistent, averaging about 3 per cent annually since 1954. As the service offered is being curtailed only very slightly, this implies a continuing drop in the number of passengers per vehicle mile, the most important factor in economy of operation. This ratio has dropped in Canada from 7.4 passengers per vehicle mile in 1946 to 5.3 in 1960, but is still substantially higher than the U.S. average of 4.25. The generally better performance of transit in Canada is probably the effect as well as the cause of lower fares.

Nevertheless, a 3 per cent absolute decrease in the face of a rapidly rising urban population indicates a rapid decrease of the share of public transit in total daily traffic. The vicious circle of decreased riding, higher cost per rider, decreasing service and increased fares, and resulting further decrease in riding, has clearly started. In many smaller communities in the U.S. and in some in Canada this vicious circle has run its full course and led to exclusive reliance on the private automobile.

It is hardly necessary to dwell here on the many reasons which have led to the rapid and continuing growth in car ownership. It may however be worth mentioning that nobody knows exactly how many cars are actually at the disposal of the inhabitants of a community at a given time. There are two sources: the annual car registrations, and the decennial census counts of cars owned by households which yield substantially lower figures. The annual registrations include all cars which are held for sale by dealers, all those which go to the scrap heap during the year, plus a possible surplus (or deficit) of cars sold to over those bought from other communities. As a result registration may overstate the number of cars actually available for operation at any given date by as much as 15 per cent. On the other hand, the census counts do not include cars registered in the name of businesses, cars for rent, and taxis. In Metropolitan Toronto, for instance, the number of registered cars per household at the present time (1960) slightly exceeds the number of households. Yet the 1961 census will probably show that about 30 per cent of all households—many of them containing second families or lodgers—have no car (in 1951 over 40 per cent had no car).

The Chicago Area Transportation Study estimates that in 1980 still 13 per cent of all "spending units." in their area, as well as in the U.S. will have no car, while the number of families with two or more cars may increase from 10 per cent to 23 per cent. Car ownership in Canada is not likely to exceed these figures during the next 20 years. Considering that different members of each family have to make different trips at the same time, it is evident that there is continuing public interest in providing transportation for a large group of citizens who have no private car at their disposal. But, in addition, growing street congestion and shortage of parking space make it evident that any attempt to solve the urban traffic problem by the private car alone is likely to be self-defeating. To the cost of streets and parking spaces and of the time losses of public transit vehicles, pedestrians, and the private cars themselves as a result of congestion have to be added the cost of accidents, of air pollution, and of nervous wear and tear. Finally, the private car is not an all-weather means of transportation. In heavy snow or dense fog only rail transportation on its own right-of-way, in particular in a subway, can move on schedule.

For all these reasons there has been in recent years a growing willingness to maintain and improve public transit by public action. There is, however, less clarity about the rôle which private and public transportation, respectively, are best suited to play.

The Role of Various Modes of Transportation

It is not too difficult to define the rôle which various means of transportation are best suited to play. The decisive factor is the density in the zones of origin and of destination of the trips.

The private automobile must serve all movements within low density areas, including travel to work in outlying factories, and travel to rapid transit and railroad stations. In addition, it must serve movements in medium density areas in unusual directions and/or at unusual times. Finally, those people who use their cars to move about during business hours have to bring them to the downtown concentration during the day.

Public surface transportation serves most movements in medium density areas, including feeder movements to rapid transit and suburban railroad stations, short and medium length movements from medium density areas to the high density downtown area, and very short movements within the downtown area.

Rapid transit serves long and some medium distance movements within medium density areas, most movements from medium density areas and some from low density areas to the downtown area, and in addition, also movements within the downtown area.

Suburban railroad lines mostly serve the movement from the more distant low density areas to the downtown area. These may travel directly to the downtown area or by transfer to rapid transit lines.

If, where, and when major outlying concentrations are developed, these may also be connected with the downtown area by rapid transit or suburban railroads.

The distinction made here between "rapid transit" and "suburban railroad lines" does not necessarily refer to the operating agencies, but rather to the type of service. The former operates on headways from 90 seconds to five minutes, the latter generally on headways from 10 minutes to one hour.

"Medium" densities are here defined as those with residential densities between 7,000 and 25,000 persons per square mile.

Public transportation requires concentration of trips not only in space, but also in time. If 1000 persons want to travel from point A to point B during the same five-minute period, it is obviously more rational to carry them in one train than in 700 cars, each carrying one or two persons. If the same 1000 persons make their trips between the same two points during 200 different such periods, they will have to use their cars.

The main concentrations in time occur, of course, during the morning and evening rush hours, as a result of the journey to and from work. It is therefore not surprising to find that transit loads are increasingly concentrated at these hours, while the private car has become more and more predominant for trips at other hours and on week-ends. While generally not more than 20 per cent of all person-miles in private cars are made during the two morning and two evening rush hours of the five weekly workdays, about 50-60 per cent of all transit rides are concentrated during these periods. This means that structures—very expensive in case of rapid transit—vehicles, and personnel are fully used only during 20 out of the 168 weekly hours during which they have to be maintained.

In Metropolitan Toronto, in 1959, about two-thirds of all trips were made by private car and one-third by transit. However, while only one out of five trips for social and recreational purposes was made by transit, two out of five of the trips from home to work were transit trips. Of the trips most highly concentrated in space and time, the rush hour trips to and from the C.B.D., transit still accounted for over 70 per cent, the same percentage as in 1929.

It is evident that private and public transportation fulfill different purposes. Movement into and out of the centre is best served by transit and within the centre by walking. However, private cars cannot be completely barred from the centre, because many of the people working there need them for the performance of their work. Probably the only feasible way to limit their number is rationing by price, by raising fees for parking, in particular all-day parking, in the C.B.D. well above the price for parking at outlying stations of rapid transit and suburban railroad lines. The remaining road traffic should interfere as little as possible with pedestrian movement. This can be achieved to some extent by creating "pedestrian islands," as has been done, on a temporary basis, in Ottawa and in a number of small American towns, and permanently in some European cities, notably Rotterdam and Coventry. Complete elimination of the conflict between vehicular and pedestrian traffic by creation of a second, upper level has been proposed for Fort Worth, Texas. The idea is far from new; in fact, it was universally practiced by our lake-dwelling ancestors more than 2000 years ago; and the last, greatest and most glorious of the lake dwellers settle-

ments, Venice, demonstrates to this day its attractiveness. Leonardo da Vinci developed a plan for a city with streets on two levels, and many similar proposals have been advanced from time to time; but so far none has been realized.

Decisive for the potential of public transit to attract riders is, in addition to speed (including headways), comfort, and price, the connection between its stations or stops and the points of ultimate origin and destination of its passengers. The great attraction of the private car is its ability to provide door-to-door service. Public transportation must always rely on some second means to assemble and distribute its riders. These means are walking, driving a private car to and from a parking facility at a station, and riding other transit vehicles and transferring. In the C.B.D.'s of big cities large numbers of passengers, sufficient to support rapid transit trains at frequent headways, can be assembled and distributed by a combination of walking and the use of elevators, a means of public transportation which is usually not considered as such. In areas of medium densities a sufficient number of passengers can be assembled by walking to support surface transportation by street-car or bus; and by combination of transfer from surface lines and walking, rapid transit stations can be fed. However, this necessitates relatively close spacing of transit stations, resulting in a relatively low travelling speed. It is therefore hardly feasible to extend rapid transit lines of this type far out into the peripheral low density areas, because total travelling time would become too long to be competitive with the private automobile. Also, the loads that can be assembled in these outer areas are too small to justify use of the long and frequent trains which are required on the inner sections of a rapid transit system. These outer areas can be better served by a different system with widely spaced stations, relying for the assembling of its passengers largely on the private automobile, the "park-and-ride" or "kiss-and-ride" method.

Such "combined" trips, using private and public transportation for different parts of the way are possible where the destinations are concentrated so that they can be reached either by walking—destinations in the C.B.D.—or by transferring to the transit system—destinations in the inner, medium-density area. However, where the destinations are dispersed, the private cars appear to be the only feasible means of transportation.

As stated, traffic to and from the centre has levelled off and traffic within the inner ring of medium density is also not increasing. As places of employment disperse, a greater proportion of work trips from these areas is bound to go to dispersed destinations. All future growth of residential population will necessarily occur in the outer rings. If it continues to take place, as it has during the past ten years, at densities averaging about four to five households per acre of residential neighbourhood, it will be impossible to provide it with the public transportation even in the main direction toward the centre. However, this type of development is by no means entirely the result of consumer preference, but largely of public policy. The Central Mortgage and Housing Corporation has encouraged home ownership of detached houses on large lots; municipalities have excluded more intensive development by zoning. As the effects of these policies are becoming evident, they are beginning to change and some increase of residential densities in the outer zones may be expected. Even so, it is inevitable that the proportion of all trips which are made by the private automobile will continue to increase because of the increasing dispersal of destinations for employment, shopping, and recreation. Peripheral "ring" or "by-pass" expressways are required to handle the increasing number of trips to these destinations. While these movements originate and ter-minate in a multitude of thin streams, they collect for a major part of their way in a mighty flow.

It is more questionable whether radial expressways are desirable, because they tend to pour even more cars into the overloaded streets and parking facilities of the centre. On the other hand, they serve a very useful purpose for trucks, for the considerable number of cars which are needed for use during the working day by persons employed in the C.B.D., and for trips outside of rush hours. However, they should terminate not in the C.B.D. but in an inner ring which also serves to by-pass the centre; and this ring should be fairly large to permit the location of a sufficient number of interchanges spaced wide enough apart to allow for weaving, acceleration, and deceleration.

Cost and Benefits of Public and Private Transportation

Both private and public transportation require substantial investments and large operating cost, and these have to be weighed in assessing their respective rôles.

According to the Gordon Commission, the total cost of a passenger car-mile averaged 10.5 cents. If a transit fare of 15 cents is assumed, this indicates that driving a car without passengers is cheaper for distances up to 1½ miles, with 1, 2, or 3 passengers up to 3, 4½ and 6 miles, respectively. It is therefore evident that in a considerable number of cases it is cheaper for the individual to drive than to ride, even if he figured the total cost. However, about three-quarters of the cost of operating an automobile consists of more or less fixed costs; and, in practice the driver counts only the "out-of-pocket" costs of operation which averages 2.8 cents per mile. So, except when he has to pay for parking, from the point of view of the individual car owner it is always cheaper to drive.

On the other hand, one bus lane carries during a peak hour 5 times, one street-car track 10 times, and one rapid transit track up to 50 times as many persons as an ordinary street lane. About 12 expressway lanes would be required to carry the volume of passengers now carried during peak hours by the Toronto subway. Transit vehicles travel 2½ to 5 times more miles annually than passenger cars. While a private automobile performs about 15,000 person-miles annually, a bus (excl. inter-urban) averages over 500,000, a street-car over 800,000, and a subway car about one and a half million person-miles annually. Thus, despite its underuse during all but the 20 peak hours of the week, one subway car performed as many person-miles as 100 passenger cars —and required no parking space.

These comparisons indicate strongly that the market may not allocate resources in the most rational way to private and public transportation, respectively. As indicated above, the greater part of the cost of operating an automobile consists of fixed costs. If public transportation is to compete with the private car, a substantial portion of its cost will also have to be transformed into fixed costs. The only practical way of doing this is by covering them out of general tax revenues. It might be objected that it is unfair to ask the auto driver to pay for a service which he does not use. However, he benefits from the fact that the transit rider, by leaving his car at home, frees the street for the driver.

Support of public transit out of tax revenues underwrites a deficit, obviously an undesirable procedure; or it assumes responsibility for all or part of the capital cost, in particular of rapid transit lines, while the operating agency must cover the operating cost out of user charges. This militates against a rational weighing of capital versus operating costs and may lead to a curtailment of surface feeder lines which frequently can only be run at an operating loss and to subsequent underutilization of the rapid transit lines and of the capital invested in them. The only sound procedure is for the municipality to pay in accordance with the service performed, that is per passenger-mile or seat mile. This method has now been adopted by the state of New Jersey for subsidizing suburban railroad service.

A strong case could be made for operating public transit as a public service free of charge. This would permit considerably faster loading of buses, resulting in greater speed and consequent economies of operation. There is a precedent for this in vertical public transportation. The entire cost of elevator service in office and apartment buildings is always assessed as a "fixed cost" as part of the rent, regardless of the amount of use of the service by the various tenants.

The question of the relative costs and benefits of the competing modes of transportation requires further research in order to develop a comprehensive transportation system which allocates to each mode its appropriate rôle.

JOHN WOLFORTH

The Journey to Work

It is only recently that the location of workplace and residence have been separated by long distances. According to such writers as Pirenne,[1] Weber,[2] and Sjoberg[3] a characteristic feature of the pre-industrial town was the close proximity of work and residence. They often in fact shared the same building and the connection between industrial and domestic life was an intimate one.[4] Even at the birth of modern industrialization, industry was often centered in the homes of the workers in the form of cottage industry, and work and living were woven into the fabric of pre-industrial and early industrial towns alike.

Urbanization and the Journey to Work

New forms of energy and industrial technology required the concentration of

workers in one location, and greater industrial specialization led to the spatial segregation of industrial activities. Thus, the individual craftsman working in his own home became increasingly dependent upon the larger organization of which he was a part. For example, "weavers who worked in their own cottages found themselves dependent upon supplies of raw materials," reports Beshers. "As new technology was introduced, they were forced to rent the new equipment, thereby relinquishing ownership of the means of production. Ultimately the technical advantages of the eighteenth century made the factory system dominant."[5] As industrial activity came increasingly to be centered in factories, the site characteristics of particular parts of the city gave them advantages of specific kinds of activity so that the city developed as a mosaic of zones each of which was associated with a particular industrial enterprise or group of related enterprises.

Even the dominant commercial areas began increasingly to make use of special situational characteristics, particularly

1. Henri Pirenne, *Medieval Cities* (Garden City, N.Y.: Anchor Books, 1962).
2. Max Weber, *The City,* trans. D. Martindale and G. Neuwirth (New York: Collins Book, 1962).
3. Gideon Sjoberg, *The Preindustrial City* (Glencoe, Ill.: The Free Press, 1960).
4. Lewis Mumford, *The City in History* (New York: Harcourt, Brace and World, 1961), p. 284.

5. James Beshers, *Urban Social Structure* (Glencoe, Ill.: Free Press, 1962), p. 72.

Adapted by the author from Chapter Two of his original manuscript **Residential Location and the Place of Work,** British Columbia Geographical Series, No. 4, 1965. Reprinted in revised form by permission of the Tantalus Research Corporation Ltd., Vancouver, B.C., 1965.

with respect to their accessibility to the mass of the urban population. In this way particular parts of the town gradually came to be associated with either industrial or commercial economic activity.

Areas which were not specifically required either for commercial or industrial uses were left to residential use and the locally directed services which residential areas support. It was in this way the city in its segregated aspects came to reflect the pluralistic nature of evolving industrial society itself. It even became possible to draw distinctions between one residential area and another, as working-class, middle-class, and upper-class areas became a feature of the urban landscape. The concentration of economic activities resulted in economies of scale for the factory owner, but these were often compensated for by diseconomies borne by the worker. "External as well as internal economies accrued to the firm," writes Lampard, "but not the diseconomies created by the firms own operations. Some of the latter no doubt fell on other firms . . . others were transferred to the household which was now separated institutionally as well as spatially from the place of work."[6]

The ability to bear these diseconomies varied with the income of the worker, a fact which has had some impact on current writings on the journey to work. In the early industrial era, when the millhand's home was still adjacent to his place of work, his long working day was not necessarily lengthened by time spent in the journey to work, nor his very low wage effectively diminished by the cost of getting there. In fact, the transportation technology of the time precluded the location of his residence beyond a reasonable walking distance from work. The mill-

owners on the other hand were usually able to avoid the unpleasant environment associated with the factory by living some distance away and travelling each day to his work by carriage.

The introduction of modes of mass transportation like the railroad and the streetcar simply extended this privilege down through the social spectrum. More recently the increase in personal prosperity and a reduction of the working day have extended this privilege to practically all workers and decreased the validity of the purely economic determinant of the length of the journey to work. The widespread use of the automobile has rendered great freedom to the worker to choose where he wants to live with less regard to his place of work than ever before.

The Journey to Work as a Social Problem

In the large modern city the costs of the journey to work are social as much as economic. It has been estimated that both in London and in New York time spent in travelling to work lengthens the work-day effectively by almost 20 percent.[7] Not only does the time spent in travelling to work not produce any economic gain but it reduces the amount of time that could be spent in leisure and recreation. It thus represents a problem for society as a whole and of which society is becoming increasingly aware. It is not surprising then that early studies of the journey to work were concerned primarily with its social implications.

One of the most influential of these was carried out by Kate Liepman[8] in London. Her work analyzed both the social and economic functions of the journey to work, and although it suggested that the

6. Eric E. Lampard, "Urbanization and Social Change," in Oscar Handlin and John Burchard (eds.), *The Historian and the City* (Boston: M.I.T. and Harvard University, 1963), pp. 225-247.

7. Howard S. Lapin, *Structuring the Journey to Work* (Philadelphia: University of Pennsylvania Press, 1964), p. 14.

8. Kate Liepman, *The Journey to Work* (London: Routledge and Kegan Paul, 1944).

increasing time spent in commuting and the consequent burdens that placed upon an already overloaded public transportation system were a cause for some alarm, it also suggested that some benefits accrued to society from a highly mobile market. Liepman suggested that there are two causes to the journey to work. First, there are what she called the topographic causes resulting from the spatial segregation of industrial, commercial, and residential areas in a burgeoning and relatively unplanned industrial society such as she observed in pre-war Britain. Second, there were the social and economic causes which carry with them important benefits to employer and employee alike. First, she suggested the economies of scale enjoyed by modern industry require a large and varied labour force, which could be supplied only from an extensive labour catchment area. "Daily travelling by the workers," Liepman reported, "has become necessary to secure the concentration of labour in plants of the size demanded by technical and economic considerations."[9] Second, a highly mobile labour requires that each worker should have access to several alternative places of work. Thus, the advantages accruing to the employer are that he may expand, reorganize, or relocate his plant without serious disruptions of his labour supply. The employee on the other hand has a greater choice of employment within the extended range of the daily journey to work brought about by public transport facilities or by the ownership of a car.

It does not follow, however, that large-scale commuting is a desirable end in itself. The advantages for both employer and employee would still exist, Liepman maintained, were alternative workplaces brought within closer reach of each employed person in a regional pattern of distinct small towns about a central nucleus. An attempt was made to put this kind of suggestion into practice in Britain's post-war development of new towns ringing London.

Later British writers added force to Liepman's argument by suggesting the existence of labour-deficient and labour-surplus areas and by commenting on the power of certain areas to attract labour from very long distances. For example, Westergaard[10] reported that in the Greater London area "the central area, and to a lesser extent the subsidiary centre depend for their labour supply on a widespread catchment area."[11] At the time Westergaard's study was done, the British Census did not include detailed data on the journey to work, and so it was not possible to comment on the occupational groups which would be drawn the longest distances to the central areas or identify the residential zones from which they would come. The existence of a complex system of surface and underground railways permits workers to commute to central London from as far away as fifty miles with comparative ease and speed, but the prohibitive costs of travelling such distances would suggest that only higher income workers are in fact able to do this. In support of this view Chaline[12], amongst others, has shown the existence of a belt of higher-income workers on the fringes of the metropolitan area in what is often called the "stockbroker belt," which takes advantage of the pleasant site characteristics of the countryside surrounding London. In the same study, it was found that those who live in the main and subsidiary centres of employment more often than not work close to home, and this also raises questions about the occupations of those for whom this observation is valid.

The questions which were left unanswered by the works of either Liepman or

9. *Ibid.*, p. 11.

10. John Westergaard, "Journeys to Work in the London Region," *Town Planning Review*, 28 (April, 1957), pp. 37-62.
11. *Ibid.*
12. C. Chaline, "Nouveaux Aspects de la Cité de Londres," *Annales de Géographie*, 70e. Année (1961), pp. 273-286.

Westergaard concern the nature of the equation between social, economic, and topographic determinants of the journey to work. Do those who both live and work in the London central area do so because they cannot afford a long journey to work or because the quality of residential accommodation available there is more appropriate to their earnings than that found in the outer suburbs?

Conversely, the studies of both Liepman and Westergaard, although not done from a geographical point of view, do suggest a division of urban areas which may contribute towards a specifically geographical understanding of the journey to work. That of Westergaard in particular suggests the existence of four distinct types of urban areas on the basis of their labour deficiency or abundance. First, his study recognized the existence of self-sufficient labour markets in which the local residents are employed exclusively and into which there is no inflow from other areas. Second, it recognized areas where the daily inflow and outflow of workers is in a state of balance, and where the number of residents who must find employment elsewhere is the same as the number of commuters coming in. Third, it recognized areas where the residential population is much greater than the available employment and therefore the inflow is greater than the outflow. And, fourth, it recognized areas where the available employment is much greater than the residential population and therefore the inflow greater than the outflow. Although Westergaard's study, like that of his predecessor, had been motivated by a concern for the social implications of large-scale commuting, there emerged from it what could be recognized as the beginnings of a geographical perspective.

The Journey to Work as a Demographic Problem

What had been recognized in both studies was in fact a problem of demography.

Some parts of the city have a larger working population than a residential population while others a larger residential population than a working population; the journey to work is the link between such areas. Several writers have focussed on the areas themselves rather than on the links between them, often because of the nature of official statistics. For example, the Swedish Census contains data on the working and residential populations of census areas and several Swedish studies have used such data to draw a distinction between areas of labour-abundance and of labour-deficiency. Kant[13] has suggested two different indices which may be employed to make such a distinction in quantitative terms, but since such a distinction is after all only between areas of industrial, commercial or residential land use it may often be made on a simple morphological basis. If a regionalization is to be of any value at a small scale, it must surely be based upon the identification of the labour catchment areas of particular workplaces or groups of workplaces.

The nature of available data often makes this kind of identification difficult. Kant[14] and Forbat[15] have stressed that more useful studies of work-residence relations would be forthcoming were information on the catchment areas of specific workplaces available from official statistics. The coarse-scale regionalization attempted by these writers leaves two questions unanswered. First, what is the importance of commuting within the areas considered? Kant calls this "pseudo-commuting," but the distinction between it and commuting across administrative

13. Edgar Kant, "Suburbanization, Urban Sprawl and Commutation," in David Hannerberg, Torsten Hagerstrand, and Bruno Odeving (eds.), *Migration in Sweden,* Lund Studies in Geography, Series B, No. 13 (Lund: The Royal University, 1957), pp. 244-309.
14. *Ibid.*
15. Fred Forbat, "Migration, Journey to Work and Planning," *Migration in Sweden,* pp. 310-319.

boundaries is really not generically different. Second, the gross figures used by both writers give no indication of the direction of commuting. For example, do the residences of a particular administrative division who find employment outside that division converge upon a specific work zone or are they distributed throughout all the work zones equally?

The inadequacies of static cartography had been pointed out by Hagerstrand. "As the human geographer produces his dot maps of population distribution," he writes, "he is fully aware that this method, however useful, gives an inadequate impression of the population in geographical space. The dot maps give a static picture, as if each individual has his given place. In reality, the reverse is the most obvious feature of the population—fluidity. Each individual has a moving pattern of his own, with turning points at his home, his place of work and his shopping centre during the week, and his recreation grounds on a holiday or Sunday."[16] It is the element of fluidity which is missing from studies based on crude and undifferentiated sets of data on commuting, or on data which refer to population distributions at specified times of the day, like the many studies of day and night populations of American cities.[17] In all of these, the functional and dynamic aspects are not apparent except by inference and the picture presented is always a static one. Geographers have traditionally distinguished between two different kinds of regions, that which has homogeneous characteristics among certain specified components, and that which is given unity by virtue of the fact that it is functionally linked to a particular node. Demographic studies of the journey to work have generally paid attention to the former rather than the latter kind of region.

The Concepts of Conflux and Dispersion

The terms conflux and dispersion occur fairly frequently in the literature and may have a potential as tools which has not been fully realized. In particular they would seem to provide a bridge between those studies concerned with the differences between labour-abundant and labour-deficient areas, and those which are concerned with drawing precise labour catchment boundaries. The terms are found first in Liepman's work where they are used as a capsule description of the movements of commuters in an urbanized area. Very simply, residential areas are those from which people disperse on journeys of different lengths towards workplaces of different types and locations. But the term implies something more than a simple description of the fact that there is net outflow; it implies also a sense of direction since one may conceive of workers dispersing from a specified residential area to one, two, three, or more places of work. Viewed from the place of work, these movements may be seen as conflux rather than dispersion, and this term too contains a strong sense of direction.

Vance[18] has used the concepts of dispersion and conflux to develop a theoretical model of labour catchment areas based on the evolutionary processes which are associated with transportation technology. He stresses that the relationship between work and residence may be explained only in terms of its historical development and postulates an original zone of conflux as the initial site of an urban area. As economic activity at this site increases so also does the labour force em-

16. Torsten Hagerstrand, "Migration and Area," *Migration in Sweden,* pp. 27-159.

17. For example, see G. W. Breese, *The Daytime Population of the Central Business District of Chicago* (Chicago: University of Chicago Press, 1949).

18. James E. Vance, "Labor-Shed, Employment Field, and Dynamic Analysis in Urban Geography," *Economic Geography,* 36 (July, 1960), pp. 189-220.

ployed in that economic activity until it can no longer be accommodated by the site itself. It is at this stage that the community divides into two distinct zones, a zone in which work is performed, or the zone of conflux, and another in which those who perform the work reside, or the zone of dispersion. The presence of a growing population itself attracts further industry and commerce, which, unable to locate at the initial zone of conflux, locates at the periphery. The effect of this is to increase the total employment of the area and to provide for secondary zones of conflux at the outer perimeter of the growing urban area. The expansion of employment, Vance argues, takes place not only through the expansion of the Central Business District as it takes in adjoining previously residential areas, but by the external reproduction of manufacturing and transportation facilities at the edges.

The changing locations and dimensions of the zones of conflux and of dispersion are a function of changing transportation technology. While in the early stages workers travelled to work either on foot or horseback, the introduction of the railroad and the streetcar results in expansion of the labour catchment areas of centrally placed workplaces through the linking together of contiguous residential zones in a linear fashion. The most recent phase of transportation technology, that characterized by the widespread use of automobiles, sees a return to the initial situation modified only by an extended range to the daily journey to work. "By breaking down the compartmentalized organization within the complex," writes Vance, "automobile transportation has made the geographical city an intimately tied economic and functional agglomeration."[19] Not all members of society are able to take advantage of each successive stage of transportation technology as it appears, however. In the present city it may well be that all three

stages—foot, streetcar and railroad, and automobile—are characteristic of different sectors of the labour force and that, consequently, different residential areas are perceived in different ways by workers of varying social and economic status. Vance's study places more emphasis upon distance as a variable and less upon the pluralistic nature of society. Its conclusion that the "areal structure of economic activity along with the dependent urban areal structure would result from two irreducible variables, (1) absolute distance from an initial or satellitic zone of conflux, and (2) transportation technology"[20] is similar to viewpoints expressed by the human ecologists of the 1920's. In his classic work on human ecology for example, Amos Hawley[21] suggested that the distribution patterns of human life are the results of the interdependence of man's activities within the limitations set by the varying character of space and by the friction of distance.

The Journey to Work as a Problem of Human Ecology

In many ways the ecological approach would seem to be the most promising towards the journey to work. Human ecology, which had its origins in the Chicago School of Sociology in the 1920's, had as its aim "to discover the principles and factors involved in the changing patterns of spatial arrangement of population and institutions resulting from the interplay of living beings in a continuously changing culture."[22] Above all it was concerned with theory. A principal assump-

19. *Ibid.*
20. *Ibid.*
21. Amos Hawley, *Human Ecology* (New York: Ronald Press, 1950), especially Chapter 13.
22. R. D. McKenzie, "Human Ecology," *Encyclopaedia of the Social Sciences* (New York: Macmillan, 1931). Quoted by Leonard Reissman, *The Urban Process* (Glencoe, Ill.: The Free Press, 1964), p. 93.

tion of the ecologists was that man exists in a competitive environment in which adjustments are made between individuals and institutions such that the city resembles a closely interrelated, functioning organic whole. The ecological perspective still features prominently in the urban literature and is believed by some to represent the closest we have come to a systematic theory of the city.[23]

Studies of the journey to work which have been done within the ecological framework have generally assumed the pervading influence of the length of the journey to work. An early study by Carrol[24] employed hypotheses largely based upon Zipf's[25] principle of least effort. They suggested that forces are in operation which tend to minimize the distance between a worker's home and his place of work, and the concentrative effect of these forces is an important factor conditioning the total residential arrangement of urban populations. In their crudest form studies of this nature exhibit a kind of "distance determinism," although they were often based on sound empirical research. A previous study for example had shown that "the bulk of factory workers live close to work, and beyond two or three miles the proportion of factory workers decreases as distances from the factory increases."[26] And the findings of both studies were summarized into three broad generalizations. These were, first, that the total urban area population is residentially distributed about the central business district of the principal city; second, that the residential distribution of persons employed in central districts tends to approximate that of the entire urban population; and, third, that the residences of persons employed in off-center workplaces are concentrated most heavily in the immediate vicinity of the place of work.[27] The pattern, in short, is a familiar one in human ecology, that of dominance and sub-dominance. It is one in which "population and the residences of central district employees are arranged about the core areas in a constantly declining density [while] off-center work concentrations, on the other hand, have residences grouped about them so that the seem to resemble nucleated sub-clusters within the larger whole."[28] The present writer's own research would seem to support these generalizations.

Schnore[29] has pointed out that the ability to minimize effort varies among the population, and it has been suggested earlier that the ability to meet the diseconomies transferred from the plant to the worker by the necessity of the journey to work are borne with varying ease by different sectors of the labour force. While the lower-income manual worker might find it necessary to minimize his journey to work, the higher-income white-collar worker has presumably greater ability to meet the costs of commuting from further afield. But both do so within the established structure of the city. Beverly Duncan[30] showed in Chicago that work-residence separation is higher for white-collar than for blue-collar workers and, specifically, that the degree of work-residence separation varies directly with the socioeconomic level of the worker, is directly related to the centralization of work-

23. Leonard Reissman, loc. cit.
24. J. Douglas Carrol, "The Relations of Homes to Workplaces and the Spatial Pattern of Cities," Social Forces, 30 (March, 1952), pp. 271-282.
25. G. K. Zipf, Human Behaviour and the Principle of Least Effort (Cambridge, Mass.: Edison Wesley Press, 1949).
26. John Douglas Carrol, "Some Aspects of the Home-Work Relationships of Industrial Workers," Land Economics, 25 (November, 1949), pp. 414-422.

27. John Douglas Carroll, op. cit. (1952).
28. Ibid.
29. Leo Schnore, "The Separation of Home from Work: A Problem for Human Ecology," Social Forces, 32 (May, 1954), pp. 336-343.
30. Beverly Duncan, "Factors in Work-Residence Separation: Wage and Salary Workers, Chicago, 1951," American Sociological Review (February, 1956), pp. 48-56.

places, and consequently is greatest for workers of high socioeconomic status with centralized workplaces. However, the question remains unanswered as to whether this is the result of those in low-wage occupations being unable to meet the higher costs of the journey to work, especially if employed in off-center workplaces with difficult public transport connections, or of the structure of the city itself.

Whiting[31] showed that Chicago families who were relocated from the "black belt" of the central area to scattered public housing projects retained an affinity for their original workplaces in the central area. What is in operation here is evidently a form of locational "preference" which is independent of the distance from the place of work. The Chicago public housing tenants may have been unable to find employment close to their new homes, but the example does bring into question the analysis of the journey to work solely in terms of cost and distance. It has been suggested by Goldner that "workers' locational preferences are not a unique and interdependent portion of the totality of the workers' labour-market preferences. A related set of propensities are those involving workers' choices between labour and leisure."[32] Proximity to shopping facilities, to parks, to theatres, to schools, and the operation of traditional patterns of residential occupance must all be taken into question. Even in the USSR, where the possibilities of the relocation of population according to rational notions of space economy would be expected to be at a maximum, Lyubovnyy[33] reports that in the industrial city of Kolomna different factories and even different departments within the same factory may be staffed with workers from completely different residential villages, some of which are traditional sources of labour for a particular industrial operation. It would thus seem that in addition to the consideration of distance as an important variable other factors must be taken into account, including the positive or negative effects of planning, the operation of bases of preference other than proximity to work, and what might be termed traditional patterns of work and residence.

Once the notion of the distance from work as a prime determinant of where people live had been dethroned, then the journey to work assumed its proper place as just one of many factors which contribute towards the complex patterns of the modern city. In more recent research emphasis has been placed increasingly on the development of more refined conceptual tools for examining the journey to work, particularly those which may have predictive value. The association which exists between the removal of constraints on the distance between work and home, and its consequences for the urban explosion have made the refinement of such tools a primary need. The planning departments of many cities as well as researchers in university departments have used gravity and potential models, probability models, and models involving systems theory. As the cities grow, suburbs burgeon, and transportation becomes more difficult, the problems associated with the separation of work-residence become more pressing and their solution more urgent.

31. R. F. Whiting, "Home-to-Work Relationships of Workers Living in Public Housing Projects in Chicago," *Land Economics,* 28 (August, 1952), pp. 283-290.

32. William Goldner, "Spatial and Locational Aspects of Metropolitan Labour Markets," *American Economic Review,* 45 (1955), pp. 113-128.

33. V. Ya. Lyubovnyy, "Some Questions Relating to the Formation of Urban Populations," *Soviet Geography,* 11 (December, 1960), pp. 51-57.

M. E. ELIOT HURST

The Structure of Movement and Household Travel Behaviour

Most urban transportation research is today concerned with the prediction of travel patterns and spatial distributions. The prediction of travel patterns assumes a given spatial distribution of human activities, usually measured in land use terms. On the other hand the prediction of a spatial distribution is usually carried out via land use models using a given transportation network and the simulated travel patterns resulting from that network. In all these efforts assumptions have been made at a macroscopic level about individual behaviour, and attempts at prediction are usually made with only a small number of behaviour-affecting functions such as car ownership, family size, and travel time and costs. An examination of overall travel movements, a description of what movements occur, at what time, at certain volumes, between particular traffic zones, presupposes that we know much more about the factors of actual travel motivation than we actually do. Apart from using explicit factors therefore a great many other attributes, varying according to group and individual values and goals, are of significant importance for most people. What we now

need to investigate are the ways in which individuals themselves view the "choice" situations in which they make travel decisions, rather than placing those "choice" situations within a much too economically rational framework. I would hypothesise that the unique particulars of these situations are at least of equal importance to the less personal characteristics normally used in travel analyses, and that the subjective and cultural values present about an individual are of more importance than the more stringent types of economic or rational control.

Current Transportation Studies

Transportation studies to date have tended to take a macroscopic view of movement patterns. Most of these studies in North America and Western Europe have been reports of individual cities, and little work has been carried out to establish any "universal" applications. Of these latter studies, most are of the correlation type, which attempt to find relationships between origin-destination data and socio-economic characteristics. One of the frequently used correlations is that of trips

From **Urban Studies**, Vol. 6, No. 1, February 1969, Glasgow, Scotland. Reprinted by permission.

from-the-home and the car ownership level, which merely produces as many regression equations as there are investigators! As a result few studies have been completed which can be directly applied to other areas.

Current studies are based on two main propositions:

1. the establishment for the present time of travel patterns and certain socio-economic variables; the concern is also with the elimination of congestion, or the provision of capacity for travel at certain levels of congestion, often arbitrarily selected from an engineering standpoint;
2. the projection of certain of these criteria to some future date.

Highly sophisticated mathematical models are now available to help determine the existing deficiences of the transportation system. These are, however, all based on the macroscopic view which considers only factual data relating to the *habits* of the individual tripmaker. Such data is in fact a record of the response of the public to that available transportation system. As noted above it has been found that this response at a given time may be strongly correlated with certain socio-economic characteristics. No attempts are made to measure the satisfaction of the tripmaker with the transportation system, and in fact the existing system may be effectively masking real desires by deliberate limitations on levels of transportation service. This may apply both to the street system as it affects usage, and to the journey-to-work as it is affected by the qualities of the equipment. Other steps in the planning process include other correlations, as between trip frequency and trip time for example, as aids in estimating trip distributions between various potential origins and destinations. In other words unlike certain other sectors dealing with the consumer, the transportation study does not to date consider the *discriminatory* attitude of the tripmaker.

The same models are used with identical parameters, but with projected socio-economic characteristics, to determine future travel patterns. However, as is now obvious, the basic data refers not to demands or desires, but to travel habits. Thus although the travel habits of today may well be correlateable with current socio-economic conditions, there is little reason to believe that the same correlations will hold in predicting travel in the future. To improve the use of these correlations, both for the present and the future, the underlying *causes* or decision factors that govern the travel motivations of the tripmaker should be examined.

The significance of these comments to the estimations of traffic flows made both in the United Kingdom and North America, is that since cause and effect are not examined or understood, little reliance can be placed on the predictive power of the models used over long terms. Even in a short period of time, say five or ten years, the relationship between trips, and for example car ownership, can alter significantly. Similar comments can be made about the methodology applied to trip distribution. Several methods are currently used to account for trip distributions between traffic zones. Distribution functions are derived by fitting curves to data descriptive of present conditions; the same distribution function is then assumed to apply to future conditions and is therefore used in determining future distribution. One example of this is the time function which relates trip frequency to trip time for various trip purposes in the "gravity model."[1] The implicit assumption is that the time function is independent both of the generation of the trip, the attraction of the trip, or the system which channels the trip. Some success has been achieved

1. See for example G. A. P. Carrothers, "An Historical Review of the Gravity and Potential Concepts of Human Interaction," *Journal of the American Institute of Planners*, 22, 1956, pp. 94-102; and A. M. Voorhees, "Forecasting Peak Hours of Travel," Highway Research Board, *Bulletin*, 203, 1958.

in simulating present-day travel patterns in this way. Several features, however, go unexplained and require adjustments to make the facts fit observed conditions. The main criticism of this method is that it does not attempt to *explain* the facts but merely correlates them in an apparently satisfactory manner. Since also the "gravity model" is based on a physical analogy there is a tendency on the part of investigators to make facts fit the formula, further obscuring the possibility of gaining much insight into the true conditions governing transportation demands. Methods other than the "gravity model" exist, but none give insight into the motivations of the individual tripmaker.[2]

Currently then there is no reliable information on the *causes* underlying travel demand or use, nor of the causes underlying consumer satisfaction with the transportation system or its elements. Furthermore there is no data on which to evaluate the way changing social and economic conditions may affect these demands. Transport study procedures tend to *freeze* the tripmakers response to the system, and to make the assumption that present *habit patterns* will reliably describe those of the future, whether it is 25 or 50 years away. Of course, some of these mathematical procedures are modified for a particular study by the subjective judgment of an individual traffic researcher, but there is no uniform approach in these modifications.

Despite these criticisms, some useful development work has been carried out in these transportation studies, and some highly refined and sophisticated models have been produced, which within certain

limits, can reliably simulate today's traffic patterns. Travel demand predictions are obtained by using these parameters describing present conditions and incorporating predicted socio-economic factors. Trip forecasting and distribution, the basis of planning for the future, thus becomes a matter of appropriately forecasting socio-economic characteristics. Since, however, neither of these, nor the parameters, are likely to be descriptive of the future, and since much of the work in predicting future land use is carried out with little understanding of the forces shaping land use, the prediction of transportation demand is obviously subject to considerable doubt.

Further research is needed into the causes of movement, one such postulate, the concept of "movement space" is considered in the remainder of this paper. Research is also required into the reasons for land use development in terms of individual and group decision making, with particular emphasis on the transport system. It is generally recognised by researchers in the field of transportation, some of whose work is reviewed below, that a great deal more knowledge of the perceptions, conceptions, and the decision processes of the individual tripmaker or household is required. To obtain this kind of information both the *habits* and the *motives* of the urban traveller must be analysed and understood.

Evaluation of Recent Literature

General systems of movement, the correlation of movement systems and land use patterns, and traffic assignment, obviously have their role to play as the considerable literature, such as that of Mitchell and Rapkin,[3] Mertz and Hammer,[4] Oi and

2. For other methods see, S. Osofosky, "The Multiple Regression Method of Forecasting Traffic Volumes," *Traffic Quarterly,* Vol. 13, 1959, pp. 423-45; M. Schneider, "Gravity Models and Trip Distribution Theory," *Papers and Proceedings,* Regional Science Association, vol. 5, 1959, pp. 51-56; R. T. Howe, "A Theoretical Prediction of Work-trip Patterns," Highway Research Board, *Bulletin,* 253, 1960, pp. 155-65; etc.

3. R. B. Mitchell and C. Rapkin, *Urban Traffic, a Function of Land Use,* New York: Columbia University Press, 1954.
4. W. L. Mertz and L. B. Hammer, "A Study of Factors Related to Urban Travel," *Public Roads,* April 1957, pp. 170-4.

Schuldiner,[5] testifies. But despite this considerable research into outward patterns of movement, we still do not really understand why this behaviour occurs. Detailed inquiry into travel motivation and travel behaviour obviously would throw further light on trip generation analysis and on the relationship of land uses. Attempts at more detailed analyses of travel behaviour have been rather cursory to date, tending to utilise certain social factors either implicitly as with Schnore[6] or Breeze,[7] or more explicitly, Huff,[8] or Marble.[9] However, during the past few years, increasing attention has been given to the role of individual perception and value judgments, by planners, sociologists, psychologists, and geographers.

A pioneer work was that of Kevin Lynch who studied "the visual quality of the American city by studying the mental image of that city which is held by its citizens."[10] Many have followed, notably Wilson,[11] Peterson,[12] Medalia,[13] and Van Arsdol, Sabagh and Alexander.[14] Schimpeler[15] has used a ranking method and game and decision theory to quantitatively assess alternative plans and community goals as perceived by panels of residents. In other fields including geography, more direct attention has been paid to the interaction of the phenomenal and behavioural environments. Kates[16] related the actions of shopkeepers and residents of a flood plain zone to their perceptions of the dangers of flooding, Lansing and Mueller[17] examined interactions between satisfaction with residential communities and household locational choices, Webber[18] contrasted varying perceptions of space and spatial organisations with culture and social rank, and most recently a symposium at the A.A.G. annual meeting considered environmental perception.[19] Finally, Murdie, has conducted a study of the factors which affected the distances travelled by two groups of consumers. These two groups, Old Order Mennonites and "modern" Canadians provided a comparison of

5. W. Y. Oi and P. W. Schuldiner, *An Analysis of Urban Travel Demands,* Evanston: Northwestern University Press, 1962.

6. L. F. Schnore, "Transportation Systems, Socio-economic Systems, and the Individual," in *Transportation Design Considerations,* Paper 29, Publications 841 NAS-NRC, 1961.

7. G. Breeze, "Urban Transportation and the Individual," in *Transportation Design Considerations,* Paper 28, Publication 841, NAS-NRC, 1961.

8. D. L. Huff, "A Topographical Model of Consumer Preferences," *Regional Science Association, Papers and Proceedings,* Vol. 6, 1960, pp. 159-73.

9. D. F. Marble, "Transportation Inputs and Urban Residential Sites," *Regional Science Association, Papers and Proceedings,* vol. 5, 1959, pp. 253-66.

10. K. Lynch, *The Image of the City,* Cambridge: M.I.T. Press, 1960, p. 5.

11. R. L. Wilson, "Livability of the City: Attitudes and Urban Development," in F. S. Chapin and S. F. Weiss (eds.), *Urban Growth Dynamics in a Regional Cluster of Cities,* New York: Wiley, 1962, pp. 359-99.

12. G. L. Peterson, "Subjective Measures of Housing Quality: An Investigation of Problems of Codification of Subjective Value for Urban Analysis," unpublished PhD. thesis, Northwestern University, 1965.

13. N. Z. Medalia, *Community Perception of Air Quality: An Opinion Survey in Clarkston, Washington,* Cincinnati: U.S. Public Health Service, June 1965.

14. M. L. Van Arsdol, G. Sabagh, and F. Alexander, "Reality and the Perception of Environmental Hazards," *Journal of Health and Human Behaviour,* V, Winter 1964, pp. 144-53.

15. C. C. Schimpeler, *A Decision-Theoretic Approach to Ranking Community Goals and to Alternative Plan Evaluation,* West Lafayette, Purdue University, 1966.

16. R. W. Kates, *Hazard and Choice Perception in Flood Plain Management,* University of Chicago, Department of Geography, Research Paper No. 78, 1962.

17. J. B. Lansing and E. Mueller, *Residential Location and Urban Mobility,* Ann Arbor: University of Michigan Institute for Social Research, 1964.

18. M. M. Webber, "Culture, Territoriality, and the Elastic Mile," *Regional Science Association, Papers and Proceedings,* vol. 13, 1964, pp. 59-69.

19. 61st meeting of the A.A.G., Columbus, Ohio, April 20, 1965, edited by D. Lowenthal as *Environmental Perception and Behaviour,* University of Chicago, Department of Geography, Research Paper No. 109, 1967.

two sub-cultural groups living within the same area. While the findings showed striking similarities for movement of "modern" goods and services, those movements of "traditional" goods and services produced strikingly dissimilar patterns.[20] Others who have added weight to this theme are Stea, Snow, Sommer and Ray.[21]

Within transport most attention, however, has been given to car drivers' route choices.[22] Campbell,[23] Claffey,[24] and St. Clair and Leider[25] have tried to quantify the values which drivers place upon benefits gained by use of toll roads, value being equated with willingness to pay. Michaels,[26] Cohen,[27] and Wachs,[28] have

tried to statistically explain the choice made between alternative routes on the basis of the driver's attitudes, which indicated that neither time nor costs, the traditional explanatory variables, were dominant. What seemed to be indicated was that drivers chose routes on direct experience, and choices were made to minimise the total stress. The tension generated on a trip was a function of travel time in that time controlled the frequency, though not the intensity, of stressing interferences. The mean tension on a freeway was found to increase lineally to about 1,400 vehicles per lane per hour, after which it increased very rapidly.[29] Although car drivers attempt to make a rational evaluation of transportation, their choice appeared "to have very little in common with the economic criteria normally used in highway transportation."[30] Apart from these studies, however, the role of individual values and perception has not yet been pursued in transportation studies in any detail.

Operational Framework

The following untested operational framework and concepts are proposed, within which travel decisions could be analysed. They are offered as suggestions at this stage, drawing on a number of general propositions identified by decision behaviour theorists.[31]

It is first necessary to identify some of the properties of tripmaking, to distinguish between the intentions that motivate trips, and the events that actually occur. A trip, "the one-way travel from one point to

20. R. A. Murdie, "Cultural Differences in Consumer Travel," *Economic Geography,* vol. 41, 1967, No. 3, pp. 211-33.
21. D. Stea, "Reasons for our Moving," *Landscape,* Autumn 1967, vol. 17, No. 1, pp. 27-28; T. J. Snow, "The New Road in the United States," *Landscape,* Autumn 1967, vol. 17, No. 1, pp. 13-14; R. Sommer, "Man's Proximate Environment," *Journal of Social Issues,* vol. 22, No. 4, 1966, pp. 59-70; and D. M. Ray, "Cultural Differences in Consumer Travel Behaviour in Eastern Ontario," *The Canadian Geographer,* vol. XI, No. 3, 1967.
22. An exception would be some of the research proposals set out in J. D. Carroll (chairman) Panel 2, *Human Values Related to Urban Transportation,* Highway Research Board Special Report No. 69, 1962, pp. 21-40.
23. M. Earl Campbell, *Toll Bridge Influence on Highway Traffic Operation,* Bureau of Highway Traffic, Yale University, Technical Report No. 2, 1947.
24. P. J. Claffey, "Characteristics of Passenger Car Travel on Toll Roads and Comparable Free Roads," *Highway Research Board, Bulletin,* 306, 1961, pp. 1-22.
25. G. P. St. Clair and N. Leider, *Evaluation of the Unit Cost of Time, and of Strain and Discomfort of Driving,* Highway Research Board, Special Report, No. 56, 1960, pp. 116-29.
26. R. M. Michaels, "Attitudes of Drivers Determine Choice Between Alternate Highways," *Public Roads,* December 1965, pp. 225-36.
27. D. A. Cohen, "The Attitudes of Drivers in their Selection of Alternative Routes, as Approaches to the Measurement of Quality of Traffic Service," unpublished M.S. thesis, Northwestern University, 1966.
28. M. Wachs, *The Evaluation of Engineering Projects Using Perceptions of, and Preferences for, Project Characteristics,* Ph.D. thesis, Northwestern University, published as Transportation Centre Research Report.
29. R. M. Michaels, "The Effects of Expressway Design on Driver Tension Responses," *Public Roads,* December 1962, pp. 107-12.
30. Michaels, "Driver Attitudes. . . ," *op cit.,* p. 235.
31. For example Cyert and Marsh, McGuire, Simon, Starbuck.

another for a particular purpose,"[32] must have an objective or *goal,* even though this may not be consciously formulated.[33] The objective is to accomplish *goal events(s)* at one or more *intended destinations,* so that the trip decision involves both the identification of an event, and a point(s) at which it occurs. To someone making the decision to begin a journey a goal event is a desired or intended action that is expected to be fulfilled at a particular point in space and time, even though the latter may be indefinite at the time of decision.

As distinct from the intentions or goals, are the actual occurrences, which may be transactions or merely modal changes. A transaction is any significant event which consciously terminates the trip, whether it be premeditated or occurring on impulse. The point at which it occurs becomes the actual destination, which may be an establishment or something like a shopping precinct, where a number of transactions will occur. Both the goal event and the intended destination, and the degree of determinateness change as the goal is approached.

Having identified terminologically the trip, goal, intended destination, occurrence, and destination point, we can turn to the initial motivation, to the isolation of the desire or tension within a traveller (conscious or not) which he hopes to satisfy in the course of a trip. That is the translation of a desire into an action decision.

We can begin with the concept of "intendedly rational" man[34] who can differentiate between courses of action by way of their relative utility, even though he has a finite ability to perceive or calculate. The tripmaker has a level of aspiration and expected attainment, adjusted by ex-

perience. This level or threshold functions as an evaluative mechanism, which allows the distinction of positive or negative net utilities.[35] Transferring this notion to the travel decision environment and to a spatial context, we can say a *positional utility* indicates the net utilities derived from the tripmaker's integration at some point in space. The threshold for the tripmaker will be a function of his experience of previous travel. The positional utility will be positive or negative indicating the tripmaker's satisfaction or dissatisfaction with the anticipated move.

Instead of a binary positional utility, we could substitute degrees of valence, degrees of attraction or repulsion, satisfaction or dissatisfaction.

Assuming then this "intendedly rational" behaviour, the generation of trips from an origin to a destination is the result of a decision process which recognises differences in utility associated with different places. The tripmaker moves to a destination whose characteristics he knows to possess, or promise, a relatively higher level of utility than at other destinations known to him. In this sense movement reflects a subjective positional utility evaluation. The move from origin to destination can be conceived in this way as proceeding from varyingly perceived stimuli, within a satisfaction-framework. Some of these processes will be relatively simple, like the decisions preceding the journey-to-work or the journey-to-school, for instance, whilst others like the decisions prior to shopping, pleasure trips, or social visits will be more complex.

A *movement space,* a perceived part of the environment within which movement occurs, can also be identified. This movement space is in many cases the specifically restricted space within which the tripmaker receives his stimuli and makes

32. U.S. Bureau of Public Roads, *Manual of Procedures for the Home Interview Traffic Study,* revised ed. 1954, p. 39.
33. Mitchell and Rapkin, *op cit.,* pp. 44-53.
34. H. A. Simon, "Economics and Psychology," in S. Koch (ed.), *Psychology, a Study of a Science,* No. 6, New York, McGraw-Hill, 1963.

35. Compare J. Wolpert, "Behavioural Aspects of the Decision to Migrate," *Regional Science Association, Papers and Proceedings,* vol. 15, pp. 159-69, especially pp. 161-3.

his responses. This concept of movement space is similar to Lewin's "life space."[36] This is a universe of space and time in which the person conceives that he can or might move about, and is only a limited portion of the environment. To the tripmaker this space about him is the more or less immediate subjectively perceived portion of the environment, within which his sets of positional utilities occur. This behavioural environment or space is the surface over which an organism moves, is dependent for its needs, drives, goals, and perceptual apparatus.[37] This subjective environment or movement space, as perceived by the tripmaker, is filtered through conscious and unconscious brain processes, programmed by his needs, desires, and abilities.[38]

Movement space could be further refined. It might be possible to identify three types of movement space:

1. A *core,* which is the frequently travelled space, with which the tripmaker is most familiar. This is the space within which regular journeys are made, frequent visits to friends, and shopping trips.
2. A *median* area, the occasionally travelled space, within which journeys to visit relatives, and holidays would be made by many people.
3. An *extensive* movement space, which is the conceived, concept-learnt, or cosmological space.

36. K. Lewin, *Field Theory in Social Science,* New York: Harper and Row, 1951. Compare also Chapin's "activity space" and Wolpert's "action space"; F. S. Chapin and H. C. Hightower, "Household Activity Patterns and Land Use," *Journal of the American Institute of Planners,* August 1965, pp. 222-31; J. Wolpert, *op. cit.,* p. 163.
37. H. A. Simon, "Rational Choice and the Structure of the Environment," *Psychological Review,* vol. 63, 1956, pp. 129-38.
38. H. and M. Sprout, "The Cognitive Aspect of Man-Milieu Relationships," in *The Ecological Perspective on Human Affairs,* Princeton University Press, 1965, pp. 117-41.

For some tripmakers all three types of movement space are virtually coterminous, for others they vary considerably. For the purposes of urban transportation studies the first type of movement space would be of the greatest importance.

The limits of the movement space, unique to a particular tripmaker, are set by his finite abilities to perceive, and by his learning experiences. Movement space will vary from the limited realm of the young child to the extensive realm of say an international movie-star. This variation occurs with the increasing number and intensity of contacts with the environment. The degree of contact could be measured, using Meier's term,[39] by knowing the rate of receipt or perception of "informational bits." The tripmaker can now be conceived within a particular space, perceiving besides his origin, a number of alternative destinations or positional utilities, between which he chooses one as a goal, according to the valence of the intended destination(s). His positional utilities, however conspicuous at any one time, will mainly include a cluster of alternate destinations within close proximity, and all positional utilities will be contained within the limits of the individual tripmaker's movement space. The wider his communication with friends and relatives, his contact with mass media and travel, the more comprehensive will be his movement space.

In Lewin's concept, behaviour is a function of life space, which in turn is a function of the person and the environment. The behaviour-influencing aspects of the external environment are represented through the life space. In a similar way movement space includes the range of choice defined by the tripmaker's personal attributes and, as will be shown later, by his position in a life cycle. So the tripmaker's movement space fashioned in this way, includes not just his origin, but a

39. R. L. Meier, *A Communications Theory of Urban Growth,* Cambridge: M.I.T. Press, 1962.

finite number of alternative destinations, presented to him through a combination of search and communication. The movement space becomes a set of destinations, intended or not, towards which the tripmaker has a set of utilities. He attaches a utility to his present position (the origin of the trip) and relatively higher or lower utilities are assigned to the alternative destinations. The variables are the number of alternative destinations and their spatial arrangement with respect to the origin. The destinations may be neighbours' homes within the same block, homes of friends in another suburb, or relatives in another urban area. Not all of these alternatives may be presented simultaneously of course, since there are other constraints such as time and cost.

Cyert and Marsh in their study of the business world[40] suggest further factors for an operational framework, which could be utilised by a detailed study of travel motivation. Such factors as sequential appearance, attention to, and consideration of alternative destinations; the order in which the movement space is searched; the minimisation of conditions of uncertainty which may lead to delayed responses; although reliance on informational feedback, and the imitation of successful travel decisions made by others, could all determine to a substantial extent the actual travel decision.

The distinction between the environmental realms of the young child and the movie-star, places a further constraint on utilities and movement space, that is a variation with life cycle.[41] Each point on the life cycle from birth, to maturity and old age, gives rise to distinct movement patterns, the expanding movement space being a function of increased contacts with "bits." Associated with this variable of age, are other variables such as sex, race, educational attainment, income, social status, all of which shape the area of movement in which positional utilities can be assessed.

This framework has isolated concepts of positional utility; movement space, life cycle, and certain other behavioural factors. In the process of actual travel decisions, this indicates that we should examine the decision processes by which goal events and intended destinations are chosen, and the cognitive aspect of potential destinations where the tripmaker is aware, believes, or hopes that a goal event can occur. The decision and cognition is shaped by utility, perceived space, point on the life cycle, habit, and role.

40. R. M. Cyert and J. G. Marsh, *A Behavioural Theory of the Firm,* Englewood Cliffs: Prentice Hall, 1963.

41. Meier, *op. cit.,* and Wolpert, *op. cit.,* pp. 164-5.

GERALD J. KARASKA

Manufacturing Linkages in the Philadelphia Economy: Some Evidence of External Agglomeration Forces

External economies of scale have been regularly noted in discussions of manufacturing location, but only a few studies have attempted to empirically identify and measure relevant characteristics of this locational factor. The availability of an intensive survey of Philadelphia manufacturers and the subsequent compilation of these original data into an input-output matrix have prompted this attempt to probe the nature of the external-agglomeration locational forces. We pursue this identification by analyzing data from the input-output matrix, and are constrained by the facts of this matrix which only describe the procurement or supply patterns of Philadelphia manufacturing. We postulate that the agglomeration forces may in part be described by procurement actions between local manufacturing firms. The strength of the linkage with the local manufacturing system is a measure of the agglomerative force exerted by the size of the local metropolitan industrial complex. This approach is obviously not completely valid in measuring the external economies as no attempt is made to evaluate and

compare the strength of other locational attractions in the metropolitan area, for example, labor, taxes, power, transportation, and so on. Nonetheless, we present this study as a first step toward better comprehension of the nature of the agglomeration forces.

The substance of the following discussion is the identification of linkages between Philadelphia industries in their procurement actions. These input linkages are first generally described, then a typology of industries is presented. This analysis of industries according to the strength of their local linkages provides some measure of the external economies of scale and an identification of industries exemplifying these characteristics.

The External Economies of Scale

A factor attributed as important in influencing the location of a manufacturing enterprise is its size or scale of operation. Certain economic advantages such as lower production costs and greater revenues often result from higher levels of production. These economic advantages, called economies of scale or agglomeration economies, may result from conditions both internal and external to the firm. Hoover[1] differentiates among the agglomeration forces as follows:

1. *large-scale economies* within a firm, consequent upon the enlargement of the firm's scale of production at one point;
2. *localization economies* for all firms in a single industry at a single location, consequent upon the enlargement of the total output of that industry at that location; and,
3. *urbanization economies* for all firms in all industries at a single location, consequent upon the enlargement of the total economic size (population, income, output, or wealth) of that location, for all industries taken together.[2]

We do not attempt here an exhaustive definition of the scale-economies as these are examined elsewhere.[3] However, since the ensuing discussion is concerned with certain aspects of this multi-dimensional force, a brief review of the topic is important.

On the one hand, the external economies relate to the more efficient technology associated with a higher level of use of the existing economic apparatus.[4] The infrastructure of large urban systems provides a more efficient technology wherein the costs of services to individual firms are minimal or appreciably lower than if separately provided by each firm. Small firms, for example, may obtain lower production costs by "pooling" certain resources with other firms—sharing suppliers, labor, utilities, and so on.

Another dimension of the external economies relates to demand aspects of the urban system. The metropolitan area acts as a large market in terms of both intermediate and final consumption. The latter refers to the large, local, final demand for certain products of the manufacturing sector. This output is subject to the highly variable and unpredictable requirements of the region's households. Lichtenberg[5] notes that the technical requirements of this production are such that producers must be able to cater to an ever-changing demand by speedily tooling-up (or rapidly drawing upon an established network of subcontractors and suppliers) and turning out their product in a short period. Lichtenberg's study of the New York Metropolitan Region described these firms as manufacturing "unstandardized products" with the following characteristics: small plants; short production cycles; face-to-face contacts with customers; low ratio of inventory to sales; a sharing of facilities, services, and labor; short-term capital commitments; and quick access to all linkages.

With regard to the large intermediate demand of manufacturing in the metropolitan area, other kinds of external agglomeration forces may appear. Lichtenberg noted that some firms are attracted to the metropolitan area because they supply a large number of customers in different industries in the region and can look forward to a steady demand for their product from the whole group, if not from individual customers.

In the context of these dimensions, we now proceed to identify and measure local input linkages of Philadelphia manufacturers. We acknowledge the complexity of the "agglomeration forces" and the complicity of linkages in such a large,

1. E. M. Hoover, *Location Theory and the Shoe and Leather Industries* (Cambridge: Harvard University Press, 1937), p. 91.
2. W. Isard, *Location and Space Economy* (Cambridge: M.I.T. Press, 1956), p. 172.
3. T. Scitovsky, "Two Concepts of External Economies," *Journal of Political Economy*, 62 (1954), 143-52.
4. Isard, *Location and Space Economy*, p. 182.

5. R. M. Lichtenberg, *One Tenth of a Nation* (Cambridge: Harvard University Press, 1960), p. 58.

interdependent, regional system. We examine only one direct linkage; namely that between one manufacturing industry and another industry. If a strong link is identified, we conclude a mutual economic advantage exists for the location of both industries within the urban system. This we feel to be the first step in understanding the urbanization economies, which we define as the total economic size of the Philadelphia manufacturing complex. Regrettably, we are not able to consider the relevance of the magnitude and composition of the service sectors of the Philadelphia Metropolitan area in defining the urbanization economies.

The Philadelphia Region Input-Output Study

In order to implement certain impact analyses, a detailed interindustry table was prepared for the Metropolitan Philadelphia economy for 1960. The input-output matrix was designed to represent manufacturing at the four-digit S.I.C. level and all other sectors at the three-digit S.I.C. level.[6] The data and information for this matrix came from three principal sources: interviews with local businesses, published and unpublished reports from state and federal agencies, and records of local governmental agencies. The business interviews were the most important source of data and produced a sample of approximately 1,000 manufacturing firms. A more detailed description of the Philadelphia Region Input-Output Study is available elsewhere.[7] It is important to note that

the data described in this paper are not those that appear in Isard, et al.[8] The latter did not attempt to compile interregional interindustry flows. The present analysis uses a different aggregation procedure wherein interregional information and flows are the primary concern.

Hypothetical Manufacturing Linkages

It is postulated here that information from the input-output table will shed some light on the complexity of the external economies. Since the input-output coefficient represents a linkage between industries, it in essence can describe locational forces within the local economic system; for, as noted earlier, one important element of the external economies is the spatial juxtaposition of mutually dependent enterprises. The input-output coefficient measures the value of a purchased input in relation to the value of an industry's (or firm's) level of output. As such the coefficient explicitly describes only the supply linkages of an industry. The demand relationships for the industry become explicit when the coefficients are viewed in relation to the regional system; i.e., in the context of an input-output table. Since the following analysis only evaluates individual coefficients, supply linkages will be measured directly while demand linkages must be indirectly measured. Hence, we postulate that manufacturing linkages as described by input-output coefficients may be of three types. The first is the local supply link of a firm for its largest input, the second is the local supply link for any input, and the third is described as the demand link to another local firm.

In essence, the first two types of linkages measure the degree to which a firm (or industry) is tied to the local economy through its supply or purchasing requirements. That is, the firm experiences a strong attraction to the local economy

6. Executive Office of the President, Bureau of the Budget, *Standard Industrial Classification Manual* (Washington, D.C.: U.S. Government Printing Office, 1956).
7. W. Isard et al., *The Philadelphia Region Input-Output Coefficient Table* (Philadelphia: Regional Science Research Institute, 1967); W. Isard, T. W. Langford, Jr., and E. Romanoff, *Philadelphia Region Input-Output Study: Working Papers* (Philadelphia: Department of Regional Science Research Institute, January 1967).

8. *The Philadelphia Region Input-Output Coefficient Table.*

because of important input linkages. The two types differ only in the strength of these linkages as measured in an input-output framework wherein one can identify either the largest input-output coefficient and the percentage of total requirements purchased locally, or any coefficient and its percentage purchased locally.

The third type of linkage looks at the same input-output coefficients, but from another perspective—the demand side. Here the linkage identifies those local firms (or industries) which experience large intermediate (manufacturing) demand from the local economic system. This demand may be measured by the number of times a local firm sells to local industry and by the relative value of the local sales.

Philadelphia Supply Linkages

Industries and their purchases were identified and aggregated at the four-digit S.I.C. level so that each firm and all of its

inputs appeared in the input-output table on this four-digit basis. The ensuing discussion analyzes the following inputs from each industry class: the largest input, the total-materials-consumed coefficient, and all inputs.

The local purchasing characteristics of 282 manufacturing industries in Philadelphia when described by the largest input of each industry showed a mean of 34.5 per cent locally purchased. Thus it may be concluded that most industries procure their largest input from nonlocal sources. Further, 44 per cent of this sample of Philadelphia industries purchased less than 10 per cent of their largest input from local industries. When the largest input is qualified according to its size as an input-output coefficient, i.e., the value of the input per dollar of output. These largest inputs are typically imported and the local inputs may be characterized as small inputs.

The preceding information is summarized in Table 1 in terms of the local

Table 1. Per Cent Locally Purchased for Largest Input

S.I.C. Number	Industry	Number of Four-Digit Industries	Mean Per Cent Locally Purchased
20	Food	26	42.6
22	Textiles	21	23.0
23	Apparel	16	6.6
24	Lumber	5	54.8
25	Furniture	10	54.6
26	Paper	12	12.7
27	Printing	15	63.6
28	Chemicals	20	26.1
29	Petroleum	4	73.0
30	Rubber	5	7.8
31	Leather	8	24.5
32	Stone, Clay, Glass	22	21.5
33	Primary metal	17	28.5
34	Fabr. metal	21	41.4
35	Machinery	29	47.5
36	Elect. mach.	17	49.6
37	Transportation	7	23.9
38	Instruments	8	62.0
39	Miscellaneous	19	23.3
Total Manufacturing		282	34.5

Table 2. Distribution of Total Materials Coefficient by Per Cent Locally
Purchased for Four-Digit Industries

Category of Per Cent Locally Purchased	Number	Four-Digit Industries Per Cent	Cum. Per Cent
0	7	2.5	2.5
01-10	52	18.4	20.9
11-20	38	13.5	34.4
21-30	38	13.5	47.9
31-40	39	13.8	61.7
41-50	25	8.8	70.5
51-60	21	7.4	77.9
61-70	20	7.1	85.0
71-80	14	5.0	90.0
81-90	14	5.0	95.0
91-99	11	3.9	98.9
100	3	1.1	100.0
Total	282	100.0	

Mean = 36.9%

Table 3. Number of Times a Four-Digit Input was Purchased Locally vs. the
Number of Times Imported, Summarized on a Two-Digit S.I.C. Basis

Two-Digit S.I.C. (1)	Total Number of Times Purchased (2)	Number of Times Purchased Locally (3)	Number of Times Imported (4)	Ratio (3) : (4)
20	102	74	78	1:1.1
22	219	125	166	1:1.3
23	23	13	22	1:1.7
24	118	90	65	1:0.7
25	12	10	8	1:0.8
26	421	356	218	1:0.6
27	55	44	23	1:0.5
28	457	334	310	1:0.9
29	41	32	22	1:0.7
30	93	68	66	1:1.0
31	22	8	18	1:2.2
32	140	88	108	1:1.2
33	583	493	370	1:0.8
34	248	204	165	1:0.8
35	115	97	83	1:0.9
36	116	89	91	1:1.0
37	9	4	9	1:2.2
38	18	12	14	1:1.2
39	45	22	40	1:1.8
Other	32	11	22	1:2.0
Unclassified	140	128	119	1:0.9
Total	3009	2302	2017	1:0.9

purchasing characteristics at the two-digit S.I.C. level. The Petroleum, Printing, and Instruments industries are seen to have important linkages with the local economy; 73 per cent, 64 per cent and 62 per cent, respectively, of the largest input of these industries is purchased locally. The Apparel and the Rubber industries are seen to have the weakest linkages with the local economy as measured by the largest input requirement, 7 per cent and 8 per cent, respectively.

The total materials coefficient is a measure which describes the sum of all material inputs purchased by a firm (here a four-digit S.I.C. industry). Table 2 shows the local purchasing characteristics of this coefficient, and reveals that when the total purchasing requirements of a firm are considered the over-all local linkages to the manufacturing sector are

somewhat stronger.[9] The mean of the sum of all inputs purchased locally is only 37 per cent, but the distribution of industries in Table 2 is more even over the range of per cent-local categories. For example, for almost half of the industries in the sample, thirty per cent of the value of the materials consumed came from local sources.

Every input to the industries of the sample was analyzed according to its degree of local linkage. When all of the inputs are treated separately, similarly strong local supply linkages may be seen

9. In analyzing the questionnaires from the Philadelphia Study, it was learned that management in responding to requests for data tended to neglect reporting the smaller purchases as inputs. The data compilation and aggregation did not completely correct for this unreported input. The total materials coefficient, hence, contains an unknown (though small) element of error.

Table 4. The Total Value of Four-Digit Inputs and the Value of Locally-Purchased vs. Imported Inputs, Summarized by Two-Digit S.I.C. in Thousand Dollars*

Two-Digit S.I.C. (1)	Total Value of Purchased Inputs (2)	Value of Local Inputs (3)	Value of Imported Inputs (4)	Per Cent Local (3):(2)	Ratio (3):(4)
20	122,191	14,470	107,721	11.8	1:7.4
22	66,552	6,321	60,228	9.5	1:9.5
23	2,673	1,025	1,649	38.3	1:6.1
24	13,585	6,612	6,972	48.7	1:1.1
25	3,063	944	2,120	30.8	1:2.2
26	262,834	31,900	230,933	12.1	1:7.2
27	6,125	3,704	2,421	60.5	1:0.7
28	155,014	26,649	128,366	17.2	1:4.8
29	22,872	6,288	16,584	27.5	1:2.6
30	11,319	2,661	8,658	23.5	1:3.3
31	4,142	1,260	2,882	30.4	1:2.3
32	25,615	7,668	17,947	29.9	1:2.3
33	255,045	94,705	160,340	37.1	1:1.7
34	69,134	25,600	43,533	37.0	1:1.7
35	36,635	7,417	29,217	20.2	1:3.9
36	51,946	12,362	39,584	23.8	1:3.2
37	17,701	1,144	16,557	6.5	1:14.5
38	2,123	834	1,290	39.2	1:1.6
39	1,938	596	1,342	30.7	1:2.3
Other	284,838	543	284,842	0.0	1:524.6
Unclassified	74,994	37,535	37,463	50.1	1:1.0
Total	1,490,890	290,246	1,200,654	19.4	1:4.1

* Value is the dollar sum of the sample of Philadelphia manufacturing firms.

Table 5. Selected Four-Digit Industries (Inputs) Frequently Selling to
Local Industries, Philadelphia Manufacturing*

S.I.C. Number (1)		Total No. of Times Purchased (2)	No. of Times Purchased Locally (3)	No. of Times Imported (4)	Per Cent Value Local to Total Value (5)
2284	thread	31	25	17	44
2298	cordage	16	12	6	17
2396	findings	17	10	17	42
2421	planing mills	42	33	23	41
2432	veneer	13	11	9	64
2441	boxes	16	16	3	75
2499	wood, n.e.c.	24	11	18	55
2643	bags	25	22	12	05
2649	paper, n.e.c.	21	17	8	43
2651	folding boxes	99	94	44	46
2652	set-up boxes	42	41	11	75
2653	corrugated boxes	63	60	24	71
2753	engraving	12	10	2	67
2813	ind. gases	13	12	4	99
2843	surface agents	11	9	6	53
2851	paints	48	41	28	25
2891	glue	41	32	25	55
2893	ink	36	34	13	33
2899	chemicals, n.e.c	17	13	8	29
2911	pet. refining	22	19	12	33
3221	containers	14	12	14	49
3241	cement	10	6	9	47
3291	abrasive prods.	13	11	6	89
3312	steel	110	102	87	41
3316	cold steel	32	31	13	29
3321	gray founds.	34	30	21	42
3322	mall. iron	13	10	8	50
3323	Steel founds.	30	28	17	54
3352	rolling, etc. alum.	57	46	34	50
3361	alum. castings	23	23	6	80
3362	casts., brass, etc.	31	30	17	24
3369	casts., n.e.c.	10	7	7	42
3391	steel forgings	20	16	13	44
3411	metal cans	14	12	11	46
3451	screw mach. prods.	17	16	13	58
3452	bolts, nuts, etc.	37	36	19	30
3471	electroplating	12	12	1	81
3491	metal barrels	14	13	10	71
3544	special dies	13	11	12	47
3591	machine shops	10	10	4	54
3622	ind. controls	12	10	6	52
3643	wiring devices	14	12	10	41

* Those local industries (inputs) which meet the following criteria: (a) provide inputs to Philadelphia manufacturing ten or more times; and either (b), column (3)
is 1.5 times or more than column (4), or (c) the value of those local sales is more
than 40 per cent of the total value of all sales, column (5).

to exist. If one arrays these inputs by their size, a revealing fact is that the imported inputs are larger while local inputs are smaller in size.

Philadelphia Demand Linkages

All of the inputs to the 282 manufacturing industries were sorted by their four-digit

S.I.C. number. These inputs (industries) are now analyzed according to whether they are local inputs or nonlocal inputs to the industries in the Philadelphia sample. The inputs first were counted to give the number of times each served as an input to the 282 industries (counted across the rows of the input output matrices). Similarly, each input was counted for the

Table 6. The Local Manufacturing Supply Linkage Classification: Four-Digit S.I.C. Industries Ranked and Grouped by Factor Scores

Highest Class 1	Class 2	Class 3	Class 4	Class 5	Class 6	Class 7	Lowest Class 8
2952	3831	2541	3272	3992	3269	2339	3444
3352	2793	2789	3569	3432	2392	3291	3442
3634	2042	2731	3221	2251	3421	2013	2011
2433	2852	3161	3843	3536	3361	2082	3111
2951	3316	2815	3995	2073	2816	2873	2072
2445	2024	2051	3961	3566	3231	3955	2654
2741	3679	3587	2293	3452	3552	3142	2337
2272	3811	3693	2512	2211	2221	3141	3259
2095	2992	3251	2761	3567	3662	3171	3255
2844	2751	3629	3621	3559	2231	3914	3317
2033	2652	3579	3613	3531	3988	2323	2711
2522	2542	3522	3273	2842	3292	2395	3312
2022	3913	3691	3423	3643	2643	3982	2397
2037	2752	3429	2291	2843	2085	3731	2284
3121	3842	2599	3493	3341	3069	3711	3911
2087	3554	2084	3722	3369	3962	3562	3275
3545	3611	2327	2032	3821	3399	2241	2721
2576	2026	2511	2271	2851	2642	2352	3721
2771	3841	3296	2645	3441	2841	3461	2341
2894	3299	3993	3861	2531	2821	3172	2621
2753	3622	2431	3729	3551	2891	3315	2328
3555	2515	2036	3323	3644	2653	2892	2282
3591	3585	3229	2261	3031	3494	2283	2096
3534	2514	3661	3953	2818	3079	3981	3011
3623	2071	3362	3321	3987	2021	3211	2911
3542	3714	3433	2641	3581	2782	3357	2259
3491	3589	2794	3281	3293	2269	3295	2893
3451	2791	3356	3271	3339	2443	2813	3131
3411	3498	2279	2631	2651	3931	3253	2351
2294	3561	2899	3941	2252	3052	2361	3274
3499	3544	2394	3799	3479	2819	2281	2871
3449	3565	3822	3949	3351	2035	3297	3021
2262	3535	3511	3642	3599	2834	2655	3964
3942	3471	3541	2732	2649	3481	2321	2062
2094	3639	2441	3621	3391	2015	2369	2299
							2393
							2591

number of times it was a local vs. an imported input. If an input was purchased only in part (per cent) from a local source, it was recorded as one local input and as one imported input. These counts (Table 3) reveal that each input was, as a rule, purchased with almost equal frequency from both local and nonlocal sources. The 282 industries purchased 3,103 inputs; local industries supplied inputs 2,359 times as compared to 2,094 times when inputs were imported (Table 3). Although not reported here, this approximately equal split was also seen at the three- and four-digit S.I.C. levels.

In contrast to the preceding table, Table 4 reports for the same set of data at the two-digit level, the value of these local vs. imported purchases. When measured by their dollar value, the imported inputs outweigh the local inputs almost five to one. Only in the Newspaper industry does the value of the local inputs significantly exceed that of the imported inputs. This same observation can be made at the three- and four-digit level of aggregation.

With respect to the major concern of this paper—the identification and measurement of external economies of scale—Tables 5 and 6 also reveal a special kind of local linkage. As described earlier, certain industries can be characterized as critically linked to the local economy when they sell to many local industries, and no one sale is significantly large.[10] If we examine the inputs to Philadelphia manufacturing and count the number of times a local industry served as an input to local manufacturing, and compare this to the number of times the same input was imported by Philadelphia manufacturing, the ratio identifies the industries linked to local manufacturing demand.

Table 5 lists the four-digit industries which most strongly show this demand-type linkage. The Table only identifies those local industries which served as in-

puts to Philadelphia manufacturing ten or more times and for which the frequency of local supply is more than 1.5 times the frequency of imported supply; or, for which the value of the local supply is greater than 40 per cent of the value of the total supply requirements.

A Typology of Philadelphia Industries According to Local Manufacturing Linkages

To summarize the above findings and to synthesize the numerous measures of local manufacturing linkages, a classification of Philadelphia industries is now presented. The objective of this classification is to aggregate the preceding measures into two separate indices. One index measures the degree to which each industry in the sample can be characterized as having local manufacturing *supply linkages*. The other index measures the degree to which Philadelphia industries can be characterized as having local manufacturing *demand* linkages. The first index then, classifies Philadelphia industries on the basis of their input characteristics (linkages). The second, classifies the inputs on the basis of their linkages with the Philadelphia manufacturing market. The aggregation and classification are performed by two separate principal components analyses.

The index of "local manufacturing supply linkage" is derived from the following five variables with the observations being the 282 industries of the sample:

1. the per cent local for the largest input;
2. the per cent local for the total materials coefficient;
3. a variable measuring the absolute size of the local largest input; specifically, the largest input-output coefficient multiplied by its per cent locally purchased (Table 2).
4. a variable measuring the relative size of the local largest input—the quotient

10. Lichtenberg, *One Tenth of a Nation*, p. 63.

of the total-materials-consumed coefficient and the largest input coefficient multiplied by the per cent locally purchased of the largest input.

5. a variable measuring the size of the local total materials consumed—the total materials consumed coefficient multiplied by the per cent local of the total materials coefficient.

The variation "explained" by the first dimension extracted from the principal components analysis is 73 per cent, and the loadings of the variables on this component are .89, .94, .77, .75, and .89, respectively. The 282 observations (industries) are ranked by their corresponding component score and arbitrarily grouped into eight classes in Table 6.

The industries scoring highest on this first component (Class 1 of Table 6) have extremely high supply linkages with the local Philadelphia manufacturing complex. For example, S.I.C. No. 2952 (asphalt felt products) purchases its largest input 100 per cent from local sources; this largest input has an input-output coefficient of .3375 as compared with a total materials consumed coefficient of .6996; and, in fact, all of its inputs are purchased from local sources. At the other extreme in Table 6, industry number 2591 (venetian blinds) purchases no inputs from local sources.

A close examination of the industries ranked in Table 6 reveals that the strongest local supply links exist in those industries which are part of the two-digit S.I.C. groups of petroleum (S.I.C. No. 29), lumber (No. 24), printing (No. 27), instruments (No. 38), furniture (No. 25), and machinery (No. 35), in that order. That is to say, four-digit industries beginning with these two-digit sets occur most frequently in the highest classes of Table 6. Conversely, those industries showing weakest links belong to the two-digit industries of rubber (No. 30), apparel (No. 23), paper (No. 26), and

stone, clay, and glass (No. 32), in that order.

The relevance of the components analysis is that it combines industries on the basis of their scores on a combination of five variables measuring local supply linkages. By contrast, the earlier tables and discussion were only able to evaluate the industries on one, or at most two, measures of local linkage. Hence, industries showing weak local linkages on some of the individual variables now demonstrate strong local linkages on the basis of the composite measure.

The index of "local manufacturing demand linkage" is based upon the demand characteristics shown in Tables 3, 4, and 5, which describe the inputs of Philadelphia industries. This index is the basis for a classification of the inputs and is derived from a principal components analysis of only two variables:

1. a measure of the number of times a *local* industry sold an input to another local industry as compared with the number of times a *nonlocal* industry sold an input to a Philadelphia industry; and

2. for each four-digit input the per cent represented by the value of local sales to Philadelphia industry as compared with the value of all sales to Philadelphia industry (column 5 of Table 4).

The first component explained 74 per cent of the variation in the two variables. The loadings of the variables on the component are both 0.86. The component score of each observation (input industry) constituted the desired index of "local manufacturing demand linkage"; the industries are ranked by these scores in Table 7.

The industries ranked highest in Table 7 have characteristics strongly identified with the demand linkages described ear-

Table 7. The Local Manufacturing Demand Linkage Classification Four-Digit
S.I.C. Industries Ranked and Grouped by Factor Scores

Highest Class 1	Class 2	Class 3	Class 4	Class 5	Class 6	Lowest Class 7
3471	2789	3292	2899	3315	3334	1459
2793	3491	2284	3241	3461	2821	3331
2441	3293	3321	3566	2816	2819	2241
2442	2654	2421	3443	3621	2751	3069
2753	2062	3391	3362	3011	3357	2631
2813	2651	3221	3351	2046	2824	3339
3361	3323	3452	2298	3494	2099	2299
2652	2532	3411	3499	3111	2295	1499
2426	3622	2499	2396	3229	2621	3333
3291	2893	3861	3429	2231	2283	2281
2791	2649	3312	3481	2641	2823	3964
2653	2891	3341	2851	2643	2655	2211
3274	2843	3561	3079	3679	2818	3295
2645	2841	3544	3317	3441	2812	2221
3399	3451	2911	1421	3356	3963	2093
2087	3599	2992	3613	3297	3255	2822
3591	3322	3643	2431	3562	2026	2291
1441	3352	3369	2861	2752	3211	2611
2842	3479	2094	2294	2815	3497	2041

lier.[11] For example, industry number 3471
(electroplating) supplied Philadelphia
manufacturing twelve times as a local
input and only once as an imported input;
also, local industry S.I.C. 3471 supplied
81 per cent of the value of the electroplating requirements of the Philadelphia
manufacturing complex. Another example
is S.I.C. 2793 (photoengraving) which
was a local input five times as compared
with a nonlocal input once, and the local
supply met 99 per cent of the total Philadelphia demand for this industry.

In summarizing the information shown
in Table 7, the following two-digit level
S.I.C. industries may be characterized as
having strong local demand linkages:
printing (No. 27), lumber (No. 24), fab-
ricated metals (No. 34), and machinery

11. These inputs classified as four-digit S.I.C.
industries, are not the same set as the 282 industries of the Philadelphia sample. Obviously,
the inputs to Philadelphia industry may be supplied by industries not represented in the Philadelphia sample.

(No. 35), in that order. Conversely, the
following two-digit industries exemplify
weak local demand linkages: miscellaneous manufacturing (No. 39), apparel
(No. 22), rubber (No. 30), food (No.
20), in that order.

The preceding has classified manufacturing industries found in the Philadelphia
SMSA on the basis of the strength of their
linkages with other Philadelphia industries. This linkage was identified and measured as the technological coefficient of an
input-output system. The intent of the
classification was to provide some insight
into those complex forces which attract
industry to a large metropolitan area.
While not totally accurate, this mutual
linkage partly describes the external agglomeration forces. In addition to describing the nature and overall strength of local
buying and selling, the discussion specifically identified those Philadelphia industries which exemplify strong local linkages—both in their supply and demand
components. The broad industry classes of

petroleum, lumber, printing, instruments, furniture and machinery have important linkages with the Philadelphia economy in both their supply and demand components. Conversely, industries such as rubber, apparel, and paper show evidence of weak linkages in their supply and demand components.

From another point of view, the overall effect of the Philadelphia economy upon manufacturing location—within the context of the external, agglomeration economies—appears to be weak. The largest inputs to Philadelphia industry are procured from nonlocal sources, and those largest inputs which are purchased locally are small in size. In fact, most of the local inputs to Philadelphia manufacturing are smaller than the imported inputs. The weakness of the agglomerative force of the Philadelphia economy is further demonstrated in terms of the "frequency of demand" of local vs. imported procurement. While Philadelphia industry frequently purchases inputs from the local economy, the value of the local inputs is considerably less than the value of the imported purchases. Of course, the strength of the Philadelphia economy in terms of the urbanization economies of scale can only be ascertained in relation to comparable effects in other metropolitan or urban systems. Finally, the strength or force of the service sectors of these urban systems must be evaluated.

DUANE F. MARBLE AND JOHN D. NYSTUEN

An Approach to the Direct Measurement of Community Mean Information Fields

The last decade has seen an increasing growth of interest in studies of the spatial structure of the diffusion process. The pioneering work of Professor Torsten Hägerstrand of the Royal University of Lund (Sweden) provided much of the original stimulus for research in this area, and his continuing research on Monte Carlo models for the stimulation of the diffusion process has provided the basic framework within which most subsequent studies have operated.[1] Among the most basic assumptions of Hägerstrand's simulation models are those which pertain to the manner in which information about the innovation is transferred from one person to another within the spatial system. The present study represents an attempt to perform some preliminary checks on the validity of the surrogate measurement techniques which have been used by Hägerstrand, and others, to generate the simulation inputs dealing with information transfer in the system.

Basically, Hägerstrand assumes that in-

formation about the innovation is spread only by telling (oral communication) at pairwise meetings of persons, and that the probability of being paired with a carrier of information about the innovation depends upon the geographical distance between the teller and the receiver in a way which may be determined by empirical estimate.[2] The first assumption, relating to the means by which the information transfer takes place, is well in line with the results of studies which have been undertaken by research workers in the fields of rural sociology and mass communications. The importance of person-to-person contacts has been pointed out in numerous studies which have investigated the factors influencing the adoption of innovations from a non-spatial standpoint.[3] One author (Rogers) feels that the impersonal information sources (e.g., mass media) are most important at the awareness stage,

1. Hägerstrand, Torsten. *Innovationsförloppet ur Koroloqisk Synpunkt,.* Meddelanden fran Lunds Universitets Geografiska Institution, Avhandlingar XXV. Lund, Sweden: Gleerupska Univ.-Bokhandeln, 1953.

2. Hägerstrand, Torsten. "On Monte Carlo Simulation of Diffusion," in W. L. Garrison (ed.), *Quantitative Geography.* New York: Atherton Press, forthcoming.

3. Lionberger, Herbert F. *Adoption of New Ideas and Practices.* Ames: Iowa State University Press, 1960.

Rogers, Everett M. *Diffusion of Innovations.* New York: The Free Press of Glencoe, 1962.

From **Papers and Proceedings of the Regional Science Association**, Vol. 11, 1963. Reprinted by permission of the Regional Science Association, Philadelphia, Pennsylvania.

and that personal sources are more important at the evaluation stage in the adoption process.[4] Katz has also stressed the growing realization, on the part of persons studying the role of mass media in our society, that person-to-person contacts retain a high level of significance in the transfer of information even when the society involved may be nearly saturated by the various mass media.[5]

In so far as Hägerstrand's simulation models are concerned, the second assumption (dealing with the relationship of geographical distance of frequency of contact) is operationally defined via the concept of the *Mean Information Field* (MIF). The MIF is designed to express the average spatial extent of an individual's short-term (i.e., non-migratory) contacts. The major difficulty which arises in the operational specification of the MIF is that no body of information is available which treats the problem of the spatial structure of non-migratory household contacts in any depth.[6] While it is generally agreed that the bulk of such contacts tend to occur at quite short distances, researchers who need to develop a MIF for a specific research situation have been forced to fall back upon one of several classes of information which appear to provide likely surrogates for the measurement of direct personal contacts in space. Hägerstrand, for instance, based the development of his MIF's largely upon local migration data. This type of information is quite readily available in Sweden and he concluded that it would provide a valid surrogate for the desired personal contact field since several recent studies of migration fields have stressed the close relationship which exists between the spatial extent of the migration field and the web of social contacts.[7] Other researchers have made use of MIF's derived from marriage distances (that is, the distance between the residences of the bride and groom prior to their marriage) since information on this surrogate is more readily available in some areas, and its links with the pattern of social contacts in space are perhaps somewhat more appealing on an intuitive basis.[8]

Whichever surrogate is utilized, the MIF is generated in a rather straightforward fashion. From mapped raw data on, say, local migration movements, a chart is constructed showing the point of origin (which is always at the center of the coordinate system) and the point of termination of each movement. A series of rings is then drawn about the center of the coordinate system and the number of points of termination in each ring is tabulated. This produces a body of directionally smoothed information of the type displayed in Table 1. A Pareto curve of the general form $Y=aD^{-b}$ is then fitted to the tabulated information by least-squares techniques. For the information presented in Table 1, Hägerstrand notes that the curve has the form

$$Y=6.26D^{-1.558},$$

where Y is the expected number of migrants per square kilometer and D is the distance from the point of origin in kilometers. A twenty-five cell grid (with each cell measuring 5×5 kilometers) is

4. Rogers, Everett M. *op. cit.*

5. Katz, Elihu. "Communications Research and the Image of Society: Convergence of Two Traditions," *American Journal of Sociology*, 65: 435-440 (1960).

6. A small amount of information on this topic is available, see sections III, IV, and V in W. L. Garrison, B. J. L. Berry, D. F. Marble, J. D. Nystuen, and R. L. Morrill, *Studies of Highway Development and Geographic Change.* Seattle: University of Washington Press, 1959.

7. Hägerstrand, Torsten. "Migration and Area: Survey of a Sample of Swedish Migration Fields and Hypothetical Considerations on Their Genesis," in Hannerberg, Hägerstrand, and Odeving (eds.), *Migration in Sweden.* Lund University Studies in Geography, Series B (Human Geography) No. 13. Lund, Sweden: C. W. K. Gleerup, 1957.

8. Personal communication from Professor Forrest R. Pitts of the Department of Geography of the University of Oregon.

Table 1. Observed Local Migration in
the Asby Area

Distance in Kilometers	Number of Migrating Households	Ring Area in Sq. Kilometers	Number of Migrating Households Per Km.²
0.0- 0.5	9	0.79	11.39
0.5- 1.5	45	6.28	7.17
1.5- 2.5	45	12.56	3.58
2.5- 3.5	26	18.85	1.38
3.5- 4.5	28	25.14	1.11
4.5- 5.5	25	31.42	0.80
5.5- 6.5	20	37.70	0.53
6.5- 7.5	23	43.99	0.52
7.5- 8.5	18	50.27	0.36
8.5- 9.5	10	56.56	0.18
9.5-10.5	17	62.82	0.27
10.5-11.5	7	69.12	0.10
11.5-12.5	11	75.41	0.15
12.5-13.5	6	81.69	0.07
13.5-14.5	2	87.98	0.02
14.5-15.5	5	94.26	0.05

Source: Adapted from Hägerstrand (1953),
page 190.

then constructed and the estimating equation is used to provide point estimates of
the expected number of migrants in each
of the twenty-four exterior cells. Because
of the Pareto curves' rather strong tendency toward overestimation at short distances, actual instead of expected numbers of migrants are entered in the center
cell. (See Table 2.) When these figures
are converted to probabilities, by dividing

Table 2. Expected Migration Grid for
the Asby Area

2.38	3.48	4.17	3.48	2.38
3.48	7.48	13.57	7.48	3.48
4.17	13.57	110.00	13.57	4.17
3.48	7.48	13.57	7.48	3.48
2.38	3.48	4.17	3.48	2.38

Source: Hägerstrand (1953), page 246. Cells
are 5×5 km.

Table 3. Mean Information Field for
the Asby Area

.0096	.0140	.0168	.0140	.0096
.0140	.0301	.0547	.0301	.0140
.0168	.0547	.4431	.0547	.0168
.0140	.0301	.0547	.0301	.0140
.0096	.0140	.0168	.0140	.0096

Source: Hägerstrand (1953), page 247.
Note: The entries in each cell denote the probability of a receiver in that cell coming in contact with a carrier of information who is assumed to originate in the center cell. Cells are
5×5 km.

each cell entry by the sum of all cell entries, the expected migration field becomes
the mean information field for the diffusion model (see Table 3). The manner in
which this information is subsequently
utilized in the simulation model has been
described in some detail by Hägerstrand
and others and need not concern us here.[9]

The question might well be raised at
this point, just what are the characteristics
of an actual personal contact field and
how well do the various surrogates represent it? The generation of an empirically
based personal contact field would require
the collection of detailed information on
all movements and contacts of a fairly
large group of persons, perhaps over a
period of several days or even weeks. The
information on interzonal transfers collected by the major urban transportation
studies appears at first glance to provide a
potential body of data for such investigations, but a closer examination reveals
certain differences in definition of trips,
etc., which would effectively prevent the
use of this information. However, in 1949
a private research group (the Traffic Audit
Bureau) undertook a study of the movement patterns of a sample of households

9. Hägerstrand, Torsten. "On Monte Carlo
Simulation . . . ," op. cit.

in and around Cedar Rapids, Iowa. All members of the sample households who were ten years of age and older were paid to keep travel diaries which recorded routes, times, location of stops, etc., for all trips made by all modes during the thirty day study period.[10] While certain biases appear to exist in this body of data (e.g., visits to gas stations and certain other specialized retail facilities appear to be underreported) it seems to be the only existing body of information which could be used to develop a personal contact field.

The Cedar Rapids travel information is currently being prepared for analysis by the staff of the Household Travel Behavior Study, a research operation conducted by the Regional Science Research Institute under the terms of a grant from the National Science Foundation. Card deck five of the HTBS provides, for each trip in the sample, the location of the residence (the point of origin of the trip) and the purpose and location of each stop which was made.[11] The nature of the locational coding on these cards is such that it is fairly easy to calculate the distance and direction of each stop in relation to the location of the residence. A computer program has been developed for the HTBS which accepts deck five cards as input and produces tabulations of the number of contacts which occur in each cell of a system of 15° sectors and 0.1 mile rings centered on the residence location.[12] When deck five is completely punched, it will provide a record of the location of all visits made within the thirty day period by the mem-

Table 4. Observed Personal Contacts in Cedar Rapids

Ring	Number of Contacts	Contacts per Sq. Mile
0.00-0.50	1661	2115.92
0.50-1.00	770	326.69
1.00-1.50	1082	275.53
1.50-2.00	442	80.41
2.00-2.50	584	82.72
2.50-3.00	301	34.88
3.00-3.50	73	7.15
3.50-4.00	80	6.79
4.00-4.50	47	3.52
4.50-5.00	4	0.268
5.00-5.50	4	0.242
5.50-6.00	18	0.996
6.00-6.50	9	0.458
6.50-7.00	8	0.377
7.00-7.50	4	0.176
7.50-8.00	0	0.000
8.00-8.50	35	1.350
8.50-9.00	2	0.069
9.00-9.50	0	0.000

Note: The mean distance of the sample households from the Cedar Rapids CBD was 1.35 miles.

bers of some 250 households (about 4/5ths of which are located within the Cedar Rapids-Marion urbanized area). At the present time about one-fourth of the urban households are completely processed; a number which appears to be sufficient for the production of some provisional figures. Table 4 presents the distance-contact frequency relationships derived from 5,128 visits made by the members of forty-nine of the sample households during the thirty day study period. Treating this information in the manner proposed by Hägerstrand produces a summary expression of the form $Y = 197.7D^{-3.035}$ where Y is the number of contacts per square mile and D is distance from the residence in miles. Hägerstrand's reported figure for Asby was, as mentioned previously $Y = 6.26D^{-1.585}$. The expected contact grid and the mean information field derived from the Cedar Rapids data are displayed in Tables 5

10. Details of the study design, sampling proceedures, etc., are reported in William L. Garrison, et. al, *op. cit.*
11. Regional Science Research Institute. *Card Format and Coding.* Working Paper No. 1 of the Household Travel Behavior Study. Philadelphia 1962. (mimeo)
12. Dr. Waldo Tobler of the Department of Geography of the University of Michigan provided valuable assistance in the original formulation of the analysis program.

Table 5. Expected Personal Contact Grid for Cedar Rapids

2.62	5.30	7.48	5.30	2.62
5.30	21.42	60.98	21.42	5.30
7.48	60.98	3677	60.98	7.48
5.30	21.42	60.98	21.42	5.30
2.62	5.30	7.48	5.30	2.62

Note: Cells are 5×5 km.

Table 6. Mean Information Field for Cedar Rapids

.0006	.0013	.0018	.0013	.0006
.0013	.0052	.0149	.0052	.0013
.0018	.0149	.8990	.0149	.0018
.0013	.0052	.0149	.0052	.0013
.0006	.0013	.0018	.0013	.0006

Note: Cells are 5×5 km.

and 6 respectively. An examination of the Cedar Rapids and Asby results (as well as those reported by Pitts[13] in Kagawa Japan) clearly reveals that the majority of personal contacts do indeed occur at very short distances, but that apparently the MIF derived from the Cedar Rapids contact data exhibits a much faster rate of decay with increasing distance.

It should be clearly recognized however that both the Asby and Kagawa MIF's were derived from surrogate measures and in areas which are rural and semi-rural in nature. Cedar Rapids, on the other hand, is an example of a medium-sized American city, and most of the observed contacts took place well within the limits of the built-up area. One possible explanation for the differences in decay rates (other explanations might be based

13. Personal communication from Professor Forrest R. Pitts.

upon supposed differences in transport technology, cultural bias, etc.) may be found in a series of central place studies which were recently conducted in this country by Dr. Brian J. L. Berry of the University of Chicago.[14] These studies have clearly demonstrated that a strong tendency toward the diminution of what we might call "mean contact distance" develops as the gross population density of the area increases. Following this notion through, we might then expect to find that the mean information field in Cedar Rapids (a relatively high density area vis-à-vis Asby) is steeper than in the rural areas. This indeed is what was observed, but the situation would be still further clarified if some firm notion were available of the type of mean information field that would be generated in an urban area through the use of one of the various surrogate measures. Ideally, a MIF for Cedar Rapids could be obtained through the use of any one of the surrogate measures, but on a practical basis it appears that only marriage distances will be available without the expenditure of excessive amounts of time and resources. It is indeed frustrating that a ruling of the Iowa Division of Vital Statistics has prevented our making use of this material at the present time.[15] There are a number of sociological studies of marriage distances in several American cities, but all of those examined to date have reported their distances in terms of city blocks of unknown lengths.[16] This, of course, effectively eliminates them as a possible source of comparative data.

14. Berry, Brian J. L. and Harold Mayer. *Comparative Studies of Central Place Systems.* Final report of project NONR 2121-18 (NR 389-129), Department of Geography, University of Chicago, February, 1962.
15. An exception to this ruling has recently been obtained, and a MIF based on marriage distances is currently being generated.
16. A number of these studies are summarized in Gunnar Boalt and Carl-Gunnar Janson's "Distance and Social Relations," *Acta Sociologica,* 2:73-97 (1957).

V

COMMUNITIES: Residential Areas and Household Behavior

Filling in the cells created by the transportation network are the city's residential sectors. Within these sectors distinctive community types may be recognized. This section examines urban communities building on previous discussions of residential land-use patterns by Nelson and Alonso, of filtering by Smith, and the outline of residential location decisions by Brown and Moore. These papers describe the processes which give rise to specific residential land-use patterns, but do not define what communities exist within these patterns and why. This section looks at communities as the spatial expression of the city's social characteristics, that is, its ecology. It begins by reviewing attempts to merge residential areas into a geographic grid or lattice of communities. This lattice is the city's social space. What is the origin of communities? What types of communities are there? How do they change? The following papers address themselves to these questions.

The study of residential areas, their location and social characteristics, may in part be subsumed under the general heading of urban social geography. To introduce the subject, Robert Murdie defines the variety of theoretical and empirical approaches to the social structure of the city, approaches which derive largely from research by urban ecologists and sociologists discussed in Section II. Other concepts of intra-urban residential structure, although previously summarized in several papers in this volume (see Form, Berry, and Hoyt), are also reviewed by Murdie in this essay. But in this case the particular emphasis is on recent developments in the analysis and identification of social or ecological areas in the

273

city. In its most general form this approach is described as social area analysis. This repetition of concepts is quite appropriate. The often cited concentric and sector models of urban structure and land use, despite assertions to the contrary,[1] were intended primarily as descriptions of residential space in the city, and not of the composite structure of all urban land uses.

Social area analysis is introduced as a logical framework for the analysis of urban communities. It provides a means of differentiating between types of residential areas within a city on the basis of three postulates or variables which, it is argued, determine the underlying social structure of our society. These variables are: economic or social status; family status or composition; and ethnic status or segregation. Combined these indices define the city's social space. Murdie discusses how the city might be systematically sub-divided into distinctive social areas, by factor analytical methods, according to the ranking of residential areas on each of these three indices. This statistical approach has recently been given the title of factorial ecology by some geographers.[2] Evaluating the spatial patterns of these indices, Murdie concludes that all three of the classical concepts of urban ecological structure, the concentric, sector, and multiple nuclei hypotheses, are necessary contributions to the description of social differentiation within urban areas.[3] His idealized spatial model (Figure 1), graphically illustrates the way in which these ecological concepts may be superimposed to give a composite view of the city.

There are many different types of communities within the city's social areas. What do we mean by community and neighborhood? A community has been described as an economic unit, a polity, a formal social system, a geographic unit of territory, or as a society on its own. Each definition, of course, was put forward with a different purpose in mind, and each has

1. See J. N. Johnston, *Urban Geography: An Introductory Analysis* (Oxford: Pergamon Press, 1967).
2. For example, among the more recent contributions in addition to Murdie's research are a number of factor analytic studies including: B. J. L. Berry and Philip H. Rees, "The Factorial Ecology of Calcutta," *The American Journal of Sociology,* LXXIV (March 1969), pp. 445-91; G. F. Pyle, "A Factorial Ecology of Rockford (Illinois) 1969," *Transactions of the Illinois State Academy of Sciences,* (December 1969); and Philip H. Rees, "The Factorial Ecology of Metropolitan Chicago, 1960," in B. J. L. Berry and F. Horton (eds.), *Geographical Perspectives on Urban Systems* (Englewood Cliffs, N.J.: Prentice-Hall, 1970), and Philip H. Rees, "Factorial Ecology: An Extended Definition, Survey and Critique of the Field," paper presented at the International Geographical Union (I.G.U.) Conference on Quantitative Methods at Ann Arbor, Michigan, August 1969.
3. An interesting review of the differing importance attached to the role of geographic space in urban social structure, between the early Chicago ecologists and the social area analysts, is given in Peter Orleans, "Robert Park and the Social Area Analysts," *Urban Affairs Quarterly,* Vol. 1, No. 4 (June 1966), pp. 5-19.

some validity. But there is no general agreement on definitions. For example, the confusion surrounding the neighborhood concept and its value as a planning device has led to considerable debate and criticism in the social planning literature.[4] The following articles in this section examine several concepts of communities in terms of their historical evolution, ethnic diversity, density, stability, and locational patterns.

One of the most distinctive of urban communities is the so-called ghetto. In the second essay, David Ward discusses the location and historical growth of one well known but poorly understood example of a ghetto, the immigrant reception areas which were so common to North American cities in the latter part of the last century.[5] He notes that such areas developed generally within similar environments and locations. Most commonly these were near the city center because of the availability of older and low-cost housing, adjacent employment opportunities for unskilled labor, tight social affinities, and of course because of rigid segregation in both housing and employment. The existence and expansion of these areas also displays a direct relationship to the physical expansion of the central business district. Although most of these immigrant neighborhoods have long since disappeared in American cities, their historical existence has left a prominent impression on our cities and a legacy of needed social reform.

Communities in general are as varied as the characteristics of the urban population they house. Greater contrasts may in fact exist between neighborhoods within the same urban area than between cities in different cultures. One only has to think of the sharply-defined contrasts between

4. A recent and thorough review of the philosophical and sociological basis of urban neighborhoods is Suzanne Keller, *The Urban Neighborhood: A Sociological Perspective* (New York: Random House, 1968). See also Lewis Mumford, "The Neighborhood and the Neighborhood Unit," *Town Planning Review*, XXIV (January 1954), pp. 256-70. Part of this debate has centered around Mumford's views of the city in general and neighborhoods in particular. He has been accused rightly or wrongly by some as being anti-urban in outlook. For example, see Morton and Lucia White, *The Intellectual Versus the City,* (Cambridge: Harvard University Press, 1962), p. 236, a discussion of the critical attitudes of the American literary elite to cities and to urban life in general. A recent summary of Mumford's views of the city is provided in Park Goist, "Lewis Mumford and Anti-Urbanism," *Journal of the American Institute of Planners*, XXXV (September 1969), pp. 340-47. Mumford's own interpretations are best illustrated in his two well known books: *The Culture of Cities* (New York: Harcourt, Brace, 1938); and *The City in History: Its Origins, Its Transformations and Its Prospects,* (New York: Harcourt, Brace, and World, 1961).

5. In a more recent paper the author, utilizing techniques of principal components factor analysis, examines the internal structure of these same immigrant districts with specific reference to New York City. See David Ward, "The Internal Spatial Structure of Immigrant Districts in the Late Nineteenth Century," *Geographical Analysis,* Vol. 1, No. 4 (October 1969), pp. 337-53.

suburban communities and inner-city ghetto communities. These areas are worlds apart. Herbert Gans discusses the social and cultural character of one type of ethnic community, the West End area of Boston. At the time of his study, this area was in the midst of a massive urban renewal and redevelopment scheme. Its very existence as a community was threatened. Gans employs the expression "urban village" to denote the intimate and spatially confined neighborhood ties typical of many such areas. This view contrasts with the conditions perceived by the outside community, conditions which initially defined the necessity for urban renewal. The lesson to be learned from Gans is that urban neighborhoods, whether they are defined as units of territory or of social organization, differ significantly in their appearance and social character, and in their importance in the life styles of people who live in them. What appear to be congested slums to some may in fact be necessary and desirable communities for others.[6] Not all slums, or even a majority, have sufficient virtues to warrant social acceptance. What Gans argues for is a more flexible and humane planning approach which maintains community relationships while improving older neighborhoods through rehabilitation and renewal. The question of whether or not spatially confined and tightly knit communities are appropriate concepts in the planning of the modern metropolis is, as Strauss noted earlier, open to debate.[7]

Segregation is a dominant process in the origin of communities. As one example, in a study of Pittsburgh, James Wheeler examines the relationship between the occupational status of a household and its location within the city. Wheeler concludes that similar occupational groups cluster together in distinct social areas, but the degree of clustering does not represent a continuum. The most segregated occupational groups tend to be at the extreme upper and lower levels of the social ladder. In light of some of the previous comments on the historical development and persistence of inner-city ghetto areas, this conclusion is not surprising. Yet the differentiation of residential areas by occupational status is only one of many segregation processes. Ward, for example, illustrated the broad

6. See Allan Pred, "The Esthetic Slum," *Landscape,* Vol. 14, No. 1 (Autumn 1964), pp. 16-18. See also Gerald D. Suttles, *The Social Order of the Slum* (Chicago: University of Chicago Press, 1969); and D. W. Minar and Scott Greer (eds.), *The Concept of Community Readings with Interpretations* (Chicago: Aldine, 1969).

7. A stimulating examination of the rapid diffusion of community boundaries in the large metropolitan area, and the declining importance of distance as a constraint on social interaction is Melvin M. Webber, "The Urban Place and the Nonplace Urban Realm," in M. M. Webber et al. (eds.), *Explorations into Urban Structure* (Philadelphia: University of Pennsylvania Press, 1964); and M. M. Webber, "Order in Diversity: Community Without Propinquity," in Lowdon Wingo Jr. (ed.), *Cities and Space* (Baltimore: Johns Hopkins Press for the Future, Inc., 1963), 23-54.

spatial patterns of residence for different ethnic groups that result from the diverse population backgrounds of North American cities. The strength and durability of segregation by ethnic background is related to the cultural distance between the social attributes of each ethnic group and those of the dominant ethnic character in the city. The importance of cultural distance in augmenting residential clustering is nowhere more evident than in the continued, and it appears increasing, segregation into ghettoes of the black population.[8]

How do these black ghettoes develop and through what means do they expand? Harold Rose looks at the Negro ghetto as one of the many social and geographical subsystems in the American city. These are defined as particular units of urban territory occupied and dominated by one distinctive social group. Territory then becomes an important part of the culture of that group. Growth of this territory reflects a game of psychological warfare in which the transfer of territory from one social group to another, in this case from white to black, is associated with a fear-safety syndrome among white residents. The result represents a retreat by the white population rather than an invasion by the black population. Segregation is clearly a two-way street.

Residential areas also change their social character in relation to changes in the housing stock. The composition and location of new housing in particular within an urban area may substantially alter the pattern and evolution of urban communities. The following paper by Bourne, examines the market factors which have contributed to the apartment construction boom typical of North American cities during the 1960's. What are the reasons for the location of apartments within the city, and what are the subsequent implications of this growth for urban form? The increased rate of apartment construction, using Metropolitan Toronto as an example, is seen as one outcome of rapid changes in land costs, building conditions, and in household formation and preferences. It is also suggested that a new spatial order of residential uses and communities is evolving because of the growth of apartments which cannot be adequately described or explained by traditional concepts of urban form and structure.

One other common expression of differences in residential areas is that of population density. Most frequently, spatial regularities in population densities have been defined as exhibiting a systematic decline with in-

8. Among the classic studies of Negro populations in cities are Karl and Alma Taeuber, *Negroes in Cities* (Chicago: Aldine Publishing Co., 1965); Otis Dudley and Beverly Duncan, *The Negro Population of Chicago* (Chicago: University of Chicago Press, 1957); and Beverly Duncan and P. M. Hauser, *Housing a Metropolis —Chicago* (Glencoe: The Free Press, 1960).

creased distance outward from the limits of the city center. Berry introduced this research in his review paper in Section II. In statistical terms, this relationship takes a negative exponential form which on log-log paper is a straight line relationship. Bruce Newling extends the analysis of this distance-density regularity to a particularly advanced quantitative level. Although far from introductory, the beginning reader will find the graphic display of urban density gradients to be of considerable value. The rationale for the existence of this form of population density gradient is similar to the arguments developed by Alonso in his theory of the urban land market in Section III.[9] Employing a quadratic equation of common form, he is able to incorporate both the very low densities found in the commercial core of the city, and the wave-like evolution of the population densities gradient over time which Boyce described in Section II, as the city and each of its zones expands in area. With densities well defined, we might well ask what the effects of differing densities are on urban residents.

Communities take form and evolve as a result of decisions by households to change their place of residence. The net structural effects of this residential mobility determine in large part the stability and composition of urban neighborhoods. These dynamic aspects are treated empirically in the next essay by Ronald Boyce. In describing a study of the spatial movements of households in Seattle, Boyce identifies the existence of a strong link between residential mobility and the resulting form of the city. He asks such questions as why people move, how frequently, and where, and subsequently what patterns of mobility emerge. There are not, he suggests, clear-cut directions of movement of population between zones in the city. Rather there appears to be a diffuse network of movements within and among such areas, and between different cities. In fact, the majority of growth in the suburbs comes from other cities. In concluding, Boyce notes the inadequacy of the concept of the filtering process or the trickling-down of housing, previously outlined in a paper by Wallace Smith in Section III, to account for such changes. The necessary basis for explaining residential mobility is more complex. Most residential movement he describes as a kind of "musical chairs" within each area of the city. The actual choice of house and location depends on many factors. It reflects individual preferences, cumulative past experience, the use and quality of information that is available to the household, and the broad spatial patterns of employment or urban activities. These latter patterns are the subject of the following section.

9. Richard F. Muth, *Housing and Cities: The Spatial Pattern of Urban Residential Land Use* (Chicago: University of Chicago Press, 1969).

ROBERT A. MURDIE

The Social Geography of the City: Theoretical and Empirical Background

Although coming from a wide variety of subfields in the social sciences, ecological research has proved to be cumulative and complementary. Frequently work initiated in one field has been developed further by scholars in closely related fields. For example, the social area analysts were originally concerned with describing the socio-economic structure of an urban population. Subsequently, the social area typology was applied to the spatial differentiation of urban populations by human ecologists such as Anderson.[1] More recently yet, this work has been integrated with that of social morphologists such as Chombart de Lauwe by urban and social geographers.[2]

1. Theodore R. Anderson and Janice Egeland, "Spatial Aspects of Social Area Analysis," *American Sociological Review*, XXVI (June, 1961), 392-99.
2. The work of geographers in this regard is meager and has usually been in conjunction with studies of phenomena other than urban ecological structure. See Brian J. L. Berry and Robert J. Tennant, *Metropolitan Planning Guidelines: Commercial Structure* (Chicago: Northeastern Illinois Planning Commission, 1965), 23-24.

Chombart de Lauwe is responsible for the most fundamental conceptual contribution linking social space to the physical space of the city. In a study of the social morphology of Paris, he suggests that social space is made up of economic, demographic, cultural, and other kinds of space which, when superimposed on the physical space of the city serve to isolate areas of social homogeneity. In this manner one is able to build up a comprehensive picture of urban social structure and to single out relatively uniform social areas for more detailed studies of social dynamics within the urban system.[3]

Chombart de Lauwe's concept of social space can be quantified using modern factor analysis. In factor analysis, the dimensions that are derived are *independent* and *additive*. Each accounts for a separate portion of the total variance of the original observations (census tracts here) as

3. P. H. Chombart de Lauwe, *Paris et l'agglomeration parisienne* (Paris: Presses Universitaires de France, 1952). For a short English summary of Chombart de Lauwe's work see Robert E. Dickinson, *City and Region* (London: Routledge and Kegan Paul, 1964), 144-52.

Adapted by the author from Robert A. Murdie, "Theoretical and Empirical Background," Chapter 2 of **Factorial Ecology of Metropolitan Toronto 1951-61**, pp. 9-26. Research Paper No. 116, Department of Geography Research Series, University of Chicago, 1969. Reprinted in revised form by permission.

279

measured by the initial set of variables (socio-economic characteristics here). In summation, the dimensions span the space of the original variables.

Anne Buttimer, who has defined social geography as the geographical study of social space, argues that social space is made up of three major ingredients:[4]

1. Formal characteristics, summarized spatially as areas and obtained by mapping socio-economic criteria.
2. Functional characteristics, summarized spatially as points which serve as major foci of social activity.
3. Circulatory characteristics summarized spatially as lines representing the flows of goods, services, people and ideas and including space perceived by individuals and specfic groups.

This formulation was influenced considerably by the work of French scholars such as Vidal de la Blache, and Max Sorre, in addition to Chombart de Lauwe.

These formulations, like much of the empirical work in the field, fail to deal adequately with change in the ecological structure of the city. Such insights into change as are available come from the classic spatial models of Burgess, Hoyt, and Harris and Ullman, and from recent studies such as that of Sweetser, for example, of the changing social ecology of Metropolitan Boston.[5]

Of course, the initial emphasis of urban research workers on cross-sectional anal-

yses parallels the development of knowledge in other scientific disciplines. For example, W. E. Moore writes:

Because by definition the observation of change takes time, and because the complex interplay of factors requires a rather elaborate "intellectual model" for analysis, all scientific fields first develop an understanding of simple, *static* relationships. These relationships rest on coexistences repeatedly observed, but with each observation essentially photographic or "cross-sectional." Dynamic models and laws require knowledge of sequences of cause and effect in a temporal order. Simple and short-term relationships tend to be established before complex and long-term ones, and relationships observed under controlled, experimental conditions to precede relationships that occur "in nature."[6]

The Concentric Zone Model

Concentric models of land use are not new. Early concepts were formulated by Plato, Aristotle, Marco Polo, von Thunen and Hurd.[7] The first person to formulate such a construct in reference to North American cities was E. W. Burgess. After a study of land use and social characteristics in Chicago, he indicated that urban patterns could be summarized in terms of five concentric zones: (1) the central business district, (2) the transition zone, (3) the zone of independent working-

4. Anne Buttimer, "Social Geography," *International Encyclopedia of the Social Sciences,* ed. David L. Sills, VI (1968), 134-45. For a more detailed discussion see Anne Buttimer, "Some Contemporary Interpretations and Historical Precedents of Social Geography: with Particular Emphasis on the French Contributions to the Field" (unpublished Ph.D. dissertation, Department of Geography, University of Washington, 1964).

5. Frank L. Sweetser, *Patterns of Change in the Social Ecology of Metropolitan Boston, 1950-1960* (Boston: Massachusetts Department of Mental Health, 1962).

6. W. E. Moore, *Social Change* (Englewood Cliffs: Prentice-Hall, 1963), p. 4.

7. De Planhol notes that ". . . at Lut, an Iranian oasis southeast of Kerman, Marco Polo described seven circles of concentric walls, protecting the various quarters, each of which was occupied by the members of a single social class. Their social importance increased as they approached the citadel. From the outside to the center they were peasants of the oasis, foreigners (Tartars, Arabs, and Jews), armorers and smiths, caravaners, tradesmen and shopkeepers of the bazaar, warriors, and doctors of law." See Xavier de Planhol, *The World of Islam* (Ithaca, New York: Cornell University Press, 1959), 10-11. See also Richard M. Hurd, *Principles of City Land Values* (New York: The Record and the Guide, 1924), 63-70.

men's homes, (4) the zone of better residences, and (5) the commuters' zone.[8] Or, in sum, he argued that socio-economic status varies directly with distance from the city center. The model was based on ecological principles of invasion and succession and, therefore, was designed as both a statement of functional zonation and of urban growth. In it, migrants settle in older housing close to the center of the city and then move outwards as their status improves. Further, neighborhood characteristics change as the result of outward expansion of lower status groups as the city grows. As a generalized scheme, the Burgess model has been criticized because it was developed from a study of only one city at one point in time, and, as a result, may not be applicable to other situations.[9]

The concentric zone hypothesis parallels three other models of urban growth and structure: (1) Colby's notions of centrifugal and centripetal forces, (2) generalizations concerning regularities in urban population densities, and (3) the more recent bid-rent models of urban land use. In a classic article, Colby suggested that there are two opposing forces which act within a city.[10] Centripetal or attractive forces tend to retain functions in the central area by stressing advantages of proximity. Centrifugal or disruptive forces, on the other hand, cause functions to migrate from the center towards the periphery, often in an attempt to avoid the congestion and high rents of the core.

Colby's ideas of centripetal and centrifugal forces have since been further developed by urban land economists in the form of mathematical models. Colin Clark has shown that population densities decrease away from the center of the city in a negative exponential fashion.[11] Urban land economists have attempted to account for this regularity by bid-rent functions. Richer people tend to value land over transport costs so that they live on relatively inexpensive land at the periphery of the city, consume a great deal of this land, and incur high transport costs in reaching the center of the city where most employment opportunities for them are located. Poorer people, on the other hand, live near the center of the city on more expensive land but consume little of it thereby creating peak densities just outside of the central business district. An exception to this generalization in many cities, though, is the development of prestige high rise apartments in the city center.

The Sector Model

The sector model was described initially by Richard Hurd in 1903,[12] and formulated by Homer Hoyt following a pre-World War II study of the movement of rental neighborhoods in a number of United States cities.[13] A more recent study by the same investigator using income data from the 1960 United States Census confirms the earlier findings.[14] In Hoyt's model, the central business district remains as a circular form at the center of the city while residential areas of similar socio-economic status originating near the

8. E. W. Burgess, "The Growth of the City," in R. E. Park, E. W. Burgess, and R. D. MacKenzie (eds.), The City (Chicago: University of Chicago Press, 1925), pp. 47-62.
9. See especially James A. Quinn, Human Ecology (New York: Prentice-Hall, 1950), pp. 116-37.
10. C. C. Colby, "Centrifugal and Centripetal Forces in Urban Geography," Annals of the Association of American Geographers (March 1933), Vol. 23, 1-20.

11. Colin Clark, "Urban Population Densities," Journal of the Royal Statistical Society, Series A, CXIV (1951), 490-96.
12. Hurd, op. cit. pp. 59-63. Hurd's book was published initially by the Real Estate Record Association in 1903.
13. Homer Hoyt, The Structure and Growth of Residential Neighborhoods in American Cities (Washington, D.C.: Gov't Printing Office, 1939).
14. Homer Hoyt, "Where the Rich and the Poor People Live," Urban Land Institute, Technical Bulletin, No. 55 (April, 1966).

center tend to migrate in sectors towards the urban fringe. Socio-economic status, then, varies according to an angular measurement about the center of the city. Better quality residences spread out along major transportation routes and higher ground while the interstices fill in with lower quality residences. Within the high rent sectors rents grade downwards from the periphery to the center of the city. Homes closer to the city center which were once occupied by high income groups filter down through the housing market until they are occupied by middle and eventually lower income groups. However, this trend is interrupted to some extent when the upper class expresses sentimental attachment to older sections of the city and when high rent apartment buildings are constructed close to the central business district.[15]

The Multiple Nuclei Model

The multiple nuclei model as applied to urban areas was first suggested by R. M. Hurd and R. D. McKenzie and later elaborated upon by C. D. Harris and E. L. Ullman.[16] The basic notion of this model is that urban land uses concentrate around several nuclei rather than a single core. The central business district is not necessarily located at the geometrical center of the city, but may be off to one side. Other nuclei may be centers of industry, wholesaling, education, etc. In sum, this model suggests that unlike the Burgess and Hoyt models there is no one basic pattern of ecological structure common to many cities.

15. Firey's study of the Beacon Hill area in Boston is a classic example. See W. I. Firey, *Land Use in Central Boston* (Cambridge, Mass.: Harvard University Press, 1949).
16. R. D. McKenzie, *The Metropolitan Community* (New York: McGraw-Hill, 1933); and C. D. Harris and E. L. Ullman, "The Nature of Cities," *The Annals of the American Academy of Political and Social Science* CCXLII (Nov. 1945), 7-17.

Empirical Verification

Since their inception all three models have been used with varied success to describe the spatial differentiation of land use patterns and population types in dozens of cities throughout the world.[17] There are many investigators who feel that the individual city is so unique that idealized models can explain only a small proportion of the total spatial variations in ecological structure within the city. The residual or unique patterns, these researchers argue, can only be explained in terms of social values and administrative decisions such as the implementation of zoning ordinances, urban renewal projects, and transportation schemes. In his study of central Boston, Firey rejects the inevitability of ecological processes such as invasion and competition, and demonstrates effectively that the use of areas like Beacon Hill, the Commons, and the North End can be explained largely by the cultural values attached to these areas by the local inhabitants. In this context Firey notes that, ". . . the very idea of a typical land use pattern holding true for every American city, is predicated upon a deterministic premise, upon a denial that social values, ideals, or purposes can significantly influence the use of land."[18] Similarly, Emrys Jones rejects the concentric and sectorial models as adequate descriptions of the ecological structure of Belfast. In a review of the concentric and sectorial patterns, he suggests that "many theories of city growth imply no more than the mechanistic adjustment of society within the urban framework."[19] Jones goes on to apply the concentric and sectorial models

17. See, for example, Maurice R. Davie, "The Pattern of Urban Growth," in G. P. Murdock (ed.), *Studies in the Science of Society* (New Haven: Yale University Press, 1937), pp. 133-61.
18. Firey, *op. cit.*, p. 7.
19. E. Jones, *A Social Geography of Belfast* (London: Oxford University Press, 1962), p. 269.

to the urban pattern of Belfast and concludes that ". . . the exceptions are too big to contemplate, and the idealized pattern, whether concentric zonal or sector, falls to the ground both as a description of Belfast and as a suggestion for the possible explanation of the pattern. There are elements in the sector theory to which we will return, but for the moment, sectors and zones must be set aside as complete answers."[20] Identifiable sectors in the Belfast urban pattern are explained to a significant degree by the social values invested in a particular piece of land rather than by physical factors alone.

In a recent evaluation of the Burgess zonal model and his own sectorial model, Homer Hoyt discusses how these idealized patterns have been distorted to some extent by growth factors, especially the increased flexibility of location provided by widespread use of the automobile.[21] With reference to the sector model, Hoyt states:

The automobile and the resultant belt highways encircling American cities have opened up large regions beyond existing settled areas, and the future high grade residential growth will probably not be confined entirely to rigidly defined sectors.[22]

The foregoing discussion is closely related to the role of deterministic and probabilistic models in the social sciences. The conflict between determinism and probabilism in geopraphic research is a familiar one and will not be elaborated upon here.[23] Deterministic or mechanistic models, as applied in their most rigid form, imply absolute certainty in the explanation of human behavior while probabilistic or behavioristic models take into

account basic uncertainties in the behavior of individuals. In the main, the models put forth by Burgess and Hoyt are based largely on deterministic principles whereas studies such as those by Firey and Jones, which rely to some extent on the identification of social values in the urban environment, are probabilistic in nature.

The present study assumes a position somewhere between the two extremes of determinism and probabilism. A descriptive model of urban ecological structure and change which takes into account social area analysis and the three classic models of intra-urban location is hypothesized. It is assumed that the model is *generally* valid for *most* large industrialized cities within the developed nations of the world. However, it is recognized that this model is an idealized pattern which, when applied to the real world, describes the structure of some cities better than others. In this context the author recognizes the importance of social values and administrative processes in shaping the ecological structure of individual urban areas and attempts to identify these as they affect patterns of ecological structure and change in Metropolitan Toronto.

In many instances, as Berry and Simmons have pointed out, the three classical models of intra-urban location have been used simultaneously as conflicting descriptions of the internal structure of the city.[24] Recent empirical evidence from the work of human ecologists such as Anderson suggests strongly that the three models complement one another with each describing a separate aspect of social differentiation within a city[25] (Figure 1).

20. *Ibid.,* pp. 273-74.
21. Homer Hoyt, "Recent Distortions of the Classical Models of Urban Structure," *Land Economics,* XL (May, 1964), 199-212.
22. *Ibid.,* p. 209.
23. For a recent discussion of the role of deterministic and probabilistic models in geographic research see Peter Haggett, *Locational Analysis in Human Geography* (London: Edward Arnold, 1965), pp. 23-27.

24. Brian J. L. Berry, "Internal Structure of the City," *Law and Contemporary Problems,* XXX, No. 1 (Winter, 1965), 111-19; and J. W. Simmons, "Descriptive Models of Urban Land Use," *The Canadian Geographer,* IX (1965), 170-74.
25. Anderson and Egeland, *op. cit.* The additive characteristic of the three models was recognized as early as 1903 by Hurd. See Hurd, *op. cit.,* pp. 56-74.

Table 1. Social Area Analysis: Steps in Construct Formation and Index Construction

Postulates Concerning Industrial Society (Aspects of Increasing Scale) (1)	Statistics of Trends (2)	Changes in the Structure of a Given Social System (3)
	Changing distribution of skills:	Changes in the arrangement of occupations based on function
Change in the range and intensity of relations	Lessening importance of manual productive operations—growing importance of clerical, supervisory, management operations	
Differentiation of function	Changing structure of productive activity:	Changes in the ways of living—movement of women into urban occupations—spread of alternative family patterns
Complexity of organization	Lessening importance of primary production—growing importance of relations centered in cities—lessening importance of the household as economic unit	
	Changing composition of population:	Redistribution in space-changes in the proportion of supporting and dependent population—isolation and segregation of groups
	Increasing movement—alterations in age and sex distribution—increasing diversity	

Constructs (4)	Sample Statistics (Related to the Constructs) (5)	Derived Measures (From Col. 5) (6)	
Social Rank (economic status)	Years of schooling Employment status Class of worker Major occupation group Value of home Rent by dwelling unit Plumbing and repair Persons per room Heating and refrigeration	Occupation Schooling Rent	Index I
Urbanization (family status)	Age and sex Owner or tenant House structure Persons in household	Fertility Women at work Single-family dwelling units	Index II
Segregation (ethnic status)	Race and nativity Country of birth Citizenship	Racial and national groups in relative isolation	Index III

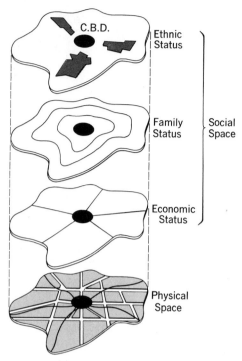

Ethnic Status

Family Status

Economic Status

Social Space

Physical Space

Figure 1. Idealized Spatial Model of Urban Ecological Structure and Change

The structural basis for these studies comes primarily from the work of the social area analysts, to which we should now turn.

Social Area Analysis

Social area analysis was developed by Eshref Shevky and a group of sociological colleagues as a technique for classifying census tracts according to three indexes: economic status, family status, and ethnic status. The technique was first applied by Shevky and Williams to a study of Los Angeles and later elaborated upon by Shevky and Bell in a study of San Francisco.[26] Since then, the technique has been

applied to a number of cities, primarily within the United States, often in conjunction with studies of such topics as crime, voting behavior, and the demand for intra-urban transportation.[27] Although the empirical relevance of social area analysis has been verified many times, the theoretical basis of the technique has been severely criticized. The monograph by Shevky and Bell provides an excellent description of this basis, and a table from that study is reproduced here (see Table 1).[28]

Social area analysis rests upon certain broad conceptual notions or postulates concerning the changing character of modern society.[29] These postulates are outlined in Column 1 of Table 1 and elaborated upon in Columns 2 and 3. In Column 2 the initial postulates are translated into three broad trends of modern society and in Column 3 these trends are illustrated by specific changes which might be expected in the structure of a given social system. These trends or changes have cross-sectional as well as temporal relevance for at any point in time a particular social system may be measured in relation to the major trends identified above. On

26. Eshref Shevky and Marilyn Williams, *The Social Areas of Los Angeles* (Berkeley and Los Angeles: The University of California Press, 1949); and E. Shevky and Wendell Bell, *Social Area Analysis* (Stanford: Stanford University Press, 1955).

27. Kenneth Polk, "Juvenile Delinquency and Social Areas," *Social Problems,* V (Winter, 1957-58), 214-17; Walter C. Kaufman and Scott Greer, "Voting in a Metropolitan Community: An Application of Social Area Analysis," *Social Forces,* XXXVIII (March, 1960), 196-204; Walter Y. Oi and Paul W. Shuldiner, *An Analysis of Urban Travel Demands* (Evanston: Northwestern University Press, 1962), pp. 116-20.

28. Shevky and Bell, *op. cit.,* p. 4.

29. See Colin Clark, *The Conditions of Economic Progress* (2d ed. rev.; London: MacMillan, 1951); P. Sargent Florence, *The Logic of British and American Industry: A Realistic Analysis of Economic Structure and Government* (London: Routledge and Kegan Paul, 1953); William F. Ogburn, "The Family and its Functions," *Recent Social Trends in the United States* (New York: McGraw-Hill, 1933), I, 661-708; and Louis Wirth, "Urbanism as a Way of Life," *American Journal of Sociology,* XLIV (July, 1938), 1-24.

the basis of these changes three factors are chosen which might be used to study a particular social system at one point in time. These are the constructs of *economic status* (social rank), *family status* (urbanization), and *ethnic status* (segregation) (see Column 4). Census characteristics related to the factors are selected as possible measures of the constructs (see Column 5) and from these characteristics derived measures which the authors deem to be, ". . . more direct measures of the constructs than the others and . . . more useful as measures of the three factors" are chosen as measures of the three indexes of economic status, family status, and ethnic status.[30]

With three indexes available, census tracts can each be characterized by three scores. Those tracts which exhibit similar scores can be grouped into relatively uniform social areas. The authors divide what they call "social space" into sixteen cells or social areas by dividing social rank and urbanization scores each into four intervals. The result is a structural rather than a spatial representation of social space with each social area corresponding to a cell in a four-by-four table. Note is also taken of tracts with high indexes of ethnic segregation (Figure 2).

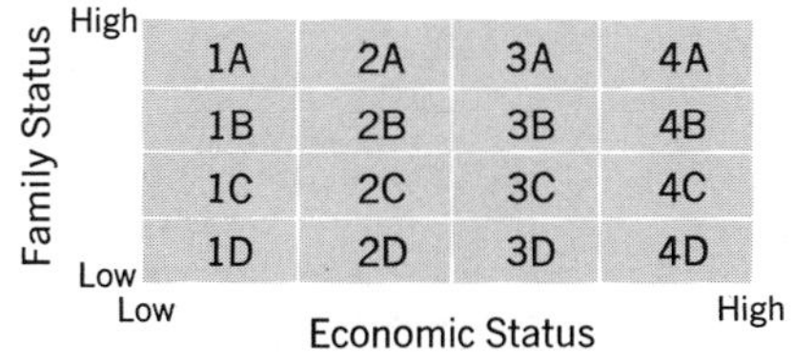

Figure 2. Social Area Key Based on Economic Status and Family Status

A study of the social structure of the San Francisco Bay Region in 1940 and 1950 demonstrates the use of the social area typology. Comparisons of the social area structure in these two years are made

30. Shevky and Bell, *op. cit.,* p. 5.

but as in most of the subsequent social area analyses very little mention is made of spatial differentiation and change. The authors explicitly leave this task to city planners, geographers, and human ecologists.[31]

Criticism of Social Area Analysis

Social area analysis has been severely criticized by Hawley and Duncan mainly on grounds that the technique lacks a carefully formulated theoretical basis.[32] They claim that Shevky and Bell have not answered the fundamental question of why residential areas within cities should differ from one another and, more specifically, they suggest that the Shevky-Bell attempt to explain the theoretical basis of the social area typology is merely an ". . . *ex post facto* rationalization for their choice of indexes."[33] Most critics would agree with Hawley and Duncan on this point although it must be mentioned that few investigators have tested the theory of increasing scale of industrial society using longitudinal data.[34]

Other criticisms of social area analysis by Hawley and Duncan are directed towards the operational characteristics of the technique and are either recognized by Shevky and Bell or are related to more general problems of using areal data. Hawley and Duncan argue that social area analysis is a prematurely closed system in that the "social areas" have no necessary geographic or spatial relevance, a

31. *Ibid.,* p. 43.
32. Amos H. Hawley and Otis Dudley Duncan, "Social Area Analysis: A Critical Appraisal," *Land Economics,* XXXIII (November, 1957), 337-45.
33. *Ibid.,* p. 339.
34. A recent study using data from the United States for the last century shows the increasing scale of the economic status and family status indexes but not ethnic status. See J. Richard Udry, "Increasing Scale and Spatial Differentiation: New Tests of Two Theories from Shevky and Bell," *Social Forces,* XLII (May, 1964), 403-17.

problem which is somewhat analogous to the geographer's differentiation between regional types and contiguous regions. Recently, Greer has attempted to interrelate Shevky's concept of social space and the classic notions of ecological space.[35] Hawley and Duncan also suggest that census tract data alone are insufficient to describe variations in urban ecological structure, a point generally recognized by urban scholars. And, finally, they are concerned with the amount of heterogeneity within census tracts, a problem recognized by geographers and others under the rubric of "modifiable units."

Researchers from disciplines other than sociology seem to have viewed the work of the social area analysts more favorably. In a reply to the Hawley and Duncan paper, the economist Tiebout suggests that many of the difficulties are really problems of interpretation.[36] Geographers have also commented favorably on the general utility of social area analysis. Berry states that:

. . . Although social area analysts began simply in a "look-see" manner, with later work facilitated by advancing computer technology, their work has now laid the basis for a spatial model of the internal socioeconomic pattern of cities in which the relevance and role of the traditional concepts is clear.[37]

In a review of the social area technique Timms concludes that:

The general significance and utility of the social area typology can only be established

by an extension of comparative studies, but it is readily apparent that the technique represents one of the most promising attempts yet available to provide a coherent and logically demonstrable frame for an analysis of urban social structure.[38]

In a recent study, Herbert applies social area analysis to British census material for the city of Newcastle-under-Lyme.[39] Newcastle was selected because its urban structure is well known and therefore the results of the social area analysis could be easily evaluated. After mapping the index scores Herbert notes three advantages of social area analysis:

The social area map is meaningful and accurately differentiates the urban structure of Newcastle thus fulfilling one claim which may be made of the approach in that it summarizes several essential aspects of the social geography of an urban area. That social area analysis is a useful comparative tool has perhaps been demonstrated by the comparisons which have been made between the results of this study and those which have been obtained from other parts of the world. The social area map and social space diagram are also held as valuable frames of reference in the context of which sample studies of selected parts of the urban area may be made.[40]

Empirical Validity

Emphasis has recently been placed on empirical testing of the social area typology and on more explicit analysis of the spa-

35. Scott Greer, *The Emerging City* (New York: The Free Press, 1962), pp. 120-37. A review of this problem is to be found in Peter Orleans, "Robert Park and Social Area Analysis: A Convergance of Traditions in Urban Sociology," *Urban Affairs Quarterly*, I (June, 1966), 5-19.
36. Charles M. Tiebout, "Hawley and Duncan on Social Area Analysis: A Comment," *Land Economics*, XXXIV (May, 1958), 182-84.
37. Berry, "Cities as Systems within Systems of Cities," *loc. cit.*, p. 129.

38. D. Timms, "Quantitative Techniques in Urban Social Geography," in Richard J. Chorley and Peter Haggett (eds.), *Frontiers in Geographical Teaching* (London: Methuen, 1965), p. 255.
39. D. T. Herbert, "Social Area Analysis: A British Study," *Urban Studies*, IV (1967), 41-60. See also D. T. Herbert, "The Use of Diagnostic Variables in the Analysis of Urban Structure," *Tijdschrift voor Economische en Sociale Geografie*, LVII (1967), 5-10.
40. Herbert, "Social Area Analysis: A British Study," *loc. cit.*, p. 55.

tial distribution of the indexes. For the most part these studies have used some form of factor analytic model to verify the existence of the hypothesized patterns of urban ecological structure and in a few cases to examine their spatial distribution.

At first these studies generally employed only the six census characteristics selected by Shevky and Bell as measures of the social area indexes. Examples include studies by Bell and Tryon who both verified the independence of the three social area indexes using 1940 San Francisco data and a more recent study of ten large cities in various parts of the United States by Van Arsdol, Camilleri, and Schmid.[41] The latter analysis demonstrated the validity of the Shevky-Bell typology in all but three southern cities where fertility was found to be associated with both the economic status and family status dimensions instead of only with the family status dimension.

Analyses were then extended to include additional variables. For example, a factor analysis by Anderson and Bean of thirteen census tract characteristics in Toledo, Ohio, confirmed the general structure of the Shevky-Bell typology except that the hypothesized dimension of family status separated into two factors identified as urbanization and family status.[42] Demonstration of the general validity of the social area indexes was not surprising be-

cause in this analysis the six variables used by Van Arsdol, Camilleri, and Schmid were included along with other characteristics carefully selected because of their possible relationship to the three indexes.

These analyses suggest that all three indexes are necessary to describe socioeconomic differentiation in an urban ecological system but do not mean that these indexes are sufficient to describe all socioeconomic differentiation within such a system. However, the results give some reason to believe that the concepts are adequate to describe a good deal of differentiation in the published census characteristics.

When the empirical existence of the social area indexes had been confirmed for United States cities interest turned to more careful analyses of the spatial distribution of the indexes and to studies of cities outside of the United States for which data were available. Initially, these studies used similar methodology to test the classical spatial models of urban growth and structure. A sample of census tracts was selected from a predefined grid of sectors and zones using slightly different criteria in each study. Social area indexes were calculated for each tract and an analysis of variance design was used to determine the relative significance of the spatial models in describing the location of each index.

The first study of this type was by Anderson and Egeland who selected four almost circular and topographically uniform United States cities for analysis and concluded that economic status is primarily distributed within sectors while family status is a concentric phenomenon.[43] More recently, similar analyses have been made for Rome, Italy, and Chicago. The study

41. Wendell Bell, "Economic, Family, and Ethnic Status: An Empirical Test," *American Sociological Review,* XX (February, 1955), 45-52; Robert C. Tryon, *Identification of Social Areas by Cluster Analysis* (Berkeley: University of California Press, 1955); Maurice D. Van Arsdol, Jr., Calvin F. Schmid, and Santo F. Camilleri, "The Generality of Urban Social Area Indexes," *American Sociological Review,* XXIII (June, 1958), 277-84.

42. Theodore R. Anderson and Lee L. Bean, "The Shevky-Bell Social Areas: Confirmation of Results and a Reinterpretation," *Social Forces,* XL (December, 1961), 119-24. Urbanization comprised variables such as type of dwelling whereas family status was made up of variables related to fertility.

43. Anderson and Egeland, *op. cit.* The cities used in this study ranged in population from 200,000 to 500,000 and included Akron and Dayton, Ohio, Indianapolis, Indiana, and Syracuse, New York.

of Rome indicated that economic status and family status are both concentric and sectorial with large families of low economic status occupying the periphery of the metropolis.[44] This finding is consistent with our knowledge of urban differentiation in relatively unindustrialized societies. An analysis of the Chicago Metropolitan Area using 1960 data produced somewhat different results.[45] Economic status and family status were concentrically distributed while ethnic status exhibited a sectorial pattern. Individual components of the indexes were then examined to determine the consistency of their spatial patterns with those of the composite index. In general, evidence from Chicago indicates that the spatial differentiation of individual characteristics is consistent with that of their respective indexes.

Aided by advancing computer technology, recent studies of the socio-economic structure of urban areas have been extended to include a much wider range of census characteristics. In most instances, characteristics are not chosen with the aim of specifically replicating the social area indexes, but rather, of isolating those dimensions which explain as much as possible of the socio-economic differentiation within urban areas. In some cases, the dimensions also serve as a basis for classifying urban areas for more specific studies. In each case, the desire is to eliminate redundancies within an inter-correlation matrix of census characteristics using multivariate statistical tools such as component analysis and factor analysis. These two techniques allow the researcher to investigate the spatial variations in urban ecological structure by mapping the scores of census tracts on the components or factors.

44. Dennis C. McElrath, "The Social Areas of Rome: A Comparative Analysis," *American Sociological Review,* XXVII (August, 1962), 276-91.
45. Dennis C. McElrath and John W. Barkey, "Social and Physical Space: Models of Metropolitan Differentiation" (Northwestern University, October, 1964). (Mimeographed.)

DAVID WARD

The Emergence of Central Immigrant Ghettoes in American Cities: 1840-1920

During the three generations of sustained and heavy European immigration into the United States, which preceded the immigration restriction legislation of the early 1920's, congested ghettoes of foreign immigrants assumed substantial dimensions within the residential structures of American cities. Most immigrants settled near the sources of unskilled employment and, although suburban industrial districts attracted considerable numbers of immigrant laborers, the majority of newcomers concentrated on the margins of the emerging central business districts. The central business district provided the largest source of unskilled employment opportunities, and many of the adjacent residential quarters had been abandoned by their original residents because of the threatened encroachment of commercial activities. Although some districts retained their middle and high-income occupants, most residential areas adjacent to the central business district were abandoned to immigrants. Vacated houses were converted into tenements and rooming houses, while vacant lots and rear yards were filled with cheap new structures. On some margins of the central business district newly established immigrant concentrations were rapidly displaced by expanding commercial activities; but because the specialized functional areas of the central business district expanded at different rates in different directions, many adjacent residential districts survived and exhibited striking variations in their relative longevity, physical quality, and social composition. Indeed, the selective adoption and subsequent characteristics of immigrant residential locations were primarily determined by the timing, dimensions, and direction of the expansion of the adjacent specialized business activity. This paper proposes first, to examine in general the competing and at times complementary claims of immigrants and commerce for central urban locations between 1840 and 1920, and second, to illustrate the relationship of immigrant residential locations to different adjacent business activities in the particular instance of Boston, Massachusetts, during the same period.

From the **Annals** of the Association of American Geographers, Vol. 58, No. 2, June 1968. Reprinted by permission.

Immigrant Residential Locations and the Urban Residential Structure

The settlement of newly arrived immigrants on the margins of the central business district has for long been closely associated with the blighting effects of commercial encroachment into adjacent residential districts. The uncertain timing and quality of future commercial developments encouraged the neglect of existing property and the departure of the mort prosperous members of the resident population. Once abandoned by their original populations, central residential districts were most frequently adopted by low-income immigrants, and the deterioration of the physical quality of the dwellings was assumed to encourage the social disorganization of the new residents. Blighted conditions thus implied not only bad housing but also pathological social repercussions. Even today, however, blighted conditions do not prevail on all margins of the central business district, and many observers have documented the considerable variations in the social and physical characteristics of the central residential districts. Although a zone of blight adjacent to the central business district formed an integral part of Burgess' concentric scheme of the urban residential structure, he was impressed by the apparently anomalous location of central high-income apartment districts and by the belt-like distribution of Negroes across the otherwise concentric arrangement of urban social groups.[1] Zorbaugh examined the development and survival of the "Gold Coast" apartment district of Chicago alongside the central business district and the slums of the Near North Side, and Hoyt recognized similar high-rent areas near to the business districts of other

American cities.[2] Zorbaugh suggested that the "Gold Coast" was artificially protected by lease conditions and would eventually yield to the competitive demands of commerce. In contrast, Hoyt proposed a sector hypothesis of the residential structure of the city which was in part an effort to recognize the variations in the quality of residential districts on the margin of the central business district.

Since surviving middle and high-income residential districts occupy only a small segment of the residential fringe of the central business district, they are often regarded as local exceptions to the widespread blighted conditions created by the threat of commercial expansion. Re-evaluations of the social organization of low-income neighborhoods have, however, also enlarged our conceptions of the physical and social conditions of central residential districts. It was for long assumed that all low-income neighborhoods were afflicted by pathological social conditions which were directly related to the unhealthy and congested living conditions of tenement housing and to the breakdown of the traditional social organization of rural people in the impersonal and anonymous world of the city.[3] Relatively few immigrants escaped the material and social discomforts of congested urban living conditions, but some immigrant groups were able to re-establish parts of their ancestral social organization in the New World and thereby facilitate their adjustment to the unfamiliar scale of American urban life. For example, Ware demonstrated that the institutions and

1. E. W. Burgess, "The Growth of the City," in R. E. Park, E. W. Burgess, and R. D. MacKenzie (Eds.), *The City* (Chicago: University of Chicago Press, 1925), pp. 47-62.

2. H. W. Zorbaugh, *The Gold Coast and the Slum* (Chicago: University of Chicago Press, 1929), pp. 1-16; H. Hoyt, *The Structure and Growth of Residential Neighbourhoods in American Cities* (Washington, D.C.: Government Printing Office, 1939).

3. R. E. Park and H. A. Miller, *Old World Traits Transplanted* (New York: Harper Bros., 1921), pp. 60-80; O. Handlin, *The Uprooted* (Boston: Little, Brown & Co., 1951), pp. 259-85.

values of the native American society seemed remote and confusing to most immigrant groups and, therefore, it was the survival of the extended family, along with local political and religious allegiances, that facilitated the adjustment of immigrants and their descendants to American urban life. Similarly, Whyte identified the distinctive internal structure of the street corner society and suggested that earlier observers had failed to recognize the presence of social organization among low income people largely because their customs and values were different from those of the more familiar society of suburban America.[4]

The suburban movement has severely depleted the populations of the original ghettoes of European immigrants; but quite recently Glazer and Moynihan have suggested that ethnic origin has also partly influenced the suburban residential choices and social life of the descendants of immigrants,[5] while immigrants from Puerto Rico and from the American South have partly compensated for the population losses created by the suburban movement. Since, however, the central business district has lost its former pre-eminence as a source of unskilled employment and since low-rent housing is no longer confined to central residential districts, the more recent immigration has had more modest effects upon the central residential pattern than that of the nineteenth century. Although urban renewal schemes have diminished the extent and capacity of many tenement districts, some authorities have suggested that the material and fiscal priorities of most public improvement schemes have obscured the social attractions of many low rent dis-

tricts to their resident populations.[6] A preoccupation with the vitality of local neighborhood life has at times degenerated into an uncritical admiration of the culture of poverty; but nevertheless there is a need to identify variations in the social and living conditions of low income residential areas.[7] Some original ghettoes have survived for several generations on the margins of the central business district and, in spite of considerable depopulation, remain attractive to the resident population. Other districts have housed either a rapid succession of diverse immigrant groups or the most impoverished and discriminated social groups in the city and, under these circumstances, pathological social conditions tend to compound the material inadequacies of the housing and neighborhood.

Firey, and Jones, in their respective studies of central parts of Boston and Belfast, have related the survival of middle- and high-income districts and the development of different types of low income areas to the sentiments and values of the occupying social groups.[8] Although this perspective provided many new insights into the attachment to a given district of a particular social group, the effect of changes in the central business district upon the original adoption and subsequent survival of the adjacent residential districts remained obscure. Indeed, most recent contributions to our understanding of the residential structure of American cities have acknowledged the locational implications of cultural preferences in

4. C. F. Ware, *Greenwich Village: 1920-1930* (Boston: Houghton Mifflin, 1935), pp. 3-8, 81-126; W. F. Whyte, *The Street Corner Society* (Chicago: University of Chicago Press, 1943), pp. 94-104, 255-78.
5. N. Glazer and D. P. Moynihan, *Beyond the Melting Pot* (Cambridge: MIT Press, 1964).
6. H. J. Gans, *The Urban Villagers* (New York: The Free Press of Glencoe, 1962), pp. 3-41; B. J. Frieden, *The Future of Old Neighborhoods* (Cambridge: MIT Press, 1964), pp. 1-5.
7. G. C. Homans, *The Human Group* (New York: Harcourt, Brace & Co., 1950), pp. 334-68; W. I. Firey, *Land Use in Central Boston* (Cambridge: Harvard University Press, 1947), pp. 170-97, 290-313.
8. W. I. Firey, *op. cit.,* footnote 7; E. Jones, *A Social Geography of Belfast* (London: Oxford University Press, 1962).

their developments of an explanatory focus pioneered some fifty years ago and
based upon measures of site costs and of
accessibility of home to employment.[9]
These considerations have provided the
most satisfactory principles for an interpretation of the extensive suburban residential additions to American cities since
the turn of the century. The emergence
and diversification of central residential
districts, however, occurred during the
course of the second half of the nineteenth
century when the suburban alternative to
central tenement residence was available
only to limited numbers of immigrants
and their descendants and when the
growth and differentiation of the central
business district most profoundly affected
the adjacent residential quarters.

Immigrant Concentration in Central Urban Locations

The dense central concentrations of immigrants were thus established at a time
when the distributional implications of
accessibility were determined not only by
the extent and density of the streetcar network, but also by the long working hours,
low wages, and unpredictable tenure of
unskilled employment.[10] Most newly arrived immigrants sought cheap accommodation partly because of their poverty and
partly because of their desire to accumulate savings to finance the passages of
relatives. The central tenement districts
provided by far the largest supply of cheap
living quarters, but because most tenements were overcrowded, badly designed,
and poorly—if at all—endowed with sani-

tary facilities, even low rents were ex-
orbitant. Tenement accommodation, however, could be obtained by the room at
fractional rates, whereas self-contained
dwelling units which possessed only the
minimum requirements for the comfort
and health of their occupants rented at
rates far beyond the means of new immigrants.[11] Towards the end of the nineteenth century, legislation was introduced
in many cities to improve the living conditions in newly constructed tenements,
but even modest structural refinements
increased minimum rents and failed to enlarge the supply of low-rent housing.[12]
The housing choices of most immigrants
were thus largely restricted to central
residential districts until either a rise in
real incomes made possible suburban
residence or public funds were provided
to subsidize rent payments.[13]

The central tenement districts also possessed the advantage of convenient accessibility to the growing employment
opportunities of the emerging central business district. Although the facilities for
local transportation were improved and
enlarged during the second half of the
nineteenth century, many immigrants
were employed in occupations with long
and awkward hours and, therefore, preferred a short pedestrian journey to work.
The tenure of unskilled employment was
also characteristically uncertain, and daily
hiring was the common procedure in general laboring and portering. Consequently,
immigrants not only faced the problems
of numerous changes in the location of
their work, but also suffered from frequent
spells of unemployment. Under these cir-

9. W. Alonso, *Location and Land Use* (Cambridge: Harvard University Press, 1964); L.
Wingo, Jr., *Transportation and Urban Land*
(Washington: Resources for the Future, 1961);
R. M. Hurd, *Principles of City Land Values*
(New York: The Record and Guide, 1903).
10. D. Ward, "A Comparative Historical Geography of Streetcar Suburbs in Boston, Massachusetts and Leeds, England: 1850-1920," *Annals,* Association of American Geographers,
Vol. 54 (1964), pp. 477-89.

11. E. R. L. Gould, "The Housing of the Working People," *8th Special Report of the Commissioner of Labor* (Washington: Government
Printing Office, 1895), p. 419.
12. E. E. Wood, *The Housing of the Unskilled
Wage Earner* (New York: Macmillan, 1919),
p. 21.
13. E. Abbott, *The Tenements of Chicago:
1908-1936* (Chicago: University of Chicago
Press, 1936), pp. 481-83.

cumstances, employment in the central business district had the advantage of a wide range of alternative opportunities when regular work was abruptly terminated. Suburban industrial districts also attracted considerable numbers of immigrants, and cheap housing was built in adjacent locations; but the variety of both industrial and commercial employment within and near to the central business district supported far larger numbers of immigrants in central residential locations. The central business district offered the largest and most diverse source of unskilled employment opportunities, and the adjacent tenement districts provided uncomfortable but conveniently located residential quarters which were within the limited financial means of new immigrants.

The first generation of immigrant groups who arrived in American cities in large numbers often provided almost the entire labor force of some activities conducted within the central business district. Irish immigrants first helped to build, and later found employment in, the warehouses and terminal facilities of the business district, whereas German immigrants found employment in the sewing machine and port supply trades which were housed in the upper stories of warehouses.[14] Italian immigrants in part replaced the Irish as general laborers, but the distribution of fresh food also attracted Italians in large numbers.[15] Jewish immigrants, equipped with long experience in the handicraft industries and local commercial life of their East European homelands, rapidly developed many branches of merchandising at a time when

the retail and wholesale segments of marketing were first firmly separated and established as distinct specialized areas within the central business district.[16] Jewish immigrants also adopted the ready-made clothing industry and, in order to achieve economies of rent and labor, reorganized production within their own residential districts. The clothing industry needed close and immediate contact with the credit and informational facilities of the central business district, and the central tenement districts possessed the advantage of adjacency to the commercial facilities of the city.[17] This ethnic division of labor was neither rigid nor exclusive but, nevertheless, encouraged the concentration of immigrants in those residential districts where they could most effectively obtain employment from their compatriots. Many immigrant business enterprises, which later served the entire city or national market were, moreover, originally founded upon the provision of the distinctive material and dietary needs of the immigrant community.

Group consciousness, as well as economic necessity or advantage, stimulated the concentration of immigrants in the central tenement districts; for once established, the ghetto provided institutions and neighborhood life familiar to the immigrant. Indeed most immigrants preferred to spend their early years in a new country and unfamiliar city in a district which housed their fellow countrymen or co-religionists if not their immediate family and friends. Many contemporary observers were inclined to ignore the positive social attractions of the tenement districts to the newly arrived immigrants, for it was assumed that the congested living conditions resulted in the social disorgani-

14. R. Ernst, *Immigrant Life in New York City: 1825-1863* (New York: King's Crown Press, 1949), pp. 17, 61-77; O. Handlin, *Boston's Immigrants: A Study in Acculturation* (Cambridge: Harvard University Press, 1959), pp. 54-87.

15. R. F. Foerster, *The Italian Emigration of Our Times* (Cambridge: Harvard University Press, 1919), pp. 332-44.

16. S. Joseph, *Jewish Immigration to the United States from 1881 to 1910* (New York: Columbia University Press, 1914), pp. 42-46.

17. J. R. Commons, "Immigration and its Economic Effects," *Report of the Industrial Commission XV* (Washington: 1901), pp. 316-26.

zation of the resident population and that the concentration of immigrants delayed and discouraged their assimilation into the native American society. In spite of the adverse living conditions, however, some immigrant groups established stable local communities and attracted deservedly laudatory reports upon the stability and moral orthodoxy of their family and neighborhood life.[18] Moreover, in the absence of effective public welfare, residential concentration provided immigrant communities with their share of the patronage of local politics, for the heavily populated ethnic wards provided a major source of voting strength in civic elections.[19] The development of local communities within the tenement districts attracted the majority of newly arrived immigrants of similar ancestry and assisted their adjustment to the unfamiliar scale and conditions of American urban life.

The social attractions and political advantages of residential concentration were not, however, characteristic of all tenement districts, nor were they shared by all immigrant groups. The adjustment of different immigrant groups to the changing conditions of residence and employment in American cities was rarely repetitive. Although southern Italian immigrants had lived in large unsanitary villages, and Jewish immigrants had lived in the congested towns of Eastern Europe, many immigrants had no previous experience of crowded living conditions. Certainly relatively few immigrants had faced the problems of residence in cities as large and as complex as those of industrial America, and some groups lacked the numbers to support their own institutions or to lay claim to their proportionate share of political patronage. Moreover,

most small immigrant groups were composed of young single men who eventually hoped to return to their homelands with the assumed profits of their American employment and, consequently, with neither a family structure nor a permanent commitment to residence in the United States, some degree of social disorganization did compound the material discomfort of their residential quarters.[20] Although the marginal economies and social advantages of scale insulated most large and well established immigrant groups from the problems faced by small groups, all central concentrations of immigrants faced the disturbing effects of displacement by the expansion of the adjacent commercial activities. Even the largest and most organized immigrant groups were unable to establish enduring communities in those tenement districts which suffered from the continuous invasion of business premises. The specialized functional areas of the central business district, however, emerged and expanded at different rates at different times and, accordingly, the effect of the central business district upon the adjacent residential areas was neither continuous nor uniform.[21]

20. Zorbaugh, *op. cit.,* footnote 2, 142-51.
21. Information on the timing and scale of the expansion of the component specialized areas of the central business district during the nineteenth century is widely scattered and rarely related to the fortunes of adjacent residential districts. J. E. Vance, "Emerging Patterns of Commercial Structure in American Cities," in K. Norborg (Ed.), *Proceedings of the I.G.U. Symposium in Urban Geography* (Lund: Gleerups, 1962), pp. 473-83, and D. Ward, "The Industrial Revolution and Emergence of Boston's Central Business District," *Economic Geography,* Vol. 42 (1966), pp. 152-71, give some indication of the developmental aspects of the problem, whereas R. E. Murphy and J. E. Vance, "Delimiting the CBD," *Economic Geography,* Vol. 30 (1954), pp. 189-222, and D. W. Griffin and R. E. Preston, "A Restatement of the Transition Zone Concept," *Annals,* Association of American Geographers, Vol. 56 (1966), pp. 339-50, from an essentially contemporary perspective indicate the diverse characteristics of different edges of the CBD.

18. W. T. Elsing, "Life in New York Tenement Houses," in *The Poor in Great Cities* (New York: Scribners, 1895), pp. 42-85.
19. T. J. Lowi, *At the Pleasure of the Mayor: Power and Patronage in New York City, 1898-1958* (New York: The Free Press of Glencoe, 1964).

The Effect of Business Expansion on Immigrant Concentration

Thus, although the residential choices of immigrants were largely restricted to central locations, and although the tenement districts fulfilled many of their more immediate social and economic needs, the development and survival of central concentrations of immigrants was primarily dependent upon the rate and dimensions of expansion of the adjacent segment of the emerging central business district. The invasion of business activities into adjacent residential districts occasionally followed so closely upon the departure of the original population that the immigrant newcomers had neither the time nor the incentive to develop a stable neighborhood life. The warehouse quarter, for example, housed both expanding small scale workshop industries and a large proportion of the growing commercial activities of the city and, during the middle decades of the nineteenth century, made greater claims upon the adjacent residential quarters than all the other segments of the central business district combined[22] (Fig-

22. N. S. B. Gras, "The Development of the Metropolitan Economy in Europe and America," *American Historical Review* Vol. 27 (1922), pp. 695-708.

ure 1). Towards the turn of the century, the demands of regional distribution had displaced most of the workshop industries and stimulated a separation of the retail and wholesale segments of marketing within the central business district (Figure 1). The emergence of a retail quarter and the continued expansion of the warehouse district as the seat of wholesale distribution increased even further the rate and scale of expansion of business premises into a broader segment of the residential fringe of the central business district. Central residential districts adjacent to these rapidly expanding segments of the central business district were most frequently occupied by the smallest or poorest immigrant groups along with remnants from older groups which had moved on to securer residential locations.[23] The residents of these districts did suffer from the social disorganization created by the problems of eviction and residential relocation.

There were, however, central residential districts which failed to attract anticipated commercial developments once they had been abandoned by their original populations. Because of the improvement in the facilities for local movement and the increase in the scale of business or-

23. Zorbaugh, *op cit..*, footnote 2, p. 127.

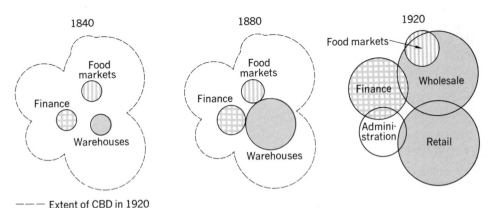

--- Extent of CBD in 1920
—— Current boundaries

Figure 1. Generalized Stages in the Development of the CBD

ganization, the location of the greatest constructional activity and commercial expansion within the central business district tended to shift during the course of the nineteenth century.[24] Consequently, residential districts adjacent to older centers of growth lost their attractiveness for commercial development. Moreover, the most attractive locations for business had often been pre-empted early by commercial activities which were unable to maintain their original choices in the face of the expanding needs of more competitive activities. Financial and administrative functions for long occupied separate and diminutive quarters, and only late in the nineteenth century coalesced and expanded their accommodations into premium locations within the existing limits of the central business district rather than at the expense of peripheral residential locations (Figure 1). Other business activities retained their small quarters throughout the nineteenth century and eventually reorganized their facilities by decentralization rather than by central expansion. The distribution of fresh food, for example, was conducted in extremely congested quarters and expanded only slightly into adjacent residential districts, partly because nearby tenements provided convenient housing for laborers who worked in the early hours of the day.[25] Under these circumstances of limited commercial expansion into the adjacent residential districts, the immigrant newcomers were able to establish enduring ghettoes which not only served their own immediate residential needs but also those of later immigrant arrivals. Districts which housed Irish and German immigrants in the middle

decades of the nineteenth century gradually passed into the possession of Italian and Jewish immigrants towards the turn of the century.[26]

The subdivision of abandoned housing and the construction of cheap new tenements in their vacant grounds were designed to extract a marginal rental income from buildings and land during the period of uncertain property values which preceded their adoption by commercial activities. Thus, the housing of immigrants was at first regarded as a temporary expedient, but it soon became clear that as long as immigrants arrived in large numbers, the provision of their housing needs would be a source of substantial profit. Once established under favorable conditions on the edge of the central business district, immigrant ghettoes resisted or at least retarded the rate of any subsequent commercial claims upon their quarters.[27] Not all central districts were converted into tenement areas, for it was also possible to obtain a substantial income from lodging or rooming house accommodation. Conversion into rooms was, moreover, less costly than the modifications required for tenement residence, whereas lodging houses tended to maintain the status of an area by catering to the needs of single white-collar people.[28] Although many single foreign immigrants were housed in the lodging and rooming house districts, the relatively high proportions of native Americans clearly distinguished the populations of these areas from those of the tenement districts and, for a brief time, the lodging house districts were able to escape the popular and often erroneous

24. L. Grebler, *Housing Market Behavior in a Declining Area* (New York: Columbia University Press, 1952), p. 113 on the up-town shift of retailing on Manhattan Island and the effects on the residential districts near to the original center of growth.
25. Zorbaugh, *op. cit.,* footnote 2, p. 166; F. E. Bushee, "Italian Immigrants in Boston," *Arena,* Vol. 17 (1896-7), pp. 722-34.

26. W. L. Warner and L. Srole, *The Social Systems of American Ethnic Groups* (New Haven: Yale University Press, 1945), pp. 33-52; K. H. Claghorn, "The Foreign Immigrants in New York City," *Report of the Industrial Commission XV* (Washington: 1901), pp. 471-72.
27. Grebler, *op. cit.,* footnote 24, pp. 106-16.
28. R. A. Woods (Ed.), *The City Wilderness* (Boston: Houghton Mifflin, 1898), pp. 35-39; Zorbaugh, *op. cit.,* footnote 2, pp. 69-86.

identification of depravity and delinquency with immigrant tenement districts.

Although almost the entire residential fringe of the central business district eventually housed low income immigrants, lodgers, or commerce, one segment occasionally retained its original high income population and resisted the competitive demands of business and immigrants. The survival of high income residential districts in part depended upon favorable site conditions and long established status. Many central locations which were at one time endowed with advantages of site and status failed to retain their original population, for the quality and needs of the adjacent business activity in part influenced the status of central residential quarters. Financial institutions and the seats of public authority attracted rather than discouraged adjacent residence by people of wealth and status. Throughout the nineteenth century many established families valued their proximity to the sources of political and economic power and the historic status of the adjacent residential quarters. Financial and administrative activities offered only limited unskilled employment opportunities and, consequently, the demand for low rent housing was more limited than on those margins of the business district adjacent to abundant sources of unskilled employment. The different directions and characteristics of the expansion of the central business district directly affected the selective adoption of central residential districts by immigrants and also in part influenced the abandonment of these districts by their original populations. Thus, during the course of the nineteenth century, not only tenement districts of varying quality but also lodging houses and substantial town houses developed on different margins of the central business districts of large American cities.

HERBERT GANS

The West End: An Urban Village

An Historical and Ecological Overview

To the average Bostonian, the West End was one of the three slum areas that surrounded the city's central business district, little different in appearance and name from the North or the South End. He rarely entered the West End and usually glimpsed it only from the highways or elevated train lines that enveloped it. From there he saw a series of narrow winding streets flanked on both sides by columns of three- and five-story apartment buildings, constructed in an era when such buildings were still called tenements. Furthermore, he saw many poorly maintained structures, some of them unoccupied or partially vacant, some facing on alleys covered with more than an average amount of garbage; many vacant stores; and enough of the kinds of people who are thought to inhabit a slum area. If he ventured inside the area, he saw some old people who looked like European immigrants, some very poor people, some who were probably suffering from mental illness, a few sullen looking adolescents and young adults who congregated on street corners, and many middle-aged people who were probably mainly Italian, Russian Jewish, Polish, and Irish in parentage.

To the superficial observer, armed with conventional images and a little imagination about the mysteries thought to lie behind the tenement entrances, the West End certainly had all the earmarks of a slum. Whether or not it actually was a slum is a question that involves a number of technical housing and planning considerations and some value judgments. . . . For the moment, the West End can be described simply as an old, somewhat deteriorated, low-rent neighborhood that housed a variety of people, most of them poor.

In most American cities there are two major types of low-rent neighborhoods: the areas of first or second settlement for urban migrants; and the areas that attract the criminal, the mentally ill, the socially rejected, and those who for one reason or another have given up the attempt to cope with life.

The former kind of area, typically, is one in which European immigrants—and more recently Negro and Puerto Rican ones—try to adapt their nonurban institutions and cultures to the urban milieu. Thus it may be called an *urban village*. Often it is described in ethnic terms: Little

Italy, The Ghetto, or Black Belt. The second kind of area is populated largely by single men, pathological families, people in hiding from themselves or society, and individuals who provide the more disreputable of illegal-but-demanded services to the rest of the community. In such an area, life is comparatively more transient, depressed if not brutal, and it might be called an *urban jungle*.[1] It is usually described as Skid Row, Tenderloin, the red-light district, or even the Jungle.

In sociological terminology, these are ideal types, and no existing neighborhood is a pure example of either. Moreover, since the people who occupy both types are poor and at the mercy of the housing market, they often may live in the same neighborhood, erecting physical or symbolic boundary lines to separate themselves. In some areas, especially those occupied by the most deprived people, the village and the jungle are intertwined.

The West End was an urban village, located next to Boston's original and once largest skid row area, Scollay Square. During the early nineteenth century, the West End had been an isolated farm area, almost inaccessible from the North End and the central business district area that then constituted Boston. Later, some streets were cut through and developed with three-story single family homes of various price levels. Following the arrival of Nova Scotian and Irish immigrants, other streets were built up with three- and five-story tenements, until, by the turn of the century, the five-story tenement became the main building type. The structures built in the latter half of the nineteenth century were intended, like those in the North End, for the poorest tenants. Apartments were small and several units

1. These are purely descriptive terms, and should not be taken too literally. They are not ecological concepts, for neither in economic, demographic, or physical terms do such areas resemble villages or jungles. They are terms that describe the quality of social life, but do not definitively identify social structure or culture.

had to share bathroom and toilet facilities. The buildings constructed around the turn of the century, however, were intended for a somewhat higher income group. Instead of three- and four-room apartments, there were five- and six-room ones, each with private bath and toilet, and kitchens equipped with a large combination heating and cooking stove. The new and the old apartments were built at high densities—more than 150 dwelling units per net residential acre—as compared today with the 5 to 8 units in the average middle-income suburb. Land coverage was high, 72 per cent of the land being covered with buildings, and, in a quarter of the blocks, buildings comprised over 90 per cent of the land.[2] Some of the streets were shopping blocks with small stores on the ground floor of the tenements. A few industrial lofts that attracted small manufacturing and wholesale establishments were scattered through the shopping streets.

Physically, as well as socially, the development of the West End followed a typical ecological process. The West End is located at the bottom of one slope of Beacon Hill. At the top of this hill are the apartments and townhouses inhabited by upper-and upper-middle-class people. As one descends the slope, the status of buildings and people decreases. The "Back of the Hill" area, once occupied by servants to the Hill aristocracy, now is inhabited by families who moved up from the bottom of the slope, and, increasingly, by young middle-class couples in modernized tenements or converted townhouses who are gradually erasing the social differences between the Back of the Hill, and the Hill itself.[3]

2. Boston Housing Authority, "West End Project Report," Boston: The Authority, 1953, p. 5.
3. For descriptions of this area, see Walter Firey, *Land Use in Central Boston,* Cambridge: Harvard University Press, 1947; and H. Laurence Ross, "The Local Community and the Metropolis," Unpublished Ph.D. Dissertation, Harvard University, 1959.

The West End is at the bottom of the slope. At one time, when the Back of the Hill was a low-income settlement, both it and the area below were called the West End. Then, with the widening of Cambridge Street in the 1920's, a physical boundary was created between the two areas that eventually led to the symbolic separation as well. Within the West End, the area nearest to Cambridge Street and the Back of Beacon Hill contained the better apartment buildings, and the two major institutions in the area—Massachusetts General Hospital and St. Joseph's Roman Catholic Church. The hospital, traditionally an extremely high status institution, is one of the teaching hospitals for the Harvard Medical School. The church, originally Congregationalist, later became one of the higher status Irish churches, which served Beacon Hill as well.[4] The area closest to Cambridge Street and that fronting on the Charles River was known as the "upper end." Then, as one descended to what was called the "lower end," dwelling units became older and the people, poorer. At one corner of the lower end, the West End fronted on the Scollay Square skid row, and provided rooming houses for the people who frequented its bars and eating places. At another corner, there were small commercial buildings which were part of the industrial and wholesaling area that separated the residential portions of the West End from the North End.

Several times during its existence, the population of the West End has changed in a pattern typical of other urban villages. The North and the South End were the primary areas of first settlement for Irish, Jewish, and Italian peoples, in that order. The South End also served the other ethnic groups that settled in Boston, especially Chinese, Greek, and Syrian. The

West End had somewhat more distinctive functions. First, it was an overspill area for those who could not find room in the North End; later, it became an area of second settlement for some of the groups who began their American life in the North End. Thus, the West End underwent approximately the same ethnic succession pattern as the North End. In the late nineteenth century, it was primarily an Irish area, with Yankees scattered through the upper end.[5] Then, around the turn of the century, the Irish were replaced by the Jews, who dominated the West End until about 1930. During this era, the West End sometimes was called the Lower East Side of Boston. In the late twenties, Italians and Poles began to arrive, the former from the North End, and they joined a small Italian settlement that had existed in the lower end of the area since the beginning of the century. Throughout the 1930's and early 1940's, the Italian influx continued until eventually they became the largest ethnic group in both the upper and lower portions of the West End. The changes in population are reflected in data taken from library registration cards.[6] In 1926, the area was estimated to be 75 per cent Jewish. In 1936, however, the library users were 35 per cent Italian, 25 per cent Polish, 20 per cent Jewish, and 20 per cent "miscellaneous."[7] By 1942, the Italians were in the majority.

5. For a detailed description of the West End around the turn of the century as it appeared to Yankee settlement house workers, see Robert A. Woods, ed., *Americans in Process,* Boston: Houghton Mifflin, 1902. For a fictional description of Jewish life in the area in the second decade of the twentieth century, see Charles Angoff, *In the Morning Light,* New York: Beechhurst Press, 1952.
6. From unpublished reports in the files of the West End Library.
7. *Ibid.* Registration figures do not reflect the population distribution with complete accuracy. In all likelihood, Jews are overrepresented among library users; and all other ethnic groups, underrepresented.

4. At one time, it was the church of the Kennedy family, and President Kennedy attended it as a boy.

A Polish church that had been established in 1930 quickly enrolled 250 families. Although it later lost some of these, the congregation was replenished by displaced persons who came into the West End after World War II. Also there were small Greek, Albanian, and Ukrainian settlements, the latter served by a Ukrainian church located in a tenement. Consequently, proud West Enders were able to claim that twenty-three nationalities could be found in the area. In recent years, small groups of students, artists, and Negroes had come into the West End, some from the Back of the Hill as rents there had begun to rise.

Numerically, the West End was at its height around 1910, when it had 23,000 inhabitants. In 1920, it had 18,500 residents; in 1930 and 1940, 13,000; and, in 1950, 12,000.[8] In 1957, the population was estimated to be about 7000 individuals in about 2800 households. The long-range population decline could be attributed to decreasing family size among the descendants of immigrant groups, and to the gradual reduction in dwelling units as the hospital expanded its facilities, and as deteriorated buildings became vacant. Between 1930 and 1950, the population remained constant, at least in total number. After that time, it decreased, partially because young families moved out to raise their children in lower density urban and suburban areas, and because of the announcement in 1951 that the area would be redeveloped.

At the time of the study, then, the population of the West End consisted of the following major groups:

1. *Second- and First-Generation Italian Households.* They included the surviving immigrants—most of them elderly—and the much larger group of second-generation people who were their children, or who had come into the area from the North End. The Center for Community Studies survey indicated that the Italians constituted 42 per cent of the West End's population.[9]

2. *First-Generation Jewish Households.* By 1930, the main Jewish population contingent had moved on to Roxbury and Dorchester. But some of the Jews who had come to America in the final wave of European immigration, 1918-1925, did remain in the West End, maintaining two synagogues, a Hebrew school, and a number of stores.[10] Most of them, however, lived in retirement—some in poverty—and spent their time in visiting, in synagogue social activities, and with their children. The Jews accounted for 10 per cent of the West End population.[11]

3. *First- and Second-Generation Polish Households.* This group consisted of immigrants who came before and during the depression, of second-generation families, and of displaced persons. They comprised 9 per cent of the population.[12]

4. *An Irish Residue.* A small number of Irish families, most of them old people, stayed either because they owned buildings in the area, or because they were active in the Catholic church and parish. They constituted 5 per cent of the population.[13]

8. Boston Housing Authority, West End Project Report, *op. cit.,* p. 18.

9. Marc Fried, "Developments in the West End Research," Center for Community Studies, Research Memorandum A 3, October 1960, mimeographed, p. 5. This, and other estimates from the Center's survey reported in this chapter and the next are based on interviews with a 473-person random sample of the West End female population aged twenty to sixty-five.
10. Most of the West End stores were owned by Jews, as were the medical, dental, and legal offices. These were largely run by second-generation Jews who no longer lived in the West End.
11. Fried, *op. cit.,* p. 5.
12. *Ibid.*
13. *Ibid.* The rest of the population was almost equally distributed among "Other Latin," "Other Slavic," English, American, and "Other" ethnic groups. Only 7 per cent of the West End sample was of American background.

5. *Other Ethnic Groups*—Albanians, Ukrainians, Greeks.[14]

6. *Pathological Households.* Each major ethnic group left behind a residue of families or individuals whose social and residential mobility had been aborted either by extreme poverty, or by physical or psychological disability. In addition, a part of the area served to house some of the Scollay Square transients.

7. *Postwar Newcomers.* When young residents left after 1950, landlords no longer could replace the vacancies left by them with tenants from their own ethnic group. In order to fill the buildings, they rented them to anyone who came along. Thus the West End attracted people who came because of its low rents—Gypsies, groups of single men, broken families subsisting on Aid to Dependent Children, and people who fled from the New York Streets Redevelopment project in the South End. Some were squatters who tried to live rent-free in vacant buildings.

8. *Middle-Class Professionals and Students.* The presence of the hospital and the availability of clean, low-rent, and conveniently located apartments attracted a number of nurses, interns, and doctors as well as students from various colleges in the city. They provided a smattering of professional middle-class culture to the area.

9. *Other Hospital Staff.* A number of hospital service workers also lived in the area because of the low rentals and the convenience. Some of these were women, wives of Italian or Polish residents, who worked in the cafeterias, kitchens, and laundries. Some were homosexuals who worked as male nurses in the hospital, and were able to practice their deviant ways in an area which disapproved of them, but which tolerated them grudgingly.

10. *The Artists and Bohemians.* A small but highly visible group of artists, would-be artists, and bohemians was scattered throughout the parts of the West End closest to Cambridge Street. While some of these were students, others worked in low-status jobs and took advantage of the low cost of living in the area.

Some other characteristics of the West End population in 1958 are available from data gathered by the Center for Community Studies survey. Like the Italians to be discussed in later chapters, the largest single group of West Enders—50 per cent—was native born of foreign parentage. A third were European immigrants, and the rest were children of native-born parents. Seventy per cent of the women were married and living with their spouses, and 10 per cent had never married. About a fifth of the sample was twenty to twenty-nine years old, half was between thirty and forty-nine, and the remainder between fifty and sixty-five.

The population's socio-economic level was low. Indeed, the sample's median income was just under $70 a week. About a quarter earned less than $50 per week; a half between $50 and $99; and the top category, slightly less than a fifth, between $100 and $175. Most of the household heads were unskilled or semiskilled manual workers (24 and 37 per cent, respectively).[15] Skilled manual workers, semiskilled white-collar workers, and skilled white-collar workers (including small businessmen) each accounted for about 10 per cent of the sample.

Data on years of schooling are available only for women respondents. The median educational level was about 10.5 years: 40 per cent had had eight years of school or less, 30 per cent had nine to eleven

14. The Center for Community Studies survey shows 8 per cent of the sample to be "Other Slavic," a category which includes some of the above. Fried, *ibid.*

15. These figures report the occupation of the past or present household head. In 18 per cent of the cases, the woman's occupation is reported, either because there was never a male household head, the husband was not in the labor force because of illness, or because his occupation was unavailable.

years, 19 per cent had graduated from high school, and 10 per cent had attended college for a year or more.

Life in the West End

As a neighborhood is more than an ecological or statistical construct, some of its qualities can perhaps be captured only on paper by the sociologically inclined poet or artist. Typical aspects of West End life and the "feel" of the area can best be described by an informal sketch of what so often struck me as an urban village.

To begin with, the concept of the West End as a single neighborhood was foreign to the West Enders themselves. Although the area had long been known as the West End, the residents themselves divided it up into many subareas, depending in part on the ethnic group which predominated, and in part on the extent to which the tenants in one set of streets had reason or opportunity to use another. For example, the social distance between the upper and lower end was many times its geographical distance.[16]

Until the coming of redevelopment, only outsiders were likely to think of the West End as a single neighborhood. After the redevelopment was announced, the residents were drawn together by the common danger, but, even so, the West End never became a cohesive neighborhood.

My first visit to the West End left me with the impression that I was in Europe. Its high buildings set on narrow, irregularly curving streets, its Italian and Jewish restaurants and food stores, and the variety of people who crowded the streets when the weather was good—all gave the area a foreign and exotic flavor. At the same time, I also noticed the many vacant shops, the vacant and therefore dilapi-

dated tenements, the cellars and alleys strewn with garbage, and the desolation on a few streets that were all but deserted. Looking at the area as a tourist, I noted the highly visible and divergent characteristics that set it off from others with which I was familiar.[17] And, while the exotic quality of the West End did excite me, the dilapidation and garbage were depressing, and made me a little fearful of doing a participant-observation study.

After a few weeks of living in the West End, my observations—and my perception of the area—changed drastically. The search for an apartment quickly indicated that the individual units were usually in much better condition than the outside or the hallways of the buildings. Subsequently, in wandering through the West End, and in using it as a resident, I developed a kind of selective perception, in which my eye focused only on those parts of the area that were actually being used by people. Vacant buildings and boarded-up stores were no longer so visible, and the totally deserted alleys or streets were outside the set of paths normally traversed, either by myself or by the West Enders. The dirt and spilled-over garbage remained, but, since they were concentrated in street gutters and empty lots, they were not really harmful to anyone and thus were not as noticeable as during my initial observations.

Since much of the area's life took place on the street, faces became familiar very quickly. I met my neighbors on the stairs and in front of my building. And, once a shopping pattern had developed, I saw the same storekeepers frequently, as well as the area's "characters" who wandered through the streets everyday on a fairly regular route and schedule. In short, the

16. One resident who had lived for thirty-five years about two blocks away from the upper end, and who had supper with relatives there at least twice a week for more than a decade, said that he knew very few people in the upper end.

17. For some of the characteristics of the tourist view of the social and physical landscape, see Kevin Lynch, *The Image of the City,* Cambridge: Technology Press and Harvard University Press, 1960; and Herbert J. Gans, "Diversity Is Not Dead," *New Republic,* vol. 144 (April 3, 1961), pp. 11-15, at p. 14.

exotic quality of the stores and the residents also wore off as I became used to seeing them.[18]

The attractions that the West End had for the people who had lived there for a long time became evident quickly. Apartments were extremely cheap. I paid only $46 for a six-room apartment with central heating. Long-time residents paid as little as $35 for one like it, and $15 to $25 for a similar unit without central heating. The rooms were large and the apartments comfortable. In buildings without central heating, the apartments were heated with the large combination cooking and heating stoves placed in the kitchen.

At first, I thought that the buildings without central heating were slums, but I soon learned otherwise. The kitchen stoves freed the West Enders from dependence on the landlords and their often miserly thermostats. Moreover, people with stoves could heat their apartments to their own specifications, making them as warm as they liked. In a cold spell, the kitchen stoves were less desirable, for the rooms furthest away from the kitchen were cool, and, when the temperature went down to 10 degrees above zero, the outside bedroom was icy. Some people placed smaller oil or kerosene stoves in these rooms, and these occasionally caused fires, although the kitchen stove was completely safe. Needless to say, central heating was cheaper in the long run, for people had to buy oil to heat the stove. Usually, the oil was purchased in quantity, and stored in the cellar. Poorer people had to buy it in smaller amounts. The apartments also were equipped with gas water-heaters, which required West End families to heat their own water, but also assured independence from landlord whims.

18. A similar change of perspective over time has been reported by a student of a working-class municipal housing estate in London. See Peter Willmott, *The Evolution of a Community*, London: Routledge and Kegan Paul, 1963, p. 4.

The apartments did, of course, have a number of faults. The buildings were old and not easy to keep clean. Windows leaked and the plumbing had its quirks. There were rats in many of the cellars—although they rarely disturbed anyone except the janitor. No one liked these faults and almost everybody wanted a modern apartment that lacked these disadvantages. However, people were happy with the low rents they were charged in the West End; modernity is not much of an advantage when it depletes the family budget.

Of course there were people, especially the very poorest, who lived in badly substandard housing where the toilets were shared or broken, the rats were a danger, the oil stove did not heat properly, and the leaks in the windows could not be sealed. Such people, who were probably also paying higher rents, suffered from all the ills of poor housing. When it comes to livability standards, there is little difference between the classes. Although poorer people do not have as high expectations as the well-to-do, they are no more willing to live with defective plumbing than anyone else.

Everyday life in the West End was not much different from that in other neighborhoods, urban or suburban. The men went to work in the morning, and, for most of the day, the area was occupied largely by women and children—just as in the suburbs. There were some men on the street: the older, retired ones, as well as the young and middle-aged ones who either were unemployed, worked on night shifts, or made their living as gamblers. In the afternoon, younger women could be seen pushing baby carriages. Children of all ages played on the street, and teenagers would "hang" on the corner, or play ball in the school yard. The West End's lone playground was fairly dilapidated, and usually deserted. Many women went shopping every day, partly to meet neighbors and to catch up on area news in the small grocery stores, and partly to buy foods that could not be obtained in the weekly excursion to the supermarket.[19] On Sunday mornings, the streets were filled with people who were visiting with neighbors and friends before and after church.

The average West End resident had a choice between anonymity and total immersion in sociability. A few people had moved into the area to hide from the world, and, while visible to their neighbors, could discourage contact, and thus feel anonymous. Generally speaking, however, neighbors were friendly and quick to say hello to each other, although more intense social contact was limited to relatives and friends. Deviant behavior, as displayed by the area "characters," the bohemians, or the middle-class residents was, of course, highly visible. As long as the West Enders were not affected personally, however, they were tolerant. Yet this tolerance was ambivalent: people objected to deviants grudgingly but explained that such kinds of people must be expected in a low-rent neighborhood. At the same time, they found deviant behavior a lively and readily available topic of conversation, which not only provided spice and variety for gossip, but also an opportunity to restate and reaffirm their own values. The bohemians and the schizophrenic characters also served as sources of community amusement, although the latter usually received friendly greetings from other West Enders, even if they did laugh at them once their backs were turned. On the whole, however, the various ethnic groups, the bohemians, transients, and others could live together side by side without much difficulty, since each was responsive to totally different reference groups. Also, at various points, the diverse cultures had common values. For

19. There were no supermarkets within the West End, but one was located just outside it. Many of the West End families with cars went supermarket shopping in outlying neighborhoods, often combining this with a visit to relatives or friends.

example, everyone liked the low rents, the cheapness of the cost of living generally, and the convenience to downtown. Moreover, as Italians like to stay up late, and to socialize at high decibel levels, the bohemians' loud parties were no problem, at least to them.

The sharing of values was also encouraged by the residential stability of much of the population. Many West Enders had known each other for years, if only as acquaintances who greeted each other on the street. Everyone might not know everyone else; but, as they did know something about everyone, the net effect was the same, especially within each ethnic group. Between groups, common residence and sharing of facilities—as well as the constant struggle against absentee landlords—created enough solidarity to maintain a friendly spirit. Moreover, for many families, problems were never far away. Illnesses, job layoffs, and school or discipline problems among the children occurred regularly. Alcoholism, mental illness, desertion, the death of a loved one, serious financial difficulties, and even violence were familiar to everyone. If they did not take place in one's immediate family, they had happened at some time to a relative or a neighbor. Thus when emergencies occurred, neighbors helped each other readily; other problems were solved within each ethnic group.

For most West Enders, then, life in the area resembled that found in the village or small town, and even in the suburb. Indeed, if differences of age and economic level among the residents were eliminated, many similarities between the life of the urban neighborhood and the suburb would become visible.

Age and class differences are, of course, crucial; they, rather than place of residence, shape the lives of people. That West Enders lived in five-story tenements and suburbanites occupy single-family houses made some—but not many—differences in their ways of life and the everyday routine. For example, although the West Enders were less than a mile from the downtown department stores, it is doubtful whether they used these more than the average suburbanite who has to travel 45 minutes to get to them. Not all city neighborhoods are urban villages, of course, and there are few similarities among the urban jungle, the apartment hotel district, and the suburb, or for that matter, the urban village.[20]

20. Similarities and differences between city and suburb are discussed in more detail in Herbert J. Gans, "Urbanism and Suburbanism as Ways of Life: A Re-evaluation of Definitions,"

Although it is fashionable these days to romanticize the slum, this has not been my purpose here. The West End was not a charming neighborhood of "noble peasants" living in an exotic fashion, resisting the mass-produced homogeneity of American culture and overflowing with a cohesive sense of community. It was a rundown area of people struggling with the problems of low income, poor education, and related difficulties. Even so, it was by and large a good place to live.

in Arnold Rose, ed., *Human Behavior and Social Processes,* Boston: Houghton Mifflin, 1962, pp. 625-648.

JAMES O. WHEELER

Residential Location by Occupational Status

Few researchers have investigated occupational distributions by residence in metropolitan areas, despite increasing availability of detailed areal data from census and transportation surveys. The traditional emphasis on land use analysis and classes of residential structure has perhaps diverted attention from spatial studies dealing specifically with occupational groups.[1] Another reason for the neglect may be the multivariate approaches of social area analysis which have emphasised the interrelationships of several socio-economic variables, including occupation, income, and educational level.[2] While a multivariate approach is valuable in providing useful generalisations of social rank differentials of individuals, families, and neighbourhoods, it is also fruitful to isolate a particular variable to examine its spatial structure and associations.

This lack of spatial research on the distribution of occupations within cities is revealed in a recent text-book in urban geography, which, although devoting a chapter to the three familiar concepts of city structure (the concentric zone, the sector and the multiple nuclei patterns), makes no specific statement regarding occupational structure within cities.[3] One is forced to turn largely to the literature of sociology for urban studies of occupational distributions.

Even here the studies are remarkably few, in spite of the concern of sociologists with correlates of status, occupational mobility, and differential migration and movement of urban residents. Several studies have compared the central city with suburban areas in socio-economic

1. Recent studies reflecting this traditional emphasis include: J. Tait Davis, 'Middle Class Housing in the Central City," *Economic Geography*, 41 (July 1965), pp. 238-51; T. L. C. Griffin, "The Evolution and Duplication of a Pattern of Urban Growth," *Economic Geography*, 41 (April 1965), pp. 133-56; and Richard E. Preston, "The Zone in Transition: A Study of Urban Land Use Patterns," *Economic Geography*, 42 (July 1966), pp. 236-60.
2. Maurice D. Van Arsdol, Jr., Santo Camilleri, and Calvin F. Schmid, "The Generality of Urban Social Area Indexes," *American Sociological Review*, 23 (June 1958), pp. 277-84; Eshref Shevky and Wendell Bell, *Social Area Analysis* (Stanford: Stanford University Press, 1955).

3. Raymond E. Murphy, *The American City: An Urban Geography* (New York: McGraw-Hill, 1966).

From **Urban Studies**, Vol. 5, No. 1, February 1968, Glasgow, Scotland. Reprinted by permission.

status.[4] The results show suburbanisation at first attracted primarily high-status occupations but that suburban areas have become increasingly heterogeneous, although status differentials continue to exist between central cities and suburbs. Other studies have focused around one or more of the three traditional concepts of generalised urban structure.[5]

The Duncans' study of Chicago remains the major empirical description of residential areas by occupational status.[6] Their ecological analysis yields "a close relationship between spatial and social distance . . .", although their "spatial distance" does not include an analysis of particular parts of the metropolitan area. Neither does it take up the social and economic forces underlying residential location. These forces have more recently been reviewed by Anderson, who in addition to the factors of population concentration and competition for land focuses on "social interaction preferences."[7] These

preferences, manifest in social rivalries and hostilities among groups, supplement economic theory in accounting for residential location by socio-economic status.

Kain, drawing on work by Alonso, Wingo and others, shows how residential location by status can be expressed as a function of income, space preference, and economic rent.[8] Assuming a declining surface of economic rent away from the city centre, a household with a given preference for space will attempt to maximise the utility of its income by locating where the marginal cost of transport intersects marginal savings in location rent. This trade-off function between transport costs and economic rent is related to the nature of urban population densities, land use zonation, and the spatial composition of socio-economic groups. Rigorous verification of the theory has been hampered by problems of empirical definition of the cost components of the model.[9]

Purpose

It is the purpose of this study to examine the general occupational structure of residential areas in the Pittsburgh metropolitan area. Based on existing theory and limited empirical findings, it is hypothesised that groups of similar occupational status will have similar patterns of residential location; and, as the status level

4. Beverly Duncan, George Sabagh and Maurice D. Van Arsdol, Jr., "Patterns of City Growth," *American Journal of Sociology,* 67 (January 1962), pp. 418-29; Sidney Goldstein and Kurt B. Mayer, "Demographic Correlates of Status Differences in a Metropolitan Population," *Urban Studies,* 2 (May 1965), pp. 67-84; Bernard Lazerivitz, "Metropolitan Community Residential Belts, 1950 and 1960," *American Sociological Review,* 25 (April 1960), pp. 245-52; Leo F. Schnore, "The Socio-Economic Status of Cities and Suburbs," *American Sociological Review,* 28 (February 1963), pp. 76-85.
5. Homer Hoyt, "Where the Rich and the Poor People Live," *Technical Bulletin,* 55 (Washington, D.C.: Urban Land Institute, April 1966); P. J. Smith, "Calgary: A Study in Urban Pattern," *Economic Geography,* 38 (October 1962), pp. 315-29; B. T. Robson, "An Ecological Analysis of the Evolution of Residential Areas in Sunderland," *Urban Studies,* 3 (June 1966), pp. 120-39.
6. Otis D. Duncan and Beverly Duncan, "Residential Distribution and Occupational Stratification," *American Journal of Sociology,* 60 (March 1955), pp. 493-503.
7. Theodore R. Anderson, "Social and Economic Factors Affecting the Locations of Residential Neighbourhoods," *Papers and Proceedings of the Regional Science Association,* 9 (1962), pp. 161-70.

8. John F. Kain, "The Journey-to-Work as a Determinant of Residential Locations," *Papers and Proceedings of the Regional Science Association,* 9 (1962), pp. 137-60; William Alonso, "A Theory of the Urban Land Market," *Papers and Proceedings of the Regional Science Association,* 6 (1960), pp. 149-57; William Alonso, *Location and Land Use* (Cambridge, Massachusetts: Harvard University Press, 1964); John D. Herbert and Benjamin H. Stevens, "A Model for the Distribution of Residential Activity in Urban Areas," *Journal of Regional Science,* 2 (Fall 1960), pp. 21-36; and Lowdon Wingo, Jr., *Transportation and Urban Land* (Washington, D.C.: Resources for the Future, 1961).
9. See Leslie J. King, "Approaches to Locational Analysis: An Overview," *The East Lakes Geographer,* 2 (August 1966), p. 7: "There has been little . . . vigorous testing of . . . urban rent-models."

widens, location of residence will become increasingly dissimilar. This hypothesis is not stated to test a specific theory, but rather is intended as a framework for empirical evaluation. Occupational status levels should have relatively distinct residential locations, which in turn will be associated with a pattern of employment locations.

Method of Investigation

There are problems of measurement associated with testing the hypothesis. The problem of categorising workers into eight occupational groups may result in certain groups representing broader ranges of status than others. In addition, the size of the areal units may modify the results, since too large a unit would not properly differentiate among status groups and too small a unit would create an artificial difference. Data used in this study are provided by the Pittsburgh Area Transportation Study (PATS); occupational classifications are taken as given, and seventy-four metropolitan zones are used for analysis.[10] Although the zones are of unequal size, their increasing size away from the city centre is inversely related to their population total.

A separate problem involves the ranking of occupations by status. Basically, the classical Edwards's grouping is used here.[11] (See Table 1.) However, Edwards combined sales and clerical workers and labourers and service workers. Another frequently used prestige rating of occupations, the North-Hatt grouping, separates governmental officials into the highest

Table 1. Residential Location Quotient and Distance

Occupation	Coefficient of Correlation
Professionals	0.04
Managers	0.43*
Sales workers	0.22
Clerical workers	−0.34*
Craftsmen-Foremen	0.34*
Operatives	−0.11
Service workers	−0.49*
Labourers	−0.33*

* Significant at the 99 per cent level.
Source: Computed from PATS data, 1958.

ranking category.[12] Public administrators in this study are included as managers. The North-Hatt rating also does not differentiate between sales and clerical workers. Other studies have shown clerical workers to be similar to sales and managerial workers in education and prestige but below craftsmen-foremen in income.[13] The groupings here are those provided by the PATS and closely follow the categories of the U.S. Bureau of the Census. Private household workers are combined with service workers, and sales workers are ranked ahead of clerical workers.

To measure residential differentiation by occupational status, locational indices and correlation techniques are employed. Specifically, location quotients are determined for each zone to indicate how far above or below average a particular occupation falls in residential concentrations among Pittsburgh zones, a value of 100 being average.[14] These locational in-

10. These data are based on a 4 per cent sample of households in the 420 square mile Pittsburgh metropolitan area and represent 92 per cent of the population of Allegheny County (about 1.5 million persons). Data were made available on some 14,000 IBM punch cards, each card representing a residential location of a member of the work force.
11. Alba M. Edwards, "Socio-Economic Groups of the United States," *Journal of the American Statistical Association,* 15 (June 1917), pp. 643-61.

12. Cecil C. North and Paul K. Hatt, "Occupational Status and Prestige," *Opinion News,* 9 (September 1947), pp. 3-13.
13. Duncan and Duncan, op. cit., pp. 502-3; and Beverly Duncan, "Factors in Work-Residence Separation: Wage and Salary Workers, Chicago 1951," *American Sociological Review,* 21 (February 1956), pp. 48-56.
14. Location quotients are computed by:
$$\frac{X_i \,/\, \Sigma \, X_i}{N_i \,/\, \Sigma \, N_i} \cdot 100$$
where X_i equals the number in occupation X residing in zone i and N represents the total members of all occupations residing in zone i.

dices for eight occupations are intercorrelated to show the degree of similarity or dissimilarity among the groups, and the indices are also correlated with distance from the central business district (CBD). The index of dissimilarity is used to show the degree to which an occupation differs residentially from another occupation.[15] The coefficient of geographic association shows how one occupation is different from all other occupations, a low value indicating a large deviation.[16]

Findings for Pittsburgh

One commonly used indication of the physical structure of a metropolitan area is the way in which some variable relates to distance from the CBD. Coefficients of simple correlation were computed relating the residential location quotients by zone with distance from the heart of Pittsburgh's Golden Triangle (See Table 1.). All occupations except professionals, sales workers, and operatives show a significant relationship to distance, although none is strong. Labourers, service, and clerical workers have significant inverse correlations with distance, since these occupations are most concentrated near the CBD. Clerical workers, of whom nearly 40 per cent work in the CBD, also reside in large proportion in the central city, in contrast to other high-status groups. The only significant positive correlations are for managers and craftsmen-foremen,

15. The index of dissimilarity is computed by:

$$\sum_{i=1}^{n} \frac{| (X_i / \Sigma X_i) - (Y_i / \Sigma Y_i) |}{2} \cdot 100$$

where X_i represents one occupation and Y_i represents another occupation residing in zone i.
16. The coefficient of geographic association is computed by:

$$1 - \sum_{i=1}^{n} \frac{| (X_i / \Sigma X_i) - (N_i / \Sigma N_i) |}{2}$$

where X_i and N_i are defined in reference 14. The coefficient has a range from zero to one.

groups with dissimilar occupational status. Therefore, although correlations are found between the relative concentrations of certain occupational groups and distance from the CBD, the coefficients are weak and do not suggest a simple relationship between residential location and occupational status, as implied by the Burgess concept of city structure.

Coefficients of variation are used with the residential location quotients to show the degree of variation among zones by occupation.[17] A high coefficient of variation, for example, would indicate that that occupational group is either well above or below the metropolitan average. Low coefficients reflect a more uniform distribution of an occupation among zones. The residential pattern of those occupations at the lowest and highest ends of the socio-economic scale is the most segregated (See Table 2.). Service workers and labourers are the most segregated occupations residentially, and these groups consist of 26 and 20 per cent Negro, respectively. Operatives, craftsmen-foremen, and especially clerical workers show a strong tendency to occupy residential zones in which there is a high degree of occupational mixture.

Table 2. Measures of Segregation

Occupations	Coefficients of Variation of Location Quotient by Zone	Coefficient of Geographic Association
Professionals	54	.761
Managers	52	.812
Sales workers	48	.836
Clerical workers	30	.881
Craftsmen-Foremen	38	.834
Operatives	40	.842
Service workers	75	.772
Labourers	71	.731

Source: Computed from PATS data, 1958.

17. The coefficient of variation is a measure of relative deviation, obtained by dividing the mean into the standard deviation.

Table 3. Intercorrelation of Location Quotients by Zones

	Profes-sionals	Man-agers	Sales workers	Clerical workers	Craftsmen-Foremen	Operatives	Service workers	Labourers
Professionals	1	.65†	.20	.04	−.26*	−.58†	−.49†	−.62†
Managers		1	.45†	−.05	−.25*	−.50†	−.54†	−.60†
Sales workers			1	−.09	−.11	−.38†	−.35†	−.36†
Clerical workers				1	−.17	−.13	−.27*	−.36†
Craftsmen-Foremen					1	.32†	−.34†	−.12
Operatives						1	.05	.24*
Service workers							1	.71†
Labourers								1

* Significant at the 95 per cent level.
† Significant at the 99 per cent level.
Source: Computed from PATS data, 1958.

Another measure of residential segregation of occupational groups is the coefficient of geographic association, which shows the degree to which each occupational group is spatially similar to all other occupations. This coefficient, also shown in Table 2, reveals that occupations occupying intermediate status positions are least segregated and are found most commonly in all residential areas. The only exception to a consistent status/segregation relationship is the reversal of craftsmen-foremen and operatives. Clearly the two highest and lowest status occupations reside in the most segregated patterns.

Coefficients of correlation were computed between residential indices for the eight occupations. Examination of Table 3 discloses a degree of regularity and occupational patterning in the Pittsburgh metropolitan area. Nineteen of the 28 intercorrelation coefficients (excluding the diagonal) are significant at either the 95 or 99 per cent confidence level, 16 of the 19 at the latter level.

Looking first at the four highest status groups, one notes that among the highest correlations in the matrix is the one between the residential index values of professionals and managers. However, no other occupation shows a statistically similar distribution to professionals, but sales workers have a residential pattern somewhat similar to managers. Clerical workers are not similar in residential structure to any other white-collar group but are significantly different from labourers and to a lesser extent from service workers, but not from craftsmen-foremen or operatives. On the other hand, each of the four lowest status occupations is significantly different from the residential pattern of professionals and managers. And the degree of this inverse relationship tends to increase as the occupational status decreases. Sales workers are different residentially from all the four lowest status groups, except the craftsmen-foremen, but these inverse correlations are not as high for sales workers as for professional and managerial workers. White-collar occupations thus tend to be similar in their residential index and generally different from the lower status groups.

While craftsmen-foremen are significantly different residentially from only professionals and managers of the high-status group, they are also dissimilar to service workers and show no meaningful correlation with labourers. Operatives, however, have a significantly similar residential grouping to craftsmen-foremen, a barely significant correlation with labourers, but no correlation with service workers. The pattern for operatives is dissimilar to those for high-status workers—

professional, managerial and sales workers —and is increasingly dissimilar as status rises. Service workers and labourers have either a positive or a negative correlation residentially with all groups except operatives and craftsmen-foremen, respectively. The correlations are mostly negative for both service workers and labourers with all the white-collar groups, and in addition different from craftsmen-foremen for the service workers. The highest correlations between the residential indices of one occupation and another is between service workers and labourers.

The index of dissimilarity is another measure of differences in residential location among occupations. The proportion of each occupation residing in each zone is computed, and the percentage difference between two occupations for each zone is summed and divided by two. Specifically, the index measures the percentage of an occupational group that would have to change residential zones to be identical with some other group. For example Table 4 shows that only 14 per cent of professionals would have to move to be consistent with residential locations by zone of managers; but 43 per cent of professionals would have to change zones to be identical to labourers. These two examples represent the smallest and largest displacements within Table 4.

If the hypothesis of this study holds, index values should increase away from the diagonal. Thus occupations with similar socio-economic ranks will have similar residential distributions, and as one increases the socio-economic separation, the residential dissimilarities will increase. This relationship obtains with only two exceptions. Clerical workers are somewhat less closely related to craftsmen-foremen than expected (or more closely related to operatives), and craftsmen-foremen are not as similar residentially to service workers as hypothesised (or are more similar to labourers). In general the four highest status groups are more similar residentially among themselves than are the four lowest status occupations.

The intercorrelation matrix derived from location quotients reflects a somewhat different approach to residential location by status from the matrix of dissimilarity indices. Both provide only partial solutions to the problem. The dissimilarity index suggests a strong and consistent relationship between status and residential location, while the correlation coefficients show a weaker association. The significant negative coefficient of correlation between craftsmen-foremen and service workers is consistent with the dissimilarity index; likewise, the greater difference than expected in dissimilarity index between clerical workers and craftsmen-foremen is

Table 4. Index of Dissimilarity

	Profes-sionals	Man-agers	Sales workers	Clerical workers	Craftsmen-Foremen	Operatives	Service workers	Labourers
Professionals	—	14	20	22	28	31	35	43
Managers		—	15	17	25	28	33	39
Sales workers			—	16	20	27	32	35
Clerical workers				—	19	17	22	30
Craftsmen-Foremen					—	15	27	26
Operatives						—	18	22
Service workers							—	20
Labourers								—

Source: Computed from PATS data, 1958.

noted by a weak negative correlation coefficient.

The findings here corroborate the Duncans' classical Chicago study and provide a firmer foundation for describing socio-economic variation within metropolitan areas. A complementary investigation might focus on the residential location of Negroes by occupational status. Much of the value in this approach lies in relating the findings to occupational employment indices and to the pattern of work-trips. Although such is beyond the purpose of this paper, a number of journey to work studies have isolated occupation as an important variable in determining work-trip length.[18] Moreover, an investigation of urban social circulation is a needed and logical extension of these findings.

18. Sidney Goldstein and Kurt Mayer, "Migration and Social Status Differentials in the Journey-to-Work," *Rural Sociology,* 29 (September 1964), pp. 278-87; Louis K. Loewenstein, *Residences and Work Places in Urban Areas* (New York: The Scarecrow Press, 1965); James O. Wheeler, "Occupational Status and Work-Trips: A Minimum Distance Approach," *Social Forces,* 45 (June 1967), pp. 508-15.

HAROLD M. ROSE

The Development of an Urban Subsystem:
The Case of the Negro Ghetto

The internal development of individual urban places has not traditionally been one of central focus in geography. This probably stems in part from the overriding emphasis on regions in general and the urban geographer's concern with the interrelationships among individual urban nodes. American geographers have only recently turned their attention to the internal structure of urban areas, no doubt an outgrowth of general interest in central place theory. Increasing interest in urban subsystems has resulted in a concommitant interest in the spatial structure of these systems. This paper attempts to provide insights on the spatial dynamics of a single subsystem within the metropolitan system, the Negro ghetto.

The Negro ghetto, as a universal and viable urban subsystem within the American urban system, has evolved with the rise of the Negro population in northern urban centers beginning with the decade prior to World War I.[1] The almost continuous flow of Negroes from both the

rural and urban South to the North and West has permitted and promoted the development of Negro ghettos in all of the nation's major population centers. By 1960 more than thirty percent of the nation's Negro population resided in twenty metropolitan areas. Whereas the Negro ghetto is found in nearly all 200 metropolitan areas in the United States, the basic concern of this study is with the processes responsible for its change in scale in northern urban centers. The previous legality of a system of racial separation in the American South served as an exogenous factor, overriding all others, in the promotion and maintenance of residential clusters based on race. For a brief period there existed laws which were specifically designed to maintain residential segregation based on race. The Supreme Court outlawed attempts to maintain a legal system of residential separation in 1917, in the case of Buchanan *versus* Warley.[2] Such a legalized role-prescription tends to reduce the fruitfulness of a be-

1. A. Meier and E. M. Rudwick, *From Plantation to Ghetto* (New York: Hill and Wang, 1966), pp. 191-92.

2. R. L. Rice, "Residential Segregation by Law," *The Journal of Southern History*, Vol. 34 (1968), pp. 194-99.

From the **Annals** of the Association of American Geographers, Vol. 60, No. 1, March 1970, pp. 1-5. Reprinted by permission.

316

haviorally oriented study, and thereby accounts for the limiting of this investigation to northern cities.

To date, only Morrill's pioneer work might be described as a spatial behavioral approach to the study of the changing state of the ghetto.[3] The model he assembled was employed to replicate the process of ghetto development in Seattle. Other researchers are beginning to show increasing concern for the general problem, with emphasis on the spatial dimension. Beauchamp recently suggested the use of Markov Chain Analysis as a means of specifying or identifying territorial units as ghetto or non-ghetto by investigating the dynamic changes taking place in the racial composition of areas.[4]

The process of the changing ghetto state has been described elsewhere as a diffusion process.[5] Diffusion models have attracted the interest of a small number of geographers who have employed them as a means of describing the spatial spread of an innovation. The more notable of these are associated with the work of Hägerstrand. The suitability of diffusion models as a means of describing the spread of the ghetto, however, is questionable. It appears that the spread of the ghetto is a phenomenon of a different type. More specifically, it appears that the spread of the Negro ghetto is a function of white adjustment to a perceived threat. The distinction between adjustment and diffusion was recently reviewed by Carlsson.[6] He averred that motivation and values transcend knowledge, in importance, in ex-

plaining certain types of behavioral change.[7] If the diffusion thesis is accepted as a means of explaining rather than describing the expansion of the Negro ghetto, then it must be assumed that each metropolitan system operates as a closed system. Since this is not the case, the adjustment hypothesis which Carlsson supports is undeniably more appealing than the diffusion hypothesis as a means of explaining the spread of the ghetto. Admittedly, whites must first be aware of the presence of Negroes if a change in their normative mobility pattern is to occur, but awareness here promotes the kind of behavior which has also become accepted as normative. Thus, the necessary adjustment is made as a means of maintaining the steady state condition. The kind of behavior inferred here was described by Zelinsky as social avoidance.[8] Morrill, who previously described the ghetto development process in terms of diffusion, now describes processes of this general type, which are interactional in nature, as quasi-diffusionary.[9]

Intra-Urban Population Mobility

The spatial mobility of the American population, both in terms of long distance moves and intraurban shifts, was intensified during the decade of the 1950's. As major metropolitan systems were the target of most long distance moves, these moves resulted in the rapid dispersion of population into what was previously part of the rural countryside. The latter phenomenon has attracted the attention of researchers from a vast array of disciplines, geographers included. Geographers have also focused particular interest on the

3. R. L. Morrill, "The Negro Ghetto: Problems and Alternatives," *The Geographical Review,* Vol. 55 (1965), pp. 339-61.

4. A. Beauchamp, "Processual Indices of Segregation: Some Preliminary Comments," *Behavioral Science,* Vol. 11 (1966), pp. 190-92.

5. Morrill, *op. cit.,* footnote 3, p. 348; R. L. Morrill, *Migration and the Spread and Growth of Urban Settlement* (Lund, Sweden: C. W. K. Gleerup, 1965), p. 186.

6. G. Carlsson, "Decline of Fertility: Innovation or Adjustment Process," *Population Studies,* Vol. 20 (November 1966), pp. 149-50.

7. Carlsson, *op. cit.,* footnote 6, p. 150.

8. W. Zelinsky, *A Prologue to Population Geography* (New York: Prentice-Hall, 1965), pp. 45-46.

9. R. L. Morrill, "Waves of Spatial Diffusion," *Journal of Regional Science,* Vol. 8 (Summer, 1968), p. 2.

centrifugal flow of population, as this flow has had the most obvious impact on the form and areal magnitude of urban systems. But to consider the latter and ignore the role of the centripetal movement weakens the analysis of population shifts within the system and of the ensuing patterns which evolve.

Movements toward the periphery of the urban system, both from within the system and from without, have been principally responsible for the increase in the size of individual metropolitan aggregates. At the same time many central cities within metropolitan systems have suffered absolute losses in their populations. Thus, the centripetal flow into the central cities of metropolitan systems has seldom been sufficiently large to offset the counter flow. The most rapid and easily observed flow into the nation's larger central cities is that of Negro in-migration, a phenomenon which has had far-reaching effects on the color composition of metropolitan areas.[10] By the mid-sixties there was official evidence that this process was continuing. The city of Cleveland, Ohio, undertook a special census on April 1, 1965. The results showed that the city had lost 91,436 white residents during the five years that had elapsed since the last census, while gaining an additional 26,244 Negro residents.[11] The Negro proportion of Cleveland's population rose by five percentage points during that period, from twenty-nine to thirty-four percent. Since the census was confined to the political city of Cleveland, it is impossible to determine the extent to which Negroes entered the stream of movers destined for suburbia.

In response to the changing magnitude and composition of metropolitan popula-tions, a network of transport links has evolved to facilitate the spatial redistribution of the population. Where an individual chooses to locate himself within the urban system is a function of occupational status, income, place of employment, and social taste. The operation or interaction of these factors has produced a strongly segmented pattern of urban occupance. A change in an individual's socioeconomic status frequently results in relocation within the metropolitan system. As the nation's occupational structure is being rapidly altered in the direction of a larger proportion of white collar workers, especially technical and professional workers, with a concomitant alteration in the income structure, spatial mobility is further accelerated. Changes of this nature tend to produce shifts in territorial status assignment in urban space. Davis, in a recent study, described the magnitude of territorial shifts in the location of middle class housing areas in a selected group of American cities.[12] With the redistribution of the population towards the periphery, there has subsequently been an outward shift of the inner boundary of the zone of middle class housing. As a consequence, these shifts frequently create gray areas which act as zones of transition or buffers between middle and lower class occupance. It is within these gray areas, with their high vacancy rates, that most of the centrifugal Negro flow is destined. The growing intensity of mobility within the metropolitan system has affected all segments of the population, although somewhat differentially. The pattern of movement of whites and nonwhites in urban space is akin to the pattern of interregional movement within the nation as a whole. In both instances nonwhite moves are characterized by short distance, whereas whites are more frequently engaged in long distance moves.

10. See H. Sharp and L. F. Schnore, "The Changing Color Composition of Metropolitan Areas," *Land Economics*, Vol. 38 (1962), pp. 169-85.

11. Special Census of Cleveland, Ohio, April, 1965, *Current Population Reports*, Series p-28, No. 1390 (1965).

12. J. T. Davis, "Middle Class Housing in the Central City," *Economic Geography*, Vol. 41 (1965), pp. 238-51.

The nature of population movement within the urban system is highly related to the magnitude and form of the set of urban subsystems which evolve. The Negro ghetto which comprises one such subsystem or social area is directly related to this process. Since spatial mobility is related both to age and income, one would expect to observe the evolution of a series of patterns which reflect the economic health of a specific metropolitan system, the nature of its economic base, and its subsequent ability to attract population through the process of internal migration; the latter phenomenon has the effect of altering the age distribution of the population. If ability to purchase was the single most significant variable influencing the distribution of population in metropolitan space, it should be easy to predict the kind of sorting-out which eventually occurs. Although this can be done in a rather general manner, purchasing ability alone is far from adequate in explaining the development of the ghetto.[13] The relative stability of the Negro's economic position vis-à-vis the white's during the last several years may have reduced or severely limited the ability of individual Negroes to cross critical rent isolines. On the other hand, the brisk hiring of Negroes to salaried positions by an increasing number of firms pledged to the goal of equality of opportunity, could have the effect of increasing the length of the individual move. It is impossible at this time to specify with any degree of precision the effect of either factor upon the pattern of Negro movement, even though they both may be significant.

Territoriality

The existence and persistence of the Negro ghetto as a spatially based social community may best be explained within the framework of the social assignment of territory. Once a slice of physical space is identified as the territorial realm of a specific social group, any attempt to alter this assignment results in group conflict, both overt and covert. Stea recently described this behavior in the following way: "We have reason to believe that 'territorial behavior,' the desire both to possess and occupy positions of space, is as pervasive among men as among their animal forbears."[14] Webber attributed this kind of behavior simply to working class groups for whom physical space is an extension of one's ego.[15]

Human ecologists have employed terms such as invasion and succession to describe the process of residential change in which members of competing groups struggle for territory. Henderson recently questioned the employment of the term invasion to describe the process of Negro entry into areas bordering on the ghetto.[16] Admittedly the term invasion appears to be appropriate only within the context of territorial conflict. Viewed outside this context, the term does not appear to be meaningful. A further point, no doubt the one which concerned Henderson, is that the term invasion not only reflects the white resident's perception of events, but the perception of the researcher as well. It has been said, "When our own tribe engages in this behavior we call it nationalism or aggression."[17] From another vantage point, it would appear that the term retreat describes the process more accurately. Since both terms, invasion and retreat, refer to territorial conflict, no major point is settled by substituting one for the other. Nevertheless, it should be

13. For a methodological discussion of this point see K. E. Taeuber and A. F. Taeuber, *Negroes in Cities* (Chicago: Aldine Publishing Co., 1965), pp. 78-95.

14. D. Stea, "Space, Territory and Human Movements," *Landscape,* Vol. 15 (1965), p. 13.
15. M. M. Webber, "Culture, Territoriality and the Elastic Mile," *The Regional Science Association Papers,* Vol 13 (1964), pp. 61-63.
16. G. C. Henderson, "Negroes Into Americans: A Dialectical Development," *Journal of Human Relations,* Vol. 14 (1966), p. 537.
17. Stea, *op. cit.,* footnote 14, p. 13.

kept in mind that the nature of the behavior which occurs within this context
does so within the context of a fear-safety
syndrome.

The territorial acquisition by advancing
Negro populations cannot always be
viewed as a gain in this game of psychological warfare, for once the territory is
transferred from one group to the other,
it is perceived by the white population as
having been contaminated and, therefore,
undesirable. The formalization or codification of this attitude is associated with the
Federal Housing Administration's policy
of promoting racial homogeneity in neighborhoods during the period 1935-1950.[18]
Hoyt's classic study on the growth of
residential neighborhoods strongly supported this position, and possibly served
to support and justify the government's
position.[19] Thus, the whole notion of
stable property values revolves around the
transfer of the status designation from a
group to the territory occupied by the
group. More recently Bailey observed in
one case that unstable property values
were associated with those zones located
in the shadow of the ghetto rather than in
the ghetto itself.[20] However, it is the slack

demand for housing in a racially changing
neighborhood that is likely to drive down
housing values. The unwillingness of
whites to compete with nonwhites for
housing in a common housing market,
coupled with vacancy rates which frequently exceed Negro demand, could
eventually lead to a lessening of values.
Thus, land abandoned by whites on the
margins of the Negro ghetto at some
single point in time is almost never known
to be retrieved by such residents.

The behavior described above is rapidly
leading to the development in the United
States of central cities within which territorial dominance is being relinquished
to the Negro population. This fact has
undoubtedly had much to do with the increasing demand by Negroes for black
power, and logically so. If one inherits
a piece of turf it is only natural for him
to seek control of the area of occupance.
Thus, both the critics and supporters of
black power have traditional white behavior and the public decisions stemming
therefrom for its overt crystallization.
Grier recently noted that it was not until
President Kennedy signed his executive
order of 1962, which treated the problem
of discrimination in housing, had the federal government ever gone on record as
opposing discrimination in housing.[21] Yet
even today, as the nation's ghettos continue to expand, public policy abets their
existence and expansion.

18. E. Grier and G. C. Grier, "Equality and
Beyond: Housing Segregation in the Great Society," *Daedalus*, Vol. 95 (1966), p. 82.
19. H. Hoyt, *The Structure and Growth of
Residential Neighborhoods in American Cities*
(Washington, D.C.: Government Printing Office, 1939), pp. 62 and 71.
20. M. J. Bailey, "Effects of Race and Other
Demographic Factors on the Values of Single-
Family Homes," *Land Economics,* Vol. 42
(1966), pp. 214-18.

21. G. C. Grier, "The Negro Ghettos and Federal Housing Policy," *Law and Contemporary
Problems* (Summer, 1967), p. 555.

L. S. BOURNE

Apartment Location and the Housing Market

Among the most prominent additions to the contemporary urban landscape is the high-rise apartment development. In the United States in 1956 over 89 per cent of all new housing completions were single-family units, only 11 per cent were apartments.[1] In recent years the proportion of apartment units has approached 40 per cent.[2] This trend has been similar, if not more pronounced, in Canada, with apartments[3] representing nearly 50 per cent of

1. W. Alonso, 'The Historical and Structural Theories of Urban Form: Their Implications for Urban Renewal," *Land Econ., XL*, 2 (May 1964), 229.
2. For example, United States Census of Housing 1960, "Components of Inventory Change," (Washington: U.S. Bureau of the Census).
3. Studies employing residential building statistics are frequently hindered by the lack of consistency in definitions of housing types. The Central Mortgage and Housing Corporation, the Canadian federal housing agency, for example, defines apartment to include ". . . triplexes, double duplexes, row duplexes and other multi-family units." Other agencies, however, such as the Metropolitan Toronto Planning Board define apartments to include only those structures consisting of several multi-family units. "An apartment (unit) is a self contained dwelling unit in a building containing six or more units which share a common means of access at street level" (Metropolitan Toronto Planning Board,

Table 1. Construction of New Housing by Type, Canada, 1950–67 (Dwelling Starts)

Year	Total Units	Single-Detached	Apart-ments*	Per centage Apart-ments
	(thousands of units)			
1950	92.5	68.7	14.5	15.6
1954	113.5	78.6	27.4	24.1
1958	164.6	104.5	47.0	45.1
1960	108.9	67.1	29.7	28.3
1962	130.1	74.4	40.9	31.6
1964	165.7	77.1	75.1	45.3
1966	134.5	70.6	51.5	38.3
1967	164.1	72.5	74.2	45.2

Source: Central Mortgage and Housing Corporation and Economic Council of Canada.
* Excludes single-attached, duplex, and row-housing units.

total residential construction starts in 1967 (Table 1). As expected in metropolitan areas the dominance of apartments in the provision of new residential space has been even higher, for example, in

Survey of Apartments 1961 [Toronto, 1962]). As a result it is often impossible to develop comparative statistics from different sources. In this paper, emphasis is given to the high-rise apartment type.

Adapted by the author from L. S. Bourne, "Market, Location, and Site Selection in Apartment Construction," **Canadian Geographer**, Vol. XII, No. 4, 1968. Reprinted in revised form by permission.

321

1967 it approached 73 per cent in Metropolitan Toronto (Table 2).[4] At the same time, the distribution of apartments within urban areas has become more widespread and variable as their dominance expands. The implications of this drastic change in the housing market, for theoreticians concerned with the evolving form and spatial structure of the modern city as well as for public policy, are considerable.

This paper attempts to merge a rather broad set of ideas and empirical analyses concerned with the accelerated rate of apartment construction, the location of this construction within urban areas, and the resulting implications for urban form and structure. The paper is divided into two sections. The first examines recent market conditions which have encouraged high-density apartment construction and evaluates the relevance of traditional residential-location theory in accounting for apartment location. In the second section, a formal set of locational parameters are hypothesized and tested against both the aggregate distribution and site selection process of apartment construction. Building-permit statistics are employed for Metropolitan Toronto through 1967, and assessment records for each apartment constructed in the city of Toronto between 1952 and 1963.[5]

Changes in the Structure of the Housing Market

Apartments, by most common definitions are distinctive within the urban housing inventory in only two regards; they are usually of high-density construction and they represent rental accommodation. Clearly neither of these criteria are in themselves distinctive as some apartments do not fit into either of these categories. Generally, however, apartments can be characterized by both criteria, and the uniqueness of apartments derives from this combination. Any discussion of the rationale for their distribution or extent must therefore dwell on the reasons for and implications of high-density construction, and the nature of both the housing industry and the rental-housing market.

Several distinct structural changes on both the demand and supply sides of the housing market have converged to accelerate the trend toward apartment construction and the provision of rental accommodation. These processes are by no means unique to the present time, similar trends were noted in the 1920's,[6] nor do they necessarily reflect long-run trends in the production or consumption of housing,[7] yet they are radically altering the

Table 2. Construction of New Housing by Type, Toronto Metropolitan Area, 1951–67 (Building Permits Issued)

Year	Total Units	Single-Detached and Others	Apartments*	Per centage Apartments
	(thousands of units)			
1951	11.9	9.7	2.2	18.3
1954	25.4	15.4	10.0	39.4
1958	27.6	14.4	13.2	41.7
1960	18.2	7.8	10.4	56.9
1962	19.0	8.7	10.3	54.2
1964	29.4	11.3	18.1	61.6
1966	28.2	9.2	19.0	67.3
1967	32.3	8.8	23.5	72.5

Source: Dominion Bureau of Statistics.
* Includes all multiple housing with 3 or more units, as well as row housing. These figures are for building permits issued rather than dwelling starts and thus are not directly comparable to those in Table 1.

4. Metropolitan Toronto as used here refers to the municipality under metropolitan government. The estimated 1967 population of Metro was 1.9 million and of the census metropolitan area 2.3 million.

5. L. S. Bourne, *Private Redevelopment of the Central City, Spatial Processes of Structural Change in the City of Toronto*, Res. Paper no. 112, Dept. of Geog. Univ. of Chicago, 1967.
6. For example, Homer Hoyt, *One Hundred Years of Land Values in Chicago* (Chicago, 1933).
7. Alonso, p. 230.

urban landscape and the evolving form of metropolitan areas.

The increasing specialization of the building industry in apartment construction results from several supply factors operating together. Rising land costs throughout, augmented by an insufficient supply of reasonably priced land on the urban fringe, have increased the pressures on residential land development. As a result, it is increasingly difficult to construct anything but high-density residential buildings or high-cost low-density units within the larger metropolitan areas.[8] For example, land costs for single-family bungalows under N.H.A. financing are estimated at over $8,300 in the Metropolitan Toronto region, and are considerably higher in Metro itself, compared to a national average of $3,200.[9] Moreover, land costs in Toronto have risen nearly 50 per cent in only two years.

This trend has markedly increased the density of apartment construction from 6 to 8 storeys in Toronto prior to 1960 to 15 to 20 storeys today,[10] as well as encouraging the shift away from low-density

construction. Costs of single-family homes have also risen sharply in concert with the price of serviced land. In fact the estimated cost index of home ownership in Canada, since 1960, has been higher and has increased much more rapidly than the cost index of rental accommodation.[11] Local municipal taxation and education costs have also been conducive to the high-density, small-family housing development. Again the trend has been strongest in the larger metropolitan areas, and particularly in the suburbs. Figure 1 illustrates the wide distribution of apartments in Toronto in 1967.

On the demand side, changes in family income, family size and age structure, and housing and locational preferences, have all combined to alter the market for new housing. Rising real incomes among all segments of society, and particularly among non-family households, have contributed to an accelerated demand for new housing space precisely at the time when increased competition for sources of capital financing and high construction costs have reduced the available supply of new housing in all but the higher income categories.[12] Among non-family households the demand has been particularly heavy for rental accommodation. The most rapidly growing age groups in the last five years have been the younger married, the single, and the older retired elements of the population.[13]

Changing social preferences have also played a significant role in the housing

8. An equally relevant consideration is the nature of the residential construction industry itself. Rapid and enormous swings are characteristic of the industry in general and of residential construction in particular following but more exaggerated than swings in the national economy. A thorough treatment of the industry is contained in Leo Grebler and S. J. Maisel, "Determinants of Residential Construction: A Review of Present Knowledge," in *Impacts of Monetary Policy*. D. B. Suits, et al. (Englewood Cliffs, N.J., 1963), pp. 475-620.

9. Central Mortgage and Housing Corporation, *Canadian Housing Statistics, 1967* (Ottawa: Economics and Statistics Division, Central Mortgage and Housing Corporation, March 1968), p. 77. In The United States the Federal Housing Authority reports a similar trend. Between 1945 and 1960 land costs for residential purposes increased by nearly 200 per cent. U.S. Housing and Home Finance Agency, *Fourteenth Annual Rept.* (Washington: U.S. Govt. Printing Office, 1961) p. 110.

10. Metropolitan Toronto Planning Board, *Apartment Survey 1965* (Toronto, 1966). p. 15.

11. Bank of Nova Scotia, "Apartment Boom in Canada," *Monthly Rev.* (Oct. 1965), p. 2.

12. The scale of the housing shortage in most metropolitan areas is evident in published vacancy figures for Metro Toronto. In 1961, slightly over 6.1 percent of apartments were reported vacant, compared to less than one percent in 1966. A vacancy rate of at least 3 percent is considered to be essential for the housing market to perform efficiently.

13. For example, Arnold Rose, "Living Arrangements of Unattached Persons," *Amer. Sociol. Rev.*, XII (Aug. 1947), 429-35.

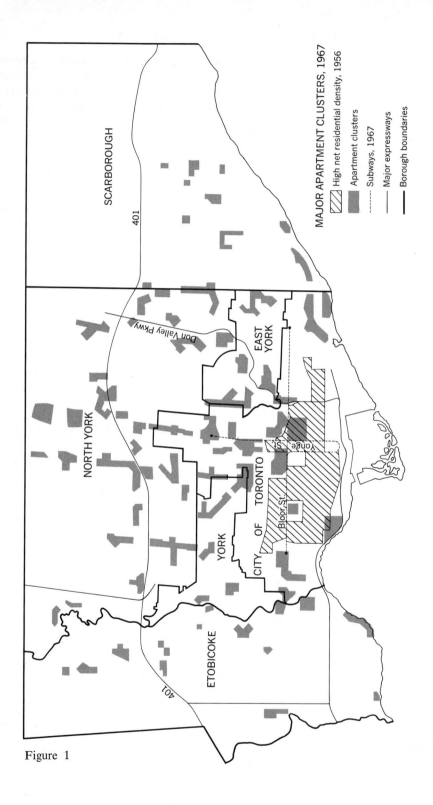

MAJOR APARTMENT CLUSTERS, 1967

- ⬚ High net residential density, 1956
- ▪ Apartment clusters
- ---- Subways, 1967
- —— Major expressways
- —— Borough boundaries

SCARBOROUGH

401

Don Valley Pkwy.

EAST YORK

NORTH YORK

Yonge St.

CITY OF TORONTO

YORK

Bloor St.

ETOBICOKE

401

Figure 1

transformation.[14] There is not only an apparent preference among the younger population for both central location and rental accommodation, but also a willingness among a larger proportion of society in total to accept apartment living. Demand elasticities for new housing have changed, but to what extent is uncertain. Nonetheless, the greater mobility provided by rental accommodation, as well as generally lower costs, built-in conveniences, and higher accessibility either because of central location or proximity to mass transit, have accelerated the shift to apartments. The range of facilities and amenities provided may not be within the financial grasp of most people in other forms of accommodation.

Many of these changes in the demand side of the housing market are, however, to a considerable extent short-term. The post-war population boom, which is now having its greatest impact in the age-specific rental section of the market, will in a few years enter the house-purchasing period. In the next decade, this growth will considerably strengthen the demand for low-density, owner-occupied housing relative to the current level. Yet the combined factors of costs, land availability, and preferences discussed above, will act to keep the level of this demand proportionally below the level of the 1950's.[15]

The rate of urban growth, particularly an excessively high rate such as that recorded by Metropolitan Toronto in recent years is also likely to alter both demand and supply in the residential market. Rapid growth is usually concomitant with

development speculation and high land values, accelerating the trend toward higher-density construction and increased housing costs. Rapid growth also invariably increases the lag between provision of local services such as transportation and educational facilities, which slows the spread of low-density construction by reducing the amount of serviced land available. On the demand side, rapid growth stimulates in-migration which tends to be age-specific to the rental housing market.

Apartment Location and the Residential Land Market

Each of these documented changes in demand and supply is reflected by a shift in the type of residential space provided toward high-density rental accommodation, which in turn alters the location of new construction and thus the form of the city. As primarily rental units catering to small families and non-family households, and consuming less land per unit than more traditional residential areas, the location of apartments should be the result of a rather unique mix of factors. Traditionally, residential location has been examined in terms of theories of land use and land value.[16] The price of land at any location is considered to be a function of accessibility to the city centre with land uses sorting themselves out in accordance with their ability to pay for each site. Thus uses which cannot compete, or are not able to operate at high densities are forced to the periphery. Apartments, because of their land-rent paying ability are therefore able to compete for almost all locations. On Figure 1 note the tendency for apartment developers to avoid the older areas of higher densities, which include the pre-

14. Bernard J. Frieden, *The Future of Old Neighborhoods Rebuilding for a Changing Population* (Cambridge, Mass., 1964), particularly pp. 173-96.

15. John R. White, however, forecasted a decline in apartment construction in the mid-1950's as a result of government mortgage procedures, zoning controls, and prosperous business conditions. "Apartment Living on the Wane," *The Appraisal Jour.* XXIV (Jan. 1956), 20-22.

16. A useful summary on residential land and housing markets is: Univ. of California, *Essays in Urban Land Economics.* In Honor of the Sixty-fifth Birthday of Leo Grebler. (Los Angeles: Real Estate Res. Program, 1966).

dominantly ethnic areas, to the east and west of the city center.

Most location theorists assume all costs to be constant allowing only land to vary as a factor price. As a result, intra-urban location differentials become simple land value differentials, and land use is automatically determined. This deterministic assumption ignores the effects of the standing stock of buildings,[17] and thus is only marginally valid for the location of urban activities particularly in the already built-up areas. Furthermore, in the case of high-rise residential construction, this assumption commonly results in the erroneous assertion that apartments will be confined to areas near the city centre. Nourse, for example, noting this concentration in the centre states ". . . As the distance increases, and rent declines, the builder will shift to duplexes, to single-family houses, and finally to single-family houses on large acreage."[18] High-rise apartments, however, are not confined to the immediate proximity of the city centre, but increasingly are found throughout the urban area, including the suburban fringe.[19] The older standing stock may approximate this direct distance relationship simply because there were fewer high-rise additions in previous years and those constructed were more spatially confined by accessibility and mobility constraints.[20]

One obvious constraint on the location of new residential construction is the quality level at which new housing is added to the inventory. As most new units are added in the upper levels of the household-income profile, and since similar social and income groups have been shown to cluster, new housing tends to be concentrated in existing high-income sectors. Grigsby[21] suggests that about 40 per cent of all households are in a position to purchase new housing. Although Smith[22] in a study of Los Angeles, attempts to prove the opposite, that housing additions are lowest, relative to demand, in the higher-income sectors, recent trends in Toronto and most other cities indicate that Grigsby's argument is correct. Although new apartments are usually rented and therefore not nearly as restrictive in income, they are nonetheless subject to the same income-stratification constraint.

Trade-offs in Residential Location

The question of exactly what is traded-off in residential location between accessibility and space costs, however, is not clear. It has been argued that, as intensive users of land, apartment developers can afford to pay a premium for sites that reduce travel time and costs between residence and place of work to a minimum.[23] It is also possible to argue that people live in apartments in order to reduce their overall housing costs. Although it is not at all

17. In a review of W. Alonso's *Location and Land Use* (Cambridge, Mass., 1964), W. C. Pendleton argues that a theory of urban residential location which ignores the effects of the standing stock of buildings in a city is suspect. See *Jour. of the Amer. Inst. of Planners*, XXXI, 1 (Feb. 1965), pp. 78-79.
18. Hugh O. Nourse, *Regional Economics* (New York, 1967) p. 114.
19. Similar trends in office-development location have been documented in several cities: in London, J. S. Wade, "Office Decentralization: An Empirical Approach," *Urban Studies*, III, 1 (Feb. 1966), 35-55; in Westchester County, N.Y., F. P. Clark, "Office Buildings in the Suburbs," *Urban Land*, no. 13 (July-Aug. 1954), 3-10. D. L. Foley, *The Suburbanization of Administrative Offices in the San Francisco Bay Area*, Res. Rept. no. 10, Real Estate Res. Program (Berkeley: Center for Business and Economic Research, 1957).

20. Wallace F. Smith, *The Low Rise Speculative Apartment*, Res. Rept. no. 25 (Berkeley: Center for Real Estate and Urban Economics, 1964).
21. William Grigsby, *Housing Markets and Public Policy* (Philadelphia, 1963).
22. Wallace F. Smith, "The Income Level of New Housing Demand," in *Essays in Urban Land Economics* (Los Angeles: Real Estate Res. Program, 1966), p. 145.
23. Homer Hoyt, "Expressways and Apartment Sites," *Traffic Quarterly*, XII, 12 (April 1958), 266.

certain that rental accommodation does reduce total housing costs in the long run, it is assumed to do so in most instances.

A third consideration, introduced by Alonso,[24] argues that individuals may choose a housing location on the periphery because of a preference for space over centrality. Accessibility and space under this hypothesis then are substitutes; both are costs which must be paid for either in money terms or time equivalent. For apartment construction to increase, particularly in the city centre, is to suggest that accessibility is again becoming of greater importance because of increases in the costs and difficulty of commuting.

Obviously all three reasons are to some extent justified and are in fact interrelated. Accessibility alone is not a sufficient explanation, in that it would mean that if all travel-time differentials between place of residence and place of work were eliminated or equalized, all persons would live in single-family housing. Clearly the rapid increase in apartment construction at the same time as both accessibility and employment are becoming more generally uniform would seem to refute this argument. Moreover, Alonso's reasoning ignores the attraction in residential location of housing quality, particularly new housing, and of environmental amenities. Decisions about high-rise residential location must therefore reflect trade-offs among accessibility, amenities, and land and building space considered simultaneously.

At this point it is necessary to draw a distinction between two types of apartment construction in the formulation of locational parameters. First, apartment construction may take the form of redevelopment, that is of replacing property already developed for urban use usually in the older, central areas, or second, new development on vacant land. This distinction is fundamental for two reasons. In replacing existing building stock, apart-

24. Alonso, p. 229.

ment redevelopment encounters extremely high land costs, as well as the considerable costs of demolition and lost income from the existing building which are not faced in suburban developments. Second, the relative mix of location factors changes since developed urban environments exert a profound effect on the potential for any site to attract new investment. The environment or neighbourhood is also relevant in a new suburban area, but it is not an overriding effect deriving from established physical and social patterns. Suburban areas generally offer newer, more pleasant, and more socially uniform environments, as alternatives to the obvious advantages of centrality. To a particular developer then potential suburban and central city sites are competitive locational choices, within the same housing market, for investment-risk capital in high-rise construction.

Each location factor, moreover, operates within given spatial parameters. Decisions of residential developers in particular tend to follow a three-level sequence of locational evaluation. First is the largely regional decision which defines location in terms of existing and anticipated land use and dwelling stock distributions, and the transportation system of the metropolitan area.[25] A second level of location decisions isolates the importance of the local environment in urban real estate transactions. For residential purposes the environment is obviously the neighbourhood unit, but a unit defined not only by social class but also by the condition of the physical structures, by adjacent and antecedent land uses and by the presence of local amenities. The third level, which follows logically only after the two previous decision criteria have been satisfied, is the site-selection process. Within a neighbourhood unit a developer

25. Northwestern Univ. School of Law, "Apartment in Suburbia: Local Responsibility and Judicial Restraint," *Northwestern Univ. Law Rev.* Evanston, Ill., (July-Aug. 1964), 143pp.

will seek out individual sites which offer sufficient space, low acquisition costs— preferably vacant land, and attractive vistas, or some combination of these factors. Often, the choice of any individual real estate parcel for development, and most development particularly in central areas has been on a parcel-by-parcel basis,[26] depends on unique externalities.[27] Ownership considerations, obscurity of titles, unwillingness to sell or invest, political pressures, and zoning constraints may act either to accelerate or retard the development process in each area.

Obviously this is only a unidirectional sequence of decisions, and in fact the sequence need not be complete. Developers need not go through the first two in selecting an appropriate site. However, the interrelationship of investment in urban real estate usually precludes substantial investment in sites outside of suitable neighbourhoods, thus necessitating at least an implicit location choice of neighbourhood.

Within this framework and from the preceding discussion, it is possible to enumerate a comprehensive set of area and site characteristics which may be expected to influence the location of apartment construction. These factors are intended to encompass both redevelopment and development aspects of apartment location, although clearly the relative importance of different factors may vary considerably between the two situations. These factors are: (1) the distribution and composition of the existing housing inventory measuring the dominant effect of the standing stock; (2) accessibility to the city centre, to employment opportunities, and to mass transit and expressway facilities; (3) existing clusters of apartment development and existing directions of growth, reflecting the agglomerative effect of a chain-reaction in developer decisions; (4) the immediate physical and social environment including the age and condition of housing, mixed land uses, as well as socio-economic status measured by income and rent levels; (5) the cost and availability of land, including the presence of vacant land, and the average size of parcels; (6) the quality and cost of local services, including simply the presence or absence of municipal services as well as the quality of educational and social facilities.

The increased rate of apartment construction and the spread of apartments to a wide variety of locations, has been shown to represent a logical extension of recent trends in housing demand and supply. Changes in family size, age structure, and personal preferences, combined with more uniform employment and accessibility opportunities, and higher land costs, have provided the stimulus for this transition. The costs of home ownership have increased substantially more than those for rental accommodation. At the beginning of the period under study, approximately 10 per cent of all dwelling units in Metropolitan Toronto were apartments, compared to 26 per cent in 1965. Over 60 per cent of all apartments in Metro have been constructed since 1952. Although construction has spread into the suburbs the higher relative concentrations remain in the city and inner suburbs. These figures indicate the scale of transformation that is possible in the urban residential inventory in a relatively short period. High-density apartment construction as it is presently evolving has shifted both the structure and the location of this inventory away from traditional patterns.

26. R. U. Ratcliff, *Private Investment in Urban Redevelopment,* Res. Rept. no. 17 (Berkeley Real Estate Res. Program, 1961), p. 3.
27. A valuable discussion of externalities in real estate investment is contained in Lowdon Wingo, Jr., "Urban Renewal: A Strategy for Information and Analysis," *Jour. of the Amer. Inst. of Planners* XXXII, 3 (May 1966), 143-54.

BRUCE E. NEWLING

The Spatial Variation of Urban Population Densities

Some years ago Colin Clark suggested that urban population densities beyond the limit of the central business district decline exponentially with distance from the center of the city.[1] Clark's work proved to be extraordinarily seminal. Others[2] adopted his generalization as the

law of spatial variation of urban population densities, and he himself published papers that elaborate on the concept.[3] It now seems clear, however, that Clark's great contribution is principally in his exposition of the idea that urban population densities are in some way spatially systematic, rather than in the identification of a universally applicable model to describe the phenomenon; for the negative exponential formulation he proposed is actually only a good approximation of a more efficient, and a conceptually more relevant, model. In the present paper an alternative hypothesis of the spatial variation of urban population densities is proposed, which views the pattern of density within and beyond the limits of the central business district as a continuum, and which can be placed in a dynamic framework to provide for the

1. Colin Clark: "Urban Population Densities," *Jour. Royal Statist. Soc.,* Ser. A, Vol. 114, Part 4, 1951, pp. 490-496.

2. At the time of its publication, the footnotes in the article by Brian J. L. Berry, James W. Simmons, and Robert J. Tennant: Urban Population Densities: Structure and Change," *Geogr. Rev.,* Vol. 53, 1963, pp. 389-405, provided a comprehensive summary of the literature in the field. More recent studies that have adopted the negative exponential in the analysis of urban densities include Bruce E. Newling: "Urban Growth and Spatial Structure: Mathematical Models and Empirical Evidence," *Geogr. Rev.,* Vol. 56, 1966, pp. 213-225; *idem:* "Teoria parcial del crecimiento urbano: Estructura matemática e implicaciones de la planeación," *in Unión Geográfica Internacional, Conferencia Regional Latinoamericana:* Vol. 1, *La Geografía y los problemas de población* ·(Mexico City, 1966), pp. 367-387; and Emilio Casetti: "Urban Population Density Patterns: An Alternate Explanation," *Canadian Geographer,* Vol. 11, 1967, pp. 96-100.

3. Colin Clark: "Transport—Maker and Breaker of Cities," *Town Planning Rev.,* Vol. 28, 1957-1958, pp. 237-250; "Urban Population Densities," *Bull. Inst. International de Statistique,* Vol. 36, Part 4, 1958, pp. 60-68; and "The Location of Industries and Population," *Town Planning Rev.,* Vol. 35, 1964-1965, pp. 195-218.

Adapted by the author from the **Geographical Review**, Vol. 59, No. 2, April 1969, pp. 242-252. Copyright © 1969 by the American Geographical Society of New York. Reprinted in revised form by permission.

emergence of a density crater in the central business district.

Revisions of the Clark Model

The first revision of Clark's model was proposed independently by Tanner[4] and by Sherratt,[5] who suggested that urban population densities decline exponentially as the square of distance such that

$$D_d = D_0 e^{-cd^2}, \qquad (1)$$

where D_d is the population density at distance d from the center of the city, D_0 is the density at the center of the city, $-c$ is a measure of the rate of change of the logarithm of density with distance squared, and e is the base of the natural logarithms. The density profile described by the Tanner-Sherratt model is thus a half-bell curve, and its logarithmic transformation produces a half parabola, concave downward. As Tanner noted, this downward concavity (owing to the squared term with its associated negative sign) approximates more closely the observed density profiles of cities than does the linear curve generated by the loga-

4. J. C. Tanner: "Factors Affecting the Amount of Travel," *Road Research Tech. Paper No. 51,* Department of Scientific and Industrial Research, London, 1961.
5. G. G. Sherratt: "A Model for General Urban Growth," *in* Management Sciences, Models and Techniques: Proceedings of the Sixth International Meeting of the Institute [of Management Sciences] (edited by C. West Churchman and Michel Verhulst; 2 vols.; New York, 1960), Vol. 2, pp. 147-159.

rithmic transformation of Clark's negative exponential model.

The Tanner-Sherratt formulation, however, is still inadequate as a general rule. It assumes that the instantaneous rate of change of density with distance at the center of the city is zero and does not recognize the possibility that the instantaneous rate of change of density at the center can be either positive (as when density first rises and then falls with increasing distance from the city center) or negative. The possibility that the instantaneous rate of change of density at the center of the city is other than zero can, of course, be accommodated by introducing a linear term in the exponent of equation (1) such that

$$D_d = D_0 e^{bd - cd^2}, \qquad (2)$$

where b measures the instantaneous rate of change of density with distance at the center of the city and can have either a positive or a negative sign (Figures 1-3). Figure 2 makes it clear that the Tanner-Sherratt model is a special case of the more general quadratic exponential model, in which the linear term is equal to zero. On the other hand, Clark's model, in which the exponent is linear in d, is an approximation of the quadratic exponential, matching its form most closely where the b parameter assumes large negative values (Figure 1), and departing from it most noticeably where the b parameter assumes large positive values and where the density profile displays

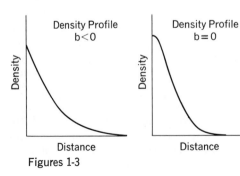

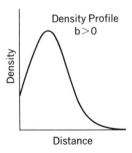

Figures 1-3

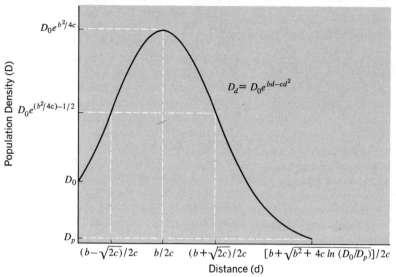

Figure 4. Urban Population Density Profile with Central Density Crater

a pronounced central density crater (Figure 3).

The Quadratic Exponential Model

The quadratic exponential density profile has several distinctive features that can be specified in terms of the parameters of equation (2). For illustrative purposes, assume that Figure 4 represents the density profile of a city with an extensive central business district. Within the central area nonresidential use preempts most of the available space, so that the profile displays a central density crater with a rim, or crest, of high density bordering the central business district. Beyond this crest density falls away to the suburbs. The profile also displays two inflection points at which the density is identical, one located between the city center and the density crest and the other between the density crest and the outer limit of the urban area. The definition of the characteristics thus identified now proceeds from the logarithmic transformation of equation (2) and the first derivative of this transformation.

The logarithmic transformation of equation (2) is written as

$$lnD_d = lnD_0 + bd - cd^2, \qquad (3)$$

where lnD_d is the natural logarithm of density at distance d, and lnD_0 is the natural logarithm of density at the center of the city. The first derivative of equation (3) is written as

$$lnD'_d = b - 2cd, \qquad (4)$$

where lnD'_d is the slope of the tangent to the curve of equation (3) at distance d. Since the first derivative of equation (3) at its maximum is equal to zero, we can set lnD'_d in equation (4) equal to zero and solve for d to obtain

$$d(D_{max}) = b/2c, \qquad (5)$$

where $d(D_{max})$ is the distance of the maximum, or crest, density from the center of the city. Substituting the solution of equation (5) in equation (2), we define the crest density, D_{max}, as

$$D_{max} = D_0e^{b^2/4c}. \qquad (6)$$

Let us specify the density at the perimeter of the urbanized area as D_p. The radius of the urbanized area, $d(p)$, is then defined as

$$d(p) = [b + \sqrt{b^2 + 4c\ln(D_0/D_p)}]/2c. \quad (7)$$

The first and second inflection points of Figure 4 lie at a distance of minus and plus $1/\sqrt{2c}$, respectively, on either side of the density crest. The distance of the first inflection point from the origin, $d(1)$, is therefore defined as

$$d(1) = (b - \sqrt{2c})/2c, \quad (8)$$

and the distance of the second inflection point from the origin, $d(2)$, is defined as

$$d(2) = (b + \sqrt{2c})/2c. \quad (9)$$

Substituting the solution of either equation (8) or equation (9) in equation (2), we define the density at the inflection point, $D_{(1,2)}$, as

$$D_{(1,2)} = D_0 e^{(b^2/4c)-\frac{1}{2}}. \quad (10)$$

The expression $e^{-\frac{1}{2}}$, the square root of the reciprocal of the base of the natural logarithms, is a constant term equal to 0.60653, to five decimal places. Hence, the density at either inflection point is approximately 60.7 percent of the crest density.

Substituting the solutions of equations (8) and (9) in equation (4), we obtain the first derivative of equation (3) at the inflection points. At the first inflection point the first derivative, $\ln D'_{d(1)}$ is defined as

$$\ln D'_{d(1)} = +\sqrt{2c}, \quad (11)$$

and at the second inflection point the first derivative, $\ln D'_{d(2)}$, is defined as

$$\ln D'_{d(2)} = -\sqrt{2c}. \quad (12)$$

These values are useful in establishing a density-profile classification of urban development.

A Density-Profile Classification of Urban Growth

Equation (4) reveals that the b parameter is a measure of the instantaneous rate of change of density with distance at the center of the city. It has been shown that where the b parameter carries a negative sign, the density profile reveals no density crater, and where the b parameter carries a positive sign, the density profile has a density crater and an associated density crest. The appearance of a density crater results from the displacement of residents from the central area by nonresidential activities. Accordingly, one associates the absence of a density crater with an early stage of development and its presence with a later stage. We can make a further distinction in categorizing the stage of development of the city, based on equations (11) and (12). If the b parameter is less than $-\sqrt{2c}$ (or, alternatively, if the sign of b is negative and its magnitude is greater than $\sqrt{2c}$), no inflection point is found in the density profile, and the city is at an early stage of development. If the b parameter is greater than $\sqrt{2c}$ (or, alternatively, if the sign of b is positive and its magnitude is greater than $\sqrt{2c}$), two inflection points, together with a crest, are found in the density profile, and the city is at a late stage of development. A four-part classification of urban growth, based on the ratio $b/\sqrt{2c}$ and the sign of the b parameter, is presented in Table 1, while Figure 5 presents graphically the density profiles characteristic of each stage of development.

Although the four-part classification presented in Table 1 is based on values of

Table 1. A Density-Profile Classification of Urban Development

$b/\sqrt{2c}$	b PARAMETER SIGN	
	Negative	Positive
>1	Youth	Old Age
<1	Early Maturity	Late Maturity

$b/\sqrt{2c}$ within specified ranges, the ratio can assume an infinite range of values and can be used for precise comparisons

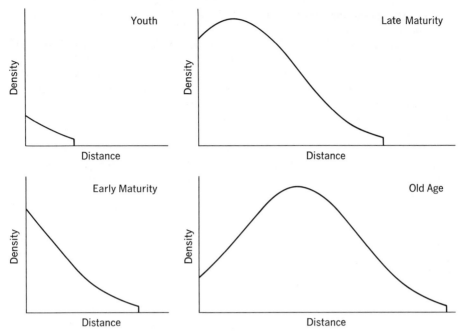

Figure 5. Urban Density Profiles at Successive Stages of Development

between cities with respect to their stage of development. This suggests, among other things, that the ratio could be used to test for systematic spatial variation of development within an entire system of cities.

It is important at this point to make explicit what is meant by the term, "population density." The population density of a specified territorial unit is defined here as the ratio of the persons enumerated as residents of that unit to the magnitude of its area. Such a definition is commonly referred to as gross residential density, and it is to be distinguished from other measures such as net residential density (persons per unit area of residential land) and floor-space density (persons per unit area of residential floor space). The measurement of gross residential density is, of course, much simpler that that of net residential density and of floor-space density, and it also happens that it is conceptually more useful: for an urban density profile ex-

pressed in terms of gross residential density is a summary statement about the spatial allocation of residents in the urban area. Such a density profile therefore simplifies comparisons between cities at any given time with respect to the spatial distribution of people within them and also makes it possible to trace the spatial structure of intraurban growth in any one city through time.

A Mathematical Model of Urban Growth

The graphical representation of the sequential development of the city (Figure 5) shows that at first density rises to a maximum at the center of the city, after which the crest moves out and a density crater forms as residential use is displaced by an expanding central business district. However, these changes in the spatial distribution of urban residents can be more efficiently and usefully described if one relates the spatial distribution of urban residents to time by means of a series of equations. In so doing, a mathematical description or model of urban growth is constructed, within the framework of which actual changes in urban population density can be examined.

The rise and decline of density at the center of the city is most simply described if it is assumed that the central density is a quadratic exponential function of time, such that

$$D_{0,t} = D_{0,0}e^{mt-nt^2}, \qquad (13)$$

where $D_{0,t}$ is the central density at time t, $D_{0,0}$ is the central density at the arbitrary zero of time, $t = 0$, m is a measure of the initial instantaneous rate of growth of the central density with time, and n is a measure of the rate of change of the rate of growth with the passage of time.

Similarly, the b parameter might be described as a positive linear function of time, such that

$$b_t = b_0 + gt, \qquad (14)$$

where b_t is the instantaneous rate of change of the logarithm of the density with distance at the center of the city at time t, b_0 is the b parameter at the arbitrary zero of time, $t = 0$, and g is the rate of change of the b parameter with time. The c parameter of equation (2) might also be specified as a function of time. For the present purpose, however, let us assume that it is constant through time, according to the equation

$$c_t = c, \qquad (15)$$

where $-c_t$ is the rate of change of the logarithm of density with the square of the distance at time t. With the c parameter constant, we can now specify density as a function of distance and time by substituting the solutions of equations (13) and (14) in equation (2). Thus

$$D_{d,t} = D_{0,0}e^{mt-nt^2+(b_0+gt)d-cd^2}, \qquad (16)$$

where $D_{d,t}$ is the density at distance d at time t.

Let us assume also that the perimeter density of the urbanized area is constant, as specified by the equation

$$D_{p,t} = D_p, \qquad (17)$$

where $D_{p,t}$ is the perimeter density at time t. The radius of the urbanized area is therefore specified by the equation

$$d(p)_t = [(b_0 + gt) + \sqrt{(b_0 + gt)^2 + 4c(lnD_{0,0}+ mt - nt^2 - lnD_p)}]/2c, \qquad (18)$$

where $d(p)_t$ is the radius of the urbanized area at time t. The size of the urbanized area is proportional to the square of the radius defined in equation (18), such that

$$A_t = \pi\, d(p)_t^2 \qquad (19)$$

where A_t is the areal extent at time t, and π is a constant factor, applicable when the urbanized area is circular. Where the urbanized area occupies less than a complete circle (as when the organizational center of the city is located on a lake or coast), the right-hand side of equation (19) is modified by an appropriate factor of proportionality.

Figure 6 is a simple model of urban growth that conforms with the equations set forth above. It is assumed that the original density profile at the arbitrary zero of time, $t = 0$, moves out at a constant speed, such that

$$lnD_{d,t} = lnD_{d-vt,0}, \qquad (20)$$

where v is the speed at which a point of constant density moves. Substituting in equation (20) from equation (3), we then obtain an equation equivalent to the logarithmic form of equation (16), with the parameters of equation (16) given by $g = 2cv$, $m = -b_0v$, and $n = cv^2$. The density at the center of the city rises and falls with the passage of time; the b parameter increases from negative to positive values with time; and the radius

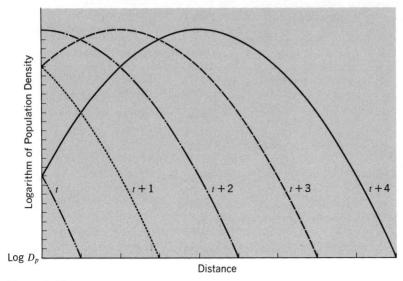

Figure 6. Simple Model of Urban Growth Population-Density Curves from Time t to t + 4

(and, inferentially, the area) of the urbanized area grows with time. Such a pattern may be described as displacement growth, since the city grows and spreads outward by the radial displacement of the density profile associated with the movement of people from the central city to the suburbs. Blumenfeld has aptly described it as "the tidal wave of metropolitan expansion."[6]

The Analysis of Density Profiles

In Clark's first article on urban densities, he presented thirty-five population density profiles for nineteen cities in Europe, North America, and Australia, with the profiles of some cities repeated at different points in time.[7] Although Clark intended his negative exponential rule to account for the spatial variation of density outside the central business district only, he nevertheless included the central

density observations in order to demonstrate how the observed data departed from the trend line when the latter was extrapolated toward the center of the city. He therefore provided a wealth of data[8] with which to test the hypothesis that population density within and beyond the central business district is a quadratic exponential function of distance from the city center, with the squared term in the exponent carrying a negative sign.

The quadratic exponential, like the negative exponential, cannot describe the spatial variation of density for unlimited distances from the center of the city: eventually rural density patterns and density patterns associated with peripheral subcenters obscure the density field of the central city. From a study of Clark's graphs, it appears that he himself ex-

6. Hans Blumenfeld: "The Tidal Wave of Metropolitan Expansion," *Journ. Amer. Inst. of Planners,* Vol. 20, 1954, pp. 3-14.
7. Clark, "Urban Population Densities" [see footnote 1 above], p. 494.

8. The data were derived by measuring the distance and the logarithm of density coordinates of the observations recorded in Clark's diagrams enlarged to ten times their published size. Some small measurement error was undoubtedly entailed in this procedure, though not enough to vitiate the results and the conclusions drawn from them.

Table 2. Density-Parameter Estimates, Density-Crest Estimates, and the $b/\sqrt{2c}$ Ratio for Urban Density Profiles Derived from Clark's Data

City and Year	Parameter Estimates			Crest Estimates		
	D_0[a]	b[b]	c[c]	Height[d]	Distance[e]	$b/\sqrt{2c}$
Chicago, 1900	28,977	0.26972	−0.08471	35,916	1.59	0.66
Chicago, 1940*	9,820	0.57500	−0.06298	36,487	4.57	1.62
St. Louis, 1900	44,331	−0.19671	−0.10525			−0.43
St. Louis, 1940*	32,068	−0.24944	−0.02521			−1.11
Boston, 1900	59,244	0.21257	−0.04138	77,817	2.57	0.74
Boston, 1940*	35,215	−0.23643	−0.00477			−2.42
Philadelphia, 1900	73,350	−0.30016	−0.05139			−0.94
Philadelphia, 1940*	43,673	−0.19554	−0.01702			−1.06
Cleveland, 1940	5,754	0.54567	−0.07520	15,482	3.63	1.41
Los Angeles, 1940*	25,838	−0.19993	−0.00419			−2.18
New York, 1900	103,552	−0.13954	−0.04865			−0.45
New York, 1910	99,917	−0.34734	0.00497			
New York, 1940	90,440	−0.13468	−0.00325			−1.67
Paris, 1817*	122,459	−0.29934	−0.37417			−0.35
Paris, 1856*	117,050	0.06447	−0.27055	117,500	0.12	0.09
Paris, 1896	181,067	−0.45996	−0.03495			−1.74
Paris, 1931	164,093	−0.26475	−0.04221			−0.91
Berlin, 1885	220,673	−0.86347	−0.05756			−2.54
Berlin, 1901	56,273	0.91675	−0.34292	103,846	1.34	1.11
Vienna, 1890	129,292	−0.66577	−0.01973			−3.35
Budapest, 1935	200,263	−0.53070	−0.07675			−1.35
Oslo, 1938	10,971	2.96112	−1.42760	50,945	1.04	1.75
Dublin, 1936	53,364	−0.31776	−0.14967			−0.58
Brisbane, 1901	10,106	−0.47926	−0.08881			−1.14
Brisbane, 1947*	8,196	0.30065	−0.16857	9,371	0.89	0.52
Sydney, 1947*	24,842	−0.22029	−0.00306			−2.81
Melbourne, 1933*	8,734	0.23848	−0.05982	11,077	1.99	0.69
Manchester, 1931	41,118	−0.36659	0.00863			
Liverpool, 1921*	18,678	1.23617	−0.33058	59,320	1.87	1.52
London, 1801*	169,551	−1.09571	−0.02056			−5.40
London, 1841*	191,236	−0.50459	−0.11184			−1.07
London, 1871*	182,726	−0.52342	−0.02323			−2.43
London, 1901*	82,319	0.08992	−0.07320	84,624	0.61	0.24
London, 1921*	61,409	0.03046	−0.03258	61,848	0.47	0.12
London, 1939*	45,430	0.03155	−0.02063	45,981	0.76	0.16

* Cases in which peripheral density data recorded on Clark's graphs were excluded in calculating the parameter estimates. With the exception of Chicago in 1940 (for which the outer seven of Clark's eighteen observations were excluded), in no case were more than three peripheral observations excluded, which leaves no fewer than four observations on which to base each parameter estimate.

[a] Estimate of the population density at the center of the city, in persons per square mile.

[b] The b parameter is the instantaneous rate of change of the logarithm of density with distance at the center of the city. It is expressed as a natural logarithm per mile.

[c] The c parameter is a measure of the rate of change of the rate of change of density with distance from the center of the city. It is expressed as a natural logarithm per mile per mile.

[d] Estimated maximum density, in persons per square mile.

[e] Radius of estimated maximum density, in miles.

cluded the peripheral densities in some cases in fitting the negative exponential function. In the present study, as noted in Table 2, some peripheral densities have been excluded in order to maximize the descriptive efficiency of the curve in the central city.

With this qualification, Table 2 presents parameter estimates and other calculations derived by fitting a quadratic exponential curve by the method of least squares to Clark's data. Several conclusions with respect to the hypothesized model of density variation and change are to be derived from this table. First, the postulated quadratic exponential model of density variation is validated in all cases except New York in 1910 and Manchester in 1931; in both instances, the c parameter carries a positive sign instead of the required negative sign, but the magnitude of the c parameter is extremely small, and a minor error in measurement would be sufficient to account for the aberrations. Second, where comparisons through time are possible, it can be seen that the c parameter is never constant (as proposed in the simple urban growth model described previously); in two-thirds of the cases, the c parameter declines in magnitude, indicating that

the urbanized area is expanding through the "flattening" of the quadratic exponential density profile as well as (or instead of) through the outward displacement of the density profile. This flattening effect has been noted by Clark, who detected it through changes in the linear term of his negative exponential model. He attributed the phenomenon to improvement in the urban transportation system, and this appears to be the most likely explanation. A third and related conclusion refers to the changes in the $b/\sqrt{2c}$ ratio. Since the outward expansion of the urbanized area is achieved both by the flattening of the density profile and by its outward displacement, the ratio does not always increase, as was postulated. In half the cases, in fact, the ratio shows a decline in value, which suggests that the density-profile classification of urban development is less useful than was earlier hoped. Finally, it is clear that the density crests were higher in the nineteenth century than they are in the twentieth. The conclusion that central city residents lived at higher densities in the last century than at present is also supported by the estimates of central density parameters presented in the table.

RONALD R. BOYCE

Residential Mobility and Its Implications for Urban Spatial Change

Residential growth is widely recognized as a major factor in understanding urban spatial structure, pattern, and change. However, it has not been treated properly at the residential unit level nor in detail sufficient to reveal the true complexity of intra-urban residential mobility.

The most general approach is to treat residential use as a mere follower of other activities such as employment, and residential development is seen primarily as a linked response to other space-setting activities.[1] In other cases, residential development has been explained by a general spread of the present pattern outward along corridors.[2] General theories of suburban residential development, whereby the suburbs are presumed to be fed by residential moves from the central city, follow this theme.[3] Still other approaches view residential response as an interplay between site and transportation cost features;[4] given improvements in transportation, it is assumed that greater freedom of choice in residential location has resulted in a movement to outlying areas. This may be generally true, but the process by which people actually move to such areas is little understood.

The missing link in most approaches is the process of residential mobility itself. Specifically, how and why do people change residence? What are the micro-patterns of mobility within the city? Is residential change easily explained by changes in workplace, family income, and the like? These questions have not been investigated in depth, either theoretically or empirically.

1. Brian J. L. Berry, "Research Frontiers in Urban Geography," in Philip M. Hauser and Leo F. Schnore (eds.), *The Study of Urbanization* (New York: John Wiley and Sons, 1966), pp. 416, 417.
2. Homer Hoyt, *The Structure and Growth of Residential Neighborhoods in America* (Washington, D.C.: Federal Housing Administration, 1939), pp. 112-122.

3. Leo F. Schnore, "The Growth of Metropolitan Suburbs," *American Sociological Review,* Vol. 22 (1957).
4. Lowdon Wingo, Jr., *Transportation and Urban Land* (Washington, D.C.: Resources for the Future, 1961).

From the **Proceedings** of the Association of American Geographers, Vol. 1, 1969, pp. 22-26. Reprinted by permission.

In order to answer such questions, data were obtained from the records of the Seattle City Light Company for more than 3,000 residency changes in the city of Seattle between 1962 and 1967. These records show previous addresses of all occupants and the new address to which all persons having previously resided at the address in question have moved. They appear to be complete and highly accurate, and it is hoped that they have provided a solid base by which detailed questions can be answered about the specific characteristics of intra-urban residential mobility.

The sampling framework included some twenty study areas, containing slightly more than one hundred households each, in low, middle, and high value housing areas. All occupancy changes for all households (some 2,254) were examined and plotted on maps by computer to reveal differential mobility patterns.

From this data base, five questions will be answered which bear directly on existing and newly developed urban spatial theory. These questions are:

1. Why do people move within cities?
2. How often do people change residence and how does this vary within the city and among housing value areas?
3. Where do people move when they change residences within the city and what general patterns result?
4. Where within the city are people migrating to Seattle most likely to reside first?
5. From where within the city are people leaving the Seattle metropolitan area most likely to leave?

Why Do People Move Within Cities

The reasons why people move from one city to another has been fairly well examined—employment opportunity appears to be the key—but intra-city residential change has been given only slight attention. Most studies have dealt with the relation of home to workplace[5] and the results indicate that residence change within cities has little do with a change in workplace.[6] Instead, residential change appears to be highly voluntary, (i.e., strictly speaking, unnecessary) and to be triggered by discontent with the present neighborhood or house. The basic force seems to be "push" rather than a "pull" feature, although upward housing mobility is almost always involved in any move.

To determine motivations for leaving the ghetto area, persons "escaping" were interviewed as to their reasons for leaving. Some 42 percent of the families listed "dissatisfaction with house and/or old neighborhood" as the primary reason. Increase in family, income, and friends in the present neighborhood also showed up as quite important. Interestingly, none of the persons interviewed listed job change as a cause for residential change.

Push factors may not be as high in more amenity-laden areas, but job change is not a significant factor for most moves within the city. The average length of an intra-city move was less than three miles, and sixteen percent were less than half a mile—hardly enough distance to be related to a job change. The short move length is even more apparent among the low value housing areas. In the Negro housing areas the average length of move was 1.2 miles, and over one-third of all movement was less than one-half mile.

That the push factors of an adverse environment play a heavy role in causing movement is demonstrated by the varying turnover rate among residences. A

5. John F. Kain, "The Journey-to-work as a Determinant of Residential Location," *Proceedings of the Regional Science Association,* Vol. 9 (1962), pp. 137-160.

6. James E. Vance, "Housing the Worker: The Employment Linkage as a Force in Urban Structure," *Economic Geography,* Vol. 42 (1966), pp. 323-325.

comparison of occupancy change for houses located along arterials (any street carrying over 5,000 vehicles daily) versus non-arterial houses showed a considerably higher turnover for arterial-located houses. For example, in the low value, predominantly Negro area, with an abundance of arterials, 35.1 percent of all houses along arterials changed occupants each year, as contrasted with 25.9 percent for all other houses in the area. The same kind of difference was noted in all areas as, for example, 35 to 24 percent in other low value areas, and 16 to 12 percent in middle value areas, but there were no arterials adjacent to high value housing in the study areas taken. In such high value areas only six percent of all houses changed occupants each year.

Other adverse site features such as corner lots, unusual set-backs, and cul-de-sac sitings also show up significantly higher in turnover than other houses in the immediate area. The end result of such environmental difficulties is often rental housing status, and rental housing has from seven to ten times the turnover rate of owner-occupied housing. Moreover, housing near rental property also turns over at a higher rate because of contamination features, so such adverse physical features are multiplied many times over in the degree of occupancy change in an area.[7]

In the predominantly Negro area 50.3 percent of housing in rental status turned over each year as contrasted with only 7.2 percent for the owner-occupied residences in the area. The same kind of relationship also applies to middle and high value housing. For example, in the high housing value areas 45.3 percent of all renter housing changed occupants each year in contrast with only 4.2 percent of the owner-occupied housing.

Other reasons why people move include the characteristics of the movers themselves. Maisel maintains that the important variables in housing status and in probability of moving are age of head of household, number of persons in the household, and income of household.[8] Rossi, likewise, has made an exhaustive study to find the major variable affecting residency change[9] but both approaches are largely a-spatial and do not cover the geographical characteristics of residential movement.

How Often Do People Move?

It is already evident that people who live in low value housing areas move much more often than people who live in high value housing areas. Thus, in cities, those who can least afford to move do most of the moving. And the amount of movement is much greater than generally believed. The general figure, derived from the U.S. Census, is that about one family in every five moves each year in the United States. However, this fails to measure most intra-city moves, because of multiple moves within a census measurement period.

The 2,254 houses examined here experienced 2,965 moves during a five year study period, and it appears that over twenty-six percent of all housing changes occupancy each year. Among the low value non-white housing areas, there was an average of 1.9 occupants per house during the five year study period—or 38 percent of all housing changed occupants each year. (In fact, all of the moves were concentrated in only about 20 percent of the housing.) By contrast, high value areas showed a turnover rate only about

7. Harvey Eric Heiges, "Intra-Urban Residential Movement in Seattle," Unpublished Ph.D. dissertation, University of Washington, 1968, pp. 87-94.

8. Sherman J. Maisel, "Rates of Ownership, Mobility, and Purchase," in Real Estate Research Program, *Essays in Urban Land Economics* (Los Angeles: University of California, 1966), pp. 93-98.

9. Peter H. Rossi, *Why Families Move* (Glencoe: University of Illinois Press, 1955).

Table 1. Frequency of Occupancy Change in Study Areas, 1962-67

Housing Type	Number of Households	Number of Occupancy Changes	Number of Occupancy Changes per House	Per cent of Housing Changing Occupancy per Year
Low Value— Negro	559	1,085	1.9	38
Low Value— other	542	1,019	1.9	38
Middle Value	506	523	1.0	20
High Value	647	338	0.5	10
Total	2,254	2,965	1.3	26

Data Source: Seattle City Light Company Records

half that of the census-reported average and less than one-third as great as the low value housing areas (Table 1).

What Is the Pattern of Movement Within Cities?

Most analyses of population change within cities have been based on crude data, and data limitations have caused researchers to focus primarily on presumed general shifts in population between the central city and the suburbs. Inasmuch as population has been growing relatively slowly, or declining, in most central cities and increasing in the outlying areas, it has been assumed that suburban growth was being fed directly by migration from the central city. Some such movement does occur, but residential movement within Seattle is complicated by short moves among and between areas in a complex network of feeder and receptor areas. There is no straight forward move pattern of central city areas feeding the suburbs. Out of 1,835 moves in the sample areas, 605 were within the same housing value area, 658 were to other housing areas within the city limits, and only 182 (or about 10 percent) were to suburban areas in the metropolis (Table 2).

The patterns of movement are vastly different among different housing value types. In the Negro central areas movement is mostly internal (percent of all moves). Movement out of the area is highly restricted and channelized to nearby and newly-forming Negro areas. By contrast, most other low value and middle value housing areas are best characterized as having a star-burst pattern. The dominant type of move in both cases seems to be to the next higher housing value rather than any suburban movement.

The high value housing moves are highly directed, but primarily to other high value areas rather than to suburban areas. High value areas are quite separated in Seattle, which may account, in part, for the longer length of move among the high value residential areas. The general movement among high housing value areas is a cross-town pattern.

The predominant movement pattern among all areas is definitely not suburban oriented. In fact, only three percent of all out-moves from the low value non-white housing is to residences outside the city limits. Likewise only 13.4 percent of white low value housing changes were to such suburbs. In none of the study types does the percentage of out-movement to the suburbs exceed 15.7 percent. However, some of the sample areas adjacent to the city limits do show much higher movements to areas outside the city. This appears to be primarily the result of proximity rather than any suburban trend (Table 2).

Surprisingly, the study areas have almost as much movement from the suburbs as to them. Over 8 percent of all

Table 2. Movement out of Sample Areas
in Seattle, 1962-67

	Housing Area Types (Per cent in Each Type)			
Movement Types	Low Value– Negro	Low Value– white	Middle Value	High Value
Within Same Value Area	58.2	24.0	3.0	17.0
To Other Areas in City	26.4	39.9	47.9	38.4
To "Suburbs"	3.0	13.4	15.7	14.5
To Other Cities	12.3	23.0	33.4	30.2
Total	99.9	100.3	100.0	100.1

N: 1835
Data Source: Seattle City Light Company Records

white low and middle value housing, and 6.4 percent of high value in-movement is from the outlying suburban areas. As might be expected, only 1.4 percent of all non-white in-movement is directly from the suburbs of the metropolis.

There is no indication that the suburban areas are being fed to any extent by inlying areas. Instead, much of the new suburban development must be the result of "new start" families (not picked up in the data used) or as the result of intercity migration. In fact, a casual survey of several suburban areas in Seattle reveals a strikingly high proportion of families are newcomers to the Seattle area. Thus, the suburbs must be the major landing place for white newcomers in the metropolis, much as the ghetto area is for Negroes.

According to the concentric zone theory, newcomers to the city, particularly new immigrants, first reside near the center of the city in the "zone of transition."[10] From this zone, through a trickling-down process whereby the lower order status and income groups occupy the cast-off housing of higher order groups, these newcomers eventually work their way upward and outward in housing quality and newness.

In some respects this supposition is true. Clearly, the more affluent members of the residential community do indeed often leave their old residences in sort of a hand-me-down fashion to the next order group. The abundance of former first class houses now cut up into apartments make this process fairly clear.

However, common observation also reveals that new housing is not just built for the elite—as witness much of suburbia. This new housing is therefore obviously occupied first by middle and sometimes low income families. Likewise, the recent trend toward urban renewal and redevelopment has created many new housing units in the inner zone of the city for both low and high income families. Even if the cast-off thesis had validity in the past it is lacking something today.[11] Finally, common sense causes us to recognize that newcomers to any given city are from many different income groups and such people will likely settle in those housing types in the city which best fit them.

The movements examined here show clearly that there is no one predominant place where newcomers first reside in Seattle. There is a tendency, however, for high value housing areas to have few newcomers (6.8 percent of all households vs. 28.7 percent for low value white areas). Nevertheless, all areas have newcomers.

From Where Do People Leave the City?

The literature is very weak on the question of from what area of a city people are most likely to "escape" the metropolis entirely. The popular notion, however, is

10. Donald W. Griffin and Richard E. Preston, "A Restatement of the 'Transition Zone' Concept," *Annals of the Association of American Geographers,* Vol. 56 (1966), pp. 341-347.

11. Homer Hoyt, "Recent Distortions of the Classical Models of Urban Structure," *Land Economics,* Vol. 40 (1964), pp. 282-285.

that migration between cities mostly occurs in the more affluent and middle class population. The data above, however, show the highest percentage of newcomers and out-goers in the white low value housing areas, but perhaps this is merely a peculiarity of Seattle (28.5 percent vs. 8.5 percent for high value areas). People appear almost as likely to escape the city from the low and especially middle value housing areas as from the high value areas. However, several of the high value housing study areas had over 40 percent of their out-moves to areas outside Seattle.

Some Implications

Analysis of residency change on a household level reveals that much theory on housing change is in need of considerable refinement, and many theoretical assumptions appear to be more myth than reality. First, there is no clear-cut movement of population between the inner zone and the outer zone of cities. To the contrary, there appears to be a complex network of channels and flows within and among areas, but Negro area occupancy change patterns show little connection with other areas. Most movement is a kind of musical chairs within the area, and the major growth of suburban areas appears to come not from the central city directly, through a process of decentralization, but from other cities.

Based on the above findings, it is clear that in order to build a satisfactory model of residential mobility, five major items will have to be considered simultaneously: (1) location of area (2) site characteristics of residences and neighborhood (3) status of housing—e.g. rental versus ownership (4) class and value of housing, and (5) the characteristics of the resident such as income, size of family, monetary and marital status. The effect of each of these items on residential mobility requires much more thorough study before any model can be developed.

VI
ACTIVITIES: Specialized Activity Patterns and Systems

The components of the city's functional structure are its activity systems. These systems represent clusters of similar activities within the commercial, industrial, and institutional sectors of the urban economy. Clusters develop because of the strength of interaction between activities. Each displays similar patterns of corporate behavior and land use. Studies of such systems may focus either on the economic sectors themselves, on the type of institutional behavior involved, or on the geographic areas of specialized activity created.

The systems of activity in a city are almost limitless in number and complexity. Many are in fact conceptual abstractions which have meaning only in reference to the objectives of any given analysis. A useful context with which to introduce such systems is given in an excellent study entitled *The Core of the City*,[1] by John Rannells. He describes these systems as representing three sequential stages of elaboration of individual and group behavior. The first stage involves fairly repetitive individual routines such as shopping and the journey to work. In the second stage, routines have become patterned, regular actions, thus taking on a permanent form which he describes as institutionalized processes. Repeated activities at given locations become urban institutions. Third, repeated and regular interactions between institutions result in the organization of processes into clusters of activity systems such as service industries, manufacturing, retailing, and government. In Rannells's terms these are connective tissues in the structure of the city. Each cluster en-

1. John Rannells, *The Core of the City: A Pilot Study of Changing Land Uses in Central Business Districts* (New York: Columbia University Press, 1956).

compasses a number of less elaborate subsystems resulting in an organizational hierarchy of both urban space and activities. The latter defines the functional systems of the city, while the former define the areas or zones of concentrations of similar activities. In this section we examine both of these aspects.

The most prominent of these activity zones is the central business district (C.B.D. or city center). As the original settlement nucleus of the city, the C.B.D. has in the past acted as the strongest single organizing influence on the spatial distribution of all other urban activities. Despite a proportional decline in recent decades in its importance within an expanding metropolitan area as a place of business, particularly in terms of retail, industrial, and warehousing functions, the C.B.D. still tends to dominate. It remains the focus of the transportation network and of traffic flows in the city, the institutional and utilities infrastructure, and the spatial structure of retail and service business.

The C.B.D. as the name implies is both a cluster of functions, that is, a sector of the urban economy, as well as an area of specialized activity.[2] The C.B.D. itself also displays a regular internal structure evident from city to city. It is possible, for example, to distinguish between the "core" of the C.B.D., the area of high-density concentrations of specialized office and service functions, and the surrounding fringe or "frame" area in which generally lower density, but still clearly central or C.B.D. functions, merge with a mixture of other non-central activities. Nesting within these two broad zones are smaller core areas which reflect concentrations of highly specialized activities such as finance and insurance, government and entertainment.

Yet the core-frame concept suggests only part of the structure of the C.B.D. As one illustration, Larry Smith outlines more detailed characteristics of the C.B.D. in the introductory paper in this section. The paper serves two functions in this volume: description and prognosis, the latter with specific reference to the problems of planning future core-area development. He documents systematic variations in rent levels, amount of space utilized, and densities between land use or activity clusters. The composition of activities in the core is shown to vary with the size of the city, as increased geographic size in itself forces the decentralization of

2. There has been an extensive literature concerned with defining and locating the exact spatial limits of the central business district. The standard reference is R. E. Murphy and J. E. Vance, Jr., "Delimiting the C.B.D.," *Economic Geography, XXX* (1954), pp. 189-222. Other examples of review papers are E. M. Horwood and M. D. McNair, "The Core of the City: Emerging Concepts," *Plan Canada,* Vol. 2 (1961), pp. 108-14; and C. E. Browning, "Recent Studies of Central Business Districts," *Journal of the American Institute of Planners,* Vol. 27 (February 1961), pp. 82-87.

certain activities toward the periphery of the city. Smith also indicates that the rate at which the dominance of the core declines relatively with increased city size is greatest for industrial functions and lowest for offices and department stores. Other forces of decentralization which would obviously accelerate these changes in location such as urban renewal, highway displacement, and entrepreneurial preferences are summarized in his conclusion.

Outside of the C.B.D., regularities in the spatial structure of commercial activity systems are also observable. An overview to these patterns is given by Brian Berry in an excerpt from his comprehensive study of commercial structure, deterioration, and change in the city of Chicago.[3] Initially, a classification of four types of concentrations of retail and service business is identified: planned and unplanned shopping centers, highway ribbons, urban arterial developments, and specialized commercial areas. Each type has a different composition of functions, exhibits a different spatial pattern and serves a different set of consumer needs. Particularly among shopping centers the identification of systematic differences in the number, variety, and sales of retail establishments indicates the existence of a hierarchy of commercial facilities. The trading area of each smaller center nests within those of larger centers, from the isolated street-corner variety store upward through the hierarchy to the C.B.D. Clearly each center also reflects its age—the time and conditions of its development and the changing character of the neighborhood that it serves.[4]

One of the components of urban retail structure are the ribbons of commercial activity stretching along major arterial streets. These are

3. This study was published as two volumes: Brian J. L. Berry, *Commercial Structure and Commercial Blight—Retail Patterns and Processes in the City of Chicago,* Department of Geography Research Paper No. 85, University of Chicago, 1963; and *Chicago Commercial Reference Handbook* (with Robert J. Tennant), Research Paper No. 86, 1963. Two other monographs also derived from this same study: James W. Simmons, *The Changing Pattern of Retail Location,* Department of Geography Research Paper No. 92, Universtiy of Chicago, 1964; and Barry J. Garner, *The Internal Structure of Retail Nucleations,* Studies in Geography No. 12, Department of Geography, Northwestern University, Evanston, Illinois, 1966. Similar research procedures have been employed in studies of Chicago suburbs by Berry and Tennant, and in Toronto by Simmons. See James W. Simmons, *Toronto's Changing Retail Complex,* Department of Geography Research Paper No. 104, University of Chicago, 1966; and Brian J. L. Berry and Robert J. Tennant, *Commercial Structure,* Metropolitan Planning Guidelines, Northeastern Illinois Planning Commission, Chicago, 1965.
4. One of the most revealing examinations of the impact of social and cultural changes in urban neighborhoods on the character of older retail centers is Pred's study of Negro shopping areas in the south side of Chicago. See A. Pred, "Business Thoroughfares as Expressions of Negro Culture," *Economic Geography* (1963), pp. 217-33.

analyzed in the following paper by F. W. Boal and D. B. Johnson. Within one of these ribbons in Calgary the authors recognize nuclei of specialized retail activity. There are indications of hierarchic differences in the composition of these nuclei similar to those in shopping centers. The respective trade areas of each ribbon depend on a strong relationship between the type and purpose of consumer traffic and the linkages between similar types of retail establishments. The trade areas are two-fold: one serves highway traffic and is linear in form while the other is confined to the immediate neighborhood. While each commercial ribbon has its own unique internal structure, there are clearly regularities different from those for shopping centers.

Another economic activity which dominates the urban landscape is the industrial sector. Unlike the commercial-oriented retail and service sectors which are predominantly responsive to the social geography of the resident population, the composition and to a lesser extent the location of industrial activities are in part externally induced. Those industries within an urban area that are most sensitive to the influence of outside markets are frequently cited as the city's economic base.[5] In Section II Berry referred to these activities as external determinants of urban structure. In Section III, Karaska documented the structural linkages within the local economy which lead to industrial agglomerations within the city. What is surprising however, is that there has been little systematic research on the intra-metropolitan location of industry. Although there is a well developed body of industrial location theory, as illustrated by the extensive bibliography of Stevens and Brackett,[6] and the recent collection of readings edited by Karaska and Bramhall,[7] its relevance to the internal structure of cities is indirect because it is primarily concerned with inter-regional industrial distributions.

One attempt to fill this gap is a review paper by Allan Pred.[8] The

---

5. For a recent review in geography of economic base studies see Harold M. Mayer, "The Economic Base of the Metropolis," *Journal of Geography,* LXVIII (February 1969), pp. 70-87.

6. Benjamin A. Stevens and Carolyn A. Brackett, *Industrial Location: A Review and Annotated Bibliography,* Bibliographic Series No. 3, (Philadelphia: Regional Science Research Institute, 1967). A parallel review paper is F. E. I. Hamilton, "Models of Industrial Location," in R. J. Chorley and P. Haggett (eds.), *Models in Geography* (London: Methuen, 1967), pp. 361-424.

7. Gerald J. Karaska and David F. Bramhall (eds.), *Locational Analysis for Manufacturing a Selection of Readings* (Cambridge, Mass.: The M.I.T. Press, 1969).

8. See also Allan Pred, *Behavior and Location,* Part I (Lund, Sweden: Gleerup Publishers, 1967). An excellent review paper in the geographical literature on manufacturing location is M. Logan, "Locational Behavior of Manufacturing Firms in Urban Areas," *Annals of the Association of American Geographers,* Vol. 56 (1966), pp. 451-66.

paper has three themes: a description of the historical evolution of industry and of industrial location in American cities; a critique of various approaches to intra-metropolitan location theory; and an evaluation of the application to manufacturing of the classical models of Burgess, Hoyt, and Harris and Ullman discussed in Section II. He concludes that neither these traditional models of urban form, nor those of regional industrial location theory, offer much insight into urban industrial location. He outlines an empirical study of locational shifts in manufacturing in which the entire industrial configuration of the urban area is evaluated in an attempt to define a spectrum of distributions in which industries range from dispersed to highly concentrated in location. With this as a study framework, the elements of a systematic intra-urban industrial location theory might be forthcoming. Combined with recent research on the behavioral aspects of location decisions, this approach offers a stimulating basis for further industrial research.

The institutional, public, and political systems of the city are even more difficult to encompass. Although an obvious component of the spatial relations and processes of change in the city, the public sector has as yet received limited attention in our research. No doubt this is due to the inherent complexity of these systems, and the paucity of adequate data. But their importance should not be underestimated.[9] Institutions and public functions occupy large expanses of urban space, in some cities as much as one-half of the developed area. Also, regulatory policies exert direct influence on the spatial patterns and the behavior of all urban activities, businesses, and residents. Public utilities provide the umbilical system, or the infrastructure, which holds the urban area together, defines the growth of its margins and the renewal of its core. Decisions regarding the location, timing, and character of public services also contribute to urban form. Similarly, political power and voting behavior has its own spatial expression and is an integral component of urban growth. The following essays examine three quite different examples of the public sector.

What are the spatial patterns of public service activities in the city? Do they exhibit regularities similar to other services? As one example, Morrill and Earickson examine variations in the location, type of service, and usage of hospitals in the Chicago metropolitan area. As part of a

9. Two excellent studies of the public sector in urban areas have been published by the Committee on Urban Economics and Resources for the Future, Inc., in Washington. These studies are: Howard G. Schaller (ed.), *Public Expenditure Decisions in the Urban Community* (Baltimore: Johns Hopkins Press for Resources for the Future, Inc., 1963), and Julius Marglois (ed.), *The Public Economy of Urban Communities* (Baltimore: Johns Hopkins Press for Resources for the Future Inc., 1965).

major regional hospital study, the authors identify a distinct hierarchy in the range of hospital services. Hospitals differ in size and specialization and in the characteristics of people that use them. A principal-components analysis summarizes these features and a grouping procedure defines a classification or typology of hospitals by location and type of service provided.

Research on the political geography of the city is introduced by Roger Kasperson in a study of voting behavior in municipal elections in Chicago. Political behavior is defined as both a consequence and a reflection of the distribution of social characteristics of a city and the geography of community attitudes. What are the important spatial considerations influencing political decision-making? What are the ties between political behavior and the city's social geography and how do politicians utilize these ties? For example, the results of a mayoralty election in Chicago displayed a marked concentricity outward from the C.B.D. similar to that noted for socio-economic characteristics in preceding papers. Variations in community values will influence both the content and presentation of political issues. In concluding, Kasperson argues convincingly for the systematic study of urban political behavior and its spatial outcomes.[10]

Are there theories of public facility location? Michael Teitz proposes a framework within which a location theory of urban public facilities may develop. He then evaluates the relevance of existing principles of regional location theory to the spatial structure of these facilities. However, there are some obvious problems in the study of public facilities. Each of these services has certain components which make them unique kinds of spatial problems. One such problem is how society prices specific services, police and fire services, for example. Moreover, as public facilities are an increasingly important sector of the urban economy they provide an ever-expanding variety of services to differing consuming populations at varying costs. All of these complexities temper the form of the facility system that emerges. Nevertheless, Teitz concludes that public facility location is worthy of further theoretical and empirical exploration.

Activity systems, such as that outlined by Teitz, are often described in the language of models. This language has been used frequently through-

10. The present paper has also been included in a new text on political geography co-authored by Professor Kasperson, which indicates the growing interest in this important field. R. E. Kasperson and J. V. Minghi, *The Structure of Political Geography* (Chicago: Aldine Publishing Co., 1969). Also indicative of the expanding research framework in urban political geography are several recent papers by Kevin Cox, "The Voting Decision in Intraurban Space" in *Proceedings of the Association of American Geographers,* Vol. 1 (1969), pp. 43-47; and "The Voting Decision in a Spatial Context," in C. Board, R. J. Chorley and P. Haggett (eds.), *Progress in Geography* (London: Edward Arnold, 1969).

out this volume and should at this point be more explicitly defined and illustrated. Increasingly, studies of the structure and growth of urban areas are concerned with the construction of analytical models which are designed to test hypotheses by replicating the operation of the real world. In its most general sense, the word model means an idealized representation or construct of reality.[11] Such representations may be of three types: physical scale or iconic models, for example an areal photograph or an architect's mock-up of a new building; physical analogy models, such as simulating the operation of an urban transit system with analogous electricity networks; or symbolic models. Those in which the concepts are symbolic usually are specified in either graphic or mathematical form. Most large-scale urban models are of this form and typically they demand the use of high-speed computers. Such models attempt to simulate some aspect or set of subsystems of the urban area by a set of computer programming procedures.

In the last paper Kain and Meyer evaluate the general difficulties in simulating urban phenomena, and the contributions of several well known urban development models. Although the paper represents an appropriate conclusion to this section and a lead into the discussion of problems, it assumes that the reader has an elementary knowledge of urban models, such as that provided by Ira Lowry in his review paper "A Short Course in Model Design,"[12] and by others.[13] The problems of model construction are enormous, and practical applications have as yet been of limited direct value in planning. The Pittsburgh and San Francisco housing and urban renewal models are employed as examples. However, the importance of models and efforts at model-building offer attractive incentives. They may improve our understanding of the many and varied spatial relationships between urban activities. Our ability to define concepts in terms which can be evaluated and tested for purposes of solving urban problems may also be enhanced.

11. The most thorough review of models and their applications in geography is Richard J. Chorley and Peter Haggett (eds.), *Socio-Economic Models in Geography* (London: Methuen and Co., 1967).
12. See Ira S. Lowry, "A Short Course in Model Design," *Journal of the American Institute of Planners,* XXXI (1965), pp. 158-65.
13. For example, among the many excellent summaries and applications of urban models are: G. Olsson, "Trends in Spatial Model Building: An Overview," *Geographical Analysis,* Vol. 1, No. 3 (1969), pp. 219-24; Britton Harris, "Quantitative Models of Urban Development: Their Role in Metropolitan Decision-Making," in H. S. Perloff and Lowdon Wingo, Jr. (eds.), *Issues in Urban Economics* (Baltimore: Johns Hopkins Press for Resources for the Future Inc., 1968); A. G. Wilson, "Models in Urban Planning: A Synoptic Review of Recent Literature," *Urban Studies,* Vol. 5 (1968), pp. 249-76.

LARRY SMITH

Space for the CBD's Functions

In an era of change probably unprecedented in its speed and scope, we are presented today with that rare phenomenon in the history of cities: a second chance. Heretofore, it has generally been an overnight calamity—an earthquake, a conflagration—that confronted a dazed citizenry with the sudden need for stocktaking and rebuilding. Very often the same old mistakes were speedily incorporated into the new municipal fabric.

Today's realization of the need to reappraise and challenge the functions being performed by our metropolitan areas and our central cities has been long in coming, but the trends toward reappraisal are recognizable; and in spite of a diversity of influences and interests that are often conflicting, there is a growing urgency to spell out the way of the future. This is our chance for a fresh start, for incorporating the lessons we have learned the hard way to achieve an intelligent, balanced, and profitable relationship between our metropolitan areas and their respective CBD's.

The chief factor behind this need to review our established concepts of the purposes and functions of the various municipal entities is the constantly increasing size of our cities. This factor is in itself both a trend and an influence, playing a major role not only in relation to the functions performed by the city but in the very location of those functions within the city structure as well.

Among the major innovations and developments that have contributed to the changing requirements for satisfactory urban living are the introduction of the automobile as a means of personal travel, the tremendous changes in the standard of living, the recent concept of national responsibility for housing standards resulting in the urban renewal program, changes in personal habits affecting the expenditure of both time and family income, and the development of new highways.

Furthermore, we have the effects of obsolescence in a large percentage of our buildings and of the deterioration of our public transportation systems.

All these influences have come under examination in one form or another, chiefly in attempts to define the relationship between the "central city" and the rest of the metropolitan area, or between the "central business district" and the rest of the metropolitan area of which it is the

From the **Journal of the American Institute of Planners**, Vol. XXVII, No. 6, February 1961. Reprinted by permission.

focal point. The first definition is predicated on the political boundaries of the central city; the second, on the functional entity which is the subject of our present concern.

In studying the functions of the CBD one is handicapped by the fact that only within the last few years has it been defined in area and recognized as a reporting unit by the Census Bureau, whereas material for the study of the "central city" has been available since the middle of the last century.

Even studies based upon the political boundaries, however, have been inadequate, if not misleading, because these boundaries and the original street pattern for most of our cities were developed on a surveyor's concept of land use related primarily to engineering considerations and limited traffic solutions, with no consideration of the economic or social uses of the land within the city area. The original focal point and the growth pattern were usually tied to the primary means of access to the city, whether by water or by rail. The city's business enterprises competed for space within the surveyor's "grid" by a typical bidding process, their proximity to the original (or subsequent) focal point depending upon whether the uses that they developed could support the payment of higher or lower prices for land.

Subsequently, with the competitive bidding for property, the land itself reached a value for an alternate use greater than the combined value of the land in its existing use and the structure already in existence, and the obsolete structure was rebuilt.

In many of our cities, notably New York, rapid economic development in recent years has permitted a very quick replacement of substantial structures that have outlived their economic use. The investment of private funds in the replacement of structures proceeds, usually, without reference to the most desirable use of the land for the city as a whole. For example, the location for such developments is often chosen without consideration of attendant traffic and transportation problems, which may impose increased service costs on the municipality out of proportion to the increased tax revenues, or, perhaps more serious, may add to the inconvenience of private business and individuals.

In developing master plans for our American cities, the planning profession is faced with both an opportunity and a challenge. It must seek to guide the further development of these cities in such a way as to contribute to the economic, social, and spiritual well-being of the residents while at the same time offering a practical economic justification for the investment of both the private and public funds necessary to accomplish the task.

Before attempting to examine the overall problem of planning for land use in the CBD, it will be necessary, first, to study the various land uses found in our American cities, keeping in mind the effect that population and the ability to pay have on the location of the various categories. Then, as a separate consideration in determining location, we must analyze the influence exerted by our increased standard of living.

CBD Uses and Their Future

Substantial work has already been done on the *classification* of metropolitan land uses, their influence on property values, and the methods of estimating street and freeway requirements.[1]

1. For example, see Raymond Vernon, *The Changing Economic Function of the Central City* (New York: Committee for Economic Development, 2nd Printing, 1959); Edgar A. Horwood and Ronald R. Boyce, *Studies of the Central Business District and Urban Freeway Development* (Seattle: University of Washington Press, 1959); Shirley F. Weiss, *The Central Business District in Transition* (Chapel Hill, N.C.: University of North Carolina Press, 1957).

Less work has been done, however, on the economic *justification* for the specific location or distribution of these functions throughout the metropolitan area and on the economic implications for both private and public investment of locational decisions that flow from the master-plan itself.

Precise and functional categories for CBD land use are difficult to establish, in part because the specific elements tend to change with the size of the city and with the other factors mentioned in this article, and in part because the purpose of an analysis may require a relatively simple classification in some instances and a greatly expanded classification in others.

The very useful Standard Industrial Classification Manual has been widely used in studying the functions of the CBD, but its organization by industries instead of by function makes it cumbersome. Within certain industrial classifications it may list functions such as headquarters offices not readily identified as CBD functions; whereas other functions, such as parking, are not segregated for study to the extent necessary for ready reference.

Shirley Weiss has suggested a functional classification for CBD land use analysis which provides an excellent starting point.[2] This classification can be expanded or condensed, depending upon the size and characteristics of the city being studied, and (even more important) upon the purpose for which the analysis is required.

The amount of land required for the efficient performance of each of the various functions within the CBD may best be calculated by determining:

(a) The total extent of the particular function in the metropolitan area, measured in economic or other terms.

(b) The share of the total function to be performed within the CBD.

It must be stressed, however, that the variables in such a situation (the size of

2. *Op. cit.,* appendix.

the city; its principal economic function or functions, whether governmental, educational, industrial, trade, or residential; and the other influences discussed in this article) make any generalization dangerous. It is necessary to bear in mind at all times the specific local influences at work in the area.

For the typical metropolitan area, however, we may expect per capita floor area requirements for certain major activities to approximate those found in Table 1.

These are not to be regarded as absolute figures, but rather as an approxima-

Table 1. Metropolitan Per Capita Floor Area Requirements for Selected Activities

Activities	Floor Area per Capita (Square Feet)
Retail	20 to 55
Office	2 to 15
Parking (on the ground or in structures)	4 to 16
Public	1 to 3.5
Quasi-public	1 to 3.5
Wholesale	5 to 15
Industrial	2 to 15
Residential	200 to 400

tion. It would be desirable if we could indicate the proportion of these various activities which are presently, or which ideally should be, located within the CBD; however, there is no set formula for determining this proportion.

I suggest, therefore, that planners and others studying the central business district in a particular city should prepare their own tabulation by measurement and observation, using whatever functional classification they may select for their specific purpose.

Information concerning the extent to which these functions are performed either in the CBD or in non-CBD areas within a metropolitan area, is normally available through statistical data compiled by the central city government, the metropolitan government, or the planning commission.

If the required data are not available from such sources, analysis by measurement or observation can be undertaken to whatever degree may be indicated for the particular purpose.

CBD Shares of Regional Growth

In recent years, range of distribution between CBD and other areas for the retail category can be related to population size. Census data were not available prior to 1949 in sufficient detail for study purposes, but studies between 1920 and 1948[3] suggested the following relationships.

Table 2. Share of Retail Business in the CBD Related to City Size

Population	Share of Retail Business in CBD (Per Cent)
0–25,000	80–100
25,000–100,000	65–85
100,000–400,000	50–70
400,000–750,000	30–55
Over 750,000	15–35

The various retail categories have their own relationship. As population increases, food and other convenience stores move to the suburbs first; general merchandise facilities show the greatest resistance to movement out of the CBD.

With the rapid growth in recent years of small cities such as Miami and Phoenix, the rate of retail growth in the suburbs has been such as to make generalizations like that made above less useful. Fortunately, data now published by the Census Bureau provide accurate information on

3. Studies of approximately two hundred cities for private clients, made by Larry Smith & Company and others.

the retail category in most of the larger cities.

For other categories and for the retail categories in smaller cities, it will still be necessary to determine the distribution of facilities between CBD and •other locations, by observation or from data published locally where they are available.

Significantly, the process of decentralization in all major categories preceded the general use of the automobile for personal transportation, although this process has accelerated as the use of the automobile has increased.

It has been observed that there is no clear, accepted definition of CBD boundaries. The area defined in the more recent censuses often does not conform to the functional CBD areas used in specific cities for planning purposes. A complicating factor, also, is the tendency of the central core itself to move with the growth of the city.

Land Uses and Values

Before the definition, function, and movement of the CBD are considered further, attention should be given to the general hierarchy of economic uses of land in the urban framework. Table 3 indicates the variety of land uses and their economic relationship, expressed in terms of the relative land cost per square foot which these various uses can support. It will be noted that the highest uses on the scale are the most central of the CBD land uses and that they characterize the denser portions of our major cities. Actually, the first two groupings form the core of the CBD.

The second series of groupings forms the frame or fringe. The extent to which these uses will occur within the CBD is determined by the degree of intensity of land use in the CBD and the amount of secondary land area available.

In cities of extreme density, many of the secondary uses have been forced out of the core area by high land cost and a

ACTIVITIES

Table 3. Hierarchy of CBD Land Uses and Land Values

Location	Land Value Supported (Per Sq. Ft.)	Land Uses	Comments
Core (office)	$50+–$25	Prime multi-tenant office Prime single occupany office (prestige) Prestige retail Financial Other mixed uses (not freestanding) Service Food (eating & drinking)	High density primary core space use; prestige a highly important factor—convenience and central location controlling factors
Core (retail)	$25–$15	Large comparison retail (department stores)* Specialty and chain retail* Multi- & single-tenant office Hotel Entertainment Banks Service and support uses Luxury hi-rise residential apartments	Somewhat lower density use
Fringe	$55–$5	Secondary retail Other centrally oriented commercial Secondary office	Necessary CBD service uses form major portion of fringe
Fringe	$5–$1	Wholesale Middle-income residential apartments Neighborhood—convenience retail Loft industrial	Marginal CBD uses
Non-CBD or suburban	$1–$0.10	Low-rise or single-family middle-income residential Low-income private & public housing Industry Warehousing Neighborhood—Convenience retail Suburban retail (shopping center) Low-rise office—other commercial	Locate in CBD only as a result of utilization of obsolete space (warehousing industry low-income housing) or as a result of public policy offsetting space differential
—	—	Civic and institutional uses	Location and land price as a question of public policy—centrality guides many locational decisions

* The table must be taken as an illustration of the relationship which frequently exists rather than an absolute statement of values, or ranking order of land values. In practically all cities, certain types of retail will be found on limited areas of land of greatest value. The size of the city under consideration will influence the absolute values.

growing market for the core-area space. Frequently secondary uses jump to suburban areas, but more often move to depressed fringe locations where obsolete structures can be found at a rental or purchase price that the type of use will justify. It is well, therefore, when considering future land use patterns within our cities, to study the various rates of growth in all uses and the economic relationship among them.

In federal urban renewal areas, the necessity of determining specific re-uses makes it imperative to recognize the "ability to pay" of the various use types. In market studies and re-use appraisals made by our office, it has been found that even with a maximum governmental absorption of land cost it is sometimes impossible, in view of the costs of new construction, to develop new fringe-type use facilities that can compete on a rental basis with existing obsolete facilities in the fringe area.

The values in Table 3 must, of course, be taken as indicative only that a relationship of economic function to land cost and location exists, rather than as a statement of absolute valuation. These values vary from city to city (particularly according to the size of the city) by scarcity due to geographical factors, by distribution of functions between the CBD and other sections of the city, and also by specific location within the generalized districts (core, fringe, etc.) in any particular CBD.

Forecasting CBD Land Uses

Estimates of future requirements for CBD's have frequently been made my projection of historic relationships which are the result of factors of growth and the special influences discussed in the sections which follow. This method of statistical calculation of future requirements is not wholly sound. Historic relationships *may* continue in the future, but modified by the various influences discussed in this article. However, the planning process should facilitate the introduction of modifications of the historic trend for the benefit of the community.

The effectiveness of a master plan in the development of specific uses in the CBD or other areas will be limited by the extent to which changes in the use of property can be brought about by zoning, building codes, highway changes, rights of access, traffic controls, condemnation practices, and other limitations on the private use and enjoyment of land.

To determine the most desirable and feasible land uses for the CBD and for other parts of the metropolitan area included in the master plan, a process of experienced analysis and judgment must be applied, one which takes into consideration not only the historic development and compromise of the various local influences at work, but also the relationships between private sectors of the economy. Consideration must also be given to the degree to which the implementation of the master plan itself may affect the location and function of the various land uses.

City Size and Proper Location

Population size is usually the primary factor affecting the distribution of facilities between the CBD and other sections of the metropolitan area. However, the *effect* of the size of the population will vary from city to city, depending largely on the following:

1. The physical characteristics of the city
2. The rate of growth
3. The timing of the period of rapid growth—whether previous to the 1950-1970 period or within that period.

In the broad sense, the relationship between the growth characteristics given above and the location of various land uses is controlled by the factor of convenience. This convenience may be expressed in terms of ready access, cost, comfort and atmosphere, availability of services, etc.— the sum total of these factors provides a test of the over-all value of the specific location to owner, tenant, or customer.

Within the general limitation of convenience, however, the physical characteristics of the city, whether natural or created by private development or governmental design, will play an important part in determining the extent of land use in any given category within the CBD as well as in other areas.

The move toward decentralization associated with a rapid population growth has resulted primarily from the inability of the CBD to adapt itself to rapid change, with a consequent change in convenience orientation.

The fragmentation of property ownership in the CBD and the holding of a substantial part of such property by trusts and estates, which are either unable or unwilling to participate in any activity involving change or increased investment, have a tendency to freeze the pattern of use. Faced with the competitive necessity for the development of increased facilities, the owner of a business may, in the absence of the right of condemnation, decide against waiting for the acquisition

of an adequate area or location within the CBD, even though such a location may be recognized as desirable in terms of cost and other convenience considerations.

There are well-known instances where business organizations, having acquired suburban locations for various facilities, particularly office headquarters, have subsequently, before construction, reviewed their decision and attempted to acquire CBD locations instead. If CBD ownership cannot furnish the land required for these improvements within the competitive time limit available to such a prospective user, he has no choice but to utilize his suburban property.

The point at which decentralization of certain major land uses is likely to occur, within the framework of present experience, is shown on Chart 1. The timing of dispersal from the CBD and the proportion of this dispersal will depend to a great degree on the influences discussed in a following section, and the modifications of these influences which might occur through the development of a master plan. In my opinion, a simple expansion of the chart on a percentage basis is justified only when the calculations are tempered by the results of study in the individual case.

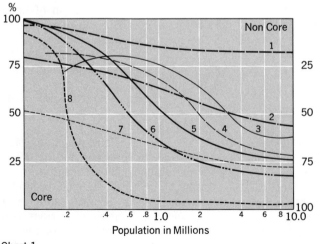

KEY

1. Major Office
2. Medical Dental Offices
3. High-Rise Residential
4. Warehousing
5. Department Store
6. Major Comparison Shops
7. Industrial
8. Food

Chart 1

Just as we have considered the general characteristics of *existing* land use, the planner or other professional, in studying any particular city, should analyze the classifications of the *proposed* land uses within the same framework.

Determination of the proper and economically feasible location of each of these functions within the CBD framework is a critically important part of the master planning process and will in itself have a substantial bearing on the degree to which the functions may flourish.

It is also important to use this approach in considering the extent and placement of functions proposed for any specific portion of the CBD, such as the area of an urban renewal project or a similar smaller area. The extent and location of such functions within the entire CBD must be considered in determining the extent to which the functions should be developed for the smaller area, because the success of the functions in the smaller area will depend upon their locational or competitive relations with similar and other functions in the entire CBD.

The availability of land for each category of use and its proper locational relationship to all other uses in the metropolitan area constitute the economic foundation on which capital investment must be predicated. A major portion of the planning effort must therefore be directed toward insuring the economic validity of the plan. Once this is accomplished, a presentation should be developed for voters, public authorities, and investment groups to indicate clearly the total financial implications of the plan and the economic justification as applied to each group from whom approval and acceptance is required.

The Effects of Other Influences

Important influences (apart from city size) affecting the distribution of facilities between CBD and other portions of the metropolitan area are discussed briefly in the following paragraphs. It is important, however, to observe that the impact of each of these influences will depend upon the particular conditions which prevail in the individual city under discussion.

1. *Decentralization.* Retail, industrial, and office facilities have developed in non-CBD areas. Stimulation initially for certain retail uses has been the geographic expansion of the city to meet the need for land suitable for residential development. The need for lower cost land for industrial development in view of climbing wage rates, the desire for corporate identity and atmosphere in offices, and the factors of convenience discussed earlier influence industrial and office facilities.

2. *Regional growth.* In some areas, smaller functioning cities with a full complement of economic uses are surrounded and absorbed. In other areas the total growth of the region has necessitated the creation of relatively self-sufficient new industrial and commercial complexes within the metropolitan framework. This type of growth would probably become evident only in metropolitan areas of more than a million and a half people.

3. *Highway programs.* Intercity highways have been developed and in many cases a system of circumferential highways within the metropolitan areas. Each influences the distribution of facilities. In this connection, a special influence could be created by the development, for example, of an inner loop whose location might define the CBD in such a way as either to encourage or to limit its improvement. It could, consequently, either inhibit or increase the rate of CBD deterioration.

4. *Access and parking.* Provision of adequate access and parking as prerequisites is an urban responsibility which must precede any large-scale improvement in a CBD by either private or public investment. The extent, location, and interrelationship of arterials and parking facilities in the CBD will be a controlling influence

in the amount and location of economically useful land for all major categories of use.

5. *Automobile and public transportation trends.* Many cities outgrew their public transportation systems before those systems became large enough or well enough equipped to serve the urban sprawl. The result is a higher degree of automobile use in these cities. There is need for a resolution of the dilemma in which the placement of downtown access and storage facilities for the automobile may strangle the CBD.

6. *Urban renewal.* The elimination of blighted areas creates both an opportunity and a responsibility for redevelopment that will benefit rather than injure the total functions of both CBD and the metropolitan area. Though generally dependent upon federal assistance, this program may be carried out in part without the benefit of federal funds.

7. *Automation.* Improved technical processes have brought changes in capital goods and equipment which have resulted in a relatively constant total manufacturing labor force despite the spectacular growth in gross national product. A transfer of employment to executive, supervisory, service, and similar functions has ensued. Automation will affect the land specifications for certain types of industry and is also likely to increase the relative need for office buildings and similar space for housing supervisory and service personnel.

8. *The investment climate.* Implementation of CBD plans depends upon the political atmosphere, the integrity of planning and of other municipal functions in a community, the assessment and taxation policies, the efficiency of municipal government, the strength of the economic base of the community and region, and all the other factors which induce capital to flow into either public or private investment.

9. *The standard of living.* The change in the standard of living affects working hours, wages, rates, expenditure patterns, use of leisure time, standards of home ownership, and so on.

10. *Entrepreneurial activity.* The investor of risk capital frequently influences the "unplanned" creation of specific industries and specific facilities through the accident of personal location or strong personal preferences and judgments. Individuals and the financial community as a whole may recognize and seize upon an investment opportunity in one community rather than in another.

Each of these influences will be exerted at any particular moment in such a way as to modify the distribution of land use within the metropolitan area. The weight of each influence and the extent to which the combined weight of all influences in any specific metropolitan area can be modified by sound planning presents a challenge and opportunity to the planner of today.

BRIAN J. L. BERRY

General Features of Urban Commercial Structure

A detailed review of the literature dealing with commercial structure of American cities[1] concludes that outside the central business district, this structure comprises four basic components:

  a) A hierarchy of business centers.
  b) Highway-oriented commercial ribbons.
  c) Urban arterial commercial developments.
  d) Specialized functional areas.

These are the results of the early twentieth century phase of growth, little modified as yet by more recent pressures toward increased specialization, and the pulls of increased mobility, changing consumer preferences, and the like.

The hierarchy of business centers appears to have at least four levels beneath that of the metropolitan central business district. In ascending order these are:

  i) Isolated convenience stores and "streetcorner" developments.
  ii) Neighborhood business centers.
  iii) Community business centers.

1. Brian J. L. Berry, *The Commercial Structure of American Cities. A Review* (Chicago: Community Renewal Program, 1962).

  iv) Regional shopping centers.

The first of these levels consists of the grocer-drugstore combination, and serves only the occasional demands of people residing within a two or three block radius of the streetcorner. A neighborhood center, on the other hand, has grocery stores or small supermarkets, drugstores, laundries and dry cleaners, barber and beauty shops and a small restaurant. To these functions are added, at the community level, variety and clothing stores, bakeries, dairies and perhaps confectioners, jewelry stores, florists, and a post office. Banks may or may not be present (outside of Illinois branch banks would be found in community centers). At the regional level department stores, shoe stores, specialized music, record, hobby and toy shops, photographic stores, and so forth are added.

Such centers may be either planned or unplanned. Most in the central city are unplanned, and usually take the form of centers focussing on some major street intersection, although the smaller ones may string out as local shopping streets. In sections of the city which have de-

Adapted from B. J. L. Berry, **Commercial Structure and Commercial Blight,** Research Paper No. 85, Department of Geography Research Series, University of Chicago, 1963. Reprinted by permission of the author.

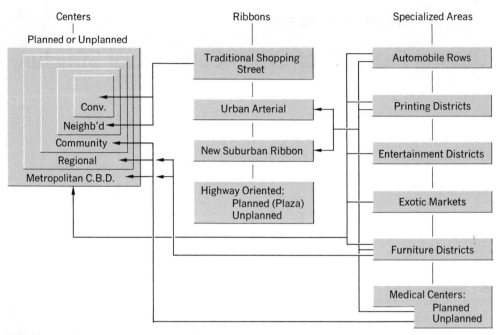

Figure 1. The Structure of Business and Commerce

veloped in the last two decades, many of the centers of neighborhood and higher levels have been planned on a unitary, integrated basis. Planning, however, affects the *design* of centers rather than their core functions. Both planned and unplanned neighborhood centers, for example, perform the same group of functions. The major difference, as we shall see later, is that in the planned centers peripheral uses are missing, and duplication of stores of the same kind is minimized.

Centers display spatial patterns that conform to the geographic distribution of consumers. Each is located centrally with respect to the maximum number of consumers it can serve, although the size of its trade area is maintained in the course of competition at about the minimum size necessary to support its most specialized functions (its threshold size, or condition of entry). The stores which cluster in such centrally-located centers at any given level of the hierarchy thus

require similar trade areas for their support, and experience mutual benefits from congregation at a central place where surrounding consumers can assemble easily. There is a pressure for stores to group, resulting from the tendency of consumers to make a single trip between one center and their homes, shopping from store to store in the center for the set of goods which they expect to be offered in that level of center. Functions at any one level are thus "linked" into nucleation by consumers' desires to visit several of them on a single trip.

The hierarchy results because (a) on the supply side, different commercial functions have different conditions of entry (thresholds), and thus demand minimum trade areas of different sizes for their support, and (b) on the demand side, consumers spend differing proportions of their income on different goods and services, and purchase them with differing degrees of frequency. Low threshold, high frequency functions are found in lower-level nucleations ("convenience goods centers"), whereas high threshold, low frequency functions are found in higher-level nucleations serving larger trade areas ("shopping goods centers"). These reasons apparently lead to the emergence of at least four groups of functions and therefore four levels of centers, from the most to the least ubiquitous, the streetcorner, neighborhood, community and regional (the CBD is, of course, the fifth and highest level). Competition between centers of any one level reduces their trade areas near to threshold, and spreads the centers throughout the city in a dispersed geographic pattern of consumer orientation, each central to its own trade area. Higher order centers (e.g., community) also perform lower order functions (e.g., of neighborbood level), and for their lower order goods have somewhat larger trade areas than centers which are exclusively of that lower level. The reason is the greater number of shopping opportunities in the higher order center, so that consumers can find additional reasons to travel somewhat further to purchase their convenience goods. Low order centers "nest" within the trade areas of higher order centers in terms of the provision of higher order goods and services to the consumers who visit the lower order centers for their offerings, and at the extreme, all outlying centers "nest" within the sphere of influence of the CBD for its most specialized functions.

Highway-oriented ribbons are natural "strip" developments. They comprise such functions as gasoline and service stations, restaurants and drive-in eating places, ice cream parlors, motels and fruit, vegetable and produce stands. These functions serve demands originating on the highways, and in general, the greater the traffic volume, the greater the demands for and density of highway-oriented uses. However, they seldom are associated functionally; most shopping stops at them are single-pur-

pose, so that use of their facilities is not combined on the same stop. Most highway-oriented developments are uncontrolled ribbons, but a few are now planned, for example the "service plazas" on the Illinois and other toll highways.

A large number of commercial functions seek out accessible *urban arterial locations* in cities. Most of these functions like reasonable access to the urban market, but because of space requirements and the ways in which consumers use them, they function most efficiently outside the nucleated business centers. Among such uses are specialized automobile repair establishments, furniture and appliance stores (including discount houses and large independents such as Sears), office equipment sales, funeral parlors, nurseries, lumber yards, establishments which provide a variety of building and household supplies, electrical repair and plumbing, radio-T.V. sales and service, etc. These are the uses for which the householder has an infrequent, specialized demand that calls for an occasional special-purpose trip to the store or a special house-call on the part of the businessman, or they may be able to attract a large market on their own, by virtue of price, variety, etc., like the discounters. The important criterion for location of such businesses is reasonable accessibility to a substantial segment of the urban market, such as is ensured by arterial orientation. A set of urban arterial uses exists because many types of business seek out similar arterial locations. Since the trips to or from such establishments are single-purpose, however, there is no functional association among stores resulting from linkage on the same trip; urban arterial uses are therefore "single-standing," even though with common arterial orientation.

Establishments of several types cluster in *specialized functional areas* for example dealers in new and used automobiles in "automobile rows," and doctors, dentists, medical laboratories, pharmacies, optometrists and related uses in special "medical districts." Such functional areas are held intact by the close linkages between establishments provided by comparative shopping, by economies in advertising in the case of automobile dealers, and by referrals and common use of specialists and special services in the case of medical districts to cite two examples. Most functional areas require good accessibility to that segment of the urban market that is required for their support, for example automobile rows to arterial highways or major intersections, and medical centers either to public transport or arterials. In the contemporary American city most specialized functional areas remain unplanned. Planning has recently entered in the case of medical districts however, with the building of modern outlying clinics, which now compete for

the patient with the older upper-floor medical complexes of the traditional unplanned major regional business centers.

This pattern is summarized in Figure 1 which distinguishes between the three main categories of business: centers, ribbons, and specialized areas. The successive boxes under the heading "center" indicate the hierarchy. Several kinds of ribbons are distinguished: highway-oriented. urban arterial, and two not previously discussed, the "new suburban ribbons" in which are found concentrations of the newer kinds of drive-in and discounting business, and the traditional shopping streets that still string out in older parts of American cities, essentially performing the functions of centers at the convenience and neighborhood levels, although with many of them today having a decided "skid road" character. Specialized areas are of several kinds. As the

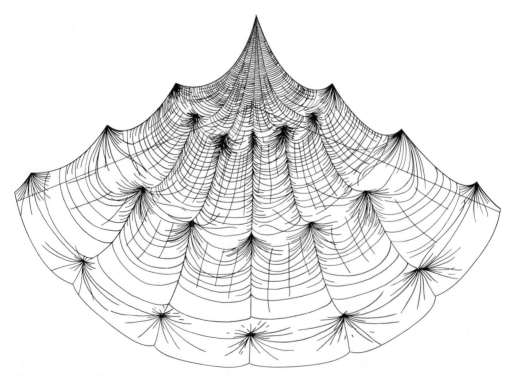

Figure 2. General Pattern of Urban Land Values

maze of lines indicate, some of them are found in centers of various levels, others in the ribbons, and some in both.

Outlying Centers

The basic features of Chicago's land value skeleton were already in existence in 1935, and they persist to this day. These features include a major cone with the CBD at its apex, ridges radiating from the CBD and extending along the grid-iron of streets, and minor peaks of land values rising at regular intervals along the ridges (Figure 2). Wherever there is a peak there is a business center; wherever there is a ridge there is a ribbon development. A map of commercial land values is thus of inestimable value to any analysis of commercial centers and ribbons, for it identifies exactly where the centers and ribbons are located. Such a map of commercial land values was the starting place of this study of Chicago's outlying commercial structure.[2]

If the profiles formed by commercial land values along major streets are examined, it is relatively easy to distinguish the peaks (centers) from the ridges (ribbons). Outer limits of the peaks are given by those points at which values turn upwards from the levels of the ridges towards the heights of the cones. If the outer edges are transcribed on to an accompanying map and joined, the center may be delineated. Given a map of land values, it is possible to delineate every business center in the city by the same process, except for the planned centers built during the last decade. Planned centers, the product of postwar forces, do not conform to the patterns of the land value skeleton which emerged prior to 1935.

The land values map of Chicago indicates several hundred peaks. Most rise barely $50 or $100 per front foot over

the prevailing height of the ridges (which usually run $200 plus or minus $50 per front foot). These minor "bumps" are the local street-corner nucleations of the city. The largest peaks, on the other hand, rise to more than $4,000 per front foot (the peak of the CBD exceeds $40,000), and are occupied by the city's largest outlying business centers. One study completed recently, which analyzed a portion of the south side of Chicago in great detail, found that few neighborhood centers had peaks that rose above $750 per front foot, whereas no centers of any higher level had peaks of less than this value.[3] To facilitate the analysis of centers which had to be completed if the study of commercial blight were to proceed speedily it was therefore decided to use this criterion value of $750 per front foot as a cut off point. All centers with peaks of $750 and over were analyzed in detail. Centers with lower peaks were analyzed on a sampling basis in conjunction with the study of ribbons described below. This decision led the analysis to focus upon the 64 largest unplanned business centers in Chicago. To these were added the 9 largest planned centers within the city limits. Of the 73 city centers, 20 perform shopping goods functions. Four of the twenty qualify to be called "major regional centers." There are twenty-eight community-level convenience goods centers. Twenty-one of the peaks rising to $750 per front foot or more contain large neighborhood centers, and the four smallest planned centers are also of this level. Six of the suburban centers, five of the major regional type and one other performing shopping goods functions, are competitors that draw off city consumers living near the city limits.

Three variants of the hierarchy. There

2. It was compiled using Olcott's 1961 *Blue Book of Land Values* for Chicago.

3. Brian J. L. Berry *et al., Comparative Studies of Central Place Systems,* Final report of Project NONR 2121-18, NR 389-126 (U.S. Office of Naval Research, 1961).

are three variants of the hierarchy of outlying business centers within Chicago. The first serves higher income sections of the city. Lower income neighborhoods are served by the second. The third comprises those planned centers built as integrated developments in the last decade, both in urban renewal areas (Lake Meadows, Hyde Park), and in areas of post-war residential expansion (Scottsdale, Chatham Park).

In higher income areas shopping goods are provided by major regional centers in the most central strategic locations, and by a peripheral ring of smaller shopping goods centers whose trade areas encircle those of the major regional centers. Convenience goods are distributed by an upper level of community centers and a lower level of neighborhood centers (we ignore for the moment the lowest level comprising widely-scattered convenience shops).

Lower income neighborhoods lack the larger type of center at both the shopping and convenience goods levels. In such areas the heirarchy is simpler, with clothing and similar goods provided by smaller shopping goods centers, and necessities sold in neighborhood level centers. The effect of the lower incomes is to eliminate the larger centers that provide greater varieties of goods, more specialized stores, greater opportunities for a full range of shopping opportunities.

There is a four level hierarchy of planned centers, also. The planned centers differ from their unplanned counterparts in that they do not have the upper floor and peripheral uses of the latter, because store sizes are larger, and because there are fewer establishments of any one kind.

A Symbolic Model for Centers

Retail and service activities are consumer oriented. Moreover, the retail and service sector is probably the most highly competitive in the American economy today. A reasonable premise upon which to build models of retail structure is thus that the numbers and kinds of retail and service activities in any area are constantly being pulled and pushed towards some condition of adjustment to the demands of the consumers residing in the area. A state of balance is hard to reach, however. Conditions are always changing on both the demand and the supply sides. The numbers of consumers, or their incomes, may change. If they do, businessmen will be quick to take advantage of new opportunities, or will have to fight hard for a share of a declining market to prevent going out of business, as the weaker among them may do. New ways of doing business may be introduced. If they are successful, businesses of the new forms will replace those of the old. Readjustments towards new equilibrium conditions may therefore be generated by changes on either the demand or the supply sides, but a stable equilibrium can seldom, if ever, be achieved, because the essence of an American city is its dynamism. Things are always changing. Retailing is always trying to adjust towards new states of balance but as it moves towards them conditions change and the goal moves further on. There is an incessant chase of a moving equilibrium.

At any point in time the retailing structure of a city may be analyzed in detail. If the foregoing argument is true, the retail structure of the city should, at that point in time, display an approximation to an equilibrium condition, but with variability. Old forms will persist because the necessary time for them to have been eliminated will not yet have elapsed. New forms will be seen, presaging future trends. Current forms will not balance neatly with demands. Certain areas are to be expected in which there will be either an over- or under-supply of facilities simply because people and their incomes are more mobile than retail and service businesses.

Nevertheless, there will be an approximation to an equilibrium, and it is this approximation which enables us to construct a model which captures the essence of the equilibrium, and permits us to specify the mathematical form of this model. Comparison of predictions based upon the model for any area of the city and the actual conditions in that area should then enable cases of over- and under-supply to be identified. Combination of the model with information on how conditions have changed and how retailing has reacted to these changes should also permit certain generalizations to be made about how the equilibrium condition has moved in the recent past, and how it is likely to move in the near future.

F. W. BOAL AND D. B. JOHNSON

The Functions of Retail and Service Establishments on Commercial Ribbons

Commercial ribbons or string streets have been the subject of a number of studies over the past ten years. Interest would appear to stem from two main sources, the first being the general disfavour with which planners and other researchers view such developments; the second and more abstract being the problem of how such developments fit into existing theoretical concepts of urban retail and service structure.

The opposition of planners is based on a dislike for the visual character of commercial ribbons and the apparently unfavourable effect these developments have on the free flow of traffic. That such streets fulfill important functions in a city's commercial structure is recognized, but it is felt that these functions could be performed by establishments located in some alternative physical form, a form that would not have the apparently built-in disadvantages of ribbon development itself. However, several writers have recently inferred that out and out criticism of commercial ribbons can be carried too

far. Wolfe has shown that many accidents occurring on ribbon streets are associated not with movements into and out from roadside shops, gas stations, and so on, but with normal traffic intersections.[1] Berry, in his studies of retail and service businesses, has pleaded strongly for the retention of the ribbon function, though not necessarily in its present form, because he found it to be of such widespread occurrence that it was obviously a fundamental part of the over-all commercial structure.[2]

Many recent studies of shopping and allied functions in cities have been based on a central place hierarchic approach, recognizing discrete levels of business centres serving nested "hinterlands." At the same time dissatisfaction has been expressed with the apparent inadequacy

1. R. I. Wolfe, "Effect of Ribbon Development on Traffic Flow," *Traffic Quat.*, XVIII, 1 (Jan. 1964), 105-17.
2. B. J. L. Berry, "A Critique of Contemporary Planning for Business Centers," *Land Econ.*, XXX, 4 (Nov. 1959), 306-12.

From **Canadian Geographer**, Vol. 9, No. 3, 1965, pp. 154-169. Reprinted by permission of the authors.

of the central place approach as an explanation of all intra-urban service areas, especially where a group of commercial establishments tends to be linear rather than nuclear in form, that is, the commercial ribbon. Both Bunge and Marble have suggested that a broadened central place approach based on a concept of linear hinterlands will prove adequate.[3,4] However, the validity of this concept depends on the ribbon functions being completely oriented to passing traffic.

The general conflict of opinion and the variety of approaches used in these studies indicate that a further examination of ribbon development is called for. The present study, consequently, attempts on the one hand to review current concepts as to the character and function of commercial ribbons in general, and on the other to examine the actual function of one such street, the Macleod Trail in Calgary, Alberta.

General Character and Function of the Commercial Ribbon

A review of the literature on commercial ribbons fails to bring out a clear consensus as to what functionally constitutes such streets. In six different studies[5]

thirty-one types of retail and service establishments were mentioned as ribbon functions, ranging from service stations to grocery shops, and from automobile dealers to drug stores. Furthermore, it is difficult to determine whether the lists of establishments were intended to be exhaustive or merely illustrative. Ambiguity over the functional make-up of a commercial ribbon is increased by the existence of a variety of definitions used to delimit such streets. Some studies include all groups of commercial establishments which have developed in a linear form, while others recognize nucleations or beads on the ribbon as separate centres. Finally, it has also been suggested that ribbon developments vary according to their location in the urban matrix:[6,7] specifically that is whether they are outgrowths from major nucleated centres, or are more isolated; and also whether they are embedded in the urban street system, or are on an inter-urban artery.

The great variety of functions found on commrecial ribbons and the considable differences in functional balance between one such street and another can be attributed to the fact that they present desirable locations to a wide range of establishments. Ratcliff, writing in 1949, sums up this idea:

The nature of the uses comprising [the principal business thoroughfare] depends upon the extent to which the street is a main automobile artery and the degree to which it is the core of a residential area. The use

3. W. Bunge, "The Location of Population, Demand, Purchasing Power and Services on Highways" (unpub. study, Dept. of Geog., Univ. of Washington, 1958).
4. D. F. Marble, Symposium Discussion in *Proceedings of the IGU Symposium in Urban Geography Lund 1960* (Lund Stud. in Geog., ser. B, Human Geography no. 24, Lund, 1962), p. 159.
5. B. J. L. Berry, "Ribbon Developments in the Urban Business Pattern," *Ann. Assoc. Am. Geog.,* XLIX, 2 (June 1959), 145-55; W. Bunge, *Theoretical Geography* (Lund Stud. in Geog., ser. C, General and Mathematical Geography no. 1, Lund, 1962), p. 154; D. H. Davies, "Investigating a Business Ribbon in the Northern Municipalities, Cape Town," *South African Geog. J.,* (1960), 41-51; W. Garrison *et al., Studies of Highway Development and Geographic Change* (Univ. of Washington Press, 1959), p. 44; P. R. Merry, "An Inquiry into the

Nature and Functions of a String Retail Development: A Case Study of Colfax Avenue, Denver, Colorado" (unpub. Ph.D. dissertation, Northwestern Univ., 1955); U.S. Dept. of Commerce, *Intra-City Business Statistics for Philadelphia, Pennsylvania* (Washington, D.C., Bureau of Census, May 1937).
6. B. J. L. Berry, *Commercial Structure and Commercial Blight* (Univ. of Chicago Dept. of Geog. research paper no. 85, Chicago, 1963), p. 73.
7. Wolfe, "Effect of Ribbon Development," p. 106.

of the street as a traffic artery attracts retail shops serving the transients—filling stations, accessory shops, automobile showrooms, quick lunches and refreshment stands, and fruit stands. The proximity of residential districts encourages convenience type outlets—drug stores, grocery stores, laundry and cleaning branches, hardware stores, delicatessens and pool halls. Since there are infinite variations in the relative importance of major streets as arteries and as the cores of residential districts, the nature of string street retail development cannot be strictly defined.[8]

However, in a study of United States Highway 41 in Illinois and Wisconsin the Grotewolds noted not only the occurrence of a wide variety of establishments, but also the fact that each establishment had a mixed functional role.[9] Many of these establishments catered almost exclusively to residents of nearby urban communities, while those providing services sought by through travellers also attracted sizable numbers of local customers.

With the exception of the above study, commercial ribbon studies tend to be morphological in character, examining what kinds of establishments are found in large-scale linear commercial developments, and then making a series of assumptions about the functional roles of these establishments. Proudfoot, examining his "principal business thoroughfare," states that "these stores manage to thrive by attracting customers from a small fraction of the passengers of . . . intercommunity traffic."[10] Ratcliff claims that filling stations, automobile showrooms,

and so forth serve "the transients."[11] Berry, in a comprehensive series of commercial studies, mentions "highway oriented ribbons" as comprising such functions as gasoline stations, restaurants, and motels which serve "demands originating on the highway."[12]

These studies indicate that commercial ribbons are composed of a great variety of establishment types, and suggest that many of them are largely dependent upon passing traffic.

Because there is such a mixing of establishment types, for the purpose of this study it will be useful to employ a system whereby the various establishments may be classified into recognizable groups. The classification developed by Berry will be used.[13] In this system he recognizes four basic conformations of retail and service activity in cities outside the central business district. Each conformation is distinguished by the types of establishments present, these in turn having specific functional attributes. The four conformations are "mutually exclusive as functional groups, but they need not be spatially exclusive."[14] Briefly, Berry's system is as follows:

(1) *A hierarchy of business centres.* Each centre in this conformation is theoretically located centrally with respect to the maximum number of customers it can serve. Functions such as grocery stores, drug stores, barber shops, variety and clothing stores, and department stores locate in these centres. There is pressure for the various functions to cluster because customers tend to shop from store to store during a given shopping trip.

(2) *Highway-oriented ribbons.* These are composed of service stations, restaurants, and motels, and they serve de-

8. R. U. Ratcliff, "Internal Arrangement of Land Uses," reprinted in H. M. Mayer, and C. F. Kohn (eds.), *Readings in Urban Geography* (Univ. of Chicago Press, 1959), p. 412.
9. A. and L. Grotewold, "Commercial Development of Highways in Urbanized Regions: A Case Study," *Land Econ.*, XXXIV, 3 (Aug. 1958), 236-44.
10. M. Proudfoot, "City Retail Structure," reprinted in Mayer and Kohn, *Readings,* pp. 236-44.

11. Ratcliff, "Internal Arrangement of Land Uses," p. 412.
12. Berry, *Commercial Structure and Commercial Blight,* p. 23.
13. *Ibid.,* pp. 14-24.
14. Berry, "Ribbon Developments in the Urban Business Pattern," p. 149.

mands originating on the highways. The establishments are seldom associated functionally because most shopping trips to them are single-purpose trips.

(3) *Urban arterial commercial developments.* These groups contain functions which seek out accessible urban arterial locations. "Most of these functions like reasonable access to the urban market, but because of space requirements and the ways in which consumers use them, they function most efficiently outside the nucleated business centres."[15] The establishments in this group are usually associated with special single-purpose trips with little customer come-and-go between them. Examples are furniture and appliance stores, automobile repair shops, radio-TV sales and service establishments, and plumbing shops.

(4) *Specialized functional areas.* These areas are characterized by the presence of several related types of establishments, notably dealerships in new and used cars in "automobile rows," and doctors, dentists, X-ray technicians, and so forth in medical complexes. "Such functional areas are held intact by the close linkages between establishments provided by comparative shopping, by economics in advertising in the case of automobile dealers, and by referrals and common use of specialists and special services in the case of medical districts. . . . Most such functional areas require good accessibility to that segment of the urban market that is required for their support."[16]

Because this system yields four sets of retail and service establishments, all of which are characterized by distinctive forms of customer usage, we can adopt it in order to classify the business located on Macleod Trail in Calgary, Alberta.

The Macleod Trail

The Macleod Trail is the main north-south artery in Calgary leading south on

15. Berry, *Commercial Structure and Commercial Blight,* p. 23.
16. *Ibid.,* p. 24.

Highway 2 to the United States border and north to the city centre, with connections to the Trans-Canada Highway and to Highway 2 north to Edmonton, the provincial capital. The city of Calgary has been noted for a very rapid rate of postwar growth, increasing from a population of 100,044 in 1946 to 249,641 in 1961. Consequently, most of the city is very new and has grown in an era dominated by the automobile as the means of intra-city transport. The growth of activities on the Macleod Trail has been equally rapid, the number of business establishments along it tripling in number between 1951 and 1963.

The segment of the Macleod Trail examined in this study lies between its intersection with 34th Avenue on the north and 90th Avenue on the south, an overall length of some three miles. Table 1

Table 1. Composition of Macleod Trail and 17th Avenue South, 1963 (Percentage)

| | Establishment Group | | | |
Street	Hier-archic	High-way-oriented	Urban Arterial	Special Func-tional
Macleod Trail	21.2	49.2	12.7	16.9
17th Avenue South	62.7	12.8	21.3	3.2

shows the percentage breakdown of the Macleod Trail establishments into the four groups recognized by Berry. The establishments located in a regional shopping centre at 66th Avenue (Chinook Shopping Centre) are not included in the content analysis, although it will be seen that they form a significant part of the study of customer use patterns. A similar breakdown is given for 17th Avenue South, providing a comparison between the Trail and a ribbon which is older, close to the central business district, and not on a major inter-city route. The actual composition of each major group on the Trail is given in Table 2, and the group distribution is shown on Figure 1.

The analysis shows that establishments

Table 2. Composition of Each Establishment Group on McLeod Trail

Hierarchic		Highway-oriented		Urban Arterial		Special Functional	
Grocery, super-		Gas station	24	Auto repairs and		Automobile,	
market, drug		Restaurant,*		accessories	11	truck and	
store, general		cafe, drive-in	14	Lumber	1	trailer sales	20
store	8	Motor hotel/		Appliances	1		
Bank, post office	5	motel	20	Home repairs	2		
Beauty/barber	3			Recreation	1		
Real estate	5						
Hardware	4						
Clothing	1						
Totals	26		58		16		20

* Berry recognizes restaurants as occurring in both *hierarchic* and *highway-oriented* conformations. In this study we have allocated the restaurants to the *highway-oriented* group because of their location on the ribbon. The wisdom of this decision is questioned later.

in all four of Berry's conformations are well represented on the Trail. It would be possible to group these establishments into a series of spatially discrete centres, as has been done in a number of recent studies on other cities.[17] However, in these studies the break points recognized between centres have been based on some standard distance measure which is usually somewhat arbitrarily selected, and which therefore would appear to have questionable validity in the present context where movement is predominantly by automobile. Consequently, it is felt that centres should be recognized on the basis of customer linkages rather than physical proximity of establishments.

Customer Movement

If we consider the establishments on Macleod Trail as falling into four distinct

17. These comprise three studies: F. W. Boal, "An Analysis of Retail Business Location and Customer Movement in Ann Arbor, Michigan" (unpub. Ph.D. dissertation, Univ. of Michigan, 1963); D. B. Johnson, "A Functional Comparison of the Central Business District with Two Regional Shopping Centers in Calgary, Alberta" (unpub. Masters thesis, Univ. of Alberta, 1963); J. D. Nystuen, "Geographical Analysis of Customer Movements and Retail Business Locations" (unpub. Ph.D. dissertation, Univ. of Washington, 1959).

groups, it follows from the classification system itself and the assumptions built into it that one should expect to find distinct customer use patterns associated with the establishments in each of the four groups. In order that the validity of these assumptions in the present empirical context could be checked, a survey of customers using selected establishments on the Trail was carried out. Because, as Foster and Nelson noted at the conclusion of their study of Ventura Boulevard, "what is really needed is a route [flow] map of actual purchasers, correlated with the additional stops made during the particular trip,"[18] the survey was designed to obtain this information, each customer interviewed being asked to trace his shopping trip route on a city map. Data on trip origins and destinations and on mode of travel were also obtained. The survey was carried out over a period of four days in July 1963. Table 3 provides information on the types of establishments, number of interviews obtained, and mode of travel used by interviewees.

The interview establishments selected

18. G. J. Foster and H. J. Nelson, *Ventura Boulevard: A String-Type Shopping Street* (Real Estate Research Program, Bureau of Business and Economic Research, Univ. of California, L.A., 1958), p. 59.

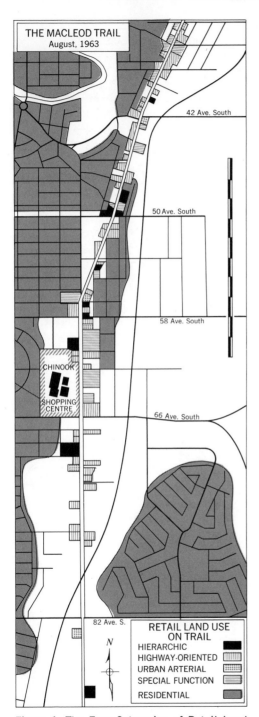

Figure 1. The Four Categories of Retail Land Use on the Macleod Trail, 1963

Table 3. Interview Establishments, Number of Interviews, and Mode of Travel to Establishment, Macleod Trail, 1963

Interview Establishment	Number of Interviews	Mode of Travel (%)			
		Auto	Bus	Walk	Other
Bank	61	68.9	1.7	24.6	4.8
Grocery	108	50.9	5.6	35.2	8.3
Supermarket	170	91.8	–	7.1	1.1
Restaurant	75	89.5	–	6.6	3.9
Inner gas station	61	90.3	–	–	9.7
Outer gas station	70	98.6	–	–	1.4
Drive-in eats	93	98.8	–	–	1.2
Used car lot	40	82.5	–	17.5	–

provide data on three out of the four groups outlined in the previous section of this paper. *Urban arterial* establishments are excluded because their low volume of customers during a given time period would not provide a sufficient sample to justify analysis. Two gas stations were selected to provide comparative data on two different locations on the Trail. The interviews were carried out over a series of two-hour periods to cover from 2 P.M. to 9 P.M. on weekdays, and Saturday mornings and afternoons. Times at the bank had to be adjusted to fit banking hours.

Analysis of Customer Use Patterns

The various studies of ribbon streets suggest that the main elements of customer use patterns are as follows: (1) many establishments serve the needs of passing traffic; (2) particularly at nodal or "bead" positions, many establishments serve surrounding hinterlands; (3) certain establishments serve neither passing traffic nor surrounding areas, but are oriented to a city-wide clientele; (4) *highway-oriented* and *urban arterial* establishments on a given ribbon are held to have no functional linkages with other establishments on the same ribbon, but the *hierarchic* and *special functional* types are expected to have linkages with other establishments in the conformations to which they belong.

Interview data from customers using the sample establishments on the Macleod Trail have been examined to see whether the above customer use patterns emerge. This examination was based on classifying the trips made by the interviewees into seven trip types. The trip classification was drawn up to enable distinction of trips associated with through traffic from those which had specific objectives on the Trail itself. In addition, the classification takes into account the extent and nature of linkages between establishments on the Trail, and whether links are pedestrian or automotive in nature. The trip categories are specified below and illustrated in Figure 2.

Trip Classification:

Sa. A special trip to interview establishment on Trail. The shopper calls only at the interview establishment and then proceeds back to the origin of the trip, or to a destination located such that the interview establishment could not be interpreted as being conveniently on the route to that destination.

Sb. Similar to *Sa* in that only one stop is made on the Trail. In this case, however, other stops may be made elsewhere in the city. The trip structure is such that a definite diversion from a more general trip is made to reach the interview establishment.

S-Lw. A trip to more than one establishment on the Trail. However, although travel to the Trail may be by any means, the travel between all establishments visited on the Trail must be on foot. Consequently, the establishments visited are in close proximity. This type of trip is interpreted as being "special" to the interview establishment's immediate area and not associated with its accessibility to passing traffic. The external relationships of this type must be the same as those for *Sa* and *Sb*.

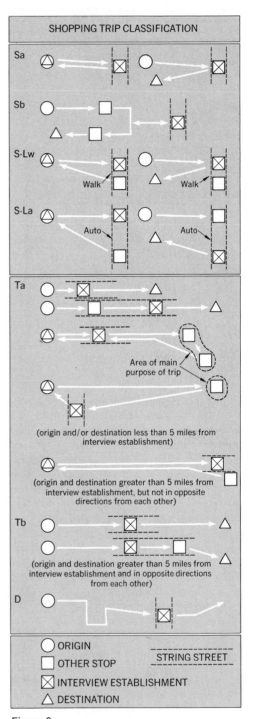

Figure 2

S-La. A trip made specially to the Trail but not necessarily specially to the interview establishment. At least two stops are made on the Trail and the establishments visited are linked by automobile. The external relationships of this trip must be the same as those for types *Sa, Sb,* and *S-Lw.*

Ta. A trip with one or more stops on the Trail. The trip structure is such that the journey can be interpreted as one using the Trail or part of the Trail as a through route. This type is associated mainly with internal traffic in the city proceeding from origin to other stops and/or destinations in such a way that the Trail provides a convenient route. Excluded from this category are the major through trips (*Tb*) as defined below.

Tb. A trip with one or more stops on the Trail. The trip structure is such that the journey can be interpreted as one using the Trail as a through route *and* such that the origin and destination of the trip are (a) each at least five miles from the interview establishment; and (b) lying in opposite directions from the interview establishment.

D. "Driving around": a person making this trip has no immediate purpose or destination in mind when he is interviewed. The route taken to the interview establishment is known, but the future route is uncertain.

The trips are recognized as falling into three basic groups: those that are interpreted as being specifically to the interview establishment or its immediate area (*Sa, Sb,* and *S-Lw*); those specially to the Trail, but not necessarily specially to the interview establishment (*S-La*); and those in which the Trail is used as a "through" route (*Ta, Tb,* and *D*). The breakdown of trip types for each of the interview establishments is shown in Figure 3 and a summary of the findings in Table 4.

The three *hierarchic* establishments (bank, grocery, and supermarket) together with the restaurant have the highest proportions of special trips. They are also the only establishments with "walking links" (*S-Lw* trips) to other establishments on the Trail. Examination of the through trips (*Ta, Tb, D*) shows that the two gas stations and the drive-in

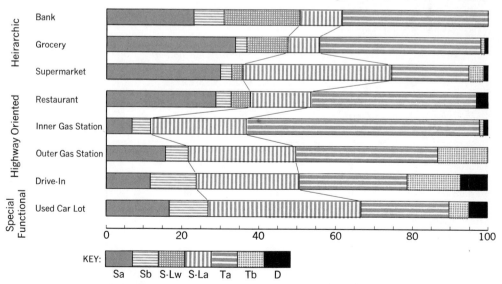

Figure 3. Percentage Breakdown of Trip Types to Each Sample Establishment (The trip types are defined in the text.)

register the highest proportions, all three being *highway-oriented* functions. The trips interpreted as special trips to the Trail (*S-La*) bring another element into the picture, the regional shopping centre. The supermarket, outer gas station, and drive-in are linked by automobile with this centre in a relatively high proportion of trips (Table 4). These linkages illustrate the important influence that a large nucleated centre has on a commercial ribbon. The used car lot is quite distinct from the other interview establishments, having a fairly good balance of special trips, through trips, and special trips to the Trail. The trip types associated with the restaurant place it in an anomalous position in that although it was originally classified as a *highway-oriented* establishment the trips suggest that it has equal affinity for the *hierarchic* group.

The trip classification thus discloses that the *hierarchic* types of establishments are those most closely associated with special trips either to the establishments itself or to some other point on the ribbon. Conversely the *highway-oriented* establishments are those most clearly associated with through trips. The restaurant, which was classified as *highway-oriented,* would appear to be transitional between that type and the *hierarchic.* In addition, the used car lot, classified in the *special functional* group, demonstrates many of the trip characteristics assumed to be associated with this group. Generally, these results confirm the findings of previous studies.

It must be noted, however, that the *hierarchic* establishments are associated with a very considerable proportion of through trips while the *highway-oriented* are in turn associated with a large number of special trips. Thus, although in terms of main emphasis, one should classify these two establishment types by association with one trip type, this procedure fails to give a true picture of the functional nature of any of the establishments studied. In fact what happens is that the *hierarchic* establishments demonstrate a considerable dependence on passing traffic, while the *highway-oriented* types gain from visits made specifically to them or to other establishments on the ribbon because of their accessible loca-

Table 4. Classification of Trips to Sample Ribbon Establishments (Percentage of All Trips)

Interview Establishment	Special Trip to Establishment (Sa, Sb, S-Lw)	Special Trip to Establishment or Special Trip to Trail (Sa, Sb, S-Lw, S-La)		Through Trip* (Ta, Tb, D)
		No Regional Centre Connection	Regional Centre Connection Included	
Bank	51	52	62	38
Grocery	48	51	56	44
Supermarket	36	40	75	25
Restaurant	38	47	54	46
Inner gas station	12	30	37	63
Outer gas station	22	26	50	50
Drive-in	24	31	51	49
Used car lot	27	60	67	33

* Ninety-five per cent confidence limits for the "through trip" percentages were calculated for those interview establishments for which the sampling ratio was available. The following ranges were yielded: bank ± 10.3; grocery ± 8.2; inner gas station ± 8.7; outer gas station ± 6.8; used car lot ± 3.9.

tion in the urban area. In sum, the two main establishment types are characterized by a very considerable functional overlap.

Linkages on the Trail

The trips thus classified can be examined further in terms of their connections with other establishments on the Macleod Trail. These data are presented in Table 5 and indicate that, on the average, about 40 per cent of all trips had at least one other stop on the Trail. The used car lot is particularly high in its level of connection with other establishments on the

Table 5. Multiple Stop Trips
(Per 100 Trips)

Interview Establishment	Stops Anywhere in City	Stops on Trail	Stops on Trail Excluding Chinook Centre
Bank	70.5	41.0	27.9
Grocery	51.8	32.4	22.2
Supermarket	64.6	51.1	6.5
Restaurant	68.0	25.0	15.8
Inner gas station	68.8	34.4	27.8
Outer gas station	67.2	39.6	8.6
Drive-in eats	73.1	41.0	14.0
Used car lot	90.0	60.0	47.5

Trail, and is obviously of quite a different nature from the other interview establishments.

When those trips with stops only at the regional shopping centre are excluded, a significant drop in contact between establishments along the Trail is observed. This decrease is most marked in the case of those establishments near the centre, namely the supermarket, drive-in, and outer gas station. These establishments functionally are strongly tied to the regional centre, though the latter exerts an influence throughout the Trail.

The linkages between establishments can be further analyzed by classifying the other calls according to the four conformation types which were described previously (see Table 6). It can be seen that none of the interview establishments have significant ties with *urban arterial* establishments on the Trail. The links with *special functional* types are also low, the used car lot being the outstanding exception. This latter feature emphasizes quite clearly that the nature of used car lot functioning on a ribbon involves a great deal of comparative shopping from lot to lot.

All of the interview establishments have somewhat stronger links with *high-*

Table 6. Other Retail Stops on the Macleod Trail According to Group
(Per 100 Trips)

Interview Establishment	Other Retail Stops			
	Hierarchic*	Highway-oriented	Special Functional	Urban Arterial
Bank	28.0 (14.7)	18.0	—	—
Grocery	30.6 (20.4)	12.0	6.5	0.9
Supermarket	52.5 (7.7)	3.5	—	0.5
Restaurant	16.5 (1.3)	5.3	9.2	—
Inner gas station	16.4 (9.8)	13.1	5.0	1.6
Outer gas station	37.1 (7.1)	7.1	—	4.3
Drive-in eats	37.5 (10.8)	2.2	2.2	3.2
Used car lot	17.5 (5.0)	20.0	92.5	—

* The numbers in parentheses are hierarchic stops which exclude those at regional shopping centre.
Note: a stop at the regional centre counts one stop even though a number of establishments may have been visited in the centre.

way-oriented establishments, but even here the contact level is never higher than twenty trips in one hundred. In fact some of the *highway-oriented* connections are probably misleading. For example, the evidence presented previously in the paper indicated that the interview restaurant had as much affinity for the *hierarchic* group of establishments as for the *highway-oriented*. This distinction is particularly important in the case of the bank and grocery, both of which are located in a cluster of shops with two restaurants attached.

The most significant contacts of the interview establishments with other establishments on the Trail are with those of the *hierarchic* type. This is true for all interview establishments with the exception of the used car lot, independent of the group to which they belong. All interview establishments have links with the regional centre, and, as noted previously, the links are much more marked for those in close proximity to this centre. Two principal kinds of contact with *hierarchic* establishments can be distinguished:

(1) Contact of *hierarchic* establishments with others of the same functional group in a nearby cluster or centre—the bank and grocery with other establishments in the cluster at 50th Avenue, and the supermarket with the regional shopping centre which is about 200 yards distant.

(2) Contact of *highway-oriented* establishments with *hierarchic* establishments in the regional centre. This linkage applies to the drive-in and outer gas station, both of which appear to have a service relationship to the centre.

The three remaining interview establishments have lower levels of *hierarchic* contact, the used car lot being linked with other used car lots, and the restaurant and inner gas station, neither of which are near to *hierarchic* groups, actually having their strongest contact with the central business district about two miles to the northwest.

These patterns, together with the types of linkages discussed above, suggest that, in so far as the interview establishments have other contacts on the Trail at all, a number of subdivisions of the ribbon may be made:

(1) The Trail functions as a "linear shopping centre" in the case of used car sales.

(2) Portions of the Trail function as shopping nuclei. The bank and grocery at 50th Avenue are functionally part of a cluster of predominantly *hierarchic* establishments, while the supermarket is linked in a similar way to the regional shopping centre.

(3) Some establishments provide service functions to shopping nuclei. Evidence is provided by the outer gas station and the drive-in showing that these establishments are linked in this way to the regional shopping centre.

(4) Some establishments have dispersed connections throughout the ribbon, no clear build up of contact occurring at any particular point. The inner gas station and the restaurant display this characteristic.

Conclusion

The most important set of characteristics to emerge from the study of the Macleod Trail are those associated with overlap in terms of both locational and functional attributes. If we employ the screening technique introduced by Rannells in his study of the city core,[19] it is possible to view the Trail, on one hand, as a series of locations with varying attributes suitable for a wide range of establishments, and, on the other, as a series of establishments characterized by a variety of functional mixes (Figure 4).

Thus, although each establishment on

19. J. Rannells, *The Core of the City: A Pilot Study of Changing Land Use in Central Business Districts* (Columbia Univ. Press, 1956), pp. 147-51.

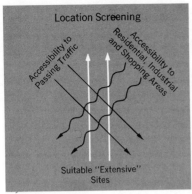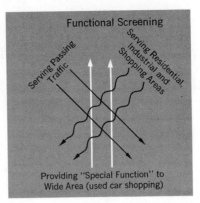

Figure 4. Locational and Functional "Screening" of Establishments on Commercial Ribbons

the ribbon may have its own particular locational emphasis, and at the same time a particular functional emphasis, location on the ribbon introduces varying degrees of functional overlap for all establishments. Each establishment serves unique combinations of passing traffic *and* nearby residential, industrial, and shopping areas. To classify any particular establishment on such a ribbon as *highway-oriented* or *hierarchic* is to express only part of the truth. In fact *hierarchic* businesses on the ribbon depend to a significant extent on passing traffic, while *highway-oriented* establishments draw considerable numbers of customers from nearby residential, industrial, and shopping areas. The *special functional* establishment, as noted throughout this study, has its own functional characteristics, but still cannot be considered in isolation from the effects of both passing traffic and nearby residential, industrial, and shopping areas.

Implications

The application of the central place concept to the commercial ribbon would seem to be quite legitimate but operationally complex because of the mixture of establishment types and their functional overlap. In the case of the Macleod Trail we are dealing neither with linear hinterlands nor with hinterlands of a nodal na-

ture, but with varying combinations of these types. In fact each establishment on the ribbon would appear to attain minimum (threshold) size of hinterland by a particular combination of these two types of hinterlands. This characteristic must be true for nearly all retail and service establishments whether on ribbons or elsewhere, but in the case of the larger nucleated centres passing traffic is probably of marginal significance, while, in the case of inter-urban highways with small surrounding populations, passing traffic provides a dominant source of customers.[20]

Clearly, commercial ribbons perform vital functions in the retail and service structure of urban areas. Planning should concentrate less on abolishing this type of linear commercial development, and more on ameliorating its obvious disadvantages (1) by trying to prevent the entry of an excessive number of establishments (principally by cutting down on the vast areas of "highway commercial zoning"); (2) by trying to achieve better design of individual establishments in terms of both visual characteristics and accessibility; and (3) by improving the over-all design of the ribbons themselves.

20. However, special trips from neighbouring areas are made in considerable volume to service plazas on the English super highway system; see *Sunday Times* (London), June 6, 1965.

ALLAN R. PRED

The Intrametropolitan Location of American Manufacturing

The ten largest metropolitan areas in the the United States, each comprised of an area of several thousand square miles and a population in excess of two million[1] (Table 1) have a distribution of manufacturing within their respective boundaries which is not only remarkable in its diversity, but also in its apparent geographical chaos. To the casual observer the landscape of the great American metropolis appears to be haphazardly peppered with manufacturing activities of every description, with factories of every magnitude. However, beneath this superficial disorder and confusion, certain spatial regularities can be discerned if the structure of metropolitan manufacturing is viewed in terms of its evolution, the local friction of distance, and broad in-

dustrial categories which express similar locational tendencies.[2]

Evolution: The Pattern Before "Industrial Revolution"

The colonial and pre-industrial revolution predecessors of the multi-million metropolis were little more than small towns. The manufacturing of each town was carried out in a relatively small circumscribed area which closely corresponds with the center of today's metropolis. This dominance of the central area has at least in part been perpetuated to the present;[3] i.e., the earliest intraurban manu-

1. Although two million may be interpreted as an arbitrary figure by which to define the lower population limits of a metropolitan area, it is not without precedent. Florence has gone so far as to term two million "a clear boundary line." See P. Sargant Florence, "Economic Efficiency in the Metropolis," in Robert M. Fisher, ed., *The Metropolis in Modern Life* (New York: 1955), p. 86.

2. The intrametropolitan distribution of all economic phenomena generally confronts the uninitiated as a "confused and baffling welter of anomalies and paradoxes." However, it has long been recognized that: "Most of the apparent anomalies and paradoxes dissolve into commonplaces when subjected to serious study and detailed examination." See Robert Murray Haig, *Major Economic Factors in Metropolitan Growth and Arrangement* (New York: Committee on Regional Plan of New York and its Environs, 1927), p. 31.

3. This observation is obviously also applicable to European metropolises; e.g., Kürfurstadt, the

From the **Annals** of the Association of American Geographers, Vol. 54, No. 2, June 1964, pp. 165-174. Reprinted by permission.

Table 1. Selected Democraphic and Industrial Characteristics of
Major American Metropolises

Metropolitan Area	1960 Population	1960[1] Population Within a 50-Mile Radius	1961 All Manu-facturing Employees	1961 Production Workers	1961 Value Added by Manu-facturing ($1,000)
New York–northeastern New Jersey	14,759,429	15,566,745	1,789,371	1,211,072	17,483,645
Chicago–northwestern Indiana	6,794,461	6,901,844	933,381	643,504	10,418,538
Los Angeles	6,742,696	7,048,004	769,317	511,875	8,325,279
Philadelphia	4,342,897	5,759,612	550,889	387,997	5,445,784
Detroit	3,762,360	4,165,910	449,578	291,468	5,138,660
San Francisco–Oakland–San Jose[2]	3,425,674	3,577,349	274,233	171,503	3,323,966
Boston	2,589,301	5,089,280	328,338	219,355	3,056,319
Pittsburgh	2,405,435	3,355,787	280,514	184,842	2,705,880
St. Louis	2,060,103	2,267,573	250,369	172,005	2,679,258
Cleveland[3]	1,796,595	3,070,692	260,406	180,121	2,806,751
		Total	5,886,396	3,973,742	61,384,080
		U.S. Total	16,347,785	11,794,536	163,801,084
		% of U.S. Total	36.0	33.7	37.5

Sources: *Census of Population,* 1960 (Washington, D. C.: 1961); "Population within 50 Miles of Selected Points: 1960," Geographic Reports, GE-10, No. 1 (April, 1963); and *1961 Annual Survey of Manufactures,* Bureau of the Census (Washington, D.C.: 1962–1963).

[1] These figures, unlike those in the first column, serve as a consistent basis of comparison.

[2] The San Jose Standard Metropolitan Statistical Area is included with the San Francisco–Oakland SMSA because there is a considerable amount of manufacturing which occurs in a continuous belt overlapping the two units. In addition, the two SMSAs have coalesced, most noticeably on the west side of San Francisco Bay, and can for some purposes be regarded as a single unit.

[3] Washington, D.C. is actually the tenth most populous SMSA but, as it is an anomaly with less than 21,000 manufacturing employees, it does not merit consideration with the more industrially complex areas discussed in this paper.

facturing districts have usually been zones of considerable inertia.

Early craft industries were largely confined to the household and nearby waterfront workshops. Because of the length of the working day, and because distance was to be overcome only by horse or foot, the gunsmith, the tailor, the printer, the chandler, and the shipwright were all forced to choose a place of residence which was near the place of work.[4] The commanding position of the waterfront derived from the fact that in every colo-

nial town "the principal industries were those that had to do with shipping and the preparation of provisions or naval stores for export."[5] Shipbuilding was quickly established as a vital waterfront activity in seventeenth century Boston, New York, and Philadelphia; and it was of initial significance in centers founded

oldest nucleus of Berlin, is partially occupied by the textile industry, and small-scale industry abounds in the heart of Vienna. See Robert E. Dickinson, *The West European City* (London: 1960), pp. 191, 242.

4. Many general statements have been made which would indicate that this phenomenon was nearly universal prior to the beginning of mechanized transport. See Harlan W. Gilmore, *Transportation and the Growth of Cities* (Glencoe: The Free Press, 1953), p. 112; and Gideon Sjoberg, *The Preindustrial City* (Glencoe: The Free Press, 1960), pp. 101-103.

5. Carl Bridenbaugh, *Cities in the Wilderness: The First Century of Urban Life in America 1625-1742* (New York: 1955), p. 182.

somewhat later, such as Pittsburgh and Cleveland.[6] Contemporary accounts of the seventeenth and eighteenth centuries relate the importance of rum distilling, sugar refining, and rope making around the tidewaters of Mill Pond in Boston, near the Hudson and East Rivers in New York, and on the banks of the Schuykill and the Delaware in Philadelphia.[7] In Chicago, where the population did not reach 4,000 until 1837, early industrial development began along the two branches of the Chicago River, and initially concentrated upon "the making of sails and spars, oars and pumps, mast loops and blocks, belaying pins and levers."[8] Of course, manufacturing was not entirely restricted to the household and the waterfront workshop. For example, by 1637 wind-powered flour mills and sawmills were operating in New Amsterdam (the Dutch antecedent of New York) and a steel furnace was producing in downtown Philadelphia prior to 1730.[9]

The Early "Industrial Revolution"

As time passes, and as there are concomitant increases in area and population, the urban industrial structure has a tendency to increase in its spatial complexity.[10]

Technological innovations and the expanding local market constantly proliferate new industries, each of which generally expresses distinctive locational characteristics. In the American experience this growing complexity became apparent with the introduction of the factory system, power-driven machinery, interchangeable parts, and other mass production techniques during the late eighteenth and early nineteenth centuries. Water power was then essential to the large-scale functioning of wool and cotton textile mills, and this prerequisite often dictated location at rural waterfall sites, such as in Waltham, Massachusetts, and in Paterson, New Jersey, many of which have since become absorbed into the Boston and New York Metropolitan Areas.[11] Whereas the development of nearby large-scale rural industries was most characteristic of the cities of the eastern seaboard, it was also sometimes associated with the centers founded later in the mid- and far west; e.g., most of the early blast furnaces operating by 1825 in the Pittsburgh area had riverside locations outside of the city.

At the same time, industries which were not dependent upon water power continued to expand in areas near the center of the modern metropolis. Fundamentally, "the factory system was a city development."[12] Even the largest production facilities were not distant from the contemporary core of the metropolis.

6. J. Leander Bishop, *A History of American Manufactures from 1608 to 1860* (Philadelphia: 1861-1866), Vol. 1, pp. 38-39, 59-60, 69, and Vol. 2, p. 89; and James H. Kennedy, *A History of the City of Cleveland* (Cleveland: 1896), p. 139.

7. For example, see the sources cited by Walter Muir Whitehall, *Boston—A Topographical History* (Cambridge: 1959), p. 48; and Bridenbaugh, *op. cit.,* p. 337.

8. Bessie Louise Pierce, *A History of Chicago* (New York: 1937), Vol. 1, p. 145.

9. Bishop, *op. cit.,* Vol. 1, pp. 105 and 119; and Carl Bridenbaugh, *The Colonial Craftsman* (Chicago: 1961), p. 84.

10. Naturally, in the process of urban growth not merely manufacturing but all land uses undergo "a development from the simple to the complex, . . ." See Robert D. McKenzie, "The Ecological Approach to the Study of the Human Community," in Robert E. Park, *et al.,* *The City* (Chicago: 1925), p. 73.

11. The eventual absorption of mill villages into metropolitan areas is a process which is not to be confused with the consolidation of medium-sized cities, such as Fall River, Massachusetts, around essentially rural mills. For a discussion of the predominantly rural origins of the cotton and woolen textile industries see Victor S. Clark, *History of Manufactures in the United States* (New York: 1929), Vol. 1, pp. 533-575; Margaret Terrell Parker, *Lowell: A Study of Industrial Development* (New York: 1940).

12. George Rogers Taylor, *The Transportation Revolution: 1815-1860* (New York: 1951), p. 233.

Typically, Philadelphia's first locomotive was built in 1828 in the heart of the modern central business district.[13]

During the earliest phases of the "industrial revolution," the limited physical mobility of the working force and the modest scale of urban agglomerations were still the keystones of intraurban industrial location. The friction of distance usually confined the industrial workers' residences to a specialized quarter adjacent to the factory.[14]

The Initial Consequences of Transport Innovations

The extension and intensification of the national railroad network in the mid- and late nineteenth century reinforced the industrial significance of the central areas in the largest urban concentrations. Although most of the cities in question had attained a population of several hundred thousand, land costs in those areas abutting upon the emerged central business districts were not inordinately high. Furthermore, the concentrations of new large-scale industries adjacent to the central business districts were logical consequences of the construction of rail terminal facilities in these same areas. Wholesaling activities rapidly became associated with rail terminal districts which offered direct access to goods brought in from distant points, proximity to the area where most business was transacted, and a location which came close to providing minimum local distribution costs. In an age when wholesaling and manufacturing were more closely associated than they are today, it was perhaps inevitable that many industrial entrepreneurs expressed

and implemented a preference for rail terminal district locations.[15] The railroad was particularly influential in the evolution of manufacturing districts near the core of midwestern metropolises; e.g., by the 1870's "The Flats" of Cleveland and the Union Stock Yards of Chicago were prominent features in their respective urban landscapes.[16]

The transport innovations of the nineteenth century also had profound ramifications for the scale and diversity of manufacturing within the growing metropolis. "Technological advances in transportation, and particularly the introduction of steam power, led to substantial reductions in the cost of transport inputs, which theoretically meant a spreading out of critical isodapanes, and an opportunity to realize previously untapped scale-economies—even in the absence of advances in production technology."[17] This extension and enlargement of the firm's market area increased the feasibility of agglomeration and large-scale production (a tendency further compounded by concurrent innovations of production technology), created the possibility of still further mass production economies, and consequently resulted in the downfall of many small-

13. John Rannells, *The Core of the City* (New York: Columbia University Press, 1956), p. 73.
14. Note Warner's recent analysis of Philadelphia's residential patterns during the 1830's. Sam B. Warner, "Innovation and the Industrialization of Philadelphia," in Oscar Handlin and John Burchard, eds., *The Historian and the City* (Cambridge: 1963), p. 68.

15. It is revealing to make a comparison with Weber's observation on the effect of railroads in Europe in the late nineteenth century. He contended that rail transport was so economical that "highways" no longer had "any independent locational significance at all; their function is rather that of a subsidiary of the railway system." Within this framework the railway station or terminal assumed pre-eminent importance in shaping local industrial location. Alfred Weber, *Theory of the Location of Industries* (Chicago: 1929), pp. 86-87. A translation with introduction and notes by Carl J. Friedrich of *Über den Standort der Industien* (Tübingen: 1909).
16. Kennedy, *op cit.*, and Pierce, *op. cit.*, Vol. 2, pp. 92-93.
17. Allan Pred, *The External Relations of Cities during "Industrial Revolution"* (Chicago: University of Chicago, Department of Geography, Research Paper no. 76, N.A.S.-N.R.C. Foreign Field Research Report no. 14, 1962), p. 31.

scale industries, particularly the rural domestic industries, serving limited local markets.[18] In short, large-scale factories ceased to be an oddity and the land pressures which later led to the decentralization of manufacturing began to mount. The greater concentration of industrial activities in large cities, coupled with an expanding population that was constantly satisfying new demand thresholds, logically meant a more varied array of products. By 1860, for example, there were 155 industries in Philadelphia which employed no less than 98,000 people in 6,314 establishments.[19]

Early Evidence of Decentralization

Even by the late nineteenth century, before the widespread utilization of rapid transit and the coming of automotive transportation, evidence was accumulating to show that the paramount industrial importance of the core of the emerging metropolises was a temporary phenomenon.[20] Land was becoming increasingly scarce and expensive in the urban core, where local taxes and nuisance legislation were also proving less conducive to the establishment of truly massive production facilities. Individual corporations began to erect plants in outlying districts during the 'eighties and 'nineties. The success of solitary establishments in such places as

Pullman, then peripheral to Chicago, and Granite City, across the Mississippi from St. Louis, quickly attracted other firms to the same suburbs.[21] However, as it was still mandatory for factory workers to travel minimal distances, the construction of residences with company funds was usually an attendant requisite to the founding of isolated suburban production facilities.

Some alteration already had taken place in journey-to-work patterns, and not all laborers still lived near their place of work. As early as the 1850's, plank roads had precipitated "tentacles" of urban growth in Chicago; commuter trains were running between West Newton and Boston in 1843; New York's five principal street railways carried about 100,000 passengers per day in 1858; Philadelphia's first street railway began operating in 1857; and similar service commenced in Cleveland in 1860.[22] In Boston, Irish laborers were encouraged to move to new residential areas by the spread of horse-car lines in the 1850's.[23] Despite these developments, short-distance commuting patterns remained prevalent. Nineteenth century transport restricted almost all commuting to a radius of a few miles around the place of work. Evidence collected in New York indicates that daily trips up to a few miles were characteristic of laborers with relatively high wages and relatively short working hours.[24]

In summary, about 1900, the absence of an intricate rapid transit network, and

18. For a more elaborate analysis of the economic forces leading to the urban agglomeration of manufacturing during this period of time see *ibid.*, pp. 29-37; Weber, *op. cit.*, pp. 124-172; Alfred Marshall, *Principles of Economics,* 8th ed. (New York: 1948), pp. 265-282; and Adna Ferrin Weber, *The Growth of Cities in the Nineteenth Century* (Ithaca: 1963), pp. 185-209—originally published in 1899.
19. Bishop, *op. cit.*, Vol. 3, pp. 14-17. Based on a revision of the Census of 1860.
20. In large metropolitan areas the relative "dominance of the major city in manufacturing employment has tended to lessen significantly since 1879." Glenn E. McLaughlin, *Growth of American Manufacturing Areas* (Pittsburgh: Bureau of Business Research, University of Pittsburgh, 1938), p. 127.

21. For greater details see Graham Romeyn Taylor, *Satellite Cities—A Study of Industrial Suburbs* (New York: 1915).
22. Homer Hoyt, "The Influence of Highways and Transportation on the Structure and Growth of Cities and Urban Land Values," in Jean Labatut and Wheaton J. Lane, *eds., Highways in Our National Life* (Princeton: 1950), p. 202.
23. Oscar Handlin, *Boston's Immigrants, 1790-1865* (Cambridge: 1941), pp. 99-100.
24. Edward Ewing Pratt, *Industrial Causes of Congestion of Population in New York City* (New York: Columbia University Studies in History, Economics and Public Law, 1911), p. 188.

the necessity for manufacturers to build even the most slipshod of laborers' quarters, often acted as powerful deterrents to the suburban diffusion of manufacturing. The metropolitan core and manufacturing were still nearly synonymous. For example, as late as 1910, 75 per cent of the manufacturing employment in New York City—*not* the entire New York Metropolitan Area—was in Manhattan, and 66.8 per cent of the employment in Manhattan was in the small area south of Fourteenth Street.[25]

Decentralization in the Twentieth Century: Order and Disorder

Only after 1900 was the pattern of downtown industrial concentration emphatically broken by the advent of new industries with new locational patterns.[26] Absolute growth of manufacturing continued within the central city but, by 1910 observers recognized the slow, persistent relative increase of manufacturing in the suburbs.[27] Decentralization has been as

apparent in metropolises founded in the colonial era, such as New York, as in Los Angeles, a child of the late nineteenth century; and in Detroit and in most of the multimillion metropolises the trend has become even more marked during the last decade.[28] The bus, the car, and the commuter railway have terminated the traditional linkage between the place-of-work and the place-of-residence and, at the same time, have magnified the quality and quantity of the individual firm's labor market; i.e., the suburbanization of a major portion of the industrial working force has engendered "intimate daily contacts of one part of the periphery with another as well as the perpetuation of old ties between the periphery and the core."[29]

Furthermore, the efficiency of local and regional movement of finished products has been improved immensely by the advent of the truck. A central location is no longer fundamental to an economically rational distribution of manufactured commodities to the metropolitan market. The multiplication of external diseconomies and the introduction of new production techniques which require "sites of such a size as to be totally impracticable near the core of the city."[30] have both been instrumental in encouraging new industries to locate at the periphery of the metropolis where they can avoid the unnecessary transport inputs associated with distribution from a point of congestion. Centrifugal forces have considerably broadened the spectrum of locational alternatives, a fact that is reflected in the

25. *Ibid.*, pp. 41-42.

26. The volume of literature on the suburbanization of manufacturing is imposing in size and only the more pertinent works are cited here: Jean Gottmann, *Megalopolis* (New York: 1961), pp. 482-487; Tracy E. Thompson, *Location of Manufactures: 1899-1929* (Washington, D.C.: Bureau of the Census, 1933), pp. 29-43; Amos H. Hawley, *The Changing Shape of Metropolitan America: Deconcentration Since 1920* (Glencoe: The Free Press, 1956), pp. 114 and 130-145; Daniel B. Creamer, *Is Industry Decentralizing?* (Philadelphia: 1935); Evelyn M. Kitagawa and Donald J. Bogue, *Suburbanization of Manufacturing Activity* within *Standard Metropolitan Areas* (Oxford: Scripps Foundation for Research in Population Problems, and the Population Research and Training Center, 1955); Coleman Woodbury, "Industrial Location and Urban Redevelopment," in *The Future of Cities and Urban Redevelopment* (Chicago: 1953), pp. 205-288; and Leo F. Schnore, "Metropolitan Growth and Decentralization," *American Journal of Sociology,* Vol. 63 (1957), pp. 171-180.

27. For example see Adna Ferrin Weber, *op. cit.*, p. 202; and Rene Maunier, *La Localisation des Industries Urbaines* (Paris: V. Giard et E. Briere, 1909), pp. 235-274.

28. See the tables in Benjamin Chinitz, *Freight and the Metropolis* (Cambridge: Harvard University Press, 1960), pp. 131 and 138; and comments in Dudley F. Pegrum, *Urban Transport and the Location of Industry in Metropolitan Los Angeles* (Los Angeles: U.C.L.A., Bureau of Business and Economic Research, 1963), p. 45.

29. James E. Vance, Jr., "Labor-Shed, Employment Field, and Dynamic Analysis in Urban Geography," *Economic Geography,* Vol. 36 (1960), p. 218.

30. Vance, *op. cit.*, p. 193.

continued decline of the percentage of manufacturing plants located at rail sidings in the New York Metropolitan Area.[31]

In addition, as the modern metropolis has coalesced, formerly rural industries have frequently been engulfed, overrun, and integrated into the new urban complex. For example, the mills of the Charles and Merrimac Valleys became part of the Boston Metropolitan Area; those of the Passaic Valley became encompassed by the New York Metropolitan Area; and the tanneries of Redwood City were drawn into the confines of the San Francisco Bay urbanized area.

Ostensibly, the intrametropolitan distribution of manufacturing has decentralized considerably and has assumed a Babel-like disorder of enormous proportions. However, not all industries have decentralized to noncentral and peripheral areas of the metropolis; nor have all of those industries decentralized identically. The forces of inertia and precedent have left a deep imprint on the industrial landscape of the modern metropolis. Therefore, two crucial questions should be answered if any order is to be attributed to the intrametropolitan location of American manufacturing: What kinds of industries remain in or near the core of the metropolis? What patterns, if any, are to be distinguished among the decentralized industries? However, if the proposed answers to these questions are to be seen in their proper perspective, it is first necessary to take a brief look at a few of the more cogent hypotheses regarding the intrametropolitan location of manufacturing.

A Critique of Previous Interpretations of Intrametropolitan Industrial Location

Some of the earliest and most time-resistant theories and empirical generalizations concerning intrametropolitan industrial location have either emphasized the

31. Chinitz, *op. cit.*, p. 136.

availability of transportation facilities or the minimization of local distribution costs (accessibility to the local market). In the extreme case, Weber implied that transportation costs are the sole determinant of industrial orientation within the metropolis by arguing that ". . . exactly the same rules of orientation will be operative in detail which determine the orientation at large for the whole country, with its extensive transportation system. Everything will simply be repeated in miniature."[32]

Similarly, some urban scholars have maintained that: "The center is the point at which transportation costs, for an enterprise serving the entire area, can be reduced to a minimum. Since there is insufficient space at the center to accommodate all the activities which would derive advantages from location there, the most central sites are assigned, for a rental, to those activities which can best utilize the advantages, while the others take the less accessible locations."[33] In a different but related framework, Lösch hypothesized that before complicating elements of price discrimination, competition, and elasticity of demand are introduced, the simplest and most efficient market areas are those which are hexagonal, and have the producer located at the center.[34] However, it is just when realistic market and competitive conditions are introduced that the minimum transportation cost-rent argument collapses. Competitors cannot monopolize a market, so distribution costs to the consumers served, rather than to the entire

32. Alfred Weber, *op. cit.*, p. 87. Weber used the term "railway station unit" instead of metropolis, but the implications are identical. The statement is made before labor orientation and agglomeration economies are introduced to the analytic framework.
33. Haig, *op. cit.*, p. 39. Wendt and others have recently criticized Haig's simplifying assumptions.
34. August Lösch, *The Economics of Location* (New Haven: 1954), pp. 105-137. Translated by William H. Woglom from *Die räumliche Ordnung der Wirtschaft* (Jena: 1940).

market, theoretically assume more importance than locational centrality. The complications of spatial competition in reality are such that Ackley[35] has "shown clearly that no precise generalized solutions emerge, even when rigid assumptions are made as to competitor's reactions."[36] In relation to the problem of intrametropolitan industrial location, the contentions of all the maximum accessibility or central location proponents, and some of the market area theorists, dwindle still further in relevance when it is realized that: The markets served by some metropolitan manufacturers are discontinuous, non-local, and distant; that transport costs are immaterial to site selection decisions in many industries; and that no account is taken of the desirability or undesirability of core locations for specific kinds of industries.

A somewhat less involved construct is one which maintains that all urban functions, including manufacturing, either expand in the center, or along and eventually between, the main transportation axes radiating from the metropolitan core.[37] This truism is valid as far as it goes; but it is inapplicable to a detailed analysis of metropolitan manufacturing because of its imprecision and failure to identify the specific locational tendencies of broad industrial groups. An oversimplified corollary of the axial growth theory is that factories outside of the central area either string themselves out along railroad lines or along water fronts.[38] This partial dichotomy may be dismissed because it ignores the fact that manufacturers "of the less bulky goods need not be located on railroads or water fronts at all, since they can be served by truck."[39]

At least four sets of generalizations regarding the intrametropolitan distribution of manufacturing have been synthesized in simple graphic form. The earliest diagrammatic scheme is associated with Burgess' well-known concentric zone conception of the city. Burgess only went so far as to delimit a zone of mixed wholesaling and "light" manufacturing abutting on the central business district.[40] Whereas it is true that such a manufacturing and wholesaling district exists in some form on the perimeter of all the major metropolises of the United States, the concentric zone hypothesis is woefully inadequate because it completely omits any assessment of manufacturing in other parts of the metropolis. In addition, it has been demonstrated that the theory as a whole has severe pitfalls and drawbacks when compared with reality, even in Chicago where Burgess collected the empirical observations which inspired him.[41] However, it is only fair to mention that some geographers have found it convenient to identify industrial zones or rings at various distances from the core of metropolitan areas in the United States and England.[42] With one exception, the lim-

35. Gardner Ackley, "Spatial Competition in a Discontinuous Market," *Quarterly Journal of Economics,* Vol. 56 (1942), pp. 212-230.
36. Walter Isard, *Location and Space-Economy* (New York: 1956), p. 165.
37. See Richard M. Hurd, *Principles of City Land Values* (New York: The Record and Guide, 1903), pp. 56-59, and 74; and Homer Hoyt, *The Structure and Growth of Residential Neighborhoods in American Cities* (Washington: Government Printing Office, 1939).
38. For example see Richard U. Ratcliff, *Urban Land Economics* (New York: 1949), pp. 386-397; and McKenzie, *op. cit.,* p. 74.
39. Edgar M. Hoover, *The Location of Economic Activity* (New York: 1948), pp. 128-129.
40. Ernest W. Burgess, "The Growth of the City: An Introduction to a Research Project," in Park, *et al., op. cit.,* p. 50.
41. Amongst the more convincing critical estimates of Burgess one might list Maurice R. Davie, "The Pattern of Urban Growth," in George P. Murdock, ed., *Studies in the Science of Society* (New Haven: 1937), pp. 133-161; and Walter Firey, *Land Use in Central Boston* (Cambridge: 1947), pp. 85-86.
42. See for example Martin W. Reinemann, "The Pattern and Distribution of Manufacturing in the Chicago Area," *Economic Geography,* Vol. 36 (1960), pp. 139-144; and M. J. Wise, "On the Evolution of the Jewelry and Gun Quarters in Birmingham," *Transactions and Papers of the Institute of British Geographers,* Vol. 15 (1949), pp. 59-60.

ited evidence presented refers to particular metropolises and there is no pretension to generalizations which might have more widespread applicability. The exception, part of a study of the total urban land-use mix, used "arbitrary" concentric circles and added little, if anything, to pre-existing knowledge on the intraurban location of manufacturing.[43]

A second diagram, devised by Homer Hoyt, is merely a graphic representation of the already discussed axial growth or sector theory. Although it is true in Los Angeles and most other major metropolises that "locational growth and expansion have followed the route patterns laid out by the railroads before the expansion began,"[44] the industrial structure of metropolitan areas is infinitely more complex than the single "light" manufacturing district suggested by Hoyt.

In delineating their "multiple nuclei" theory of urban structure Harris and Ullman intimated that all urban manufacturing is found in "light" manufacturing districts, "heavy" manufacturing districts, or industrial suburbs.[45] The location of metropolitan manufacturing in discrete integral districts, according to Harris and Ullman can be attributed to a combination of four causes: Certain activities require specialized facilities; certain like activities agglomerate because they profit from cohesion; certain unlike activities are incompatible; and certain activities are unable to afford the high rents of the most desirable sites. Although one might contend that a considerable amount of manufacturing occurs at isolated or non-district sites, a more basic weakness underlies this theory. The Harris-Ullman theory implies, and the Burgess and Hoyt

hypotheses suggest, that all industries are either "light" or "heavy," and that the two types are spatially segregated. The distinction between "light" and "heavy" manufacturing has apparently never advanced beyond a dichotomy of small-scale non-nuisance industries versus large-scale nuisance industries,[46] and this fuzzy notion has been unthinkingly perpetuated by land economists, city planners, and geographers alike.[47] Assuming that one was actually willing to accept that "heavy" and "light" manufacturing could be distinguished from one another meaningfully, a field check would usually show these two types of activities to be intermixed in the manufacturing and wholesaling district contiguous to the central business district, as well as in most other industrial districts. Whereas this amounts to a clear indictment of the manufacturing propositions of Harris and Ullman, it should not be overlooked that their thinking on the formation of districts is a useful contribution.

Finally, Isard presents a scheme which is unique because it is not couched in terms of "light" and/or "heavy" manufacturing (Figure 1). The generalizations diagrammatically offered are part of an optimal urban land-use pattern which in the author's own words "represents one of many possible brews of (1) intuition, (2) logic and analytic principles relating to the interaction of general forces gov-

43. Louis K. Loewenstein, "The Location of Urban Land Uses," *Land Economics,* Vol. 39 (1963), pp. 413-415.
44. Pegrum, *op cit.,* p. 33.
45. Chauncy D. Harris and Edward L. Ullman, "The Nature of Cities," *Annals of the American Academy of Political and Social Science,* Vol. 242 (Nov., 1945), pp. 7-17.

46. Haig has come closest to making an explicit and logically consistent distinction between "light" and "heavy" manufacturing, but in so doing he was actually attempting to catalogue the characteristics of those industries which cling to central locations as opposed to those which abandon core sites. See Haig, *op. cit.,* pp. 104-105.
47. For example, see Rannells, *op. cit.,* p. 76; William T. Chambers, "Geographic Areas of Cities," *Economic Geography,* Vol. 7 (1931), pp. 181-182; Robert E. Dickinson, *City Region, and Regionalism* (London: 1947), pp. 125-127; and Harland Bartholomew, *Land Use in American Cities* (Cambridge: 1955), pp. 52-53, and 111.

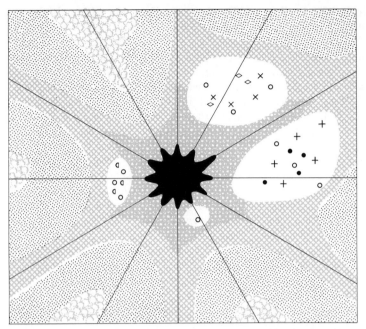

Figure 1. Isard's Optimal Urban Land-use Pattern (Six different industries are represented by a like number of dissimilar symbols. White areas represent industrial districts.)

erning land use, and (3) facts. It is not a rigorous theoretical derivation."[48] Isard's diagram is a cousin of the "multiple nuclei" depiction insofar as all manufacturing is segregated into districts. Perhaps the most significant aspect of the diagram is the concentration of all producers of a given commodity in the same district, except for those commodities which are of a miscellaneous nature or are composed of ubiquitous raw materials. This is a step toward recognizing that individual industries have intrametropolitan distribution patterns which cover a spectrum ranging from highly concentrated to highly dispersed. However, the step falls short because it collapses the spectrum to a dichotomy of completely concentrated and completely ubiquitous industries. Isard's proposal is also unrealistic because there is no manufacturing district immediately adjacent to what appears to be the central business district.

48. Isard, *op. cit.*, p. 280.

There have been countless studies of the manufacturing structure of cities. Few of these have attempted to interpret the entire industrial configuration of a major metropolis from a locational standpoint, and still fewer have made such analyses free from the constraining fetters of the traditional division between "light" or "intensive" industries and "heavy" or "extensive" industries.[49]

Only recently has a more perceptive, yet simple and comprehensible, basis for analysis been devised and implemented. In analyzing the location-elements of what is probably the largest and most involuted arrangement of manufacturing in

49. Of the earlier non-traditional surveys made by geographers, the cooperative work of Swedish scholars on Stockholm is outstanding. See Hans W:son Ahlmann, *et al.*, "Stockholms inre Differentiering," *Meddelanden från Geografiska Institutet vid Stockholm's Högskola,* No. 20 (1934); and a terser statement by W. William-Olsson, "Stockholm: Its Structure and Development," *Geographical Review,* Vol. 30 (1940), pp. 430-433.

the world, the New York Metropolitan Area, Chinitz sorted industrial plants into three broad types: (1) those serving markets which are predominantly local; (2) those serving markets of national extent; and (3) those plants localized by external economies and by definition not subsumed under (1) or (2).[50] The second type was subdivided into finer, more distinct groups, i.e., small plants, and large plants with low-value, medium-value, and high-value products. Also, more specifically, local market industries by definition shipped more than half of their tonnage to points inside the New York Metropolitan Region; and conversely, national-market industries shipped at least half of their tonnage to markets outside the Region.

Since each type and sub-type has different transportation requirements, or different abilities to absorb transport outlays, singular, but not exclusive, locational tendencies emerge. The rationale underlying the grouping by Chinitz is

therefore manifest; but although the typology yields a result which is unquestionable in its penetration, it is not without shortcomings. No appraisal is made of the role of raw material sources and linked wholsaling functions in influencing the location of certain local-market industries; there is little elaboration upon those external-economy industries which frequently exhibit tendencies toward non-central clustering; waterfront industries are neglected as a single cohesive entity; and specific industries, or groups of industries, are not cartographically plotted. Moreover, the work of Chinitz does not represent an effort to generalize for all of the multi-million metropolises of the United States. Nevertheless, a modification of the approach employed by Chinitz offers an excellent starting point from which to answer the two questions previously posed on an earlier page in concluding the evolutionary synopsis: What kinds of industries remain in or near the core of the metropolis? What patterns, if any, are to be distinguished among the decentralized industries?

50. Chinitz, *op. cit.,* pp. 129-157.

RICHARD L. MORRILL AND ROBERT EARICKSON

Variations in the Character and Use of Hospital Services

Some outside observers of the health system are tempted to view hospitals as offering a homogeneous service, patients as having common needs, and the "hospitals problem" as one of the ratio of capacity to demand. Those who are called upon to evaluate in detail the hospital needs of a specific area, however, know that hospitals are not alike, nor are their patients. The Chicago Regional Hospital Study,[1] which aims to provide criteria for evaluation of existing hospital systems and future needs, realized that a first step must be an understanding of the significant variations among hospitals and among their patients that affect their location and use. In a metropolis like Chicago, the more than one hundred hospitals vary greatly in size, specialization, control, religious affiliation, and location; and populations in turn vary in their preference for hospitals of different kinds,

1. de Visé, P. *The Chicago Regional Hospital Study*. Working paper III.1, Chicago Regional Hospital Study, 1963.

their ability to pay, and their location with respect to hospitals.

Two studies are briefly reported here:
1. Estimation of the hierarchy of hospital services—that is, the level of service offered.
2. General classification or grouping of hospitals based on hospital characteristics, service areas, and relative location.

The first study reveals significant distinctions in the level of service offered; facilities and services, kinds of residence and intern programs, size of medical staff, and overall size are the major differentiating characteristics. The second undertakes a principal-components analysis, in which many variables involving hospitals and their patients are reduced to a few major dimensions of variation and hospital groups are then classified on the basis of these dimensions. Groups reflect especially variation in volume of service offered, relative location of hospitals and patients, and scope of service.

From **Health Services Research,** Vol. 3, Fall 1968. Copyright © 1968 by the Hospital Research and Educational Trust, Chicago. Reprinted by permission.

391

Hierarchy of Hospital Services

Hospital services do not constitute a homogeneous output. Some hospitals, typically the smaller ones, have a limited range of facilities and perform a smaller range of services. A few hospitals, usually large, have highly specialized diagnostic and treatment facilities and personnel and are able to handle unusual and difficult cases. Hospitals of the latter type in fact have a partially different output; they provide a higher level of service, in addition to the more usual services. Their patients are likely to come from greater distances, partly because hospitals closer to home may be unable to provide these services. A more complex output is, of course, one explanation for apparent diseconomies of scale—that is, higher average costs per patient with increasing size. Returns to scale probably obtain for hospitals within a similar group.

The level of service of a hospital is a simple function of the presence or absence of various specializations. Schneider,[2] in a study of Cincinnati hospitals, suggested a three-level hierarchy: the few very large hospitals had a virtual monopoly of Type A services (dermatology, plastic surgery, psychiatry, neurology, thoracic surgery); and large and medium-size hospitals shared a second level of specialties, absent in smaller hospitals. (It should, of course, be borne in mind that even the small hospital is itself at a fairly high level in the entire health system.) In the absence of data on specializations, the level of service can be estimated from the facilities. The facilities available are listed (though with little regard to quality or quantity) by the American Hospital Association in the Guide Issue of its journal, Hospitals.[3] The num-

2. Schneider, J. B. Measuring the Locational Efficiency of the Urban Hospital. Discussion paper 11, Regional Science Research Institute, Philadelphia, 1967.
3. Hospitals, J.A.H.A. Annual Guide Issue.

ber of residencies and internships, by hospital and by specialty, and the number of paramedical staff members of hospitals are also available.[4]

Figure 1 graphically portrays the relation between number of beds and an "index" of specialization—actually the sum of the number of facilities and the number of specialties with interns and/or residents. The long-term governmental institutions are set apart, since they are less concerned with care of acute illness and therefore have many beds but few services or facilities. The large university hospitals are also set apart, as they contain typically both more beds and many more services and facilities. The very small hospitals (with a few exceptions) have a minimum number of services.

CORRELATIONS BETWEEN HOSPITAL SIZE AND SERVICE

The relation between bed complement, facilities, and number of intern or resident specialties was subjected to regression analysis. Table 1 indicates the fairly

Table 1. Coefficients of Correlation Between Hospital Size and Services

	All Hospitals	Higher Level*	Community
Facilities and services	.77	.76 (.82)	.73
Facilities only	.82	.63 (.95)	.73
Intern/resident programs	. .	.72 (.87)	. .

* Figures in parentheses are values obtained when governmental hospitals were excluded.

strong positive relation between size and scope. From these correlations it can be concluded that Figure 1 describes not one relation but two fairly strong ones. For the hospitals with a higher level of services, the number of intern and resi-

4. Directory of Approved Internships and Residencies. Chicago: American Medical Association.

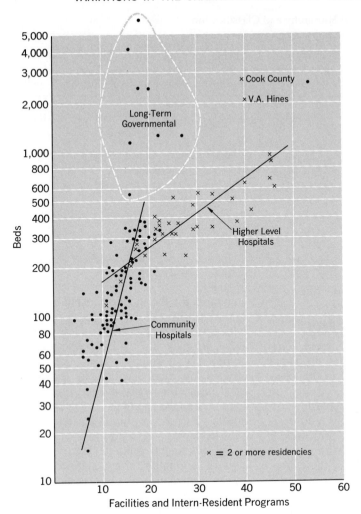

Figure 1. Hospital Size, Facilities, and Programs

dent programs increases fairly rapidly with size, after a threshold size of about 200 beds. This emerges clearly when predicted values are computed from the regression in Figure 1. The general relation between size and scope may also be seen from Table 2, based on American Hospital Association listings, which groups the hospitals of various sizes according to levels of service. It may be observed that the large majority of hospitals are intermediate in size and service.

Table 2. Number of Hospitals at Various Service Levels, by Size*

Number of Facilities & Services	Bed Complement		
	Under 100	100–399	400 and Over
12	26	6	0
12–24	6	80	1
25 and over	0	6	13

* Data from American Hospital Association listings.

Table 3. Summary of Hospital Hierarchy and Classification

Classification	No. of Hospitals	Mean No. of Beds	Mean No. Facilities	Mean No. Intern/ Resident Programs	Mean No. Total Services	Mean No. Medical Staff
Group A: Teaching and research hospitals	10	995	24	17	41	180
Group B: Regional and district hospitals, intermed. service level	24	360	20	5	25	30
Group C: Community hospitals	67	205	15	0	15	3.3
Group D: Very small hospitals	24	64	10	0	10	1
Group S: Long-term institutions	25	800	16	1	17	12
All hospitals	150	362	16	2	17	19
Groups A,B,C,D	125	270	16+	2	18	22

HIERARCHICAL CLASSIFICATION

On the basis of these data, a more complete classification is suggested in Table 3. The hospitals of Group A in this classification are uniformly large, possess the widest range of facilities (particularly specialty programs for interns and residents), and have the largest professional staffs. They are all affiliated with medical schools. With two exceptions, these hospitals are all central in location. All the Group B hospitals have some medical school relationship and have moderately large medical staffs. The majority of this group are rather close to the city center, but a few major suburban hospitals are included. These provide an intermediate level of service, not too far from home, for many patients. Group C, the largest group, consists of the many moderate-size community hospitals. They are the most widely and evenly spaced. They may be considered the norm, equipped to handle most normal needs and situated fairly close to most patients. But since they have extremely small house staffs and few approved intern or resident programs, they do not meet the theoretically desired standards for the modern hospital. Group D, arbitrarily defined as those hospitals with fewer than 100 beds, is less typical. Here we may distinguish between those community hospitals whose size is restricted by their location in less-populated, semirural areas and the small, perhaps hospitals, perhaps restricted to a special purpose within Chicago proper (for example, Negro hospitals).

Subject to the validity of the assumption of normality, some statistical tests of the significance of the classification in Table 3 were carried out. Differences in the means of Groups A, B, C, and D in beds, facilities and services, intern and resident programs, and medical staff are all significant at the 95 percent level (except, obviously, interns and residents for Groups C and D, both 0).

When hospitals in these groups are mapped (Figure 2), one can observe the concentration of the higher-level hospitals near downtown Chicago or in older, larger satellite cities or suburbs. Whether this degree of concentration is necessary or desirable is difficult to say. However, if only about 10 percent of patients, even in a large hospital, require more specialized services, then the threshold popula-

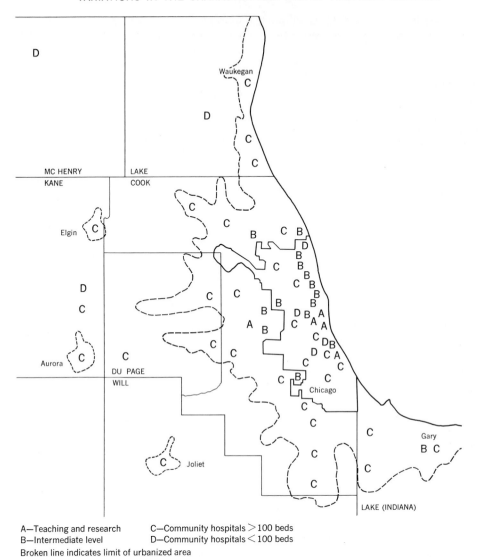

A—Teaching and research   C—Community hospitals > 100 beds
B—Intermediate level   D—Community hospitals < 100 beds
Broken line indicates limit of urbanized area

Figure 2. Functional Hierarchy or Levels of Care in Chicago Area Hospitals

tion for entry for such specialized services must be on the order of 500,000 to 1,000,000 people. Considered in this context, the present pattern is not surprising. Hospitals with high service levels are located close to centers of transport and population, where they can share a regional market. These hospitals have a wider drawing power and their patients travel a longer mean distance. Also as would be expected, they have less definable service areas. Whereas community hospitals tend to separate and seek a somewhat protected trade area, higher-level hospitals cluster together so that their service areas cover much of the metropolitan area. All but 6 of the 34 Group A and Group B hospitals are part of clusters, but only 27 of 67 Group C hospitals are in clusters, and 10 of the 27 are shared-market hospitals in satellite cities, themselves isolated from competition.

Principal-Components Analysis of Variations

Hospitals vary in many ways; they may be arrayed according to other factors than size and facilities. For example, hospitals differ in their willingness to accept Negro patients and in the domination (proportion of an area's patients attracted to the hospital) that they exert over nearby communities.

There may be relatively few, if any, really independent dimensions of variation. Data were collected for 123 of the Chicago area's hospitals on 99 variables concerned with patient capacity, quality and service, costs and means of payment, patient population, hospital service area, relation to other hospitals, change over time, and occupancy and length of stay. Factor analysis, appropriate for problems in which there are many interrelated variables, yielded one possible set of variations, emphasizing the relation of hospital and patient rather than the internal operation of the hospitals.

The principal-components method, analyzing the degree of correlation among variables, was used to reduce variations among the 99 variables to nine major components or independent dimensions of variation, each representing a set of related variables. The hospital scores or values on the nine component dimensions —that is, composite variables—were then used for a grouping analysis. This resulted in a classification of hospitals with high similarity within groups but significant differentiation between groups.

PRINCIPAL COMPONENTS

These nine significant dimensions accounted for two-thirds of the variance among all 99 variables. Highly correlated variables reduced to fewer composite variables. The remaining variance is accounted for by peculiarities of individual hospitals or by relations involving few variables and hospitals. Since the dimensions are composite, they cannot be precisely defined, but the following descriptions reflect the variables comprised.

1. This dimension arrays hospitals by *amount or volume of service,* especially medical-surgical. Highly represented variables include those measuring number of admissions, patient days, expenses, payroll, and personnel, all of which were highly correlated. This dimension accounted for 26 percent of the explained variance in the battery of variables. Such a ranking, essentially by number of admissions, is of course the most obvious form of variation. Personnel and payroll are much better predictors of capacity than number of beds, according to this result.

2. This dimension (accounting for 15 percent of explained variation) is spatial, ranking hospitals by the *character of the service area and the relative location* of the hospital. Highly represented variables include the proportion of a hospital's patients (medical-surgical or obstetric) coming from its own community and its own hospital district and the distance of the hospital from the Loop (city center). All these variables had been highly correlated. High-ranking hospitals on this dimension are those whose patients are concentrated locally and which tend to monopolize care in their communities —most typically, hospitals in widely separated satellite cities or distant suburbs. Since population density declines outward from the city center, service areas on the outskirts are also likely to be higher-ranking on this dimension. At the low end of the ranking are special-purpose hospitals and large teaching hospitals, which attract patients from the entire metropolis but

do not dominate their local area.

3. A dimension (accounting for 13 percent of variation) that arrays hospitals according to *length of stay and quality or scope of service*. Highly represented variables include length of stay (for various groups), facilities and services of hospitals, intern and resident programs, expenses per admission, and type of ownership or control. This dimension reflects the longer stay and greater expense associated with patients requiring more specialized kinds of treatment. Highest-ranking hospitals are the Veterans Administration hospitals, then the major teaching and research hospitals. The typical low-ranking hospital is small, often private, and has many Negro patients.

4. This dimension (accounting for 12 percent of variation) orders hospitals by the *importance of obstetric and pediatric care*. Represented variables, all correlated, include obstetric and pediatric beds, admissions, patient days, and occupancy rates. This dimension indicates that hospitals tend to reflect, in their patient emphasis, the demographic characteristics of the communities around them. This and the preceding dimension illustrate distinct forms of variation: an increase in overall capacity does not necessarily mean an increase in quality or importance of obstetric care.

5. The fifth dimension (8 percent of variation) arrays hospitals according to their *recent dynamism*, ranging from newer, growing hospitals to older, stagnant ones. Represented variables are those which measure changes in beds, admissions, or patient days and population in the periods 1950-60 and 1960-65, as well as age of hospital. In general, the most dynamic are newer suburban hospitals; the least, older institutions in the city, especially public hospitals in areas of stagnant population. The dimension is signif-

icant because of patients' apparent preference for newer hospitals.

6. A dimension (8 percent of variation), also spatial, that ranks hospitals according to their *competitive position*. Highly represented variables include distance to the nearest and next nearest hospitals, community population, and proportion of the community's patients visiting local hospitals. High-ranking hospitals are those in highly competitive clusters in large close-in communities; low-ranking hospitals are quite isolated ones.

7. This dimension (7 percent of variation) orders hospitals by their *propensity to admit nonwhite patients*. Represented variables are those that reflect Negro community conditions (lower income, lower average age) and the proportion of Negro admissions. This dimension is important because the Negro community does not have free access to the hospital system.

8. This dimension (6 percent of variation) distinguishes between hospitals with high *personnel and expenses per bed and proportions of patients on public aid* (Veterans Administration and county hospitals) and the proprietary (for-profit) type, which reduce costs to a minimum and rely on full ability to pay.

9. Dimension 9 (5 percent of variation) orders hospitals by the *importance of elderly patients*. Again, the dimension indicates that the hospitals tend to reflect the age distribution of the population.

These results are complementary to those of Rosenthal,[5] who used principal components in an analysis, for states rather than hospitals, of the ways the using population varies and the relative importance to hospitals of various classes of the population.

5. Rosenthal, G. D. Factors affecting the use of short-term general hospitals. *Am. J. Pub. Health* 55:1734 November 1965.

GROUPING OF HOSPITALS

The above nine dimensions are new or composite variables that can substitute for most of the original 99. Grouping analysis finds those hospitals which are most similar in their scores or values in terms of these new variables. The method is sequential. The two hospitals that have the smallest differences in scores are found, then the next pair, and so on. Gradually all hospitals are added to a group, with progressively weaker links, until all are grouped. The significance of groups is found by comparing the variation within them with that between groups. Since the dimensions involve both internal characteristics of hospitals and external characteristics of their service areas, this grouping is more complex than the classification by size and scope of services alone.

Ten groups and eight "isolates" were identified. The largest group brought to-gether hospitals that occupied middle positions on most dimensions and thus might be considered typical. Most of the other groups and isolates, then, represent extreme positions on various dimensions (Figure 3).

The largest group of most typical hospitals, designated "medium city," includes most medium-to-large city and inner suburban hospitals with small-to-moderate staffs, good facilities, and a few interns and residents. They are characterized by competitive overlapping service areas. Although they rank intermediate on most dimensions, they are rather low on dimensions 2 (compactness of service areas) and 7 (nonwhite) and high on 6 (competitive position). A particularly close core group contains mostly older hospitals; peripheral subgroups include a few city hospitals of moderately high level (that is, more interns and residents), special-clientele hospitals, and a few newer hospitals in the city.

The grouping of hospitals according to

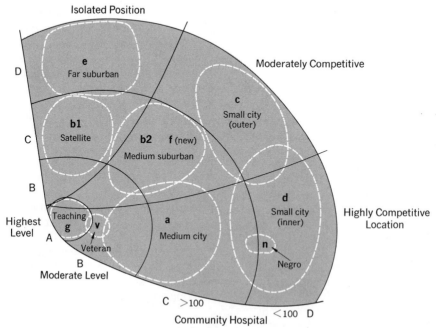

Figure 3. Graphic Summary of Hospital Grouping in Relation to Hierarchical Level of Services

the principal dimensions of variation provides a summary statement of the degree of complexity in hospital and patient characteristics that must be taken into account in any realistic evaluation of the present system. In the dense Chicago core, patient differences in race, ability to pay, age, veteran status, religion, and other characteristics are reflected in similar hospital differentiation, and the sheer mass of demand justifies specialization of purpose and division by level of service. In low-density far suburban areas, where much less differentiation is possible, the problem is simplified.

ROGER E. KASPERSON

Toward a Geography of Urban Politics: Chicago, a Case Study

Although the interest of the urban geographer has been channeled into diverse approaches to the city, one important dimension—the political geography of the city—has remained grossly neglected. Indeed, despite the incontestable importance of public decision-making for a wide variety of urban functions, a researcher is hard-pressed to unearth more than a handful of geographical studies upon this subject.[1] There are surely a number of reasons for this neglect, but one may well cite the association of urban geography with economic geography and the focus of political geography upon the national state as leading factors. The conviction that our understanding of urban problems would be greatly augmented by

a fuller realization of their political attributes has generated the present research.

An inherited problem for any initial geographical interpretation of city politics, then, is the paucity of prior research. This underlines the constant need for drawing upon the findings of related disciplines. A "building-block" progression of research is necessary, not only to permit sound generalization but to provide a body of thought with which to interpret material gathered in the field. In the case of the geography of urban politics, this body of thought must be derived from the works of political scientists and sociologists.

It is beyond the scope and intent of this paper to summarize the findings of political scientists and sociologists upon urban politics, but several brief observations relevant to the present research are noteworthy. First, since the early 1950's, political scientists have become acutely aware of the shortcomings of viewing urban politics as the inefficiencies of city

1. H. J. Nelson: The Vernon Area, California: A Study of the Political Factor in Urban Geography, *Annals Assn., of Amer. Geogrs.*, Vol. 42, 1952, pp. 177-191; Malcolm J. Proudfoot: Chicago's Fragmented Political Structure, *Geogr. Rev.*, Vol. 47, 1957, pp. 106-117; Peirce F. Lewis: A Geography of the Politics of Flint (unpublished Ph.D. dissertation, University of Michigan, 1958).

From **Economic Geography**, Vol. 11, No. 2, April 1965, pp. 95-107, Clark University, Worcester, Massachusetts. Reprinted by permission of the publisher and the author.

government and administration.[2] The inadequacies of a strictly formalistic approach to city politics are well illustrated by Chicago, which possesses a decentralized formal government, but whose politics are highly centralized in a powerful political machine.

Second, the elitist model formulated in the community power studies of sociologists has been criticized effectively by political scientists on both theoretical and methodological grounds. Political scientists have countered this view of a stable, ruling elite[3] with a pluralist one of shifting, ephemeral coalitions of power.[4] In the latter approach, the career public official participates more actively in the decision-making process. Although the pluralist interpretation is also subject to criticism, the writer would contend that it represents a more sophisticated understanding of the diffusion of power within the city.

Third, although no single interpretation of urban politics is complete in itself, useful guide posts for research can be found in classic statements on the governmental process and group and urban politics.[5] Together with the geographical characteristics and the individual ethos of the city, these statements will form the foundation of any interpretation.

Problem

Within most American cities, there are certain areas in which political support and opposition are concentrated. The cores of these conflicting areas may be apparent, but their boundaries are blurred and in a constant state of flux. Indeed, the very flexibility of the zones plays an influential role in the politician's decision-making process. Moreover, since there is a constant struggle for political support in many of these areas, this competition has far-reaching implications for the politician's very existence in public life. To maintain or further his position, he must strive to maximize his political power at the expense of his opponents.

The way in which city issues are decided, then, operates within a spatial framework that is too often overlooked by the political scientist and the geographer. Can areas of conflict be determined and systematically arranged in a study of the geography of urban politics? What are the implications to the decision-making process of the existence of such areas?

Assumptions

Several factors are assumed in the following analysis. First, by politicians is meant those politicians who function on a city-wide base of power (i.e., a mayor or city treasurer), as opposed to those who

2. See Lawrence J. R. Herson: The Lost World of Munipical Government, *Amer. Pol. Sci. Rev.,* Vol. 51, 1957, pp. 330-345; Allen Richards: Local Government Research: A Partial Evaluation, *Public Administration Review,* Vol. 14, 1954, pp. 271-277.

3. The elitist approach can be found in Floyd Hunter: Community Power Structure, A Study of Decision Makers (Chapel Hill, University of North Carolina Press, 1953); A. A. Fanelli: A Typology of Community Leadership Based on Influence Within the Leader Subsystem, *Social Forces,* Vol. 34, 1956, pp. 332-338; Harry V. Kincaid: Interviewing the Business Elite, *Amer. Journ. of Soc.,* Vol. 63, 1957, pp. 304-311.

4. For criticism of the elitist model and statements of the pluralist alternative, see Robert Dahl: A Critique of the Ruling Elite Model, *Amer. Pol. Sci. Rev.,* Vol. 52, 1958, pp. 463-469; Robert Dahl: Who Governs? (New Haven, 1961); Lawrence J. R. Herson, In the Footsteps of Community Power, *Amer. Pol. Sci., Rev.,* Vol. 55, 1961, pp. 817-831; Herbert Kaufman and Victor Jones: The Mystery of Power, *Public Administration Rev.,* Vol. 14, 1954, pp. 205-212.

5. *E.g.,* David Truman: The Governmental Process (New York, 1951); Chester Barnard: The Functions of the Executive (Cambridge, 1956); Arthur F. Bentley: The Process of Government (Chicago, 1908); George C. Homans: The Human Group (New York, 1957).

operate on a more localized base of power (i.e., a ward alderman). The second assumption is that each politician, when faced wtih alternatives, chooses the one which he believes will return him the greatest benefits in terms of political advantage and the realization of certain goals. In actual situations, this choice will not always be conscious and such a rational maximizing of benefits and costs oversimplifies the decision-making process.[6] The assumption is necessary, however, for an initial assessment of the role of geographical differences in urban politics. Finally, when discussing the characteristics and political implications of the voting zones, it is assumed that zones are discrete and homogeneous units, though this is clearly not the case in reality.

Electoral Background and Zonal Delimitation

With its fifty wards, Chicago typifies the "small-ward" American city, a characteristic which has important ramifications for Chicago politics. Chicago aldermen, elected from relatively small wards of 20,000-70,000 registered voters, have direct contact with a sizable number of their constituents. In addition, the coincidence of the location of wards with comparatively homogeneous ethnic and eco-

nomic groups reinforces this link between the aldermen and the electorate.

In terms of formal governmental structure, Chicago's 50 aldermen comprise the ruling force in the city's politics.[7] Each is an independent representative of his own ward and is elected for a four-year term. Since he is elected from a localized base of power, his first duty is to the welfare of the population of his ward. City-wide issues are of secondary importance to the alderman. This decentralized governmental structure doubtlessly would produce an ineffectual political system if informal controls were not present to centralize this dispersed power. Meyerson and Banfield recognize two chief sets of such informal control.[8] First, a handful of powerful Democratic aldermen, usually working with the mayor, effectively control the City Council when key issues are at stake. This is accomplished largely by controlling committee assignments, especially those of the important Finance Committee. Second, the presence of the ward committeeman, the party leader in the ward, forces the alderman to toe the line. The ward committeeman decides who will run on the party's ticket in the ward, appoints and dismisses precinct captains, and distributes patronage.

By means of this informal integration, the Democratic machine has sustained itself in power since 1931. During the late 1940's, however, the machine under Mayor Kelly underwent heavy fire from a number of reform-demanding civic groups. Widespread scandals and corruption had convinced party leaders that some internal changes were mandatory. In 1947 Martin Kennelly, a Democratic businessman, was chosen to run for Mayor on the understanding that he

6. Any such simple calculation would depend upon the extent of knowledge and the accuracy of perception of decision-makers. In municipal problems, such as urban renewal, the social background of the public official is an important factor in his perception. See Donald R. Mathews: The Social Background of Political Decision-Makers (Garden City, 1954). Many decision-makers probably do not "maximize" but "satisfice" by reducing alternative choices into broad classes of satisfactory outcomes. In urban decisions, considerable satisfaction is derived by merely playing the game of politics, and this modifies any rigid rational explanation. See Herbert Simon: Theories of Decision-Making in Economics and Behavioral Science, *Amer. Econ. Rev.*, Vol. 49, 1959, pp. 253-274.

7. Martin Meyerson and Edward C. Banfield: Politics, Planning and the Public Interest: The Case of Public Housing in Chicago (Glencoe, Ill., 1955), pp. 64 ff.
8. *Ibid.*

would not become party leader. His subsequent election ushered in the politics of the 1950's.

To interpret the spatial aspects of the politics of this decade, voting returns have been mapped by wards and grouped into political zones based upon consistency of voting habits. Returns for the mayoral elections of 1951, 1955, and 1959 serve as data bases. Two principal considerations determined the choice of 1951 as the base year: (1) between the 1947 and 1951 elections, a major change was made in the distribution of wards, and (2) 1951 touched off a decade that has been characterized by urban politics as being of a nature different from that of the preceding two decades. The flagrantly corrupt administration of the traditional Chicago machine had become increasingly incompatible with the ethics of a modern American metropolis.

Based upon an analysis of area voting patterns for the three election years, Chicago can be divided into four political regions. The *core area* includes the wards in which the Democratic Party obtained over 80 per cent of the votes cast. The *inner zone* contains those wards in which 60-80 per cent of the electorate cast its vote for the Democratic Party. The *outer zone* consists of the wards in which the Republican Party received 60 per cent or more of the votes cast. The crucial area between the outer and inner zones is the frontier *zone of competition,* where no party received 60 per cent of the vote. The critical limits of these regions were chosen arbitrarily, but minor alterations would not seriously affect the over-all results of the study.

The voting patterns that led to the re-election of Mayor Kennelly in 1951 are shown on Figure 1. The chief area of Democratic support was centered in the populous heart of the city with an important sub-center in the Calumet area. The frontier zone of competition was composed largely of the outlying wards

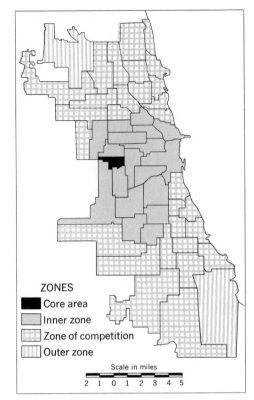

ZONES
- ■ Core area
- ▨ Inner zone
- ▦ Zone of competition
- ▥ Outer zone

Scale in miles
2 1 0 1 2 3 4 5

Figure 1. Zones are based on the mayoral election of 1951. Source: Board of Election Commissioners, City of Chicago.

north and south of the inner zone. Despite Kennelly's re-election, the Democratic machine increasingly came to regard him as a liability.[9] His drive to strengthen the civil service system had incurred a loss of important sources of patronage. In addition, Kennelly's role as a "ceremonial" mayor with weak leadership encouraged factional quarrels which threatened the internal coherence of the machine. With these and other grievances, 1955 ward leaders nominated Richard Daley as their mayoral candidate. Kennelly contested the primary with strong

9. James Q. Wilson: *Politics and Reform in American Cities* (Reprint Series, Joint Center for Urban Studies of the Massachusetts Institute of Technology and Harvard University, 1962), pp. 44-45.

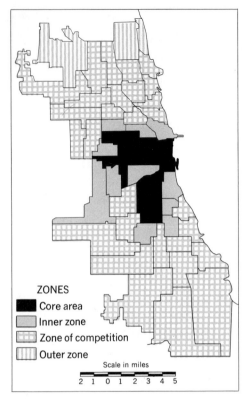

Figure 2. The zones are based on the mayoral election of 1955. Source: Board of Election Commissioners, City of Chicago.

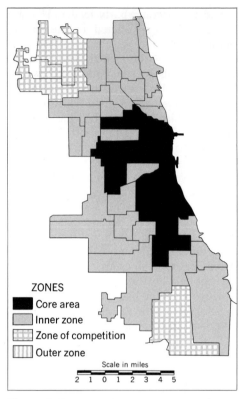

Figure 3. Based on the mayoral election results of 1959. Source: Board of Election Commissioners, City of Chicago.

support from the newspapers and good-government groups, and Daley's victory shifted much of the Kennelly's former support to Robert Merriam, the Republican candidate. Nevertheless, receiving strong support from the key Democratic wards of the core area (Fig. 2), Mayor Daley won the election. The inner zone reveals the divisive effects of the election and the loss of the Calumet sub-center.

When Mayor Daley assumed office, there was a widely-held suspicion that Chicago was destined to return to the machine politics of Mayor Kelly. Daley, however, incorporated a number of reform programs into his administration and operated under the slogan "good government is good politics."[10] Public ap-

10. *Ibid.*, p. 45.

proval of this shotgun wedding may be inferred from Figure 3. In the election of 1959, Mayor Daley faced weak opposition and garnered the support of newspapers, good-government groups, and prominent business and civic leaders. The core area expanded from seven to 19 wards, while all but three of the remaining 31 wards fell into the inner zone. The outer zone disappeared, for in no ward did the Republican candidate receive 60 per cent of the vote. The flexibility of the voting zones in these three elections is immediately apparent, and its significance will be examined later in the study.

For purposes of analysis, it was necessary to arrive at a composite set of regions from the three elections. The most satisfactory method of regionalization,

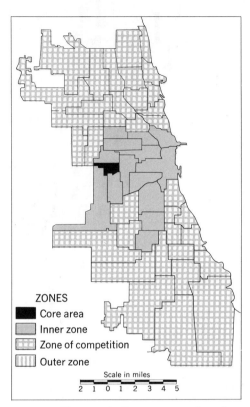

ZONES

■ Core area

▨ Inner zone

▦ Zone of competition

▥ Outer zone

Scale in miles

2 1 0 1 2 3 4 5

Figure 4. The composite zones are based on the results of the mayoral elections of 1951, 1955, and 1959.

though admittedly imperfect, was to delimit the wards of the core area and the inner and outer zones according to the aforementioned percentages for all three elections. For a ward to warrant inclusion in the core area, then, its electorate must have cast over 80 percent of its votes for the Democratic Party in all three elections. The overlapping area which resulted was delegated to the frontier zone of competition, to which it more correctly belonged. The composite map (Fig. 4) thus constructed enabled the researcher to examine the social and economic characteristics of the zones and to evaluate them in relation to the urban politics of Chicago.

Social and Economic Characteristics

The concentric character of the voting zones is readily apparent in the electoral maps. The pattern immediately suggests a possible relationship to Burgess's concentric zone theory of land use.[11] In 1950, the beginning of the period in question, most of the core area and inner zone, corresponding roughly to Burgess's transition area and zone of independent workingmen's homes, had a median income per family of less than $3000, as compared with the city mean of $3956. These zones also contained large immigrant and Negro minorities. A low percentage of owner-occupied housing units and a high population density per dwelling unit are also characteristic of the inner zone. In contradistinction to these characteristics are those of the frontier zone of competition and the outer zone, which generally correspond, respectively, to Burgess's zone of better residences and zone of commuting. Higher income per capita, lower population density per unit, better housing conditions, and a higher percentage of native-born whites all combine to distinguish these zones from the core area and the inner zone. This general pattern is confirmed by the census tract data for 1960.

A final significant zonal distinction revealed by a comparison of 1950 and 1960 census data is the character of population change within the city. The core area and inner zone have experienced serious population declines, often in the order of 10-50 per cent of the total population of the community area. During the same period, community areas in the zone of competition and the outer zone revealed markedly smaller population losses, and many areas, particularly in the

11. Ernest W. Burgess: The Growth of the City, Robert E. Park, Ernest W. Burgess, and Roderick D. McKenzie, edits.: The City (Chicago, 1925), pp. 47-62.

western portion of the city, experienced relative increases in population. These demographic changes hold far-reaching implications for Chicago politics.

The differing social and economic features of the voting zones are not to be interpreted as determinants of voting behavior. The spatial distinctions do contribute, however, to explanations of the varying types of appeals with which politicians court the zones, of the different interests in city issues, and of varied conceptions of the public interest on the part of the electorate of the zones. Finally, they provide an ecological setting against which the interplay of urban politics becomes more meaningful.

Implications for Public Decision-Making

The relative importance of each zone is constantly changing. Population changes are increasingly forcing the politician to rely upon the zone of competition and the outer zone for support. The political efficacy of the core and inner zones, the traditional areas of Democratic support, is constantly being undermined by the population losses in these areas and by the rapid population increase in the outer areas of the zone of competition. These demographic changes find expression in the changes in voter registrations over the past decade (Fig. 5). The core area and inner zones showed major declines between 1950 and 1960, whereas the chief increases occurred in the outer ring of wards encompassing the city. The vital statistics are summarized in Table 1. The entire city showed a decline of 7 per cent in voter registrations, but the losses did not occur uniformly in all sections of the city. The core area and inner zone showed a drop of 13 per cent, whereas the frontier zone of competition had only 4 per cent fewer registered voters in 1960 than in 1950. Because of these geographical changes in registrations, the Democratic

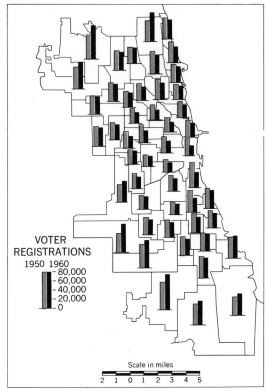

Figure 5. Changes in voter registration show a marked decline in the central portions of the city. Source: Board of Election Commissioners, City of Chicago.

politician is increasingly torn between his obligation to the core and inner zones and the need to capture votes in the zone of competition. This conflict is creating far-reaching changes in the character of Chicago politics.

With the increase of voting power in the frontier zone of competition, middle class ethics and values are becoming more influential in determining public policy. Here resides the politically conscious electorate which views government as a means of enacting general principles which should be of city-wide rather than of local neighborhood scope. Here the political process is conceived as necessitating farsighted planning rather than factional dispute and political bargaining. In

Table 1. Changes in Voter Registrations, 1950-1960

Zone	1950	1952	Year 1954	1956	1958	1960	Percentage change 1950-1960
Core area and inner zone	526,216	522,733	457,324	454,263	420,320	429,807	−13
Zone of competition	1,561,354	1,648,062	1,473,883	1,539,428	1,427,730	1,506,167	−4
Chicago total	2,087,570	2,170,795	1,931,207	1,993,691	1,848,050	1,935,974	−7

Source: Board of Election Commissioners, City of Chicago.

short, this is the citadel of good government policy, urban planning, social welfare groups, and public reform. Because of such concerns, these areas are characterized by a responsiveness to the mass media. In fact, many of them have been dubbed, rather derisively, "newspaper wards" or "silk-stocking wards."[12] Professional politicians are acutely aware of the influence of the press in these areas and seek to maintain cordial relations with reporters and editors.

The inner zones, by contrast, shun many of the programs espoused by the outer zones and are less sensitive to the mass media. Here greater value is placed on neighborhood needs, material gifts and favors, and family and ethnic ties. In the past, politicians capitalized on the poverty-stricken and more transient population of this area to erect a political machine with its accompanying corruption.[13] Significantly enough, good government groups, such as the League of Women Voters, continue to post observers at polls in these wards in an attempt to eliminate possible electoral manipulations. Even with observers, however, it is noteworthy that most of the accusations of voting irregularities in the 1960 Presidential election were directed at these wards. Special objects of attention have been the so-called "river wards," located along the Chicago River in the core area and inner zone. A cultural antagonism exists between these zones which is more fundamental than voting data reveals.

The zonal differences in social and economic values have partially contributed to different methods of assembling political support in Chicago. To secure maximum support, the politician often varies his type of voter appeal to suit the values and interests of the particular ward. In the frontier zone of competition and in the outer zone, public support tends to rely more effectively on good government and reform programs than on patronage. This type of appeal can be termed intangible as opposed to tangible.[14] Tangible appeals are more widely used in the core area and inner zone where the electorate has a low per-capita income and material benefits have real value. As the wife of one machine committeeman put it, "The system for becoming a leader is based on the number of favors a politician can do for

12. Meyerson and Banfield comment that in the newspaper wards "voters usually split the ticket in the way a newspaper advised. The alderman in the 'river wards' could afford to be contemptuous of the newspapers; in their wards editorials were words wasted." Meyerson and Banfield, *op. cit.,* p. 77.

13. Harold F. Gosnell: Machine Politics: Chicago Model (Chicago, 1937). For a colorful and informative portrait of one such ward, see William Braden and Art Petacque: The Wayward First Ward, *Chicago Sunday Sun-Times,* February 10, 1963.

14. This distinction is based upon the discussion of material and immaterial incentives in Chester I. Barnard: The Functions of the Executive (Cambridge, 1956), pp. 142-160.

the people in his ward. Needy people can't turn to their bank account, and they're appreciative of small things. In a silk-stocking ward, there's not much a politician can do except keep the streets clean. The people don't need small favors and so they have a different kind of politician."[15] Thus, political support in the inner zone is maintained by a system of carefully distributed city jobs and local favors. Even retribution of a tangible nature can be, and is, employed—fire inspections, police investigations (or lack thereof), and city ordinance enforcement.

The danger of adopting any one approach is that it may well boomerang on its originator. A politician's adoption of a particular appeal for one area may well create repercussions in other wards throughout the city. Consequently, the politician must weigh the relative areal benefits he will receive against the drawbacks incurred. In some situations, the methods of obtaining support in different zones is not irreconcilable. A particular appeal which generates nearly maximum support in one area may simultaneously appeal to a certain strata or segment in another. A controversial political issue recently resolved in Chicago exemplifies some of the spatial overtones of public decision-making.

Since the establishment of the Chicago Undergraduate Division of the University of Illinois in 1946, there has been considerable interest in establishing a Chicago campus.[16] The subsequent struggle

15. Mrs. Florence Pacelli, quoted in Braden and Petacque, op. cit. Another ward committeeman said, "What I look for in a prospective captain is a young person—man or woman—who is interested in getting some material return out of his political activity. I much prefer this type to the type that is enthused about the 'party cause' or all 'hot' on a particular issue. Enthusiasm for causes is short-lived, but the necessity of making a living is permanent." Meyerson and Banfield, op. cit., pp. 70-71.
16. The following discussion is based upon Edward C. Banfield, op. cit., pp. 159-189; Peter B. Clark: The Chicago Big Businessman as a

over the location of the campus reveals the interplay of geography and politics in public decision-making. Miller Meadows, a county forest preserve in a western suburb, was one of the earliest sites under serious consideration. Strongly recommended by a real estate research organization which had been hired to recommend sites, its chief advantages were that it was inexpensive ($.29 per foot with a total cost of $3 million) and had reasonable accessibility (55.4 per cent of the potential students were only an hour away by public transportation). Furthermore, Miller Meadows boasted the added attraction of scenic beauty. On June 27, 1956, in the face of powerful opposition from the Advisory Committee of the Board of Forest Preserve Commissioners, the Board of Trustees of the University of Illinois selected Miller Meadows as the site for the new campus.

Legal difficulties and political opposition persistently hamstrung plans for this location, however, so that in early 1959 the Board of Trustees concluded that the adjacent Riverside Golf Club should be the site. At this juncture, Mayor Daley intervened. At a meeting of the Board of Trustees on February 23, 1959, he announced that the City of Chicago would defray any extraordinary cost arising out of the selection of alternative sites in Chicago as compared with the cost of the Riverside Golf Club location. In effect, this action allowed for a large number of alternative sites which were formerly economically unfeasible. A proposal to use Meigs Field was rejected because the city wanted to retain its services as an airport. When the Board of Trustees selected Garfield Park, Mayor Daley again

Civic Leader (unpublished Ph.D. dissertation, Political Science Department, University of Chicago, 1959); pp. 254 ff.; Chicago Daily Tribune, February 11, 1961; The University of Illinois at Congress Circle (Chicago, 1961); Department of City Planning, City of Chicago: Area Plan for West Central Community, Interim Report (Chicago, 1961).

countered with a successful proposal to locate the campus on Chicago's near west side.

In terms of political benefits, the near west side location possessed several important advantages. Strong support for this site was provided by local business interests, such as Sears-Roebuck Company, whose main plant was threatened by neighborhood deterioration. Second, inhabitants of the core area and inner zone gained the advantage of a sizeable new source of employment and ease of accessibility for attending the University. Finally, the approved plan pleased many voters in the frontier zone of competition and the outer zone because the plan included an extensive urban renewal and conservation plan which would eliminate the city's worst slum district and supplant it with an intellectual center. Moreover, two-thirds of the financing necessary for the project would be provided by federal sources.

Mayor Daley's adroit political maneuverings serve to illustrate the effectiveness of the politician's tools. To obtain a favorable decision on his proposal of the near west side site, his administration took the following actions. First, the city arranged for the University to secure more than twice the amount of frontage along the Congress Expressway than was originally planned. In addition, elimination of a portion of the site originally proposed prevented the campus from being split by a major thoroughfare. Second, the city administration and the Chicago Land Clearance Commission pledged a new urban renewal program for the provision of new private apartment buildings in the area. Third, Mayor Daley guaranteed that city housing agencies would "push" a large community conservation program to the west of the campus. Finally, Mayor Daley's proposal conveniently received support when prominent business and civic groups announced that the city would contest the legality of the

alternative area (Garfield Park). A visible grain of truth can be found in the angry remark of Sam K. Lenin, President of the Garfield Park Chamber of Commerce. "Our Garfield Park site has been overpowered by the downtown money interests and outmaneuvered by the Chicago politicians."[17]

While the politician is concerned with the potential voting capacity of a particular area, he must also consider its flexibility. If one ward is relatively inflexible, the politician can profitably risk alienating some of his support there in order to realize larger gains in another, more flexible ward. An examination by ward of zonal voting characteristics for all three elections affords some understanding of the variation among wards. It was found that the frontier zone of competition showed greater flexibility than the inner zone and core area.

The signifiance of this flexibility is illustrated in the 1959 election. Mayor Daley mobilized the Democratic machine to its fullest capacity and produced an overwhelming endorsement of his administration. In so doing, he gathered the support of the usually recalcitrant opposition press, voluntary associations, prominent business and civic leaders, and other typically Republican groups. It is not insignificant that his most impressive gains occurred in the zone of competition, not in the inner zone and core area (Figure 4). In fact, some wards of the inner zone betrayed signs of a possible upper voting limit.

Another variation among voting zones may be related to the different types of appeals made. In the inner zone, rigid party control through patronage compels the ward alderman to toe the line. In the outer zones, however, the alderman is less dependent upon the political machine for patronage votes and more dependent upon his ability to appeal to mass media and local voters. Thus, there

17. *Chicago Daily Tribune*, February 11, 1961.

may well be a weakening of party loyalties in various areas which will confront the city-wide politician with labyrinthine problems. By garnering more total votes through intangible appeals, he is less and less likely to have a loyal disciplined party of aldermen.

The spatial aspects of politics are implicit in a number of other city issues. For example, Mayor Daley is appointing more and more "blue-ribbon" candidates to public office, Police Superintendent Wilson being one of the more recent of a large number of academic and professional figures. With every "blue-ribbon" appointment, one more patronage job, and perhaps indirectly more, is lost to the party. Another issue is the entire activity of urban planning and urban renewal. Urban planning receives much of its impetus, drive, and personnel from the frontier zone of competition and the outer zone, while the core area and inner zone often vehemently oppose it. The fact remains, however, that city politicians are increasingly recognizing the advantage of city planning in assembling and maintaining political support.[18] Doubtless, this is one important reason why the 1951-1961 decade has witnessed more political support for planning than have past decades, even though the cultural background of the politician himself may motivate him to oppose the general philosophy embodied in urban planning.

Conclusions

There are important spatial considerations influencing political decision-making

18. See Norton Long: Planning and Politics in Urban Development, *Journ. of the Amer. Inst. of Planners,* Vol. 20, 1959, pp. 163-169.

and shaping public policy. The study set forth should be regarded properly as a series of hypotheses rather than an accumulation of well-established generalizations. Hopefully, however, this study presents a spatial framework within which to view voting habits and the political behavior of decision-makers. Certainly, further comparative investigation is required to test adequately the over-all results. Chicago represents but a single American city—a large city with a well-defined nucleus, a small-ward system, partisan politics, and a powerful political machine. Moreover, this study represents but one aspect of the political geography of the city. Other topics such as metropolitan political organization, the provision of urban functions, zoning, electoral geography, and urban renewal are all of potential value and should not be overlooked in a comprehensive study.

Nevertheless, geographers have long neglected the interplay of geography and politics in the city. There is evidence of an increase in attention to these problems,[19] but research upon this subject cannot be delegated to the political geographer alone. Unless urban geographers assume the responsibility of viewing urban politics as something more than an obstacle to planning, a serious deficiency will continue to thwart our understanding of the geography of American cities.

19. Encouraging in this respect is the informal conference on political geography and urban problems held at Yale University in March of 1962. For a brief summary of the proceedings, see Stephen Jones: Conference on Political Geography and Urban Problems, *Prof. Geog.,* Vol. 14, May, 1962, p. 28. A provocative set of essays on this theme can be found in Arthur Maass, edit.: Area and Power: A Theory of Local Government (Glencoe, Ill., 1959).

MICHAEL B. TEITZ

Toward a Theory of Urban Public Facility Location

Location theory has come a long way from von Thünen and Weber. In recent years, we have witnessed its formalization and codification by Isard[1] promptly followed by two kinds of radical change. The first of these, typified by formal theories of consumer residential choice and advances in analysis of urban retail location, comprises an expansion of the theory's substantive domain. The second change consists of the adoption of computable models, ranging from hill climbing algorithms for the classic Weber problem to complex land use models in transportation studies. Although the latter may be a shift primarily in technology, it appears to be so far reaching that its inevitable feedback to theory has hardly begun to take shape.

Both of these developments contribute to the subject of this paper. Its aim is to suggest a further area of substantive concern for location theory, namely, urban public facility location, the application of which will call for computable models.

Although it is not entirely true to say that location theorists have ignored the

1. W. Isard, *Location and Space Economy* (Cambridge: The M.I.T. Press, 1956).

problem of public facility location in cities, their concern has been slight. Isard,[2] for example, briefly mentions urban public facilities in the context of a discussion of urban scale economies but does not consider their location at all. Elsewhere,[3] he deals with them as instruments for participation. Other locational analysts have usually dealt with public facilities by assuming either that their location could be considered determined by residential location or a special case of commercial and retail location. Even in the modern development of central place theory, consideration of public facilities has been marked by virtually no concern with their public rather than market mechanism for determination of scale and location. Berry[4] discusses planning applications of central place theory but cites only one instance of rationalization of public services, and that in a nonurban and nontheoretical context. Similarly, Berry and

2. Ibid., pp. 182 ff.
3. W. Isard et al., *Methods of Regional Analysis* (New York: John Wiley & Sons, Inc., 1960).
4. B. J. L. Berry, *Geography of Market Centers and Retail Distribution* (Englewood Cliffs, New Jersey: Prentice-Hall, Inc., 1967).

From **Papers and Proceedings of the Regional Science Association,** Vol. 21, 1968, pp. 35-44. Reprinted by permission of the Regional Science Association, Philadelphia, Pennsylvania.

411

Pred[5] give virtually no theoretical references pointing toward public facilities, and, although a section of their bibliography is devoted to medical services, no mention is made of others.

On the other hand, the problem has not been totally unconsidered. The relationship between public welfare concerns and the minimum average cost solution to the Hotelling ice cream vendor problem has often been noted. Tiebout,[6] in an important paper, outlined some major components for a theory of urban public expenditure decisions but assumed away most location problems. Suggestive papers have appeared in the recent literature in local public expenditure economies, especially in Schaller.[7] Haggett[8] cites empirical work on school location and district boundaries. Alexander[9] has put forward some suggestive ideas on urban highway spacing. And finally, in this brief catalogue, the literature on medical facilities offers a number of recent works, notably by Schneider.[10]

Why a Theory of Urban Public Facility Location?

The failure of location theorists to consider publicly determined facilities is quite

5. B. J. L. Berry and A. Pred, *Central Place Studies: A Bibliography of Theory and Applications* (Philadelphia: Regional Science Research Institute, 1961).
6. C. M. Tiebout, "Economic Theory of Fiscal Decentralization," in *Public Finances: Needs, Sources and Utilization* (National Bureau of Economic Research, Princeton: Princeton University Press, 1961).
7. H. Schaller, *Public Expenditure Decisions in the Urban Community* (Baltimore: Johns Hopkins Press, 1963).
8. P. Haggett, *Locational Analysis in Human Geography* (New York: St. Martin's Press, 1966), pp. 248-50.
9. C. Alexander, "The Pattern of Streets," *Journal of the American Institute of Planners,* XXXII (1966), pp. 273-78.
10. J. B. Schneider, *Measuring the Locational Efficiency of the Urban Hospital* (Philadelphia: Regional Science Research Institute, Discussion Paper Series No. 11, 1967).

surprising when one comes to consider the role of those facilities in shaping both the physical form of cities and the quality of life within them.

Modern urban man is born in a publicly financed hospital, receives his education in a publicly supported school and university, spends a good part of his life travelling on publicly built transportation facilities, communicates through the post office or the quasi-public telephone system, drinks his public water, disposes of his garbage through the public removal system, reads his public library books, picnics in his public parks, is protected by his public police, fire, and health systems; eventually he dies, again in a hospital, and may even be buried in a public cemetery. Ideological conservatives notwithstanding, his everyday life is inextricably bound up with governmental decisions on these and numerous other local public services.

Implicitly, we seem to have assumed as theorists that the character and location of public facilities simply reflect the overwhelming nonpublic decisions on residential, commercial, and industrial location. Furthermore, we have assumed that since market-based competitive models of the latter should lead to Pareto optimal location patterns under atomistic decisions, the public decisions accompanying them should likewise be optimal. It is sometimes hard to take market-based location theory seriously in the real world. Even if it does hold, one is hard put to see why the political process should respond in an optimal way. Yet, by and large, government has in the past responded sufficiently well to give rise to virtually no theoretical speculation about the nature of the response and its implications for the city.

Urban planners, for all their shortcomings, have recognized the problem in practice. But the lack of a theoretical basis for action has left their response mechanical and inadequate. Rules of thumb about size and location of facilities have been developed but, for the most part, without ways to evaluate the results or to stimulate invention of new systems. With services locked in mazes of standards and without powerful competitive pressures for innovation, only crisis has precipitated demands for reevaluation of urban services. And even then, the response tends to be a shotgun scatter of proposals—not a remarkable result, given that no framework for evaluation exists. In this context, it is interesting to note the current urban crisis in America. With it has come the usual plethora of proposals, this time including measures emanating from the federal level that could drastically change the pattern of urban public services. The schools are the first target, but no doubt others will face similar problems.

Beyond these questions lies a further uncharted territory. Although theorists may have assumed that public facilities followed private decisions, a powerful feedback of public decisions on private also seems likely. If government can use public facilities as instruments to shape urban growth and social and economic behavior, then a new level of evaluation is superimposed on the usual considerations for public services. Of course, planners have been advocating this for many years, but only now does it begin to seem a serious possibility for reasonably scientific investigation. However, even if such larger aims are not now achievable, the drive toward PPB, systems analysis, and cost-benefit at the local level suggests a rising interest in more efficient and effective utilization of resources in urban services to achieve the direct public ends for which those services were instituted. For this alone, some theoretical structure might be invaluable.

Public and Private Location

These considerations suggest that urban public facility location is worth some theoretical exploration. They do not demon-strate that such a theory is unified, feasible, or significantly different from other components of location theory, including central place theory. In the remainder of this paper, it is scarcely possible to develop a full-blown theory of public facility location. Rather, we shall try to indicate its unique characteristics and sketch out some of its most interesting component problems.

The first question that we shall examine concerns the relation of a theory of public location to conventional location theory. There are several important qualitative differences between them. Both location and the scale of expenditure on urban public facilities are determined by some sort of public or quasi-public process. This central fact gives rise to some important characteristics. It suggests that public location theory may bear a relationship to conventional location theory similar to that between the expenditure side of public finance or welfare economics and conventional economic theory. In each case, the former focuses upon public decisions and government budgets in response to some welfare criterion in a mixed market-nonmarket setting. The latter emphasizes the role of choice, taste, and utility or profit maximization in a predominantly market context. Under assumptions of competition and many decision units, the result should be Pareto optimal allocations. Public expenditure theory constantly seeks some equivalent framework in a situation of one or few decision units and restricted personal choice.

One should not carry the analogy too far. Several writers on local public expenditures have pointed out the asymmetry between national and local public finance resulting from large numbers of governments at the local level. Tiebout[11] used this property of local finance as a

11. C. M. Tiebout, "A Pure Theory of Local Expenditures," *Journal of Political Economy,* LXIV (1956), pp. 416-24.

basis for a consumer behavior oriented theory of local public expenditures. We recognize the existence of many local governments but, for purposes of analysis, will begin by treating public facility location on the basis of a single government.

If a single government is responsible for provision of some service over a given area, then a second powerful contrast with conventional location theory emerges. Location theory of the firm or consumer asserts that many decentralized decisions have produced an observed pattern of locations. The pattern may be described positivistically as a system by central place theory, but its locational efficiency is not usually evaluated in system terms. For example, retail location analysts may count the number of supermarkets in an area and describe their pattern. Usually, they do not ask whether the individual markets are too small or too large. If the market is operating effectively, such questions are automatically taken care of.

For public facilities, in contrast, these are central questions. Even if we accept an incrementalist view of government budgeting, the problems of the appropriate scale and location of new facilities remain. If a more general position is adopted for theoretical investigation, the over-all scale of operation, i.e., the determination of the budget, becomes critical. Such a view has powerful implications for locational analysis. The theorist of public facility location finds himself inevitably drawn away from the problem of location of the individual facility and toward the structure and location of the entire *system* of facilities within the area over which the government exerts jurisdiction.

Location theory has not concerned itself much with multiple location systems. Operations researchers have analyzed multifacility location problems in practice; location theorists have dealt little with the theory of the multiple facility firm. Yet many interesting problems arise as

soon as one begins to look at location from a system viewpoint. For example, one might ask for an appropriate retail location strategy for supermarket chains of different sizes. Or, again, what happens to the Hotelling problem under multiple unit assumptions? To my knowledge there is very little theoretical discussion of these or similar questions.

System location is not a single problem, as will be shown below. But in one form or another, it does appear crucial in most considerations of public facilities. Before we go on to examine in detail some of these manifestations, some further characteristics of public facility systems and decisions need to be identified.

PUBLIC FACILITY SYSTEMS

In order to talk about public facility location, it is desirable to characterize public facilities. Presumably, we mean those components of the city whose primary function is to facilitate the provision of goods and services declared to be wholly or partly within the domain of government. The range of such goods and the degree of government involvement vary greatly over time and place. Almost every function has been run at some time or place by government. For purposes of the present discussion, we will take the set of governmental urban functions in western countries, particularly the United States and Canada, as our purview. No attempt will be made here to establish a list of such functions or their associated goods and services in detail. In the understanding of urban systems, such a list may eventually be necessary and might bear a relation to public location similar to that of the complete classification of industry to the theory of industrial location. Or perhaps a better analogy might be the relation of anatomy to human biology.

For preliminary discussion, some first approximations to classes of functions and facilities may be invaluable. We will approach this through the description of generalized ways of making such distinctions. A first cut at the problem follows the theory of public expenditures in classifying outputs and associated facility systems as public or collective use goods, zero short-run marginal cost goods, or merit goods. An air pollution monitor system is of the first kind, a noncongested street network of the second, and, so far as one can tell, a public library system of the third. This is a well-understood basis for discrimination and may have significant utility in the study of location. But, for the moment, we shall not explore it further here except to note its influence on the classifications below.

A second distinction applies to facility systems rather than to goods and services and focuses on their geometric properties. Since theorization and model building imply abstraction, we would do well to look at the most likely abstractions of facility systems. They appear to take two common forms, point patterns and networks. Point patterns characterize a variety of distributive services in which the final phase of distribution is flexible and intermittent. Medical centers, post offices, libraries, police, and fire systems are of this type. On the other hand, many services call for continuous connections in space. For these a network characterization seems more suitable. Examples might be water, sewer, electric power, gas, telephone, and highways. Let it be emphasized that these are merely suggestive distinctions. Clearly, for any urban function the abstraction is technologically influenced and often more properly described as a mixture than a pure form of one or the other. In the present context, it is useful because we will be concerned more often with point-representable than network-representable systems.

Related to the formal geometric property is another quality which combines geometry and behavior. It often appears useful to characterize point-representable

facility systems by the direction of interaction associated with each point in the system and by the abstraction of its relationship to the city, itself abstracted as a point pattern or surface. A system of facilities representable by a point pattern may take this particular form as a compromise between scale economies in operation and economies in distribution. However, there are interesting differences observable in the distribution process itself. We might distinguish on the basis of direction of flow, for example, among systems involving physical movement, between those that are distributors and those that are collectors. In a formal sense, though, these abstract to the same thing. Rather more interesting might be a distinction among distributional systems on the basis of the formal representation as mappings of their relationships with the city. If we represent the city as a point set or surface, the relations between the facility system as domain and its sphere of concern as range may be one-one, one-many, or many-many. Which of these is appropriate seems to be a function of the technical properties of the system, its status as a public good, and the role of consumer choice in consumption of its output. An example involving the first and third of these is offered by the post office. The collection and distribution facilities of the post office are asymmetric. Ideally, each letter entering the system must find a unique destination, namely its addressee, and all letters must be delivered. To achieve these ends effectively, and retain security, an obvious solution is to assign a unique one-many mapping between post office substations and addresses. Thus, at the last stage of its trip, any letter to a particular address comes from exactly one substation. Admittedly, other methods could be employed and perhaps should be examined, but this one appears to be universal. In contrast, the collection arm requires no such form. Because all letters must go into a common sorting process, there is no need for any letter to enter at a unique point. Additionally, part of the collection cost may easily and without significant loss of security be passed on to the consumer. The result is a mailbox system as the lowest order subsystem on the collection side. It exhibits a many-many relation to the set of addresses in the city and consequently is not a mapping in the strict mathematical sense.

At the risk of belaboring this point excessively, we might point out that the form of relation determines whether the city must be divided into regions for any particular function. Post office substation delivery regions exist; mail box collection regions do not. Not uncommonly, regions are established administratively with no such functional basis. Large urban public libraries offer examples of such exhaustive and disjoint region systems. They also may exhibit inconsistency in boundaries and general disregard for their existence. Given the character of the library function, this is not surprising, and, in fact, it is probably more healthy than the creation of such regions in the first place. A similar problem appears in efforts to delineate hospital market areas.

A final characteristic of public facility systems that we must mention is their hierarchical property. Almost universally, hierarchical elements appear in the technical structure of public facility systems. At least two sources contribute to the generation of hierarchies. For spatially continuous or regularly periodic distribution and collection systems, the logic of aggregation and system control calls for attenuation of capacity as the consumer is approached. Thus, electrical distribution requires a decline in voltage which is best attained in discrete steps with a transformer station at each stage. Simultaneously, the number of branches in the network increases. Water and sewer pipe capacities likewise propagate steplike attenuation and dendritic properties.

A similar effect in point-representable systems arises from variation in the functions they perform and concurrent scale variations in requirements necessary to support specific functions, either due to cost or infrequency of demand. This effect parallels the orders of stores and goods in a central place system. Every firehouse may have an engine and ladder company, but a specialized heavy rescue company will be much rarer, although located at some firehouse in the system. Whether the outcome for any system is a pure hierarchy depends on the degree to which the higher order system elements include all functions of lower order. For public services, this may not necessarily be the case, especially where specialized components reflect local peculiarities in the demand structure, such as an alcoholic treatment unit in the local medical center catering to skid road.

Empirical information on hierarchical structure in public facilities is scarce and sometimes misleading. There seems to be confusion between technical requirements and standards. In many cases, the existence of an apparent hierarchy reflects the earlier acceptance of some system of standards that may be of dubious value. Where such standards no longer reflect technology, cost, and social objectives effectively, the observed hierarchy may be quite misleading. Nevertheless, incorporation of hierarchical properties into public location models remains important.

PUBLIC FACILITY DECISIONS

Its concern with systems sets off public from conventional location theory in terms of units. The fact of being governmental similarly shifts the emphasis in the structure of optimization, that is, objective functions and constraints.

We have previously mentioned the general problems raised by governmental allocation—the need for a social welfare function, the absence of a competitive price system, and the problem of appropriate levels for allocation and optimization. The response of public expenditure economics to these problems has been cost-benefit analysis. In military systems analysis, the heavier emphasis on system design and the impossibility of attaching dollar values to some components of the cost-benefit expression, even though they are quantifiable, has led to a form of cost-benefit in which multiple effectiveness criteria are substituted for the single benefit measure. If we lump these together, calling them cost-utility analysis, they provide a technical framework for decision comparable, if theoretically inferior, to simple profit or utility maximization under competition.

Having said this much, most of the interesting problems still remain. We shall briefly comment on some broad questions first, then pursue those especially germane to public facility location. Governments and their component agencies operate under a budget allocation system. This implies at least three major levels of decision, although they may not be separable in practice. Society decides as a whole what part of its resources will be allocated to objectives whose machinery for realization is administered or heavily influenced by government. Within this over-all allocation, government allocates resources to what we will call major program areas. These we will take to be clusters of objectives of a similar type. Within these program areas, in turn, resources must be allocated to particular programs and their associated systems of facilities. At this point, we will not consider the validity of this description in terms of behavior, nor will we speculate on the direction of determination, that is, whether the real world budget represents a sectoring of a pie or a plate of cookies. We assume that some allocation process exists whereby a quantity of resources becomes available for a program, loosely defined. This assumption is dangerous in

that it tends to lead toward the specification of the system location problem in a constrained budget-effectiveness maximization form. Such a form predicates that the entire budget for the program must be used up, a view consistent with agency behavior but lacking elegance and clearly inefficient unless exactly the right amount has been allocated to ensure equality of marginal net social return in all programs. The latter, to be known, implies that the pattern of expenditures and benefits is known in each program. Thus, the problem is circular. Optimal over-all allocation presumes optimal program allocation which, in turn, requires an over-all allocation for its calculation, especially if interprogram spillovers are taken into account.

We could look at the process as a time-free iteration or a sequential response over budget cycles. In any event, it makes little difference where we enter except insofar as emphasis is placed on achieving optimality at the higher, government-wide, or lower, program-facility system, level. And, of course, it is the latter in which we are chiefly interested. For the former, it might be that a constrained effectiveness-budget minimization form proves more appropriate. On the other hand, the use of multiple nonequivalent effectiveness measures would lead to choice of this form for the system problem.

Another general problem which faces facility location, in common with local expenditure allocation, is the absence of a social welfare function. Even lacking such a function, we might be willing, if all benefits and costs could be quantified in dollar terms, to accept an aggregate net benefit outcome that appeared large enough. Without monetarily quantifiable benefits, we are inevitably forced to consider in detail the distributional consequences of an outcome both over space and over population groups. Where government policies specify "target groups" this is a desirable result. Yet, at the local level, it may lead to political complexities beyond manageability.

Given these difficulties, we may now consider relevant variables for public facility system decisions. Evidently, we need to know what it is about systems that influences their cost and effectiveness, however measured. In part, the answer depends on the form in which the public location problem is posed, a topic taken up below. In general, however, we may immediately identify the opposing forces of economies of scale and advantages of dispersion.

This is a refrain familiar to location theorists. Of particular interest here is its formulation in system terms in a context which lends itself to effective measurement. For a point-representable facility system, we might hypothesize that the effectiveness of an individual component depends upon its scale and the disposition of the rest of the components in the system. The effectiveness of the system as a whole depends upon the scale of its components and their combined relationship to each other. Under an unconstrained budget, system effectiveness should increase or at least not decrease with the number of components, since new additions do not interfere with the scale of the old. The improvement might increase almost indefinitely, although with decreasing marginal gain. For example, if response time were a measure of fire system effectiveness, then any new fire house would decrease first response time up to the point where every structure in the city became a fire house. If the budget for the system is constrained, this is no longer true.

Under a constrained budget, several variables begin to interact. Let us assume that a distinction is made between capital and operating outlays but that the system structure is highly flexible. The first result of a budget constraint is that addition of a new component to a given facility system reduces the resources available to the previously existing components. Where the resources come from remains indeterminate. We could reduce the capital outlays, i.e., the scale of all or some facilities or reduce their operating expenditures, i.e., output. However, we must also take into account the interaction between these in turn.

Public facilities produce a variety of goods and services and their relationship to the consuming population varies greatly. Two important sources of variation are individual choice and pricing in the consumption of the outputs. At one extreme are those goods for which consumer choice is virtually nonexistent and direct price zero. These include most police and fire services as well as pure public goods. When a man's house is on fire he rarely pauses to consider whether or not to call the fire brigade. Nor, in our present system, is he usually presented with a bill for fire protection service that varies with the size of fire that he enjoyed during the previous year. Thus, once some communal decisions about form and quantity of expenditure on fire service have been made, the form of system will depend upon the expected scale and pattern of fires, the technology of surveillance and response, and the measures of effectiveness employed. If a measure such as response time dominates, then for a given surveillance system the result should be maximum dispersion. However, since there are some widely accepted minimum operating scales—the engine company— dispersion must be tempered by the need to retain this minimum scale of operation. This represents the present pattern of local response in fire systems. Overlaid upon this level are higher order fire suppression and rescue functions that will increase the scale of investment and operations for some system components. Additionally, the fire system incorporates many phenomena that derive from its peculiar relationship to standards established by the underwriters. Since compliance with the standards rather than empirical fire experience determines insurance rates in most cases, their influence on the configuration of facilities is immense. Other criteria also influence fire control facility location, particularly high fire risk and life risk situations such as oil refineries and hospitals, respectively. Thus, for this type of service, the existing pattern of facilities represents a series of compromises plus a certain amount of political and organizational maneuvering —the more fire houses, the higher the prestige of the chief. Consumer choice in the usual sense plays little part in determining the shape of the system.

Urban services for which consumer choice is significant but price zero present a different picture. Libraries provide a good example of such a function. In general, the larger the scale of a unit in such a system, the more consumers it attracts by virtue of providing better or more varied services, for example, by carrying a larger book stock. Since entry is free for members of the community and they commonly travel to the facility for the service, travel cost, including time and inconvenience, represents the major real cost to the consumer. Under these circumstances, we would expect to find a distance decay effect on usage. If the budget is fixed but the number of facilities variable, then a larger number of outlets implies a smaller scale at each but greater aggregate access to the population. The scale effect and the distance effect then conflict. An optimal system must solve for both scale and location.

One further complexity should be noted. We have not defined scale precisely, implicitly assuming it to involve relatively fixed cost components of total cost for any facility. But in public facility systems, as any others, variable costs depend on the volume of services rendered. Since price is zero, this volume depends on demand which, in turn, depends on the spatial structure and scale of facilities. The system is in a curious position of being able to generate demand by organizing itself appropriately, but, at the same time, its variable costs will increase and must be constrained within the budget. Demand and supply are tightly interlocked, indeed so much so that it may be impossible to talk about actual quantity supplied except in terms of the amount demanded.

In practice, many of the influences mentioned earlier temper the form of facility system that emerges. Locations of outlets for "free" services are not easily moved in the face of opposition from citizens who know well that they are not free. The influence of standards pervades system evaluation and perception by participants. Often, little or nothing is known about potential response to changes in location as against other elements that influence demand. A general theoretical form may be extremely useful in pointing up the effect of these distorting factors.

The chief aim of this paper has been to make a case for a field of location theory specifically devoted to urban public facilities. Such an endeavor appears to be worthwhile both for its theoretic interest and its probable utility. Theoretical problems derive chiefly from the system character of the unit of location and the public decision aspect of objective functions and constraints. Practical applications are suggested by recent attempts to improve the quality of local resource allocation through such devices as PPB.

For the most part, we have catalogued problems. Several important ones remain unconsidered. Foremost among them is the question of multiple jurisdictions providing the same services within a larger area. This can occur in two ways. Multiple governments exert jurisdiction over spatially disjoint territories within most larger urban areas. The allocation of resources under such circumstances has been examined by Tiebout[12] and Williams.[13] Within any government, there is typically functional overlap between agencies or departments. This problem has been discussed chiefly in a nontheoretical way in the PPB literature. Both are likely to influence facility system location.

12. Ibid.
13. A. Williams, "The Optimal Provision of Public Goods in a System of Local Government," *Journal of Political Economy,* LXXIV (1966), pp. 18-33.

Finally, we should be well aware that public decisions are made in the political system. Political variables will enter any decision on a facility system, especially since public facilities are so often the visible symbols of delivery of public goods to particular groups in the city. We have not considered political variables here, being more concerned with an efficiency approach, but their power may be attested by any official who has ever tried to close an existing facility.

JOHN F. KAIN AND JOHN R. MEYER

Computer Simulations, Physio-economic Systems and Intraregional Models

While the development of computer simulations has proceeded rapidly in many fields and might be expected to spread soon to new applications, the impact on regional and urban economics has been particularly pronounced. There seem to be at least two reasons for this: urban and regional economics is largely an applied, policy-oriented field, which arose (albeit with a lag) in response to "real" policy problems; and urban and regional analysts found they needed to manipulate large quantities of empirical data.

Indeed, it quickly became apparent that simply adding a locational subscript to the usual economic entities vastly multiplied the number of variables and observations. The handling of these large quantities of data caused urban and regional researchers great difficulty, but these data also provided opportunities. Complex and highly interdependent systems could be modeled that economists studying a single national economy were not even able to contemplate. For these national economies, only a few "historical" experiments recorded in highly aggregative data were normally available.

While it is beyond the scope of this paper to discuss or even enumerate all of the urban and regional models that have been spawned by the burgeoning computer technology, several major classes can be identified. These are:

1. *Regional Models of a Single Region.* One of the first and best known of these in the post-World War II period was that developed by Hoover, Vernon, and associates for the New York metropolitan area, an effort only slightly influenced by computer technology.[1, 2] More recently, there have been the Pittsburgh and the Upper Midwest regional studies, which were rather strongly computer-oriented.[3, 4] In general, these models were intended to

1. Edgar M. Hoover and Raymond Vernon, *Anatomy of a Metropolis* (Harvard Univ. Press, 1959).
2. Raymond Vernon, *Metropolis 1985* (Harvard Univ. Press, 1960).
3. Pittsburgh Regional Planning Association, *Region with a Future, Economic Study of the Pittsburgh Region,* Vol. 3 (Univ. of Pittsburgh Press, 1963).
4. James M. Henderson and Anne O. Krueger, *National Growth and Economic Change in the Upper Midwest* (Univ. of Minnesota Press, 1965).

From the **American Economic Review**, Vol. LVIII, No. 2, May 1968, pp. 174-181. Reprinted by permission of the author and the American Economic Association, Evanston, Illinois.

421

evaluate and forecast the condition of particular regions and to propose policies that would improve the regional condition.

2. *Metropolitan Growth Models.* These have typically been inspired by and executed in conjunction with metropolitan transportation studies. The models developed by the Chicago, Detroit, Puget Sound, Boston, Philadelphia (Penn-Jersey), and Southeast Wisconsin Transportation Studies are among the best examples.[5, 6, 7, 8, 9, 10] These modeling efforts were strongly influenced by engineers and transport planners who initially developed elaborate computer simulations to evaluate highway networks and, in particular, new expressway networks. As noted above, development of computer models for forecasting the determinants of urban travel, e.g., land use, seemed a simple and logical extension of these methods. The observation about large quantities of empirical data applies with special force to these studies. A number of "academic" efforts aimed at the development of regional metropolitan simulation models should also be mentioned. The Lowry model, developed at the Pittsburgh Regional Economic Study and completed at the RAND Corporation, and the University of North Carolina model are two of the most successful of these efforts.[11, 12, 13]

These academic modeling efforts have both been strongly influenced by and in turn have influenced the models developed by comprehensive transportation studies. For example, the Lowry model is calibrated largely on travel and land use data obtained from the Pittsburgh Area Transportation Study and a modified version of the model has been developed for use in the Bay Area Transportation Study.

3. *Community Renewal Programming (CRP) Models.* Over 160 communities have participated in Community Renewal Programs and have developed a programming model of some kind. However, computer and simulation methods have thus far had much less impact on Community Renewal Programming. Thus, only two CRP's, for Pittsburgh and San Francisco, are sufficiently well reported in the literature and involve "explicit" enough modeling to be considered in this survey.[14, 15, 16]

4. *Regional Economic Models Developed for Use in River Basin Studies.* The Susquehanna river basin study is among the most advanced of this class.[17, 18]

To meet space and time requirements,

5. Chicago Area Transportation Study, Vol. II, *Final Report* (Chicago, 1960).

6. Detroit Metropolitan Area Traffic Study, Part II, *Future Traffic and a Long Range Expressway Plan* (Detroit, 1956).

7. Charles H. Graves, *Forecasting the Distribution of 1985 Population and Employment to Analysis Zones for Plan A,* Staff Report No. 15 (Puget Sound Regional Transportation Study, Aug., 1964).

8. Donald M. Hill, "A Growth Allocation Model for the Boston Region," *J. of the Amer. Inst. of Planners,* May, 1965, pp. 111-20.

9. Penn-Jersey Transportation Study, Vol. 2, *1975 Projections, Foreground of the Future* (Philadelphia, Sept., 1964).

10. Pittsburgh Area Transportation Study, Vol. 2, *Forecasts and Plans* (Pittsburgh, 1963).

11. F. Stuart Chapin, Jr., Thomas G. Donnelly, and Shirley F. Weiss, *A Probabilistic Model for Residential Growth* (Center for Urban and Regional Studies, Univ. of North Carolina, 1964).

12. Chapin, Donnelly, and Weiss, "A Model for Simulating Residential Development," *J. of the Amer. Inst. of Planners,* May, 1965, pp. 120-25.

13. Ira S. Lowry, *A Model of Metropolis* (RAND Corp., Memorandum RM-4035-RC, Aug., 1964).

14. Arthur D. Little, Inc., *Model of the San Francisco Housing Market,* Technical Paper No. 8 (San Francisco Community Renewal Program, Jan., 1966).

15. Ira M. Robinson, Harry B. Wolfe, and Robert L. Barringer, "A Simulation Model for Renewal Programming," *J. of the Amer. Inst. of Planners,* May, 1965, pp. 126-33.

16. Wilbur A. Steger, "The Pittsburgh Urban Renewal Simulation Model," *J. of the Amer. Inst. of Planners,* May, 1965, pp. 144-49.

17. H. R. Hamilton, *et al., Final Report on a Dynamic Model of the Susquehanna River Basin* (Battelle Mem. Inst., Columbus, Ohio, Aug. 1, 1966).

18. Arthur Maass, *et al., Design of Water-Resource Systems* (Harvard Univ. Press, 1962).

we will focus most of our discussion on metropolitan growth models and community renewal programming (CRP) models, and particularly the former. Both seek to explain or project the intraregional distribution of activity and should be highly complementary to one another. Metropolitan growth models focus on the metropolitan periphery and primarily attempt to explain the extensive (marginal) growth of metropolitan regions; CRP models focus on central city real estate markets and primarily attempt to explain the demand for housing in built-up, relatively old and centrally located areas.

Metropolitan Growth Models: Problems and Deficiencies

Despite very great strides, metropolitan or intraregional growth models remain seriously deficient in at least three important dimensions: in modeling (1) industry (employment) location, (2) the housing market, and (3) the effects of housing market segregation. Not surprisingly, these three areas are also among the most difficult and most intractable areas of urban analysis, especially from an empirical standpoint.

In the broadest sense, the usual purpose of metropolitan growth models is to predict changes in metropolitan spatial structure and the location of residential and nonresidential activity within the region. Virtually all models postulate a recursive structure in which certain "basic" or nonpopulation serving employers choose locations within the region. These choices in turn become inputs into the location decision of employees of these firms, who, *ceteris paribus,* are assumed to live as near work as possible. So-called "linked" employment activities behave as the households since their costs or revenues, by definition, are favorably influenced by proximity to the basic employers. These location decisions by households and linked employers in turn influence or determine the location of population serving

employment within the region.[19] While there may be important differences in the way in which models treat these linkages, all metropolitan growth models have a structure of this general kind. Sketching this causal mechanism serves to point up the critical function of basic employment in metropolitan growth models. Relatively small shifts in the location of metropolitan employment will cause pronounced differences in the location and density of linked employment, households, and population serving employment.

Given the "critical" nature of basic employment in these models, it is difficult to understand why so little research has been done on the determinants of industry location. It cannot be because these activities have been "stable" or because there have been no important shifts in the underlying distributions. Though the data leave much to be desired, they leave no doubt that there have been major changes in industry location within U.S. metropolitan areas. Between 1954 and 1958 manufacturing employment declined in the central cities of thirty of the forty largest metropolitan areas.[20] The decline amounted to nearly 1.7 percent per year. During the period 1958-63 manufacturing employment declined in twenty-eight of these same forty SMSA's. During the period 1954-58 suburban manufacturing employment increased by 7.4 percent per year. Similarly, wholesaling employment, much of which could be included in the basic category, declined in twenty-one of the central cities of the

19. These "basic" or nonpopulation serving industries are generally handled exogenously. In the Lowry model, for example, exogenous employment accounted for 361,000 jobs, while the endogenous population serving sector accounted for 191,000 jobs. The Lowry model determined the location of 191,000 population serving jobs and 470,000 households, given a predetermined distribution of the 361,000 basic or nonpopulation serving jobs.

20. John F. Kain, "Distribution and Movement of Jobs and Industry," in *The Metropolitan Enigma*, ed. James Q. Wilson (Chamber of Commerce of the United States, 1967).

largest metropolitan areas between 1958 and 1963.

Little effort thus has been made to explain the existing pattern of industry location. Even less attention has been devoted to explaining changes in this pattern. Most studies hypothesize a high degree of stability: existing basic employment activities (especially large ones) are presumed to remain at their existing locations (although possibly expanding somewhat). Heavy reliance on cross-section data and the *ad hoc* methods of projecting employment changes used in metropolitan growth models have biased these models toward underestimating the amount of change in existing distributions of employment and overestimating employment levels in built-up areas, particularly dense central areas. Forecasting errors of this kind can have, among other consequences, an enormous and erroneous effect on capital investment choices in transportation.

This bias toward overestimating employment levels within central areas is symptomatic of a more general shortcoming of metropolitan growth models. This is a failure to model, or even seriously contemplate, the adjustment processes by which the stock of residential and nonresidential structures is adapted to new uses over time. Metropolitan growth models have concentrated on explaining or projecting the determinants of housing demand and particularly on projecting the extent and density of new residential development. Thus, they have all but ignored the determinants of supply or the manner in which the housing stock adjusts to changes in demand. Yet questions of stock adjustment are obviously central to any analysis of housing markets or to the design of programs to modify the characteristics of the housing supply. New construction accounts for only a fraction of the supply during any time period and tends to be sharply limited in its location. Despite the im-

portance of stock adjustment and adaptation in metropolitan housing markets, almost no research exists on the way in which units are modified, upgraded, and downgraded.

It would be expected that CRP studies would have been more concerned with these questions. However, they also focus on the demand for housing and virtually ignore supply relationships. Thus, we have virtually no idea how expenditures for maintenance and renovation vary by type of property and by type of household. While the meager research does not permit us to be very specific about changes in the housing stock, we do know something about the magnitude of this activity. Census data indicate that over four million dwelling units were upgraded from substandard to standard condition, while nearly one million went from standard to substandard between 1950 and 1959.[21] Similarly, expenditures for residential upkeep and improvement during 1965 were an estimated $11.4 billion of which $4.7 billion were for additions and alterations and $5.0 billion for maintenance and repairs. This compares with the $21 billion spent during that year on new housing units.[22] It is clear that adequate structural modeling of metropolitan growth and development requires a more explicit treatment of the process of investment, disinvestment, and modification of the housing stock. Until some better understanding of these processes is obtained and, more ambitiously, some modeling of these changes is executed, metropolitan growth models will be next to worthless as either predictive or analytical devices for built-up areas. These deficiencies are even more serious where the

21. Bernard J. Frieden, "Housing and National Urban Goals: Old Policies and New Realities," in *The Metropolitan Enigma*, ed. James Q. Wilson (Chamber of Commerce of the United States, 1967), p. 156.
22. U.S. Bureau of the Census, *Statistical Abstract of the United States: 1967*, 88th Ed. (Washington, D.C., 1967), p. 715.

models are intended as guides to government housing policy.

Nearly all metropolitan growth models are also color blind. While the impact of housing market segregation on metropolitan development is not adequately understood, there can be no doubt that its effects are substantial.[23, 24] The rapid growth of Negro ghettos in metropolitan areas creates a massive entrapped demand for low-quality housing within the ghetto. The ghetto's growth similarly displaces a large number of low-, middle-, and high-income whites that might otherwise locate in central cities. The result is a much different pattern of housing demand by income groups than might exist in the absence of segregation; specifically, a much more homogeneous residential location pattern by income groups than might otherwise be expected.

Some Observations on Data Requirements and the Present State of the Art

Any large-scale effort at computer simulation creates, of course, special data and information requirements, as well as a need to estimate particular behavioral parameters. Computer simulation models are demanding in their data input requirements. One common fallacy is to argue that these models are therefore beyond the present state of the art. Actually, large-scale models of this type, which systematically check economic and physical data against one another, can provide an invaluable set of consistency checks on the accuracy and quality of data obtained from diverse sources. Such models also provide useful insights as to where data ignorance is likely to be most penalizing

23. John F. Kain, "The Big Cities' Big Problem," *Challenge,* Sept.-Oct., 1966, pp. 5-8.
24. John F. Kain and Joseph J. Persky, "Alternatives to the Gilded Ghetto," paper prepared for the Economic Development Administration Research Conference in Washington, D.C., Feb., 1968.

in terms of decision quality. Indeed, the development of such models is almost a necessary prerequisite to better specifying data requirements and information systems for public investment evaluations. The alternative, incidentally, of asking only the questions that can be answered directly by the available data often smacks of weak rationalization for avoiding the important or relevant questions.

This need for a better definition of objectives in data gathering is well illustrated by experience with urban transportation studies. Disproportionate shares of the budgets of these studies have been devoted to the collection and processing of huge quantities of cross-section data on urban travel and in making "assignments" to highway networks. By comparison, budget allocations for the development of metropolitan growth models, while increasing considerably in recent years, remain pitifully small. In part these allocations are a reflection of what study staffs regard as important. However, they are also the result of an inherent conservatism. Changes from the "standard" method require extensive justification (particularly to the Bureau of Public Roads and state highway agencies) and assurances (difficult to provide) that the results obtained from a new and untested method will be better than, or at least as good as, those obtained from the standard method. Obviously, the first step in providing the needed justifications is development of better models.

Standardization also has an impact on the kinds of data available. Data availability has, in turn, strongly influenced not only the modeling activities of transportation studies' research staffs but the research focus of academic researchers. Thus, because urban travel and household data have been plentiful (although there have been some annoying deficiencies), computer modeling activities have emphasized relationships between household characteristics and travel choices to the exclusion of analyses for which data are not so easily available; e.g., employment location and the behavior of the housing market. In short, lacking a good model to better illuminate data needs, data availability has become a major factor conditioning and perpetuating model designs, with all their inadequacies.

Lack of attention to important behavioral problems, such as industrial location, housing stock adaptation, and the effects of housing market segregation in metropolitan growth models and CRP studies can also be explained by their having taken place as part of rather specific policy planning projects. Far more progress would have been possible at the same cost if these efforts had been placed in a somewhat different institutional structure. Transportation studies have been carried out in over 200 and CRP studies in over 160 metropolitan areas since World War II. Virtually all of the transportation studies developed some kind of a metropolitan growth model. Admittedly, in many instances these models were nothing more than crude, *ad hoc* projections. But in an ever increasing number of instances, somewhat more ambitious modeling efforts have been undertaken. At any rate, the amounts spent on model building in the aggregate have been large. But for any one project, they have tended to be too small to permit really significant gains in the state of the art. When significant advances were obtained they were frequently poorly reported (e.g., due to limited publication budgets) or withheld because of "proprietary interests." Progress would have been more rapid if even a small portion of the resources devoted to these many individual model building efforts had been pooled and used for much larger scale efforts in a few metropolitan regions.

The model building or research activities have also been expected to keep pace with the difficult time schedules of the project planners. This creates substantial tensions between the researchers (or model builders) and the project planners that sharply constrain the amount and kinds of development that can be undertaken. Invariably, both the research and the planning suffer. Anyone engaged in research appreciates the deleterious effects of unrealistic deadlines. A clearer distinction seems needed between project planning and research and, in particular, between the actual planning process and model development.

In sum, large-scale physio-economic models are admittedly not easy to build. Frustrations have been known to attend such efforts. The basic requirements are: (1) a good deal of specific engineering; (2) an advanced computer technology and capability; (3) experience with the design and empirical estimation of economic growth models; and (4) an ability to estimate behavioral parameters relating changes in economic and physical phenomena to changes in the socioeconomic system. Nevertheless, the approach is much too appealing and correct to be abandoned. The alternative of limping along with partial analytical techniques can "succeed" only by begging many relevant questions.

VII

PROBLEMS: Perspectives on Research and Policy

Each of the preceding sections contains implicit reference to the problems that beset cities in this the post-industrial age. This section encompasses two sets of what we referred to as "problems" in the introduction. One is concerned with the problems involved in theory, research, and policy formulation, and the second with broader social and economic issues. Most problems of theory are either implicitly or explicitly intermeshed with these issues. Among the latter, most readers will agree the critical problems of the city are those of persistent poverty, housing and renewal, rapid growth and sprawl, pollution, and the quality of urban life and urban government.[1] Each of these problem areas is of course the subject of a book. Nevertheless there are important geographic dimensions to these problems which follow logically from the materials previously covered in this book. The papers in this section were selected to illustrate some of the spatial and environmental aspects of these problems and to emphasize the importance of both theory and policy.

By what standards do we judge the contemporary city? How do we identify the problems in the forms of cities that seem to be developing and in the environments that this growth creates? In an extract from a larger

1. Among the most critical issues in American cities is obviously the racial problem. Excellent bibliographic sources are included in Nathan Glazer and Daniel P. Moynihan, *Beyond the Melting Pot: The Negroes, Puerto Ricans, Jews, Italians, and Irish of New York City* (Cambridge, Mass.: The M.I.T. Press, 1963); *Journal of the American Institute of Planners*, "The Cities, The Black and the Poor," Special Issue, Vol. XXXV, No. 2 (March 1969); *American Behavioral Scientist*, "Urban Violence and Disorder," Special Issue (March 1968); *Report of the National Advisory Commission on Civil Disorders* (New York: Bantam Books, Inc., 1968); Donald Canty, *A Single Society: Alternatives to Urban Apartheid* (New York: Praeger Publishers, 1969); and Roger Miller (ed.), *Race, Research and Reason: Social Work Perspectives* (New York: National Association of Social Workers, 1969).

paper, Hans Blumenfeld establishes one set of criteria to evaluate what might be called the "natural" pattern of cities. The criteria relate to the variety of choice in accessibility, communication, employment, and community stability and change, each of which were themes of previous sections in this book. What solutions exist and what opportunities do the present forms of cities offer? The essay concludes with an engaging challenge to the criteria of contemporary urban planning and to prevailing social values and philosophies, particularly in the dedication to private and profitable land ownership, which typify North American society. Are the ideal patterns proposed for our cities in direct conflict with democratic ideology? Is it possible to have both private land ownership and a clean efficient urban environment? Will we have to choose?

Alonso takes up the issue of theory in discussing the conceptual premises underlying the urban renewal program in the United States. The formulation of this program, Alonso contends, rests on certain critical assumptions about the attitudes of urban residents, particularly their housing and location preferences, which derive from the traditional ecological views of the city. Some of these assumptions, as outlined in general terms in Section II and in more detail in Section V, according to Alonso are fundamentally incorrect. The assumptions in question concern the preferences of most urban residents for open space and new housing and for central city or suburban living. He argues that people move to the suburbs in order to buy larger quantities of space and not, as seems to be implicit in the classical ecological models of urban structure, for new housing.

The philosophy of urban renewal programs appears to assume similar preferences because of its emphasis on the construction of new high-density housing in areas designated for renewal. Alonso concludes that on this basis urban renewal programs are doomed to failure, and an expensive failure at that. What is needed in fact is a policy based on the provision of more land and housing space in urban renewal areas in order to attract middle-income residents back into the central city. This position may well be disputed as housing preferences have not been adequately measured. Yet it does challenge our knowledge of basic urban spatial concepts and our ability to apply these to realistic policy problems.

The application of theory to urban problems is beset with difficulties. Charles Tiebout identifies two serious limitations of intra-urban economic location theory in this regard. The first is the inability of existing location concepts, given their origin in agricultural studies, to adequately treat the complex interrelationships, defined as externalities, which permeate the urban landscape. He draws an analogy between attempts to remove these spill-over effects in rural and urban property. Increasing the amount of space utilized for any given crop may neutralize or at least reduce the effects of externalities on other crops grown in the vicinity. In the crowded urban environment, however, what happens to one property inevitably exerts greater influence on surrounding properties. The construction of fences is not sufficient to eliminate the effects of neighborhood deterioration or pollution as examples. The second deficiency, identified earlier by Teitz, is the lack of attention given to the effects of location decisions made in the public sector in forming the urban environment.

Urban renewal is one of the important policy decisions influencing the structure of the city. Recently, both the results and strategy of public renewal programs have been subjected to severe and open questioning, and by all evidence rightly so. As there are now several excellent summary volumes on the subject, particularly on the complex issues of legislation and financing,[2] only one article on renewal was selected for inclusion here. In this paper David Wallace reviews both the concepts and strategies of urban renewal in the United States as well as the relevance of urban theory and research to renewal policy. In so doing he emphasizes the concern expressed by Alonso that existing theories of urban growth and structure may not provide a substantive basis for public policy. He outlines a parallel plea to that of Tiebout that policy decisions should be a logical component of these theories. In part the many problems and criticisms of urban renewal stem from the diversity of strategies which have appeared in the absence of a consensus on goals and approaches. Wallace classifies these strategies into five groups, each reflecting the views of individual interest or pressure groups on the value of renewal to the city. In evaluating criticisms of renewal, which usually relate to procedure (relocation) and impact,[3] or the degree of attainment of welfare criteria and economic goals,[4] he concludes that improvement in goal specification and in the

2. J. Q. Wilson (ed.), *Urban Renewal: The Record and the Controversy* (Cambridge, Mass.: The M.I.T. Press, 1966); and J. Bellush and M. Hausknecht (eds.), *Urban Renewal: People, Politics, and Planning* (Garden City, New York: Doubleday and Co., 1967). Comparative experience in urban renewal in North America is summarized in *Urban Renewal,* papers presented at the Inaugural Seminar of the Centre for Urban and Community Studies, University of Toronto, 1968, from which the present paper has been taken. Recent European experience in urban renewal is discussed in Leo Grebler, *Urban Renewal in European Countries: Its Emergence and Potentials* (Philadelphia: University of Pennsylvania Press, 1964).
3. The results of this study should be contrasted with the results of a recent study in the Hyde Park-Kenwood community in Chicago. See B. J. L. Berry, S. Parsons, and R. Platt, *The Impact of Urban Renewal on Small Business* (Washington, D.C.: Small Business Administration, 1968).
4. An excellent summary of economic analyses of urban renewal programs and strategies is Lowdon Wingo, Jr., "Urban Renewal: Objectives, Analyses, and Information Systems," in W. Z. Hirsch (ed.), *Regional Accounts for Policy Decisions* (Baltimore: Johns Hopkins Press for Resources for the Future, Inc., 1966), pp. 1-29.

formulation of theories of urban structure and growth are necessary and complementary tasks to be solved if renewal is to become an effective policy instrument.

The impact of the public sector is nowhere more apparent than in the provision of urban transportation facilities. As one illustration, Ruth and Edward Brecher provide a critical evaluation of contemporary transportation planning with reference to the journey to work (see Section IV). The Brechers introduce their critique with a description of a massive traffic snarl in Boston which developed during one unusual evening rush hour and lasted for five hours. The message seems clear that the city cannot accommodate the automobile. They then set out to evaluate the comparative costs of expressways and transit systems and to propose alternative transportation plans as guidelines for increased public awareness and action. The increasing public outcry against expressway construction in North American cities illustrates the need for such evaluations.

Subsequent essays treat other dimensions of the urban "problem": slums and blight, urban sprawl, land speculation, environmental pollution, and the deteriorating quality of urban living. The existence of urban slums and widespread physical blight have been of concern to social activists since cities began. Yet why do these conditions still persist?[5] The reasons why blight, slums, and ghettoes exist in the first place are complex and as yet ill-defined. There is no doubt that such conditions reflect a convergence of factors, rather than one central force. They derive from social attitudes, taxing and zoning policies, housing policies, technological change, spill-over effects in the real estate market, and the like. Most of these considerations, as in the case of the existence and persistence of Negro ghettoes in most large American cities, tend to be interlocking and self-reinforcing. What may start as a problem attributable to a single source tends to quickly become a set of problems which require a multitude of solutions. Urban slums are concurrently a social problem, in terms of social pathologies, a poverty problem because of low incomes, a housing problem in regard to space shortages and deterioration, and a spatial problem because of the geographic position of such areas relative to areas of growth within the metropolitan area. These factors are discussed in detail in an extensive and growing body of literature.[6] One critical problem in

5. For example, David R. Hunter, *The Slums: Challenge and Response* (New York: The Free Press, 1964). A number of the volumes of readings on housing, renewal, and planning referenced in the Introduction also include numerous papers on urban slums. One of the best known and most provocative reviews of planning approaches to the slum problem is Jane Jacobs, *The Death and Life of Great American Cities* (New York: Random House, 1961).

6. For example, G. E. Berger, "The Concept and Causes of Urban Blight," *Land Economics,* Vol. XLIII, No. 4 (November 1967), pp. 369-76; Anthony Downs,

American cities, that of race and residential location was reviewed by Harold Rose[7] in Section V, and is not emphasized here.

Each of the above papers illustrates the interlocking nature of spatial and environmental problems in urban areas. Urban blight, for example, may be defined as a level of both social and functional depreciation of real property which is unacceptable to the community at large. The interrelationships which permeate the urban landscape, the externalities noted by Tiebout, accelerate the negative effects of obsolescence resulting from changes in land use, technology, and rising social aspirations. The market system of our cities locks in these negative effects because of the vulnerability of urban property to any environmental change and to the unstable behavior of real estate owners. The critical dilemma of the housing market is the uncertainty of real estate investment. The result is that all owners will minimize risks by minimizing maintenance investment, and in the example of the Negro ghetto, by rapidly turning over the racial composition of a neighborhood once the tipping-point has been reached. The outcome is increasing social segregation, block-by-block geographic expansion of the ghetto, and the encouragement of slum development. Not all ghettoes are of course slums by any definition, yet the withdrawal of maintenance investment tends to be more pronounced in such areas.

Within the specific definition of a slum as a social problem there are recognizable differences in social characteristics. John Seeley views typical urban slums as encompassing a number of types of communities. Some are based on tight kinship and informal personal relations, while others are virtually receptacles for society's unwanted, unacceptable, unfit, and unknown. The various functions of each he contends must be understood if public policy is to be an effective and humanly sensitive method of improving life in these problem areas. All too often the broad descriptive label of slum is applied to all of the older inner-city residential areas which contain substandard housing. A typical example of the misapplication of this term is reported in Herbert Gan's study of the West End of Boston in Section V. Clearly what is needed are planning policies which are equated to the nature of the social problem at hand.

"Alternative Futures for the American Ghetto," in "The Conscience of the City," *Daedalus,* Vol. 97, No. 4 (Fall 1968), pp. 1331-78; Jay W. Forrester, *Urban Dynamics* (Cambridge, Mass.: The M.I.T. Press, 1969); John F. Kain, "Coping With Ghetto Unemployment," *Journal of the American Institute of Planners,* XXXV (March 1969), pp. 80-89; John F. Kain, and J. J. Persky, "Alternatives to the Gilded Ghetto," *The Public Interest* (Winter 1969), pp. 74-87; and E. Smolensky, S. Becker, and H. Molotch, "The Prisoner's Dilemma and Ghetto Expansion," *Land Economics,* XLIV (November 1968), pp. 419-30.

7. See also Harold M. Rose, *Social Processes in the City: Race and Urban Residential Choice,* Commission on College Geography, Resource Paper No. 6, Association of American Geographers, Washington, D.C., 1969.

Opposite to the inner-city slum is the discontinuous development typical of the urban periphery. As noted in Pryor's paper in Section I, the area commonly described as the rural-urban fringe, at least in most North American cities, has distinctive and generally unfavorable characteristics. Robert Harvey and William Clark take issue with some of these widespread interpretations and with the confusion that surrounds the definition of sprawl, its causes and consequences. They recognize several forms of sprawl rather than one, each of which may be attributed to varying combinations of monopolistic competition in the land market, rugged physical terrain, misdirected taxing policies, rigid attitudes to land ownership, and transportation and housing policies. Speculation, however, is not considered a serious catalyst. In evaluating the different costs and benefits that may be attached to this growth they conclude that sprawl occurs because it is economical. The question we might raise is whether economics are a sufficient excuse.

Among the other outcomes of the variety of human behavior, attitudes, and activities previously described in these pages is the pollution of the natural environment. It is a problem perceived by everyone, but like the slum it persists.[8] Joseph Fisher supplies a provocative summary of the multiple pollution problem, involving water, air, noise, landscapes and so on, that typifies and often degrades life in our cities. To this list of well known types of pollution he adds poor planning, inadequate and unstimulating architecture and construction, inefficient city management and undisciplined civic behavior, all of which do contribute to an unpleasant urban environment. The way people perceive, develop, and utilize this environment tells much about the quality of urban life.[9] He concludes by offering suggestions for approaches to meeting some of these problems. The solutions proposed are many, but the available means of public action and administrative equipment appear to be insufficient. Yet increased social awareness and the trend toward administrative reorganization in urban areas may provide the necessary stimulus for action on and implementation of pollution controls. That such reorganization, particularly in

8. A recent review and bibliographic summary on pollution is provided in Robert Ayres and Allen Kneese, "Pollution and Environmental Quality," in Harvey S. Perloff (ed.), *The Quality of the Urban Environment: Essays on New Resources in an Urban Age* (Baltimore: Johns Hopkins Press for Resources for the Future, Inc., 1969); and in Allen V. Kneese, "Economics and the Quality of the Environment—Some Empirical Experiences," in M. E. Garnsey and J. N. Hibbs (eds.), *Social Sciences and the Environment* (Boulder: University of Colorado Press, 1967), pp. 165-293.
9. An interesting reference in urban geography to environmental perception is Frank Horton and D. Reynolds, *Urban Environmental Perception and Individual Travel Behavior*, Special Publication No. 2, Department of Geography, University of Iowa, Iowa City, Iowa, 1969.

our government structures, is necessary is clearly illustrated by what Daniel Moynihan[10] calls the "crisis of confidence." There is a general feeling that existing institutions are inadequate to solve urban problems. This may be the challenge for the future.

10. Daniel P. Moynihan, "A Crisis of Confidence," *The Public Interest,* No. 7 (Spring 1967), pp. 3-10.

HANS BLUMENFELD

Criteria for Urban Form

This volume has dealt, in generalized terms, with the "natural" pattern of the contemporary metropolis, as it develops without the benefit—or "malefit"—of planning. Is it "good"? How do we judge urban form? In attempting to establish criteria of judgment, we have to resort to a series of pairs of contradictory desiderata.

(1) *Minimize need and maximize opportunity for commuting to work.* As people come to the metropolis primarily "to make a living," it is important that they can find work close to their homes but also that they can avail themselves of the wide choice of jobs available in the metropolis. It is equally important to employers to be able to draw on the full range of skills available anywhere in the area.

(2) *Access to center and to periphery.* As Ebenezer Howard put it, people are attracted by two magnets, "city" and "country." They want easy access both to central facilities and to open land.

(3) *Separation and integration of functions.* Intermingling of different uses such as industry and housing tends to conflict. But complete isolation of different functions from each other threatens to narrow the horizon of the inhabitants of the metropolis and break it up into sterile and monotonous precincts.

(4) *Identification with a part and identification with the whole.* People want to identify with and take part in the life of the community in which they live and which they can easily grasp and understand. But there is an equal if not greater need for understanding, interest, and pride in relation to the metropolis as a whole.

(5) *Continuity and change.* Identification with any environment becomes impossible if it loses its identity. But change is the very nature of the metropolis, and possibilities for change and growth must be kept open.

Finally, whatever demands may be derived from these or other criteria, they must be satisfied at the least possible cost.

From "The Urban Pattern" in **The Annals of the American Academy of Political and Social Science,** Vol. 352, March 1964. Reprinted by permission of the author and the American Academy of Political and Social Science, Philadelphia, Pennsylvania.

434

Form of the Metropolis

In the light of these criteria, we may try to evaluate the developing form of the metropolis and proposals for its modification.

The need for commuting can be minimized by providing employment in every part of the metropolitan area. This requires the reservation, by zoning or by creation of industrial "districts" or "estates," of land for industry. But, with a growing majority of the labor force employed in services, the location of these assumes even greater importance. Service employment outside the central business is growing, but it is scattered. Much could be gained by concentrating into major subcenters or "secondary downtowns" retail, consumer, public, professional, and retail services. Probably, manufacturing plants of those labor-intensive industries which can operate on small lots might be located in their proximity. Around and possibly also within these centers, housing at relatively high densities could be developed. The concentration would, in turn, make possible the establishment of higher-order services.

Such centers would also satisfy the criteria of variety and of integration of functions and would be identifiable focal points, continuous as to location and basic arrangements but changing in detail, of the districts which they serve. There is no certainty about the most desirable size of such districts. However, it is pertinent to note that the estimates of the minimum population required for a self-contained urban unit have been steadily going up. Ebenezer Howard thought of 20-30,000 for his "garden cities." The English "New Town" program started with a limit of 50-60,000 but subsequently has raised it to 100,000 and more. American planners now talk of a quarter million. It may be that the half-million, which we specified as the minimum population

of a metropolis, is required to support a really vital and attractive secondary downtown.

The concentration of many potential trip destinations would reduce the number of trips and also make it possible to provide good public transportation. This is likely to result in substantial economies in transportation costs.

While such centers would also, to some extent, increase the choice of jobs, maximization of opportunity requires primarily a relative compactness of the entire metropolis which can be effectively served by an economical transportation system.

Compactness also facilitates access to the metropolitan center. However, complete compactness would make access to open country very difficult. At the same time, the frequently advocated proposal to isolate each urban unit by a "green belt" would increase the distances to the center as well as to other units and would increase the cost of transportation and of public utilities. Increasing distances would also result from a "linear" scheme, which would line up its urban units along one axis.

It seems preferable to line up such units along a greater number of shorter lines, which would radiate from the metropolitan center. This would result in a "stellar" or "finger" scheme, with easily accessible wedges of open country between the fingers. It would, by its orientation to the metropolitan center, facilitate identification with the metropolis as a whole, while the centers of the districts, out of which the fingers are composed, would encourage identification with the district. Growth would be possible by adding new districts at the ends of the fingers, but it would be gradual, preserving continuity with the previous district.

Ends and Means

It appears that some modification of the "natural" pattern of the metropolis could make it "better." However, such modifications are hardly possible without some fairly substantial institutional changes.

Deliberate modification of the pattern of the metropolis presupposes that its area is brought under one jurisdiction, by annexation, federation, or any other means—if there are others. Separate municipalities, each hard pressed to balance its budget and with the real estate tax as the main source of income, must of necessity, like the private real-estate owner, attempt to get those land uses which produce the highest revenue and require the least operating cost—industry, commerce, and wealthy residents, preferably without children. They can hardly be expected to provide open space for the recreation of their neighbors nor to house and educate workers to produce added value in the factories and spend their money in the stores of the next municipality.

A metropolitan government could, legally, implement a land-use pattern by zoning. But zoning transfers development rights from some property owners to others. If a strong secondary downtown is to be created, values from other sites which might be chosen by its occupiers would be transferred to its area. If an area is to be kept open, its development value is transferred to all sites in the development fingers. The blatant inequity of such a procedure makes it unfeasible. Substantial development rights can be shifted around only within the same ownership, which, in this case, means ownership by a metropolitan authority.

Such an authority could become the owner of all or most of the land within its boundaries only if it could tap the very substantial income generated within its boundaries far more effectively than our present three-level tax structure permits.

These three measures would make it possible to modify the general metropolitan pattern. They could not, however, deal with the most serious inadequacy of the present pattern, the exclusion of the low-income groups from the expanding outer zones of the metropolis. This could be accomplished only by assumption of public financial responsibility for standard housing. It is self-deception to talk of "socially balanced" new neighborhoods or "New Towns" when one-third of the population cannot possibly afford to live in them.

Metropolitan-wide governments with commensurate financial resources, public land owership, housing financed, though not necessarily owned or managed, by and for the public, not token ghettos for the poor—these are all "radical" innovations in terms of current American thinking. However, in different forms and degrees, all of them have been adopted, singly or jointly, within the framework of democratic capitalism by the countries of northwestern Europe.

The American and Canadian people are faced with a dilemma. They want, and want badly, two things. They want to live in an efficient, convenient, healthy, and pleasant environment, and they want, as individuals and collectively as municipalities, to be able to make an honest dollar out of every piece of property they happen to own. The two are basically incompatible. Sooner or later they will have to decide which one is more important to them.

WILLIAM ALONSO

The Historic and the Structural Theories of Urban Form: Their Implications for Urban Renewal

An explanatory theory of urban form has been developing in recent years that provides an alternative to the classic theory developed by R. Haig (1926)[1] and by Park and Burgess (1925).[2] The new theory has emerged so gradually and it differs from the older theory in apparently so slight a degree that it has gone unrecognized as being in conflict with the older theory. Yet the difference is a most important one not only from a scientific point of view but also for the vast urban renewal program that is so vigorously being pursued by our cities. This program is implicitly based on the older theory, and depends on its validity for its success. Should the new theory prove more nearly correct, there is grave danger that much of the current renewal effort will fail.

Both theories are interested in a broad

1. Robert M. Haig, "Toward an Understanding of the Metropolis," *Quarterly Journal of Economics,* May 1926.
2. Ernest W. Burgess, "The Growth of the City" in *The City,* editors, R. E. Park and E. Burgess (Chicago, Illinois: University of Chicago Press, 1925).

range of urban phenomena but it will be useful to focus on a paradox that has intrigued students of American cities since the turn of the century. This is that land values tend to drop with distance from the center of the city, while family income tends to rise with distance. The paradox is, then, that the well-to-do live on cheap land while the poor live on expensive land.

The older theory explains this phenomenon in terms of the passage of time, and may be called an *historical theory.* In brief, it holds that as a city grows the houses near the center of the city become old and therefore unsatisfactory to high-income families. The rich then build new houses where open land is available which, of course, is on the periphery of the city. Those of lower income then move into the vacated houses. The moving parts of this theory are the aging of structures, sequential occupance by income levels, and population growth, for the number of low-income families must increase to provide a demand for the houses vacated by the well-to-do. The urban area grows much like a tree in

From **Land Economics,** Vol. XL, No. 2, pp. 227-231. Copyright © 1964 by the Regents of the University of Wisconsin. Reprinted by permission.

cross-section, by means of a growth ring which leaves behind old, rigid tissue. Land values do not play an essential part in the argument and seem to receive slight mention in recent statements of the theory although earlier writers placed emphasis on speculation to explain high central land values. Homer Hoyt, whose sector theory is an important variant of this type of theory, explains: "The wealthy seldom reverse their steps and move backwards into the obsolete houses which they are giving up. . . . As they represent the highest income group, there are no new houses above them abandoned by another group. Hence the natural trend of the high rent [high rent for dwellings: it should not be confused with high land values] area is outward, toward the periphery of the city."[3]

In spatial terms the clearest statement of the historical theory remains the "concentric zones hypothesis" of Burgess. The Burgess theory is the spatial equivalent of the filtering process or trickle-down theory of the housing market according to which new houses are built only for the well-to-do but in time pass on to those of lower income. Thus, society provides housing for the poor not by building directly for them but by letting the wealthier absorb most of the depreciation costs before the house is handed on.

By the historic theory, then, the location of the rich depends on the availability of land. Residential urban renewal, whatever its original statement of intentions, has taken on a typical form. It clears decayed housing in the center of urban areas and replaces it with more expensive housing, confident that the newness of the buildings will attract those of high income. The previous low-income residents are thus displaced and move elsewhere, typically away from the center. In effect, it

3. Homer Hoyt, *The Structure and Growth of Residential Neighborhoods in American Cities* (Washington, D.C.: Federal Housing Administration, 1937), p. 116.

makes land available in the center for high-income housing, while still endorsing the trickle-down view of the housing market. If correct, this means that Americans will no longer follow each other like lemmings from the center to the suburbs and then to the exurbs as population grows and buildings age. Rather, this centrifugal expansion will now be turned inward and the growth ring will be near the center. The suburbs, as time goes by and buildings age, will become available to those of lower income. But of course the new central housing built by urban renewal will in time age also and the wealthy will once again be on the move. If they are not to go to the suburbs again urban renewal will have to provide them with buildable land near the center. Logically this should be the land ringing the areas now being renewed, which will by then be occupied by the oldest structures. Following this reasoning, urban renewal in the long run will be a ring expanding outward *through* the urban mass, leaving behind a gradient of housing that ages toward the center and pushing against the oldest housing of the urban area until the center is once again the oldest and the process starts again. Thus, the simple movement outward of high income to the suburbs will be replaced by a convection flow like that of boiling water in a pot.

This is a very simplified view of the distant future of urban renewal. It is clear that the moving ring of renewal cannot always be of the type used today. Institutional devices may be modified to permit renewal by the free market and less direct governmental intervention. Depending on a host of factors, such as the quantity and condition of the housing stock and the structure of the demand forces, rehabilitation may become more important. For the process to work there must be a balance of the rates of population growth, new construction, aging of buildings, and the structure of demand, according to income, age, and type of families. If there is, for instance, a very rapid increase of low-income demand, the filtering process may not deliver enough dwellings to the lower sector of the market and overcrowding, invasion, and accelerated social obsolescence will result. In the extreme case, as in the developing countries, there would result a complicated alternation of high- and low-income rings. If, on the other hand, population growth slows down or the structure of income rises rapidly at the bottom, there would be a softening of the demand for old, central accommodations so that the centrifugal growth may leave a hole in the center, manifested in high vacancies, lower densities, reconversions, and the other phenomena of "gray areas." This appears to be the case in metropolitan areas and of course is the ideal situation for urban renewal according to the historical theory.

But the practice of urban renewal is based on the assumption that if high-cost housing is offered in the center, it will attract high-income people. Recent investigators have suggested that the peripheral position of the rich may be the result of the structure of market forces rather than the consequence of historical development. That is to say, that the rich may be in the suburbs because they prefer to be there rather than because they have nowhere else to go. In the words of Vernon and Hoover, "higher-income people use their superior purchasing power to buy lower density housing, but at the cost of a longer journey-to-work."[4] Note that in this explanation it is lower density rather than newness that makes the suburbs attractive to the wealthy.

The reason for the preference for ample space over shorter journey-to-work becomes clear by the simultaneous consideration of the value of land, the cost of commuting, and travel and space preferences. Most Americans prefer to have ample land, as shown by the popularity of the single-family home and as anyone can learn merely by talking to people. As with all desirable things that can be bought, the wealthy tend to buy more land than the poor, all other things being equal. Coupling this greater purchasing power with lower land prices away from the center, it is clear that the savings in land costs are far greater for the rich than for the poor. For instance, if one would buy 10,000 square feet and the other 2,500, a drop in price of 50 cents per square foot would mean a savings of $5,000 for one and only $1,250 for the other.[5] Consider now that such a move would cost $500 per year in added commuting costs: this would represent 20 cents per square foot for the poor man but only 5 cents per square foot for the wealthy one.[6]

If typical American tastes are a liking for ample land and a relative willingness to commute, it is clear that more distant but cheaper per-square-foot sites are more attractive to the wealthy than to the poor. Accessibility, which diminishes with increasing distance, behaves as an "inferior good;" that is to say that, although accessibility is desirable, people as they become wealthier will buy less of it because they prefer to substitute for it something else (land). Such inferior goods are not rare: for instance, the per capita consumption of wheat and its products has declined steadily in this country as people in their affluence prefer to substitute meat and other foods for bread.

This explanation of the more-land-but-

4. Edgar M. Hoover and Raymond Vernon, *The Anatomy of a Metropolis* (Cambridge, Massachusetts: Harvard University Press, 1959), p. 169.

5. Of course, greater quantities will be bought at the more distant location because of price elasticity, but the essence of the argument is unchanged and it is simpler to view the quantity of land bought by each individual as unchanging with location.
6. The analysis of the effect of income on location is developed more fully in my *Location and Land Use* (Cambridge, Massachusetts: Harvard University Press, 1964).

less-accessibility phenomenon may be called *structural* to distinguish it from the Burgess-Hoyt historical explanation in that it represents the working out of tastes, costs, and income in the structure of the market. It does not rely on the historical process although this process is undeniable and has been a strong influence reinforcing the structural forces. To put it another way, the structural theory says that a city which developed so quickly that the structures had no time to age would still show the same basic urban form: low income near the center and high income further out. The structural theory is not an alternative to the historical theory; rather, they are complementary. Thus far, both have acted in the same direction. But now urban renewal, relying entirely on the logic of the historical theory, has set them at odds for, while it provides central land, it cannot afford sufficiently low prices to permit low densities[7] so that the structural forces will continue to pull high-income people (and therefore new construction) to the suburbs.

Under these conflicting circumstances the net result of urban renewal will be unclear, particularly because the structural forces depend on tastes and these are very difficult to evaluate. For instance, the fragmentary evidence I have seen of societies where apparently no great value is placed on ample land for the home (*i.e.,* societies in which the rich do not occupy very much more land than the poor) suggests that there the rich tend to live near the center. This is in agreement with the

---

7. Even in cases in which extraordinary subsidies (in excess of 90 percent) afford the redeveloper central land at a price comparable to that of suburban land in order to permit low densities, the resulting pattern has been more urban (ten or more families per gross acre) than suburban (four or less families per gross acre). The subsidy per family of providing 100-by-100-foot lots at suburban land prices in a renewal area would be in the order of twenty to forty thousand dollars.

structural theory because, as there is no attraction in the substitution of space for accessibility, greater purchasing power is used to buy accessibility. Indeed, there is in the United States a substantial minority of the well-to-do that does prefer accessibility to space and this minority lives in luxury apartments or town houses in the central areas. Much of the demand for the new construction of urban renewal is undoubtedly attributable to previous neglect of this sector. It is also instructive to follow the location of middle-class families through their life cycle: the young couple lives in a central apartment, moves to the suburbs as the family grows, and returns to the center after the children leave home, thus reflecting their changing space-preferences with changing family size.

Taste or preference for space are possibly words too weak to denote what is really meant by this key variable of the structural theory. Rather, the nature of the demand for space in this country seems to be a deeply ingrained cultural value, associated not only with such functional needs as play space for children, but also with basic attitudes toward nature, privacy, and the meaning of the family. A preference so deeply rooted in a culture is not likely to change suddenly. But in the last three years there has been a startling increase in the proportion of new dwellings in multiple structures and it has been suggested that this reflects such a change of taste. Whereas from 1954 to 1956, 89 per cent of new dwellings were single-family homes and only some 11 percent of new dwellings were in multiple structures, the current rate is well over 30 per cent. Have the well-to-do, who are the consumers of most new housing, begun to prefer accessibility to space? In a sense this may be the case: as metropolitan areas have grown bigger and roads more congested it may be that some have come to feel that the commuting trip is too long and have returned to central locations. However, the prospective vast road building and mass transit improvement programs may again reduce time-distances (much as the popularization of the automobile did in the 1920's) and re-establish the almost complete preponderance of the single-family house.

But there is another explanation, more powerful than that of distances, for the increase in apartment construction. We have mentioned the convection-flow life cycle of the American middle-class family. The young and the old need apartments while it is those in their thirties that power the demand for single-family homes. Those reaching the age of thirty these days are those who were born in the Great Depression when the birth rate fell dramatically. Thus, in the 1960 to 1970 decade there is less demand for single-family homes because there are 9 per cent fewer people coming into their thirties than in the 1950 to 1960 decade. But this situation will change sharply in 1970: there will be an increase of almost 40 per cent among those reaching their thirties in the 1970-1980 decade over the 1960-70 decade. Thus, we may attribute much of the shift from single to multiple dwellings to temporary changes in the age composition of the population rather than to fundamental changes in taste and we may expect that these changes will be short-lived.

Urban renewal is a magnificent opportunity to reshape our cities. Today there is money, public support, legal power, and human energy of a scale that could not have been imagined a few years ago. The urgency of urban problems and the many years of frustration of those concerned with them have naturally led to a rush of activity now that the means are available. In spite of the conviction of the planning profession as a whole that comprehensive planning is necessary, too often urban renewal has consisted of one project and then another, with no overall plan. It is precisely this lack of a comprehensive urban (*i.e.,* metropolitan) plan that has obscured the implicit theoretical structure of renewal, for a comprehensive plan is the marriage of the goals of a community with an understanding of the structure of the community. The implicit exclusive reliance on the historical theory (which is incomplete without the structural theory) raises the danger of large-scale failure through a lack of understanding of the workings of the urban system and a misinterpretation of the structure of demand. It is a false empiricism to scoff at theory as too abstract. Empiricism requires an evaluation of results and it will be many years before the long-range effects of current experiments in urban renewal become clear. At a time when we are so vigorously rebuilding our cities it is important that we be as intelligent as possible about it. We must make explicit the theories of urban structure under which we are proceeding. If the historical theory by itself is correct, current renewal procedures stand a good chance of success. But if it needs the complement of the structural theory, current renewal projects are skimming a narrow and specialized sector of demand which will soon dry up. In many cities stand acres of cleared land awaiting development and investors face time lags of years from the inception to the completion of development. The reaction-time of the urban renewal process is too slow to permit a purely pragmatic approach. Vacant land and vacant buildings are frightening possibilities.

CHARLES M. TIEBOUT

Intra-urban Location Problems: An Evaluation

This paper is concerned with one aspect of intra-urban location problems: the potential of intra-urban location theory to the solution of urban problems. No attempt is made to develop a theory of intra-urban locations. Rather, what is sought is a current appraisal: What are the urban problems? What can we say about them? Finally, where do we go next? It is important to consider such questions as these, for regardless of the state of our theoretical models, planners are planning, developers are developing, and highway engineers are pouring ever more concrete.

After a few words pleading the case for urgent attention to intra-urban location problems, this paper considers: a pure-market, intra-urban, "location assignment" problem, the approach to a solution via agricultural location theory which, in turn, highlights the crucial role of governments in intra-urban locations and suggests, possibly, the most important void in the theory of the urban structure.

The Intra-urban Location Assignment Problem

The nature of a pure, intra-urban, location theory assignment problem may be con-ceptualized in the spirit of von Thünen and Lösch.[1]

Imagine a bounded nonagricultural region. A large population engaged in a set of productive activities is introduced. Included in these activities are dwelling units.

To keep things simple, eliminate all considerations of geographical terrain; i.e., activities are located on a smooth un-differentiated surface. Further, assume a transport surface exists. This implies that the transport costs of a good are constant for any given distance in any direction. (This says nothing about the level of transport costs; they may be high or low.) In general terms, the task is to find a general equilibrium solution which allo-cates these activities in urban space. The resulting patterns, leaving the term "pat-terns" and their measurement undefined,

---

1. Johann H. von Thünen, *Der isolierte Staat in Beziehung auf Landwirtschaft und National-ökonomie* (Hamburg: Fr. Derthes, 1826); August Lösch, *The Economics of Location,* trans. by William Wolgom with the assistance of Wolfgang Stolper (Yale Univ. Press, 1954). The term "assignment" is not used here in the tight technical sense, but as shorthand for spatial allocation of activities.

From the **American Economic Review**, Vol. LI, No. 2, May 1961, pp. 271-278. Reprinted by permission of the American Economic Association, Evanston, Illinois.

represent the spatial allocation of urban activities via pure market forces.

One approach to the assignment of economic activities in urban space has been to apply agricultural location analysis.[2] Consideration of agricultural theory not only provides some insight into urban patterns but, in addition, points up certain difficulties which suggest new areas for investigation.

Agricultural Location Analysis

Agricultural location theory has been relatively well explored.[3] Many of the explorations are variations on a theme by von Thünen. Von Thünen imagines a central city surrounded by farm lands. Some distance away from the city is an impenetrable circular forest bounding the farm lands. His task is that of assigning agricultural crops to various zones.

In essence, transport costs to market for the various products taken in conjunction with demands allocate land to various product belts. In this analysis, the belts are concentric rings around the central city. The technical details of the analysis are not relevant for purposes of this discussion. What is relevant are two of the assumptions common to discussions of agricultural location theory.

One assumption is that of a transport surface, just as Weber and Lösch assume a transport surface for their nonagricultural analysis. True, modifications of simple "cost proportional to distance and weight" analysis have been introduced, but these modifications do not vastly distort the patterns of location. How unrealistic is the assumption of a transport surface?

Let me suggest that for the United States it is not unrealistic. Between the railroads, highways, and waterways, we have a grid that approaches a transport surface. Whole areas are not inaccessible. In consequence, we do see broad belts; cities surrounded by truck garden crops; milk, cream, and butter zones; and other patterns, explicable in terms of transport-demand considerations.

A second assumption, standard in most discussions of market forces, is the absence of externalities; i.e., private costs and benefits are equal to social costs and benefits. In the agricultural sector, this seems to be a reasonable assumption. Robert Frost is our witness. In his "Mending Wall," Frost's neighbor argues that "good fences make good neighbors." His stand is adamant despite Frost's declaration that:

> He is all pine and I am apple orchard
> My apple tree will never get across
> And eat the cones under his pines.

Less elegantly, Mr. Frost sees no externalities.

These assumptions plus others combined with market forces enable transport cost-demand variables to assign rents such that agricultural zones are created. A simple piece of casual evidence suggests that the theory and the assignment of agricultural locations is not bad. While we have heard many discussions of agricultural problems, the "problem of bad locations" does not arise.

How does this analysis apply in intra-urban space?

Intra-urban Location Patterns via Agricultural Location Theory

Agricultural location theory does suggest some spatial patterns in terms of the

2. See William Alonzo, "A Theory of the Urban Land Market," *Regional Sci. Asso. Papers and Proceedings,* 1960, pp. 149-57; Walter Isard, *Location and Space Economy* (Technology Press, M.I.T., and Wiley, 1956), pp. 200-06.
3. See Edgar S. Dunn, *The Location of Agricultural Production* (Univ. of Florida Press, 1954) and the references cited therein.

intra-urban location assignment problem specified above.

Given an urban core of some kind, we would expect to find located in that core activities where: (1) face-to-face requirements are high; (2) specialized human labor inputs are needed which may be available outside of the core's large labor pool; and (3) the market is the whole region; i.e., speciality, consumer oriented activities. Outside the core, the single storied manufacturing activities which cannot afford high land rents could be expected. Mingled in with these manufacturing activities are some residential units. And probably the furthest distance from the core would contain the "estate dwellers."

In terms of key variables, these patterns emerge as the result of: (1) technology; e.g., the technology of mass, assembly line production which requires a low single storied manufacturing plant; and (2) communications; e.g., the need for face-to-face contacts versus telephone communication. Transportation facilities and technology are a third key variable. Recall that for our assignment problem a transport surface has been assumed. To the extent that transport costs on the transport surface are low or high, patterns may be expected to expand or contract. Congruent with these patterns, of course, is a rent map of the urban area.

All of this suggests, so far, that the application of agricultural location theory is relevant for intra-urban regions. These patterns are pretty much those described by Hoover and Vernon for the New York metropolitan region.[4] Given the objective of the Hoover and Vernon analysis, which is evidently to take a broad look towards the future, an agricultural type of analysis seems satisfactory.

Yet it does not distract from this type of analysis to suggest that this is not

4. Edgar M. Hoover and Raymond Vernon, *Anatomy of a Metropolis* (Harvard Univ. Press, 1959).

enough. Policy-makers, whoever that group may be, seem to require more specific information; i.e., more detail as to locational patterns. Here an agricultural type of location analysis breaks down.

The difficulty in applying agricultural location theory to the intra-urban region may be simply stated: the assumptions simply do not fit reality. First, urban areas are not transport surfaces and, therefore, simple rings do not emerge. Second, a more critical assumption: the lack of externalities is not valid. Externalities are omnipresent.

The absence of a transport surface. Urban regions, clearly, are not transport surfaces. Even Los Angeles is not an undifferentiated sea of concrete, in spite of the efforts of highway engineers. More often than not, major and minor arteries lead out from the core of cities.

As a result of arteries, urban regions become combinations of rings and arterial spokes; i.e., star shaped. To consider an urban region only in terms of rings can be very misleading. For example, consider the twenty-five to forty mile spoke out of mid-Manhattan running through Connecticut. This segment includes the commuter towns of Greenwich, Stamford, and Darien. If the segment is moved counterclockwise, a less densely populated region emerges, until the eastern shore of the Hudson River is approached. As even the reader unfamiliar with this area can guess, these denser strips lie along the commuting railroad lines.

This is not the place to ask if there is some optimal number of arteries. Whether a five, six, or n numbered star appears is not relevant. What is relevant is the simple realization that the patterns of urban development we see are not those that emerge from market forces operating on a transport surface. The patterns that result are dependent upon a transport network.

The transport network can well be included as an endogenous variable in any model relying on market forces; e.g., as Lösch has done. No doubt, many intra-urban bus routes are determined by market demands. Yet, the real world is full of imperfections; bridges take time to build; intra-urban railroads may temporarily provide "indequate" service in the absence of certain tax advantages; some cities may rely on rapid transit for the movement of people while others read the demand of mobility as a call for more freeways. In short, intra-urban location patterns reflect a transport network, and not a transport surface. Thus, agricultural patterns are modified. The transport network may well result from nonmarket as well as market forces. Hence, patterns are further distorted.

Perhaps the greatest difficulty in applying agricultural location analysis to the urban economy arises when externalities are considered.

Externalities in intra-urban space. The usual rules of the game allow only market forces in solving general equilibrium problems. Thus, in imagining any solution to the pure intra-urban location assignment problem stated above, no restrictive governmental actions are allowed. This implies no zoning, control of air pollutions, and other such governmental restrictions and activities. Obviously, it is difficult to imagine what sort of locational patterns might emerge, given the large number of externalities.

The presence of a substantial number of externalities in the urban area arises, in part, in the nature of externalities. Externalities have a spatial extent. While Farmer Jones's chickens and pigs may smell up his barnyard, they do not bother Farmer Brown. Space can isolate or internalize externalities. Yet, as any resident of Chicago can testify, the wafts from the stockyards on ripe days are something less than invigorating. In the case of urban areas, they simply do not have the space to internalize externalities.

Of course, externalities may be positive.

Whereas Farmer Jones's attractive front lawn may mean little to Brown, who rarely sees it, in an urban environment the whole neighborhood may enjoy one homeowner's striking landscape.

Geographically, externalities are of varying size. Some are confined only to a neighborhood; e.g., the attractive lawn. Others cover the whole region; e.g., air pollution.

Given the large number of externalities, suppose we seek a stable solution to the intra-urban location assignment problem without government restraints such as zoning. What would be the result? Without rigorous proof, it seems likely that an unending game of musical chairs would result. Maximizing its own advantage, a manufacturing firm may locate in the middle of a residential neighborhood. In turn, the residents may move only to find later another manufacturer in their midst. In short, I am suggesting that a problem exists with even more destabilizing elements than in the simple location assignment problem tackled by Koopmans and Beckmann.[5] Yet, their simple assignment problem had no stable solution.

The achievement of more stable solutions which recognize social costs and benefits may be accomplished when government action is introduced. The control of externalities in the urban region, which can only fall upon governments, removes some of the destabilizing elements. Unlike Frost's view on rural fences, we may analogize that zoning, for example, seeks to make good fences because good fences do make good urban neighbors.

Urban patterns then, to a much greater degree than agricultural patterns, are molded by governmental decisions. The form and mode of transport and the policies to control externalities are all important. In turn, the elements of urban

5. Tjalling Koopmans and Martin Beckmann, "Assignment Problems and the Location of Economic Activities," *Econometrica,* Jan., 1957, pp. 53-76.

problems are more clearly seen if we reconsider intra-urban location patterns as a joint product of government plus market decisions.

The Intra-urban Location Problem Reconsidered

The twofold source of urban problems is analogous to the sources of error in national income forecasting models. Two sources of error are possible: (1) the endogenous relations are less than perfect; e.g., the consumption function predicts poorly; and (2) exogenous variables are set incorrectly; e.g., government expenditures are higher than assumed.

Suppose we want to solve some urban problem, say traffic congestion. A "good" solution requires: (1) an ability to predict market reactions to an exogenous change; e.g., shopping behavior after the introduction of new one-way streets; and (2) that from the set of possible actions the government chooses the proper action; e.g., new one-way streets versus a new parking lot with shuttle bus service. Errors from either the first or the second imply a degree of nonoptimality.

Stated positively, good solutions require an ability to predict patterns which result from market forces, given governmental actions. Here new theories as well as the extensions of agricultural location theory can help to build better predictive tools. Good solutions simultaneously require appropriate governmental actions. It is the latter requirement that is much neglected and really involves a theory of the spatial aspects of urban finance. Examples will indicate the nature of the problems involved in evaluating the government component.

Consider an urban renewal program. Suppose slums are replaced by low-income housing. Assume part of this program is paid for by taxes on the rich.

In turn, the rich regroup in a suburban tax colony. As a result of both actions, urban patterns are altered. The slum has been removed, and, hopefully, the neighborhood reclaimed. The rich, now further out in the urban landscape, require commuting facilities. Other ramifications can be imagined.

The question is: Have we a good solution to an urban problem? Clearly, this action has resulted in a redistribution of income. Hence, the goodness or badness of the solution must, at least, consider local governments' function in income redistribution.

Recently, there has been an increased call for area-wide planning as a solution to urban problems. This is a subtle issue.

Area-wide planning is necessarily ineffective in the absence of area-wide government for the functions involved. With area-wide government, such solutions are good only to the extent that, through the political process, the government has somehow ascertained voters' views on the externalities involved. Without ascertaining preferences, we cannot be sure that governmental actions are solving urban problems consistent with consumer-voter sovereignty.

In summation, the solution to problems involving the organization of intra-urban space (1) requires a recognition of the role of the government in controlling externalities and influencing the transport network and (2) given governmental restraints, a theory which can predict location patterns. Both are important.

Yet this study, which originated in an attempt to evaluate the possible contribution of intra-urban location theory to the solution of urban problems, leads to the concluding judgment that, in terms of ordering research priorities, further studies on the role of the government win hands down.

DAVID A. WALLACE

The Conceptualizing of Urban Renewal

After twenty years—fifteen of them with
the federal loan and grant programme—
urban renewal is involved in a major
period of criticism and review. On the
one hand, its protagonists are seeking,
through intensive research and planning,
to give it a new and much needed intellectual thrust and long-range sense of
direction. On the other, its critics are
mounting serious, and often well-de-
served, attacks, based on the experience
to date.[1] Urban renewal's ability to with-
stand and survive depends, I believe, on
a renewed consensus on more carefully
formulated goals and a more sophisticated
set of concepts and strategies than have
existed up to now. Survival also depends
on a careful analysis and correction of
the programme's many current deficiencies. It is high time for a review. In
general, and with rare exceptions, planning for urban-renewal projects has been
poor, execution worse, and the final results decent, safe, and sanitary, but little
else.

1. E.g., Jane Jacobs, *The Death and Life of
Great American Cities* (1961).

Projects Without Strategy

It would be more accurate to call any
given city's urban-renewal activity a collection of projects rather than a programme. Projects have been initiated as
the result of local pressure to get rid of
the worst blight first, to satisfy special
interest groups, to clear areas with great
market potential, or to combine renewal
with other capital improvement programmes. In very few cases has there been any
effort to tie the projects to a city-wide
strategy.

Planning for these projects and programmes has been fragmentary and op-
portunistic until recently. It has suffered
because of the absence of over-all conceptualization, because of inadequate
understanding of the urban phenomenon
as a system, because of limited knowledge
of the consequences of even the first-
round effects of intervention in this system, and because of a concentration on a
"brick and mortar" short-run set of
goals. These last are largely irrelevant to

From the **University of Toronto Law Journal**, Vol. 18, No. 3, 1968, pp. 248-258. Reprinted by
permission of the author and the University of Toronto Press.

the majority of people affected by the urban-renewal action programmes.

Although, in the above sense, we don't know very much about what we are doing, we are doing it anyway. Across the nation most of the projects that can be processed within the technical and financial capacity of the cities involved are already somewhere in the renewal pipeline. An examination of their nature shows many that would undoubtedly make sense under any circumstances of adequate planning and conceptual framework; however, the majority of these same projects are recognized as the "easy" ones, the ones that have dramatic results, for which wide local support can be mobilized, and which rely almost solely on the investment market for new construction. Either their end product is hoped to be so good, or the slum conditions to be eliminated are so bad (in rare cases, both) that consensus on their validity is easy to obtain.

As these "easy" projects are processed and completed—and the rate is growing— the bureaucratic machinery of urban renewal begins to nibble at the tough problem areas for which planning has as yet no solution, nor are there even very effective ways of coping. These are the "gray areas" in which human problems, particularly those of poverty and minority groups, overshadow environmental problems.

The number of cities that are beginning to grapple with these is growing. Realization is also growing that the traditional focus of urban-renewal property and housing must shift and aim at the human problems more directly. In Oakland, Philadelphia, Boston, New Haven, New York, and other centres, new approaches are being hammered out—experimental approaches that are either only indirectly related to traditional urban-renewal action, or use various aspects of urban renewal as points of departure and the basis for access to people.

This shift in emphasis is long overdue

but it is still in its infant stage and time will not wait; the renewal programme's critics are basing their attacks on the extent to which urban renewal has not met its stated objectives, or goals imputed to it. The programme sails along in an ever-broadening sea of controversy about what it ought and ought not to do and be. Its friends have the somewhat uneasy feeling of "where do we go from here?"

A Major Flaw of the Renewal Programme

To understand the criticism it is first necessary to consider the diverse value-frameworks on which they are based. The fact that these bases vary widely points to one of the fundamental weaknesses of urban renewal—it is a multi-purpose programme with a major flaw.

Twenty years ago two interest groups that had been battling since the 1930s temporarily joined forces to support the urban-renewal enabling legislation. One group was a constellation of business interests, the other of social welfare. Each saw the need for and desirability of urban renewal from a different value framework or set of goals. Internally each group was divided into those primarily concerned with the physical environment—the architects, engineers, and city planners—and those interested in either the flow of money or the human problems of slum dwellers. To make national legislation possible, their goals had to be reduced to the most common denominator, no mean feat. In the federal Housing Act of 1949[2] this was done.

The Declaration of National Housing Policy stated the nation's major objective as: ". . . the realization as soon as feasible of the goal of a decent home and a suit-

2. Public Law 171, 81st Congress of the United States; 42 U.S.C.A. Ch. 8A s. 2. See also earlier state legislation such as Pennsylvania's Urban Redevelopment Law of 1945 (PL 991).

able living environment for every American family." The mercantilist philosophy clearly shows through the social welfare veneer in the additional qualifications that a high rate of housing production and related community development are necessary ". . . to enable the housing industry to make its full contribution toward an economy of maximum employment, production, and purchasing power."

The Act which follows these statements has been progressively broadened over the years since, to permit almost any kind of "reasonable" programme and approach. This kind of broadening is considered by each of the various interest groups as desirable, for its separate purposes. Nevertheless the continued broadening every year brings to a sharper focus urban renewal's major flaw and dilemma—it has to be all things to all people. Transportation, defence, education, or agriculture are comparatively single-purpose programmes that can be easily conceptualized, while urban renewal is a multipurpose programme in much the same way as is the Tennessee Valley Authority. Yet, unlike TVA, it does not have a central unifying and organizing concept, such as the "seamless web,"[3] that gave the valley programme its focus, intellectual coherence, and rationale. This lack of conceptualization has a two-fold aspect. We do not understand the nature of the urban phenomenon—the very thing we are so vigorously trying to renew. We understand neither its structure nor its growth, nor have we yet achieved any widespread agreement on what we want it to be.

The Problem of Conceptualizing

It is a not very constructive truism that there is need for an adequate theory of city structure and growth that both explains the present urban phenomena, and

3. See David E. Lilienthal, *TVA, Democracy on the March* (1944), at 54.

serves as a guide for future action. Nevertheless it is this lack that is at the root of many of our problems in urban renewal.

Why is theory so important? For one thing, if we had an adequate theory it would serve as a means of testing the long-range implications of intervention in the system. As a result, programmes that are objected to because of their short-range negative impact could be judged instead on a long-range perspective. In the absence of adequate theory we find difficulty in achieving consensus on goals except at the very high level of national housing policy. At lower levels of the goals-means scale, we are forced to an *ad hoc,* short-run, and "muddling through" approach. Many of the current criticisms are based on negative short-run reactions, with little understanding of the long-range consequences that might justify or invalidate any particular project. Thus theory would serve the important need for a method to discount the utility of the future in the present.

The theory that does exist is meagre, mostly descriptive, and not very useful. It postulates the city as a system—that is, a phenomenon whose elements are united by some form of regularized interaction. We observe and understand limited forms of such interaction in transportation and shopping patterns, housing markets, and industry. These latter are sub-systems and their relations with each other and with all the other elements have been the subject of a number of efforts at descriptive theory, and a few attempts at normative theory. These theories are heavily weighted toward economic explanations of reality. They all see the evolving pattern of land uses and activities as constantly tending toward a state of dynamic equilibrium. The problems of urban land-use are seen as resulting from maladjustments between the relatively rigid physical urban structure, and the changing needs of a dynamic society. Ratcliff says: "The redevelopment (renewal) of cities is an ancient and basic process by which the urban structure painfully and imperfectly, but continuously, moves to adjust itself to the ever changing needs of the community."[4]

The normative "model," the concept of what ought to be, which underlies most of this economic theory is that of Robert Murray Haig[5] who said that activities should be assigned to areas to minimize the costs of friction, of which transportation and site rental were the most important. Later modifications by Homer Hoyt elaborated but did not basically change this model except to borrow the Burgess' concepts of the process of segregation to the pattern.

These basic formulations underly much of the rationale of business groups in their concepts of the city, and therefore in their approach to, and expectations from, urban renewal. They consider renewal, as a public activity, to be intervention in a market and competitive system and to be justified by the need to make up for imperfections in the market mechanism that impede the adjustment process, to eliminate conditions which are economic or social liabilities. Adam Smith's "unseen hand" has to be helped out.

In contrast to business groups with their economic justification for urban renewal, social-welfare interests see the general raising of living standards as the prime rationale for public intervention in the urban system. In these latter groups opinion on the techniques of intervention is divided, with environmental determinists predominating until recently. Mounting evidence has demonstrated the fallacy of the premise that improvement in environment basically influences people's lives for the better, and massive—but still symptomatic—treatment of the

problems of the poor and the culturally deprived is now being mounted in conjunction with renewal efforts. The expectation still is that there will be significant improvement in the environment and housing possible by marrying the "human" approach with rehabilitation, conservation, and code enforcement, that is, urban renewal.

A Classification of Strategy Concepts

The expectations, or explicit and implicit goals, and the assumptions of fact and concepts of intervention of all interest groups can be classified under five general headings.[6] These are essentially long-range strategy concepts—in fact philosophies, partly of what is, partly of what ought to be—that embody goals and implicit (sometimes explicit) assumptions. These strategy concepts are not necessarily mutually exclusive. In the absence of consensus on theory and conceptual framework, discussed previously, they serve as a partial theory for the interest groups involved.

REPLACEMENT AS A STRATEGY

Replacement strategy is the simplest concept. Worn-out parts of the system are removed through clearance; in the urban system they are replaced by sound development. The assumption is that structural quality and environmental deficiencies as defined by standards of "eligibility" will determine areas to be renewed. Implicit in this strategy is the assumption that elements that are worn out are no longer a working part of the system.

In the early days of the programme, many areas were cleared on this basis with the expectation that market forces

4. Richard U. Ratcliff, *Urban Land Economics* (1949), at 427.
5. Robert Murray Haig, "Toward Understanding of the Metropolis" (1926), *Quarterly J. Economics*.

6. The writer is indebted to Dr. William G. Grigsby of the University of Pennsylvania, Institute for Urban Studies, for suggesting the organization of the concepts on this basis.

would automatically operate to provide investment on the vacant land. Both business and social-welfare groups supported this basic strategy at first, but this is no longer the case. Often those removing the worn parts did not recognize that they were still working parts of the system, and so the necessary preconditions for their replacement were not established. Thousands of still vacant acres across the country, acres whose development potential is very dim, are evidence of the inadequacy of this concept of strategy. This is common knowledge and need not be elaborated. The strategy remains, with a kind of simple logic that has appeal.

GUIDING URBAN GROWTH THROUGH INVESTMENT

Guiding urban growth principally through new investment combines elements of a replacement strategy with market forces. Areas of action are a function of existing quality, trends, and the economic feasibility of desired renewal. They are classified by degree of renewal potential, or renewability. Basic to this strategy are concepts of self-renewal and continuous renewal. A fundamental belief is that through carefully selected clearance and re-investment, the private market can be triggered to respond and generate private investment. New spores will grow of themselves and, at a theoretical extreme, the city can be made to be self-regenerating and adapting.

This strategy has behind it primarily economic goals such as maximizing investment, and the efficiency of the urban pattern. Dyckman[7] developed it as a theoretical strategy, and in at least one major American city, Detroit, it is implicit in the renewal programme.

Two contrasting examples of how this strategy affects programmes are the

7. John W. Dyckman and Reginald R. Isaacs, *Capital Requirements for Urban Development and Renewal* (1960).

Charles Center in Baltimore, and the area north of Connecticut Avenue in Washington, D.C. Charles Center was conceived of as necessary to halt the deterioration of the entire downtown area and to create a new investment climate. It only belatedly depended for its public purpose on the elimination of blight within its own boundaries. The area alluded to in Washington is eminently suited to conservation treatment but, so far, local interests have prevented its becoming an active area. The reason is that it is looked at by Georgetown-type rehabilitators as the next Georgetown. They feel that renewal would stabilize the Negro population which they would like to displace. These examples point to a major element of the strategy—the replacement of structures in key areas where the market potential is great to set the stage for subsequent action.

THE FILTRATION STRATEGY

Another concept of strategy sees major additions to the housing supply (and office supply) as setting the stage for the eventual depopulation of the slums and their ultimate clearance. It relies on elements of the previous strategy but adds conservation. It also includes programmes to open up the suburbs to slum occupants, the location of housing on vacant land or formerly non-residential areas (often central business district (CBD) or near-CBD location) and has the major additions to the housing supply added at upper- or upper-middle-income levels.

The underlying assumption of this strategy is that the filtration system operates to move the slum occupants up the quality ladder as they inherit the dwellings left by occupants of the new housing. As a result, preconditions of high vacancy and low acquisition cost will be established that will ultimately make possible the massive elimination of obsolete and deteriorated housing. A cycle of renewal similar to the original growth pattern of the city will ensue. Variations on this strategy include heavy commitments to industrial, institutional, and commerical renewal to take advantage of their investment thrust and aid the filtration.

Philadelphia's programme from 1957 through the present is based on this concept, with minor local variations. The CURA report[8] framed the basic policy as subsequently adopted by the office of the development co-ordinator. It represented an agreement between business and social welfare groups that further frontal attacks on slums were of limited potential success and should wait on the preconditions mentioned above. Social welfare interests—particularly the environmentalists —had to be content with delay in the realization of the goals until a more opportune moment.

This philosophy or thesis is one of the major rationales for the proposal to dramatically lower densities, later embodied in Philadelphia's comprehensive plan. However there is some question as to whether the city's conservation programme is consistent with the thesis, since one of its probable effects, if it materializes, will be to undercut the market for new construction.

The filtration strategy is a more system-oriented approach than most, and is the one which, potentially at least, has most promise for meeting the goals of all interest groups.

THE BOOT-STRAP STRATEGY

In contrast to the relative balance, at least over time, of the filtration strategy, the basic concept of the boot-strap strategy

8. Philadelphia Redevelopment Authority, *CURA Report* (1956). See also, William L. C. Wheaton, "The Feasibility of Comprehensive Renewal," *Ends and Means of Urban Renewal* (1961), 68. The recently completed Renewal Program Study recommends in effect carrying out the CURA recommendations not already implemented.

is to conserve and upgrade existing property, but without displacing the occupants. It is the concept that everything is improvable, and worth improvement, in place. Public housing, code enforcement, low-standard rehabilitation, and self-help conservation programmes all combine to raise the minimum standards of housing, hopefully to acceptable levels. This strategy is logically combined with "human" renewal and social-service programmes to retain the rich texture of social organization of the city.

It has a wide-spread appeal for a variety of reasons that reach to the goals of all groups. It not only keeps slum inhabitants where they are, but also may use their housing stock more efficiently. It presumes to teach them habits of thrift and concern for property, good middle-class traits they must learn before they can be acceptable in better areas. If the occupants are Negroes, the boot-strap strategy assuages the consciences of us all that things are being done for them, but that these things won't upset the rest of the city too much. In its early history urban renewal frequently has had this self-help philosophy, according to which houses don't grow obsolete, at least not if treated properly. It is a concept that leaves to other capital programmes the job of restructuring the city, and is consistent with notions of a laissez faire economy except for the very poor.

SOCIAL PLANNING AS A STRATEGY

The last strategy concept to be considered could almost be classed as non-renewal, although urban renewal serves two functions for it. This strategy makes people rather than property the central object. The nation's anti-poverty programme, supplemented in some cities by Ford Foundation funds and programmes, deals mostly with symptomatic treatment. At city-wide and national levels, basic causes of poverty and cultural deprivation are being studied, but to date symptomatic treatment predominates.

This strategy uses traditional urban renewal to some extent to provide room for industry, to improve the economic base, and, hopefully, to provide more jobs. The more important use of urban renewal is, however, the access to people that it provides. Gaining access to people in ways that they will find acceptable is always a problem for social welfare. Relocation and rehabilitation and conservation programmes provide such access. In this context, relocation is considered a major reason for renewal, not a burden and barrier to it as Dr. Grigsby points out. It becomes an opportunity for cities to offer social services and programmes, to help solve human problems that pre-exist relocation but that are uncovered by it.

This last strategy is based on a non-geographic concept of system and is looked at by groups oriented towards social welfare with considerable hope. The environmentalists among them see the possibilities for upgrading property, and the rest see the potential for the immediate improvement of social conditions.

In fact, cities now have one or another, or combinations, of these strategic concepts implicit in their over-all programmes. And, of course, they are not necessarily mutually exclusive, although certain aspects of them are obviously contradictory.

Evaluating Implications of Urban Renewal Programmes

Combining such strategic concepts in an over-all, logically consistent, yet practical programme for any city requires the kind of sophisticated effort envisioned in Pittsburgh and San Francisco, and a number of other cities. Various forms of models of the urban system and its sub-systems were developed in an attempt to set up trial relationships between elements. Alternative forms of intervention based on

different urban-renewal strategies and tactics were to be introduced and the results observed.

Hopeful though these sophisticated methods are, the evalution of implications of urban-renewal intervention will still pose problems because of the diverse values of the various interest groups involved. Traditional cost-benefit analysis methods have little usefulness here.[9] After model making, which can test programmes through the first round of effects, there must be theory to carry the programme further. What is needed is a renewed consensus on the objectives of urban renewal, and a basic conceptualization, like the "seamless web," to give the programme intellectual coherence and focus. The development of both descriptive and normative theory of city structure and growth is critical to the future of urban renewal.

Evaluation of urban renewal must range across the full scope of both programmes and goals to be valid. The current set of critics, in every instance, select, as points of departure, the objectives of renewal that fit their own value structure. Criticisms can be divided into two classes: those that deal with problems of process, and those that deal with goals. These latter can be grouped into the two major interest constellations discussed before, and within each of these into environmentalists, and functionalists, as subcategories.

Problems of Process

There is no question about the validity of the criticism that urban renewal takes too long from initiation to completion of projects. Explanations of the reason for the minimum five-year life cycle of the fastest projects leave much to be desired. The most valid is that any shorter period would require reducing the various steps and notices necessary to adequately pro-

9. E.g. Nathaniel Lichfield, *Cost Benefit Analysis in Urban Redevelopment* (1962).

tect the public interest and the rights of individuals. Since we are not clear what the first is, we lean heavily on the faith that a democratic process to achieve ultimate consensus will develop it, as well as protect the second.

What is equally clear is that the frequently unconscionable lengths of time required for the majority of projects is not in the public interest. The uncertainty for local residents and business men, the cost to cities in lost taxes, and the long-term disruptions of the social fabric of communities, are evidence that the price of progress is awfully high. Whether the price is considered too high will be decided by weighing the results achieved. Since this can only be done over time, it is likely that the two elements—cost and benefit—will not be considered in the same accounting system.

One major group of criticisms of process are concerned with the adequacy of compensation. The original guideline: paying people only what the city could get away with, has shifted to a greater concern for equity. Payments now include a good many things beyond actual real estate—relocation, good will, etc. Some observers say that the complaints could easily be silenced by simply paying people enough but the question is then: what is enough? Would the renewal programme become a bad business bargain for cities if the costs rise substantially? It would seem that this decision must be political, on the assumption that the democratic process will be the basis of the decision.

Problems of Welfare Goals

The more important criticisms concern the goals of the business and social welfare constellations of interests. William Grigsby points out that the early emphasis on providing decent housing for low-income people has almost disappeared. Only a few cities—most notably Norfolk, Virginia—have a reasonably high proportion of relocatees in public housing. Most cities have relocated from ten to twenty per cent in public housing, although many claim that the older units occupied by relocatees are substantially better than their former homes. This is statistically true but deceptive. It lends argument to the criticism that urban renewal has simply moved slums. The old distinction between slums as created by people and blight as an economic concept tends to disappear when considered in the light of experience. That is, the relocatees have moved under terms and conditions of income and minority status that put pressures for accelerated deterioration on the housing to which they move. Since, until recently, the move was without the benefit of extensive social help, it is very likely that the criticism is largely true.

The parallel criticism that the social fabric of communities has been torn asunder is equally true for the majority of programmes. While again this cannot be quantified, Gans' study[10] of the Boston experience does give it enough dimension to raise the hackles of any who see the great value to a community of its cohesive and organizing elements. The current community renewal programmes are giving detailed study of this as a factor in decisions concerning projects and treatment. The environmentalists among the critics—most notably Jane Jacobs—also point to the sterile, drab, and uninspired physical patterns that replace the slums, patterns that seem to prohibit any very rich new social textures developing.

Problems of Economic Goals

The environmentalists among the supporters of business interests are equally concerned about the sterile results of the new downtowns and the seeming disintegration of any sense of urbanity in most projects.

10. Herbert J. Gans, *The Urban Villagers* (1962).

Their concern is submerged under the functionalists who say that urban renewal doesn't really revitalize the city's economy, that it deals with symptoms rather than causes, and that it does not add taxables at the rate needed to provide the city with a sound economic future, and on these grounds generally damn the whole programme as unsound.

Facts are few in any over-all sense, although it is clear from partial evidence that the payout time is longer than had been hoped for. In Philadelphia, by 1963, the city was receiving in taxes from new construction more than has been lost by property torn down. The balance is going to get better in the next few years. Philadelphia, however, has one of the most vigorous programmes, and has cleared relatively little area. Norfolk, Virginia and Trenton, New Jersey, and a host of other cities, are not in such a happy situation. The fact that many programmes are heavily weighted to institutional and non-taxpaying uses has been, along with slow marketing, a major reason.

Equally valid are the criticisms that renewal programmes have helped big business at the expense of small—big business that needs no help. This is certainly the case, as example after example shows large single users taking over areas previously occupied by many small firms which are, in turn, either shoved to other areas, or go out of business. But the facts are not all on one side. One study[11] showed that fewer firms went out of business than the national average, and most got satisfactory quarters in adjacent areas whose economic viability was enhanced by the influx of relocatees. This particular situation was part of a planned strategy of area improvement.

General Appraisal of the Urban Renewal Programme

Nevertheless, the sum and substance of the above criticisms indicates a renewal programme whose results are less than exciting, whose methods are crude and slow, and whose objectives have yet to be reached to any marked degree. It is the thesis of this paper that the programme's critics are imputing particular goals to the programme without considering the total goal structure within which the programme operates.

Until a more sophisticated conceptual framework exists, with a general normative as well as descriptive theory of city structure and growth as its basis, these criticisms will continue—and should continue. Such criticism is an important device for shaping urban renewal's future.

11. Baltimore Urban Renewal and Housing Agency, *The Displacement of Small Business from a Slum Clearance Area* (June 1959).

RUTH AND EDWARD BRECHER

Getting to Work and Back

Monday, December 30, 1963, was a black day for Boston. Bruce Talford, who surveys Boston traffic conditions for radio station WHDH every afternoon from a helicopter, was among the first to note that something was seriously amiss.

"It was quite obvious when we took off from the heliport at 3:45 P.M.," he wrote the next morning in the *Boston Traveler,* "that we were in for an unusual afternoon. The northbound side of the Central Artery was already showing congested traffic at that early hour. We decided to track the congestion to its source and found traffic backed up through Leverett Circle underpass. . . . Then we swung over the Boston Public Gardens and Boston Common. . . . Traffic was literally bumper to bumper and completely stalled. . . . At each of the intersections traffic looked like something you'd expect to see in a cartoon. . . . By 4:45 P.M. the entire downtown area . . . was completely snarled. We began to refer to [it] as an emergency area."

In Boston each afternoon, as in most other large American cities, drivers are accustomed to find the *outbound* lanes of their freeways clogged up as the peak

hour approaches. But on this afternoon a relatively new phenomenon made its appearance. The ordinary downtown streets were so burdened by cars trying to get onto the new Southeast Expressway and other "fast" routes home that the relatively few cars coming into the city at that hour found it impossible to get *off* the expressways. Hence the inbound routes also clogged up. "It was then," Talford reported, "that we started referring to our traffic jam as the biggest of them all."

What caused this colossal snafu? Nothing very dramatic. Boston's traffic commissioner later told CU that a somewhat greater number of shoppers than usual drove into town that day; street capacity was a little below normal owing to snow from a few days before; there was more double-parking that afternoon in the financial district than was customary; and many cars started home earlier than usual because of the approaching New Year holiday.

Out of such commonplace factors the crisis rapidly burgeoned. At 7:40 P.M., Talford noted, downtown traffic was "still at a near standstill." At 8:10 P.M., "the downtown area looked like a typical 5 P.M. rush-hour period." Not until after 9 P.M., more than five hours after the emergency began, were near-normal conditions restored.

Reading of Boston's "happening," you may feel sorry for her sorely tried residents and suburbanites. But in point of fact, the events of December 30, 1963, marked a beneficent turning point in the city's transportation history. Bostonians rebelled. They demanded action, and in less than a year they got it. The state legislature increased cigarette taxes by 2¢ per pack and earmarked the proceeds for improvements in public transportation. Boston's Metropolitan Transit Authority, serving the city and 13 suburbs, was superseded by a new agency with responsibility for improving transit service for the city and 77 suburbs. Planning programs were launched to provide the entire metropolitan area with a high-quality, balanced rapid transit and freeway system.

Last month, in Part 1 of this series, CU documented the arguments for and against such a combination of (1) high-quality rapid transit for the bulk of the rush-hour trips to and from work in a heavily built-up central business district and (2) well-planned freeways for the many other errands that make up the modern American family's life. The evidence pointed to the conclusion that many if not most cities are in dire need of something on the order of San Francisco's Bay Area Rapid Transit (BART) system to help unclog the vast system of Federally financed urban freeways begun in 1956 and scheduled for completion in 1972. The BART system is slated to open in 1969, with stations and ample parking out in the country between suburbs, 80-mile-an-hour top speeds, average scheduled speeds of 50 miles an hour (including 20-second stops), average platform waits of only a minute or two between rush-hour trains, comfortable seats, good lighting, air-conditioning, noise control, and other conveniences and amenities—all for a fare significantly less, and for some riders dramatically less, than the current cost of freeway commuting and parking.

A dozen other large North American cities, as CU noted last month, have rapid transit plans in various stages of preparation—either for building new systems approaching San Francisco's in quality or for upgrading their existing systems. But most of these plans are today stymied by the same obstacle: tax subsidies are required for the construction of high-speed, high-quality transit systems—and except in San Francisco, Montreal, and Toronto the subsidies have not yet been secured.

All city and suburban residents should be directly concerned with these transit plans, whether or not they themselves commute on transit lines. For if urban transportation problems are not solved, their cities are likely to suffer traffic jams like Boston's; and if transit systems are subsidized, the money will have to come directly or indirectly out of their pockets. In many cases, moreover, referendums will be held at which residents will be asked to approve or disapprove transit subsidies. To vote wisely, an understanding of the alternatives is important.

"Automobile commuters pay for the roads *they* use through gasoline and other taxes," opponents of transit subsidies insist. "Why shouldn't transit riders pay their own way, too? There must be something wrong with a transit system that can't finance itself out of the fares it collects."

This argument, however plausible superficially, is based on a widespread misunderstanding. At first blush it may appear that automobile commuters really are paying their own way. Under the Interstate System financing plan, for example, vehicle owners pay a billion dollars in gasoline and other taxes for every billion dollars' worth of Interstate System freeways built. But the fallacy becomes apparent if we take a closer look at a typical commuter route—the 15-mile Kennedy (Northwest) Expressway into downtown Chicago. Here is an analysis prepared by the New York engineering firm of Parsons, Brinckerhoff, Quade & Douglas, well-known transportation consultants:

The Northwest Expressway was built at a cost of about $238 million. If placed on a financing basis equivalent to that presently typical for public transportation improvements, allowing interest at 4 per cent and depreciation over about 50 years, capital charges can be said to amount to $11.1 million a year. It is estimated that fuel and other related taxes paid by vehicles operating over the Expressway will amount to approximately $3.8 million per year.

Thus user taxes, the consulting firm concludes, cover only about one-third of the capital cost—and nothing is left over to cover the expressway maintenance costs, the operating costs, the costs of traffic control, and other annual charges. The automobile commuters who use the expressway are very heavily subsidized. Where does the money come from? "The balance of the capital, maintenance, and operation costs must be met," the PBQ & D analysis continues, "by taxes on fuel consumed by vehicles operating over roads and streets already completed, some for decades."

Where a freeway built to handle peak-hour urban commuting costs $2,000,000 per lane mile, Dr. Lyle C. Fitch of the Institute of Public Administration, estimates the tax on gasoline burned on the freeway at peak hours would have to be increased by 75¢ a gallon to cover the cost of the road.

An even higher estimate has been made by the Regional Plan Association for the Greater New York area, based on studies by Professor William Vickrey of Columbia University:

The subsidy to rush-hour motorists on typical urban expressways and streets is about 10¢ a mile per automobile. The person driving 25 miles to work during rush hours in a metropolitan area is subsidized about $5 a day (or perhaps 50¢ or $1 less if he passes toll gates) . . . if [commuter] railroad and subway riders received the same subsidy as automobile commuters, the government would have to pay each rider handsomely to step onto the train.

Parking, too, is being subsidized. Free parking on streets, low-cost parking in city-owned or city-subsidized parking lots and garages, and parking provided free or at low cost by employers as an employee "fringe benefit," all reduce the out-of-pocket price of automobile commuting below the economic cost.

Against this background, the need for a transit subsidy becomes more understandable. A transit system, no matter how popular, how badly needed, or how well planned and operated, can hardly be expected to woo commuters off the freeways without a subsidy so long as the urban freeways themselves, and the parking at their downtown end, continue to be lavishly subsidized.

Another factor that tends to make a transit subsidy virtually necessary is the belief of many commuters that using their automobiles costs only as much as the transit fares do. These people tend to underestimate the latter. When asked, some car owners set the cost of driving to work as low as 3¢ or 4¢ a mile. They are thinking, of course, of the day-to-day out-of-pocket cost of driving a car one additional mile—assuming that the car itself is already paid for, insured, garaged, and in good running condition. The full cost, in contrast, averages more than 10¢ per mile driven. "If commuters' cars came equipped with taximeters that ticked off 10¢ each mile to remind drivers of their actual costs," one expert has commented, "these people might adopt a more realistic attitude toward the relative costs of driving and public transportation—and it might then be possible to raise transit fares high enough to permit new high-quality construction without a subsidy."

Some economists oppose on principle raising transit fares to cover the full cost —even if it could be done without driving more commuters onto the highways. They argue that transportation is a public "good" like education, parks, and public health; and they therefore consider it sound public policy to make transportation available below cost, or even free of charge.

The fine points of all these ideas need not be argued here. For the blunt fact is that, whether warranted or not, subsidy to peak-hour commuting by car is far too deeply imbedded in the economics of our large cities to be wrenched out at this late date. And if freeway and parking subsidies continue, the corollary inevitably follows that high-quality rapid transit will also require a subsidy.

The following five proposals, accordingly, are all concerned with ways in which a transit subsidy might be secured.

Proposal 1. Harvest the "Unearned Increment"

When the city of Stockholm, Sweden, years ago foresaw the future need for new suburbs, it bought low-priced land beyond the city limits. Now it is extending high-speed modern rapid transit lines into these undeveloped areas and building carefully planned new communities along the routes. The rapid transit lines enormously increase the value of the outlying land, of course—and the income from this land can thus be tapped to help pay for the rapid transit. Stockholm in effect thus harvests the land-boom bonanza that the new transit lines create.

American cities experience the same enormous inflation of peripheral land values when improved transportation becomes available. Russell E. Singer, executive vice president of the American Automobile Association, cited some star-

tling examples in *Traffic Quarterly* for April 1964:

In Houston, during a five-year period, land values along the Gulf Freeway increased 65 percent more in dollar value than land distant from the facility. A study by Texas A & M College of the Central Expressway in Dallas described the increase in tax valuation of abutting property as "astounding"—a gain of 544 percent in fourteen years. Communities along the route of Boston's circumferential freeway report property value increases as high as 700 percent. In Atlanta, undeveloped land rose from $100-$400 per acre to $1200-$1400 per acre after the freeway was built. Along the Eastshore Freeway in California average raw land values soared from $500 to $21,000.

Similar land-value increases occur when new transit lines are built, as Toronto's experience has shown.

It is not necessary for a government body to buy land on the Swedish pattern in order to tap these unearned increments. Much the same result might be achieved by taxing the land-value increase that results when a freeway or rapid transit line is opened up, and using the proceeds to pay for the freeway or transit line.

Proposal 2. Subsidize from Local Taxes

The three North American cities that have to date committed tax funds for new rapid transit systems are all financing them in large part out of local tax funds. The San Francisco BART system, for example, is being financed largely through a $792,000,000 bond issue; interest and amortization will be paid by local taxpayers in San Francisco and the two neighboring counties served by the system. The bond issue was approved in a referendum by 61.2% of the area's voters, even though they knew it would increase the tax on a modest home by an estimated $27 a year for many years to come. (Even some precincts that will receive no service whatever from the new BART system voted in favor of the bond issue.) In Montreal a mayor who urged that a new city subway be dug at the expense of city taxpayers was overwhelmingly elected in 1962, and the subway is now being dug. Toronto's new subway system is similarly being financed in considerable part with local taxes.

Transit subsidies by local governments can be justified on the ground that the annual value of the benefits will exceed the annual cost of the subsidy—and that the benefits will accrue to the entire area rather than merely to those who commute on the transit system. Benefits to the San Francisco Bay Area from the BART system, for example, have been estimated as follows:

Savings in travel time	$40,810,000
Savings in accident costs	630,000
Savings in automobile insurance	1,287,000
Savings in parking charges	5,850,000
Savings in freight handling costs	2,128,000
Savings in traffic control costs	242,000
Total	$50,947,000

This total is greater than the annual cost of the system to the Bay Area's taxpayers.

It seems unlikely, however, that voters in the area were much swayed by such dollar estimates. Rather, local observers report, voters approved the bond issue because they loved their city and their suburbs and wanted to protect them from more freeways and parking lots.

The basic objection to subsidizing out of local taxes, of course, is that the burden falls squarely on shoulders already overburdened by real estate and sales taxes levied for other purposes. That San Francisco, Montreal, and Toronto residents were willing to shoulder the added tax load for transit says much for their love of their cities, but their precedent is one not likely to be enthusiastically adopted by many other cities.

Local tax subsidies are further blocked by the fact that the benefits of a modern high-speed transit system will be shared by a city and its dozens or scores of suburbs—more than 500 independent governmental units in the case of the greater New York area, for example. This country lacks a pattern of metropolitan organization adequate to distribute the cost equitably among the local units and to persuade or require each of them to carry its proper share. However, San Francisco, Boston, Philadelphia, and Atlanta seem to be making some progress in this direction.

Proposal 3. Subsidize from State Taxes

Here Massachusetts has taken the U.S. lead with its new 2¢-per-pack cigarette tax increase earmarked for public transportation improvements. North of the border, legislators in the province of Ontario are also alert to the general benefits provided throughout a region whose central city has good transportation. Though a portion of the cost of the new Toronto subways is being borne by city taxpayers, part has also been assumed by the provincial government.

In many American states, however, state aid to metropolitan transit is unfeasible because the state legislatures are dominated by rural interests. The redistricting required by recent Supreme Court decisions may change this picture, but even so, most states are short of funds for such essential public functions as education. Like the cities, they would prefer to have some other agency supply the transit subsidy.

Proposal 4. Subsidize from Federal Taxes

The main justification for a Federal subsidy to local transit systems is the fact that the Federal government is already providing a 90% subsidy in many cases, and a 50% subsidy in others, for urban expressways and freeways that compete with transit systems. As a result, cities and their suburbs in effect lose their freedom of choice. If they don't choose a freeway solution to their problems, a cry goes up from the automobile clubs and sometimes from other segments of the "highway lobby" that they are "throwing away money" by letting the preferred Federal freeway subsidy slip away to other cities that did choose to build freeways.

President Kennedy had this warping of urban transportation patterns very much in mind in 1963 when he urged Congress to provide Federal transit assistance so that urban areas might "freely decide for themselves the proper balance of local public investment in highways and in mass transportation systems." The Kennedy proposal suggested $500,000,000 in Federal assistance as a "first installment" on a program for "revitalization and needed expansion of public mass transportation." Under the proposal the $500,-000,000 would have been available to pay up to two-thirds of the total subsidy required for each project; the remaining third would have been raised locally. This two-to-one ratio is smaller than the nine-to-one ratio for Interstate System freeways, but more favorable than the one-to-one ratio for other freeways. A two-to-one ratio is preferable, in CU's opinion, to nine-to-one because it is less likely to encourage overbuilding. To bring freeway and transit subsidies into balance, it may therefore be better to reduce the nine-to-one Interstate System subsidy rather than match it with an excessive transit subsidy.

Congress passed the Urban Mass Transportation Act of 1964, based on Kennedy's proposal, despite the fact that Congressional districts have for decades been heavily weighted in favor of rural voters. Some farm Senators and Congressmen, eager for city support of their farm-aid programs, were willing to reciprocate to a degree by voting for the bill. But only $375,000,000 in appropriation was authorized for the first three years—a meager drop in a very large bucket. As states revise their Congressional district boundaries to secure more equitable urban representation, future Congresses are likely to view more favorably Federal transit subsidies comparable in scope to Federal freeway subsidies.

How much money will be needed? Estimates differ. In some cities, a part of the construction cost can no doubt be paid for out of the fare box without raising fares so high as to drive away too many passengers. Some estimates suggest $10,-000,000,000 as a reasonable subsidy for construction costs over and above those that can be covered out of the fare box. A more generous estimate would peg the mass transit subsidy at the same level Congress selected for urban Interstate System freeways: $18,500,000,000, of which two-thirds would come from Federal taxes and the balance would be locally raised.

An $18,500,000,000 subsidy in one year, of course, would be unthinkable—and unnecessary. Two ways might be considered for spreading the cost over a period of years. The first is a pay-as-you-go program similar to the Interstate System plan, with construction spread over a 16-year period. This could be done if Congress pledged $771,000,000 a year for 16 years as the Federal two-thirds of the $18,500,000,000 subsidy. The second alternative is patterned after the Federal public housing subsidy program, with some modifications. Local agencies might be authorized to issue 50-year tax-exempt bonds, and the Federal subsidy committed to pay the interest and amortization on these bonds. If this pattern were followed, the Federal two-thirds of the $18,500,-000,000 (assuming a 4% interest rate) would cost $493,200,000 a year. Though the annual cost of such a program would be low, the total cost over the 50 years would be double the pay-as-you-go cost because of the interest.

Proposal 5. Provide a Combined Subsidy

Another modified pay-as-you-go proposal is perhaps most sensible—though highly explosive politically. It would provide in effect that sums collected via gasoline, oil, and tire taxes, excise taxes on new cars, and car registration fees be devoted to improving transportation facilities generally—freeways and transit alike—instead of merely building new freeways.

Out in the country where new freeways are needed, they would be built, as they are at present, with these "highway user taxes." In the cities, too, some new freeways could be built with these user funds, and modern computerized traffic-control systems could be installed to speed traffic through city streets. In cases where subsidy of parking makes sense, the funds could be used to expand parking facilities. For the peak-hour journeys to and from work in densely developed urban districts, however, the fund would be devoted primarily to rapid transit improvements.

This kind of proposal makes such good sense that, in isolated instances, it has been adopted without much opposition. San Francisco's Bay Bridge, for example, jams up severely every workday morning and evening. To lessen congestion, a new highway bridge could be built for an estimated $280,000,000. San Francisco has chosen instead to use $133,000,000 of bridge tolls paid by drivers to help finance a new transit tunnel—part of the BART system. Fast, safe commuting at moderate cost on the new BART system can help relieve the congestion on the Bay Bridge. Thus the "diversion" for transit construction of tolls paid by motorists will benefit all concerned. (Even the San Francisco automobile club supported such use of tolls.)

Consider, for another example, Chi-

cago's Kennedy (Northwest) Expressway. Users of this $238,000,000 road, as we have seen, pay only one-third of its capital cost and nothing toward its operation and maintenance. And this expressway also jams up each morning and evening.

A second freeway to eliminate congestion on this one would no doubt cost more than $238,000,000, since the least expensive right-of-way is already occupied. Thus users of other roads would have to provide an even lusher subsidy to unclog the Kennedy Expressway by building a new expressway. In contrast, a properly designed high-speed rapid transit system down the median of the Kennedy Expressway—which was built wide for this purpose—would cost much less and would accomplish as much or more toward decongesting the Kennedy Expressway at rush hours. Why not use the smaller amount out of highway funds to build the transit line? One answer is that the "highway lobby," and particularly the automobile clubs, fight such "tax diversion" proposals tooth and nail.

In 1959, the engineering firm of W. C. Gilman & Company recommended for St. Louis a new "busway" rapid transit system that would cost $190,000,000. To finance it, the Gilman report proposed that the annual registration fee for automobiles be raised by $20 per year—but that automobile users who chose to use the new transit system be given a $24 annual credit toward the cost of transit passes. Thus car owners who changed over to the transit system would in effect gain $4 a year while those who continued to use the freeways would pay $20 a year, as their share of the cost of getting other drivers off their freeways and streets and out of their parking places.

The plan was brilliant in conception, but it was expected to arouse such intense opposition that this portion of the Gilman report was hardly even publicized. Few residents of St. Louis outside of official circles know of its existence.

Similarly in California, the state legislature in 1963 authorized county commissioners to levy an additional 0.5% tax on automobiles and to devote the proceeds to transit improvements—but automobile clubs and highway interests opposed the tax, which has never been levied.

In 27 states, the "highway lobby" has secured constitutional amendments prohibiting the use of motor vehicle or gasoline taxes for nonhighway purposes. That automobile dealers, gasoline and tire companies, highway contractors, and other such interests should oppose using highway taxes for rapid transit is understandable. But why do the politically influential automobile clubs agree? Their members are not immune from the traffic jams that today clog the core of almost every large city each workday morning and evening. Their members have a deep interest in getting to work and back as quickly, as comfortably, and as safely as possible—whether by car or by transit. In blindly opposing proposals to devote gasoline tax revenues for this purpose—unless the project calls for highway construction—the

executives who control our automobile clubs may be serving the goals of the other highway groups, with whom they have long cooperated, rather than their members' interests.

As of today, proposals to finance urban transportation on a coordinated basis, with highway user taxes available for any project that will supply more and better transportation per tax dollar, are as politically explosive as proposals to raise the cost of using urban freeways so that drivers will really pay their own way. But political winds can shift. Automobile commuters themselves might approve the use of gasoline taxes for better transit if the advantages to drivers as well as to transit riders were fully publicized.

As a practical matter, of course, the five proposals reviewed above are not mutually exclusive. San Francisco's BART system is being financed through a combination of Proposals 2 and 5, Toronto's by means of 2 and 3. All five might be combined to spread the cost. The problem is to find a combination acceptable to your own community.

JOHN R. SEELEY

The Slum: Its Nature, Use, and Users

To cling to a dream or a vision may be heroic—or merely pathetic. Slum-clearance, slum renewal, or, more grandiosely, the extirpation of the slum, is for many planners just a dream: brightly imagined, cherished, fought for, often seeming —but for stupidity here or cupidity or malice there—at very finger-tip's reach. To ask how realistic this orientation is, what is possible at what costs and to whose benefit, is almost as idle-seeming an enterprise to many as it would be to raise doubts about the sanctity of American motherhood or the soundness of the American home. If a direct challenge to the orthodox view seems too bold, let us tease at the fabric of the dream only a little, to see how it appears—and perhaps still shimmers—in the cooler light of moderately disinterested curiosity as against the warm glow of programmatic commitment.

The very notion of a "slum" depends on a number of more primitive notions. We must invoke at least—(and I believe only)—the notions of

Space

Population

A value-position defining "goods" and "ills"

Dispersion in the distribution of any good (or ill) among the population so that, in that respect, all men are not equal

Correlation[1] among goods (or ills) so that one good tends to be attended by another, rather than offset by an ill

Concentration (in space) of those who have the most (and also those who have the least) of what there is to get

Any alteration in any of the realities that lie behind these six terms changes what "the slum problem" is; the elimination of any corresponding reality eliminates slums; and anything short of that guarantees the slum's survival. It cannot be overemphasized that no change in the plane of living—as for example, the doubling of all real incomes—would remove the problem. It is not a matter of absolutes. In a society where nearly everyone walks, the man with a horse is a rich man, and the man without is a poor man; in a society where nearly everyone has (or could have) a car, the man who can only afford a bicycle is *by that much* disadvantaged, and, potentially, a slum dweller. The criteria for what is a slum—as a social

1. "Positive correlation," of course.

From the **Journal of the American Institute of Planners,** Vol. 25, No. 1, February 1959, pp. 7-14. Reprinted by permission.

fact—are subjective and relative: for one brand of mystic this world is a slum (relative to the next) and for another there *is* no slum, because the proper objects of desire are as available in one area as another.

Since, for the planner, space is an eternal datum and population is also given, at least in the moderately long run, any attempt to "deal with" the slum must turn on affecting in some way one of the other factors. Since, commonly, the value-position from which goods or ills are to be defined is uncritically received from the culture or projected by the individual planner, this too appears as something given—although this unexamined acceptance undoubtedly leads to much of the defeat and frustration which the planner encounters and manufactures. We shall have to return to this question of values later, but for the moment we may ask, what is possible if indeed a single value-scheme—the value-scheme of middle-class materialism—is applicable? The answer, if the analysis is correct so far, is obvious: we can attempt an attack on any one or on all of the remaining factors: dispersion, correlation, and concentration. These are discussed in decreasing order of difficulty.

To attempt to diminish the dispersion in the distribution of any one good—say, money—is actually a matter of high politics rather than "planning" in the customary sense. Two courses are classically open politically: the periodic redistribution of goods gained; and the blocking of opportunities to gain them. An example of the first is the combination of income taxation or succession-duties with "equalizing" distribution of the proceeds —as, for instance, by differential "social security benefits." An example of the second—insofar as it is effective at all —lies in antitrust or antimonopoly proceedings, more particularly in the form which they have taken in recent years, that is, the prevention of particularly blatant potential concentrations before they

actually occur. Not only is this whole route attended by vexing ethical and political problems, but also limits are set for it by the culture and, in the ultimate analysis, by economics itself. We may or may not be anywhere near those limits in North America, but it is obvious that dispersion-reduction beyond a certain point may, in fact, reduce the total of what there is to distribute—may, in fact, reduce it to the point where the least advantaged are in absolute, though not relative, terms more disadvantaged than before. We may discover limits and optimum points by trial-and-error or experiment in the course of history, but this clearly falls outside the planning procedure. This leaves us with correlation and concentration to examine.

An attack upon the correlation of goods with goods and ills with ills, in the life of any person or group, is notoriously difficult. Nothing multiplies like misfortune or succeeds like success. As the work of Bradley Buell[2] so unequivocally demonstrated for the whole range of problems with which social work deals, disaster is so wedded to further disaster in the lives of families that the combined case-load of innumerable separate agencies in a city is very largely represented by only a small core of "multi-problem families," families in which economic dependency may be the child of poor nutrition and poor physical health and the father of overcrowding and desperate family relations and poor mental health—and so, in a new and horrible incest, in turn the father of its own father, more economic dependency . . . and so on. And what Buell finds for social work problems is not restricted to that field. Within single problem-fields themselves, diseases tend to follow diseases in the field of medicine, just as one bungled social relation generally follows another, as students of society observe,

2. See Bradley Buell, *Community Planning for Human Services* (New York: Columbia University Press, 1952).

and one psychological catastrophe is the ancestor of the next in the case history of almost any psychiatric patient. Every social agency, every "caretaker institution,"[3] is concerned to break up or diminish these correlations or to palliate their effects; but the whole apparatus can deal with only the few, worst cases; and nothing short of a society quite different from any yet seriously contemplated is likely to make sensible inroads upon the fact of correlation itself. In any case, this too falls outside the domain of local, or even regional, planning. So we are left with geographic concentration as our last point, seemingly, of promising attack. And it is at this point, if I am not mistaken, that the weight of the planners' planning has so far largely fallen.

The problem of "deconcentration" may be seen as the problem of moving from the present state of a heterogeneity of neighborhoods each homogeneous within itself to a homogeneity of neighborhoods each heterogeneous within itself. Upon succeeding, we should no longer be able to write of *The Gold Coast and the Slum*[4] but only, perhaps, of the gold coast within the slum and the slum within the gold coast. It is hard to doubt that—if we are willing to pay the price—here we *can* be successful. And it is equally hard to doubt that some increases in positive goods and some diminutions in positive evils would follow upon such a geographic transfer of the "variance" in fortune from the "between communities" label to the "within communities" one.

No one, perhaps, has put the case for the positive benefits so well as Catherine Bauer who brings knowledge, experience, vision, and passion to her task.[5] She argues,

in reality, from the full depth of her feelings, but, in form at least, from primitive democratic principles against the one-class, one-occupation, one-economic-level community and for the broad-spectrum neighborhood where a child may at least encounter the aged, the ethnically strange, the poorer, the richer, the better, the worse, the different, and, therefore, the educative and exciting. The essence of her argument, I think, is that since the efficacy of our type of democracy depends on the achievement of consensus even in a highly differentiated society, whatever militates against "understanding" diminishes the national welfare. This is a telling point, especially if lack of direct exposure does militate against "understanding," and if increased exposure promotes it.

Another argument for "deconcentration" can be made, I believe, on negative grounds; and for some it may have considerable force. The argument is that the very concentration of evils or ills is itself an additional ill or evil—quite separate from the mere sum of the evils concentrated. I think this is a valid point. Anyone who has watched a child checking quite equally his separate bruises and scratches before bedtime, only to be suddenly overborne emotionally as their totality dawns upon him, will know what is meant at an individual level.[6] The pervasive air of squalor of a Tobacco Road or any of its innumerable counterparts is, I think, differentiable from the separately existent miseries that otherwise go to make it up.

However, even at this level of analysis, things are not so simple as they seem. If it is true that the concentration of the defeated and despairing casts a pall, a psychological smog, of defeatism and despair, it is also true that "misery loves company" and that support to bear the hurt comes chiefly from the hurt. Beyond this, awareness of one's disabilities and

3. To use the phrase of Erich Lindemann.
4. See Harvey Zorbaugh, *The Gold Coast and the Slum* (Chicago: University of Chicago Press, 1937).
5. See, e.g., Catherine Bauer, "Good Neighborhoods," *The Annals of the American Academy of Political and Social Science*, Vol. 242 (1945), pp. 104-115.

6. Cf. Bruno Bettelheim, *Love is Not Enough* (Glencoe: Free Press, 1950).

disasters is heightened if they must be borne in the presence of the able and successful; and this awareness—unless it can lead to a remedy—is itself an additional, and perhaps disabling, disaster. It is also to be noted that to the extent that compresent misery adds to misery at one end of the scale, the "slum," compresent abundance adds to the sense of abundance and security at the other end, the elite community or "gold coast." Thus, at the very least, "deconcentration" is not likely to be an unmixed good to anyone or even a mixed good to everyone.

Things are much less simple again if we are willing to be realistic and to recall for re-examination one of the premises accepted for the sake of argument earlier: that the question may properly be examined at all in the light of the planner's value-system, or the one he assumes to represent the society at large. The first possibility we shall not even examine; few would argue seriously that an urban plan should rest ultimately purely on the private preferences of the urban planner who plans to please himself. The second is worth some study.

It is a persistent illusion characterizing, I believe, only the middle-class meliorist, and only the middle-class meliorist in America—where it is least true!—that there is some particular case-applicable value-system that may be ascribed to the society at large. I do not doubt that *at a very high level of abstraction* consensus around value-statements can be obtained: America believes in justice; it simply divides on segregation. America believes in due process; it divides, however, on the propriety of what happens at many a Congressional investigation. What is at issue regarding the slum is a case and not an abstraction, and around it Americans divide, not simply in terms of slum-dwellers versus non-slum-dwellers, but within as well as between both groups.

It must be recognized at the outset, I believe, that the slum is almost as much a "social necessity" for some sizable segment of the elite as is, say, an adequate, centralized, and appropriately located medical center. I do not mean this only in the relatively trivial sense, referred to earlier, in which those who enjoy the greater proportion of social goods also desire protection against the debris entailed in their production. I mean it in the quite literal sense that, like the supermarkets in its locus, or the central business districts in its locus, the slum provides on an appropriate site a set of services called out by, produced for, delivered to, and paid for by the self-same elite whose wives are likely to adorn with their names the letterheads of committees to wipe out or "clean up" the slum. Many of the services provided by the slum are not within the monetary reach of slum people: the bulk of the bootlegging, the call-girl services, a great part of what some feel able to call "vice," the greater part of the gambling, and the whole set of connections that connect the underworld with the overworld serve the latter rather than the former, and are as much a response to effective (that is, money-backed) demand as is the price of a share of A.T.&T. or General Motors.

Given this "effective demand," taking it for granted that such demand will indeed call out "supply" somewhere, the question for the planner—at least in the moderately long run—must not be *whether?* but *where?* To the degree that the services are highly specialized, as many of them are,[7] there seems no economically appro-

7. Compare, for instance, the (twelve at least) institutionalized sets of provisions for sex satisfaction demanded and supplied in a large mid-Western metropolis simply out of the changes to be rung on gender, race, and activity as against passivity. Omitting further variations and refinements, and using an obvious code, we have: (*MNA-MNP*), (*MNA-MWP*), (*MNP-MWA*), (*MWA-MWP*), (*FNA-FNP*), (*FNA-FWP*), (*FNP-FWA*), (*FWA-FWP*), (*MN-FN*), (*MN-FW*), (*MW-FN*), and (*MW-FW*).

priate locus for them too far from the core of the central city proper. To the degree that the services are not so specialized, they will generally have already found their way—by a combination of economic logic with police pressure—to the ring of satellite municipalities immediately outside the city itself.

If these services, and a whole chain of other "opportunities" that the slum presents, were solely of interest and profit to an elite group who already had most of what there was to get, a case might be made out for the abolition of the slum (if possible) as being in the public interest. (There is a sense in which this is true just as, no doubt, sinlessness or prohibition are in the public interest.) But this view of a one-sided exploitative interest in the maintenance of the slum by *outside* landlords or "service" users simply will not fit the facts. The facts are that the slum-dwellers also have sizable investments, of interest, of sentiment, and of opportunity, both in the site of these services and its appurtenances and in the way of life that goes on there.

Slums differ, of course, and I have lived intensively only in one, Back-of-the-Yards, Chicago, in the early 'forties, and, together with others,[8] have studied another, "Relocation Area A" in Indianapolis. I do not intend to give in detail any account of the former, especially as the main features of a somewhat similar area were sketched in William Foote Whyte's *Street Corner Society*.[9] Something of the intensity, excitement, rewardingness, and color of the slum that I experienced is missing from his account of his slum, either because his *was* different or because sociological reporting militates against vibrancy of description (or, perhaps, because we cut into the material of our participant-observer experience in different ways). In any case, I would have to say, for what it is worth, that no society I have lived in before or since, seemed to me to present to so many of its members so many possibilities and actualities of fulfillment of a number at least of basic human demands: for an outlet for aggressiveness, for adventure, for a sense of effectiveness, for deep feelings of belonging without undue sacrifice of uniqueness or identity, for sex satisfaction, for strong if not fierce loyalties, for a sense of independence from the pervasive, omnicompetent omniscient authority-in-general, which at that time still overwhelmed the middle-class child to a greater degree than it now does. These things had their prices, of course —not all values can be simultaneously maximized. But few of the inhabitants whom I reciprocally took "slumming" into middle-class life understood it, or, where they did, were at all envious of it. And, be it asserted, this was not a matter of "ignorance" or incapacity to "appreciate finer things." It was merely an inability to see one moderately coherent and sense-making satisfaction-system which they didn't know, as preferable to the quite coherent and sense-making satisfaction-system they did know. This is not analogous to Beethoven versus boogie-woogie, but more nearly to the choice between English and French as a vehicle of expression. (I will not even say which is which.)

Possibly I can give a clearer impression of the variety of dwellers in one slum and the variety of uses they make of it by quoting at length from the published report of the Indianapolis area that we studied. The rest of this paper is accordingly taken from that report.[10]

8. Mr. Donald A. Saltzman and Dr. B. H. Junker.
9. Second edition (Chicago: University of Chicago Press, 1958).

10. *Redevelopment: Some Human Gains and Losses* (Indianapolis: Community Surveys, 1956), pp. 48-59. Field work by Mr. Donald A. Saltzman and others; report by Mr. Saltzman, Dr. B. H. Junker, and the author in collaboration.

Types of Slum-dwellers

There are always, of course, innumerable ways of classifying a population so immensely various as that of the slum, or, perhaps, of any urban area. We were struck again and again (both when we examined the way in which these people thought about themselves and when we examined behavior objectively) by two major differences: the difference between necessity and opportunity, and the difference between permanence and change.

Quite obviously, for many the slum constitutes a set of opportunities for behavior which they want (at least at the conscious level) to indulge in or to be permitted. For others, equally obviously, the slum constitutes a set of necessities to which, despite their wants, they have been reduced.

Similarly—though changes are *possible* —some are in the slum and feel they are in the slum on a temporary basis only, and others are there and feel they are there to stay. These distinctions establish four major types:

1. The "permanent necessitarians"
2. The "temporary necessitarians"
3. The "permanent opportunists"
4. The "temporary opportunists"

The meaning of these terms[11] will become clear as we proceed. Schematically, these might be represented as follows:

Table 1. Principal Slum Types: Area "A"

| Time | Relation | |
	Necessity	Opportunity
Permanent	1	3
Temporary	2	4

Within each of these primary types, the data cast up a dozen or more fairly obvious subtypes whose characteristics are worth recording. Table 2, which locates some twelve of these, fills in some details

11. The distinction—like other human distinctions—must not be "overworked." The difference between necessity and opportunity is largely subjective—a necessity welcomed with joy is often regarded as an opportunity; an opportunity accepted only with regret may be construed as a necessity. Even "permanent" and "temporary" refer largely subjectively to expectations and intentions, though they also partly (on that account) refer objectively to probabilities of later behavior.

Table 2. Types and Subtypes of Slum-Dwellers: Area "A"

| Likeliest Term of Involvement | Primary Reason for Slum Involvement | |
	Necessity	Opportunity
Temporary	1. a. The indolent b. The "adjusted" poor c. Social outcasts	3. a. Fugitives b. Unfindables c. "Models" d. "Sporting Crowd"
Permanent	2. a. The respectable poor b. The "trapped"	4. a. Beginners b. "Climbers" c. "Entrepreneurs"

for Table 1 and gives an orderly way of arranging what is to follow in this section.

1. THE PERMANENT NECESSITARIANS

Those in the slum permanently and by necessity evidently include at least three subtypes: the "indolent," the "adjusted poor," and the "social outcasts." In Area "A," these three subtypes seem to constitute the greater part of that "hard and unmovable core," which in turn constitutes about half of the population still living in Redevelopment Commission property. These are the people who feel they "cannot" leave the area, and who will or can do nothing to find alternative housing.

The "indolent" are those whose most striking characteristic[12] is a general apathy or immobility. Whether from inherited characteristics, disease, maleducation, malnutrition, the experience of perennial defeat, religiously founded "resignation," or mere valuation of other things—these are the do-nothings, those who "have no get up and go," those whose immobility is grounded now in their very physique or character.

Whatever the cause for the "indolence," and no matter what miracles feeding, better care, or therapy (physical or psychological) could accomplish for such people in the very long run, at least in the short run no plan looking to them for even moderate effort or initiative is a feasible one. "Care" and "custody" are the only public-policy alternatives to neglect;[13] rehabilitation, if possible at all, would be a long, hard, slow process of uncertain outcome or economy.

12. It should not be overlooked that we have classified only by the most obvious characteristic. Many people have several characteristics, e.g., one could find examples of the "indolent-adjusted poor" or the "adjusted poor and trapped."

13. "Neglect," as used here, means "leaving them alone" or "not interfering" with the "natural" process by which these people are able to get along and to subsist.

The *"adjusted poor"* represent similarly, though likely less immovably, a population living in the slum by necessity but adapted by deep-seated habit (and now almost by preference) to its ways. This group represents the concentration in the area of the destitute, or nearly destitute, whose adaptation consists in "acceptance" of the nearly unfit-for-human-habitation shacks and shanties, holes and cellars of the area—provided only they be available at "that low rent." Among them are many of those who value independence fiercely enough that they would rather cling to this most marginal physical existence in independence than accept relative comfort in dependency—even supposing they could have the latter. (At least this is their first and habitual reaction. Some few who were persuaded later to move into Lockefield Gardens are now glad they made the exchange of relative independence for relative comfort.) In this group are many of the very old, the "single" women with many dependents, and other persons prevented in one way or another from working continuously enough or at pay high enough to qualify for a more respectable poverty. Many, if not most of these, are still in the area in Redevelopment Commission property, "unable to move" and unlikely, in the absence of harder necessity than they yet know, to do so.

The last subgroup among the "permanent necessitarians" are the *"social outcasts."*[14] Police evidence, tradition, and common gossip have it that these people were relatively prominent in Area "A" at one time, but left when redevelopment became imminent or even earlier. These people included the "winoes," the drug

14. They are so classified although some of them belong no doubt among the permanent opportunists (those who feel they *chose* the slum as a place of operation rather than that they were excluded from better areas) and some (those few who find their way to "respectable" roles) among the "temporary necessitarians." The peculiar arrow in Table 2 symbolizes this difficulty of classification.

addicts, peddlers and pushers, the "hustlers," prostitutes and pimps, and others whose marginal, counter-legal, or "shady" activities both excluded them from better-organized neighborhoods and made the slum a more receptive or less rejecting habitat.

In any case, by 1955 these had largely disappeared from the area. By that date, all that was left of this group seemed to be those living in common-law relationships, a handful of "winoes," and a few others living habitually in unconventional ways, for whom the slum provided escape, refuge, sympathy, tolerance, and even some stimulation by the very fact of their being together.

2. THE TEMPORARY NECESSITARIANS

The *"respectable poor,"* who are in the slum by necessity but whose residence there is or may be more temporary, usually spend a good part of their lives in it—now in and now out, although mostly in. Though slum-dwellers, and often as poor financially as the "adjusted poor," these people are unadjusted or unreconciled to the slum in the sense that all their values and identifications and most of their associations are outside it. They pay their bills, mind their own business, remain well inside the law, hold the aspirations and, within their means, practice the lifeways of a socially higher class, most of whose members far outrank them economically.

Some of these wind up in public housing, but more often than not they resist such a solution, hoping that "things will take a turn for the better," a turn that will permit them to live more nearly where they feel they belong and how they feel they should. For many of these, redevelopment provided either the money (if they owned their homes) or the incentive or both that made that "turn for the better" reality rather than wish.

The *"trapped"* are people who, having

bought a home (or had one left to them by a parent or relative) at a time when the area was not so run down, one day find themselves living right in the middle of a slum. Blight filters insensibly in and around them, destroying the value of their property. Though many remain, through a program such as redevelopment many more are induced finally to get out.

3. THE PERMANENT OPPORTUNISTS

Those who are in the slum to stay, primarily because of the opportunities it affords, are the fugitives, the unfindables, the "models" and the "sporting crowd."

The *fugitives* are really of two types: those whose encounters with the law or the credit agency have led them into a life of subterfuge and flight, more or less permanent; and those whose nature or experience has decided them to flee the exigencies of rigorous competition in a better area in their own business or profession.

The former, probably not numerous, are really using the possibility of anonymity which the slum offers. To them it offers literal sanctuary or asylum, a cover or protection from the too-pressing inquiries of the more respectable world. These people, poorly circumstanced for the most part, had also left Area "A" in large numbers before our study began.

The latter, seeking escape from the status struggles of the world outside, or looking for a more easily maintained economic niche, occupied some of the best property within the area, and when catapulted out by redevelopment, found successful ways to maintain themselves and even to enhance their position outside the area. Many of them were merchants, doctors, lawyers, or other professionals who had served that part of the population that was later to migrate to the "better neighborhoods" with them. (They resembled the "climbers" discussed below, except that they did not want or expect to escape from their refuge in the slums.)

Somewhat like the first group of fugitives are the *"unfindables."* By definition, we had no contact with them, although we did have contact with those who had had contact. From their descriptions, there is suggested the presence in the population (before the advent of redevelopment) of a sizable "floating population," who could not readily be located, rarely got counted in any census, and lived a shadowy kind of existence both in terms of location and social identity. These were not so much people in flight as people whose individualism of outlook and whose detachment from urban ways led them to seek no clear social identity (or to operate under many). Some could be found by laboriously following a chain of vague touch-and-go relationships, some only by sorting and tracing down a variety of "names" and nicknames under which each had serially or simultaneously lived. Most could not be found at all—with our resources or the census-taker's. These, too, had mostly disappeared by the time we came, although some were left, and the memory of others was still green.

The *"models"* constitute a rare but interesting type. These are people who have somehow become, or conceived of themselves as, social or religious missionaries. They are people who stay in the slum (actually, or as they interpret their own behavior) primarily in order to "furnish an example" or "bring a message" to "the others," the "less cultured," or the "unsaved." Some of them are people who were first among "the trapped," but who have adapted further by finding a satisfying permanent life in the slum; the satisfaction consists in bringing culture or religious light to "those still less fortunate." Some of them patently find some martyr-like satisfaction in such "service," but others more soberly find genuine relatedness and utility in this adaptation.

Some of these remained in Area "A"; some went early. Those who went seemed shortly to find themselves cast in the same role in their new neighborhoods.

Finally among the (relatively) permanent opportunists are the members of the *"sporting crowd."* This term, in local use, evidently connotes a range of characters noted primarily for their jollity and informality—perhaps a certain breezy offhandedness is their distinguishing characteristic—rather than for any necessary inference for illegal or marginal activities as such. They live in the slum for a complex of reasons. First, living in the slum leaves them more money to spend on "other things"; second, having spent a large share of their incomes on those "other things," what is left is only enough for slum rents; third, the slum is the place to meet others similarly situated; fourth, the slum itself provides (or, rather, in the case of Area "A," did provide once) facilities for their pursuits, such as taverns, bookmaking and other betting facilities, and so on. Marginal to this type are those who have been described to us as ranging from "the roughnecks who make it unsafe for others to be in the area" to the less violent types who just create nuisances, which, as one woman explains, ". . . cause you to be afraid to have a friend visit, because you never know whether someone is going to walk in on you without any clothes on." The informality, rather than roughness or nudity as such, is the hallmark of this group.

These, too, by now have mostly fled the area.

4. THE TEMPORARY OPPORTUNISTS

It remains to describe the temporary opportunists, a most important group both because of their numbers and because the slum of these people is a way—perhaps the only way—to the pursuit of those things that American culture has taught them are worth pursuing: "self-improvement," independence, property, a savings account, and so on. It may be only for this group that the general reader will feel fully sympathetic, and it may be only here that he will ask himself, "How are these people to get where we want them to get, if we systematically destroy the slums which are the traditional, if unspoken-of, way of getting there?" The question is a good one, and the study leaves its answering to the wisdom of the agencies, public and private, charged or self-charged with such responsibility.

We find that in this group there are three subtypes: the "beginners," the "climbers," and the "entrepreneurs."

The *"beginners"* are mostly the unattached immigrants to the city who have neither helpful kin nor access to powerful agencies of assimilation, such as churches and ethnic associations. The slum is simply their "area of first settlement" where they rest on arrival in the city not for "the pause that refreshes" so much as for the pause that instructs, the pause that permits them a precarious period in which to "get oriented," find a first job, and learn the elements of urban living. Many of these are young married couples, some with first children, trying to learn simultaneously to be citizens, husbands and wives, and parents in the urban manner. Their slim resources, financial, educational, and psychological, necessitate a place to stay that will not strain these resources much further; the slum furnishes an opportunity to rest, to gather fresh forces, and to prepare for moving on as soon as may be—if disease, misfortune, or the fortune of more children does not exert more "drag" than can be overcome. From this source the city replenishes its labor force at the lower economic levels, and its "respectable poor" and other types at the lower social rungs.

The *"climbers"* are somewhat similar to the beginners except that they may have been in the city for some time and that their plans are somewhat more long-term and ambitious. These are the ones who live in the slum in what amounts to a period of apprenticeship, self-denial and self-sacrifice with a view to accumulating enough goods, money, and know-how to leap later into a much "better" area, a considerably higher standard of living, and a much more "respectable" way of life. They are "saving"—out of the very stuff of their own lives—the material and nonmaterial means of achieving better housing, greater status, "success," and home-ownership.

For many of these, the period of stay becomes protracted because the dream tends to become embellished even as savings accumulate, and the time to move seems always "a little later, when we have a little more." Redevelopment, for many of these, helped toward a settlement with reality by putting period to an unduly prolonged stay in the slums or overextended plans; for a few, it cut off the possibility of any great "improvement" at all, insofar as it caught them in the initial phases of their plans. Some of those thus "caught" simply moved into neighboring slums to begin again. Some abandoned plans for ownership and became renters outside the area.

Last are the *"entrepreneurs,"* a special class of climbers, oriented similarly to the climbers, mostly more ambitious, but saving out of businesslike enterprises—rather than their own miseries—the wherewithal to escape misery in due time. Beginning usually as people of small financial means, they establish a small business or, more frequently, make the slum itself their business. They somehow (frequently by a kind of financial skin-of-your-teeth operation) get hold of a duplex or house that can be "subdivided." That part of it in which they do not themselves reside must, if possible, pay the costs of the whole, and moreover, yield "a little something" so that more property can be bought as time goes by. Often they purchase property, first, in the slum and, later, in better neighborhoods. In the case of at least one person in the area, a drug store was eventually purchased out of the money thus saved by living in the slums.

This kind of person lives a large part of his life in the slum, but usually leaves about the time he reaches fifty. He may by then own enough slum property to live very comfortably in a better neighborhood; or he may, out of his small-scale slum business operation, develop a larger business in a different area, becoming thus an undifferentiable element of the respectable business community.

If the earlier part of this paper made—or even labored—the point that in no way within reach of local planning could the slum be "wiped out," and if the second part drew attention via a particular case to the general situation of a vast variety of people coexisting in the slum's complex fastnesses, what, it may be asked, happens when planned steps are nevertheless taken to "do something" about an area, in this case to "redevelop" it. No general answer can be given—it depends on the steps and the people—except that the greater part of what happens is a redistribution of phenomena in space. We say "the greater part of what happens" because, as is evident from the original report,[15] this is not all that happens: in the very act of relocation *some* "positive" potentialities that were formerly only latent are released or actualized. As far as the redistribution in space is concerned, it is hard to say whether it should be viewed as "deconcentration": it is rather like a resifting and resorting, a speeding up of the city's "natural" ecological processes, with results both "good" and "bad," certainly unintended as well as intended. In this process, opportunities are created for some and destroyed for others, or very often for the same person; certainly, lifelong adjustments or habituations, comfortable and uncomfortable, productive and nonproductive, are overset, disturbed, interrupted, or destroyed. Moreover, in most cases one population is advantaged and another further disadvantaged, and it is not at all clear that the balance is tipped in favor of those who initially had least—perhaps, rather, the contrary.

15. *Ibid.*, pp. 67-143.

ROBERT O. HARVEY AND W. A. V. CLARK

The Nature and Economics of Urban Sprawl

The stimuli for this paper came from four distinct characteristics of the literature on sprawl. First, sprawl in all its forms is seldom satisfactorily defined. Urban sprawl is often discussed without any associated definition at all. The term "sprawl" has been used frequently to describe merely the extensions of the urban fringe, i.e. the general expansion of the city. For example:

So the growth of metropolitan cities will continue to take the form of continuous expansion around the edges, with a belt of land always in process of conversion from rural to urban use. This transitional zone is the scene of urban sprawl, and has been well named the area of urban shadow.[1]

Alternatively Gottman writes:

Some scattering of residences around centres where business congregates has almost always existed. . . . The exploding suburban sprawl, the rapid changes of the distribution of population within Megalopolis, especially since 1920, are all consequences of the greater freedom of access obtained as

a result of these economic and technical achievements.[2]

Sprawl is sometimes described as the scattering of urban settlement over the rural landscape. Gottman uses this definition when he writes:

Where two cities are close together the intervening rural space becomes peppered with new developments. This kind of leap frogging sprawl outflanks some farms while it covers others.[3]

While portions of today's suburbia grow up like Green Knolls as tight complexes with no reserves of open space for future woods or recreational areas, other portions are scattered like shot from a blunderbuss without the slightest umbilical tie to their maternal metropolises.[4]

Some writers make no attempt at definition while others engage in little more

2. J. Gottman, *Megalopolis, The Urbanized North Eastern Seaboard of the United States* (New York, New York: The Twentieth Century Fund, 1961), p. 247.
3. *Ibid.*, p. 334.
4. E. Higbee, *The Squeeze, Cities Without Space* (New York, New York: William Morrow, 1960), p. 119.

1. Humphrey Carver, *Cities in the Suburbs* (Toronto, Canada: University of Toronto, 1962), p. 55.

From **Land Economics**, Vol. XLI, No. 1, pp. 1-9. Copyright © 1965 by the Regents of the University of Wisconsin. Reprinted by permission.

than emotional rhetoric, as in "the great urban explosion (which) has scattered pieces of debris over the countryside for miles around the crumbling centre . . . a destruction of the qualities of the city."[5]

Second, in no one place have the many causes of sprawl been brought together and discussed as a unit. Third, more often than not sprawl is treated as a static phenomenon, when in fact areas described as sprawled are typically part of a dynamic urban scene. Finally, the literature is vague and unsatisfactory on the subject of the costs of peripheral urban development.

A basic attitude implicit in this paper is that peripheral growth too often is incorrectly described, and implicitly classed as a detriment to society.

The physical pattern of sprawl. Sprawl, measured as a moment of time, is composed of areas of essentially urban character located at the urban fringe but which are scattered or strung out, or surrounded by, or adjacent to undeveloped sites or agricultural uses. A sprawled area has a heterogeneous pattern, with an overall density greatly less than that found in mature compact segments of the city. Sprawl areas are less dense than would be found if the areas developed for housing would be if they were developed with the discipline exercised in the assembling of jig-saw puzzles by adding pieces only from the bottom up.

Sprawl occurs in three major forms. The first of these, low density continuous development, is the lowest order of sprawl and, to many, the least offensive. Low density sprawl is merely the gluttonous use of land in opposition to a value judgment about a higher density which would have been more appropriate. Ribbon development sprawl is composed of segments compact within themselves but which extend axially and leave the interstices undeveloped. At the time of devel-

5. N. Pearson, "Hell is a Suburb," *Community Planning Review,* September 1957.

opment, ribbon sprawl may be more expensive than low density sprawl. A third type of sprawl is leap-frog development, which is the settlement of discontinuous, although possibly compact, patches of urban uses. Leap-frog sprawl is the type of development most often attacked by observers of the urban scene and probably is the form of development in which the greatest capital expenditures are required to provide total urban services at the time of development.

Sprawl occurs at the periphery of expanding urban areas. Often sprawl lies in advance of the principal lines of growth and is most noticeable during periods of rapid urban expansion and around the most rapidly growing cities.

Causes and catalysts of sprawl. One cause of sprawl is the independence of decision among monopolistic competitors, each acting independently and without collusion. The competitors hold a variety of expectations about the future and a variety of demands for the rate of compensation. Rapid expansion of the economic base of a housing area tends to prompt many developers to respond to the demand for housing and produce a variety of discontinuous unrelated developments. The more rapid the rate of growth of an area and the greater the number of business firms operating in the housing market area, the greater the number of fragmented randomly located projects.

Speculation is sometimes blamed for sprawl in that speculation produces withholding of land for development. Speculation is blamed for the premature subdivision also. It might be presumed, then, that the offering of a subdivision next to a settled area which, in fact, is promptly taken from the market is not speculation. But, speculation is a motivation of the growth process. All incremental additions to the urban fringe are speculative ventures. The independence of placement and timing of these ventures permits a sprawl pattern. It is the lack of coordination of the decision to speculate which produces sprawl and not the speculation itself.

An investor may hold securities and dispose of them at a generally regarded optimum time in the market; the same investor dealing in land may find the measurement of performance in the market a great deal more difficult than in the case of the organized security markets. In addition, many restraints on the disposition of land are emotional. The institutional attitude of land hunger, that is, a deep desire for the ownership of soil, leads to what many observers would describe as irrational behavior in the holding of land.

A third cause of sprawl is physical terrain which is not suited for continuous development. The sprawl landscape may be a product of physical necessity produced by the existence of mountains, rivers, swamps, oceans, or underground deposits of minerals. The developmental pattern tends to utilize the land which is most readily and economically available. Quite often that which appears to be sprawl and is alleged to be uneconomic is simply the least cost expression of available development sites. The pockets of development in the San Francisco Bay Area, both north of the Golden Gate in Marin County and south of San Francisco in the Santa Clara Valley between San Francisco and San Jose—and also Seattle, built on the hills and valleys around Puget Sound, Lake Washington, and Lake Union—are examples of physical responses to attractive but difficult terrain.

Dead land, a concept originally suggested by Aschman to describe the blighted vacant land in the city of Chicago, cannot be thought of as a direct cause of sprawl. Aschman[6] and Berk-man[7] have pointed out that, although dead land exists in the center of the city, developments take place at the edges to provide sufficient living space. The dead or vacant land remains idle because of clouded titles, tax delinquencies, or obsolete subdivision designs. Obviously, the development of the inner vacant areas might prevent some peripheral development; but it is likely that the opportunities for peripheral development obviate the need for removing the obstacles to the redevelopment of the so-called dead land.

Public regulation contributes to sprawl by imbalancing the attractiveness of competing areas. For example, differences in land use controls inside and outside of corporate limits make the lesser controlled area more attractive. Perhaps the major problem with respect to public regulation of land use in sprawl is that a regulatory body may not have control over an entire housing market area. For example, city zoning and land use controls may extend only to the corporate limits or, at best, one, two, or three miles depending upon the state regulations. If the standards of building and land use within the controlled area are greatly more stringent than common practices in the building industry, the standards themselves may impel the development of housing units outside the controlled area and thus contribute to sprawl. The public is sometimes permissive with respect to sprawl by failing to enact land use controls or by adopting controls which fail to prevent heterogeneous land uses.

Transportation circumstances are catalysts of sprawl. Trolley and bus lines produce strip developments and the rapid transit lines have only extended the strips. Primarily, however, it is the auto which permits access to remote areas and

6. F. T. Aschman, "Dead Land," *Land Economics,* May 1949, pp. 240-245.

7. H. G. Berkman, "Decentralization and Blighted Vacant Land," *Land Economics,* August 1956.

provides the essential condition which allows sprawl to occur. The construction of expressways and super-highways has caused both congestion in the central areas, and the rapid spread of the city at the edge. The development of a highway system often creates land parcels economically unsuited to farming or housing and encourages an unfortunate heterogeneity of uses.[8]

Public policy which has supported the single-family home as a suburban environment has accentuated peripheral single-family development and contributed to sprawl. Public policy on housing in the United States has been biased in favor of the suburban single-family home as opposed to central city multiple development or even redevelopment.

The taxation of gains from land development and the mechanics of determining taxable income from real estate developments have emphasized subdivision creation in small and discontinuous increments. The seller of land to a developer may find it to his advantage to offer land only on an installment contract which could minimize the tax levied against his gains. The tax laws in the United States allow for installment contracts, provided that in the year of sale less than 30 percent of the purchase price is received by the seller. In the case of installment contracts, a tax levied on only that share of annual receipts which represent gain. The proportion of annual receipts subject to the income tax would be the same as the proportion of the total gain to the total purchase price. If the profit on a transaction is 40 percent and the deal calls for an installment contract, 40 percent of each annual installment is taxed. Thus, by dividing a sales contract over a period of years, the gain realized in any single year is reduced. Sellers of

land held as an investment for long periods of time are subject to a capital gains tax which does not exceed 25 percent. It is possible for installment contracts to produce gains which would be taxable at rates of less than 25 percent. The installment contract is particularly significant for a seller of property which may not qualify for capital gains treatment. The net result is that the tax law supports an installment sale of property which in turn tends to produce incremental development which is quite often described as sprawl.

The tax influence on the seller tends to restrict him to a single buyer-developer at a time. Furthermore, the subdivision developer is quite likely to want control of the development of land beyond his initial undertaking. Consequently, once an an owner commits the sale of land to a single developer, another developer is not likely to be able to buy the land in the line of city growth belonging to the original seller. A would-be buyer then is compelled to seek another seller, which seller may have land located in some remote or discontinuous part of the urban scene. The process of matching sellers with buyers tends to produce a sprawl pattern.

The real property tax also tends to produce discontinuous development. As soon as farm land is platted for a residential subdivision, it is taxed at the higher values normally attributed to urban plots. Accordingly, the developers of subdivisions avoid excessive platting and development in advance of actual development and sale of the urban lots.

The burden of income taxes on subdividers also tends to produce discreet and discontinuous units. Subdividers are taxed for gains on each lot on the basis of per lot allocations of development costs. However, in the year of sale the sellers may have a paper profit but no cash gain. In order to avoid having to pay income taxes on paper profits which have not

8. Evidence of this type of activity is found in a case of peripheral development in Urbana, Illinois, W. A. V. Clark, 1961.

been realized in terms of a cash flow, developers tend to minimize the amount of land developed in a single year.

Subdividers and developers of land are subject to the ordinary income tax rates; therefore, it is typical for developers to limit their programs for any taxable year in order that they do not find themselves in tax brackets which could be avoided if they merely allocated their sales program over two, three or four years.

The discreet discontinuous development in response to tax factors is far more common that the very large land projects of the 1920's which were created in an environment which was very much different with respect to both optimism and taxation.

The credit and capital markets within the United States only scarcely formally recognize the economic process of land acquisition and development and consequently encourage the fragmented development which can be effected in discreet, presumably easily completable segments.

Federally chartered savings and loan associations are the only lending institutions with formal authority to make land purchase and development loans. Other institutions engaging in land acquisition and development financing, principally commercial banks and life insurance companies, make their loans to developers largely on the basis of personal assets as opposed to the worth of the land being developed. When land acquisition development loans are made, usually the borrower must have an equity of 40 to 50 percent; consequently, most borrower-developers are limited to relatively small discreet tracts. From the point of view of the lending institutions they are likely to be interested in diversification among builders, developers, and projects, and accordingly will avoid committing to one particular builder and perhaps to one particular geographic area so that they will not suffer losses from a concentra-

tion of risks in a single project, builder, or area. Moreover, in many instances, loans to a single builder are limited by charter and statute as well as by lending policy and practice.

Most lenders supporting subdivision development demand that projects be organized in completable units which will not extend beyond one or, at best, three building seasons. Such limitations tend to produce discreet discontinuous fragmented development.

The heterogeneous ownership of land which is compatible with United States public policy of land holdings has made land ownership dispersed instead of concentrated and, accordingly, lands became available for subdividing on a discreet rather than a continuous basis. Multiple ownership resulting from inheritance frequently produces indecision and disagreement with respect to offering land in the market for development.

Several specific factors compel sellers to offer small increments of land: for example, a sale to eliminate a particular debt, a sale of a small tract to derive funds for a particular cause, or a sale of land to be rid of a site marginal for its present use.[9] Often the land to be disposed of is close to streams and bush, or with trees or contains other physical characteristics desired by the consumer seeking the rural environment.

Sprawl is sometimes a product of a buyer seeking a particular environment. Some suburban sprawl occupiers seek a housing environment of a special character, for example, similar to that of their childhood environment.[10] Others seek an area separate from the main urban scene because it offers the amenities preferred. Others seek a suburban sprawl location just because it is different from the main urban scene. The suburban scene is not without its imperfections

9. *Ibid.*
10. *Ibid.*

but oftentimes the suburban sprawl occupier prefers to trade the kinds of imperfections found in the periphery for those found in the central city.

The sprawl time span.[11] Sprawl is measured and described as of a moment of time, usually as if it were a static, unchanging thing. Actually, sprawl is a form of growth. The duration of sprawl in a particular area is largely a function of the economic base of the housing area. The sprawl of the 1950's is frequently the greatly admired compact urban area of the early 1960's. An important question on sprawl may be, "How long is required for compaction?" as opposed to whether or not compaction occurs at all.

To illustrate, 160 acres on the periphery of a city may be subdivided and built upon at a rate of 40 acres per year. Assume that the tract is in the form of a square and the segments developed are fourths of it. If the segments most distant from the established areas are created first, there is sprawl. If the segments next to the established areas are settled first, growth is presumably orderly and compact. The net results to society, however, are not significantly different.

The concept of the time span is important in the identification and measurement of sprawl. The application of static measures to dynamic areas can easily result in the misidentification of an area as sprawl when it is in reality a viable, expanding, compacting portion of a city. Furthermore, a static or very short-run view on urban development permits an exaggeration of development costs per unit, which costs may in fact be modest on a unit basis once the development is viewed as a complete entity.

The costs of sprawl. Sprawl is usually accepted as being inordinately costly to

11. For similar ideas see J. Lessinger, "The Case for Scatteration: Some Reflections on the National Capital Region Plan for the Year 2000," *Journal of the American Institute of Planners,* August 1962.

its occupants and to society. Among the types of costs which are alleged to be extreme are those involved in the development of capital facilities. The arguments usually represent that costs per person per dwelling unit are higher than the costs per corresponding unit in higher density areas. The actual cost per unit must be related to the number of units developed to take advantage of a given capital facility over a span of time. Costs per unit early in the development span of an area obviously tend to be greater than the costs per unit after the area has reached maturity. Further, the costs differ in various areas. Quite often the development costs of the periphery are high because of the necessity for the development of a new private utility such as a sewage disposal system because the system serving the main segment of the settled area cannot be expanded for technical or financial reasons.

The most common case in urban development is the extension of utilities to new, not fully developed areas. Suppose that the utility organization is free to decide whether or not to extend the utilities. The questions are then: the immediate cost of development, the time period for completion, the ultimate number to be served and finally, the cost per user. The simplest, most efficient case is that in which the utility is a privately owned corporation operating on a public franchise. Here the utility is supposedly free to tap the capital market for financial resources and offers its services essentially "on a payment by those served" basis. Under such circumstances the effective decision makers for the extension of utilities are the developer-consumers who are ultimately required to pay. The utility entity itself may ask the developer-users to pay for the entire cost or if the utility believes the area is one which will experience additional growth, it can invest in larger lines which will permit the continued expansion in the direction of the current development.

Capital costs associated with land development and utilization can be shifted from the land owners to society only in those peculiar cases in which publicly owned utility corporations are willing to install sewer and water systems for the benefit of the individual occupants without levying a charge sufficient to cover the costs of the installation. In order for the cost of development to be shifted to society under such circumstances, there would have to be maladministration in the public sector. By far the most common equitable approach to the payment for the installation of urban capital facilities is for the developer to pay to the utility company, whether it be publicly or privately owned, the actual costs of installation.

If an area is developed on the periphery of a city without adequate streets, sanitary and drainage facilities, and subsequently the inadequate facilities are to be replaced by more desirable ones, the costs of the actual construction typically are paid by assessments levied against the property owners served by the new facilities. It is interesting to note that the only cases in which adequate facilities are subsequently replaced are those cases in which the facility comes under the jurisdiction of a public body. Poor administration or the absence of public administration, not sprawl, may produce costs to society which might properly be borne by the individual.

Given a situation in which a potential urban area is required to have standardized capital facilities and a utility which is free to invest in the capital program if it appears economically sound, the cost of sprawl, if in fact there is a cost, is borne by the ultimate consumers and by the developing entity and the utility organization. If utilities are wanted in a low density, scattered area for which the prospects are not bright, the cost of the utilities will be inordinately high and paid for by the current users. To the extent that the developers or current users are unwilling

to finance the capital program, utility extension becomes a deterrent to sprawl. In this same circumstance, however, if potential land uses are free to be developed outside of the area in which utility standards are operative, the economics of utilities may induce sprawl in the uncontrolled periphery.

Another type of cost is the alleged loss of agricultural land. However, "the seriousness of long-term agricultural shortages depends primarily upon a race between technology and population. The loss of agricultural land in the short run can hardly be considered a blow to society.[12]

Foremost among those worried by the spectre of vanishing food supplies are the planners and the agriculturists. Gregor, a geographer, points out that the question is not just one of how much land is taken out of production, but that the urban areas prejudice agricultural land beyond the built-up area.[13] Gillies and Mittelbach, however, calculate that there are new agricultural lands available to replace the losses from urban expansion throughout the next sixty years; moreover, acreage losses are more than offset by increased yields.[14] They also point out that there is nothing precious about the area of any particular use; allocations for agricultural purposes are determined by market forces. Moreover, if the price of citrus fruits or some other agricultural specialty became sufficiently high to yield a return on the land higher than that earned under an urban use, then a transfer from urban to agricultural uses would take place in contrast to that which typically occurs.

While the market organism is not perfect in allocating land uses, standards for superior public control are lacking. Before the market is judged as inadequate,

12. *Ibid.,* p. 168.
13. H. Gregor, "Urban Pressures on California Land," *Land Economics,* 1957, pp. 311-325.
14. J. Gillies and F. Mittelbach, "Urban Pressures on California Land: A Comment," *Land Economics,* 1958, pp. 80-83.

cost studies such as those performed by Wibberly are needed to determine the relative costs of bringing alternative lands into production.[15] Analysis of the total costs of keeping suburban lands in production as compared with transferring urban developments to other sites or cities is needed.

A third kind of cost is that attributed to the waste in time of passing vacant land en route from the central city to the sprawled suburb. It is not clear that the passing of vacant land involves unwanted cost on the part of the population. To many, passing vacant land is less irritating and destructive than passing a smoggy and congested panorama of the compact city. It does seem that people willingly locate in agricultural areas in order to enjoy the rural scene.

A fourth type of cost which may be the most serious for society is the loss in values and amenities of urban real property from the development of conflicting, undisciplined land uses on the periphery of cities. Conflicting land uses are not the exclusive province of sprawled areas or even the product of sprawl, but sprawl and scatteration most often occur in peripheral areas which are frequently without the discipline of planning and zoning.

Notwithstanding the alleged and real costs of sprawl, there is an important characteristic of sprawl which must be remembered. Sprawl, by any definition, refers to *settled* areas no matter what their characteristics may be. Accordingly, at the time the sprawl occurred, the cost was not prohibitive to the settler. It provided a housing opportunity economically satisfactory relative to other alternatives. If sprawl were in fact economically unsound, it would occur only by the action of housing seekers artificially restricted from free compacted markets, but who could and would pay a premium for freedom to be found only in the sprawl. Sprawl occurs, in fact, because it is economical in terms of the alternatives available to the occupants.

15. G. Wibberley, *Agriculture and Urban Growth,* A Study for the Competition for Rural Land (London, England: Michael Joseph, 1959).

JOSEPH L. FISHER

Environmental Quality and Urban Living

The injunction to see life steadily and to see it whole applies with special relevance to life in the city, where babel and confusion seem always on the verge of taking over. Plato put the essential question long ago: How can we arrange things so that each individual can become one instead of many, and so that their city can become one instead of many? The answer, of course, is not monotony and sameness, but rather it is the search for unity and cohesiveness in the midst of richness of diversity.

The matter can be approached from several directions: from the vantage points of urban psychology, urban planning, urban government, urban education. My approach will be through a consideration of the natural environment of the city.

A city's natural environment by itself does not determine the quality of urban life. On the other hand, the ways in which people perceive the natural environment of their city and develop and use it tell much about the quality of ilfe. A city in which land is fouled and desecrated, in which water and air are polluted to the point at which health is endangered and

aesthetic sense violated, and in which the whole urban arrangement is haphazard and messy is not likely to support individuals who meet Plato's integrated personality test, however high their level of material welfare and comfort may be.

Pollution for All

In this country we seem to have crossed a threshold: practically everyone has heard about, is talking about, and would like to do something about pollution. Judging from the Sunday supplements, the popular weekly magazines, and the world of TV and radio, things are really pretty bad. Tom Lehrer's lament on the subject is apropos:

> *If you visit American city,*
> *You will find it very pretty.*
> *Just two things of which you must*
> *   beware:*
> *Don't drink the water and don't breathe*
> *   the air.*

Not only is there water pollution, air pollution, land pollution, and scenery pollution separately, there is also multi-

From **Planning 1967**, pp. 178-186, the American Society of Planning Officials, Chicago, Illinois. Reprinted by permission.

ple pollution through which the various single types are interrelated, frequently reinforcing one another. Automobiles pollute our air and clog our cities. Refining the gasoline they run on adds pollution to some streams and to the nearby air. Once the automobiles wear out, or people think they are worn out, there is the problem of what to do with the remains. The problem is made worse when the automobile dies at the city curb and the owner can't be found to hire an undertaker to take charge of the burial. The web of interrelations stretches unbelievably far: crude oil in a tanker destined for the refineries of Europe is now defacing, perhaps damaging permanently, the coast of Cornwall. Recently John Kenneth Galbraith wrote an essay with the title, "The Polipollutionists," in which he brings out the many possibilities for the ingenious perpetrator of pollution. Unfortunately most of the pollution problems come to roost in the cities, which is not surprising, since this is where the people and the action are.

In fact the whole matter has reached a stage which our journalists and commentators call a crisis. Using this word may be overdoing it a bit, but it does serve to register the matter strongly in the public mind. The trouble with the word crisis, whether applied to pollution, population, foreign policy, youth, or anything else, is that it seems to call for massive, undisiciplined, and unplanned action of the "damn the torpedoes" kind. And this is, or it should be, anathema to planners who necessarily will prefer a rational, deliberate approach.

Furthermore, pollution is not a newcomer on the scene. In 1661 John Evelyn wrote in his diary of the mist and filthy vapor, obnoxious and corrupting the lungs, so that "Catharrs, Coughs, and Consumptions rage more in this one city [London] than in the whole Earth besides." Two centuries later in this same city Disraeli noted that it was necessary to hang sheets soaked in lye in the corridors of the Houses of Parliament, so bad was the summertime stench from the Thames nearby. But if pollution isn't worse than it used to be, certainly the possibility of doing something about it is greater and people now expect action.

This does not mean, of course, that things are not pretty bad at the present time. A look at some of our streams, a whiff of some of our city air, and an exposure to some of our landscape are all that is needed to convince most persons that there is a problem. However, it should be noted that very few people die nowadays in this country from typhoid resulting from the drinking water. Despite much ugliness both our urban and rural landscapes offer quite a bit that is inspiring, exciting, tasteful, beautiful, or serene, suitable to whatever mood one may be in. The pollution picture is a mixed picture: very bad in spots, quite good in other places, moderately poor in general.

Pollution in urban areas takes certain forms and has certain characteristics which are important to note explicitly. The sheer amount of waste materials is increasing rapidly. The water, air, and land have to absorb, dilute, carry away, and otherwise to take care of much of the throw-off of modern society. In fact, this constitutes one of the most important uses of the natural environment and has to be entered into any reckoning. The different kinds of pollution are interrelated; programs for dealing with pollution therefore have to be carefully interrelated. Modern technology both produces much of our pollution and holds the promise for abating it. One reason why the pollution problem seems to have come upon us so suddenly is that people are now demanding higher quality water, air, and landscape than ever before. This results partly from higher incomes and more leisure time, partly from the belief that new technology can improve the quality of the natural environment, and partly, one hopes, from a rising aesthetic sense.

Before going into some of the specifics of policy and planning for pollution abatement, what about the general magnitude of the problem? What is it likely to cost to make significant headway? Information is not available to support definitive estimates. A round-up in the April 3, 1967, issue of *U.S. News and World Report,* quoting the Chase Manhattan Bank, indicates that outlays by industry and government for "controlling air and water pollution" will run to more than $300 million between now and the year 2000, with the annual cost doubling within a few years. Additional sums will be spent for solid waste disposal. According to a recent *Harvard Business Review,* the cost split among water pollution, air pollution, and solid wastes may be about 40-40-20. These figures are perhaps as good as any others, although they may underestimate the mess and clutter that will be caused by more people, more industry, and more stuff to discard.

The burden of paying for this very big job will fall mainly on the people generally, as most such burdens do. Some of it will be felt in higher prices for cars, higher electricity bills, higher rents, higher water and sewer charges, and higher prices for many industrial items as producers step up their efforts to reduce pollution (whether on their own initiative or under government compulsion). Some of the cost undoubtedly will be taken out of profits. And much of the rest of it will be met from higher taxes to pay for government grants, concessions, construction, and other expenditures.

Here is a curious paradox: all of these outlays—public and private—are counted in the gross national product. Increases in GNP are the most common measure of economic growth for which Americans strive so hard. In this odd way effluents contribute to affluence, and the gross national pollution adds to the gross national product instead of being subtracted from it. We should be more concerned with the concept of net social product which does not include outlays for taking care of the mess we make, it has a more profound meaning. Let me turn to some comments on water pollution, not that it is very different from air or any other kind of pollution in its essential economic or social aspects, but rather because planners and others have had more experience with it.

An Approach to the Water Pollution Problem

Water pollution, like the other kinds of pollution, has now become a much bigger and more complicated situation than it used to be. It is no longer the simple matter of a city's running a pipe out into a nearby lake or stream and taking in the water it needs with no more than elementary filtering and chlorination, or of dumping its sewage through an outfall line with no thought of treatment. Cities have been growing rapidly, and clearly they will continue to grow rapidly, with virtually all of the increased population locating in a couple of hundred or so metropolitan areas. Most of the new and enlarged industrial plants will be in the urban areas also.

Furthermore, city people want water recreational facilities within metropolitan regions, and they want river, lake, and ocean side drives of scenic beauty within their cities. In my metropolitan area many people want to fish, boat, and swim within the District of Columbia limits; and the President has proclaimed making the Potomac swimmable as a national objective. In fact around half of the $300 or $400 million program of the Army Engineers for development of the Potomac has to be justified in terms of recreation and scenic amenity on the river, principally in the Washington area.

In the northeast corridor, the cities from

Boston through Washington, all look to a few rivers for their water supply. The time is upon us when the coastal rivers from Maine to Virginia will have to be interconnected in various ways in a water supply network. Other such networks will come into existence elsewhere. One grandiose scheme involves the whole western part of North America. The business of thinking about water supply and waste disposal has to be considered in the very large terms of the huge megalopolis and of the extended system of interrelated rivers.

We have on our hands a systems problem of gigantic proportions. Multiple sources of water supply have to be linked with multiple uses in one or several large metropolitan areas in such a way that quantity requirements and quality standards are matched against a number of developmental and management possibilities. Optimum and least-cost systems have to be found which will supply the water services that are wanted most efficiently and will be paid for most equitably.

The experience of the Delaware River Basin Commission is instructive. This is a federal-interstate organization established recently with planning, construction, operating, and financing authority for dealing with water quality management in the Delaware basin. It was realized from the outset that the planning and development of water quality management for this region would be an extremely complex undertaking. The systems analysts were brought in from hydrology, engineering, economics, public health, and other fields. Some five so-called "objective sets" were established to bracket in the range of standards for water quality that could be practically considered. The standards had to do with oxygen content of the water, turbidity, coliform count, sediments, and solid materials. For each objective set, specified standards for each of the identified quality variables were put forward. Then, for each set a variety of control and management measures were considered, and for each one costs were estimated. In addition, benefits were estimated that would be associated with each of the sets of standards. This proved to be quite difficult because such a large fraction of total benefits involved recreation and scenic aspects of the river. Recreation benefits included boating, fishing, and swimming, none of which can be readily measured in monetary terms.

Out of all this emerged a fairly well-organized display of analyzed data and information which was then fed into a process of public hearings and discussions in which various individuals and groups had a chance to react to the possibilities and to bring forward additional information and points of view. Whether all this will lead to decisions which will be more rational and socially useful remains to be seen; but at this time the prospects are encouraging.

I mention this instance merely to indicate the way in which water quality management can now be approached so as to embrace the full scope of the problem and to make use of advanced kinds of analysis. Perhaps the most interesting feature is the effort being made in the Delaware basin to bring together data and systematic analysis with a decision-making process which involves the public. The public is not given one solution to react to, but is given several possible solutions with costs and benefits estimated for each, and each related to certain objectives and standards for water quality.

Among the techniques for water quality management, in addition to licensing and other more typical forms of regulation, is the use of incentives by government to induce private users of water to pay more attention to water quality. One of my colleagues has investigated the use of effluent charges in the heavily populated and industrialized Ruhr Valley of Germany and in a few other places to see what could be learned that might be adaptable in this country. The idea here is for a public body to levy charges against industrial plants, municipalities, and other water users who discharge waste and pollutants into lakes and streams. The schedule of charges varies according to estimates of the damages and inconveniences. The charges provide an incentive to polluters to clean up their effluents before discharging them into the streams or otherwise they have to pay the charge, which is then used by the public body to abate the pollution. The possibility of using effluent charges in this country has been under detailed study in the federal government for some time and has been considered by committees of Congress. Rapid investment amortization or other tax benefits can also prove useful in hastening the installation of pollution abatement and technology in industry.

One thing that seems to emerge clearly from a consideration of effluent charges and other incentives and policies for dealing with water quality is the need for new or altered institutions through which the policies can be made effective. Inevitably, this points in the direction of some regional organization, frequently as large as a river basin, or several river basins, and including a number of urban clusters.

Most metropolitan areas are made up of dozens of separate political entities, frequently including quite a few that deal only in water and sewage problems. It seems clear that a piecemeal approach to water quality management will prove impossible or, at best, exceedingly awkward. Larger scale authorizations will be necessary. Fortunately, in this case most people can understand readily the need for regional approaches. Here is a case where the planners will have to go quite far from their customary business of creating physical plans into the subtle reaches of economic policy, political organization, and public administration. More than this, they will have to be concerned with the social effects of the systems they are planning and, of course, the constraints of public acceptability and willingness to pay. And, increasingly, precious local autonomy will have to be surrendered to larger-scale arrangements.

Some Other Kinds of Pollution

Air pollution shares many of the difficulties of water pollution. One has to think in terms of an air shed, frequently covering a metropolitan area or several such areas. The movement of air is much more whimsical and less predictable than water; it does not stay within any defined river banks and can flow uphill as well as down. The present approach is to set general standards for smoke emissions, automobile exhaust, refuse burning, and so on. The standards being followed are mostly physical standards relating to ash and particulate matter, chemical compounds such as sulphur oxides and carbon monoxide, and the like. There is no very direct way of linking in the harmful effects on individuals except as health and comfort are correlated with these physical characteristics.

With air pollution, as with any kind of pollution, there can be interventions at various stages between the source of pollution and the human being. For example, individuals may wear gas masks or spend most of their time inside, breathing filtered air. Contraptions may be installed in the exhaust pipes of automobiles and in the smokestacks of industry to reduce the amount of pollutants discharged. Or, whole industrial processes and materials may be altered so as to reduce air pollution. The options are numerous and the tradeoffs difficult to appraise. Selective regulation of a few heavy polluting sources may be much more economical than trying to enforce general regulations on all, although the problems of equity and public acceptance may be greater.

Perhaps one of the first things needed is a set of indicators by means of which not only the physical and economic but also the social effects of air pollution, or any kind of pollution, can be traced over time. We need to know more about pollution trends and whether we are gaining on the problems or losing. Already, progress is being made in standardizing and compiling physical indicators such as dissolved oxygen and coliform count for water, and particulate matter and sulfur oxide for air. Also, cost estimates for preventing or treating water and air pollution are beginning to be made available on a more systematic basis. But much work remains to be done in creating social indicators by means of which the physical and economic aspects can be related to the health, comfort, and well-being of individuals and groups. An interagency committee under the leadership of the Department of Health, Education, and Welfare is at work on this, not only for pollution, but for health, education, crime, and many other aspects of society. A bill has been introduced into Congress calling for a council of social advisors which would take in hand the preparation of such social indicators. Also, a few articles have been published on the subject. There is some risk at the present time that federal money for combating air and water pollution may outrun capacity for spending it wisely. Planners, of all people, will support research and efforts to provide pollution indicators and to measure consequences, since this is the way to establish a better basis for formulating and advancing their plans for dealing with the problems.

Solid waste disposal is another problem of environmental quality which plagues cities. To some extent wastes can be put to useful purposes as landfill, to provide heat, and even in the composting of garbage into fertilizer material. But for the most part getting rid of the solid waste that is discarded in a modern city is a great big headache. My own suburban community of Arlington, Virginia, has to maintain a small fleet of mammoth trucks that operate round the clock hauling stuff far out into the Virginia countryside for dumping. Every few years we have to find a new place to dump and this leads into complicated intergovenmental negotiations.

To some extent solid waste disposal through conventional dumping can be converted into a water or air pollution problem—a frying pan into fire kind of thing. That is, some of the stuff that starts out as solid waste can be incinerated and discharged into the atmosphere, while some it can be sluiced away into the rivers. As new organizational arrangements are created to cope with any one kind of pollution, they will have to deal intimately and at many points with organizations created to deal with some other kind of pollution. The possibilities for an integrated attack should be considered carefully.

This is not the end of the pollution story. Pesticides used in excess or applied sloppily not only can damage the countryside and the ponds, but also can be harmful to city people. The harm can arise whenever too much of certain chemicals gets into the food supply. Chemical residues can also be a concern to city people who want to go out into the country for recreation. Radioactive substances in the general atmosphere, which like pesticides can get into the food supply, are another form of pollution of concern to people wherever they live, but the damages will be greatest where the most people are, namely in the cities. Here the matter of setting standards, limiting and controlling the explosions which are the source of the trouble, enforcing of programs, and all the rest are matters of international concern and can hardly be dealt with on any smaller scale.

Increasingly, the most disturbing part of the natural environment of cities is the noise created by trucks and automobiles, trains, airplanes, industrial operations, and just the normal activity of people. As an elected official serving on the governing board of my county, I know that I get many more squawks from people who are upset by urban noise than by water or air pollution. I suppose a tally of my gripe mail on the pollution subject would run three to one of complaints about noise over all other kinds of pollution combined. Perhaps this is exacerbated in Arlington because it is a small county close to the center of the metropolitan area and has Dulles National Airport within its boundaries. Here again the approach by means of which physical standards are set in terms of decibels of noise at different locations may be rather clumsy; perhaps one has to get much closer to the source of noise and abate the nuisance there. The convenience of those who travel in jet planes seems to be overbearing the comfort, and perhaps sanity, of a much larger number of ground-dwellers in our metropolitan areas. There is much interest in noise abatement in most cities and a few Congressmen have begun to dig into the legislative possibilities at the federal level. I have been much interested in the suburban Chicago community not far from the end of the runway of the O'Hare airport which apparently records the noise made by planes as they go over its territory, takes pictures of the planes to identify them, and then notifies offending companies whose planes have made noise in excess of the established standard. Perhaps some headway can be made by giving full publicity to efforts like this. My impression is that the public would follow eagerly newspaper reports naming flight numbers and airlines which gave offense.

I have left untouched the disfigurement of the urban environment which results from poor planning, architecture lacking in form and beauty, slipshod construction, inefficient city management, and undisciplined civic behavior. This too is a kind of pollution, perhaps the most pervasive of all; it degrades both the city and its citizens.

In Conclusion: A Suggested Approach

The environmental and pollution problems of cities are like many other problems such as education, health, and transportation: no one jurisdiction is large enough geographically, financially, administratively, or in any other way to cope with the problems. The approaches are well known: enlarge the city by annexation, develop special authorities on a metropolitan basis for particular problems, wait for the federal government to devise a metro-wide program to supplant the miscellaneous. collections of jurisdictions in a metropolitan area, work through councils of government, and so on. I don't know what the best answer is with regard to the various kinds of pollution; probably there is no one best solution.

My suggestion here is for each metropolitan area, acting under the best leadership it can find, to develop a strategy for making progress in abating pollution. The strategy should be directed first toward preparing a systematic analysis of the problems and setting forth a range of feasible solutions in the form of programs that would achieve specified objectives in an efficient and socially acceptable way. The second part of the strategy is to initiate a process of review and discussion by means of which all interested parties can be drawn into the planning decision process. The various programs offered should include not only physical structures and activities but also the incentives, regulations, and educational campaigns required to put them into effect. And the third part of the strategy is to assign the responsibilities for planning and carrying out the selected program in a way that would fit best with the possibilities for metropolitan-wide cooperation in each particular metropolitan region. Public acceptance plus financial and administrative feasibility are essential; otherwise, even the best of plans will fail.

In my own region I think this kind of approach could best be accomplished through the metropolitan council of governments which includes all of the general governmental units in the region in a voluntary association. A concerted approach through such a council has two advantages: the entire metropolitan region can be covered and the various types of pollution can be included in the program. To the extent possible, particular chores and responsibilities should probably be passed back to local jurisdictions, but the same system of incentives, penalties, regulations, and standards should prevail over the whole area. The federal government can offer its support to a council of governments or whatever organization seems to offer the best chance for developing and sustaining a good regional program. The main thing is to get cracking with the strategy, the planning, and the action.

Planners and public officials generally may be lagging behind what the people want and will support in the matter of pollution abatement. The dramatic and visible nature of water, air, and land pollution may well provide the popular basis for the practical application of planning and governmental activity on the metropolitan scale that planners have long been looking for. The nettle should be grasped. A concerted regional attack on pollution in its several interrelated forms can do much for the improvement of the quality of urban living, thereby contributing to progress toward Plato's goal of well-integrated persons at home in harmoniously composed cities.

VIII
PROSPECTS: Toward an Improved Urban Future

It has been said that recent metropolitan trends have all but destroyed traditional concepts of urban form and structure. All available evidence, as Strauss noted in Section I, points to a continued articulation of new forms in the future. These trends present a challenge to which the urban community as a whole must respond.[1] The following papers introduce some of the questions that must be answered in understanding, shaping, and improving our urban future.

In discussing the future spatial organization of our cities several problems arise immediately. One is the partial and incomplete knowledge that we have about the contemporary city and about recent trends. In evaluating future urban alternatives present concepts and analytical procedures are even less adequate. Numerous attempts have been made to extrapolate past trends into the future and to assess their implications.[2] But these are based on fairly weak evidence. The second problem involves the specifica-

1. For example, Lowdon Wingo, Jr. (ed.), *Cities and Space: The Future Use of Urban Land* (Baltimore: The Johns Hopkins Press for Resources for the Future, Inc., 1963). A more recent set of papers on the same general theme as the above is B. J. Frieden and W. W. Nash, Jr. (eds.), *Shaping an Urban Future: Essays in Memory of Catherine Bauer Wurster* (Cambridge, Mass.: The M.I.T. Press, 1969). See also Anthony Downs, "Alternative Forms of Future Urban Growth in the United States," *Journal of the American Institute of Planners*, XXXVI (January 1970), pp. 3-11.

2. The papers contained in three recent issues of *Daedalus*, the Journal of the American Academy of Arts and Sciences, provide excellent forays into the changing environments of urban life and the projections of these trends into the future. See "America's Changing Environment," Vol. 96, No. 4 (Fall 1967); "Toward the Year 2000: Work in Progress," Vol. 96, No. 3 (Summer 1967); and "The Conscience of the City," Vol. 97, No. 4 (Fall 1968). Equally relevant are a collection of papers directed to future environments over the next fifty years commissioned by the American Institute of Planners, and edited by W. R. Ewald, Jr., *Environment and Policy: The Next Fifty Years* (Bloomington: Indiana University Press, 1968); *Environment and Change: The Next Fifty Years* (Bloomington: Indiana University Press, 1968); and *Environment and Man: The Next Fifty Years* (Bloomington: Indiana University Press, 1967).

tion of goals. This raises the all important question of what the city is and what it means to its residents. To some residents it is simply what is. They accept it as inevitable and even in some cases desirable. Yet for those who wish to improve the quality of our cities in the future, a necessary step in the identification of priorities in research and policy is the classification of social goals and the means that are available or are needed to achieve these goals. The aimless chaos of contemporary metropolitan areas must in part be attributable to our inability to encourage the communication of social preferences, and subsequently to agree on explicit goals.[3] We must first decide what kind of cities we want before setting in motion the machinery to alter the present evolutionary processes. In the absence of such guidelines, policies will often be inappropriate, conflicting, and in the long-run possibly fruitless.

Is a new order of urban society emerging? In the first essay Melvin Webber presents a challenging view of the contemporary city, its problems and futures. Improvements in transportation and communication have altered the basic cohesiveness that has been typical of the spatial organization of our society. The traditional image of the urban community as a tightly knit spatial unit is rapidly disappearing as people become more mobile and their interests and activities broaden. How do we plan for these changes in cities of the future? Webber suggests that we do not even have an appropriate language to describe the organization of society and of cities that will exist if present trends continue. This has lead to considerable confusion in identifying urban trends and problems, and in searching for future alternatives. One of our first priorities might then be the review of information, such as that contained in this book, with a view to devising a way of thinking about the future which is different from our thinking about the past.

Defining the future environment that urban residents desire demands explicit knowledge of social attitudes, preferences, and individual perceptions. In the second essay William Michelson introduces one method of evaluating social preferences in physical environments. These are then used to identify the relationships between social variables and the ideal urban environment.[4] The perspective of each individual depends on his social and spatial experience, that is, his own personal space. Michelson argues

3. One result of an interdisciplinary approach to the identification of goals in urban design and the social sciences is Brian J. L. Berry and J. Meltzer (eds.), *Goals for Urban America* (Englewood Cliffs, N.J.: Prentice Hall, 1967).
4. In more recent papers Professor Michelson has added to this conceptual model of man's relationship to his physical environment. See William Michelson, "A Parsonian Scheme for the Study of Man and Environment, or What Human Ecology Left Behind in the Dust," *Sociological Enquiry*, Vol. 38 (Spring 1968), pp. 197-208; and *Man and His Urban Environment* (Reading, Mass.: Addison-Wesley, 1970).

that the physical environment must be reduced to its basic level, that is, to the perception of the individual, if it is to be understood and the future planned effectively. At the local community level at least, it is possible to plan for a diversity of environments in order to accommodate personal space preferences and individual patterns of behavior, and thus to maximize social benefits. As Gans[5] has also noted, urban planning must redirect its emphasis in order to be more responsive to social needs and social aspirations. The increasing interest in neighborhood participation in the planning process is a logical step in this direction.[6]

One suggestion for the future is the experimental city. Athelstan Spilhaus offers a potpourri of ideas, criticisms, concepts, and proposals for the improvement of urban life: waste disposal and education, zoning and recreation, culture and services. In his outline of an experimental city he anticipates that the size of the urban area, the quality of urban services, and types of housing would be planned from the outset to meet the demands and aspirations of a given and limited cluster of population. Such cities would be planned as complete entities, and as entities within a larger urban system. We build hotels, theatres, and schools for a given number of people, why not the same for cities? The size of the city would be small enough to identify with, but large enough to offer a sufficient range of choices for employment and leisure time. All social services would be improved and expanded in comparison to the contemporary city. For example, communication of all descriptions would be enhanced, in what the author calls "the wired city," by the integrated use of modern telecommunications systems. The new city in its entirety would be a total experiment in the social sciences, human ecology, and environmental engineering, facilitating the creation of a planned environment as free as possible from pollution and stress. This would be a city in which planning attempts to master rather than submit to technological change. Although most of the ideas in this paper on new communities are not unique—they can be traced to such figures as Constantinos Doxiadis, Buckminster Fuller, and Ebenezer Howard—his unusually broad formulations are nonetheless stimulating.[7]

5. See H. J. Gans, "Planning for People, Not Buildings," *Environment and Planning,* Vol. 1 (1969), pp. 33-46.

6. For example, numerous urban community organizations have sought through public protest to alter plans for urban renewal and expressways particularly those affecting their neighborhoods. See Gordon Fellman, "Neighborhood Protest of an Urban Highway," *Journal of the American Institute of Planners,* XXXV (March 1969), pp. 118-22.

7. The arguments for and against the establishment of new towns have been widely published. For example, Clarence Stein, *Toward New Towns for America* (Cambridge, Mass.: The M.I.T. Press, reprinted 1966). The traditional arguments in support of new towns are summarized in Sir Frederic Osborn and Arnold Whittick, *The New Towns: Answer to Megalopolis* (New York: McGraw-Hill, 1963).

What are the research problems in setting out a desirable urban form? Professor Britton Harris takes the point of view of a research analyst in the next essay in outlining the difficulties of specifying an appropriate design theory for the spatial structure of the city, and the complex analytical problems which are involved in finding solutions to these difficulties. It is obvious that as the number of criteria that are necessarily involved in the planning process increases, the number of combinations of design alternatives available expands prohibitively. The definition of an optimal spatial design, or designs, he concludes is a task so beset with analytical problems itself that it is unlikely to be achieved even in a limited or partial sense. Most readers will sense this. Yet it also raises the question of whether an optimum city is a tenable objective in the first instance. Nevertheless, Harris argues in convincing detail that the role of the spatial designer, and the planner in particular, is to attempt to outline alternative solutions and futures, which may or may not be optimal by whatever criteria one wishes to apply, but which indicate explicitly the outcomes of given actions and the feasibility of different solutions. With such available, we may better see the road ahead.

The city is the total environment for most North Americans. A look to the future suggests that a metropolitan environment will be the home of even larger proportions of our population. In the last essay, Kevin Lynch discusses the city and the urban environment that is possible in the future.[8] This city must be responsive to the contemporary demands for mobility, diversity, and openness, but it must also provide a richly varied and humane environment. This environment is more than a system of land uses and buildings. It also has certain geographic and social qualities and attributes, real and perceived, which, Lynch argues, act to order and to give meaning to the various parts and activities of the city's spatial structure.[9] Planning of the future city must be sensitive to these complex

---

The genesis of the new-town movement in British planning is described in William Ashworth, *The Genesis of Modern British Town Planning* (London: Routledge and Kegan Paul Ltd., 1954). The idea of employing new town concepts in urban renewal programs is explored in H. S. Perloff, "New Towns in Town," *Journal of the American Institute of Planners,* XXXII (1966), pp. 155-60.

8. A substantial review of contemporary planning problems in anticipating the future is Melvin M. Webber, "Planning in an Environment of Change," *Town Planning Review,* Part I, "Beyond the Industrial Age," Vol. 39, No. 3 (October 1968), pp. 179-95; and Part II, "Permissive Planning," Vol. 39, No. 4 (January 1969), pp. 277-95.

9. Among the most useful references on planning, design, and social attitudes is Robert Sommer, *Personal Space: The Behavioral Basis of Design* (Englewood Cliffs, N.J.: Prentice Hall, 1969); and the special issue of the *Journal of Social Issues,* Vol. 33, No. 4 (October 1966); and the first issue of *Environment and Behavior,* Vol. 1, No. 1 (June 1969).

attributes and attitudes. It is possible, for example, to identify those social elements in the technological cityscape which are relevant in specifying solutions to the complex problems of contemporary urban life.[10] In addition to those problems already discussed, there are others: architecturally monotonous developments, the extreme perceptual stress in the environment borne by urban residents, the lack of visual identity, illegibility and confusion of form and function in design, and the lack of open space through planning rigidity.[11] He argues that human behavior in the city changes rapidly, and that physical form and design may be used symbolically to stabilize and stimulate it.

The experimental solutions suggested by Lynch and others in this volume, offer one set of approaches to improving large-scale environmental quality and personal identity within urban communities, and thus to creating cities fitted to human purposes. Whether these solutions are sufficient is a question that remains to be answered.

10. The critical issue of technology in the future development of urban areas is discussed in a compilation of papers prepared for the U.S. Government's Panel on Science and Technology. See U.S. House of Representatives, Committee on Science and Astronautics, *Science and Technology and the Cities* (Washington: U.S. Government Printing Office, 1969).

11. See also, Kevin Lynch, "The City as Environment," *Scientific American,* Vol. 213 (September 1965), pp. 209-19.

MELVIN M. WEBBER

The Post-city Age

We are passing through a revolution that is unhitching the social processes of urbanization from the locationally fixed city and region. Reflecting the current explosion in science and technology, employment is shifting from the production of goods to services; increasing ease of transportation and communication is dissolving the spatial barriers to social intercourse; and Americans are forming social communities comprised of spatially dispersed members. A new kind of large-scale urban society is emerging that is increasingly independent of the city. In turn, the problems of the city place generated by early industrialization are being supplanted by a new array different in kind. With but a few remaining exceptions (the new air pollution is a notable one), the recent difficulties are not place-type problems at all. Rather, they are the transitional problems of a rapidly developing society-economy-and-polity whose turf is the nation. Paradoxically, just at the time in history when policy-makers and the world press are discovering the city, "the age of the city seems to be at an end."[1]

1. The phrase is Don Martindale's; it closes his "Introduction" to Max Weber's *The City*

Our failure to draw the rather simple conceptual distinction between the spatially defined city or metropolitan area and the social systems that are localized there clouds current discussions about the "crisis of our cities."[2] The confusion stems largely from the deficiencies of our language and from the anachronistic thought-ways we have carried over from the passing era. We still have no adequate descriptive terms for the emerging social order, and so we use, perforce, old labels that are no longer fitting. Because we have named them so, we suppose that the problems manifested inside cities are, therefore and somehow, "city problems." Because societies in the past had been

(New York, 1962), p. 67. The theme is being sounded in many quarters nowadays. See especially, Scott Greer, *The Emerging City* (New York, 1962); Kenneth Boulding, *The Meaning of the Twentieth Century* (New York, 1965); York Willburn, *The Withering Away of the City* (Tuscaloosa, 1964); and Janet Abu-Lhughod, "The City Is Dead—Long Live the City" (Center for Planning and Development Research, University of California, Berkeley, 1966, mimeo).
2. John Friedman presents a crisp clarification of the distinction in "Two Concepts of Urbanization," *Urban Affairs Quarterly*, Vol. 1, No. 4 (June, 1966), pp. 78-84.

From **Daedalus**, Journal of the American Academy of Arts and Sciences, Boston, Massachusetts, Vol. 97, No. 4, Fall 1968, pp. 1093-1099. Reprinted by permission.

spatially and locally structured, and because urban societies used to be exclusively city-based, we seem still to assume that territoriality is a necessary attribute of social systems.

The error has been a serious one, leading us to seek local solutions to problems whose causes are not of local origin and hence are not susceptible to municipal treatment. We have been tempted to apply city-building instruments to correct social disorders, and we have then been surprised to find that they do not work. (Our experience with therapeutic public housing, which was supposed to cure "social pathologies," and urban renewal, which was supposed to improve the lives of the poor, may be our most spectacular failures.) We have lavished large investments on public facilities, but neglected the quality and the distribution of the social services. And we have defended and reinforced home-rule prerogatives of local and state governments with elaborate rhetoric and protective legislation.

Neither crime-in-the-streets, poverty, unemployment, broken families, race riots, drug addiction, mental illness, juvenile delinquency, nor any of the commonly noted "social pathologies" marking the contemporary city can find its causes or its cure there. We cannot hope to invent local treatments for conditions whose origins are not local in character, nor can we expect territorially defined governments to deal effectively with problems whose causes are unrelated to territory or geography. The concepts and methods of civil engineering and city planning suited to the design of unitary physical facilities cannot be used to serve the design of social change in a pluralistic and mobile society. In the novel society now emerging—with its sophisticated and rapidly advancing science and technology, its complex social organization, and its internally integrated societal processes—the influence and significance of geographic distance and geographic place are declining rapidly.

This is, of course, a most remarkable change. Throughout virtually all of human history, social organization coincided with spatial organization. In preindustrial society, men interacted almost exclusively with geographic neighbors. Social communities, economies, and polities were structured about the place in which interaction was least constrained by the frictions of space. With the coming of large-scale industrialization during the latter half of the nineteenth century, the strictures of space were rapidly eroded, abetted by the new ease of travel and communication that the industrialization itself brought.

The initial counterparts of industrialization in the United States were, first, the concentration of the nation's population into large settlements and, then, the cultural urbanization of the population. Although these changes were causally linked, they had opposite spatial effects. After coming together at a common place, people entered larger societies tied to no specific place. Farming and village peoples from throughout the continent and the world migrated to the expanding cities, where they learned urban ways, acquired the occupational skills that industrialization demanded, and became integrated into the contemporary society.

In recent years, rising societal scale and improvements in transportation and communications systems have loosed a chain of effects robbing the city of its once unique function as an urbanizing instrument of society. Farmers and small-town residents, scattered throughout the continent, were once effectively removed from the cultural life of the nation. City folks visiting the rural areas used to be treated as strangers, whose styles of living and thinking were unfamiliar. News of the rest of the world was hard to get and then had little meaning for those who lived the local life. Country folk surely knew there was another world out there somewhere, but little understood it and were affected by it only indirectly. The powerful anti-urban traditions in early American thought and politics made the immigrant city dweller a suspicious character whose crude ways marked him as un-Christian (which he sometimes was) and certainly un-American. The more sophisticated urban upper classes—merchants, landowners, and professional men—were similarly suspect and hence rejected. In contrast, the small-town merchant and the farmer who lived closer to nature were the genuine Americans of pure heart who lived the simple, natural life.[3] Because the contrasts between the rural and the urban ways-of-life were indeed sharp, antagonisms were real, and the differences became institutionalized in the conduct of politics. America was marked by a diversity of regional and class cultures whose followers interacted infrequently, if ever.

By now this is nearly gone. The vaudeville hick-town and hayseed characters have left the scene with the vaudeville act. Today's urbane farmer watches television documentaries, reads the national news magazines, and manages his acres from an office (maybe located in a downtown office building), as his hired hands ride their tractors while listening to the current world news broadcast from a transistor. Farming has long since ceased to be a handicraft art; it is among the most highly technologized industries and is tightly integrated into the international industrial complex.

During the latter half of the nineteenth century and the first third of the twentieth, the traditional territorial conception that distinguished urbanites and ruralites was probably valid: The typical rural folk lived outside the cities, and the typical urbanites lived inside. By now this pattern is nearly *reversed*. Urbanites no

3. Richard Hofstadter, *The Age of Reform* (New York, 1955) and *Anti-Intellectualism in America* (New York, 1963). Morton and Lucia White, *The Intellectuals Against the City* (Cambridge, 1964).

longer reside exclusively in metropolitan settlements, nor do ruralites live exclusively in the hinterlands. Increasingly, those who are least integrated into modern society—those who exhibit most of the attributes of rural folk—are concentrating within the highest-density portions of the large metropolitan centers. This profoundly important development is only now coming to our consciousness, yet it points up one of the major policy issues of the next decades.

Cultural diffusion is integrating immigrants, city residents, and hinterland peoples into a national urban society, but it has not touched all Americans evenly. At one extreme are the intellectual and business elites, whose habitat is the planet; at the other are the lower-class residents of city and farm who live in spatially and cognitively constrained worlds. Most of the rest of us, who comprise the large middle class, lie somewhere in-between, but in some facets of our lives we all seem to be moving from our ancestral localism toward the unbounded realms of the cosmopolites.

High educational attainments and highly specialized occupations mark the new cosmopolites. As frequent patrons of the airlines and the long-distance telephone lines, they are intimately involved in the communications networks that tie them to their spatially dispersed associates. They contribute to and consume the specialized journals of science, government, and industry, thus maintaining contact with information resources of relevance to their activities, whatever the geographic sources or their own locations. Even though some may be employed by corporations primarily engaged in manufacturing physical products, these men trade in information and ideas. They are the producers of the information and ideas that fuel the engines of societal development. For those who are tuned into the international communications circuits, cities have utility precisely because they are rich in information. The way such men use the city reveals its essential character most clearly, for to them the city is essentially a massive communications switchboard through which human interaction takes place.[4]

Indeed, cities exist *only* because spatial agglomeration permits reduced costs of interaction. Men originally elected to locate in high-density settlements precisely because space was so costly to overcome. It is still cheaper to interact with persons who are nearby, and so men continue to locate in such settlements.[5] Because there *are* concentrations of associates in city places, the new cosmopolites establish their offices there and then move about from city to city conducting their affairs. The biggest settlements attract the most long-distance telephone and airline traffic and have undergone the most dramatic growth during the era of city-building.

The recent expansion of Washington, D. C. is the most spectacular evidence of the changing character of metropolitan development. Unlike the older settlements whose growth was generated by expanding manufacturing activities during the nineteenth and early-twentieth centuries, Washington produces almost no goods whatsoever. Its primary products are information and intelligence, and its fantastic growth is a direct measure of the predominant roles that information and the national government have come to play in contemporary society.

This terribly important change has been subtly evolving for a long time, so gradually that it seems to have gone unnoticed. The preindustrial towns that served their adjacent farming hinterlands were essentially alike. Each supplied a standardized array of goods and services to its neighboring market area. The industrial cities that grew after the Civil War and during the early decades of this century were oriented to serving larger markets with the manufacturing products they were created to produce. As their market areas widened, as product specialization increased, and as the information content of goods expanded, establishments located in individual cities became integrated into the spatially extensive economies. By now, the large metropolitan centers that used to be primarily goods-producing loci have become interchange junctions within the international communications networks. Only in the limited geographical, physical sense is any modern metropolis a discrete, unitary, identifiable phenomenon. At most, it is a localized node within the integrating international networks, finding its significant identity as contributor to the workings of that larger system. As a result, the new cosmopolites belong to none of the world's metropolitan areas, although they use them. They belong, rather, to the national and international communities that merely maintain information exchanges at these metropolitan junctions.

Their capacity to interact intimately with others who are spatially removed depends, of course, upon a level of wealth adequate to cover the dollar costs of long-distance intercourse, as well as upon the cognitive capacities associated with highly skilled professional occupations. The intellectual and business elites are able to maintain continuing and close contact with their associates throughout the world because they are rich not only in information, but also in dollar income.

As the costs of long-distance interaction fall in proportion to the rise in incomes, more and more people are able and willing to pay the transportation and communication bills. As expense-account privileges are expanded, those costs are being reduced to zero for ever larger numbers of people. As levels of education and skill rise, more and more people are being tied

4. Richard L. Meier, *A Communications Theory of Urban Growth* (Cambridge, 1962).
5. I have elaborated this thesis in "Order in Diversity: Community Without Propinquity," in Lowdon Wingo, Jr. (ed.), *Cities and Space* (Baltimore, 1963), pp. 23-54.

into the spatially extensive communities that used to engage only a few.

Thus, the glue that once held the spatial settlement together is now dissolving, and the settlement is dispersing over ever widening terrains. At the same time, the pattern of settlement upon the continent is also shifting (moving toward long strips along the coasts, the Gulf, and the Great Lakes). These trends are likely to be accelerated dramatically by cost-reducing improvements in transportation and communications technologies now in the research-and-development stages. (The SST, COMSAT communications, high-speed ground transportation with speeds up to 500 m.p.h., TV and computer-aided educational systems, no-toll long-distance telephone service, and real-time access to national computer-based information systems are likely to be powerful ones.) Technological improvements in transport and communications reduce the frictions of space and thereby ease long-distance intercourse. Our compact, physical city layouts directly mirror the more primitive technologies in use at the time these were built. In a similar way, the locational pattern of cities upon the continent reflects the technologies available at the time the settlements grew.[6] If currently anticipated technological improvements prove workable, each of the metropolitan settlements will spread out in low-density patterns over far more extensive areas than even the most frightened future-mongers have yet predicted. The new settlement-form will little resemble the nineteenth-century city so firmly fixed in our images and ideologies. We can also expect the large junction points will no longer have the com-

6. For example, the first-generation jet airplanes, like the first railroads, accelerated the growth of the largest settlements. The big jets could land at only those airports with long runways and specialized facilities. The second- and third-generation jets are fast equalizing accessibility among settlements, recapitulating the accessibility effects of the railroads and then the highways.

munications advantage they now enjoy, and smaller settlements will undergo a major spurt of growth in all sorts of now-isolated places where the natural amenities are attractive.

Moreover, as ever larger percentages of the nation's youth go to college and thus enter the national and international cultures, attachments to places of residence will decline dramatically. This prospect, rather than the spatial dispersion of metropolitan areas, portends the functional demise of the city. The signs are already patently clear among those groups whose worlds are widest and least bounded by parochial constraints.

Consider the extreme cosmopolite, if only for purposes of illustrative cartooning. He might be engaged in scientific research, news reporting, or international business, professions exhibiting critical common traits. The astronomer, for example, maintains instantaneous contact with his colleagues around the world; indeed, he is a day-to-day collaborator with astronomers in all countries. His work demands that he share information and that he and his colleagues monitor stellar events jointly, as the earth's rotation brings men at different locales into prime-viewing position. Because he is personally committed to their common enterprise, his social reference group is the society of astronomers. He assigns his loyalties to the community of astronomers, since their work and welfare matter most to him.

To be sure, as he plays out other roles —say, as citizen, parent, laboratory director, or grocery shopper—he is a member of many other communities, both interest-based and place-defined ones. But the striking thing about our astronomer, and the millions of people like him engaged in other professions, is how little of his attention and energy he devotes to the concerns of place-defined communities. Surely, as compared to his grandfather, whose life was largely bound up in the affairs of his locality, the astronomer, playwright, newsman, steel broker, or wheat dealer lives in a life-space that is not defined by territory and deals with problems that are not local in nature. For him, the city is but a convenient setting for the conduct of his professional work; it is not the basis for the social communities that he cares most about.

Indeed, we may not be far from the time when the vernacular meaning of "community" will be archaic and disappear from common usage. It has already lost much of its traditional meaning for a great many of those on the leading edge of the society. If it is retained, it may be restricted to the provisions of children and of those adults who have not gained access to modern society.

The demise of the city is associated with far more subtle and powerful changes than the expansion of market areas for firms and the collaboration among scientists in distant nations. Behind these developments lies the internationalization of society generated by the knowledge explosion.

WILLIAM MICHELSON

An Empirical Analysis of Urban Environmental Preferences

The planning professions rely heavily on the assumption that the urban physical environment which surrounds particular types of people influences social life. While recent studies have begun to investigate the relationship of man to his environment more carefully than in the past,[1] the literature in this area is fragmented and unsystematic; its primary importance has been the suggestion of social variables thought to be related to the urban environment, the most pervasive of which are: social rank or status,[2] stage in the life cycle, that is, age, nature of family,[3] life style,[4] and value orientations.[5]

The crucial question for planners—which of these are necessarily connected with variations in the planned environment—has for the most part been left unanswered.

The data reported below attempt to shed light on the systematic association of social variables and ideal physical environment. Ideal environment should of course reflect the consideration of many other types of variables as well, but the data of this study attempt to isolate, for the purposes of analysis, the sociological variables only that are relevant. Before turning to these data, however, I want to

1. See, for example, F. Stuart Chapin and Henry C. Hightower, "Household Activity Patterns and Land Use," *Journal of the American Institute of Planners,* XXXI (August, 1965): 222-31, and Robert L. Wilson, "Livability of the City: Attitudes and Urban Development," in F. Stuart Chapin, Jr., and Shirley Weiss (eds.), *Urban Growth Dynamics.* (N.Y.: John Wiley and Sons, Inc., 1962), pp. 359-99.
2. See, for example, James Beshers, *Urban Social Structure.* (New York: The Free Press of Glencoe, Inc., 1962).
3. See, for example, William H. Whyte, Jr., "Are Cities Un-American?", in the Editors of

Fortune, *The Exploding Metropolis.* (Garden City, New York: Doubleday Anchor Books), pp. 1-31.
4. See, for example, John M. Mogey, *Family and Neighbourhood.* (London: Oxford University Press, 1956), and Wendell Bell, "Social Choice, Life Styles, and Suburban Residence," in William M. Dobriner (ed.), *The Suburban Community.* (New York: G. P. Putnam's Sons, 1958).
5. See, for example, John R. Seeley, R. Alexander Sim, and Elisabeth W. Loosley, *Crestwood Heights* (New York: Basic Books, Inc. 1956).

From the **Journal of the American Institute of Planners**, Vol. XXXII, No. 6, November 1966, pp. 355-360. Reprinted by permission.

outline what I consider to be a fruitful conception of the urban physical environment for this context.

Urban Physical Environment

In recent years, several attempts have been made to construct conceptual schemes for the urban physical environment.[6] There seems little need to improve on some of the criteria Lynch and Rodwin set forth:

the categories of analysis must:
1. Have significance at the city-wide scale, that is, be controllable and describable at that level.
2. Involve either the physical shape or the activity description and not confuse the two.
3. Apply to all urban settlements.
4. Be capable of being recorded, communicated, and tested.
5. Have significance for their effect on the achievement of human objectives and include all physical features that are significant.[7]

These integrating schemes succeed in clarifying greatly the nature and range of phenomena to be captured in the urban environment. However, the concepts put forward typically fail to account for *both* microcosmic and macrocosmic elements in cities, and different concepts within the same schemes are meaningful only with reference to different levels of scope.

What must be captured? Strauss suggests that few people besides zoners and planners ever envision all the elements of an area the size of the whole city. Instead, they select partial areas with which they are familiar, according to the groups to which they belong and the activities which they perform. As Strauss puts it, ". . . the various kinds of urban perspectives held by the residents of a city are constructed from spatial representations resulting from membership in particular social worlds."[8]

When investigating the relationship of the urban environment to individual people, people must be part of the formulation of concepts. Very basically, *all people are separated in space from other people and from objects.*

Despite the fact that they will interact with other people elsewhere in the city, we primarily envision people as near or far from the homes of others. Their homes commonly involve more of their time than any other single place in the city.[9] More activities in a man's life and in that of his family begin and end in his home than in any other location. Residences cover more of the area of cities than any other land use.

Thus, as a beginning, where a person lives is separated by space from where other people live. Each person is near or far from a particular number of other people. Objects are places where people can go once they leave their housing units. They have a variety of uses—commerical, recreational, occupational, and so forth. They differ in scale according to the number of people upon which they draw. Each person is separated by space from many objects. Indeed, such objects are separated from each other as are people, but it is people who go to them; they do not go to each other.

A basic conceptual model for the urban environment, then, involves the separation in space of a person, others, and objects.

Space refers here to two different aspects of separation: perceptual distance and accessible distance. Perceptual dis-

6. See, for example, Hans Blumenfeld, "A Theory of City Form, Past and Present," *Journal of the Society of Architectural Historians,* VIII (No. 3-4, 1949): 7-16. Lynch, "The Pattern of the Metropolis," *Daedalus,* XC (Winter, 1961), 80. Kevin Lynch and Lloyd Rodwin, "A Theory of Urban Form," *Journal of the American Institute of Planners,* XXIV (Fall, 1958), 201-14.
7. Lynch and Rodwin, *op. cit.,* p. 204.

8. Anselm L. Strauss, *Images of the American City.* (N.Y.: The Free Press of Glencoe, Inc., 1961), p. 67.
9. See, for example, the data in Chapin and Hightower, *op. cit.*

tance implies the degree of proximity between two places according to whether the distance between them is symbolically conducive to being traversed; the doorway around the corner from yours may be the closest in physical distance, but it is not the closest in perceptual distance if you never see it or have no reason to go near it.[10] Accessibility describes the distance as implied by the ease (or lack of costs) with which a particular distance can be traversed. Perceptual and accessible distance are semi-independent of common physical distance (the total distance between two points as determined by a standard measure).

The urban environment is thus built from the separation of a person from others and objects in perceptual, accessible, and ultimately physical space.

But what are some measurable dimensions of the various separations of self, others, and objects? A first is housing type. If a person lives in a single-family, detached home, he begins without common walls or doors with any others. Others may in fact be accessible, but they are perceptually absent; with respect to their dwelling units, others do not impinge upon him. As one progresses to multiple dwellings of increasing complexity, from garden apartments to walkups to high rise apartments, the number of shared facilities —walls, ceilings, floors, hallways, lobbies, stairs, elevators—tends to rise. Perceptual and accessible distance are affected differentially by the nature of the buildings.

But other things affect an individual's personal space. A second measurable dimension is private or semi-private outdoor space—door to door, window to window. This is a matter of separation from those living under separate roofs and those living in multiple dwellings. These first two dimensions, housing type and separation

10. See the data on this phenomenon in Leon Festinger, Stanley Schachter, and Kurt Back, *Social Pressures in Informal Groups*. (N.Y.: Harper and Brothers, 1950).

from others' homes, tell much about the combination of perceptual and accessible distances a person experiences from others.

If buildings and grounds separate a person from others, what separates him from objects? A third measurable dimension of environment is perceptual distance to objects. He is perceptually separated if he cannot see an object, or hear it, or smell it. This would, in its extreme form, mean that all objects are with all other objects, completely separated from the person's home. Normally, however, distinctions are made between objects deemed perceptually close and those desired at a distance.

But even given a particular perceptual distance from objects, still a separate dimension of environment is the differential accessibility of various objects. A person may desire some objects more accessible than others. By the same token, objects which are equally accessible may differ as to their perceptual distance.

Accessibility may be measured on an explicit continuum of time. Perceptual space, however, is less explicitly continuous. In fact, a much better case might be made here for the presence of a dichotomy, for there may be merit in defining the concept neighborhood as including just those objects which are perceptually close.

What I am suggesting, then, is the reduction of the urban physical environment to its most basic level, the view of each individual. Cross-culturally, the relevant types of others and objects will differ; but once they are specified, the various persons' views regarding others and objects, as measured according to dimensions of housing type, separation from others' homes, perceptual and accessible distances to various objects, and scale of objects, will build a picture of urban environment applicable to any scope desired—the microscopic as well as the macroscopic.

How would we build a city, with its different levels of urban form, based on these simple concepts? We start with the separation of self from others in housing types. People's choices of perceptual and accessible distance to others will be reflected by distinct housing types from whatever stock of housing is practical, depending upon the area of the world in which the city is to be located. From all the various individuals, then, we obtain a distribution of types of housing which will be found in the metropolitan area; for all similar individuals, we have the distribution for their immediate residential area. This gives us ideas of building type and capacity. Similar considerations of personal preference for distance to others give us lot sizes and, hence, the density of buildings to each other. When objects defined as perceptually close are entered to this picture, we have an idea of what elements are in the neighborhood; and when accessibility is added, the notion of the mixture of objects and others around the neighborhood[11] is established, together with the minimum size of the neighborhood.

A particular neighborhood reflects the complementary notions of a number of relatively similar persons. If more people support the existence of a particular type of neighborhood than its size can tolerate, then a city will have more than one neighborhood of the same type. There is, of course, no necessity that an urban area contain more than one type of neighborhood, repeated as often as necessary, but differences among individuals would imply the formation of different types of neighborhoods.

But our definition of neighborhood excluded certain objects. Depending upon the accessible distance from the individuals, these objects become of larger scale and serve as focal points of more than one neighborhood or, in case of very large scale, of the entire city. The number and importance of focal points will depend on the number of objects defined as percep-

11. Corresponding to the concept "grain," in Lynch and Rodwin, *op. cit.*

tually distant, their scale, and their differential accessibility to the person.

If a description of the entire city is desired in general terms, above and beyond the details of home, immediate dwelling area, and neighborhood, one can now piece together the number and sizes of distinct neighborhoods, the number and scale of focal points, and the means of accessibility to present a large-scale picture of the environment of the macroscopic area.

The research described below attempts to shed some preliminary and tentative light on *one,* the relationship of these basic dimensions of urban environment to a variety of social variables characterizing people, and *two,* the feasibility of attempting to plan on the basis of the above conceptual scheme of urban form.

The Study

To obtain data on the systematic association of people's preferences in urban environment to their social characteristics, in a manner affected as little as possible by extraneous factors, I conducted lengthy interviews with a sample of 75 respondents with general level dominant orientations previously determined by means of the Kluckhohn Value-Orientation Schedule,[12] who otherwise represented great variation. Their distribution among diverse categories of education, occupation, age, and the like were independent of the value orientation categories, which had been used so as to have some a priori control over a major social variable. All the respondents were either Italian- or Irish-Americans, so as to assess ethnic differences as well; this type of difference was also independent of individuals' value orientations.

12. A somewhat revised schedule for urbanites was used. The most complete statement of this general endeavor, however, may be found in Florence R. Kluckhohn and Fred L. Strodtbeck, *Variation in Value Orientations.* (Evanston, Illinois: Row, Peterson, and Co.), 1961.

The people interviewed were given photographs of buildings and neighborhoods unambiguously representing variations within each of the above mentioned dimensions of environment as stimuli for open-ended and undirected responses, much as in psychological projective testing. The photographs were also compared and ranked with respect to one another, with valuative rationales demanded after every choice. A content analysis was made of transcripts of tape recordings of these free-flowing answers, which provided data on the value orientations expressed with respect to each variation of environment for each person;[13] these value orientations were of a lower level of generality than those gathered by the Kluckhohn schedule, applying only to the realm of urban habitation.

Each respondent also planned his ideal urban environment piece by piece, mapping his choices simultaneously, again explaining his reasons for each step. When dealing with basic dimensions of form, starting with the dwelling unit and progressing outward through the other dimensions, people were easily able to diagram the communities they preferred. While out of scale, the physical plans they drew located all land uses vis à vis each other with distances labeled.

Finally, each person provided data on his interpersonal activities on the nature and his own use of his present and past neighborhoods.

The Relationships of Physical and Social

To begin, I shall discuss several findings of relevance to the first of the questions raised earlier: the relationship of the basic dimensions of environment. and social variables characterizing people.

1. Of the many social variables ascer-

13. Independent codings agreed more than 90 percent of the time, surpassing the customary standard for reliability of content analyses.

tained, the one which explains the most variance in the amount of separation people choose from others' homes is the distance people now live from their personal friends (other than relatives and formal neighbors). Those whose friends currently live relatively far away tend to choose greater separations from neighbors; those living close to friends want lesser separations. Thus, those with cosmopolitan friendship patterns transform their personal independence from neighbors into spatial patterning as well.

Separation from others' homes also bears a statistically significant relationship to three other variables, but none is as strong as the aforementioned one. This amount of separation varies directly with people's scores on individualistic value orientations (such as privacy, lack of impingement from others), inversely with scores on instrumental value orientations (such as goal attainment, convenience), and directly with the extent to which people emphasize communal order and self-protection in their lives rather than economic acquisition and consumption.

2. The amount of accessible distance from objects which people choose varies directly with the instrumental value orientation score. Not surprisingly, people who emphasize convenience throughout their lives want to be relatively close to the facilities they must or desire to visit. Those low on this score desire greater amounts of this type of distance to objects. Varying less strongly with accessible distance, but still significantly, is the frequency with which a person sees acquaintances; those currently with highly active interaction patterns desire great accessibility from their homes to various objects.

3. Perceptual distance to objects, on the other hand, varies significantly with the extent to which people currently make selective use of the objects available to them. People who are relatively cosmopolitan in their choice of stores, who do not patronize an establishment merely be-

cause it is the closest one, are more apt to desire objects perceptually separated from their homes than people with currently local orientations.

4. Finally, the scale of objects desired varies inversely with expressions of class consciousness. People who want small stores, churches, and the like tend generally to speak of economic and social inequalities and their personal desire to limit interaction to their own class. Scale of objects also varies directly, although less strongly, with the amount of intimate contact a person has with relatives and neighbors, as if intimacy in public and commercial institutions might be desired to compensate for a lack of intimate contact otherwise.

5. Along one dimension of environment, housing type, there is no variation in the characteristics of people who choose one alternative or another. The popularity of the single family house is so great that its choice is independent of any variable analyzed.

6. Two major types of variable are conspicuous by their failure to vary systematically with ideal choices of environment. One is social rank, and the other is stage in the life cycle. This suggests that much of our current segregation in cities by income and family size represents the rigidities of the housing market and of conceptions of what cities should look like, and not the socially based desires of the people involved. The choices people would make are not a simple function of their age or status (nor, in addition, of ethnic position per se), but of more subtle influences—their values and styles of life.

These findings have implications greater than the specific substantive relationships discussed. In no case did the social variable which was related most closely to choices within a particular dimension of urban form occupy the same importance with respect to any other dimension. This suggests two major points. First, the dimensions of environment are independent of one another, even though they combine with one another to create high levels of environment. Second, since the dimensions of environment are independent, it is fruitless to attempt to explain the existence or popularity of some combination of them all by any single non-physical variable.

On Planning the Environment

A second type of datum in this study is addressed to the practical implications of the conception of the physical environment presented above.

First, the respondents were asked, following their choices of environment and the location of its elements on a sketch map, to indicate which of the two choices in all possible dichotomous combinations of home, block, neighborhood, and city, on their sketch map, was most important to them. By combining the six choices thus obtained, an overall ranking of these four levels of form is found. Among the 75 respondents, the neighborhood was considered most important; it was ranked first by more people (27) than was any other level, and it had a higher average rank than did any other level (1.9). A close second in importance is the type of housing unit, with 25 first choices and an average rank of 2.1. Following far behind these two are the whole city, with 7 first choices and an average rank of 3.0, and the block, with only 4 first choices and an average rank of 3.0.[14] These data provide a measure of proof to the assertions of others that the crucial intermediate residential unit between self and the whole metropolis is indeed salient to ordinary people.[15]

There is also limited evidence from one cluster of this selectively small sample that illustrates the possible planning of residential units on the basis of complementary

14. The total of first choices does not add up to 75 because of ties, which were eliminated from consideration.
15. Wilson, *op. cit.*, p. 382.

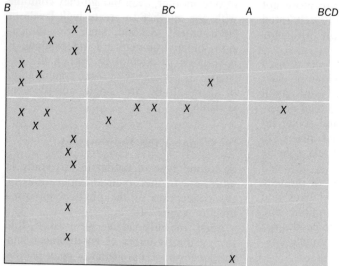

| B | A | BC | A | BCD |

KEY

X: Each house
A: Church, elementary school
B: Drug store, grocery store,
   clothing store, post office,
   medical care
C: Restaurant, movie theatre,
   high school
D: Jobs (offices, factories)

Scale: 1 inch = 5 minutes' travel

Sketch 1. Ideal Residential Unit for 21 Respondents

preferences of individuals. Twenty- one respondents (or 30 percent of the sample) designed ideal neighborhoods which were purely residential. All objects were desired to be perceptually distant. Furthermore, all wanted to live in single family homes, although with spacing between houses which varied slightly; 15 of the 21 wished substantial but not extensive separation. Moreover, 20 of the 21 desired that a number of facilities be placed in a major shopping center, rather than in individual locations. Can a neighborhood be designed which will provide the above and also satisfy the time choices to each object stipulated by each of these respondents?

The following four combinations of land uses were selected for differential distribution around the area to satisfy the preferences of these people along the several dimensions of environment.

A. church, elementary school

B. drug store, grocery store, clothing store, post office, physician's office, (one or a group)

C. restaurant, movie theatre, high school

D. occupations (offices, factories)

Given the marked differences between these groups of land uses in the accessible distance, *these* respondents locate them away from their homes, as well as their common perceptual distance, the neighborhood outlined in Sketch 1 appears appropriate. All objects are arrayed on the perimeter of this neighborhood, presumably shared with residents of the next residential unit, assuming some similar conceptions of ideal urban form. Land use group A is never located with B, but both are found more frequently on the perimeter than are C and D. According to this arrangement, a person's home may be close to A or B without necessarily being close to any of the other three alternatives, if he does not desire this. On the other hand, proximity to C or D presupposes proximity to everything that comes before (that is, A and B)—an appropriate design for these people.

Each "x" represents the best compromise location for a person's home with respect to the desired distances to A, B, C, and D. In only 3 of the 21 cases did a desired distance to a land use group differ from the ideal distance by as much as five minutes; and this happened with respect to only one of the four groups. Thus it was possible to place 30 percent of the present sample into a residential unit designed so that of the 84 travelling times thus assigned, 81 were less than five minutes deviant from what the respondents considered as ideal.

This is not, however, to say that 21 people could fill such a neighborhood; but if 21 of every 75 residents of our urban areas had similar ideas of urban forms, many such neighborhoods could exist in cities. Indeed, many do now.

Little more can be added about the form of other workable types of residential units. The size of the sample does not justify it. Yet, brief mention of a second cluster may be instructive. Another 13 percent of the sample agree on a single family house, but desire a grocery store, post office, drug store, physician, church and elementary school *within* their own neighborhood and everything else outside, which would lead to a residential unit with a far different appearance from the previous one or the location of these people in a far different pattern in Sketch 1 than most of the others already plotted. However, no more than two types of residential

unit would be necessary to satisfy the demands of 43 percent of the sample. Study of a much larger sample in an American metropolitan area might indicate the number and variations of residential units which would be necessary to complete the form of the whole city.

The data also suggest the presence of a rank ordering of objects with respect to perceptual distance. In strict statistical terms, the 13 items chosen to be the objects in this study do not form a significant scale. Yet, as Table 1 demonstrates, a powerful pattern is formed by the choices of the respondents in this sample. The chances are very high that if any given object is desired by a respondent to be within his neighborhood, every other object farther down the scale, (that is, "higher" land use), will also be desired within the neighborhood by that respondent. Proceeding on this knowledge, one would be from 67 to 94 percent correct in predicting subsequent choices, depending on the object with which one starts. If, for example, ten people want a clothing store in their neighborhood, eight of them will also want a physician perceptually close, nine will want a post office, grocery store, drug store, and high school, and all

Table 1. Additional Objects Chosen as Perceptually Close by Respondents Selecting Given Objects to be Perceptually Close

Objects	Number of People Choosing Each Object as Perceptually Close Among Those Choosing Object to the Left of Parenthesis as Close (Read Down)												
Factory	(3)												
Office	1	(5)											
Job	3	4	(7)										
Restaurant	1	3	4	(9)									
Movies	2	4	6	7	(10)								
Clothing Store	2	3	6	6	8	(10)							
Grocery Store	2	3	6	6	8	9	(16)						
Post Office	2	4	5	7	8	9	11	(17)					
Drug Store	2	4	6	7	8	9	16	16	(27)				
High School	3	5	7	9	9	9	9	12	15	(29)			
Church	2	4	6	8	9	10	14	15	23	22	(33)		
Physician	2	4	6	7	7	8	12	13	21	20	25	(34)	
Elementary School	2	4	6	8	9	10	15	16	25	26	32	31	(39)

ten will want a church and elementary school perceptually close. Thus, respondent choice of perceptual distance to specific objects forms a pattern such as to suggest possible combinations of land use once a given floor has been established below which land uses will not fall.

The data from this research, no matter how tentative, urge the understanding of social diversity and the future utilization of physical diversity in planning cities. They point out two elements of social diversity in the population as prominent for planning physical aspects of the city: value orientations and the nature and extent of social interaction. While their relevance is restricted to segmented dimensions of environment, no one variable being crucial to all of them, these two social characteristics account for great differences in the lives of people which must be taken into consideration by planners, along with more traditional concerns.

Furthermore, the conceptual scheme proposed and the data bearing on it suggest the viability of planning for diversity by concentrating on the basic unit of the individual. Since basic dimensions of environment may be independent of each other, numerous combinations may be constructed from among their variations which will not only accommodate the affected people more expertly, but which on the metropolitan level can present an endless kaleidoscope of forms for cities which ought necessarily to resemble each other no more than their residents do.

Diversity is not an end in itself. But when in cities it represents the minimization of social costs and the maximization of benefits to individuals, it represents a goal to cherish no less than others.

ATHELSTAN SPILHAUS

The Experimental City

The Experimental City suggested some years ago is now being planned. Started from scratch, the Experimental City will be unlike other cities or towns that have been built in this way. It will not be a bedroom satellite of an existing city, as some of the New Towns in England have become; nor will it attempt to be an instant utopia. It will be neither a single company town—Hershey, Pennsylvania—nor a single occupation town—Oak Ridge, Manned Space Center, Los Alamos, Chandrigar, Brazilia, Washington, D.C. The Experimental City should not be confused with "demonstration" or "model" cities that attempt to show what can be done temporarily to renew old cities. Yet it will experiment with extensions of many of the assets and experiences of these. It will attempt to be a city representing a true cross section of people, income, business and industry, recreation, education, health care, and cultural opportunities that are representative of the United States.

The Experimental City will be carefully planned for the specific purpose of people's living and working, but, like a machine, it will be planned for an optimum population size. When it reaches this capacity, its growth will be stopped, just as

machines are not overloaded when they reach their capacity. Even bacterial cultures stop growing when their size is such that they can no longer get rid of their waste metabolites. Man has not only the products of his own metabolism but what James Lodge calls the metabolites of his labor-saving slaves. Buckminster Fuller estimates that each of us has the equivalent of four hundred slaves. As technology proceeds, more and more of these mechanical slaves are used. In turn, waste metabolites increase, and cities should decrease proportionally in size. . . .

Such considerations led me to urge the Experimental City project. This will provide a laboratory for experimentation and a prototype for future dispersed systems with separated cities of high concentration and controlled size. As yet, no one has studied what the best size for a city is, nor attempted to keep a city to a certain size. Chambers of Commerce uniformly believe that bigger is better. We must get away from this conventional thinking and realize that bigger than an undetermined optimum size is not better.

A city of one hundred thousand may be too small for the diversity of cultural, recreational, educational, health-care, and

From **Daedalus,** Journal of the American Academy of Arts and Sciences, Boston, Massachusetts, Vol. 96, No. 4, Fall 1967. Reprinted by permission.

work opportunities that make for a virile self-contained community. Eight or ten million has, however, been amply proved to be too big. Somewhere in between lies an optimum number.

Once we have decided on a city's optimum size, how do we prevent the uncontrolled growth that leads to many of today's urban problems? The answer is *not* to control individuals, but to design a mix of industrial, commercial, and other employment opportunities that keeps the population in a healthy equilibrium. In the absence of better information on the proportion in a healthy mix, perhaps we should start with a cross section of the United States. But what about regional differences? A healthy mix in the Northwest might be quite different from the comfortable mix in the Southeast. Social scientists have a challenge to define these mixes. The whole concept behind the Experimental City begins and ends with people. Profiles of employees in various enterprises can be studied by wage level, group preferences, and any other factors important to a healthy representative sample, including the right quota of those dependent on welfare, the very young, and the old and retired. Here again, regional differences of employee preferences must be considered in relation to the industrial mix.

A city grows because business and industry concentrate there, providing people with diverse opportunities for work and a variety of life styles. If an Experimental City is to be built to preserve a better quality of urban environment, industry and business must build it, but in a planned way.

Although the Experimental City would be planned as much as possible, it would be designed and built so that it could change easily. In a way, the city would be designed backwards, starting with innovations in the newest engineering systems conceived for a certain number of people and no more. It would be designed to remove the burdens of chores and filth,

which modern technology can do. It goes without saying that one designs for man and his society and, in general, the planning of transportation, communication, feeding, and other networks comes later. In this case, one would use technological innovation to reduce physical restraints, which would hopefully allow man and his society more freedom to thrive. The crux is to remove the pollutants of chores, filth, noise, and congestion from the city in the hope that this will free the city dweller for a greater choice and diversity of individual human activities.

People congregate in the city because it is a gathering place for work and social interaction. Thus, working and living must be compatible, but often the factories for work make the environment for living unpleasant or unbearable. Clearly the most dramatic role of industry in the Experimental City is to show that places of work need not pollute the environment with congestion, fumes, dirty water, and noise. If living and working conditions are compatible, then people will not have to travel so much. Because of pollutants, cities are divided into separate residential and industrial areas. With the pollutants removed, industrial, commercial, residential, and educational institutions could exist side by side, reducing the human waste of commuting to and fro. If the technology of the Experimental City succeeds, there will be no need for zoning. In the interim, we should recognize four-dimensional zoning which adds a time dimension to space zoning. An example of this is the control of noise at airports, where planes are prevented from taking off during the night.

Improved communications also reduce the need for travel. As a start, an information utility could be devised that would link by broad-band coaxial cables all points now connected by telephone wires. The information utility, possibly with two-way, point-to-point video and other broad-band communication, would remove much of the obvious waste in the present conduct of business and commerce, banking and shopping. (Housewives would have bedside shopping and banking, and tele-baby-sitting when they went to visit a neighbor.) City-wide improved communications with access to the central hospital open up the possibility of less costly, less intensive services and better, more abundant home care. These, of course, are not radical ideas—but extensions. (Pediatricians today ask mothers to have their children breathe into the telephone receiver.) Los Angeles is already planning emergency helicopter-lifted hospital units that go to the scene of an accident, drop the hospital pod, and then lift the wreckage out of the way so that traffic can resume.

As a total experiment in social science, human ecology, environmental biology, and environmental engineering, the Experimental City would lend itself to a totally new concept of modern preventive medicine. Instead of healing the sick, doctors would contribute to the public-health concept that emphasizes the building up and banking of a capital of health and vigor while young, and the prudent spending of this capital over a lifetime without deficits of ill health. They would concentrate on eliminating ailments in early life rather than on repairing later ills. Their dedication, somewhat less personal in public health, would be, in a sense, what Dr. Walsh McDermott calls "statistical compassion."

Moreover, broad-band interconnections with other cities would provide smaller areas with wider access to national medical centers. Also, the educational, scientific, artistic, and entertainment opportunities would be far greater than a city of limited size would be able to offer otherwise. Point-to-point video, providing improved surveillance, should enable police to spend less time catching criminals after the event and more time preventing crimes.

Due to the present furor over the use of bugging and wire tapping, the information utility immediately invokes the specter of Big Brother and a Brave New World. In their best use, such devices can preserve and improve the quality of the urban environment, but like any other device they can also be misused by unscrupulous people. If the masses of information filed in our necessary public bureaus—the Internal Revenue Service, the National Institutes of Health, the Census Bureau, and the F.B.I.—were combined by an unscrupulous dictator, they would provide a potent coercive weapon against any individual. We cannot *not* use such devices, although we must set up adequate safeguards against their misuse. On the other hand, the information utility provides survey mechanisms for an instantaneous city census and flexible city management exactly analogous to methods of data collection used in weather forecasting.

The information utility and the mixing of living and working areas would reduce transportation needs, but it would still be necessary to experiment with new forms of mass transportation. People like automobiles because the automobile respects their desire to go directly from where they are to where they want to be without stopping where others want to stop. But the automobile produces polluting fumes and occupies parking space when the owner is not in it—which is about 90 per cent of the time.

Many suggestions have been made for a mass transportation system that retains the automobile's advantages without incorporating its disadvantages. One such scheme calls for pneumatically or electrically driven small pods with propulsion in the track. The pods may be computer-controlled to the common destination of a few people. After indicating your destination to the computer on entering the turnstile, you would wait X minutes or until, let us say, the six-person pod fills up—whichever is shorter—and then go nonstop to your destination. The pods would be small enough to pass noiselessly through buildings with normal ceiling heights. There are no motors in the pods, and because they are inexpensive small shells, we could afford many of them.

In order for there to be no air-burning machines within the city limits, connections to intercity and existing national transportation systems might be made at the city's periphery. Alternatively, air-burning machines might come into the city in underground tunnels with fume sewers. These would also provide connections to the Experimental City's airport, located at a distance and in a direction so that landing patterns are over not the city, but the noninhabited insulating belt.

The main public utilities could be accessible in the vehicular and other underground tunnels, thereby abating the noisy digging up and remaking of streets common to all American cities. The interconnecting utility tunnels would double or multiplex as traffic tunnels and utility trenches for the transport of heavy freight, for telephone lines, for power and gas lines, water and sewer mains, and for the rapid transit of emergency vehicles—police, fire, and medical rescue. All would be below the city for increased mobility and less noise.

The sewers, with a view to conserving water, might be pneumatic as in the English and French systems. To save the immense areas occupied by present sewage-treatment plants, we might treat the sewage in transit in the sewer. All this presupposes that we can throw away the old-fashioned codes stipulating that telephone and power lines, and water mains and sewers be separate. Modern technology permits messages to be sent over power lines, and pure water pipes to be concentric with sewer mains. Just as garages can be housed under parks, all services can be underground, even to the extent of going hundreds of feet down for heavy manufacturing, storage of storm water, and snow and waste heat.

The Experimental City could also provide opportunities for test-marketing new products, building materials, and postal systems. New materials would give architects a tremendous scope in developing new forms. No traffic at ground level and no land owned by individuals or individual corporations would offer a degree of freedom not possible in cities where ownership of property delimits plots. Even the materials used in the buildings themselves would be such that they could be taken down and reused if found to be obsolete or inferior. Architecture, with its emphasis on form and the visual environment, is fundamental to the success of the Experimental City. Architects would be freer to exploit the mutuality of function and form in producing a visual environment *with* other improved qualities. In Philadelphia, for example, the planners have done a magnificent job improving the visual environment, but their work is mitigated by the stench of oil refineries.

In the Experimental City, we will seek a total optimum environment without hampering diversity of architectural forms and combinations. We will experiment with enclosing portions of the city within domes that will be conditioned as to temperature, humidity, fumes, and light. It is, of course, not at all certain that people want a perfectly controlled climate. The sense of beauty and well-being involves exposure to some degree of variation. Artists know this in their play with light and shade and with colors that clash. Slight breezes and variations of temperature might be necessary to transform even clean air into fresh air that stimulates our sense of health.

The advantage of leasing and not owning land, combined with those of the new technologies, would free architects from rectilinear or stereotype ground plans that ownership of plots dictates. Space might be leased in a three-dimensional sense, and the forms the architects use in three dimensions might be emphasized by paths and foot thoroughfares, there being no wheeled traffic at ground level. Today, streets and plot plans too often predefine form. In the Experimental City, the architect will face the challenge of providing new ways for people to find face-to-face relationships in an environment that does not *require* wasteful movement.

Ralph Burgard has suggested that creative artists today are not so much concerned with the fixed audience-performer relationship. Many artists feel that art centers, now so much in fashion, are already outmoded, and that the newest forms of music, art, theater, and dance have very little to do with exhibit galleries, proscenium stages, and conventional auditoriums. Increased leisure should lead to active participation in all the arts instead of passive exposure. For this is needed an arts-recreation space completely flexible in lighting, sound, television, film, and electronic devices and in physical dimensions.

Where does one locate an Experimental City? It should be far enough away from urban areas so that it can develop self-sufficiency and not be hampered by the restrictive practices of a dominant neighboring community. Extremes of climate, far from being a disadvantage, would provide the kind of all-weather test facility needed for experimenting with technological innovations. There must be enough land for an insulating belt around the city; otherwise, conventional uncontrolled encroachments and developments would soon nullify the experiment. A density of one hundred people per acre in the city proper would mean a city area of 2,500 acres. To preserve its identity, character, cleanliness, and experimental freedom, it might need a hundred times this area as an insulating belt.

Federal and state governments are presently acquiring large tracts of unspoiled forests and lands for conservation. This is a worthy objective if done for some purpose. What better purpose is there than providing open space around cities? Such lands would be most suitable for the insulating belts between controlled-size, dispersed cities. The insulating belt would include forests, lakes, farms, outdoor museums, arboretums, and zoos. Such a mixture would make the enjoyment of the open surroundings not only attractive aesthetically and physically, but intellectually profitable. Part of the insulating belt might be devoted to hobby farms and gardens—the system so enjoyed by the Germans, who leave the city and camp in little gardens. This minimum rustic setting enables them to retain the smell and touch of the soil. There might also be high-intensity food farming and high-rise finishing farms. Fresh foods might be brought to farms in the insulating belt from starting farms farther out, and dairy cows could be fed in high-rise sterile buildings at the edge of the city to ensure the freshest, purest milk.

The legal codes and governmental structures of a city built with private funds on ground leased by a nonprofit corporation will be different from those of existing cities. Revenues to manage the city will come from leases rather than real-estate taxes. The laws and controls in the Experimental City will center on the new recognition of an individual's right to a clean environment. Though regulations will be different, there may be fewer of them because many of our laws evolved to protect us from the evil and nuisances precipitated by urban overgrowth. As the stresses of dirt, noise, and congestion are removed, other origins of antisocial behavior may be clarified.

Do people want dirt, noise, and congestion removed? Most of us assume so. But, like everything else in the Experimental City, we will have to see. The ideas and directions that have been suggested here are merely possible pieces of the total experiment, any one of which is likely to change and develop as the experiment itself develops.

BRITTON HARRIS

The City of the Future: The Problem of Optimal Design

This paper draws attention to a major distinction between planning design on the one hand and analysis, theory building, and simulation of human social and economic systems on the other hand. The distinction revolves around questions of policy-making and optimality, and in the course of examining it, I think I shall be able to demonstrate that there is at least one major aspect of purposeful social activity which is somewhat intractable and not fully responsive to systematic and scientific approaches. If this be true, there is an important residuum of art in the practice of planning that may resist the efforts of regional science to systematize the world.

For purposes of illustration, I shall later develop this distinction with the example of the city of the future as a specific instance. Meanwhile, I maintain that the process of planning has common features that apply equally well to the engineering design of a bridge, the architectural design of a building, the design of the city of the future, or the design of a viable and effective program of national economic development.

We may distinguish three main but overlapping phases in this planning or design process. The first is design proper or the delineation of a selected set of feasible alternatives. The second phase might be called plan testing or forecasting the outcome of policy and the impacts of its parts, severally and jointly. These effects are often very complex and difficult to trace, and the understanding of the relationships that govern them is perhaps the central focus of a great deal of academic research. The third phase is one of evaluation of and selection between alternative designs or plans based on more or less general social criteria applied to the delineated outcomes.

We must, of course, regard this process as cyclic. The outcomes and evaluations of one set of designs will lead us back to the drafting board for improvements and amendments. The evaluative criteria themselves will reflect social goals that will influence the very first step of select-

Adapted by the author from **Papers and Proceedings of the Regional Science Association,** Vol. XIX, 1967, pp. 185-195. Reprinted in revised form by permission of the Regional Science Association, Philadelphia, Pennsylvania.

ing interesting alternatives and, indeed, may suggest some of the elements which go into these alternatives.

The strongest coincidence between the process of planning and the process of scientific investigation arises in the area the planner might call testing alternatives and the scientist, predicting the outcomes of alternative policies. These two activities are, in fact, identical and involve relevant theories of the real world embodied in models competent to make accurate projections that discriminate between the effects of differing policies and groups of policies. When we consider the nature of these theories, we discover one of the main sources of confusion and difference between the two fields.

Many social scientists have come to the conclusion that one of the moving forces in social and economic life, and in location, is a tendency toward equilibrium arising out of the actions and decisions of individuals in a free or partially free market. This line of argument is not seriously damaged by the assumption that in a dynamic society equilibrium is always sought but never achieved. It is also true that the conditions of equilibrium frequently correspond with the conditions for the existence of an extreme value of a welfare function. Most often this extreme value is an optimum, but, occasionally, as in the case of the prisoner's dilemma, it may be a "pessimum."

There are two essential distinctions to be made between the economic or social optimum related to the equilibrating process which the scientist can identify and the optimum or best plan which the planner or engineer seeks to generate. The first point is that the scientist's optimum is not normative but refers to the state of a system and an optimum measured by a social or economic objective function which is defined by the nature of the system. The optimum can be given a normative interpretation only if society accepts the scientifically defined objective function as a desirable goal. In the second place, the scientist's optimum exists with the structure of the problem defined at least in part outside of the system of interest. Thus, laws, customs, and the existing cultural artifacts must be in general taken as givens. The planner, in turn, is concerned with the conscious change of these given elements and consequently is seeking to optimize a different problem. We will now turn our attention to that problem in some detail.

The problem of optimizing the operation of a complex system by changing or redefining its structural characteristics is essentially a problem of design. Quite generally, design might therefore be defined as a process of inventing new elements and recombining known or existing elements so as to produce a desired whole. The terms "elements" and "whole" are purposely left undefined except for their hierarchical relationship; viewed from one aspect, an element may be a lower-level whole consisting of still smaller elements, and the whole for one design purpose may be an element in a larger whole for other purposes. At the moment, I also leave undefined the term "desired," not specifying whether this to be judged by standards of optimizing or satisficing. The idea of combining elements can readily be extended to the idea of combining policy measures, activities, and like entities in variable amounts. Thus, the design process is defined in terms of the process of invention and the process of combination. A determination to include an element in the whole at any specified level will be called a design decision. It is unlike a real-world decision in that it can be revised or reversed without cost.

The essential difficulties in the analytic treatment of the design process are twofold. First, owing to the possibility of inventing new elements, the design decision space is not bounded and, in fact, has an unknown dimensionality. This fact in itself guarantees that we can never state unequivocally that a given design or proposed policy is the best. Quite aside from the uncertainties introduced into life by technology, changes in taste, war, famine, and pestilence, the best policy may be immediately available and feasible yet never have been discovered. This might be called a technological uncertainty of the policy design process itself. A second, and in some ways more intriguing, difficulty arises from the fact that the predictable effects of design decisions, if they become settled policy, are not mutually independent. Policy A in combination with policy B may and most probably will have effects which differ from the sum of the effects of policies A and B taken individually. Perhaps this problem is more intriguing because it seems that it should be susceptible to straightforward analysis and thus teases us more unmercifully than uncertainties about which we know we can do little. In order to explore the nature of this problem somewhat more fully, I propose to develop a few specific and easily comprehended examples.

I am indebted for the first example to Professor Zofia Dembowska of the Instytut Urbanistyki i Architektury, Warszawa, who encountered it in the course of planning for the expansion of an existing Polish metropolis. Let us assume that the expansion will occur in a planned fashion along a number of radial fingers from the existing body of the metropolis. The areas in which this expansion may be planned are not developed in any urban uses and do not contain any urban engineering improvements. In order to accomplish the expansion, each new district will have to be served by transportation routes and utility lines that will follow a corridor outward from the existing body of development. The costs of these installations depend in part linearly on the distance of the farthest developed precinct from existing development and in part on the number of precincts actually developed along each corridor. The incidence of

these costs on the development is roughly inverse to the number of precincts developed. Normally, this is a problem in marginal analysis, but we introduce the fact that the terrain is not uniform and that costs of development vary between areas, with some lower site development costs occurring farther out in certain corridors. Thus, a decision not to develop a close-in precinct may save on land development costs but throw a heavier burden for the provision of urban services on the remaining precincts. It appears that for any given corridor, the optimum combination for the development and nondevelopment of precincts can only be determined by a complete enumeration of combinations. If, for example, there are ten possible precincts, there will be 1,024 combinations, of which perhaps half will be worthy of examination. Considering, say, half a dozen different corridors and the constraint that all the anticipated population must be located, there is obviously an additional level of analysis, in that a selection of the best combinations for each corridor must somehow be made under an over-all optimizing criterion.

I have purposely omitted from this example many additional complications that could be included without any distortion of the problem. For example, the outlying precincts will in general incur higher travel costs to their residents, but, on the other hand, under certain circumstances, groups of these precincts may develop subsidiary business centers that will reduce these costs. The addition of these and others would greatly complicate the process of costing out the very large number of combinations that the simplest problems of this type can generate.

My second example is even more striking; it was first clearly defined by Roger L. Creighton, Director of the Transportation Planning and Programming Subdivision, New York State Department of Public Works, and represents a special case of a general and very important problem which might be called the optimum network problem. Imagine a state containing 20 major cities of various sizes currently connected by a highway network providing 30 m.p.h. service. The state proposes to upgrade this network by the provision of a number of links providing 60 m.p.h. service. To simplify the problem, we may assume that we have defined a subset of 40 out of all possible direct city-to-city links, such that these 40 links define a generally satisfactory network configuration. The state is operating under budget constraints that make it impossible to build, say, more than half of the mileage of the high-grade links defined by this network. The problem may be simply stated: what subset of the 40 links will satisfy the budget constraint and provide the greatest benefits to the state?

In order to examine this problem more explicitly, we may assume that an objective function for maximizing benefits can be formulated and even, for purposes of simplicity, that it is linear in the policy variable, travel time between cities. Such an objective function, for instance, might be

$$\text{Max} \sum_i \sum_j - P_i P_j T_{ij} .$$

Any straightforward analytical solution to this deceptively simple problem founders, because the addition of any link of improved facilities to the system effects the variable T_{ij} which depends on the precise links previously added to the improved system. Once again, the only possible thorough approach is to denumerate all possible combinations, in this case 2^{40}, or a million million. Even if we assume that only one in a million combinations is at or near the budget constraint and that these combinations can be rapidly and cheaply identified, there still remain a million combinations to be evaluated. At a most optimistic estimate of one second per evaluation on a high-speed computer, these would require nearly 300 hours!

So far, we have dealt with examples of optimal design decisions in which all of the choices are binary, either yes or no. This restriction has enabled us to lay bare the essential nature of the problem. The usual case is indeed much more complex because the policies available to the designer usually represent a mixture of binary and continuous variables. Thus, for example, budget allocations for many activities are frequently regarded in analysis as continuously variable, and this may be a useful artifice in spite of the fact that the budgets apply to programs which are indeed lumpy and discontinuous. In the general case where all policy variables are continuous, we rarely find that the connections of policies with outcomes are independent and linear. Some policies reinforce each other and others conflict. Consequently, even if all relations are clearly defined and analytically tractable, the conventional processes of optimizing lead only to local optima. Since it is to be expected that the criterion function is not unimodal in the policy space, this result is unsatisfactory.

The usual approach to this problem is to select a number of widely separated points in the policy space, that is, a number of plans or sketches differing as widely as possible from each other, and to explore their implications. This is becoming accepted practice in metropolitan planning and transportation planning.

There are other approaches to the problem of planning which are perhaps more popular, but to me less appealing than the examination of widely separated alternatives. The first of these is sequential planning or sequential decision-making, in which it is assumed that the decisions in the planning process are strongly hierarchical and that a very large number of minor and intermediate decisions depend upon and are shaped by certain primary decisions. This approach precludes discovering the richness of new combinations. A variation on this approach by Christopher Alexander and others organizes decisions hierarchically on the basis of the strength of their interactions. The most strongly interacting decisions are lowest in the hierarchy and their conflicts are resolved or optimized first. This method can also lead to inadequate attention to new combinations. A final method of some importance is to place major emphasis on minimum standards rather than on optimum performance. If these standards are very strongly defined, there may indeed be a problem even of finding a feasible solution. In this case, the importance of trade-offs, substitutions, and innovation are strongly circumscribed and the real planning decisions are taken in the course of setting the standards.

After this overview of the problem of design in principle, and of selected examples, we may turn briefly to the relation between these issues and the design of the city of the future.

The general context in which most of these problems have come forcibly to my attention is that of rapid and pejorative change in the American urban environment. Our cities are growing mightily in population, in wealth, and in geographic extent but with social and environmental consequences which most of us find distasteful. Our general view of society suggests that by conscious intervention in this developmental process we can change its course and invent a more desirable future than presently seems likely. It is also clear that the changes we can bring about may take many decades to effect. Likewise, we may assume that big problems may require drastic remedies. Thus, it is possible that the present framework of social, economic, legal, and technological arrangements of our cities and metropolitan areas may be the object of major change and modification.

Considering the commitment of resources that any society must make to urban living arrangements, we must, I think, concede that the design process must seek some sort of social optimum. We may now usefully review the extent to which regional science, urban economics and sociology, and related analytical disciplines can and cannot solve these problems of optimization.

Quite clearly, the process of theory building and analytical understanding of the metropolitan area is of key importance in the whole planning process. Without this understanding, it is impossible to predict the consequences of policy decisions and hence impossible to evaluate alternative bundles of policy. At least equally important, a direct engagement in analytic research provides a wealth of insights into urban processes which may be of critical importance in suggesting new policy designs and in guiding the process of evaluation. Therefore, although I have tried to make a conceptual distinction between analysis and design and between analysis and planning, I think that we could usefully consider means by which these processes can maintain an intimate connection in the real world. Nothing is more self-defeating than a design effort which is not based on an intimate knowledge of goals, of means, and of interrelationships.

There are at least two directions within the strict limitation of theory and analysis in which the preceding discussion suggests directions for improvement. When we examine in detail the problem of designing the future city, we find that in many aspects this becomes the problem of designing a setting for all society. Insofar as this difficulty must be faced, it suggests that economic models of equilibrium and optimization are not enough, and, indeed, that the objective function and the means by which it is maximized must cover a wider range of social forces and social values. A second aspect which deserves consideration is the importance of nonlinear and possibly of time-dependent systems. Even elementary economic considerations regarding economies and diseconomies of scale, as well as considerations of individual behavior, suggest that interactions in the urban system are strongly nonlinear. Yet we still cast much of our analysis in linear terms because these systems are more tractable. As an addendum, perhaps a third point could be made regarding the importance of exploiting equilibrium considerations more explicitly as a basis for theory building and analysis. Steps have been made in all of these directions, but perhaps they could be longer and more firm.

In contrast to the possibility of direct contributions to planning by theory, we must identify certain areas in which the contributions will be indirect and where, in fact, an independent approach to the theory of design may be required. In the discussion of these cases, we will again assume away those circumstances that are the consequence of general uncertainty and focus only on those inherent in the design process itself.

Policy planning, in the first instance, may be devoted to changing the rules of the game and thus the structure of the world to which analysis and theory apply. Mortgage insurance, urban renewal, and the interstate highway program may be taken as examples of the type of structural change greatly influencing the development of urban areas. Prior to their invention, they were not in general a part of the world which the analyst examined. In the future, we may expect that to deal with urgent urban problems, many new devices of similar magnitude will have to be invented. Frequently, perceptive analysts may actually originate these suggestions. In general, even though basic qualities of human behavior and economic reality will persist, we may expect that some such changes will so drastically alter the structure of urban affairs that they may even call for new theories and certainly for new models.

A second problem, somewhat peripheral to design but of great interest to economists, is the fact that the objective functions used in equilibrating a market or submarket may not coincide with the objective functions proposed for measuring social welfare. This is quite clearly the case, for example, when we consider the environmental effects of transportation improvements, which have become an important issue in the urban highway construction program. The fact that present engineering criteria for optimality do not take into account the externalities of highway construction might suggest to the economist that there is an imperfection in the market. He might then recommend either a new objective function which places arbitrary prices on externalities, or an actual revision of the effective pricing system, with a similar but more explicit effect. It might thus be suggested that a careful examination of mismatches between broad social and narrow economic optimizing procedures could reveal important means for improving efficiency by redefining market relations. In this context, economists could participate directly in some of the innovative aspects of policy planning design.

A narrow line divides the invention of new policy measures, our third area of difficulty, from the process discussed above of changing the rules. It might be suggested, for example, that entirely new methods of taxation of real estate could be devised with anticipated effects radically different from those of existing tax policies. Yet it is quite conceivable that the analysis of these proposals could proceed in the existing framework of economic theory and partial equilibrium treatment of the system. Despite the fact that such measures are analyzable, it would indeed be a rash economist who would suggest that he has reviewed all such possible innovations. It would be even more rash to suggest that all such measures are arranged in a continuum (of however many dimensions) and that their exploration can be made a matter of systematic search and of pushing presently known concepts to the limit. However useful this technique may be, it is clearly not exhaustive.

We come, finally, to the most troublesome aspect of exploring the consequences of alternative bundles of policies, the combinatorial aspect which has been stressed in the preceding discussions. The design of a future metropolis probably involves several hundred interdependent decisions, many of which can already be delineated. These include the sites, future land uses, and methods to be used for urban renewal; zoning over scores of districts and including the location and densities of many classes of activities and residence; and the provision of transportation facilities. They also include operating policies regarding taxes, prices, and the provision of public welfare services such as health, education, and social service. Quite apparently, the interactions of these decisions are nontrivial; for example, in a multitude of ways both large and small, the designation of land uses and the design of transportation systems interact with each other. In spite of our best efforts to restructure and simplify the problem, it seems likely to me that there exist for any given city many thousand defensible alternatives with a wide range of as yet unpredicted costs and benefits. Even assuming that we had adequate analytical methods for examining alternatives, it is quite clear that practicality and economy would dictate that we must select a restricted subset for detailed examination. When, for example, four plans are selected for detailed study out of perhaps a possible thousand, the planner puts a substantial emphasis on his professional ability to select useful alternatives. It is indeed a fearsome responsibility for the regional scientist or the plan-

ner to take the initiative in circumscribing the problem or recommending short-cut methods, since these steps are tantamount to excluding a wide class of combinations from further consideration.

The solution to this problem requires much more careful and explicit consideration of the processes involved in design and the selection of designs for testing. At the same time, it requires a detailed knowledge of the policy space in which design is proceeding and some intuition as to the probable effects of jointly determined design decisions. Thus, the design process stands with one foot in an increasingly self-conscious creative effort and the other foot in an increasingly detailed scientific knowledge of society's relation to its environment. It would indeed, I think, be foolish for people on either side of this fence to maintain that they can operate without the other side.

The acuteness of this problem is being daily increased by a variety of trends in relation to our policy toward our cities. The increasing determination for action, the increasing recognition of the importance of a long-range view, the growing willingness to use new policy measures, the increasing flexibility and virtuosity of our technology, and the increasing affluence of our society all tend to create additional degrees of freedom within which the problems will hopefully be solved. These added degrees of freedom greatly increase the complexity of the design process and its intractability under ordinary economic or behavioral analysis. I hope, therefore, that this effort to delineate the inherent nature of the problem will arouse a constant awareness of its existence and stimulate efforts to reduce its intransigencies.

KEVIN LYNCH

The Possible City

We can expect the metropolis to be the normal environment of the future: the realized desire of those seeking space, better services, congenial neighbors, and a home of their own. Present estimates are that 80 percent of our population will be living in such regions by the year 2000, and that the largest of these metropolises will coalesce into four giant megalopolitan regions—on the Atlantic seaboard, along the lower Great Lakes (these two may even grow together into a single belt), in Florida, and in California—four regions containing 60 percent of the U.S. on 7½ percent of its land. The horror of critics is unjustified: This is a superior environment by past standards. It doesn't "eat up" land, nor will it cause the end of civilization. It frees large areas of the country for rural and recreational uses. The apparent threat of extended urbanization can in fact be turned to our great advantage—can be but may not be. The metropolis has serious problems. Social groups are increasingly segregated in space. There is a lack of diversity and a lack of identity. If you have no car, you are stranded. There are no concentrated centers. But none of these difficulties is inherent in the metropolitan form.

If you ask anyone to imagine a city of 50,000 square miles, 600 miles long (as the Californian megalopolis is projected to be), he feels desperate because he imagines a mechanical enlargement of the present city. But one need not feel lost in a region, simply because it is encompassing. Setting limits is only one way of structuring. Such a region could be a very diverse place, it could be clean and open, the quality of its life could be pleasant and challenging. It could be a homeland, a beloved landscape. We cling to the notion of the rural-urban dichotomy —small cities in a rural hinterland, a world with an outside and an inside. That world is fading before our eyes. The sense of being at home depends neither on size, nor on traditional form, but on an active relation between men and their landscape, a landscape which they made and which speaks to them. How can we achieve this in such vast areas?

Guiding the development of these great regions will be a staggering task, considering our difficulties in managing the growth

From E. W. Ewald Jr., (ed.), **Environment and Policy: The Next Fifty Years,** 1968, pp. 139-148. Reprinted by permission of the Indiana University Press, Bloomington, Indiana.

of much smaller and less complex areas. Even by 1975, we can expect new construction to double the present rates. The sheer quantity of new environment, which will be most striking at the fringe but also substantial in the city interiors, is an opportunity and a threat. There will be a growing body of used environment, which must be continually adapted and maintained, or painfully rebuilt, while attending to a great diversity in user wants and needs. If anything, this diversity appears to be increasing. No central agency can direct the details of this process.

The most effective opportunities for environmental quality are at the point of development. One such opportunity is at the edge of the metropolis, where public (or mixed public and private) authorities might assemble and plan large chunks of undeveloped land for diverse urban uses, which would then be transferred to private and public development agencies for actual construction. These would not be "new towns" in the old sense. The authorities would work with the normal urbanizing process, much as several large private land developers are doing today, but on a far more comprehensive scale. The private developer works under severe limitations of market and political control, yet his product is the environment of the future.

Here at the growing edge our evolving ideas for clusters of mixed low density housing, for the maintenance of ecological balance, for intense diversified centers or continuous open spaces, for new modes of transport or the control of climate, light, and sound, could most easily be put into practice. Any existing social, or built, or natural identities could be preserved. The authority could create a sense of place by specifying particular environmental characters to be built into various zones. The region would become a mosaic of distinctive and well-fitted districts, a human landscape built from the beginning. No one is building it today. All large devel-

oping areas at the metropolitan fringe should pass through the hands of capable public authorities, but not through a single central authority. It should be a public responsibility to see that an adequate supply of land for development is constantly available throughout the metropolitan region, that it is well planned, well serviced, and free of speculative surcharge.

This public power must only be used if it will reduce the growing segregation of our population by race and class. Rather than straining to entice the middle class to return to the central city they have left behind, we should make it possible for others to move out to the suburbs that they would like to reach. This will be a long effort, contending with resistance from the suburbs and fear on the part of the movers. It will require concerted action on jobs, housing, and transport—a massive resettlement. It will mean the construction of substantial quantities of new housing within the reach of lower income groups. Technology promises future reductions in building costs, and we should press to realize those promises. Until they are realized, the construction of housing must be subsidized. We must create development agencies which can take on those resettlement tasks, in the newly organizing areas, but also in scattered locations throughout the inner and outer zones. They will necessarily be engaged in the provision of social services, the improvement of transportation, and the distribution of employment, as well as in building houses. Grants to local authorities to pay for the additional services required must accompany these movements, to make them politically palatable. "Sister" relations between inner and outer districts, with exchanges of services and visitors, might precede permanent population movements. It may be unrealistic (even undesirable) to hope for a fine-grained mix of social groups, but we must destroy the one-color school district and the single-class town. We are already building the future metropolis. If we refuse to intervene decisively, that future is an even suburbia and a frayed interior. It will have its amenities. It will have its costs—not least being a denial of growth to a sizeable number of people. And it will be a splendid opportunity gone by.

The System of Centers

Strenuous efforts are being made to "save the downtown" as a last vestige of concentrated urbanity. Indeed there is something lost, if we should no longer have places of intense activity, of diverse services and opportune encounters. The outward dispersion of high intensity activities to widely scattered sites deprives us of social and visual meeting points, as well as of the opportunity to live close to the action or to enjoy a rich array of supporting facilities. But to maintain a single center as the dominant focus of employment and services is to swim against the flood. As far as it is successful, it will preserve commuter congestion and the ghetto.

We have a better opportunity: to channel high density housing; services such as health, education, shopping, culture, and entertainment and concentrated and interlinked employment, such as offices and business services into a galaxy of metropolitan centers, each large enough to provide substantial diversity and to support a local transit system, provided with structures linked at many levels, pedestrian carriers, and climate control. To the extent that these centers had a special character of activity and form, they could stand for differentiated areas of the region, and might encourage social interactions over a broader geographic base, less tied to class and race.

In and near these centers people might live who, by choice or necessity, wished to be close to work and services. The centers might also serve as points of reception for families escaping from the central ghetto. Centers could be built out of older in-

complete foci, or encouraged to coalesce in the regions of new growth. Their range of activity and their physical character could be guided in a way which would be impractical over larger areas. Building or rebuilding the important focal points is another crucial development task which might be undertaken by public authority. There are significant advances to be made in the design and maintenance of such intensive locales.

Change and Renovation

Activities that occupy the older areas are constantly changing, and we have burned our fingers in trying to manage that change. Even the oldest areas are rarely completely abandoned, but become specialized for other activities, often more diverse than the original ones. The contrast of activity and setting can be quite evocative. If we do anything here, it should be to facilitate these shifts in use, to assist in the gradual specialization and decrease in density of the central areas. The danger lies in the attempt to cling to the present—to save the downtown, for example, or to congeal our problems by rebuilding at higher densities. We must encourage the central areas to open out, to become the locus for particular uses and institutions, the residence of people with special tastes, or attractive vacation areas in which open space and intense urban activity are closely mingled. Some concentrations of high density housing will persist, particularly at the core, but we can expect to see apartment living widely distributed throughout the metropolitan region. Areas of particular historic interest or environmental character should of course be conserved, but they occupy a small fraction of the land. The central ghettos might be transformed, not only into centers of political power and social reconstruction, but also into settings of prestige, the symbolic centers of cultures newly visible in our society. As a prerequisite for unlocking this process of change, its costs must be openly accounted for and justly allocated. The burden now falls on deprived and powerless people.

One promising avenue for dealing with the existing city is the search for underused space and time, and its readaptation for a desired activity. We can explore the use of streets as play areas, or the possibilities for using roof tops, empty stores, abandoned buildings, waste lots, odd bits of land, or the large areas presently sterilized by such mono-cultures as parking lots, expressways, railroad yards, and airports. We may find room for new modes of transit, additional housing, schools, or special recreation.

Another strategy is to find ingenious ways of adapting or reconditioning the existing environment with a minimum of disturbance to existing users. Rehabilitation techniques have not yet proved very promising, except where the degree of improvement desired is small, or where it has been done piecemeal by the user-owner, employing his own labor and capital, and making a fit to his own particular desires. New techniques which aided this latter process—packaged amenities which are easy to insert; tools, power, and materials for use by the individual; training and guidance in rebuilding—would all be useful. Technical services and information must be made available directly to the user of environment, particularly to those who presently have no voice in political and developmental decisions.

Perhaps we can organize a rebuilding and maintenance industry, and begin to conserve our still-useful environmental stock in a more systematic and efficient way. Renewal-and-rehabilitation has traditionally focused its attention on the oldest parts of the central city. The problem for the future is the conservation and improvement of what are now the new suburbs. Surely there are ways in which sophisticated technology could be employed in such essential tasks as the clean-ing or refacing of outdoor surfaces, the modification of noise and climate, routine housekeeping, the prevention of fire, the removal of waste, the provision of local communal services or the insertion of small gardens or micro-reaction facilities. It is just this kind of environmental renewal that can provide jobs for many of the lowest skilled or racially excluded workers. Maintenance technology should be designed to make use of such men, and then to train them in more complex skills.

We will always be concerned with the problem of obsolescence. Technology and styles of life will shift in the near future at least as rapidly as they have done in the near past. One reasonable response is to make sure that any new environment is highly adaptable, able to accommodate new functions at low economic or social cost. We know very little about how to do this. We can only make vague guesses: building at low density, providing growth room or surplus capacity; providing a high capability for circulation and communication; separating functions and structures that are likely to change from those likely to be permanent; using temporary or movable structures (only if we are later able to control their disposal, however); establishing a neutral grid to regulate locations and connections; setting up a monitoring system which will call for adaptation at the first signals of change. We have much to do to develop and test these ideas. The urgency and permanence of the problem would make full-scale research worthwhile. For example, we would like to be able to specify levels of adaptability as performance standards for new construction.

Mobility and change add novelty and adventure to living, but exact an emotional price. The sense of continuity with the past, the feeling of "home," of belonging and commitment, has some relation to geographical fixity. Change must be made psychologically tolerable. One may be trained to live in a changing place and with changing social relationships. One may shift his point of reference from a small spatial community to a larger unit (a metropolis, a nation), or to a stable but spatially shifting social unit (the traditional solution of the nomad), or to a stable set of connections with persons who are dispersed and shifting in space, or even to a symbolic home occasionally visited (a function that summer cottages may be taking on for some of our mobile middle class).

In any case, environmental form must take account of these stresses: providing clear orientation for the newcomer, with a proportion of familiar sterotypes; clarifying the image at larger and larger scales, so that the individual may feel that he is only moving about within his permanent "home"; providing symbolic landmarks of continuity with the past; making change legible in itself. Behavior changes rapidly; physical form may be used symbolically to stabilize it and give it continuity, as well as to support it functionally. By expressing what shifts are going on, how they arose out of the recent past and are likely to continue into the near future, the environment can help us to live with change, and even to enjoy it.

It will also be necessary to establish and protect areas of little change, of archaic ways of life, for those who do not choose to follow the common pattern. Tenure of a second home in a stable setting may make change elsewhere more acceptable. In a shifting world, one must know how to forget and how to remember, how to conserve and how to dispose of environment. The problems of change and mobility will be fundamental ones for the future city. They tempt us with new possibilities as well.

An Open Environment

It is crucial for our purpose that the future environment be an "open" one—which the individual can easily penetrate, and in which he can act by his own choice. Development of the individual has been an historic role of the city, but it has never been articulated as a conscious goal of environmental policy. The growth of leisure, the economic demands for high skill, the danger of leaving a section of our population behind in helpless ignorance combine to make this humane ideal an urgent social requirement. An education is gained in many ways, not least via the city itself.

The provision of a new kind of open space would be one strategic and yet tolerable way of building an educative city. Here also there is a tradition of government action, although I am not speaking just of the spaces colored green on official maps, but of the areas which are open to the freely chosen and spontaneous activity of city people. I include vacant lots, sandbanks, and open dumps, as well as parks, woods, and beaches. I do not mean tennis courts or baseball diamonds, which, however desirable, are designed for standardized activities, but the uncommitted complement to the system of committed uses which make up an urban region—the ambiguous places of ill-defined ownership and function. There are many possible kinds: pits, mazes, raceways, heaths, woods, thickets, canyons, beaches, allotments and do-it-yourself cabins, rooftops, hobby yards, caves, marshes, canals, dirt piles, junk yards, aerial runways, undersea gardens, ruined buildings. The zones between contrasting regions are of particular value, because of their ambiguity, flux, and range of choice: shore lines, quiet gardens in city centers, the edge of woods, the meeting of salt and fresh waters. This kind of open space may even be within doors: in barn-like buildings where people can organize various activities at temporary stands.

Space of this kind extends the individual's range of choice, and allows him to pursue his purposes directly, without elaborate prior planning or community constraint. Since social investment is low, he has a chance to demonstrate mastery and to participate actively in a way usually denied him in the protected and expensive, committed environment. Here he can act at his own pace and in his own style. Open space is a place of stimulus release, withdrawal and privacy, in contrast to the intense and meaning-loaded communica-tions which confront him elsewhere. Modern information techniques threaten to submerge our privacy and individual autonomy. In a preferred environment, one can deny communications, as well as seek them—one can protest, even rebel. The guerrillas of the future will need a base of operation.